For Reference

Not to be taken from this room

Charter School Movement

History, Politics, Policies, Economics and Effectiveness

Charter School Movement

History, Politics, Policies, Economics and Effectiveness

Second Edition

Danny Weil

Grey House
Publishing

PUBLISHER:	Leslie Mackenzie
EDITORIAL DIRECTOR:	Laura Mars-Proietti
EDITORIAL ASSISTANT:	Kristen Thatcher
MARKETING DIRECTOR:	Jessica Moody
AUTHOR:	Danny Weil
COPYEDITOR:	Marguerite Duffy
COMPOSITION & DESIGN:	DSCS Datastream Content Solutions, LLC Composition & Publishing Services

Grey House Publishing, Inc.
4919 Route 22
Amenia, NY 12501
518.789.8700
FAX 845.373.6360
www.greyhouse.com
e-mail: books @greyhouse.com

First edition published 2000
Second edition published 2009

Publisher's Cataloging-In-Publication Data
(Prepared by The Donohue Group, Inc.)

Weil, Danny K., 1953-
   Charter school movement : history, politics, policies, economics and effectiveness / Danny Weil. -- 2nd ed.
      p. : ill. ; cm.

   "The first edition (Charter Schools: A Reference Handbook) was published by ABC-CLIO in 2000."--p. xix.
   Includes bibliographical references and index.
   ISBN: 978-1-59237-289-8

1. Charter schools--United States—Finance. 2. Charter schools—Political aspects—United States. 3. Charter schools—United States—Evaluation. I. Title. II. Title: Charter schools.

LB2806.36.W45 2009
371.01/0973

This book is dedicated to all the great remaining newspaper journalists in America, both locally and nationally. Without their dedication to excellent journalistic work I could never have written this book.

This book is also dedicated to the children of Katrina and the millions of students and their parents who wish only the best education and future for their children. I hope this book has helped shed light on the concept of charter schools.

Table of Contents

Preface

In early 1995 while working with public school teachers in Arizona, attempting, as we were, to infuse critical thinking within classroom curriculums, I met Sandra Potter. Sandra was a sixth grade public school teacher in Tucson, Arizona with high hopes for all children. Sandra enthusiastically came to me with an idea one day while working with teachers. She wanted to start what she called a "charter school," and she was beginning to work towards making it a reality. Would I be interested in working with her in both setting up the school and working with teachers, as well as serving on the board once the school was started?

Intrigued with the idea, I asked her to explain the concept to me. Sandra said that her students, mostly from poor, working Latino families, were being under-served and that her desire to innovate on behalf of the children was being thwarted by a dilapidated public school system disconnected from community concerns, student and teacher realities and democratic decision making. She told me that a "charter school" would be a school where there would be a collective, social, and economic purpose: a community school where both students and their families could participate in the hiring of teachers, the development of curriculum, and the actual democratic ownership and day-to-day operations of their school. I was delighted with the idea and welcomed the chance to participate. Sandra then began the process of chartering her way toward what was to become Pimeria Alta School Charter School.

Pimeria Alta School is a high school located in Nogales, Arizona, two blocks from the border with Mexico. The superintendent of schools for Santa Cruz County, Robert Canchola, and Sandra Potter established the school in June 1995. This was one year after Arizona passed the state's charter legislation. The school opened with 13 students and by 1999 had grown to 248 students. It served from 14 to 22 students in grades 7 through 12.

According to the school's mission statement drafted at its conception, the goal of Pimeria Alta School was "to provide opportunities for historically disenfranchised students to obtain a valid high school diploma through flexible, innovative and creative means, and to provide students and community members with options for transition into various lifestyles which would further their efforts to continue as lifelong students" (Pimeria Alta School 1996). Frustrated by a lack of schools in the surrounding area that serviced disenfranchised adolescents, especially Hispanic youth, both Canchola and Potter saw charter legislation as an opportunity to create an educational environment that would provide an alternative to what they saw as a public school system that was failing local youth. They wanted to provide a safe and positive learning environment for students that would engage them and show them the importance and relevancy of education in their daily lives. A huge percentage of the young people in Santa Cruz County were idle and not attending any school, either having been expelled or having simply dropped out of education altogether. These young people saw no relevance in their educational experience and, in fact, their past experience in the traditional public schools had left them marginalized, bored with schooling, and unable to connect to academic pursuits.

When the school first opened in October 1995, 60 percent of the students at Pimeria Alta were adjudicated by the criminal court system. Only seven of the students were female, because the school was looked at as a school for "bad boys" and the community was leery of sending its girls to be a part of such a student body. This situation, however, changed. According to an interview with Sandra Potter, by March 2000, only 6 percent of the students in attendance were adjudicated through the court system, and 52 percent of the student body was female. At that time, the school was the third-largest high school in the county of Santa Cruz, Arizona.

Shortly after the experience of having helped set up the original school site, having worked with teachers and having served on the board, I decided to write a book about charter schools. I wanted to explore what other states were doing in the area of charter schools, and if the concept of the charter school would, in reality, actually provide for an equitable treatment of all children, as well as of the teachers who teach them. I wanted to see if the charter school movement, as it was now known, could provide a community school for all its neighborhood members, regardless of race, class or gender, a school with full disclosure and transparency that would allow for community governance of the school, as Albert Shanker had called for in 1988 when he embraced the charter school concept as the head of the American Federation of Teachers. I sought to see if these new schools that were springing up all over the country were motivated by a desire to shape a curriculum that would allow students to understand how power and morality influences their lives, if they could help students become life-long learners and citizens, and wisely able participants in democratic decision-making. I also was interested in how these schools began, the legislation that motivated them, how they were governed, and by whom.

In 1998 when I began the first edition of *Charter Schools: A Reference Handbook,* there were 1,100 charter schools serving one quarter of a million students in the United States. There are now over 4,600 charter schools in the United States educating 1.5 million students, and the number grows daily (The Center for Education Reform, "All About Charter Schools"). Charter schools are growing at such a rapid pace (the 2008-2009 school year saw 355 charter schools open in 40 states and the District of Columbia), that needless to say, the charter school movement has taken on a life of its own. Yet unlike the initial conception of Pimeria Alta Charter School, most charter schools today are run by large for-profit and nonprofit Educational Management Organizations (EMO's) or what has now been coined in some educational parlance as Charter Management Organizations (CMO's) and they are predominately found in large urban cities within the United States.

This second edition of the *Charter School Movement: History, Politics, Policies, Economics and Effectiveness* (new title), seeks to examine and discuss the swelling charter school movement and the particular controversies that surround what has been called "public choice" and the notion of charter schools as an educational reform movement. This edition looks at what has motivated the development of the charter school movement—from the frustration of parents, teachers and students, to the hopes and aspirations of community members, educational policymakers, and the burgeoning business and philanthropic interest in charter schools. Yet unlike many books on charter schools that seek to continuously compare charter school performance on standardized tests with traditional public schools, this book does something quite different. Using the work of some of America's best newspaper reporters throughout the United States, the book virtually goes directly into many of the communities that have charter schools and looks at them from a local vantage point—from the bottom up. Much of what the reader will find in this book is not available in any other book on charter schools for it is a localized look at the issues that swirl around the movement, which rarely receive coverage in the national news, nor in academic treatises on the subject. Furthermore, though it is specific in its investigations of various charter schools state-by-state and city-by-city, the book systematically and abstractly attempts to place these understandings within a broader conception of the sociopolitical and economic issues that surround the movement.

The book examines the political economy of the charter school movement, the history of charter schools, the development of specific charter school laws within each state, especially New Orleans. It also examines the growth of the virtual charter school movement, charter schools and the claims to innovation, competition and markets, admission policies, public disclosure and transparency, segregation, religion, No Child Left Behind and its impact on charter schools, as well as briefly looking at the curriculum and organizational model of various charter schools. The reader will find discussions on the rapid development of for-profit and nonprofit EMO's and CMO's, as well as on the issue of teacher's unions and their role in participating in charter schools. Finally, the book contains a directory of organizations, associations and government agencies associated with the charter school movement. It also contains a bibliography of print and non-print resources, and a set of primary documents important in understanding charter schools as an ideological concept.

The issues facing American education as it enters into the 21st century cannot be boiled down to simply whether students are able to compete for jobs with India or China in the new global economy. Readers are also asked to think of education as a moral imperative for any democratic system to function. Charter schools are not only about individual choice, they are about a system of democracy, economic relations and the role of education in creating opportunities for students to become competent citizens, capable of participating in democratic life. As a reader, keep in mind these questions:

Does the public school system, through its use of charter schools, provide a more equitable treatment of all students, regardless of class background, race or gender?

Do charter schools provide access to all students or do they selectively submit students?

Do charter schools further the public purpose of education so as to foster citizenship participation in democratic life?

Do charter schools enhance diversity both in terms of their populations of students and in their curriculum?

Do charter schools provide full transparency and accountability so that parents and students can actually make an informed public choice about whether to attend a charter school?

Do charter schools provide a system for innovation that can be used to bolster traditional public schools?

With national health care on the minds of all Americans, the public debate about public schools and charter schools must, and will, now begin in earnest. The questions above, and many more, are just some queries that educational stakeholders will need to wrestle with if the impact of charter schools on public education is to be understood. The issues that educational policy makers grappled with at the beginning of the 20th century—social functionalism, progressivism, goals and purposes of education, education of newly arriving immigrants, multiculturalism, race, gender, culture and democracy—remain central in the charter movement debate today. In fact, these controversies, in one way or another, have nurtured the development of charter schools as a national reform movement.

Whether charter schools will live up to their stated claim, which is to improve the performance of all United States schools in the public educational system, or whether they will remain discrete and elitist enclaves or transform into large national nonprofit or for-profit retail educational chains, has yet to be decided. I am hoping that readers of this book will be able to enter into the logic of the issue, the myriad points of view that comprise the debate and come to your own conclusions as to the veracity and future of charter schools.

Danny Weil, PhD

I wish to acknowledge Joe Kincheloe for his belief in my ability to discuss educational concerns in writing. Although Joe has passed, he was the inspiration for my writing and I will always remember him with fondness.

I also wish to thank Holly Anderson for her work in helping edit this book and especially in assisting in the development of the bibliography and references for the work.

Introduction

This edition of the *Charter School Movement: History, Politics, Policies, Economics and Effectiveness* is the first published by Grey House Publishing. The first edition *(Charter Schools: A Reference Handbook)* was published by ABC-CLIO in 2000. This significantly revised work has a substantial amount of new material and features, with a new name that better reflects its expanded content.

Triple the size of the first edition, *Charter School Movement* has been completely revised and includes new chapters on the economics of charter schools, a new compilation of Primary Documents, and new and expanded Appendices. Its comprehensiveness and currency is unparalleled, with detailed discussions of opposing viewpoints, results of several recent charter school studies published by Stanford University, and the latest on the controversial decision by the Los Angeles Department of Education to charterize 250 of its public schools.

Also completely updated are the last two chapters of the work. They provide a comprehensive directory of resources on the charter school movement—with 69 organizations and agencies, 87 print resources, and 85 nonprint resources.

The brand new section of **Primary Documents** comprises nearly 100 pages of original documents that offer detailed background on the charter school movement: about Ray Budde, considered the founder of charter schools; actual charter applications and parent contracts; interviews with charter school teachers; recent articles that address the views of the Obama administration's Secretary of Education Arne Duncan and those of the "Instigator" in Los Angeles Steve Barr, and results of recent charter school studies.

These 15 enlightening documents, combined with the author's thorough coverage, give the reader the most current information on a subject that continues to pick up controversy.

The five **Appendices** are all about comparisons. Here you will see, in clear, tabular format, how states compare with each other on numbers (of charter schools, charter school students, and charter school teachers) and achievement (test scores, and graduation rates). You will also be able to compare charter schools with traditional public schools regarding teacher qualifications.

This edition of the *Charter School Movement: History, Politics, Policies, Economics and Effectiveness* ends with a detailed **Index.** The work is available in both print and ebook formats.

Chapter One
Introduction

THE EMERGENCE OF CHARTER SCHOOLS

Shortly after the start of the 1990s, the American public witnessed one of the most significant and controversial developments in public education: the emergence of the charter school movement. Until 1991, there was no such thing as a charter school (a public school under contract) in the United States. The idea, in its embryonic state, had not been embraced by any state in the union, and, in fact, no state had passed charter school legislation. Yet since 1991, 40 states, the District of Columbia and Puerto Rico have signed into law charter school legislation. States in which a charter school law has not been passed include: Alabama, Kentucky, Maine, Montana, North Dakota, Nebraska, South Dakota, Vermont, Washington, and West Virginia (U.S. Charter Schools, under "Charter School Legislation").

By 1998, more than 1,100 charter schools had emerged and were educating more than a quarter of a million students. There are now close to 4,000 charter schools operating in America educating over 1,000,000 students (Center on Reinventing Public Education, under "Charter Schools Operating in America").

The states involved in the charter school movement allowed the public to begin the charter school experiment, while simultaneously freeing many charter schools from state laws and standard school district policies and regulations. The idea was relatively simple in its inception, although complex in its controversial implications—for charter school proponents claimed they were looking to stimulate new and innovative educational opportunities and to provide parents and communities with alternatives to traditional public schooling through "choice." *Choice* is the buzzword for market-based economic and social policies of deregulation and privatization that commenced in the late 1970s and continues unabated today. Charter school advocates argued that charter school legislation and the development of local charter schools would stimulate competition among all schools, thereby raising the level of quality instruction for all schools, raising educational standards throughout public schools, allowing for local community and neighborhood governance, and stimulating meaningful reforms and improvements throughout the entire educational system. Many educational constituencies within numerous communities—ranging from parents to teachers, pundits to principals, educational entrepreneurs to nonprofit organizations, union leaders to Wall Street—argued that charter schools should be decentralized, community-based public schools and that they uniquely hold the promise of breaking up large, factory-style schools along with the burdensome and often nonfriendly educational bureaucracies and administrations that govern them. The problem was the "government," argued most charter school advocates. The "free market," they argued, held the Houdini key to escape the bondage of underperforming public schools. Interestingly, this was the argument leveled at all "social programs" of which education was simply labeled as one among many.

Politicians, from governors to state legislators, looked to charter schools as an antidote to what they saw as the failure of public schools, lack of educational innovation, barriers to parent and student involvement, and lackluster educational accountability. They also clamored to seize on the issue for purposes of self-promotion, constituency building, and campaign fodder as well. Many conservative politicians and activists, for example, saw the idea of charter schools as a further movement towards and return to the market-based policies begun shortly before the Reagan era. Consequently, the idea had great currency within conservative think tanks such as the Heritage Foundation, American Enterprise Education, The Fordham Foundation, and a multitude of similar advocacy groups. The proponents of charter schools, be they conservative or simply wedded to an animosity for public schools and government, argued that charter schools would serve as a magical cure in an era of public school mediocrity and top-heavy educational bureaucracies. The idea became, and still is, a popular and hotly debated one among a diverse community of educational workers, parents, local neighborhoods, and students.

Part of the widespread appeal of charter schools lies in the perception, right or wrong, that the public schools are not serving the needs of their students, the teachers that labor within them, the parents of the students that attend them, nor the community at large that supports them. Proponents of charter schools argue that politics, coupled with public schools mired in burdensome bureaucracies and historically top-heavy administrations that grind along seemingly resistant to change, simply will not and cannot reform the school systems within which they are implicated. They also single out teachers' unions blaming them for everything from the impoverishment of students to failures on standardized tests. Also active in the thinking of many charter advocates is the assumption that public schools will not reform unless they are challenged with market "competition" and that this competition must come from both charter schools and private educational vouchers. The ideology of competition within an "educational market-place" has continuously been set forth as a solution to the problems besieging schools; charter schools are simply part of this ideological reform movement.

Conservative politicians and their adherents admire the charter idea because, they insist, charter schools provide a way to avoid oppressive government regulations, teachers' unions, and can operate under the auspices of competition and parental choice. Allegedly, they claim charter schools produce educational results superior to those produced by the current public school systems and collective bargaining agreements. They are also fond of the idea for it is part and parcel of the conservative ideology of privatizing all if not most public institutions, from roads to health care. But the argument for charter schools is not simply about government and the horrors of top-down bureaucracy; they are also recently being looked at by progressive thinkers as a way to promote a new national politics regarding education. Some progressive politicians promote charter schools as a way to use freedom from regulation to create innovative centers of learning that are community based and can serve as a source for revitalized community participation in local schools. These progressive political advocates look to the charter idea as an opportunity born from the historical struggle to personalize learning, promote educational self-management, and make the educational curriculum relevant to students through small schools with small class sizes. They view charter schools as an environment that has low teacher-to-student ratios and in which there are many personal opportunities for contact between students and teachers—an environment in which experimentation with a wide range of instructional techniques, including individualized and cooperative approaches to learning and critical thinking, can be undertaken with the aim of upgrading the general quality of instruction.

Progressive educational writer, Jonathan Schorr, argues:

> *Charters ought to be on the agenda for the left, in part because of their potential to serve as tools of racial and economic justice. Nationally, 52 percent of charter school students are nonwhite, compared with 41 percent of students at other public schools. Charters also serve a population that is slightly poorer than average. But the relationship between charter schools and children of color varies widely from state to state. In California and Colorado, for instance, charter school student bodies are whiter and wealthier than those of regular public schools. (Schorr 2000)*

Racial concerns are evident in the charter controversy as well. Many non-white constituencies, such as African American parents and students, support the charter school concept precisely because, as many of them claim, traditional public schools have consistently failed their communities and students and appear unwilling to change. These segments of society argue that allowing parents or guardians to choose what kind of school their children will attend will ensure that their children will be given an equal opportunity to learn. (Rose and Gallup 2000).

As we shall see, many proponents of charter schools also argue that such schools create educational options in terms of curriculum development and delivery that cannot be found in the current public school approaches, and they also maintain that charter schools provide neighborhoods with the chance to govern their own community-based schools through decentralization and site-based management principles. These factors, they argue, provide elements of control, ownership, and democracy that are not found in the massive, unbalanced, bureaucratic, and system-wide public school districts. They reason that a smaller class size, the ability to pay individual attention to students, and relevant, personalized learning are just some of the benefits of charter schools. Thus, many of the concerns charter school advocates share go beyond simple "party lines" or ideological persuasions. The area is far more controversial and ripe than a simple, or cursory categorization of opponents or proponents of charters as being "here or there" on some political spectrum. Again, Schorr is salient in describing one charter school, The Neighborhood House Charter School located in Boston, Massachusetts:

There, in a building one could easily miss while searching for a school, a remarkable story is unfolding. Inside the warm, cozy classrooms of the Neighborhood House Charter School, the 180 students enjoy class sizes of 18 students—and two teachers. The student-teacher ratio, at less than 10 to 1, would be the envy of some expensive private schools; the typical public school ratio is 17 to 1. Founded by the local settlement-house network—a movement that has long offered services to ease the transition of new immigrants—the school serves as a center for healthcare, social services, after-school activities and adult education. A local newspaper reports, "Collaboration has been expanded beyond the building walls, and the entire community is recognizing the benefits." (Schorr 2000)

New families are welcomed by a coordinator in the school's parent center, who visits homes and helps connect parents to services they need. The coordinator also oversees the "family learning contracts"—a parent's promise to help with their child's studies, get their kid to school on time, and help develop the child's "Individual Learning Plan." An independent evaluation notes:

Every teacher in the school makes detailed observations about each of his or her students every day. The teacher-student ratio is so low that most teachers have totally internalized the ILP of their individual advisees. Students attend school from 8 am until as late as 6 pm, when adult education begins. And they attend with a vengeance, posting an impressive 97 percent attendance rate. No child has ever been expelled from Neighborhood House. (Schorr 2000)

The description above serves to define a "full-service school," an innovative idea of organizing an institution normally associated narrowly with education around many sundry human needs that people confront when living in a complex society. An idea such as this, a full service school, could not be done in traditional school models inherited as they have been from industrial models of education (Weil 1998).

Among the many progressive educators who support charter schools, one also finds the argument that charters are a way to prevent the privatization of schooling sought through conservative calls for vouchers and so-called subsidized school choice. In an economic and social environment in which deregulated markets and the privatization of social institutions are looked at as solutions to social problems, these educators look to the charter school idea as a stopgap to prevent total market domination of education; a capitulation of sorts. Some veteran community activists embrace charter schools, as do other newly minted community activists and talented educators. They insist that public schools can work, and work well, if they are constructed correctly and arranged for the interest of the communities and the students they purportedly serve; and this, they argue must include the notion of charter schools as meaningful educational reform. These progressive educators promote charter schools as a public reform measure in the interest of collaborative experimentation and a creative implementation of new ideas—as a way to save public education through reformation and change.

Because charter schools are governed by private boards, often nonprofit in nature though increasingly managed for profit as we shall see in subsequent chapters, advocates also argue that such schools are a way to assert community ownership of and control over schools and allow parents and educators to participate in and indeed compose, the agenda and curriculum development of schools. This, they say, is real ownership, real empowerment if you will. Many educational policymakers of all political stripes will also argue that charter schools provide a way to implement reforms without mandating them hierarchically within politically mired public school districts laced with tenured political strife and turmoil. These policymakers claim such school districts often fail to implement necessary reforms and changes owing to the highly charged and diverse educational debates that run rampant among the various constituencies that compose them; for them charter schools offer an answer.

WHAT IS A CHARTER SCHOOL?

To begin with, just what is a charter school? Charter schools are public schools under contract—called a charter. These contracts, or charters, are granted from a public agency to a group of parents, teachers, school administrators, nonprofit agencies (like but not limited to a school board), for-profit management groups, organizations, or businesses that wish to create an alternative to existing public schools. Charter schools receive public money and cannot legally discriminate or exclude students. They are also publicly accountable; thus, they are not private schools (National School Boards Association). This important distinction is often missed and it is also important to realize that charter schools are not alternative schools. Rather, they are legal entities that exist under a legal public contract and anyone who wishes to start a charter school must negotiate the contract, or charter, with the local school district or state body that is empowered to approve the charter. Charter schools are held to the educational accountability standards that have been adopted in their state and district in accordance with the federal No Child Left Behind (NCLB) Act of 2001.

Nearly all charter schools are either "conversions" (preexisting public schools or, less commonly, private schools transformed into charter schools) or more commonly start-ups (new schools that would not otherwise exist). Data from 2006-2007 reports the percentage of start-up and conversion charter schools and can be found in the National Charter School Research Project (NCSRP) study. Figures are from the 2006-2007 school year unless otherwise noted (Center on Reinventing Public Education, under "Data from 2006-2007 Reports").

Typically, contracts, or charters, are granted for a three - to five-year period but this can vary as we will see, state by state. The charter school receives public funding at or around the per-pupil level of other public schools in the district in which it operates, although debate abounds here as well. Charters are not allowed to charge tuition and they are funded according to enrollment. States such as Alaska, Colorado, Minnesota, and New Jersey, receive less than 100 percent of the funds allocated to their traditional counterparts for the operation of public schools. In other states, like California, additional funds or loans are made available to them. In most states, charters do not receive capital funds for facilities. They are entitled to federal categorical funding for which their students are eligible, such as Title I and Special Education monies. Federal legislation provides grants to help charters with start-up costs (Center on Reinventing Public Education, under "Federal Funding").

In the charter itself, the applicants must delineate and explain how the school will operate, what courses and curriculum will be offered, what outcomes will be achieved by students, and how state standards and assessment will measure these outcomes. The charter school must eventually marshal evidence, as a form of accountability, that students in the school have gained the knowledge and skills indicated in the charter. All charter schools operate within state guidelines, in accordance with No Child Left Behind.

Who Can Legally Authorize Charter Schools?

State law governs the provision of charter school authorization and because charter schools are a creature of state law, the rules and regulations that apply to them can vary greatly from state to state. From the type of authorizers allowed (school districts, universities, state boards of education, for-profit entities, municipalities, or other institutions), to the pace and process of charter school growth, each state has its own unique legislation establishing the charter environment for their citizens. For example, in Idaho the 1996 charter school law allows for local boards of trustees to authorize a charter school; in New York the law is more complex: for conversions, local school boards can be authorizers where for start-ups, the State University of New York Board of Trustees can act as the authorizer for up to 50 start-ups. The New York State Board of Regents can authorize up to 50 start-ups as well and for the New York City Public Schools, the local chancellor charters conversions and start-ups (U.S. Charter Schools, under "Charter School Legislation").

What Does "Public" Mean in the Context of Charter Schools?

In his book *What's Public about Charter Schools,* educational researcher Gary Miron notes that the issue regarding the "public-ness" of charter schools is far from academic and indeed has important consequences for how we think about the public realm as well as charter schools and their role. In Michigan, where three quarters of all charter schools are operated by private educational management companies, or what Miron in his work and others as well refer to as Educational Maintenance Organizations (EMOs), the issue has been the subject of court rulings (Miron 2002).

For example, on November 1, 1994, the issue of "what is a public institution" nearly stopped Michigan's experiment with charter schools dead in its tracks. The court declared that public school academies that operated in Michigan as charters, in spite of their name, were not public at all for they utilized an EMO to run and maintain their academies. Thus, the result of the court's decision was that public funding of the so-called "public schools" was therefore unconstitutional, the rationale being they were not really public schools. The "parochiad" amendment to the Michigan constitution, which was approved by referendum in 1970, clearly stated:

> No public monies or property shall be appropriated or paid or any public credit utilized, by the legislature or any other political subdivision or agency of the state directly or indirectly, to aid or maintain any private, denominational, or other nonpublic, preelementary, elementary, or secondary school. (Michigan State Constitution)

The plaintiffs in the case argued that the charter school law in Michigan violated this provision of the constitution for it allowed the use of private EMOs to govern and run the public schools outside the regular transparency of public school oversight. They were sustained. They also argued that the charter law represented an unconstitutional delegation of authority over public schooling, another argument that was also sustained by the court. Two years later, a Michigan appeals court upheld the lower court's decision, concluding that the schools are "run by an essentially private entity, outside the realm of public control" (Michigan Court of Appeals 1996), thus ruling the Michigan Charter School law actually violated the law.

Taking the issue up in 1996, the Michigan Supreme Court reversed, coming to a completely opposite decision in their judicial review of the 1996 appeal. The majority of the court disagreed that the charter school law constituted an improper delegation of authority to a private entity, EMOs, and went on to argue that schools are "public" not simply by virtue of the "exclusive control" of the state. They argued that "there is, in fact, no requirement that those schools be under the government's 'exclusive control.'" So, having now effectively rejected and dismissed the idea that schools must remain under the exclusive control of the state or government, the court went on to iterate three mechanisms by which the state maintains effective partial control and as a result why this partial control confers legality to the charter school law.

To begin with, the court argued, a school's charter can be revoked by the authorizing board if it does not live up to its promises. Second, because the authorizers of charter schools are themselves inventions of the state, this invention and subsequent jurisdiction of the state comprises in and of itself an effective form of partial state control and finally, the court noted that it is the state that controls the source of money to charter schools. In closing, the court in addressing the plaintiff's argument that charter schools are under the control of private boards or EMOs and thus really not "public," arrived at the judicial finding that *control over the process* provides a reasonable opportunity and thus legal basis for state control and that the state can change this process anytime it wished through legislation. What both the lower court and Supreme Court held in common was that a charter school is public as measured by the extent that the community and their legislative representatives have control over them. The Michigan Supreme Court decision provided an important precedent setting distinction that said although the government should *support* education, there is no need for the government to *run* it.

This distinction between "supporting a school" and "running a school," Miron argues, is crucial to understand the court's legal distinction when analyzing charter schools and he goes on to name the distinctions between the *formalist* views of public education and *functionalist* views of public education. The *formalist* definition of "public-ness" argues:

> *Since issues and delegation and control are properties of institutional forms, we refer to this view as the formalist point of public-ness. This view holds that schools (or other institutions) are public if they are either publicly owned or controlled by citizens or their duly constituted representatives. On this definition a charter school is*

public if there is some chain of political authority and influence that links voters to school decisions. This linkage may be mediated through various elected representatives, including school board members, state legislators and others. (Lubienski 2001)

Choice proponents, however, suggest a more flexible *functionalist* definition of public-ness. According to this view, a school (or any other institution) is public not by virtue of lines of authority and chains of influence, but by whether it performs important public functions. This view is fully consistent with the notion of "public use of private interest"—no matter who owns charter schools and no matter who controls and manages them they are public so long as they serve public purposes (i.e., produce positive externalities) such as raising Student achievement (Miron 2002). So would this then mean that corporate-owned hospitals would be "public"? After all, it could be argued they too serve a public purpose. Or corporate owned prisons? The court did not address this.

The definitions are not purely semantic, as the court noted, but instead offer real and tangible consequences and implications for the opening up, or deregulation of public institutions that have been traditionally considered private entities, in an effort to spur and enhance privatization of, in this case, public education. In this way, the argument proceeds, private schools can serve the public interest in the same way that for-profit media or for-profit fire stations or for-profit police stations would ensure the public interest. Arguably, if one adopted this theory in the same way, it would seem, private vouchers would also legally serve the public interest. Or, in the words of former Michigan State Board of Education president, W. Clark Durant:

. . . We must also have multiple educational providers who have the motivation of ownership and accountability. Let's have public corporations for a new kind of public education. Let's allow educational entrepreneurs to raise capital in public markets . . . enormous resources are available. Banks and financial service companies might start a school of business and finance. Automobile makers and their suppliers might start a school for engineers and other related professions. Our houses of faith can create and/or expand existing schools to offer a program to touch the heart and not just the mind. (Durant 1997, 363-364)

Using this logic, of course, one would, could, and does argue that McDonalds or Burger King could and can become providers of public education. But is this really public schooling or a legalistic maneuver to redefine private, for-profit interests as social public interests in an attempt to socialize the costs of education while privatizing the profits and opening a huge market for private investors and entrepreneurs? And what is the impact of the Michigan Supreme Court ruling on entrepreneurialism and commercialization in public schools in general? Does it, or will it unleash the veritable privatization of public schools under the formalistic definition established by the Michigan Supreme Court? If so, in what forms might it appear or in what forms has it already appeared? These questions and arguments go to the heart of charter school debate and will be examined closely in this book.

WHO SELECTS CHARTER SCHOOLS?

On average, the charter schools in most states seem to serve the same types of students that are found in regular public school systems. Studies have found that most charter schools are relatively small. Average school sizes state by state can be seen in the Charter School Research Department's state comparison data for 2006-2007 (Center on Reinventing Public Education, under "State Comparison Data"). As the data shows, other than Missouri the average size of a charter school is less than public schools state by state.

Charter schools can have an average of 41 students, as in the case of New Hampshire or as high as 547, as in the state of Illinois (Center on Reinventing Public Education, under "Size of a Charter School").

Data from 2006-2007 reports the percentage of start-up and conversion charter schools and can be found in the NCSRP study. Figures are from the 2006-2007 school year unless otherwise noted. Zeros indicate no schools in the category; blanks indicate that the state department of education did not respond to this part of the NCSRP survey (Center on Reinventing Public Education, Ibid.).

Numerically, the number of minority students enrolled in charter schools can be found in the NCSRP study as well. The figures provided are state aggregates and are from the 2006-2007 school year unless otherwise noted. Public school data includes all students in the state, not just students in districts near charter schools. Because most charter schools are located in urban areas with a higher proportion of minority students, this comparison is likely to overstate the difference between the types of schools. Zeros indicate no students in the category; blanks indicate that the state department of education did not respond to this part of the NCSRP survey. While in states like Louisiana 91 percent of their charter school students are minority students, the figure can be as low as 3 percent in states like New Hampshire (Center on Reinventing Public Education, under "State Comparison Data").

The average age of charter schools themselves are also revealed in the NCSRP study of 2004-2005 and represent an average age of one year to seven years, nationally, depending on the state (Ibid.).

Nationwide, the number of charter schools opened in the 2006-2007 school year was 336, almost ten percent of the total of all charter schools in existence, with the greatest proliferation of charters seen in Ohio, where 34 charter schools were open during the 2006-2007 school year alone (Ibid.).

DOES EVERYONE SUPPORT CHARTER SCHOOLS?

No, certainly not; there are many people who are not sold on the idea of charter schools at all. Many progressive educational policy analysts criticize charter schools for their potential to further stratify schools as well as communities along racial, socioeconomic, and other ethnic - and class-based lines. Many feel that charter schools may be the first step toward the privatization of education and are concerned that charter schools will skim, or "cream off," predominantly white, privileged students from public schools and thus contribute to the segregation of schools in the United States (Schwartz 1996, 4). They also argue that the propensity for charter schools to cream off students results in ethnically concentrated schools of choice and they are concerned about the ability of charter schools to provide services for all students, such as students with disabilities and special educational needs. And they are worried that exclusionary and selective admission policies and practices might contribute to racial and class imbalances among schools and promote the return of the concept of "separate but equal" along racial lines in the United States (Cobb and Glass 1999). Furthermore, they also level the claim and as well as surface the fear that this situation has the propensity to be accomplished institutionally through public policy measures such as charter school legislation, just as well as through an overt return to racial segregation.

Others argue that the growing array of educational venture capitalists and for-profit corporations that privately serve schools are driven not by educational concerns, but by the hopes of profitable business opportunities and the money to be made off the "educational market," which has increasingly been open to an eager group of entrepreneurs. These corporate forces, they argue, are joined at the hip with conservative politicians and right-wing market fundamentalists and ideologues who view charter schools as the "thin wedge" that will prepare American society for greater privatization in all walks of life; especially educational privatization—accomplished through the transformation of public schooling through vouchers and charters into a market driven by "consumer demand," not citizen needs. As we shall see, many argue that the "consumer demand" is served by emerging corporate, educational franchise chains that will bode well for corporations seeking to profit off private education, but will regrettably reduce if not destroy public educational opportunities for U.S. students. Of course these concerns are responded to by charter advocates and we will critically examine these arguments in full detail in subsequent chapters.

One institutional concern that is highlighted by progressive policymakers in the charter debate and which is disturbingly absent from charter school reform discussions, is the issue of transportation for inner-city students who often have to travel long distances to attend charter schools. On the issue of transportation, a Carnegie Foundation report in 1992 points out that for all public schools the median distance between families and their closest school is two miles, the median distance to the next closest school is four and a half miles, and for one in four families, the next closest school is between ten and eighty miles away (Carnegie Foundation 1992). This problem has now only exacerbated with the more than decade-long surge in suburban development bringing with it long hours spent in traffic to get to and from institutions.

Transportation is a large issue for charter schools for three reasons: one, the increase in the amount families must pay to send their children to charter schools in the form of higher gasoline prices and rising public transportation costs; two, the amount of time that children are forced to spend in transit to and from these schools, often sitting in buses in both the heat and cold depending on the state involved; and three, long commuter time for parents as well as the emergence of barriers to parental involvement in building strong local schools (Buckley and Schneider 2006).

Both scholars found that:

Simply put there are geographic differences in the way in which choice in New York and Washington D.C. is structured, and these differences may explain different outcomes. While the District of Columbia is blessed with an excellent public transit system (paid for with money from taxpayers throughout the country) and is a small city compared to New York, as a whole the city is larger than the individual school districts around which New York's school system is organized. The citywide nature of choice in D.C. affects the accessibility of schools to children and parents. As an indicator of how this factor affects choice, we found that the reported commuting time for D.C. charter students was almost 50 percent longer than that of public school students. (Buckley and Schneider 2006, 59)

The authors continue:

Clearly, the longer commuting time is a burden that is most heavily felt by the children who attend school everyday. The simple fact of geography may pose a difficult trade-off for advocates of school choice—small neighborhoods may not have the capacity to support many alternative schools, yet eliminating neighborhood-based schools to create a larger choice set may weaken parental involvement, one of the primary supports of quality education. (Buckley and Schneider 2006, 60)

Districts that have absorbed the cost of transportation have found that subsidizing transportation for charter schools can cost thousands of dollars or more in face of steep and rising oil prices. And just where is this money to come from? Many educators leery of charter schools claim that transportation is one of those institutional issues that must be vigilantly watched if charter schools are not to become an unassuming partner in a further stratification of society along racial and class lines through their impact on frail transportation structures and options.

Clearly, though, much of the bipartisan approach to charters continues to exist, ironically pointing to some interesting bedfellows in the movement. However, as we shall see many progressive educators argue that research has indicated, on average, that there has been little or no positive effect on student achievement nor on increased improvement in public schools although there have been unintended consequences, many which will be discussed in a later chapter (Carnoy et. al. 2005). Several studies also show increased student segregation, not simply by race, but also by test scores, socioeconomic class, and special education status (Bifulco and Ladd 2006; Cobb and Glass 1999; Howe et. al. 2001; Howe and Welner 2002). Along with these arguments many educational policymakers would also argue that among the unintended outcomes of the charter school movement are adverse budgetary consequences to local public school districts (Plank and Sykes 2003).

The debate regarding charter schools, although arguably still in its infancy forces many crucial questions that need to be asked. Some of the questions are: Do charter schools have a responsibility to parents and students to offer a diverse community of learners? Will charter schools lead to a further segregation of U.S. schools and the privatization of education? Are "market driven choices" really good for students, parents, society, and education? Will competition really increase educational performance both within charter and among public schools? Will charter schools truly provide choice to all constituencies regardless of ethnic or class background, disability, or ethnicity? Will transportation to and from these schools be subsidized by districts or paid for by the students and their parents? Does choice really help bring about reform in public education in the myriad of ways proponents claim? Will charters put pressure on the entire public school system to engage in self-corrective practices and policies? Are charter schools really community-based schools and are they really accountable to their communities? Should we allow public schools to be run as educational maintenance organizations by for-profit companies? Do charter schools have a civic obligation to achieve the ethnic representation of the community, given that they are schools of choice with no local attendance boundaries to confine their ethnic compositions? In what ways should the state intervene in cases of de facto segregation or inequity? What should the admission policies look like? These, and no doubt many more questions, are just a few of the important issues that must be addressed as we assess the impact and implications of charter schools as an educational reform movement.

Whether supported as an innovative idea or rejected as a debilitating fancy it is certain that the growth of charter schools can claim to be one of the most interesting and controversial experiments in education for many decades. In many ways, the growth of the charter school movement parallels a movement away from traditional, mass industrial approaches to educational problems and controversies. The movement can really be said to be part of a postmodern, decentralized attempt to wrestle with educational controversy by promoting the fundamentalism of markets—a call for a shift from centralized systems of public control and organization to a more decentralized, market-driven devolutionary environment. But is it simply a reform that will die on its own accord or will it transform the educational landscape to the betterment of community and educational stakeholders? According to charter school researcher, Amy Wells, the slow growth of charter schools since 1991 has led her to claim:

> *Thus, I speculate that charter school reform is a late 20th century, laissez faire reform that will die on its own weight sometime early in the 21st century. This is not to say that all the existing charter schools will fold; many of them could continue for years, as have some public alternative schools from the 1960s to the 1970s. But it is very clear to anyone who spends a great deal of time in charter schools that this is not a public policy that will transform the public educational system into a more effective, efficient, or academically accountable system. (Wells 2002, 2)*

The success or failure of the charter school movement is subject to important debate and will continue to have unimaginable implications for the way we, as a nation, think about education and organize schooling. Improvement in student achievement; local control; issues of equity, teaching for citizenship and critical thinking issues of race, gender, and class; and the impact of charter schools on public school systems—all of these issues and more still remain to be explored and analyzed. It may take years to actually trace, analyze, and understand the impact of charter schools but we do have much information after more than seventeen years of state-by-state experimentation. With charter laws in existence in more than forty states and the District of Colombia research is becoming available and people interested in education—from teachers to students and from parents to politicians—are looking at this controversial educational movement with watchful eyes. In later chapters, this book will examine the public policy questions surrounding the charter school movement in more depth.

HOW DO CHARTER SCHOOLS DIFFER FROM OTHER REFORMS?

It is important for our discussion to distinguish between charter schools and other educational reform movements, with which they are often confused.

Vouchers

Although both charter schools and the voucher proposal demand choice and argue that competition is the key to increased public school performance and accountability, the charter school concept is significantly different from the voucher movement. For example, the charter school reform concept provides parents with a *public* choice as to which school they wish their children to attend—

not a *private* choice. Families who are given private vouchers for a specific amount of public money are thus given a *private* choice. They can use the money to pay tuition at their choice of school—be it public, parochial, or private. Although numerous voucher proposals have been put forward, and many of them have been implemented in one or more states (Friedman 1973), they differ dramatically from the charter school concept in four distinct ways (Nathan 1996, under "Early Lessons").

First, and generally, charter schools cannot be sectarian. Vouchers allow students to attend either a public or a private parochial school, but public funds, which pay for charter schools, cannot be used for sectarian or private school education. Second, in most states, charter school legislation does not allow schools to pick and choose among applicants on the basis of previous achievement or behavior. This restriction differs dramatically from the voucher concept as voucher plans state that schools may choose the students who will attend the schools in any way the schools wish. This difference in admission policy has been one of the key reasons why charter schools have been accepted and embraced as an idea for educational reform by many public school defenders. However, how this restriction translates into practice—as mentioned earlier regarding race, equity, "skimming," "creaming," and other selective admission policies—is the subject of debate.

Third, voucher proposals permit private and parochial schools to charge as much tuition as they wish, above and beyond the public money given to parents for their children, and parents must then pay the difference with their own money. Charter schools, on the other hand, cannot charge any tuition beyond the state allocation they receive.

The final difference between vouchers and charter schools is the explicit responsibility for documenting student achievement. To keep and renew their charters, charter schools are held publicly accountable to state educational standards and the No Child Left Behind (NCLB) Act and must demonstrate that their students are improving their skills and expanding their knowledge base. Voucher schools, on the other hand, have no public accountability requirements and no responsibility to publicly document or assure student achievement other than that proposed by the school itself.

However, voucher and charter schools share at least two important and essential characteristics that distinguish them from conventional public schools:

1. Admission by choice—No student is assigned to attend either a charter or voucher school. Students and parents choose such schools.
2. Market accountability—The choice to attend a voucher or charter school is partially or completely subsidized by public funds that are tied to student enrollment. This means funds reach charter and voucher schools as a result of both public policy and a family's decision to enroll a child in such schools.

Magnet Schools

Magnet schools are public schools with specialized curricula designed to attract particular students from within a given school district. They are often found in urban districts as part of a desegregation or student-at-risk program. Their stated intent is to bring students together from distinct and diverse racial and cultural backgrounds to share a common educational experience. Unlike other public schools, many magnet schools have admission tests and requirements (Steel and Levine 1994). Also, the amount of money spent on a magnet school within a local school district can be far more than that spent on other schools in the same district. Surveys have found that magnet schools in Chicago, Philadelphia, Boston, and New York received extra resources beyond those given to other local public schools in the same state (Hughes 1988). Magnet schools are often given greater funding because they are often perceived as being experimental and innovative. Their intention is not to create communities of learning that will compete with other public schools; they are part and parcel of the public school process and offer innovation within the system.

By contrast, a key distinction in the charter school strategy is that charter schools do not receive more than the state per-pupil average spent on education. This distinction becomes, for charter school advocates, a case of financial equity. Many charter school proponents argue that if charter schools are really to meet the challenges of educational innovation and thus show the value of public school choice, they should do so with the same per-pupil financial resources the other public schools receive. In other words, the public choice competition should occur on a level playing field with regard to funding. However, the costs of beginning and starting a charter school can be high, and these costs are often met through obtaining private grants and corporate sponsorship.

Also, magnet schools are under no requirement to demonstrate that the skills and knowledge of their students have improved whereas charter schools are held publicly accountable for student achievement and student improvement through their contractual relationship with the public. Finally, magnet schools are started exclusively by school districts while charters can be sponsored, depending on the state, by a host of patrons.

School-Based Management

On-site school-based management (SBM), or what is often called shared *decision-making,* differs from the charter concept in one important manner—accountability and responsibility for student performance and achievement. Although charter schools are required to document and demonstrate improvement in the achievement and performance of students, there is no accountability requirement with regard to the school site-management concept. Since the 1960s, SBM has been operating in various schools throughout the nation.

Although the SBM reform has taken on many forms and purposes, it seems that the core goals are decentralization of authority and the management of budgetary issues, along with on-site decision making at schools (Corwin and Schneider 2007). The SBM idea derives from the belief that if schools are run by the faculty, administrators, and parents, in a partnership so to speak, the schools will be more effective because educational decisions will be made by the educational stakeholders. Delegating authority to on-site councils, site-management advocates claim, will increase student achievement and have a direct and positive impact on how schools are run and operated. Critical decisions about budget, personnel, curriculum, and instruction can be made by on-site management councils or similar governing bodies made up of diverse interested parties, and this fact, advocates maintain, puts the politics of education and educational decisions directly where they belong—in the hands of parents, teachers, administrators, and students. However, as we shall see, this function is increasingly being contracted out by many public schools to for-profit, school-based management companies.

And although many charter school advocates probably would agree with decentralizing control and power to the school site, they argue that along with the power to make decisions, must come the power to be held accountable to some set of educational standards. Furthermore, they argue, on-site management, by itself, has done little to achieve effectiveness and higher educational performance (Summers and Johnson 1994).

For most charter schools, on-site management is relevant in how these schools organize their decision making and problem solving regarding educational issues. For charter advocates, on-site management within charter schools is seen more as a way of governance than as an end in itself.

WHY CHARTER SCHOOLS?

There are many reasons why the charter school movement has become so popular. The idea of allowing parents and teachers to create the types of schools they feel will work for them and their communities, is just common sense according to charter advocates. When that fact is coupled with the myriad of competing philosophies as to what education should be accomplishing, the content of curricula, and what students need to know, charter schools seem like a good idea to some. Also, many, if not most people believe that public schools should and could do a better job of helping our nation's young increase their knowledge acquisition and develop critical-thinking skills and the argument that market competition will reform existing public schools is widely appealing. And while the debate rages over the efficacy of the job public schools are doing, the impetus for the charter school movement, in large part, rests on the assumption that the public schools are not doing enough; indeed, that they are failing.

A Nation at Risk, a highly controversial report published in 1983 by the U.S. Department of Education, was highly critical of student achievement in the country's public schools, and in addition to this popular and media-sensationalized report, many educational stakeholders, from parents to teachers, from administrators to students, have historically been concerned that the public school system is not serving the needs of low-income families, varied racial constituencies, and the newly arriving immigrant populations that have increased dramatically since the 1980s. We will look at the incentives and controversies that surround the political realities of the charter movement in a subsequent chapter, but to answer the question: why charter schools? It is important to examine the philosophical tenets of the movement (A Nation at Risk, 1983).

EDUCATIONAL CHOICE

As noted earlier, the impetus for the charter school movement can be found in the idea of "educational choice." The concept is quite simple. The central argument of advocates of choice is that market competition provides the best or most efficient way to change the way public schools function. Arguing that removing regulations, dismantling educational bureaucracies, and decentralizing schools will produce better schools, charter school proponents say they look to such schools to be both beacons for a new alternative to public schools and a force to move the public schools toward greater levels of excellence. The Hudson Institute has stated the case for charters succinctly:

> The charter concept is simple but powerful: Sound school choices can be provided to families under the umbrella of public education without micro-management by government bureaucracies. Independent schools that are open to all, paid for with tax dollars, accountable to public authorities for student learning and other results, and subject to basic health, safety, and nondiscrimination requirements, are legitimate public schools even if they are governed or managed by a committee of parents, a team of teachers, the local Boys and Girls Club, or a profit seeking firm. (Hudson Institute 1997, pt. 6, 2)

From the viewpoint of many liberals and conservatives, charter schools are based on the concept that market competition, and only market competition, will drive reform and educational change. Therefore, they (charters) must be seen within the privatization of education. Veteran charter proponent and pioneer in the movement, Ted Kolderie has written:

> The intent of charter schools is not simply to produce a few new and hopefully better schools; it is to create dynamics that will cause the mainline system to change so as to improve education for all students. (Kolderie 1993, 1)

Joe Nathan, another leading reformer in the charter school movement nationwide, adds:

> *The goal of the charter movement is not just to establish innovative schools, but also to help improve the public education system. Charter schools provide families with choices and give skilled, entrepreneurial educators an opportunity, with accountability, to create more effective public schools. They also allow fair competition for public school districts. (Nathan 1996, xxviii)*

The primary assumption behind the dynamic then, is to put competitive pressure on conventional schools—or so it is stated, with the dramatic expectation they will improve. Many charter school advocates argue that school districts without charter school programs find it easier to ignore the demands for the development of responsive schools that are continually improving and changing. Thus, the argument goes charter schools "light fires" under overly bureaucratic and failing school districts. But is this really the goal? Or is the goal to do away with public schools entirely by moving towards a model of outsourcing of educational services, from management of schools to construction?

The people who are wary of the charter idea would argue that upon closer scrutiny, it seems that the market competition envisioned by charter school advocates as a result of charter school choice is designed to fiscally punish the conventional public schools by imposing costs on the school districts, thus seeking to dismantle them. After all, they argue, when students choose to attend a charter school, that fact removes money from conventional districts as the fiscal system is so designed that the public funding follows the students. As a result, it is likely that school districts will alter their practices, adopt new ideas and innovations, confront financial difficulties, or all of the above (Hassel 1999, 6). That the charter school reform is "designed" to bankrupt traditional public schools is an argument that we will examine more closely in subsequent chapters.

But just who are the charter school advocates? According to Tom Watkins, director of the Detroit Center for Charter Schools, charter school advocates fall into one of three categories:

1. Zealots, who believe that private is always better than public, market systems are always superior to public systems, unions always cause problems, and students at private and religious schools outperform their public counterparts;
2. Entrepreneurs, who hope to make money running schools or school programs; and
3. Reformers—students, parents, and teachers—who want to expand public school options and improve systems of education (Watkins 1995, 40). The list provides an interesting mixture of bedfellows.

It is undoubtedly entrepreneurial educators who have provided a large impetus for charter schools through neoconservative foundations, think tanks, philanthropic organizations and networking associations that use their media savvy in an attempt to sell the idea of market competition and charter schools to the general population. This has been going on since the 1980s through such think tanks as the Heritage Foundation, The American Enterprise Institute, The Thomas Fordham Foundation, and other advocates of educational markets.

According to the Education Industry Association, a trade association of educational entrepreneurs:

Education is rapidly becoming a $1 trillion industry, representing 10 percent of America's GNP and second in size only to the health care industry. Federal and State expenditures on education exceed $750 billion. Education companies, with over $80 billion in annual revenues, already constitute a large sector in the education arena.

The Education Industry plays an increasingly important role in supporting public education by meeting the demand for products and services that both complement and supplement basic education services. These include after-school tutoring providers, school improvement and management services, charter schools, alternative education and special education services, professional development for teachers and administrators, educational content providers and suppliers, as well as rapidly growing private providers of undergraduate and graduate education.

Early entrepreneurs from these organizations turned to each other for peer support, networking, professional development and advocacy and formed the Association of Educators in Private Practice (AEPP) in 1990. In 2002, the organization was renamed the Education Industry Association (EIA) to reflect the breadth of enterprises engaged in market-based education services.

Today, the EIA, with over 800 corporate and individual members, is the leading professional association for private providers of education services, suppliers and other private organizations who are stakeholders in education.

EIA is a broad-based organization that represents the collective strengths and contributions of the multifaceted education industry—an organization that projects a reasoned and positive voice for innovators in the supply of academic services. (Education Industry Association, under "Organization Information")

A look at EIA's board of directors reveals a list of entrepreneurial organizations such as EduVentures, Nation Heritage Academy, Scholastic, the Milton and Rose D. Friedman Foundation, Edison Schools, Educational Services of America, The Aspen Education Cooperative, and many more that we will cover in chapter five (Education Industry Association, under "Board of Directors").

In a "White Paper" prepared for the Education Industry's Leadership Board in 2002, speaking about the Association of Education Practitioners and Providers (AEPP), a think tank and network organization launched in 2002 by EIA, educational entrepreneur, Michael Sandler, noted that:

As the industry association, the AEPP is a valuable resource for networking and professional development. Through its members, AEPP provides professional contacts, technical support, business advice, operating models, and encouragement for entrepreneurs. The AEPP has also established a sister foundation, The Educators in Private Practice Foundation (EPPF), that both provides a funding vehicle for industry research and education coordinates activities of The Education Industry Leadership Board.

Writing about charter schools, the same report goes on to state:

The charter school movement provided an important stimulus to market growth by creating a more favorable environment in which schools could contract with private providers. Prior to charter school legislation, most state laws did not prohibit contracting by schools, but school boards typically did not want to face the inevitable grievances from local teacher's unions, which would entail costly litigation. Under charter school legislation, charter schools were better able to contract with private providers without facing union barriers. This provided a critical driver for education companies seeking to work with public schools. As opportunities in the education market increased in the mid-1990s on the wings of the charter school movement, many existing educational entrepreneurs discovered new opportunities in the charter field. Lavelle and Hall launched new companies (Total Education Solutions and Education Management Systems), while others such as Ombudsman expanded their existing offerings to the charter field. Smaller companies such as AEPP President Lynne Master's Learning Disabilities Clinic and Sue Fino Learning Styles began doing business with charters as providers of education services.

Not surprisingly, along with organizations like EIA, such political think tanks as the Hudson Institute, the Heritage Foundation, the Thomas Fordham Foundation, the Cato Institute and many, many more, have combined with leading financial institutions such as Montgomery Securities, Salomon Smith Barney, Lehman Brothers, Banc of America, CSFirst Boston, Parchman and Vaughn and Capital Market, to name a few, to carve out a new and distinct "single industry" for a burgeoning and now close to one trillion dollar business interest in education (Education Industry Association, under "Think Tanks and Financial Institutions").

Yet many if not most parents and their children have no idea of the booming business in, nor the development of, an educational industry. From the point of view of parents and students, the main political attraction of the charter school movement lies in the fact that it promises to give people of various social, political, cultural, and philosophical backgrounds who are disconnected from the educational system in one way or another an alternative to the regular public schools, i.e., a choice. This demand for "choice" among educational stakeholders led to more than 1,000 charter schools nationwide in just eight years (Wells et al. 1999, 3). Currently, the number of charter schools that have been launched has risen to 3,000 (U.S. Charter Schools, under "Charter Schools Launched").

Nor, as we shall see, does everybody agree that market competition as a result of choice is the prescription for what plagues public schools. Critics of the idea not only claim that charter schools have the propensity to cream off the best and the most motivated students but also they argue that the charter school idea leaves regular public schools unable to compete. They maintain that the public schools will suffer from race and class segregation and that charter schools will find ways to deny students with special needs in an attempt to stave off high costs. These people also contend that those schools not chartered will suffer from shoddy educational practices and that charter schools will serve only a handful of students while siphoning off resources that could be devoted to improving the public schools. So, claim critics, school reform that is separated and disconnected from the larger context of financial inequality and power relations in society—the institutional organization of power, control, and authority, cannot hope to work and can really only exacerbate existing problems.

According to this line of reasoning, because of the uneven distribution of material resources across communities, charter school reform essentially serves to fragment or atomize public education into smaller entities—so many bee-bees in a bag, so to speak; the creation of chains of "schools," as opposed to districts. Also, such reasoning maintains that the isolation and separation of poor communities from each other and from rich communities is actually exacerbated by charter schools (Wells et al. 1999, 19; Wells 2002; Corwin and Schneider 2007; Miron and Nelson 2002). By segregating and separating the wealthy from the non-wealthy, critics claim it is difficult for members of poor, isolated communities to build coalitions based on mutual interests with people who have both the political and the economic means to invest in public services such as schools (Massey and Denton 1993).

In a work entitled *School Choice* (1992), for example, the Carnegie Foundation has argued that advocates for choice have overwhelmingly concentrated their focus on its alleged benefits to individuals and have paid little, if any, attention to how education serves communal and civic purposes. The book states: "Adopting a language of the marketplace, education is portrayed as a solitary act of consumerism. Under systems of choice, advocates say, one can shop around for a school, much as one shops for a VCR, or a new car. The purpose of the enterprise, we are told is to satisfy 'the customer'" (Carnegie Foundation 1992, 86). The report goes on to argue for the importance of a neighborhood school and is less interested in the ability of students to move freely from one school to another than in the freedom for schools to make their own decisions without webs of regulation.

Ronald Corwin and Joseph Schneider go further, arguing that we live in an individualistic society segregated by wealth and race—consequently, schools continue to struggle to find innovative ways to educate poor children who come to schools without the advantages of their more affluent classmates. Without acknowledging this fact, they argue, the current educational system cannot count on the growth of freewheeling charter schools to reform or ameliorate the educational problems associated with schooling in a class society (Corwin and Schneider, 2007). In fact, some would argue they can only aggravate the problem facing education in America.

The Privatization and Deregulation of Schools

As we have discussed, advocates of charter schools claim that one of the central objectives of charter schools is to empower classroom teachers, administrators, and parents by giving them the opportunity to create the schools that they feel will serve and help students learn. However, as noted researcher and educational writer, Amy Wells notes:

> *There is yet another political theme that shaped the demand for charter school reform and that is the age-old call for decentralization and giving more control over governance and decision making to the local school community. Like the market metaphor the call for greater decentralization is, for some anyway, an attack on government—at least federal and state government—involvement in education. The political theme also more closely links charter school reform to what have become known as "new social movements," because it represents localized activity around issues of recognition, identity, difference, voice, and empowerment. (Wells 2002, 7)*

Whereas corporate privatization by vouchers seeks to remove control from teachers and parents and place this control within those private companies who run these schools, charter schools, so the argument goes, seek to place control of the schools directly in the hands of the educational stakeholders. At least, that is the stated claim of many proponents (Kolderie 1993, 1). But does the rhetoric match the evidence?

The movement toward market-driven solutions for perceived public educational problems has fostered the reemergence of a private voucher system that was first advocated about 1955. Market-driven solutions to educational issues promise that unregulated free choice between private and public schools will serve as a panacea for what ails education in the United States. Market-reform advocates argue that allowing parents to choose between a private and a public school will increase competition among the schools and benefit educational reforms systemwide. They advocate giving parents public vouchers so the parents can choose any school—sectarian or nonsectarian, private or public.

Charter schools are a form of public choice only, which means that charter schools remain public schools and are thus held to public accountability standards as well as being accountable to state and federal laws regarding equal protection and separation of church and state. Public choice differs from private choice when parents are able to choose among public schools, some of which are charter schools. Under charters, parents are not given public money that they might use to send their children to private schools.

The privatization of education as an answer to what ails U.S. schools has been hotly debated within the educational and political system for some time now. And although the debate has focused primarily on providing public vouchers to send children to private schools, the hiring of private companies to run public schools is also closely associated with privatization, and, as we will see, private companies are increasingly being used to manage and run charter schools. This social and economic arrangement allows for the payment of public monies to these private companies because they are contracted to run and thus manage public schools. These commercial educational companies appeal to local school districts to give them contracts to run and operate public charter schools within the designs, concepts, and curricula developed by the private companies. The companies then hire the teachers who carry out the formulated educational curriculum and plans. This practice seems in theory to be precisely the opposite of the goals of charter schools because the great majority of charter schools claim to be based on a philosophy that is the opposite to that of privately run public schools. Whether this difference actually exists in every case is another question that this book promises to explore further.

Those that advocate a market metaphor for school reform embrace charters, arguing that the best way to improve public education for all students, not just students in charters, is to force schools to compete. This is done, so market advocates argue, by metaphorically looking at students as "consumers" of education and providing greater opportunities to students and their parents through charter school choice. This argument is the backbone of the argument market proponents for educational reform make precisely because it contains one underlying moral and economic value: that by acting as self-interested individualized consumers and rational profit maximizers in the private choice-driven market of education, improvement of the educational system will be freed from the constraints of large bureaucratic regulatory systems (Chubb and Moe 1990; Cookson 1994; Friedman 1973) and parents and students will emerge victorious. The symbolic appeal of "choice" simply cannot be underestimated in the current educational policy arguments that prevail today.

At points there is a redrawing of liberal concerns into conservative political policies. The call for choice is an illustration—a political and economic metaphor that maintains a broad symbolic appeal regardless of partisanship. In the presidential election year of 2008, both candidates, Barack Obama and John McCain, favored bolstering charter schools nationwide. Democrat Barack Obama promised to double funding for charter schools (Pickler, Nedra Associated Press) while Republican John McCain supported expanding virtual learning through virtual charter schools. Like market reform proponents, both candidates argued that if parents chose the school that their children attend, market forces will produce motivation and achievement among those who previously had no choice (Popkewitz 2007, 141).

It is also important to note that the franchise model of education is related to privatization occurring in most all other sectors of economy, culture, and politics. The advocacy of market-based reforms as a corrective in educational reform by exercising individual choice has been closely aligned with the deregulation of many social institutions over the past thirty years, or what some sociologists and political economists call "neoliberal" economic and political policies. For the last thirty years individualized "choice" approaches have been advocated for everything from pensions and retirement, to educational savings accounts for colleges and secondary schools, to the privatization of health care. The fall of the former Soviet Union as well as the fall of communism in Eastern Europe only strengthened this economic policy view among powerful public policy elites. Thus, it is of little wonder that in 1996 Lester Thurow, a leading neoliberal economist, remarked, in accordance with Milton Friedman, that: The market, and the market alone, rules. No one doubts it (Thurow 1996, 1).

There is little doubt that the urge for deregulation and privatization of public bureaucratic systems exhibited in the last thirty years has been one of the most prominent themes in the charter school debate (Yergin and Stanislaus 1998, Wells 2002).

Yet as we shall discuss in depth, not all economists agree. David Kotz argues:

> *Nor is it (neoliberalism) a paragon of the economic rationality that offers the best "route to optimum efficiency, rapid economic growth and innovation, and rising prosperity for all who are willing to work hard and take advantage of available opportunities. (Kotz 2003)*

Educator, activist, and writer Henry Giroux, argues that on the contrary:

> *. . . neoliberalism is an ideology of politics buoyed by the spirit of a market fundamentalism that subordinates the art of democratic politics to the rapacious laws of a market economy that expands its reach to include all aspects of social life within the dictates and the values of a market-driven society. (Giroux 2004)*

Since the 1980s, inarguably, privatization has become the dominant economic ideology of not just national capitalism, but of global capitalism as well. Under these policies and institutions the world has witnessed the rise of monetarism, privatization, and deregulation. Nowhere can this be more evident than in the new "direction" of public policy as it relates to education and charters in particular. Whatever political, socioeconomic position one takes, neoliberalism has indeed become the broad-based political and cultural movement of our times and nowhere can this be evidenced more than in the rapid and transformational effects this form of social and economic policy has had on our nation's schools. Charters are thus as much an outgrowth of current and historical economic transformations as they are a pacesetter in the dominant ideology towards "deregulating" schools. They are, thus, historically birthed "creatures," if you will, and only time will tell if they offer any "reforms" to the problems that plague public education and its constituencies.

The Debate over Educational Standards and Assessment

With the reauthorization of Elementary and Secondary Education Act and the passage of the No Child Left Behind (NCLB) Act in 2002, the federal government revised the existing federal accountability framework for education to apply to all public school districts within the fifty states. The passage of the new law introduced new measures, specifically mandated tests, stated to make schools more accountable for academic outcomes. Some aspects of the revised law require not only annual assessment of student learning by virtue of standardized testing, but also a timeline specifying consequences for schools not meeting state-determined proficiency targets, consideration of significantly more dramatic school restructuring options, and a much stronger impetus for improvement from the federal rather than state level.

One of the particular provisions of NCLB provides that schools that fail to make adequate yearly progress (AYP) for five consecutive years must engage in restructuring of some form. Districts have several options for restructuring these schools. Although they may be constrained to choose an option that is consistent with existing state law, some of the things districts can do to restructure under the No Child Left Behind Act are:

- reopen the school as a public charter school;
- replace "all or most of the school staff (which may include the principal) who are relevant to the failure to make adequate yearly progress";
- contract with "an outside entity, such as a private management company, with a demonstrated record of effectiveness, to operate the school";
- turn the "operation of the school over to the state educational agency, if permitted under State law and agreed to by the State"; and
- engage in another form of major restructuring that makes fundamental reforms, "such as significant changes in the school's staffing and governance, to improve student academic achievement in the school and that has substantial promise of enabling the school to make adequate yearly progress" (U.S. Department of Education 2003 under "No Child Left Behind").

The chartering option under the NCLB Act needs to be distinguished from simply contracting, which refers to an agreement under which an outside organization delivers comprehensive educational and management services to a school (The Center for Comprehensive School Reform and Improvement 2005). Conceptually contracting is similar to chartering but differs in the legal relationship between the district and the entity that governs the school. In a contracting relationship, an external entity provides food services or educational and/or management services to a school according to the terms of a contract with the district. The governing board of a charter school, on the other hand, receives a charter—enabled and often partly defined by state law—from the district, and it may or may not choose to contract with an external provider for educational and management services (Ibid., 2005).

So, given the debate that is currently raging regarding the type of standards and assessments that should be used in public schools, the question arises as to the difference between the concept of charter schools and the standards and accountability debate itself. If charters are held to the same standards as traditional public schools, then where is the innovation, where is the deregulation? First, it is necessary to understand the federal law; the No Child Left Behind (NCLB) Act which governs educational accountability for public schools.

Charters are public schools that are subject to the accountability requirements of NCLB. If the charter school fails to meet adequate yearly progress set forth under the NCLB Act (AYP), then the charter school authorizer must take actions as required and specified by NCLB.

According to the Department of Education:

> *If a child attends a Title I school that has been designated by the state to be in need of improvement or unsafe, parents can choose to send the child to another public school. Districts must let parents know each year if their child is eligible to transfer to another school, and districts must give parents at least two transfer schools to choose from. Additionally districts must pay for students' transportation costs, giving priority to low-income, low-achieving students if there are not enough funds available to pay for all students. (U.S. Department of Education, under "Parents School Choice")*

The NCLB also provides money for extra educational assistance for poor children in return for improvements in their academic progress. NCLB is the most recent version of the 1965 Elementary and Secondary Education Act. Under the U.S. Constitution, states have the primary responsibility for public education. However, if states want to receive federal NCLB funds, they must agree to the law's requirements specifying that they:

- establish learning standards, that is, statements of what children in that state should know and be able to do in reading, math and other subjects, at various grade levels;

- create annual assessments (standardized tests, in most states) to measure student progress in reading and math in grades 3-8 and once in high schools;
- set a level (cut-off score) at which students are considered proficient in tested areas; and
- report to the public on what percentage of students are proficient, with the information broken down by race, income, disability, language proficiency, and gender subgroups (U.S. Department of Education, Ibid.).

The goal of the law, or so it is stated, is that all students will score at the "proficient" level in reading and math by 2014 on largely standardized tests. States are required to set annual targets for the percentage of students scoring proficient with the final goal of 100 percent proficiency by 2014. Each year, students in every subgroup must reach the target or there are consequences for schools.

For example, under the law after one year, schools failing to make annual yearly progress (AYP) are placed on a "school improvement" list. Students attending schools that do not make AYP for two years in a row are given the option to transfer to another school. Schools on the list for three consecutive years must provide supplemental services for their students, such as tutoring or after-school programs. After four years on the list, schools must, in addition to the above, do at least one of the following: replace school staff, use new curriculum, decrease school management authority, appoint outside experts, extend the school year/day, or restructure completely. After five consecutive years, schools face restructuring, such as firing staff, privatization, charter school management, state takeover, or other comparable changes; districts also face similar sanctions. So, if the state's charter laws allow a public school to convert to charter status, this is not only allowed under NCLB, but actually encouraged.

Section 1111(b)(2)(K) of the Elementary and Secondary Education Act of 1965, as amended by the No Child Left Behind Act of 2001 (NCLB) and Section 200.49(f) of the final Title I regulations (67 Fed. Reg. 71710, 71727, to be codified at 34 C.F.R. Pt. 200) require accountability for charter schools to be overseen in accordance with State charter school law. Thus, a State's charter school law determines the entity within the State that bears responsibility for ensuring that charter schools comply with the Title I, Part A accountability provisions, including AYP. The charter authorizer is responsible for holding charter schools accountable for Title I, Part A provisions unless State law specifically gives the SEA direct responsibility for charter school accountability. We do not expect the LEA in which the charter school is located to be this entity, unless it is also the charter authorizer (U.S. Department of Education 2003, under "No Child Left Behind").

NCLB requires that authorizers monitor their charter schools to ensure they are meeting the state's AYP definition. If they wish, authorizers may incorporate the AYP definition into their charter contracts. Charter authorizers have the responsibility for oversight of the NCLB Act. State charter laws currently require charter schools to participate in the state's assessment system for public schools in the state (U.S. Department of Education 2003, Ibid.).

The debate over standards and educational accountability varies depending on whom one talks to on the political spectrum yet one thing is clear: As long as the federal law mandates that students reach specific educational goals that are measured by standardized tests, charter schools will continue to have to meet these goals or face the economic and political consequences. Charter schools attempt to influence this debate about standards by providing educational choices for parents and students in terms of how their children will meet the standards, but the standards are largely dictated by the No Child Left Behind Act.

So, instead of creating their own standards for accountability, charter schools are held to the educational standards adopted by a particular state and local district (National School Boards Association). Thus, they may participate in the state, district, or federal debate regarding standards and assessment, but they cannot create their own assessment outside of the state or district purview and of course this purview is commandeered and mandated by the NCLB Act.

Although most states require charter school students to participate in statewide assessments, some authorizers, like the Chicago Public Schools, also require their charter schools to participate in districtwide assessments. Charter school operators thus need to work closely with their authorizers to understand exactly what is required in terms of accountability. According to U.S. Charter Schools it is important to ask questions such as:

> What assessments will actually measure whether that curriculum has been learned? Ideally, a combination of portfolios; projects; simulations; and norm-referenced, criterion-referenced, or other assessments will provide a rich picture of student learning. Consider instruments that appropriately measure important student objectives, reflect the vision of the school, and do not adversely affect the learner. (U.S. Charter Schools)

Many charter schools adopt unique and innovative ways of measuring student progress other than the traditional standardized tests—though those are used as well. For example, in a May 1999 study, the U.S. Department of Education assembled a cross-state comparison of the estimated percentage of schools using various types of assessment instruments. The study indicated that in an attempt to meet state standards and assess and evaluate student performance:

> Most charter schools reported that they used standardized assessments of student achievement 86 percent of the time, and 75 percent of the charter schools used tests as part of the state's assessment program. Most charter schools reported using stu-

dent demonstration of knowledge as a way of measuring the school's achievement. Seventy-nine percent used student portfolios and 70 percent used performance assessments to measure student progress. (U.S. Charter Schools, under "Accountability: Standards, Assessment, and Using Data")

The study also found that assessment methods were generally consistent for both newly created and preexisting public schools. The study found that preexisting private schools were slightly less likely to use performance assessments, student portfolios, parent surveys, and behavioral indicators to evaluate student performance. On the other hand, preexisting public schools were slightly more likely to use student surveys and behavioral indicators (U.S. Department of Education, under "The State of Charter Schools: National Study of Charter Schools"). Thus, charter schools, arguably provide unique and varied opportunities for children to meet state educational standards as they are aligned with the No Child Left Behind act.

In sum, charter advocates argue that market driven educational choices will create a climate of competition among public schools so that all public schools will feel the need to increase their students' performance and knowledge as measured by standardized tests under NCLB. Arguing they are putting pressure on the traditional public schools to raise their expectations of students and test scores through competition, many charter school advocates declare the charter movement is essential in improving the country's educational performance. The assumption is that students do better on standardized tests when they are driven by competitive schools to do so.

WHY EDUCATIONAL STAKEHOLDERS CHOOSE CHARTER SCHOOLS

In the 1980s, the development of school choice was believed to be a conservative market educational reform recommendation and for many, it still is. At that time, opinion polls consistently showed majority support for school choice, but it depended a lot on who was asked. In 1986, for instance, a Gallup poll showed that 54 percent of nonwhites supported publicly funded private school choice (Brighouse 1999, 22). Yet, arguably as we terminated the first decade of the new millennium, choice continued to receive a boost from the conviction held by many individuals of all political persuasions that public education is mired in bureaucracy and failure, particularly in the large cities, and from the hope that allowing families to choose their children's schools might be one way to undermine this educational stranglehold.

Parental Frustration

One of the biggest impetuses for the charter school movement is the frustration experienced by parents of students of all ethnic groups, cultures, and socioeconomic classes regarding the state of the country's current public schools. Although they have very different political reasons and educational priorities, they all desire the same thing: the best possible education for their children. What "the best possible education" means to each and every person, however, varies.

Using data from a four-wave panel of parents with children in the D.C. public charter and district sectors Jack Buckley and Mark Schneider of Boston College and Stony Brook University respectfully, examined the effect of charter school enrollment on parental satisfaction. They found that charter school parents evaluated their children's schools more highly than did parents with children in the traditional Washington, D.C., public schools and that they were more satisfied with their schools' emphasis on values and size of their child's school and class. They also found, however, that the parents examined were not more satisfied with classroom discipline. The study found that over time, charter parents' satisfaction with the charter schools to which their children attend generally declines and by the end of five years there is only a small difference between charter and district school parental satisfaction (Buckley and Schneider 2006). Then why does the media tell us that parents are clamoring to enroll their children in charter schools?

Just because many parents have become charter school advocates does not mean that they seek to dismantle public schools; in fact, the contrary can be claimed. By looking to control the public schools through charters, many parents believe they are defending public schools, albeit in a different form. One of the findings that appear to support this contention is an opinion poll regarding "choice." Those that answered "yes" on the "choice" question also answered "yes" when asked whether private schools receiving public funds should be regulated by the state like public schools (Hudson Institute 1997, pt. 1, 25).

However, the impetus for charter schools among parents derives from many factors, not just parent involvement; in fact, it is a combination of institutional factors such as greater sense of community, less regulations, ongoing educational and staff development and reform, assessment, and decentralized governance (Smrekar 1996). It is significant to note some of the frustrations that parents have expressed because of the current state of the public schools in order to understand the rapid development of charter schools. In 1988, the Education Commission of the United States released a report indicating what reform efforts might improve the scholastic performance of students in inner city high schools. Among many things, the report found that what was needed was to:

> . . . *establish purposive partnerships in the outside community (with parents, community organizations, private-sector business, colleges and universities, and social service deliverers) as a way to expand resources available to the school, to build a broader constituency for public education, to empower parents and community, and to create access to opportunities (jobs, postsecondary schooling) beyond the schools. (Education Commission of the States)*

Instead, parents do not feel they are truly considered a part of the educational process in many public schools, and many of them feel they are left out of the decision-making process that defines education for their children. Parents perceive of themselves as outsiders who are not communicated with but are instead communicated to. Many charter schools say they are designed to improve the relationships between administrators, teachers, parents, and students. The fostering of good interpersonal relationships between members of a charter educational community arguably has an influence on the academic performance of students through developing shared values and closer community alliances (Bryk and Schneider 2002). But are parents more involved in charter schools than traditional public schools? Are the improved relationships between educational stakeholders a consequence of charter schools?

In *The Power of Their Ideas: Lessons for America from a Small School in Harlem* (1995), author and educational activist Deborah Meier argues for school choice and educational innovation. She talks about the frustration of parents because of the enormity and size of urban public schools and the depersonalized learning that too often takes place within their walls. She speaks to parents who express frustration at the lack of respect they receive from the administrators and school personnel of large urban schools, and she narrates the parents' frustration at what they envision as large, factory-style bureaucratic machines that seek to control, rather than give ownership to, parents, teachers, and students. She also discusses the parents' frustration with the type of instruction their children are receiving, the curricula they are subjected to, and the knowledge they are attaining (Meier 1995).

The lack of what many parents see as "humanity" in large city schools has certainly been one of the catalysts that have promoted the charter school movement. Parents have sung the praises of charter schools because, they argue, they are able to make democratic and collaborative decisions in small, personal school sites. Knowing the students' names, understanding their needs, and personalizing their learning are matters that parents believe cannot be done in large, centralized schools where the parents perceive, rightly or wrongly, that they have no control or participation in the decision-making process. Educational communities of manageable size that are governed by people who have a stake in the public schools, parents argue, is something that can be accomplished in the smaller charter schools. According to the Cato Institute:

> *The ultimate key to school reform is the parent. Once parents assume the responsibility of advocating for and supporting their children's education, they will become partners with educators to create the schools their children need. State legislators should seek policies that return control of education to parents through mechanisms like tax cuts and universal tuition tax credits. The adoption of such measures promises to increase parental involvement and bring other important benefits to children. (Cato Institute 2000)*

Scott A. Imberman, an economist at the University of Houston, has come up with some interesting research regarding why parents choose charter schools. The research is based on his review of testing, attendance, and disciplinary data from a large, unidentified school district that has experienced a huge growth in its charter schools since 1997. Based on Imberman's report, parents who choose charters in the school district he studied may be "more concerned with discipline, safety, and student satisfaction than academic performance" (Imberman 2008).

A 1997 study of parental involvement in charter schools seems to support the fact that parents who send their children to such schools are much more involved in how the school operates. The findings of the study conducted by an independent researcher and presented at the annual meeting of the American Educational Research Association examined parental participation in one urban and one suburban charter school in the northwestern part of the United States. The study focused on data gathered from interviews with ten parents (six urban and four suburban), a questionnaire filled out by eighteen parents (eight urban and ten suburban), and journals kept by two parents (both urban). The parents cited curriculum, technology, and character education as the reasons for sending their children to charter schools (Anderson 1997). The study also found that in the charter schools studied, especially the urban schools, staff and teachers were encouraged to get parents involved at all levels, which included communicating with them by e-mail, weekly newsletters, and a promise that every phone call would be returned within twenty-four hours (Anderson 1997, 4). The mother of two boys who both attended a charter school commented on one of her sons:

> When he was first in the charter, I thought "something new again." But then I saw him flourish, and the teachers took such an interest in him. And in me. They called me, and we worked together. The charter has given me something to connect to. Through it I became interested in the school and really, that was part of why I was willing to serve on the governance council at our high school. I feel it is my school, now, too. (Fine 1994a, 13)

Parental frustration at a lack of relationship with teachers seems to be a universal complaint among parents interviewed. The above study illustrated that having scheduled open communication with teachers and the opportunity to express ideas about the curriculum and philosophy of the schools made parents feel treated as partners in their children's education.

Parents as partners in the classroom is hardly a novel concept, yet many parents assert, with respect to large, urban schools, that they are treated more like den mothers than partners in the classroom. Engaging families in the education of their children and treating them as equals in the classroom, many parents contend, goes a long way in building trust and community commitment and has been found to create long-term and far-reaching results (Scherer 1998).

But parental frustration with large public schools does not end with simply a call for community-based schools that are intimate and small. Another motive for parental support for the charter school idea is dismay about what parents see as crime, gangs, and school violence in the large urban schools; thus, they seek refuge in small, charter schools. Urban charter schools in low-income communities are seen by parents and educators as safe havens from the other nearby public schools, which they often perceive to be dangerous.

Frustration is also expressed at the type of instruction that is found in many large urban schools. Parents around the country have expressed frustration with the kind of learning that is taking place in the schools; the type of instruction and strategies that are employed, from worksheets to fill in the blanks; and the lack of motivation among many of the teachers in these schools.

Many nonwhite parents also argue that instructional strategies employed in many public schools fail to include the contributions of diverse cultural and racial groups in the materials and discriminate on the basis of socioeconomic class. For instance, members of a working-class African American community may want to turn their local public school into a charter school to ensure that their children are exposed to a back-to-the-basics curriculum via the use of technology (Wells et al. 1999, 9).

Parents have also been instrumental in promoting and creating urban, ethnocentric, and grassroots charter schools. Wishing to create a "safe space" or a "home place" for students of a particular racial or ethnic group who live in the surrounding community, parents, educators, and community members in many localities have set up Afro-centric, Chicano-centric, or Native American-centric curricula. These charter schools are born of the frustration of parents in marginalized communities who often feel that the educational system has failed to take their knowledge, their history, and their experiences seriously (Collins 1991). A study by the U.S. Department of Education found that one quarter of all charter schools are targeted towards certain populations (Nelson et. al. 2000). In 2002 Texas served more black students, more at risk students, and more non-Anglo students than traditional public schools in the state (Greene et. al. 2003).

Grassroots charters, advocates argue, allow for parental involvement in the process of organizing and founding the charter school and therefore can help low-income parents and community members of color create and sustain new social networks that can be used for political organizing and gaining a political voice within the larger society. The argument advanced is that by chartering schools within low-income neighborhoods and among people of color, the process will afford the promise of forging connections between disempowered parents and the education system by enhancing parental participation in the education of the children.

A teacher at one urban grassroots charter school noted that she saw improvements in her students over the school year: "We know our own history; nobody has to tell us., we know it. And they're developing a sense of pride. And I can see it's taken a long time, but it's happening slowly" (Wells et al. 1999, 12). At one charter school in a Latino community, the founder explained that one of the motivating forces behind the effort to start the school was the way Latino students whose English proficiency was limited were being treated in public schools:

> *Some of our students who were not English speaking, who were getting close to fluency but not quite there yet, many of them were put in ESL [English as a Second Language] programs. And sometimes the kids never progressed out of ESL, you know, they just continued at the junior high and high school level. And [one of the school's founders] had been at a junior high where she saw the kinds of classes where some of the students wound up. They wound up in huge classes and they worked straight out of grammar books, and she just felt there could be another kind of program for these kids. (Wells et al. 1999, 17)*

Many parents have started parent-led charter schools in which a core of extremely devoted and involved parents works with educators to move toward charter school status and is intricately involved in the writing of policies and procedures for the charters. Most of these parent-led charter schools are found in wealthy communities in suburban or exclusive urban areas (Wells et al. 1999, 12), and the parents at these schools govern the school, raise money through private fund-raisers, do volunteer work, and help the school define the terms of the financial and legal agreements.

Patty Yancey, an educational researcher at the University of San Francisco found that:

> *Considering that the demands on families' lives today, as well as the difficulties educators cite in eliciting parent involvement in schools, it seems like that a parent-run charter school would not have widespread appeal. However, because of the more visible positive facts—such as the location or the small size of a charter school—parents and guardians enroll their children regardless of parent involvement clauses. Until more public school choices are available to middle- and low-income families, this is a reality that must be considered. (Yancey 2000)*

Yet, not all state charter laws allow parents to be founders and chief operators of charter schools. For some charters, parent involvement is not the central issue due to the mission of the charter or the population served (residential foster care programs, teenagers referred by juvenile courts, etc.). Nevertheless, the National Study of Charter Schools reports that nearly fifty percent of charter schools surveyed require some sort of parent or family involvement (Yancey 2000), and this family involvement can come in the form of volunteer hours and service that are far more extensive than what is expected of parents in mot public, private, and parochial schools (Yancey 2000, 17). See the Primary Documents, page 570 for parental agreements.

Frustration among parents has also led to the creation of homeschooling charter schools, or the "virtual charter school." Under this arrangement, homeschooling advocates draw together under one charter "umbrella," and each umbrella is usually made up of a cluster of families and parents that have been homeschooling their children prior to the creation of the charter school. According to the U.S. Department of Education:

> *Homeschooled children may be taught by one or both parents, by tutors who come into the home, or through virtual school programs conducted over the Internet. Some parents prepare their own materials and design their own programs of study, while others use materials produced by companies specializing in home school resources. Accountability for homeschooling is coordinated with the state in which the family resides. (U.S. Department of Education, under "Parents School Choice")*

Motivations for homeschooling charters can vary, but they include religious, practical, pedagogical, and philosophical reasons. The families that are associated with a charter and operate as homeschoolers under a district school charter can run the political gamut from the extremely conservative to the more progressive. A homeschooling charter school does not force parents to adopt any particular formula, ideology, or curriculum; parents make their own pedagogical decisions as to what they wish to adopt as instructional methods and techniques. Still, it is important to remember that these home school charters, or "virtual charter schools" are subject to accountability under state educational standards.

Generally, the majority of the homeschooling students and parents enrolled in the home-schooling charter schools are white and for the most part, middle class (Wells et al. 1999, 13), and it is usually the nonworking mothers who do the instructing. As a result, those families or parents that homeschool typically have the time and economic resources to take advantage of the freedom from the traditional public school system.

A lack of educational innovation, dehumanization, discrimination on the basis of race or socioeconomic class, inadequate teaching strategies, fear of school violence, and lack of input into the control and authority of curriculum and school affairs have all combined to create parental frustration with the current traditional public schools. And parents are not alone in their frustration.

Teacher Frustration

Many teachers also experience deep frustration with the current public school system, and numerous charter schools have emerged from the dreams of educational leaders and teachers who want to do things differently. Teachers encounter intense bureaucracy, increasing levels of paperwork, and time-consuming clerical duties. Many argue that their schools offer no educational leadership, lack a vision of what students should be doing and what they should know, and fail to adopt innovation and creativity as the cornerstone for educational reform and improvement. Many teachers argue that the large public schools are unnecessarily bureaucratic and unresponsive and simply cannot meet the challenges of educating the nation's children. Along with parents, teachers argue that the inordinate class sizes they are forced to handle make teaching and learning difficult and often impossible tasks.

These frustrations are not confined to urban schools, for a national study of rural schools found that those schools experienced similar problems. Despite their smaller class sizes, the study found that the rural schools studied seemed to encourage and formed a bureaucratic style of governing and thinking, thus creating impersonal relationships—from the classroom to the lunchroom.

In *Chartering Urban Reform,* Michelle Fine quotes an urban high school teacher:

> It was "do your own thing" before charters. Teachers rarely shared their strategies and programs. Meetings were all administrative, no pedagogy going on. In charters with colleagues, in department or interdisciplinary meetings, there's a lot more strategizing. There was no opportunity to talk to my colleagues before. There was no reason to talk to colleagues before. Teaching interdisciplinarily, it's compulsory. I am certainly learning from colleagues, and colleagues ask me for help. Last week a teacher who has never in 35 years of teaching broken his class into groups, did so. He's not [even] in a charter. (Fine 1994a, 7)

Much like the parental frustration discussed earlier, teachers find that impersonal administrations coupled with inadequate teaching strategies have reduced the effectiveness of public schools. They point to the lack of educational and professional growth opportunities. One teacher in a charter in Philadelphia recently noted: "I always thought of myself as a good teacher; but not always so creative. I have never enjoyed teaching as much as I do now. I am learning from my colleagues in the charter and, the most amazing thing, I never thought my students wanted to see themselves as students! We would all give the class away to the most disruptive students. Now the students tell Charlie to 'shut up and let us learn'" (Fine 1994a, 11). Henry Giroux, educational pioneer, has consistently made the argument, as have many teachers, that what teachers want is simply to be treated as professionals and intellectuals in the classroom, not as clerks and technicians (Giroux 1988).

Fine, in studying high schools in the urban America, found that what she called silencing occurred at the high schools she studied. This silencing was, according to Fine, the inability to engage student thinking on major controversial issues they faced. As she noted in 1988:

> *Now I work with this major urban restructuring effort. By dismantling large anonymous bureaucratic structures of high school, educators and parents are inventing educator-designed, parent-involved, and student-empowered communities of learning called charters. Through my work with these high school educators, parents and students and work with Chicago, New York and Baltimore reform, I have come to see how thoroughly silencing defines life inside public education bureaucracies. The risks attached to speaking aloud, raising critique, voicing possibility, questioning traditional practices, and challenging social injustices are felt to be enormous. In many major cities, educators echo horror stories about what happens if you are not "loyal." The adverse consequences can be devastating. (Fine 1994b, 81)*

According to many educators, charter schools have also given teachers a new respect for the students they teach. Commenting about her experiences with students in a charter school in Philadelphia, one teacher stated that in a charter school:

> *You get to know more about kids—everything including their blood type. When you thought about it, there we were with kids from 7:47 to 2:46—all those hours, four years, and nothing. It had to be wrong. Knowing a smaller group of students intimately has to change our relationship with them. The charter structure was a place in which we could change and accept our share of the responsibility for student achievement and failure. (Vanderslice and Farmer 1994, 89)*

Another teacher, commenting on her new understanding of the students she teaches and the lives they live, noted with some fear:

> *OK, Michele, you told me you wanted to get to know these kids. Now we do. And we know what is going on with them. The kid that used to flash the lights on and off in the back of the room isn't just a discipline problem, he's a young man with a crack-addicted mother, or she is homeless. These students have hard lives. Other than taking them home, I don't know what to do with them. You need to get me some help. (Vanderslice and Farmer 1994, 89)*

It seems that for many teachers, arguably charter schools have given them an opportunity to understand the larger society within which they operate and the Dickensian lives that many of their students are forced to live.

For quite some time, teachers have mourned the lack of cooperative planning time they have together. In many charter schools, where there is an opportunity to discuss everyday interactions between themselves and students, teachers sometimes take risks with their students, share power with their colleagues, and confront the consequences of isolation and disempowerment that are part of many large school districts. Many teachers have found that collaboration is enhanced in charter schools. One high school teacher in Philadelphia noted the problems associated with collaboration among staff members:

Thinking that the most workable pair [for team teaching purposes] would be English and world history, I asked the history teacher, the long-term substitute, to do an interdisciplinary unit with me; he agreed . . . I kept a journal, elicited written responses to questions from my partner, and got journals and test results from the students. These pieces of writing show me that the students benefited greatly from the synergy of the collaboration. They also show that our collaboration was unequal, that most of the problems that occurred were solved by one person, that the expectations both of each other and of the students varied, and that the perception of the need for the structure was different for each teacher. Problems with collaborating remain. The type and amount of planning needed must be negotiated at the beginning of the partnership. I feel that we were very far apart on this issue. In my next collaboration, at the beginning, I will insist that we negotiate how often we meet, who calls the meetings and what we should get accomplished at the meeting. (Lytle et al. 1994, 176–177)

For many teachers, charter schools offer an opportunity to forge collaborations that previously did not exist. By creating and delivering education in small, intensive units with low ratios of teachers to students and plenty of opportunities to forge relationships among colleagues, many teachers argue that they, for the first time, now have the opportunity to use a wide range of instructional techniques, collaborate successfully with colleagues, create individualized instruction, and upgrade the general quality of their instruction.

Here are just some of the comments offered by teachers at various charter schools about the opportunities those schools afforded them:

You see someone with a rigid teaching style who's not yet open to a variety of kids' learning styles. But there is no room (in traditional schools) for repair through collaboration.

When we meet as a team to talk about students, we can brainstorm on how to handle problems. It makes a great deal of difference when I can say to that student, "Well your other teachers said this about you." We are working as a team and students know that.

I'm more aware of who their other teachers are and what they're doing. I tell students to watch how their teachers teach. That can help students study. It's better for individual teachers because theirs is not the only viewpoint on a student or class. They get ideas on how to handle a class because everyone has the same group.

Our idea was creating a safe place, an atmosphere of acceptance. There's no anonymity in a charter—that's why insecure teachers avoid them. Vulnerabilities hang out. That's where the charter is good because then vulnerabilities are accepted and teachers start developing strengths to start overcoming those vulnerabilities. In dealing with students holistically, as we can in the charter, we are dealing with teachers holistically as well. (Fine 1994a, 12)

One teacher at a charter high school offered:

Finally I can teach students in ways that allow me to engage with them and other faculty, and hold onto them for their entire secondary school experience. (Fine 1994a, 10)

Yet another teacher, who was also a charter coordinator in Philadelphia, described the experience:

Being in a charter, especially with the social work interns, has changed all of my work. So I, and other teachers, are being advocates for students. I was so delighted to hear my principal say, "academics have to drive the rosters, not rosters driving the academics." That's a major change. One more thing: with charters, parents are really involved. We invited 22 parents in for a Family Night, 17 showed up. (Fine 1994a, 11)

One of the results of the increasing teacher frustration with traditional public education has been the development of teacher-led charter schools. These schools are started by groups of teachers who tend to focus on the type of instructional techniques and the instructional programs they feel are important as their primary motivation for going to charter status. They generally are motivated by an educational philosophy and strongly held convictions as to how students should learn. Running the gamut from progressive to multi-age, from open classrooms to more traditional programs, these teacher-led charter schools are built on the idea that teachers know what is best for the students they serve. In these educational settings, the teachers are attempting to gain control of the pedagogy and curriculum in order to develop effective learning and teach in the interest of the student. These schools often become sites of innovation and imagination.

One example of a teacher-initiated charter school is the Constellation Community Middle School in Long Beach, California. This school was started by two public middle-school teachers who felt frustrated because of an inability to change the traditional educational system. Wanting to give their mostly minority students a world-class education, these teachers felt that the charter school idea provided them a way to put restructuring into practice.

Another group of teachers did the same thing at the Sierra Leone Educational Outreach Academy in Detroit, Michigan. This group was composed of former special education teachers who were opposed to the conventional "dumping ground" aspect of traditional special education programs, and they started their own school; just another example of frustration on the part of teachers being translated into teacher-led charter schools.

Although some of the teacher-led charter schools have been started with the help of teachers' union affiliates such as the National Teachers Association, others have been independently started by a handful or a group of teachers. Much like employee-owned companies, these teacher-led charter schools are supportive of public education in general. Their concern is making decisions and judgments as to educational philosophy and corresponding curriculum and instructional tactics in the best interest of the students they teach.

Even though charter school teachers vary from site to site in terms of their educational philosophy and curriculum orientation, a 1997 Hudson Institute study of teachers' personal fulfillment and professional rewards found that over 90 percent of the charter school teachers are "very" or "somewhat" satisfied with their charter school's educational philosophy, size, fellow teachers, and students. The study also found that over 75 percent of the teachers interviewed are satisfied with their school's administration, level of teacher decision making, and the challenge of starting a new school. Only 2.7 percent of charter school teachers say they "hope to be elsewhere" in the future (Hudson Institute 1997, pt. 1, 2). However, this study has been recently debunked by a new and more comprehensive study of charter school teachers.

In a new 2007 study entitled *Teacher Attrition in Charter Schools,* by Gary Miron and Brooks Applegate of the Western Michigan University Evaluation Center, the report indicates that as many as one out of every four charter school teachers, nearly 40 percent of newer charter school teachers, flee for other jobs leave their schools each year, which is double the typical public school attrition rate (11 percent). Moreover, attrition among new teachers in charter schools is close to 40 percent annually, a figure that is critical for charter schools given that their percentage of teachers under 30 (37 percent) is more than three times that of traditional public schools (11 percent).

Miron and Applegate also noted that their study differs from most of the existing satisfaction research that often excludes from data collection the actual efforts those teachers who are leaving or have left charter schools. For Miron and Applegate the report clearly demonstrates:

> *The high attrition rates for teachers in charter schools constitute one of the greatest obstacles that will need to be overcome if the charter school reform is to deliver as promised.*

The researchers found that teachers more likely to leave were those who reported less satisfaction with their charter school's mission, its ability to achieve that mission or its administration and governance. Also more likely to leave were uncertified teachers and those who taught in upper grades.

As a result, they recommend that:

- *Discrepancies between teachers' expectations for charter schools and those schools' realities should be identified, and strategies for narrowing the gaps should be designed and implemented.*
- *Efforts should be made to strengthen teachers' sense of security as much as possible.*
- *Efforts should be made to increase teachers' satisfaction with working conditions, salaries, benefits, administration, and governance. (Miron and Applegate 2007)*

Student Frustration

Students also declare their frustrations with public schools as they are traditionally organized. Students have continually expressed dissatisfaction with everything from school violence to school curriculum. Patterns of frustration can be detected among students throughout the nation from the elementary schools to the high schools.

Students at one charter school in Philadelphia described their frustrations at the failure of traditional education to promote confidence in learning. One high school student noted: "If I were asked in tenth grade whether I was going to college, I would have given a straight 'no.' I was never one who tried to do or accomplish anything. I know now I have abilities. . . . The school has changed me. I feel as though if I study criminal justice, I can probably make a change" (Cohen 1994, 98).

Another student, "Paul," was in the fifty-ninth percentile of his high school class, but when he was allowed to attend the University of Minnesota program, his grades averaged 4.0. "Jon," described as a disruptive, hostile, and highly argumentative individual, failed seven of his eight classes in high school before he dropped out. Nine months later, after starting in the Minnesota program, he was earning an average grade of A while taking courses in philosophy, English, and political science. Two unnamed girls had set the record for absences from their high school, but when they transferred to a nontraditional program outside their district, they planned to not only graduate from high school but also to go on to postsecondary institutions.

Many students observe that within large, depersonalized, and factory-type schools, their teachers do not care about them or have the confidence that they will learn. For many students, teachers do not have faith in their students at all, and yet, as Asa Hilliard has argued:

The risk for our children in school is not a risk associated with their intelligence. Public school failures have nothing to do with poverty, race, language, style, and nothing to do with children's families. All of these are red herrings. When re-

searchers study them, we may ultimately yield to some greater insight into the instructional process. But at present, these issues, as explanations of school failure, distract attention away from the fundamental problem facing the United States today. We have one primary problem: Do we truly see each and every child in this nation develop to the peak of his or her capacities? (Hilliard 1991, 31–35)

Charter schools, argue proponents, offer these students and their teachers opportunities to personalize learning, develop relationships, and examine assumptions about learning and scholastic ability. Such schools offer a systematic change that might allow teachers to develop more respect for their students as they begin to interact with them in a more personal way.

At one high school in Brooklyn, New York, the following were just some of the frustrations with the traditional public school expressed by its urban students.

Officials are more interested in impressing students' parents than addressing school problems such as violence:

- Gangs are taking over the hallways
- Cultural history fails to be acknowledged
- Teachers don't care
- Administrators don't serve students
- Standards need to be higher
- Classes are too crowded
- Curriculum is boring and repetitive (Sarah J. Hale High School Students 1999, 14).

Such frustrations, like those of teachers and parents, are serving to bolster calls for smaller charter schools. According to some proponents of charter schools, students' experiences with charter schools have been an educational lifesaver. A Hudson Institute study of charter schools found that when charter school students were asked what they liked about their charter school, the most frequent answers were "good teachers," 58.6 percent; "they teach until I learn it," 51.3 percent; and "they don't let me fall behind," 38.5 percent (Hudson Institute 1997, pt. 1, 2). The study also found that when the students' teachers were compared to the teachers in their previous school, three students out of five surveyed (60.7 percent) said that their charter teachers were "better" (Hudson Institute 1997, pt. 1, 2). However, this study has been refuted by Buckley and Schneider who found in their study that students in D.C. charter schools and students in traditional D.C. public schools are remarkably similar in their evaluations of their schools. The study showed that charter school parents are more enthusiastic about the charter schools than the children who actually attend them. In short, the study indicated that there was scant evidence to support the notion that charter schools changed the dynamic of student life. The children in the D.C. study were no more proud of their schools and no less likely to wish they attended a different school than their counterparts in traditional public school. Furthermore, the study found that peer groups seem to be pretty much the same across the two sectors (Buckley and Schneider 2006, 202).

In contrast, at KIPP Academy, a charter school in Houston for example, students travel as a class from one subject to the next, working as a team in their 80-minute core classes: language arts, history, science, and math. They also take 45-minute classes, including physical education, art, music, and Spanish. Students eat lunch with their entire grade in the cafeteria, as teachers conduct informal meetings. With 90 students per grade, there are three sections of 30 students each (U. S. Charter Schools, under "Charter School in Houston").

Another issue motivating both students and teachers toward charter schools is the importance of personalized learning. Students, like teachers, argue that large class sizes depersonalize learning and fail to allow the necessary time for teacher-student relationships to develop and flourish. Many teachers do not even know the names of some of their students. One high school student in Philadelphia commented on the personalized learning of the smaller class size: "We're in the ninth grade. We should act more mature. We need to make the groups [learning groups] smaller. You get more answers and questions from the girls like Sonia and them" (Waff 1994, 199).

Because charter schools are usually small, they offer opportunities for teachers and students to form relationships that translate into personalized, relevant learning. For example, a student I shall call "Susan" benefited greatly from school choice. In the bottom 25 percent of her regular high school class and undergoing therapy for depression, she was allowed to attend the University of Minnesota special program where her university grade point average was 3.2 percent compared to her high school grade point average of 1.78 percent (all of these examples are from letters sent to Daryl Sedio at the University of Minnesota). "Sam" attended the University of Minnesota special program after having dropped out of high school where he felt he never "fit in." Although his high school grades were D+/C-, he maintained a B+/A- average in the university program.

At the Peace Academy, a charter school located in Minnesota, teachers work with the same students for two years in a row, which is a practice called "looping." In the elementary school, each teacher is supported by an ESL specialist, a classroom aide, and a shared special education teacher. For grades seven and eight, teachers team by math and science and by language arts and social studies; each teacher teaches the two subjects to the same two groups of 24 students for a two-year cycle. This looping, whether at the elementary grades or in junior high school, provides continuity and allows teachers to develop strong connections with students and families. Additionally, teachers feel that when they identify a critical student need, there is support to make things happen quickly. As one teacher comments, "I see change happen here when we need it." (U.S. Charter Schools, under "Charter School in Houston")

As more and more students continue to experience overcrowded classrooms, unsafe schools, repetitive and boring classes, and lack of educational innovation, the impetus among students for charter schools will remain strong.

SUMMARY

Charter schools remain very popular with their primary constituents. The driving force to create a charter school arises from very different quarters and is motivated by varying and diverse interests—from those entrepreneurs seeking to profit off the provision of educational services to parents seeking the best school for their kids. Families and educators seek out charter schools for primarily educational reasons: high academic standards, small class size, a focus on teaching and learning, educational philosophies that are close to their own, and designing innovative approaches to curriculum and instruction are all reasons shared by parents, teachers, and students who have embraced the charter school movement. Private interests and the growing educational market see charters as educational "deep pockets," with both the privatization and deregulation of public schools and thus as rich source of emerging profits and business opportunities. What is clear to all participants in the charter debate is that conceptually, as well as structurally charters represent a radical departure from the notion of the "common school" model of public education that has been the basis of the American educational system for the last century and a half. Charters can only be understood within an ideology that argues that individual family choice, unfettered economic markets, competition, and the nongovernmental operation and regulation of schools can be the only system that can produce more effective outcomes for students and American educational endeavors in general.

REFERENCES

A Nation at Risk: The Imperative for Educational Reform. Washington, D.C., April 1983. http://www.ed/gov/pubs/NatAtRisk/risk.html.

Anderson, J. "Parent Involvement in a Charter School." Paper presented at the annual meeting of the American Educational Research Association, Chicago, 4, 24-28, March 1997.

Bifulco, R., and H. Ladd. "Institutional Change and Coproduction of Public Services: The Effect of Charter Schools on Parental Involvement." *Journal of Public Administration Research and Theory,* 2006.

Brighouse, H. "March of the Vouchers." *Against the Current,* (September–October) 1999.

Bryk, A.S., and B. Schneider. *Trust in Schools.* New York: Russell Sage Foundation, 2002.

Buckley, J., and M. Schneider. "Are Charter Parents More Satisfied with Schools? Evidence from Washington D.C." *Peabody Journal of Education* 81 (1) (2006): 57-78, 270.

Carnegie Foundation. *School Choice.* Princeton, NJ: The Carnegie Foundation, 1992.

Carnoy, M., R. Jacobsen, L. Mishel, and R. Rothstein. *The Charter School Dust-up: Examining the Evidence on Enrollment and Achievement.* New York: Teacher's College Press, 2005.

Cato Institute: *More than Grades: How Choice Boosts Parental Involvement.* Washington, D.C.: 2000.

The Center for Comprehensive School Reform and Improvement 2005. http://www. centerforcsri.org/index.php?itemid=5&id=204&option=com_content&task=view.

Center on Reinventing Public Education. National Charter School Research Project, University of Washington. Charter Schools Operating in America. http://www.ncsrp.org/cs/csr/print/ csr_docs/37?question=1. Data from 2006-2007 Reports. http://www.ncsrp.org/cs/csr/print/ csr_docs/37?question=8. Federal Funding. http://www.ncsrp.org/cs/csr/print/csr_docs/ index.htm. Size of a Charter School. http://www.ncsrp.org/cs/csr/print/csr_docs/37? question=3. State Comparison Data. http://www.ncsrp.org/cs/csr/print/csr_docs/states.htm.

Chubb, J., and T. Moe. *Politics, Markets and America's Schools.* Brookings Institution Press, 1990.

Cobb, C., and G. Glass. "Ethnic Segregation in Arizona Charter Schools." *Education Policy Analysis Archives* (peer-reviewed scholarly electronic journal) 7, no. 1 (14 January 1999).

Cohen, J., "Now Everybody Wants to Dance." In M. Fine, *Chartering Urban School Reform,* 98. New York: Columbia University Teachers College, 1994.

Collins, P.H. *Black Feminist Thought: Knowledge, Consciousness, and the Politics of Empowerment.* New York: Routledge, 1991.

Cookson, P. *School Choice: The Struggle for the Soul of American Education.* New Haven, CT: Yale University Press, 1994.

Corwin, R., and E.J. Schneider. *The School Choice Hoax: Fixing America's Schools.* Lanham, MD: Roman and Littlefield Education, 2007.

Durant, W.C. "The Gift of the Child; The Promise of Freedom: Creative Approaches to Learning, Teaching, and Schooling." *The Freeman,* 47 (6), 1997.

Education Commission of the States. Denver, CO: http://www.ecs.org/

Education Industry Association. Board of Directors. http://www.educationindustry.org/ blistings.asp?sid=16.

———. Think Tanks and Financial Institutions. http://www.educationindustry.org/EIA/files/ ccLibraryFiles/Filename/000000000062/EIA%20Special%20Report%20on%20Emerging% 20Ed%20Industry.pd.

———. Organization Information. http://www.educationindustry.org.

Fine, M. *Chartering Urban School Reform: Reflections of Public High Schools in the Midst of Change.* New York: Columbia University Teachers College, 1994a.

———. "Silencing, Inquiry, and Reflection in Public School Bureaucracies." In *Chartering Urban School Reform,* 81. New York: Columbia University Teachers College, 1994b.

Friedman, M. *Capitalism and Freedom.* Chicago: Chicago Press, 1962.

———. "The Voucher Idea." *New York Times Magazine,* 23 September, 1973.

Giroux, H. *The Terror of Neoliberalism.* Boulder, CO: Paradigm Press: 2004, xxii.

———. *Teachers as Intellectuals: Toward a Critical Pedagogy of Learning.* Granby, MA: Bergin and Garvey, 1988.

Greene, J., G. Forster, and M. Winters. *Apples to Apples: An Evaluation of Charter Schools Serving General Student Populations.* Center for Civic Innovation at the Manhattan Institute, Education Working Paper No. 1., July 2003. http://www.manhattaninstitute.org/pdf/ ewp_01.pdf.

Hassel, B.C. *The Charter School Challenge: Avoiding the Pitfalls Fulfilling the Promise.* Washington, DC: Brookings Institute, 1999.

Hilliard, A. "Do We Have the Will to Educate All Children?" *Educational Leadership,* (September 1991): 31—35.

Howe, K., and K. Welner. "School Choice and the Pressure to Perform: Déjà vu for Children with Disabilities?" *Journal of Remedial and Special Education,* 23(4), (2002): 212—221.

Howe, K., M. Eisenhart, and D. Betebenner. "School choice crucible: A Case Study of Boulder Valley." *Phi Delta Kappan*, 83(2), (2001): 137-146. (Condensed and reprinted, 2002, under the title "Research Scotches School Choice." *Education Digest,* 67 (5), 10-17. Reprinted, 2002, in A. Kohn & P. Shannon (Eds.), *Education Inc.: Turning Learning into a Business*, pp. 146-166. Portsmith, NH: Heinemann.)

Hudson Institute. *Charter Schools in Action Project.* Final Report, pts. 1, 2, 6, and 25. Washington, DC, 1997.

Hughes, T.J. "Magnets' Pull Weakens in Suburbs." *St. Louis Post Dispatch,* 25 February, 1988.

Imberman, S. *The Effect of Charter Schools on Non-Charter Students: An Instrumental Variables Approach.* New York: National Center for the Study of Privatization in Education, 2008.

Kolderie, T. *The States Begin to Withdraw the Exclusive.* Public Services Redesign Project. St. Paul, MN: Center for Policy Studies, 1993.

Kotz, David, "Neoliberalism and the U.S. Economic Expansion of the 90s." *Monthly Review* 54:11 (April 2003): 16.

Kozol, J. *Death at an Early Age.* Boston: Houghton and Mifflin, 1967.

Lubienski, C. "Redefining Public Education: Charter Schools, Common Schools, and the Rhetoric of Reform." *Teacher's College Record*, 103(4), 2001.

Lytle, S., J. Christman, J. Cohen, J. Countryman, B. Fecho, D. Portnoy, and F. Sion. "Learning in the Afternoon: When Teacher Inquiry Meets School Reform." In M. Fine, *Chartering Urban School Reform,* 157–80. New York: Columbia University Teachers College, 1994.

Massey, D., and N.A. Denton. *American Apartheid: Segregation and the Making of the Underclass.* Cambridge, MA: Harvard University Press, 1993.

Meier, D. *The Power of Their Ideas: Lessons for America from a Small School in Harlem.* Boston, MA: Beacon Press, 1995.

Michigan Court of Appeals. *Council of Organizations and Others for Education about Parochaid v. Governor.* 216 Mich. App. 126; 548 N.W. 2d 909. Decided March 29, 1996.

Michigan State Constitution. Article VII, Sec. 2

Miron, G., and B. Applegate, *Teacher Attrition in Charter Schools.* Kalamazoo, MI: Western Michigan University Evaluation Center Great Lakes Center for Education Research and Practice, 2007. http://www.greatlakescenter.org/docs/Research/Miron_Attrition.htm.

Miron, G., and C. Nelson. *What's Public about Public Schools.* Thousand Oaks, CA: Corwin Press, Inc., 2002.

Nathan, J. *Charter Schools: Creating Hope and Opportunity for American Education.* San Francisco: Jossey-Bass, xxviii, 1996.

———. "Early Lessons of the Charter School Movement." *Educational Leadership* 54, no. 2 (October 1996): 19-21.

National School Boards Association. Council of Urban Boards of Education, Alexandria, VA. http://www.nsba.org/cube.

Nelson, B., P. Berman, J. Ericson, N. Kamprath, R. Perry, D. Silverman, and D. Solomon. *The State of Charter Schools: Fourth-Year Report.* Washington, DC: Office of Educational Research and Improvement, 2000. http://www.ed.gov/pubs/charter4thyear/.

Pickler, Nedra. Associated Press. http://ap.google.com/article/ALeqM5iT—F725ypsNTaN rulnuCGd8vt0QD9336D180

Plank, D.N., and G. Sykes. *Choosing Choice: School Choice in International Perspective.* New York: Teachers College Press, 2003.

Popkewitz, T. *Cosmopolitanism and the Age of School Reform: Science, Education and Making Society by Making the Child.* New York, NY: Routledge, 2007.

Rose, L., and A. Gallup. "The 32nd Annual Phi Delta Kappa / Gallup Poll of the Public's Attitudes Toward the Public Schools, Phi Delta Kappa International (September 2000).http://www.pdkintl.org/kappan/kpol0009.htm#I.

Sarah J. Hale High School Students. "Crossing Swords." *Journal of the Society for Social Analysis* 7, no. 1, Summer/Fall 1999.

Scherer, M. "Let the Dialogue Begin." *Educational Leadership* 55, May 1998.

Schorr, J. "Giving Charter Schools a Chance." *The Nation* (June 5, 2000). http://www.the nation.com/docprint.mhtml?i=20000605&s=schorr.

Schwartz, W. "How Well Are Charter Schools Serving Urban and Minority Students?" *ERIC/CUE Digest* 119 (November 1996): 4.

Smrekar, C. *Impact of School Choice and Community.* Albany, NY: State University of New York Press, 1996.

Steel, L., and R. Levine. *Educational Innovation in Multiracial Contexts: The Growth of Magnet Schools in American Education.* Palo Alto, CA: Prepared for the U.S. Department of Education, 1994.

Summers, A.A., and A.W. Johnson. "Review of the Evidence of the Effects of School-based Management Plans." Paper presented at the conference Improving the Performance of America's Schools: Economic Choices, Washington, D.C. (October 1994): 12-13.

Thurow, L.C. *The Future of Capitalism: How Today's Economic Forces Shape Tomorrow's World.* New York: William Morrow and Co., 1990.

U.S. Charter Schools. Charter School Legislation. http://www.uscharterschools.org/pub/uscs_docs/sp/index.htm. Charter Schools Launched. http://www.uscharterschools.org/pub/uscs_docs/o/movement.htm. Charter School in Houston. http://www.uscharter schools.org/pub/uscs_docs/scs/full.htm?page=3#third. Accountability: Standards, Assessment, and Using Data. http://www.uscharterschools.org/pub/uscs_docs/r/account.htm.

U.S. Department of Education. No Child Left Behind, The Impact of New Title I Requirements on Charter Schools, March 2003. http://dpi.state.wi.us/sms/doc/03ncguid.doc

U.S. Department of Education. Washington D.C. http://www.ed.gov/nclb/landing.jhtml.

———. http://www.ed.gov/parents/schools/choice/definitions.html.

———. The State of Charter Schools: National Study of Charter Schools. http://www.ed.gov/pubs/charter3rdyear/index.html.

Vanderslice, V., and S. Farmer. *Transforming Ourselves: Becoming an Inquiring Community.* In M. Fine, *Chartering Urban School Reform.* New York: Columbia University Teachers College, 1994.

Waff, D. "Girl Talk: Creating Community through Social Exchange." In M. Fine, *Chartering Urban School Reform,* 192-201. New York: Columbia University Teachers College, 1994.

Watkins, T. "So You Want to Start a Charter School." *Education Week* 40, 6 September 1995.

Weil, D. *Towards a Critical Multiculturan Literacy.* Vol. 50, Counterpoints, Studies in the Postmodern Theory of Education. New York: Peter Lang Publishing, 1998.

Wells, A. *Why Charter School Policy Fails.* New York: Teacher's College Press, Columbia University, 2002.

Wells, A., A. Lopez, J. and J. Holme. "Charter Schools as Postmodern Paradox: Rethinking Social Stratification in an Age of Deregulated School Choice." *Harvard Educational Review* 69, no. 2: (Summer 1999): 1–28.

Yancey, P. *Parents Founding Charter Schools: Dilemmas and Empowerment and Decentralization.* New York: Peter Lang Publishing, 2000.

Yergin, D., and J. Stanislaw. *The Commanding Heights.* New York: Simon and Schuster, 1998.

Chapter Two
Chronology of U.S. Educational Reform

SEVENTEENTH CENTURY

1635—Boston Latin School, the first Latin Grammar School, was established in Massachusetts. Latin Grammar Schools were designed for the sons of the upper classes who were expected to occupy leadership positions in the church, state, or in the courts. It is the oldest public school in America with a continuous existence and is still in operation today. The curriculum of the school was and is centered in the humanities, its founders sharing with the ancient Greeks the belief that the only good things are the goods of the soul. From its inception, Boston Latin School has taught its scholars dissent with responsibility and has persistently encouraged such dissent. This philosophy was consistent with the period in history known as the Enlightenment, which spurred the founding of the United States.

—The first public "free school" in Virginia is opened.

1647—The Massachusetts Law of 1647, also known as the Old Deluder Satan Act, is passed. The law decreed that every town of at least 50 families must hire a schoolmaster who would teach the town's children to read, write, and learn scripture and that all towns of at least 100 families would have a Latin grammar schoolmaster who would prepare students to attend Harvard College. The funding was to be provided by the masters of children, their parents, or the community in general.

EIGHTEENTH CENTURY

1734—Christian von Wolff describes the human mind as consisting of powers or faculties. The theory guiding the philosophy is that the mind is a separate entity from the body. According to this model, the mind was considered somewhat analogous to a muscle and the role of education was thus to exercise and strengthen the intellect to the point where it could control the will and emotions. Referred to as "Faculty Psychology," the doctrine holds that the mind can best be developed through "mental discipline" or tedious drills and repetition of basic skills and then much later the eventual study of abstract subjects such as classical philosophy, literature, and languages. This viewpoint greatly influences American education throughout the nineteenth century and beyond and can still be argued to be the theoretical cornerstone of national policy towards standards, assessment and education in the nation's schools.

1779—Thomas Jefferson submits to Congress an amendment to the Constitution to legalize federal support in support of education. Jefferson thought of public education in essentially political terms—as an auxiliary of free government, a necessity for an informed citizenship. For Jefferson, only an enlightened people could assure democracy and this enlightenment was a product of education. In associating freedom with education, Jefferson was in the forefront of his time. It was his belief in universal suffrage, democracy, and freedom that inspired his belief in universal education (Archiving Early America).

1791—The Bill of Rights is passed by the first Congress of the new republic of the United States. The Tenth Amendment to the Constitution states that powers not delegated to the federal government "are reserved to the States, respectively, or to the people." Thus, the passage of the Bill of Rights serves to assure that education falls within the jurisdiction of the state rather than that of the federal government.

NINETEENTH CENTURY

1800—After failing to move the legislature to extend public education to black children, a citizen, Prince Hall, invites black families to start a private school in his home. In 1808 the school moves to the African Meeting House on Beacon Hill in Boston.

1821—The first public high school, Boston English High School, opens its doors. It is the oldest high school in the United States and serves a diverse population of over 1,200 students from more than 40 countries (English High School Association).

1827—The state of Massachusetts passes a law requiring any towns of more than 500 families to have a public high school that is open to all students who apply.

1829—Horace Mann originally brings forth the issue of humane treatment and accommodations for the insane; he is then appointed chairman of a committee to investigate the practicability and expediency of erecting or procuring, at the expense of the Commonwealth, an asylum for the safekeeping of lunatics and persons furiously mad (Hospitals of Massachusetts). The importance of this would be felt in succeeding years and finds its modern understanding within special education programs.

1836—The first of William Holmes McGuffey's readers is published; this is one of America's first primers or textbooks. The secular tone of the "reader" sets them apart from the more Puritan texts of the day. The McGuffey Readers, as they came to be known, are among the most influential textbooks of the nineteenth century and after the Civil War they became standard schoolbooks in thirty-seven states (Havighurst 1984).

1837—Horace Mann becomes Secretary of the newly formed Massachusetts State Board of Education. As an educational reformer and believer in universal free education, Mann worked throughout his tenure for increased funding of public schools and better teacher training. As the editor of the *Common School Journal,* his belief in the importance of free, universal public education awakens the interest of the nation and continues the educational and democratic traditions of Jeffersonian democracy.

—Eighty students arrive at Mount Holyoke Female Seminary, the first college for women in the United States. The founder and president of the college is Mary Lyon who believed that women should have the same higher educational opportunities as men (Lyon).

1839—The first state-funded school designed specifically for teacher education (known then as "normal" schools) opens in Lexington, Massachusetts. The motivation behind the schools is simple: to provide a public school education for all children and this belief was fueled by both the desire to indoctrinate students with religious teachings to assure the continued existence of a devote and moral populace (and regular church attendance) as well as the belief in the need to educate for social, economic, democratic, and national reasons (The Normal School).

1848—Hervey Wilbur helps establish the Massachusetts School for Idiotic and Feebleminded Youth, the first school of its kind in the United States (Hospitals of Massachusetts).

1852—Massachusetts enacts the first mandatory school attendance law in the United States. By 1885, 16 states have compulsory-attendance laws, but most of those laws are sporadically enforced if at all; by 1918 all states have them. The law included mandatory attendance for children between the ages of eight and fourteen for at least three months out of each year—of these twelve weeks at least six had to be consecutive. The penalty for not sending your child to school was a fine not greater than $20 and the violators were to be prosecuted by the city. The local school committee did not have the authority to enforce the law and although the law was ineffective, it did keep the importance of school before the public and helped to form public opinion in favor of education (Compulsory Education).

1856—The first kindergarten in the United States is started in Watertown, Wisconsin. The school is founded by Margarethe Schurz. Four years later, Elizabeth Palmer Peabody opens the first "formal" kindergarten in Boston, Massachusetts. The system was quickly adopted throughout the United States (Wisconsin Department of Justice).

1857—The National Education Association (NEA) is founded by forty-three educators in Philadelphia. Its strength as a teacher's union has consistently grown over time.

1862—The First Morrill Act, also known as the "Land Grant Act" becomes law. The law donates public lands to states, the sale of which will be used for the: endowment, support, and maintenance of at least one college where the leading object shall be, without excluding other scientific and classical studies and including military tactics, to teach such branches of learning as are related to agriculture and the mechanical arts, in order to promote the liberal and practical education of the industrial classes in the several pursuits and professions in life (About the Land-Grant System).

Passage of the First Morrill Act (1862) reflects a growing demand for agricultural and technical education in the United States. While a number of institutions had begun to expand upon the traditional classical curriculum, higher education was still widely unavailable to many agricultural and industrial workers. The Morrill Act was intended to provide a broad segment of the population with a practical education that had direct relevance to their daily lives.

1881—Booker T. Washington becomes the first principal of the newly-opened "normal" school in Tuskegee, Alabama, now known as Tuskegee University (Booker T. Washington National Monument).

1890—The Second Morrill Act is enacted. The Act provides for the more complete endowment and support of the colleges through the sale of public lands creation of 16 historically black land-grant colleges (Historically Black Colleges and Universities).

Although the First Morrill Act provided for land grant colleges, few were open, nor inviting to African Americans. The second Morrill Act specified that states using federal land-grant funds must either make their schools open to both blacks and whites or allocate money for segregated black colleges to serve as an alternative to white schools. Part of this funding leads to, through the sale of public lands, creation of 16 historically black land-grant colleges (Historically Black Colleges and Universities, Ibid.).

1892—An important example of judicial preference for private interests came in 1892 with the case of Homer Plessy. While traveling on the East Louisiana Railroad, Plessy, a black man, sat in a car designated for whites only. He was subsequently arrested and put in jail. He took his case all the way to the Suprme Court and in *Homer Adolph Plessy v. The State of Louisiana,* Plessy's lawyer argued that the 1890 Louisiana Separate Car Act violated the 13th and 14th Amendments to the Constitution. The trial ended with a judgment against Plessy. In 1896 the U.S. Supreme Court in *Plessy v. Ferguson* found Plessy guilty. This case would serve to legally justify racial segregation for the next half century.

TWENTIETH CENTURY

1916—Louis M. Terman and his team of Stanford University graduate students complete an American version of the Binet-Simon Scale. The Stanford Revision of the Binet-Simon Scale becomes a widely used individual intelligence test, and along with it, the concept of the intelligence quotient (or IQ) is born.

—John Dewey's *Democracy and Education: An Introduction to the Philosophy of Education* is first published. Dewey's views helped advance the ideas of the progressive educational movement. Progressive education seeks to make schools more effective agents of democracy and citizenship education. The term "progressive education" has been used to describe ideas and practices that aim to make schools more effective agencies of a democratic society. Although there are numerous differences of style and emphasis among progressive educators, they share the conviction that democracy means active participation by all citizens in social, political and economic decisions that will affect their lives. The education of engaged citizens, according to this perspective, involves two essential elements: (1) *respect for diversity,* meaning that each individual should be recognized for his or her own abilities, interests, ideas, needs, and cultural identity, and (2) the development of *critical, socially engaged intelligence,* which enables individuals to understand and participate effectively in the affairs of their community in a collaborative effort to achieve a common good (John Dewey Project on Progressive Education).

1925—*Tennessee vs. John Scopes* ("the Monkey Trial") captures national attention as John Scopes, a substitute high school biology teacher, is charged with the crime of teaching evolution. The trial ends in Scopes' conviction. The evolution versus creationism controversy persists to this day and the latest 2005 court decision in Dover, Pennsylvania is just one example.

1926—The Scholastic Aptitude Test (SAT) is first administered. It is based on the Army Alpha test. It was first administered experimentally to a few thousand college applicants in 1926 (Secrets of the SAT).

1929—The Great Depression begins with the stock market crash in October. The U.S. economy is devastated and public education funding suffers greatly, resulting in school closings, teacher layoffs, and lower salaries.

1935—Congress authorizes the Works Progress Administration (WPA). Its purpose is to put the unemployed to work on public projects, including the construction of hundreds of school buildings throughout the nation. The Civil Conservation Corps (CCC) is founded during this time as well and finds expression today in AmeriCorp.

1944—The G.I. Bill officially known as the Servicemen's Readjustment Act of 1944, is signed by FDR on June 22. Some 7.8 million World War II veterans take advantage of the G.I. Bill during the seven years benefits are offered. More than two-million veterans attend colleges or universities, nearly doubling the college population. About 238,000 of these students become teachers. Because the law provides the same opportunity to every veteran, regardless of background, college education is now available to all social classes, not just the wealthy (Our Documents).

1946—At one minute after midnight on January 1, Kathleen Casey Wilkens is born, the first of nearly 78 million children born this year. This begins the "baby boomer" generation that results in unprecedented school population growth and tremendous social change.

1947—In the case of *Everson v. Board of Education,* the U.S. Supreme Court rules by a 5-4 vote that a New Jersey law that allowed reimbursements of transportation costs to parents of children who rode public transportation to school, even if their children attended Catholic schools, did not violate the Establishment Clause of the First Amendment.

1954-1959—The U.S. Supreme Court affirmed equal access to public accommodations, especially schools, in the decision rendered in *Brown v. Board of Educa-*

tion. The ruling overturned the long-standing "separate but equal" decision in the Plessy case of 1896. Immediately following the court ruling, segregationists in Virginia devised a "freedom of choice" policy to allow white students to transfer out of schools slated for integration. When Prince Edward County whites finally exhausted their legal bag of tricks in 1959, they shut the public schools down and set up a foundation to support the education of whites only.

The white school foundation moved rapidly to raise money to establish the Prince Edward Academy of Virginia that used a variety of facilities beginning in fall 1959. Permanent academy facilities for both elementary and secondary students were built soon after. Essentially all of the white children in Prince Edward County were enrolled in the Academy in the next few years. Some of the poor whites in the county were provided scholarships to pay their children's tuition to attend.

The haste with which southern whites established private schools after 1954 throughout the United States has been characterized as "white flight." Whites in the North would react in much the same way when their turn came, opting out of the cities entirely to invest their taxes in quality schools for their own children in the suburbs. Those who remained in places like Boston chose private education over integration. This controversy is alive and well today and finds deep roots in controversies over schools.

1962—In the case of *Engel v. Vitale,* the U.S. Supreme Court rules that the state of New York's Regents prayer violates the First Amendment. On a vote of six to one, the ruling specifies that "state officials may not compose an official state prayer and require that it be recited in the public schools of the State at the beginning of each school day . . ." (Legal Information Institute, under "State Prayer").

1963—In the cases of *School District of Abington Township, Pennsylvania v. Schempp* and *Murray v. Curlett,* the U.S. Supreme Court reaffirms *Engel v. Vitale* by ruling that "no state law or school board may require that passages from the Bible be read or that the Lord's Prayer be recited in the public schools . . . even if individual students may be excused from attending or participating . . ."

—Samuel A. Kirk uses the term "learning disability" at a Chicago conference on children with perceptual disorders. He suggested the term be used to describe "children who have disorders in development of language, speech, reading, and associated communication skills." They enthusiastically agreed and shortly thereafter in 1964 established the Association for Children with Learning Disabilities. The concept caught on and today nearly one-half of all students in the United States who receive special education have been identified as having learning disabilities.

1964—The Civil Rights Act becomes law. It prohibits discrimination based on race, color, sex, religion, or national origin.

1965—The Elementary and Secondary Education (ESEA) Act is passed. The ESEA was passed as a result of the struggles of the civil rights movement. It established the precedent for a supportive federal role in public education and it has led to the funding of Title I and other programs. Traditionally, the bill has financed educational opportunities for poor children and expresses a federal commitment to education. Recently, in 2002 it was amended to allow for No Child Left Behind (NCLB).

—The Higher Education Act (PL 89-329) is signed at Southwest Texas State College on November 8. The Act increases federal aid to higher education and provides for scholarships, student loans, and establishes a National Teachers Corps.

—Project Head Start, a preschool education program for children from low-income families, begins as an eight-week summer program. Part of President Johnson's *War on Poverty,* the program continues to this day as the longest-running antipoverty program in the United States.

1966—The Equality of Educational Opportunity Study, often called the Coleman Report because of its primary author James S. Coleman, is conducted in response to provisions of the Civil Rights Act of 1964. It comes to the conclusion that African American children benefit from attending integrated schools and this in turn sets the stage for school "busing" in an attempt to achieve desegregation.

Public Law 358, the Benefits Readjustment Act of 1966 is passed and it provides not only educational benefits, but also home and farm loans as well as employment counseling and placement services for Vietnam veterans. More than 385,000 troops, serve in Vietnam during 1966. From 1965-1975, more than nine million American military personnel are on active military duty, about 3.4 million of whom serve in Southeast Asia. On June 30, 2008, President Bush signed the new G.I. Bill into law. The Bill provides among other benefits, tuition monies for college.

1968—The Monkey Trial is revisited. In the case of *Epperson et al. v. Arkansas,* the U.S. Supreme Court finds the state of Arkansas' law prohibiting the teaching of evolution in a public school or university unconstitutional (Freedom of Speech in the United States).

1969—Herbert R. Kohl's book, *The Open Classroom,* helps to promote open education, an approach emphasizing student-centered classrooms and active, holistic learning. An "open education" emphasizes the ways in which teachers can implement a humanistic view towards education. Some of these include allowing the student to have a choice in the selection of tasks and activities whenever possible, helping students learn to set realistic goals, having students participate in group work, especially cooperative learning in order to develop social and affective skills, and helping students act as facilitators for group discussions when appropriate as well as learning how to be a role model for humanistic attitudes, beliefs and habits (Educational Psychology Interactive). The conservative back-to-the-basics movement of the 1970s begins at least partially as a backlash against the open education and what they see as permissive educational tactics.

Early 1970s—In Michigan, many parents who supported the expenses of their children at private schools and who also supported government schools demand taxpayer-funded support for private schools. The increasing costs of operating the public school system and paying for private schools created significant support for partial taxpayer funding of private education. The Michigan legislature then passed Public Act 100 of 1970, the school aid bill for the year, which provided direct support to eligible private schools, which could be used only for instruction in nonreligious subjects. Michigan's law was similar in concept to those passed in a handful of other states, including Pennsylvania and Rhode Island.

The Michigan Supreme Court quickly upheld the law, ruling in an advisory opinion that "the Constitution of the State of Michigan did not prohibit the purchase with public funds of secular educational services from a nonpublic school."

The passage of the law then provided impetus for a campaign to amend the 1963 Constitution to prohibit state funds from being used to support education at private schools. A petition drive was mounted by the "Council Against Parochiaid" to place an amendment on the ballot. The petitions were thrown out after a finding by the attorney general, and later the board of canvassers, that the petitions did not let the signers know whether the amendment would abrogate the education section of the Constitution. A split panel of the Court of Appeals, and then a 5-2 majority in the Michigan Supreme Court, then ordered the issue placed on the ballot.

However, a concern for maintaining institutional separation between church and state and avoiding "excessive entanglement" by preventing tax dollars from flowing to religious schools was probably not the only force which drove the ballot initiative. There was a heightened awareness of religious differences at that time in the state of Michigan, and with it came the concomitant concern that state dollars might be used to promote not just private education in general, but a specific religion. Thus, the specter of what is known as "parochiaid" was born.

The campaign itself was rancorous and bitter, with the effect of the proposal unclear to the voters as well as to public officials. However, the amendment (Proposal C on the November 1970 ballot) was approved by a margin of 338,098 votes: 1,416,838 to 1,078,740. The new language added to Article VIII, Section 2 provided the following:

No public monies or property shall be appropriated or paid or any public credit utilized, by the legislature or any other political subdivision or agency of the state directly or indirectly to aid or maintain any private, denominational or other nonpublic, pre-elementary, elementary, or secondary school. No payment, credit, tax benefit, exemption or deductions, tuition voucher, subsidy, grant or loan of public monies or property shall be provided, directly or indirectly, to support the attendance of any student or the employment of any person at any such nonpublic school or at any location or institution where instruction is offered in whole or in part to such nonpublic school students.

The Courts and political leaders are faced with massive public opposition to school busing. Congress allocates millions of dollars to create "magnet schools" as one way of promoting racial integration. These schools offer special, sometimes enhanced curricula to hopefully attract a racially diverse student body. They are designed by central school districts as opposed to groups of parents and educators and become the source of political controversy. These schools have selective admission tests and the per-pupil cost is considered often more than that for neighborhood schools. This controversy continues today with the advent of charter schools, which seek to do much of the same although they are distinctly different in approach.

1970—The case of *Diana v. California State Board* results in new laws requiring that children referred for possible special education placement be tested in their primary language (Educational Psychology Interactive).

1971—In the case of *Pennsylvania Association for Retarded Children (PARC) v. Pennsylvania,* the federal court rules that students with mental retardation are entitled to a free public education (Ed Law Online Library).

1972—The case of *Mills v. the Board of Education of Washington, D.C.* extends the *PARC v. Pennsylvania* ruling to other students with disabilities and requires the provision of "adequate alternative educational services suited to the child's needs, which may include special education . . ." Other similar cases follow (Touro Law Center)

—The U.S. Supreme court handed down a landmark decision in *Brusca v. Missouri State Board of Education,* denying the use of public funds to pay for private tuition costs and ruling unconstitutional a Missouri state statute that authorized public funds for such use. The case involved parents of children attending religious schools in Missouri. They argued that the Free Exercise and Equal Protection Clauses of the fourteenth amendment require subsidization, with public tax funds, the cost of their children's tuition. The Brusca decision has been used to deny such relief in later decisions.

—Parents of parochial school children brought suit against the state of California, arguing that the lack of a system of "tuition grants" for parents who wished to educate their children in nonpublic elementary and secondary schools violated their rights of free exercise and equal protection stipulated in both the California and U.S. Constitutions. The court rejected the claim.

—Title IX of the Education Amendments of 1972 becomes law. Though many people associate this law only with girl's and women's participation in sports, Title IX prohibits discrimination based on sex in all aspects of education. This is now being challenged with the rise of all male charter schools and all female charter schools.

1974—Federal Judge Arthur Garrity orders busing of African American students to predominantly white schools in order to achieve racial integration of public schools in Boston, MA. White parents protest, particularly in South Boston.

1975—The Education of All Handicapped Children Act (PL 94-142) becomes federal law. It requires that a free, appropriate public education, suited to the student's individual needs and offered in the least restrictive setting be provided for all "handicapped" children. States are given until 1978 (later extended to 1981) to fully implement the law (Education for All Handicapped Children Act of 1975).

—The National Association of Bilingual Education (NABE) is founded. It is dedicated to representing Bilingual Learners and Bilingual Education professionals and will prove to have a large impact on issues of bilingual education and educational equity.

—*Newsweek's* December 8 cover story, *Why Johnny Can't Read,* heats up the debate about national literacy and the back-to-the-basics movement, which is in direct challenge to the open school movement. The opening paragraph of the article outlined the problem from the point of view of *Newsweek:*

> *If your children are attending college, the chances are that when they graduate they will be unable to write ordinary, expository English with any degree of structure and lucidity. If they are in high school and planning to attend college, the chances are*

less than even that they will be able to write English at the minimal college level when they get there.

The article was one of the media events that launched the back-to-basics movement in education (Enotes, The Literacy Crisis).

Early 1980s—The development of private voucher philosophies is an organizing concept for the conservative wing of the Republican Party. Because the idea appealed to the Christian Right's family values agenda and coupled nicely with the belief in the primacy of markets, school choice was held up as a national political, cultural and economic issue that galvanized a new generation of conservative activists.

Innovative public schools, state to state, find that they do not have the control over budgets and faculties they need to make public education work. Debates among administrators, parents, and teachers begin over the future operation and control of schools.

1982—In the case of *Board of Education v. Pico,* the U.S. Supreme court rules that books cannot be removed from a school library because school administrators deemed their content to be offensive (First Amendment Center, under "School Library"). This is a large victory for the first amendment rights of the nation but it leaves a disgruntled constituency that would go on to struggle on curriculum issues, vouchers for private schools and charter schools.

1983—The publication *A Nation at Risk,* expresses dissatisfaction with schools in the United States, capitalizing on the controversies above. Specific dissatisfaction is expressed at the public schools and is the catalyst for the development of the privatization of education movement that will gain momentum in succeeding decades. The report begins its introduction:

Our Nation is at risk. Our once unchallenged preeminence in commerce, industry, science, and technological innovation is being overtaken by competitors throughout the world. This report is concerned with only one of the many causes and dimensions of the problem, but it is the one that undergirds American prosperity, security, and civility. We report to the American people that while we can take justifiable pride in what our schools and colleges have historically accomplished and contributed to the United States and the well-being of its people, the educational foundations of our society are presently being eroded by a rising tide of mediocrity that threatens our very future as a Nation and a people. What was unimaginable a generation ago has begun to occur—others are matching and surpassing our educational attainments." The argument is keeping with the back-to-basic argument of the 1970s (A Nation At Risk).

1985—In the case of *Wallace v. Jaffree,* the U.S. Supreme Court finds that Alabama statutes authorizing silent prayer and teacher-led voluntary prayer in public schools violate the First Amendment (Legal Information Institute, under "Alabama Statutes").

Mid 1980s—The California public alternative school group, Learning Alternative Resource Network (LEARN), develops a proposed legislative bill that responds to issues of control and authority in innovative schools. It stipulates that if thirty or more parents and/or pupils request a new school and the teachers within the district choose to teach in it, and if the operating costs are no more than those of programs with equivalent status for the same pupils, the district "shall establish a public school or program of choice responsive to the request." The proposed bill is never introduced or adopted but it has strong traces of the charter school movement and the "choice" movement that was to emerge in the 1990s.

—In Minnesota, Governor Rudy Perpich introduces proposals for several public school choice programs. His 1985 proposals are strongly supported by an unusual coalition that includes the Minnesota Parent-Teachers Association, directors of the War on Poverty agencies in Minnesota, individual teachers, administrators, and parents, and the Minnesota Business Partnership (MBP).

1987—In the case of *Edwards v. Aguillard et al.* the U.S. Supreme Court strikes down a Louisiana law requiring that creation science be taught along with evolution in the science classroom (Supreme Court of the United States).

1988—The Minnesota legislature adopts key parts of Governor Perpich's "choice schools" proposal. The postsecondary option adopted by the legislature allows public high school juniors and seniors to take all or part of their coursework in colleges and universities. The option to attend other public schools is included in the adoption by the legislature. Known as the Areas Learning Center Law and High School Graduation Incentive Act, this law, which passed in 1987, allows teenagers and adults who have not previously succeeded in school to attend public schools outside their district boundaries for the first time. The bill also allows students to attend private, nonsectarian schools if a local district contracts with those schools. Thus, begins the educational "slippery slope" of "school choice."

The open enrollment portion of the legislation is finally passed in 1988 and this allows students from kindergarten through twelfth grade to apply to attend public schools outside their districts as long as the receiving district has room and the transfer does not increase racial segregation. This now becomes the first real state experience with choice programs, and these programs begin to receive media publicity and growing support throughout the United States.

1988, continued
—Ray Budde, a retired teacher and expert on school district reorganization, proposes that a school board directly charter teams of teachers to establish new, innovative programs within a district for a three- to five-year period. His book, *Education by Charter: Restructuring School Districts,* begins the first public debate regarding charter schools.

In the 1970s Budde first suggested the term "charter" to a local New England school board as an education reform movement in which local school boards give small groups of teachers contracts or "charters" to explore new educational approaches. In 1988 Budde put the concept in writing in a report titled *Education by Charter: Restructuring School Districts.* He proposed: a more rigorous course of study and more stringent graduation requirements; teachers accounting for their students' outcomes; provision of child care and preschool programs for young parents; and the incorporation of applicable training to prepare young people for the realities of the workplace. Budde's model allowed the local school board to grant a charter to a group of teachers who would manage the school in exchange for a heightened degree of accountability of their failures and successes (National Charter School Clearing House).

—In an address at a Minneapolis conference on improving public schools, American Federation of Teachers president Albert Shanker supports the idea of giving teachers a chance to create innovative new programs and charter schools and goes even further to suggest the creation of entire new schools. He suggests that both the school board and the majority of teachers working in a school be required to approve the new school. On March 31,1988, Shanker makes a speech to the National Press Club in Washington, D.C., in which he endorses these ideas again. Later that year the *Peabody Journal of Education* published "*Restructuring Our Schools.*" Shanker's report points out our academic failures as a nation. Shanker states that, "We live in a technologically sophisticated society, but the main technology of schooling is still 'talk and chalk.'" Shanker also cites the traditional school's limitations in terms of methods and activities that teachers can employ to tailor instruction to accommodate individual differences (Shanker, 92, 98).

The "charter" according to Shanker would be voluntary. He wrote:

No teacher would have to participate and parents would choose whether or not to send their children to a charter school. . . . For its part, the school district would have to agree that so long as teachers continued to teach in the charter school and parents continued to send their children there and there was no precipitous decline in student achievement indicators, it would maintain the school for at least 5-10 years. Perhaps at the end of that period, the school could be evaluated to see the extent to which it met its goals, the charter could be extended or revoked." (Shanker 1988, 98)

—The 1988 annual convention of the American Federation of Teachers endorses the charter school idea at the urging of Shanker. Paying tribute to

Budde's idea, Shanker advocates that local school boards and teachers' unions jointly develop a procedure to enable teams of teachers to establish autonomous public schools within school buildings. He calls these schools within schools "charter schools."

Early 1990s—The back-to-basics and accountability movement in education, along with a climate of economic deregulation, decentralization, the movement toward on-site management, local control issues, restructuring of schools, issues of teacher empowerment, and discussions of more local district control all contribute to the mushrooming of the charter school movement.

The growing threat of private school vouchers propels the charter movement closer to the forefront in an effort to provide choice within a public school context and from the point of view of some progressive educators, stave off the call for school privatization. Charters are seen as a compromise by adhering to the idea of public education while embracing the market fundamentalist call for school competition.

1990—Public Law 101-476, the Individuals with Disabilities Education Act (IDEA) is passed. The Act, renames and amends Public Law 94-142. In addition to changing terminology from "handicap" to "disability," it mandates transition services and adds autism and traumatic brain injury to the eligibility list.

—The Milwaukee Parental Choice program is initiated. It allows "students, under specific circumstances, to attend at no charge, private sectarian and nonsectarian schools located in the city of Milwaukee." So begins the first real experiment in school vouchers and educational "choice" (Wisconsin, Department of Public Instruction).

1991—Minnesota becomes the first state to pass charter school legislation. The law is limited in scope, authorizing no more than eight charter schools statewide and requires that local school boards approve each charter. The original law is later amended to permit forty charter schools and allow the state board of education, upon appeal, to authorize a charter school after a local district has turned it down.

1992—City Academy High School, the nation's first charter school, opens in St. Paul, Minnesota.

—California passes legislation that allows up to 100 charter schools in the state.

1993—Colorado and Massachusetts pass strong charter school laws.

1994—A $2 million dollar grant from the Walton Family foundation launched CEO America, another national private scholarship program in the United States dedicated to privatizing education.

—The U.S. Supreme Court significantly narrowed the opinion that it had rendered in the 1961 case, *Swart v. South Burlington Town School District*. A Vermont statute directed each school district to furnish a high school education to children within the district by either funding the high school or paying tuition at a school of the student's choice. The statute did not explicitly exclude religious schools from the program, but that is how the Vermont State Board of Education interpreted the statute. A parent in a school district that did not provide a public high school sued the state, arguing that his request for reimbursement of tuition for an out-of-state parochial school was illegally denied. The high court virtually overruled its earlier decision in *Swart* and ruled that the statute did not exclude religious schools from the reimbursement policy. The court went on to analyze arguments that claimed such an interpretation of the statute would violate the Establishment Clause, ruling that allowing tuition grants to the plaintiff in the case did not violate the Establishment clause.

—Eleven states have legislation that allows charter schools. A federal Public Charter Schools Program is made law as part of the 1994 amendments to the Elementary and Secondary Education (ESEA) Act. The program is designed to help charter schools in states where they are legally allowed.

In 1994, Congress reauthorized Title I to emphasize accountability for the academic learning of students served through that program.

—On November 1, 1994 the issue of "what is a public institution" nearly stopped Michigan's experiment with charter schools. The court declared that public school academies, in spite of their name, were not public at all. Thus, the result of the court's decision was that public funding of the schools was unconstitutional.

1995—Eight more states pass charter school legislation (Alaska, Arkansas, Delaware, Louisiana, New Hampshire, Rhode Island, Texas, and Wyoming).

—Starting with $6 million in fiscal year 1995, the U.S. Department of Education has provided grants to support states' charter school efforts.

1996—Connecticut, Florida, Illinois, New Jersey, North Carolina, and South Carolina pass charter school legislation and the movement begins to gain real momentum throughout the United States.

—In October, Secretary of Education Richard Riley announces the award of $17 million in the form of grants to seventeen states and Puerto Rico and the District of Columbia to support the start-up and development of hundreds of additional charter schools.

1997—The Michigan Supreme Court comes to an opposite decision in reviewing the 1997 appeal of Michigan's charter school law. The majority of the court disagreed that the charter school law constituted an improper delegation of authority to a private entity and went on to argue that schools are "public" not by virtue of the "exclusive control" of the state. They argued that "there is, in fact, no requirement that those schools be under its 'exclusive control.'"

—The momentum for charter school legislation continues as Pennsylvania and Mississippi pass charter legislation; seven states, including Virginia and Nevada, turn down similar legislation.

—The U.S. Congress increases federal funding for the Public Charter Schools Program to $51 million in fiscal 1997 and then President Clinton asks the congressional appropriations committees to double the funding to $100 million by 1998.

—By the summer, nearly 500 charter schools are operating in twenty-seven states and the District of Columbia.

—The Universal Tuition Tax Credit (UTTC) plan for Michigan is proposed in 1997.With a tax credit like the UTTC, the taxpayer pays tuition for a student at a public or nonpublic school and when she calculates her taxes, she subtracts the amount paid in tuition (subject to a maximum limit of 50 percent of what public schools receive per student) from her tax liability. The UTTC would offset a portion of private or public school tuition and would be claimed against state tax liabilities.

—In his 1997 State of the Union Address, President Clinton called for the creation of 3,000 charter schools by the year 2002.

—On November 10, the U.S. Senate refused to vote on H.R. 2646, the so-called "A+ Education Savings Account Bill." The bill would have created tax-free educational savings accounts for familes earning up to $160,000 annually to use for payment of expenses associated with private, religious, or homeschooling.

1998—The Higher Education Act is amended and reauthorized requiring institutions and states to produce "report cards" about teacher education (See Appendix A).

—By the end of 1998, thirty-four states and the District of Columbia have passed charter school legislation.

1999-2000—The Center for Education Reform reports that 1,682 charter schools will open their doors to approximately 350,000 children in thirty-one states and the District of Columbia for the current school year.

TWENTY-FIRST CENTURY

2000—In yet another case regarding school prayer *(Santa Fe School District v. Doe)*, the U.S. Supreme Court rules that the district's policy of allowing student-led prayer prior to football games violates the Establishment Clause of the First Amendment (Legal Information Institute, under "Student-led Prayer").

2001—The controversial No Child Left Behind (NCLB) Act is signed into law by President George W. Bush. The law, which reauthorizes the Elementary and Secondary Education Act (ESEA) of 1965, holds schools accountable for student achievement levels through standardized testing and provides penalties for schools that do not make adequate yearly progress toward meeting the goals of NCLB (New York State Education Department).

—The National Education Association adopts a resolution supporting charter schools. The organization argues that in order for charter schools to fulfill their intended purposes they should be designed to (1) serve as experimental laboratories for field-testing curricular and instructional innovations, with an eye to whether those innovations can be incorporated into "mainstream" public schools, or (2) provide educational alternatives for students who cannot adequately be served in mainstream public schools. It follows from these purposes that a charter should be granted only if the proposed charter school intends to offer students an educational experience that is qualitatively different from what is available to them in mainstream public schools, and not simply to provide a "choice" for parents who may be dissatisfied with the education that their children are receiving in mainstream public schools (Iowa State Education Association, under "News & Information").

2002—In the case of *Zelman v. Simmons-Harris,* the U.S. Supreme court rules that certain school voucher programs are constitutional and do not violate the Establishment Clause of the First Amendment (First Amendment Center, under "School Voucher Programs").

—President Bush called for $200 million to support charter schools. His proposed budget called for another $100 million for a new Credit Enhancement for Charter Schools Facilities Program.

2003—The Higher Education Act is again amended and reauthorized, purportedly expanding access to higher education for low- and middle-income students, providing additional funds for graduate studies, and increasing accountability.

—The Wisconsin, Northern Ozaukee School District contracted with K12, Inc. a Delaware corporation, to provide a curriculum for its new virtual charter school, the Wisconsin Virtual Academy (WIVA). K12, Inc. sent books and other materials to the students and also provided curricular materials via the Internet. Under the direction of their parents, the WIVA students are expected to study the materials and complete various assignments in accordance. As of 2004, the majority of WIVA students lived and studied outside the District. The open enrollment payments transfer from these students' home districts covered the district's cost to operate WIVA and provided the District with an "oversight fee." The remaining revenue was then paid to K12, Inc.

2004—H.R. 1350, The Individuals with Disabilities Education Improvement Act (IDEA 2004), reauthorizes and modifies IDEA. Changes, which take effect on July 1, 2005, include modifications in the Individualized Education Program (IEP) process and procedural safeguards, increased authority for school personnel in special education placement decisions, and alignment of IDEA with the No Child Left Behind Act of 2001.

—In January, individual citizens and the Wisconsin Educational Association Council (WEAC) filed suit against the Northern Ozaukee School District and Superintendent arguing that the District violated the charter school open enrollment and teacher licensing statutes set up by the state by contracting with K12, Inc. the Delaware corporation, to provide a curriculum for the District's new virtual charter school, the Wisconsin Virtual Academy (WIVA).

2005—In the latest incarnation of the "Monkey Trial," the U.S. District Court of Pennsylvania rules in the case of *Kitzmiller v. Dover Area School District,* that teaching "intelligent design" as an alternative to evolution is a violation of the First Amendment (The TalkOrigins Archive).

2006—In March, the circuit court of Wisconsin state granted summary judgment to the Northern Ozaukee School District in its legal battle with the Wisconsin Educational Association Council (WEAC) over the issue of the legality of the Wisconsin Virtual Academy (WIVA).

2007—In the cases of *Parents Involved in Community Schools v. Seattle School District No. 1* and *Meredith v. Jefferson County Board of Education,* the U.S. Supreme Court ruled 5-4 that race cannot be a factor in assigning students to high schools, thus rejecting integration plans in Seattle and Louisville, and possibly affecting similar plans in school districts around the nation (On the Docket).

2007, continued
—On December 5, the state of Wisconsin Appeals Court ruled that the Northern Ozaukee School District, which had established the Wisconsin Virtual Academy (WIVA) as a charter school, was not being operated in accordance with the charter school open enrollment and teacher licensing statutes set up by the state. The court advised the legislature to change the statutes as currently written if they wished to provide for virtual charter schools. The Wisconsin Virtual Academy served pupils across the state by providing curricular materials to students in their homes via Internet and mail. The great bulk of WIVA's funding came from open enrollment transfer payments to the District from the pupil's home districts.

—In August, there were 24 programs in 13 states and the District of Columbia that provide financial assistance in the form of voucher or voucher-like tuition assistance, tax credits and tax deductions, compared with seven programs in seven states in 1997.

2008—Chancellor of New York schools, Joe Klein and self-proclaimed civil rights leader, Al Sharpton, start an ambitious venture they call the Education Equality Project, and they vow in a Washington press conference in 2008 to lead a campaign to close the decades-old achievement gap between white and black students. In the mission statement for the new group they state:

> The Education Equality Project is a non-partisan group of elected officials, civil rights leaders, and education reformers that has formed to help ensure that America finally brings equity to an educational system that, 54 years since Brown v. Board of Education, continues to fail its highest needs students. (Education Quality Project)

—More than 100 new teachers and principals announced they are prepared to enter Orleans Parish public schools in August of 2008, bringing with them years of experience and transforming the way students learn. With 63 people enrolled in the TeachNOLA fellows program, designed for uncertified teachers, and 58 certified teachers, program graduates will be spread through new and existing schools to help as many students as possible (*New Orleans City Business*).

—The Center for Education Reform created a survey that was sent out to approximately 4,100 schools, with a 20 percent response rate, and presents an intense view into the context for, and environment surrounding, the operation of the nation's charter schools (Center for Education Reform).

—The American Federation of Teachers, the USA's second-largest teachers' union, announced on September 9, 2008, that it will put up $1 million and seek

2008, continued

additional philanthropic funding to help school systems try "sustainable, innovative and collaborative reform projects" developed by AFT teachers over the past several years. AFT has more than 1.4 million members; half of which currently work in schools. Among the efforts the fund likely will support, peer-review teacher evaluations such as those developed in Toledo, Ohio, union-run charter schools similar to those in New York City, and pay-for-performance plans as developed in Denver. The money would be earmarked to pay for implementing programs, lobbying school boards or even supporting union-friendly candidates who favor teacher-generated reforms (*USA Today*).

—Margaret Spelling, the U.S. Secretary of Education under George W. Bush, announced final regulations to strengthen the No Child Left Behind Act. Under the new regulations, all states will use the same formula to calculate how many students graduate from high school on time and how many drop-out. The final regulations define the "four year adjusted cohort graduation rate" as the number of students who graduate in four years with a regular high school diploma divided by the number of students who entered high school four years earlier, adjusted for transfers, students who emigrate, and deceased students. The data will be made public so that educators and parents can compare how students of every race, background, and income level are performing. The final rules also require that parents must be notified in a clear and timely way about their public school choice and supplemental education service options. The regulations seek to ensure that states make more information available to the public about what tutoring providers are available, how these providers are approved and monitored, and most importantly, how effective they are in helping students improve (U.S. Department of Education).

—Two years after it lost collective bargaining rights in New Orleans schools, the city's teachers' union seeks a small foothold in the handful of schools still under School Board control. Board administrators and the United Teachers of New Orleans came up with a recently revised collective bargaining proposal that could move to a board committee soon. The political prospects for a contract approval, however, remain uncertain. Two School Board members publicly supported granting the union a contract. Two members argued that any vote on returning the union's power to the district should be delayed until a newly elected School Board takes office in January of 2009. If an agreement does win approval, it would cover only the five schools directly controlled by the board, not the dozen charter schools the board oversees or any traditional or charter school in the state-run Recovery School District. The union boasted close to 5,000 members before the storm. Today, it has about 1,460 dues-paying teachers, para-educators and clerical staff—more than half of whom work in the schools operated by the state-run Recovery School District. More than 170 members work in board-operated schools and about 70 members work in the city's charter schools, according to the union (*Times-Picayune*).

2009—More than 80 teachers, parents and supporters of a revered Lower 9th Ward New Orleans charter school descended on the state Capitol on Wednesday, January 17, 2009, to object to a proposal to renew the school's charter contingent on submitting a plan to increase the number of enrolled special needs students. The charter for the Dr. Martin Luther King, Jr. Charter School for Science and Technology was renewed without the provision. King Charter was one of 17 New Orleans charters that state education officials were recommending for charter extension (*Times-Picayune*).

—The National Alliance for Public Charter Schools called for states to overhaul and expand laws governing charter schools. The nation's leading charter school organization unveiled a proposal aimed at overhauling the wide range of state laws that govern the publicly funded schools, as well as establishing charter laws in the 10 states that don't yet allow the schools to operate. Several features of the model law relate to facilities and access to capital for charter leaders. The alliance's blueprint envisions that states would provide an array of support to charters for securing and paying for facilities, including a per-pupil facilities allowance that would be based in part on what states spend on traditional school facilities over five years. A similar method is used by the District of Columbia. Also, the model law calls for giving charters access to grants and loans, as well as granting them bonding authority (*EdWeek*).

—The National Council on Teacher Quality (NCTQ) released its 2008 State Teacher Policy Yearbook, titled "What States Can Do To Retain Effective New Teachers." The report issued a series of policy recommendations for raising teacher quality. The AFT disagreed with the report, believing that bold actions must be taken to improve teaching in order to ensure that every child receives a world-class education (American Federation of Teachers).

—President Barack Obama called for tying teachers' pay to student performance and expanding innovative charter schools, embracing ideas that have provoked hostility from members of teachers unions. He also suggested longer school day—and years—to help American children compete in the world. In his first major speech on education, Obama said the United States must drastically improve student achievement to regain lost international standing. His solutions included teacher pay and charter school proposals that have met resistance among members of teachers' unions, which constitute an important segment of the

2009, continued

Democratic Party. Despite their history on the issues, union leaders publicly welcomed Obama's words, saying it seems clear he wants to include them in his decisions in a way President George W. Bush did not (*The Huffington Post*).

—Six states; Massachusetts, New Hampshire, Utah, Arizona, Delaware, and New Mexico, have committed to the "Tough Choices or Tough Times" education reform agenda created by the new Commission on the Skills of the American Workforce. The Commission argued that today's education system in the United States fails to prepare workers for global competition, and U.S. graduates are "mediocre" against international competition in the labor market. The Commission suggested that many improvements to the U.S. education system are needed including lean, performance-oriented management systems, and more high quality tests. Six states commit to the "Tough Choices or Tough Times" education reform (Mission Measurement).

—The *New York Daily News* reported that Joe Klein and Al Sharpton started an ambitious venture they called the "Education Equality Project," and they vowed in a Washington press conference in 2008 to lead a campaign to close the decades-old achievement gap between white and black students. However, according to reporter Juan Gonzalez, what the two men never revealed is that the National Action Network, Sharpton's organization, immediately received a $500,000 donation for its involvement in the new effort. The huge infusion of cash—equal to more than a year's payroll for Sharpton's entire organization—was quietly provided by Plainfield Asset Management, a Connecticut-based hedge fund, where former Chancellor Harold Levy is a managing director. The money came at a critical moment for the National Action Network, when Sharpton was then settling a long-running IRS investigation of his organization. As part of that settlement, he agreed in July to pay $1 million in back taxes and penalties both he personally, and his organization, owed the government. The $500,000 from the Connecticut firm did not go directly to National Action Network. Levy funneled the cash to another nonprofit, Education Reform Now, which allowed his company to claim the donation as a charitable tax deduction. The money was then transferred in several payments to Sharpton's group, which does not have tax-deductible status because it is a lobbying organization. Sharpton and Levy confirmed the contribution (*Daily News*).

—Legislation introduced in Salem, Oregon proposed restrictions on Oregon's virtual charter school industry. The bill pitted the state's most powerful education organizations, including the teachers' union, against online schools and parents. The battle had produced rallies on the Capitol steps, a flurry of lobbying, the birth of a parents' group, and 19 revisions of the bill (The *Oregonian*).

2009, continued

—Illinois Senate Bill 612 (Charter School Reform Act of 2009) is passed and considered by its originators to be a significant step in the growth of Illinois' charter public schools. After four years and countless hours of lobbying and deliberation, SB 612 passed the House of Representatives without opposition and the Illinois Senate by a vote of 45-10. The lifting of the restrictive cap will allow 120 charter schools with limited geographic constraints. This will include 40 new charter schools in Chicago, 15 for downstate Illinois and five new schools allocated for dropout recovery. The bill will also call for a task force to examine independent charter school authorizing in Illinois. The task force will report its findings to the General Assembly on January 1, 2010.

—A circuit court judge quashed an effort by the Chicago Teachers' Union to prevent a virtual public charter school from receiving tax money. In a 2006 lawsuit, the union argued that the Chicago Virtual Charter School is a home-based school and that it fails to supervise students as required by state law. Cook County Circuit Court Judge Daniel A. Riley rejected both arguments. He wrote that although the school shares attributes of home schools, it is not a home-based school. Further, he said, because it is a charter school, it may define supervised instruction differently from state law. On the issue of supervision, Riley looked to state law as well as the virtual school's own charter. First, he found that because it has a charter, the school is exempt from a provision in the Illinois School Code that defines days of attendance and outlines what is direct supervision. Second, he pointed to the school's own standard for supervision—defined as five hours of schoolwork per day—and found that it fulfills that standard with a combination of on- and off-site instruction (*Chi-Town Daily News*).

—A national study released in June by Stanford University's Center for Research on Education Outcomes (CREDO) gives high marks to Louisiana's charter schools, when compared to the state's traditional public schools and to charter schools in 14 other states and Washington, D.C. The report was issued prior to the decision by the Senate Education Committee to support a measure that would remove Louisiana's cap on the number of charter schools permitted to operate in the state. The Stanford report revealed that in Louisiana, the growth demonstrated by charter school students in reading and math during their first year of enrollment in a charter school was equal to the gains made by traditional public school students. However, in subsequent years, the study claimed that charter school students showed greater gains in both subjects—with the largest increases made in years two and three (Recovery School District).

—The American Federation of Teachers' New York City affiliate and Green Dot Public Schools announced a three-year contract agreement for teachers at Green

Dot New York Charter School in the Bronx, an agreement that AFT President Randi Weingarten said proved that unionized charter schools can be collaborative, innovative, and good for students and teachers. The three-year agreement between Green Dot and the United Federation of Teachers was ratified by the school's faculty and by the Green Dot New York Charter School Board (American Federation of Teachers).

—The Pennsylvania Senate passed SB 687, legislation to protect the tax-exempt status of public charter schools. SB 687 was introduced by Senate Majority Leader Dominic Pileggi. The bill now must go to the state House of Representatives for consideration. The legislation attempts to reinforce the fact that Pennsylvania's charter schools are what they are: public schools. The argument claims that as public schools, charter schools are clearly exempt from real estate tax bills. While most taxing authorities throughout the commonwealth understand this principal, there remain a few authorities that do not. As a result, several charter schools have been forced to fight costly legal battles with funds that could otherwise have been used to educate students (*Erie Times News*).

—President-elect Barack Obama nominated superintendent of Chicago schools Arne Duncan as Secretary of Education. For the past seven years, Arne Duncan served as the Chief Executive Officer of the Chicago Public Schools. Prior to joining the public school system, Duncan directed the Ariel Education Initiative, a program that seeks to create educational opportunities for inner-city children on the South Side of Chicago. In 2006, the City Club of Chicago named Duncan Citizen of the Year. Duncan comes from a family of educators; his mother founded and has run a notable Chicago tutoring program for 48 years. Duncan graduated magna cum laude from Harvard University (Change.gov).

REFERENCES

A Nation At Risk. April 1983.
    http://www.ed.gov/pubs/NatAtRisk/risk.html.
About the Land-Grant System. West Virginia University.
    http://www.wvu.edu/%7Eexten/about/land.htm#what.
American Federation of Teachers.
    http://www.aft.org/presscenter/releases/2009/013009a.htm.
———. http://www.aft.org/presscenter/releases/2009/062309.htm.
Archiving Early America.
    http://www.earlyamerica.com/review/winter96/jefferson.html.
Booker T. Washington National Monument. Hardy, VA.
    http://www.nps.gov/archive/bowa/tuskin.html.
Center for Education Reform.
    http://www.edreform.com/_upload/CER_charter_survey_2008.pdf.

Change.gov.
   http://change.gov/newsroom/entry/president_elect_obama_nominates_arne_duncan_as_
   secretary_of_education/.

Compulsory Education.
   http://www.nd.edu/%7Erbarger/www7/compulso.html.

Dieckmann, A.B. "Six States Commit to 'Tough Choices or Tough Times' Education Reform."
   Mission Measurement, LLC. 17 March 2009.
   http://www.missionmeasurement.com/content/thought-capital/thought-scraps/
   2009/03/17/six-states-commit-tough-choices-or-tough-times-education-ref.

Ed Law Online Library.
   http://www.faculty.piercelaw.edu/redfield/library/case-parc.pennsylvania.htm.

Education Equality Project.
   http://www.educationequalityproject.org/content/pages/about/.

Education for All Handicapped Children Act of 1975.
   http://asclepius.com/angel/special.html.

Educational Psychology Interactive.
   http://chiron.valdosta.edu/whuitt/col/affsys/humed.html.

English High School Association. Jamaica Plain, MA.
   http://boston.k12.ma.us/english/alumni/EHShistory.htm.

Enotes, The Literacy Crisis.
   http://www.enotes.com/1970-education-american-decades/literacy-crisis.

First Amendment Center. Washington D.C. School Library.
   http://www.firstamendmentcenter.org/faclibrary/case.aspx?id=849. School Voucher Programs.
   http://www.firstamendmentcenter.org/faclibrary/case.aspx?case=Zelman_v_Simmons_Harris.

Freedom of Speech in the United States.
   http://www.bc.edu/bc_org/avp/cas/comm/free_speech/epperson.html.

Gonzalez, J. "Rev. Al Sharpton's $500G link to education reform." *Daily News,* 1 April 2009.
   http://www.nydailynews.com/news/2009/04/01/2009-04-01_rev_al_sharptons_500g_
   link_to_education_.html.

Graves, B. "Oregon Senate Would Take Virtual Charter Schools Offline for Two Years."
   The *Oregonian,* 3 May 2009.
   http://www.oregonlive.com/news/index.ssf/2009/05/oregon_senate_would_take_virtu.html.

Havighurst, W. *The Miami Years.* New York: G.P. Putnam and Sons, 1984.

Historically Black Colleges and Universities.
   http://www.collegeview.com/articles/CV/hbcu/hbcu_history.html.

Hospitals of Massachusetts.
   http://www.1856.org/historicalOverview.html.

Iowa State Education Association. "NEA Policy on Charter Schools as Adopted in 2001."
   http://www.ia.nea.org/hot/charter/neacharterpolicy.html.

John Dewey Project on Progressive Education. University of Vermont.
   http://www.uvm.edu/%7Edewey/articles/proged.html.

Jones, Jr., L. "Charter Schools Must Remain Tax-Exempt." *Erie Times-News,* 25 June 2009.
   http://www.goerie.com/apps/pbcs.dll/article?AID=/20090625/OPINION02/906249985/
   -1/OPINION.

Legal Information Institute. Cornell University Law School. State Prayer.
   http://supct.law.cornell.edu/supct/html/historics/USSC_CR_0370_0421_ZS.html.
   ——. Alabama Statutes.
   http://www.law.cornell.edu/supct/html/historics/USSC_CR_0472_0038_ZO.html.

———. Student-led Prayer.
  http://www.law.cornell.edu/supct/html/historics/USSC_CR_0530_0290_ZS.html.
Lyon, Mary.
  http://www.mtholyoke.edu/marylyon/noframes/founding.html.
Maloney, S. "Agents of Change." *New Orleans City Business,* 7 July 2008.
  http://newschoolsforneworleans.org/downloads/7.7.08.AgentsofChange.CityBusiness.
  Maloney.pdf.
Maxwell, L.A. "Model State Charter School Law Unveiled." *EdWeek,* 23 January 2009
  vol. 28, no. 36.
  http://www.edweek.org/ew/articles/2009/06/23/36charterlaw.h28.html?tkn=
  XZSFPL1etvTstew9EmXDB1iYKkg4Yhcmbt11&print=1.
National Charter School Clearing House.
  http://www.ncsc.infp/newsletter/may_2002/history.htm.
New York State Education Department.
  http://www.emsc.nysed.gov/deputy/nclb/parents/facts/eng/eng-overview.html.
The Normal School.
  http://www.nd.edu/%7Erbarger/www7/normal.html.
On the Docket.
  http://docket.medill.northwestern.edu/archives/003697.php.
Our Documents.
  http://www.ourdocuments.gov/doc.php?flash=true&doc=76&page=transcript.
Quaid, L. "Obama Education Plan Speech: Stricter Standards, Charter Schools, Merit Pay."
  Huffington Post, 10 March 2009.
  http://www.huffingtonpost.com/2009/03/10/obama-education-plan-spee_n_173405.html.
Recovery School District.
  http://www.rsdla.net/Media/PressRelease/aspx?PR=1307.
Secrets of the SAT.
  http://www.pbs.org/wgbh/pages/frontline/shows/sats/where/history.html.
Simon, D. "Teachers' Union Seeking to Regain Foothold in New Orleans Schools."
  Times-Picayune, 10 November 2008.
  http://www.nola.com/news.index.ssf/2008/11/teachers_union_seeking_foothol.html.
———. "Lower 9th Ward School to Keep Charter." *Times-Picayune,* 18 June 2009.
Shanker, Albert. "Restructuring Our Schools." *Peabody Journal of Education* 65, No. 3 (Spring
  1988): 92, 98.
Supreme Court of the United States. *Edwards, Governor of Lousiana et. al. v. Aguillard et. al.*
  http://www.law.umkc.edu/faculty/projects/ftrials/conlaw/edwards.html.
The TalkOrigins Archive.
  http://www.talkorigins.org/faqs/dover/kitzmiller_v_dover.html.
Toppo, G. "Teachers' Union Initiates School Reform Plan." *USA Today,* 10 September 2008.
  http://www.usatoday.com/news/education/2008-09-10-aft-plan_N.htm.
———. "Young, Inexperienced Teachers Recruited to New Orleans." *USA Today,* 11
  September 2008.
  http://www.usatoday.com/news/education/2008-09-10-new-orleans-teachers_N.htm.
Touro Law Center.
  http://www.tourolaw.edu/patch/Mills/#jd.
Uribarri, A. "Court: Virtual Charter School Can Receive Public Funds." *Chi-Town Daily News,*
  12 June 2009.
  http://www.chitowndailynews.org/Chicago_news/Court_Virtual_charter_school_can_
  receive_public_funds,28382.

U.S. Department of Education.
> http://www.ed.gov/news/pressreleases/2008/10/10282008.html.

Wisconsin Department of Justice.
> http://www.doj.state.wi.us/kidspage/fun_facts/kindergarten.htm.

Wisconsin, Department of Public Instruction.
> http://dpi.state.wi.us/sms/choice.html.

Chapter Three

Charter Schools and the Law

For many charter school advocates, charter schools are not so much about individual schools as they are about reforming districts and school systems through competition in the marketplace. In fact, many charter school supporters would argue that charter schools are all about trying to change the system of education in the United States by allowing for public choice within public schools. The public policy argument that choice advocates offer in support of charter schools is that their creation will provide innovation that will spread throughout traditional public schools in general. The argument seems to be, from at least some quarters, that innovation is what is lacking in traditional publicly run schools and that the charter schools will work to provide models of success, best practices so to speak, that will pour over into traditional public schools thus raising the standards of the entire public school system. But is this the real goal? We will look more closely at this argument in chapter 5 where we consider the arguments, pro and con, for the charter school concept. However, in line with this theory, the claim is that choice improves schools through two distinct mechanisms (Hoxby, 2000).

According to the argument, the first mechanism for improvement and innovation comes with competition, "choice" and the "free market," as opposed to the public sector. Most charters are subsidized by allocations that follow the student so, if a student chooses to attend one charter school or another then that school will receive revenue in a fixed-sum payment. The theory postulates that those schools that fail to attract students or retain them will, in theory, go out of business much like any for-profit endeavor. Since charter schools cannot control their "prices," albeit lower the cost, the argument continues, schools must compete primarily on the plateau of "quality" (Solomon, Block and Gifford). With this in mind, the argument put forward is clear and simple: "free market" competition for students will raise the quality of all schools through the mechanism of parental choice and those public schools that cannot compete will fail and close and those that can compete will do so due to the innovations and reforms as a result of newly formed public charter schools.

The second argument in favor of free market fundamentalism and public education is "choice," and it was originally put forth by choice advocates Ray Budde and Moe and Chubb who argue that choice works through a sorting process. The argument is still popular among many educational policymakers and their constituents today, arguing that where there exists a wide variety of schools to choose from, "customers" will choose the schools that cater to their relatively narrow educational preferences. This, Moe and Chubb argue, reduces the amount of time schools spend on resolving conflicts between stakeholders, freeing these stakeholders to devote more time and energy to developing exceptional educational programs (Chubb and Moe, 1990).

At the center of the charter school concept is government deregulation or deregulation, really, of any kind. The core idea is that charter schools will receive a greater level of autonomy over curriculum, instructions and operations in exchange for high accountability results and deregulation and this will then produce greater education and test scores for students. To provide for this "autonomy," or deregulation, a "contract" or "charter" is created between the charter school and an "authorizer"—the public body in each state that actually grants the charter. Within the charter the applicant spells out the conditions under which the school will operate and the goals and objectives it must accomplish in order to remain a viable entity. It is important to note that because charters operate state by state, any discussion of legal issues regarding charters must be undertaken with the understanding that the charter movement is a "living mosaic"—one that is susceptible to change at any given moment through the enactment of state or federal legal statutes.

How charter schools are chartered, that is the legal status and independence given to them, has a great deal of effect on the day-to-day operations of each charter school. Many pundits and generally the more conservative educational reformers argue that charter schools must have greater autonomy to innovate and act independent of their school districts and state legislatures if the charter school experiment is to be authentically implemented and studied; they, in fact, exhort districts to relax all regulations in entirety. However, what each state does is to consider the complexity of its own particular educational and political environments and then design charter laws that meet the needs of the citizens and communities. This is the subject of political debate in all states and accounts for the reason for the disparity in legal status and the operation of charter schools among states.

Take for example the state of Colorado. In April of 2008 numerous parents stood before the Denver school board, holding up newspaper articles about a high-performing public charter school in the Denver area and asking why their children were unable to receive the same education in public schools that those students in the charter did. One parent, Luci Saenz commented:

We want this for our kids and our families. We are ready to fight. We believe in our children, and we believe they deserve it. (Denver Post, May 7, 2008)

Like other urban districts around the country, Denver Public Schools has had difficulty in educating the city's poorest students in its traditional public school system. In the wake of this problem, some public charter schools in the community are claiming success. At least a dozen public charter schools are being planned for the city over the next decade based on what are called "high-performing charter school models." And a group of public charter advocates is planning to add dozens more public charter schools to teach low-income urban youth on Colorado's Front Range (Ibid.). So here, as elsewhere it is important to note that the competition among parents and their students is for more public charter schools, not for improvement in the traditional public school system.

Citizens in some states use the electoral initiative process and then draft referendums and state statutes that would constrain a local school board's discretion so that a charter must be granted to any group that can meet established criteria. These citizens advocate the development of what they term "objective standards and criteria" that would be used to protect qualified charter advocates from school boards that seek to restrain the development of charters. The idea is total deregulation aimed at revolutionizing existing traditional public educational systems, allowing for a multitude of charters and hybrids.

Another aspect of charter school laws and their legal status is the scope of the actual exemptions from state laws and regulations such schools receive. As previously noted, charter school advocates argue that in order to be truly effective, charter schools must receive automatic exemptions from a variety if not all state laws and regulations (with the exception of provisions regarding health, safety, nondiscrimination, secular, and other core public school laws—though it is not altogether clear whether some market fundamentalist reformers might not embrace this as well). Exemptions from what charter advocates deem government bureaucratic regulations are a central demand of the charter movement. But if they receive exemptions from public regulations and oversight then where is the democratic nature of these institutions? Where is there a "democratic process" for monitoring transparency and accountability within the educational system that all educator stakeholders need in order to make critical educational decisions regarding accountability and student learning? Or is it even important?

As we will see, certain specific provisions of state laws impact the development and operation of charter schools. Some of the legal issues that arise involve funding, district revenues, collective bargaining issues, admission policies, autonomy, equity, and accountability and express varied educational ideologies.

CHARTER SCHOOL BASICS AND THE LAW

There is no national or federal charter school policy, although No Child Left Behind arguably advances the goals of charter school advocates, as we shall see. Charter schools vary from state to state, not only because the individual charters set out unique mission and goal statements, but also because state charter laws, which significantly influence the development of charter schools, also vary. The state laws exhibit perceivable patterns that cover seven basic policy and legal areas:

Charter Development: who may propose a charter, how charters are granted, the number of charter schools allowed, and related issues.

School Status: how the school is legally defined and related governance, operations, and liability issues.

Fiscal: the level and types of funding provided and the amount of fiscal independence and autonomy.

Students: how schools are to address admissions, nondiscrimination, racial/ethnic balance, discipline, and special education.

Staffing and Labor Relations: whether the school may act as an employer, which labor relations laws apply, and other staff rights and privileges.

Instruction: the degree of control a charter school has over the development of its instructional goals and practices.

Accountability: whether the charter serves as a performance-based contract, how assessment methods are selected, and charter revocation and renewal issues (U.S. Charter Schools, under "Charter School Basics").

Most chartered schools, managed by their own governing boards, are legally independent entities. Eleven states grant them independence outright and eight others permit them to be independent. The thirteen states that require their charters to operate as part of the local school district account for only 12 percent of the nation's 3,400 charter schools (Corwin and Schneider 2007, 2-3). For example, in New Hampshire, local boards are the approving agencies and sponsors, and state boards operate for appeal purposes. New Jersey approves charters through a state commissioner, and in Florida, the approving agencies are local boards and universities and colleges. New Mexico approves charters through state boards, and Arizona has a state board for charter approval.

In Michigan, the law lays out three paths to charter school status. The idea is to provide an atmosphere or an environment of deregulation and market fundamentalism that is designed to create autonomy for charter schools. Charter schools in Michigan may be converted public schools or they may be converted private schools, or they could be new start-ups. The Michigan law is seen by many as somewhat permissive as compared to Mississippi, where only public conversions are allowed. Contrast this with the law in Georgia that allows public conversions and start-ups but not private conversions (Miron and Nelson 2002).

In Arizona, one of the most permissive charter school states, the state board for charter schools is an established governing agency consisting of the following members: the Superintendent of Public Instruction, six members of the public, at least two of whom shall reside in a school district where at least sixty percent of the children who attend school in the district meet the eligibility requirements established under the national school and lunch child nutrition acts (42 U.S. Code §§ 1751-1785) for free lunches who are appointed by the Governor, two members of the business community who are appointed by the governor, and three members of the legislature who shall survive as advisory members and who are appointed jointly by the president of the senate and speaker of the house of representatives.

The state board for Arizona charter schools is responsible for exercising general supervision over charter schools sponsored throughout the state, by the board and recommend legislation pertaining to charter schools to the state legislature. The board also grants charter status to successful qualifying applicants for charter schools. The Arizona law explicitly allows charter operators to open multiple school sites with the same charter.

If an applicant seeks to establish a charter school in Arizona they must submit a written application to a proposed sponsor for the school. The requirement states that the application include a detailed "business" plan for the charter school, a mission statement for the charter school, a description of the charter school's organizational structure and governing body, a financial plan for the first three years of operation of the charter school, a description of the charter school's hiring policy, the name of the charter school's applicant or applicants and requested sponsor, along with a description of the charter school's facility and the location of the school, a description of the grade levels being served as well as an outline for the criteria designed to measure the effectiveness of the school. The Arizona law provides that a sponsor of a charter school may contract with a public body, private person, or private organization for the purpose of establishing a charter school and the sponsor of a charter school may be either a school-district governing board, the state board of education, or the state board for charter schools (Charter School Law, Ariz. Rev. Statutes Education Codes A 15-81 to A 15-89).

If a charter application is denied by the approving agency, many states have an appeal process, but many do not. In Arizona there is no appeals process, if the charter application is rejected the law provides a process for improving the application and technical assistance, but there is no formal appeals process. Arizona approves or denies a charter school through its state board of education or its state board of charters. California, on the other hand, approves charters through local boards and does have an appeal process for denial that is handled by a county panel (Ibid., A 15-181, 15-189).

Many states "cap" the number of charters that are allowed in a state and can also cap them by districts. In Colorado local boards can "reasonably limit" the number in each district, but there are no formal "caps." In Alaska in October 2002, a legal amendment increased the cap from 30 to 60 total schools in operation. Wisconsin has no caps on the number of charter schools that can be developed and operated, but it provides in the law that the University of Wisconsin-Parkside, may only sponsor one charter school. In Nevada there is a cap on the number of "non-at-risk" charter schools that may be formed: 21 throughout the state, with some geographic restrictions. The law provides for an unlimited number for charter schools serving at-risk students (U.S. Charter Schools, under "Charter School Caps").

WHO AUTHORIZES CHARTER SCHOOLS?

The answer is "authorizers," and authorizers are simply legal entities approved by state law that legally sanction new charter schools, oversee their ongoing performance and evaluate their performance, as to continuing operational issues. They also have the responsibility to make charter renewal decisions for charter schools as they arise. And so, "authorizers"—whether state or local boards of education, universities or colleges, special-purpose boards, municipal bodies or nonprofits—oversee a charter school's accountability in face of the law, as well as uphold the performance agreement each school signs. In these ways, authorizers also are arguably said to protect the public interest by exercising oversight, transparency, and regulatory functions.

Not surprisingly, the rise in charters throughout the United States has also led to a mushrooming of private charter consultants that, for a fee, will do everything for the charter applicant and eventual "authorizer." Developing, nurturing, and sustaining, "authorizers" has become big business. One such consultant organization is the National Association of Charter School Authorizers. NACSA boasts that:

> *Genuine reform through charter schools happens with the interplay of three principles: choice, autonomy and accountability. Good authorizers protect choice and autonomy and demand accountability. Schools excel when these core principles are present.*
>
> *NACSA works with local experts to create the conditions needed for quality schools to thrive. We push for high standards for authorizers and the environments*

in which they work. High standards beget high achievement. It's true for students and it's true for the adults who work with charter schools. (U.S. Charter Schools, under "Consultant Organization")

Of course this "consulting and sustaining" is often done at the expense of the taxpayer through public funds expended for such private services. Yet, other nurturing practices that might be provided for the authorizer can and has also been funded through seed monies provided by philanthropic organizations, corporate donations, personal donations, bake sales, and the like.

CHARTER SCHOOL AUTONOMY AND THE LAW

Autonomy, or what can be construed as a code for freedom from regulations in favor of free market fundamentalism, is a critical issue in determining the rights and responsibilities of charter schools—how they operate and how they govern. The degree of charter school autonomy can influence the way charter schools and local districts interact and thus can be indicative of success or failure. The states with "stronger" charter legislation grant broad autonomy to charter schools by waiving many state regulation requirements, offering a number of sponsorship options and providing an appeal process when an applicant for a charter is denied. Some states even see fit to grant what they call a "super-waiver," which sweeps away volumes of legal and regulatory red tape for the newly formed charter schools. In states that do not have such detailed legislation, the charter schools must legally remain part of a school district and may be afforded no greater autonomy than a traditional public school.

Some charter school proponents and free market fundamentalists argue the autonomy of charter schools is *the* critical issue and actually advocate that state laws should:

- Not set limits on the number of charters within a state or district
- Set few or no limits on who can apply for a charter
- Authorize a large number of entities to grant charters, such as education boards, colleges, universities, and local school boards
- Treat individual charter schools as if they were separate local educational authorities
- Provide financial and technical assistance in acquiring facilities for the schools and for start-up costs and state aid programs
- Specify that charter schools are qualified to receive federal, state, and even local revenues
- Waive a variety of state and local regulations that govern public schools
- Not require staff and teachers to meet state certification requirements that would apply in public schools

- Allow flexibility and room in the selection of accountability criteria to be used for renewal of the charter
- Assure that admission practices are not selective and that they promote racial diversity (Nathan 1996, 167-205; Hassel 1999)

As we shall see, these legal issues are the subject of never-ending debate and controversy state-by-state and they promise to continue well into the future. What direction a state law takes has a great deal to do with the efficacy of charter schools and their proponents and the strength of the opposition to the idea. And although most if not all charter schools are released from many public regulations through public legislation, they are still subject to federal and state constitutional law as well as to federal and state discrimination laws. They are also subject to the federal law: No Child Left Behind (NCLB), in terms of standards and accountability. So is this really a release from burdensome government regulations if federal bureaucrats in Washington mandate state testing and accountability for states that authorize charter schools? For some the answer is yes, for some the answer, as we shall see, is no.

Issues regarding waivers from most state education laws and regulations vary from state to state as well. Although Rhode Island forces charter schools to apply for waivers, North Carolina waives state laws and regulations automatically. So, for example, in states where many charter laws grant charter schools waivers from a wide range of regulatory requirements, in the state of Michigan charter schools are forced to seek such waivers on a case-by-case basis. Many other charter school laws require that charter schools only comply with health, safety, and civil rights laws (Miron and Nelson 2002).

Charter schools are governed by local boards whose powers are spelled out in the charter for the school. Unlike traditional public schools, where board members are elected by voters, charter school board members are in fact appointed by the authorizer. This process means that board members are often selected by the school's founders or other vested interests. Often school founders actually recommend themselves to the board and then as vacancies on the board arise they appoint new board members, giving rise to the argument that the link between voters and charter schools is far weaker than in the public school model where cronyism and nepotism are less possible.

Furthermore, many state charter school laws grant local school boards a great deal of say concerning the creation of charter schools in their jurisdictions. For example, in the state of Ohio not only school districts and what are known as "educational service centers" have the right to authorize charter schools, but so do any nonprofit organizations that apply to become an authorizer. Not only can nonpublic entities apply to the state for charter school authorization status, the law in Ohio virtually guarantees that these entities or nonprofits will not be held accountable to any sunshine laws or transparency by the public. According to Leigh Dingerson of the Center for Community Change in Washington, there are no public record laws that apply to nonprofits granted authorization status in the state of Ohio. What this means is that there is no public mechanism for transparency, no public oversight, and no public information regarding these schools (Interview with L. Dingerson, July 18, 2008).

Although many pundits and charter school devotees argue that having to comply with state public record laws impede the creation and operation of charter schools, many boards argue that without the ability to monitor and control charter schools through public information and accountability standards, the charter school experiment would essentially be unregulated, which could mean unwanted fiscal and political consequences and implications. Tension concerning theories of regulation and transparency are just some characteristics of the charter movement.

CHARTER SCHOOL ACCOUNTABILITY AND THE LAW

Even though charter schools are often exempt from many state and local laws through the use of legal waivers, they are still subject to some restrictions and regulations. First and foremost, charter schools remain subject to federal laws, which states cannot waive. The schools must provide free and appropriate education to children with special needs, respect students' constitutional rights, maintain nondiscriminatory policies in admissions and other areas, and refrain from teaching religion. Second, most state charter school laws leave at least some state-level school laws in place for charter schools. For example, some charter school laws require that each charter school submit an annual report of its activities (Hassel 1995, 161). Charter schools must also fulfill a host of state reporting requirements to assure compliance with state charter laws and other federal and state laws.

As we noted, charter school advocates would like to frame the issue of educational accountability as one of parental choice. Real accountability, they argue, is imposed by competition in the marketplace and charter schools provide this competition through parental choice. Parents, who know what is best for their children and are empowered to choose schools, will send their children to schools that actually function, argue many charter school proponents; the rising tide will lift all boats, is the argument. Thus, many charter school proponents are not eager to embrace nor are they very interested in accountability through standardized state testing. This is not true for all charter proponents but it is for a great deal of parents who select charters to detach themselves from what they look at as "government schools." Although this reasoning has a resounding populist appeal, the decision where to send one's child to school is far more complex than simply basing the decision on academic excellence and market choices.

One's economic class, race, gender, proximity to the school and work, transportation (as we saw earlier), work schedules, availability of child care, as well as the type of extracurricular activities and socialization opportunities that are available to children also have a bearing on where parents send their children to school (Molnar 1996, 4). Taking this all into consideration, as we shall see, for many charter school advocates and critics the social and economic issues that face parents, students, and teachers cannot be separated from the issues of choice, who gets it, under what circumstances it is executed and how the issue is framed.

In principle, each charter school signs a contract with its charter-granting agency or "authorizer" that spells out the academic results the school is expected to achieve throughout the term of the charter. And, of course, each school must set out a plan as to how they will meet state academic standards as adopted in accordance with No Child Left Behind. To illustrate this, let us take the following example. A school might promise that a certain proportion of its students would perform above grade average or level on a particular assessment over a specific period of time. When it comes time to reconsider the granting or the renewal of the charter, the charter-granting agency can evaluate the school's progress relative to specifically spelled out and articulated standards as well as its performance in meeting state standards. The school can then have its charter either regranted based on its performance or denied because of nonconformity with prearticulated and state-mandated goals.

One of the strengths of public bureaucracy is that it provides mechanisms to assure that public funds are being used appropriately, i.e., an oversight through checks and balances. Because many states grant charters immunity from most state laws that govern public school districts, bureaucratic oversight and public accountability for public funds can be crippled or circumvented; and in many cases they have been. According to Ronald Corwin, professor emeritus of sociology at the Ohio State University, and E. Joseph Schneider, distinguished senior fellow at the National Policy Board for Educational Administration in Washington, D.C, commenting on failed charter schools:

> *Most of these schools have been shut down or penalized financially for a variety of violations, including: failure to serve special education students; grossly inflating enrollment and attendance figures; violating state guidelines; fiscal mismanagement; failure to keep proper records; misusing or stealing millions of dollars; chronic complaints about lack discipline; indebtedness reaching millions of dollars; hiring felons and former convicts; failure to pay teachers or to pay into the teacher retirement system; teaching religion and illegally converting private schools to charters; and hiring un-credentialed teachers (in states where prohibited) ... Some schools have spent huge sums of money without ever opening, while others have folded without notice, displacing hundreds of students and producing an avalanche of litigation. (Sugarman, 1999)*

Chester E. Finn Jr., Senior fellow at the Hoover Institution, president of the Thomas B. Fordham Institute and chairman of Hoover's Task Force on K-12 Education and Free-market proponent in the advancement of Charter School policy, even noted publicly:

Whereas boosters and advocates, myself included, once supposed that charter schools would almost always turn out to be good schools, reality shows that some are fantastic, some are abysmal, and many are hard to distinguish from the district schools to which they're meant to be alternatives. Merely hanging a "charter" sign over a schoolhouse door frees it to be different but doesn't assure quality—or even differentness. Those running the school need to know what they're doing—and be good at doing it. Too many well-meaning (or, sometimes, greedy) folks set out to create charter schools that they aren't competent to run. (Finn 2006)

The bitter truth is that a number of charter schools have closed or have had their charters legally revoked because of financial problems or mismanagement since the inception of the charter revolution. The Jos-Arz Therapeutic Public Charter School, located in Washington, D.C., was shuttered in 2007 after spending nearly $40 million per year in public dollars. Its projected attendance was 190 students, but it never enrolled more than 50. A grand jury is now probing the school. According to Gina Arlotto of the Save Our Schools Coalition, a nonprofit group that advocates for traditional public schools:

I'm not totally opposed to all charter schools. But the reality is that some of these charter school operators are hustlers, quite a few of them are outright criminals and a lot of them are doing a big bait-and-switch. (Myers 2007)

In Ohio, an ongoing investigation by the state auditor's office revealed that in 2003 the former head of a Cincinnati charter school, the W.E.B. Dubois Academy Charter School, stole monies from the school. The former head of the school was indicted on six felony counts of theft, two felony counts of unauthorized use of property, two felony counts of tampering with records, and two felony counts of telecommunications fraud (Channel Five WLWT.com).

In California, sixty charter schools collapsed in August of 2004 leaving six thousand students with no where to attend school in the fall of 2004. The California Charter Academy, the largest educational retail charter chain of publicly financed but privately run charter schools in the state slid into insolvency in 2004. The businessman, who founded the educational chain of charters, C. Steven Cox, a former insurance executive, managed to collect $100 million in state financing to build a small retail chain of 60 mostly storefront charter schools. In 2004 as bankruptcy seemed to be the last resort for the powerful businessman, Cox abandoned the schools refusing to answer phone calls while terrified parents scrambled to find educational opportunities for their displaced children. Thousands of students' immunization and academic records, along with school equipment had been virtually abandoned all across the state of California at various Charter Academy school sites (Dillon 2004).

Texas boasts 206 charter schools and as of 2008, ninety-three of them were in hot water for bilking the state out of millions of dollars by overstating their enrollment, seemingly the preferred scam among charter theft artists. The Dallas Morning News reported:

> *Texas charter schools have reaped $26 million in undeserved state money by filing incorrect student attendance reports, according to state financial records. The Texas Education Agency, which oversees public education in the state, is working to recover $17 million of the $26 million from nearly half of the charters now operating in Texas. TEA records show that 20 schools went out of business before the state could recover its money, leaving taxpayers holding a $9 million bag of debt. (Smith 2008)*

As overstating enrollment seems to be the preferred method employed by most crooked charter schools, research has found the success of the scam is directly proportional with the amount of oversight that is employed by, yes, government regulators. According to Jack Ammons, a former school superintendent who works with troubled charter schools on behalf of Texas Educational Association, charters can succeed—but only with strong supervision.

> *If taxpayers knew how much of their tax money was going to charter schools and what the actual return on their tax money was in some charter schools, they would see that the Legislature address the whole charter school concept. (Ibid.)*

The irony, of course, is that it is precisely oversight and regulation that charters seek to avoid. In the state of Florida, Jim Warford, former K-12 chancellor at the Department of Education, told local reporters in 2004 that his bosses actually discouraged oversight of charter schools. According to Warford, when he asked the State Department of Education about the need for oversight and accountability:

> *The only good answer I got was there is accountability because the parents are free to choose. It was intellectually indefensible that you could take a student out of a high-accountability district school and turn them loose into the Wild West of the free market that had no accountability. (St. Petersburg Times 2007)*

Not all charter problems are caused by outright corruption and fraud. Some problems with charter schools have to do with the fact that many people who wish to charter schools for altruistic reasons find they have little experience and must rely on the for-profit secondary industry that has mushroomed around the development of charter schools. A case in point is that of James Huger from New Orleans. After Katrina hit, James Huger, a 39-year-old real estate investor, and the advocacy organization he cobbled together, Choice Foundation, saw a chance to test their ideas regarding allowing families to choose their schools and giving schools autonomous boards. So the group applied for a charter for Lafayette, a classic red-brick schoolhouse that includes kindergarten through seventh grade. Having no experience in school management, Choice hired Mosaica; a Manhattan-based firm started 10 years ago by a businessman whose expertise was in childcare. Mosaica, with 78 American schools on its business ledger, bills itself as the nation's third-largest operator of charter schools.

Mr. Huger admits that he was beguiled by Mosaica's advertised promise that it would deliver "a tuition-free classical education worthy of the finest private schools" and that he did not perform background checks on the company as he should have. According to him he believed Mosaica's promises that extra tutoring would be promptly provided for remedial readers and laptops handed out to all teachers. All Mosaica wanted in return was 12.5 percent of the $6 million in state and federal revenue for Lafayette, or roughly $723,000 a year (Berger 2007).

According to an article in the *New York Times* regarding the incident, within weeks Mr. Huger came to the conclusion that Mosaica was not only failing to deliver the champagne education they promised but also couldn't even provide a roadside beer. According to briefs filed in arbitration and interviews conducted with teachers, school hallways were caked with dirt and smelled of urine. There were too few buses for transportation. Textbooks sat in warehouses, and there was no copier for printing substitute materials. Computer programs for reading were never installed nor were the promised laptops ever passed out, and eight laptops even managed to disappear. Tutoring did not begin until January of 2008. On the upper-grade floors, students ran freely through the hallways. By year's end, 21 of 37 teachers had quit. When fourth graders took the required Louisiana test, only 36 of 98 passed. In March, Mosaica dismissed the principal, but the new experts proved unfamiliar with the school, the city and even Mosaica, according to the Choice Foundation's brief (Ibid.).

These and other unforeseen crises with regard to certain charter schools argues how important the local school board's oversight role can be and how crucial experience is in managing charter schools. It seems to also point to the need for continued regulation and monitoring of charter schools. Reviewing, monitoring, and otherwise overseeing a charter school can be hard work. For charter schools to become a central part of the educational picture, they must have clear and reliable relationships with the community agencies that serve to authorize the charters and guarantee funding, develop effective communication channels, and hold school operators accountable to their promises. In essence, there must be regulation and oversight; but the dilemma seems to be that this is precisely what charter school advocates say they wish to avoid. To be fair, most charter schools are not plagued with corruption and fraud but this does not erase the necessity for public transparency and oversight.

Charter-granting agencies in various states are still struggling with how charter schools should fit into the existing structure of legal standards and testing processes. Questions as to what to precisely implement to achieve charter school goals and accountability, how to handle accountability, and what actions to take before a school's charter renewal date are all being continually debated. Until charter-granting agencies have clear processes in place with detailed policy and mission statements can taxpayers and parents feel confident that charter schools will be held to accountability standards. And will those processes be public or private?

The need for such oversight processes has also, and not surprisingly, led to a burgeoning business in accountability consultancy. Chicago Public Schools, for example, enlisted a local charter school resource center, Leadership for Quality Education, to help create an assistance program called the Chicago Charter Schools Standards and Assessment Project. From privately raised funds, charter schools received competitive grants, ranging from $5,000 to $13,500, which could be used for staff research and expert assistance in developing unique school standards and assessments exceeding the requirements of state law to align their performance contracts more fully with their school missions. Massachusetts used part of its federal charter school grant monies to provide each school with $10,000 to hire an "accountability facilitator" in 1996. The Charter School Office provided a suggested list of such facilitators but schools were free to choose their own facilitators to help them develop their accountability plans. Once initial drafts were submitted, the state hired a contractor to create a common template and to help all schools complete their plans (U.S. Charter Schools, under "Accountability Plans").

Even market fundamentalists and conservative charter advocates argue that from the perspective of the charter schools themselves, a lack of clearly stated accountability procedures is threatening because there are no specific alternative accountability systems the charter schools can rely on. Holding charter schools accountable for results is one of the big issues facing those schools and the states that license and charter them. The issue is whether in the future this accountability will be public or private and how it will be constructed.

CHARTER SCHOOLS, TEACHERS, AND THE LAW

A charter school's bargaining unit can bargain only with the governing board of the charter school, and not with the local school board. Many of the state laws regarding charter schools are unclear about collective bargaining, retirement benefits, and other issues that affect both teachers and school boards. In some states and the District of Columbia, teachers at charter schools are bound by school district collective bargaining agreements. So, for instance in California a charter school's teachers have the same option to form a union as other school district employees. The drafters of the school's charter decide whether they will remain covered by the school district's collective bargaining agreement or have the right to organize independently. If they are independent, they are generally subject to the state's education collective bargaining laws. In Idaho, on the other hand, staff of the charter school is considered a separate unit for purposes of collective bargaining. In Massachusetts the issue is even more complex; here, what are designated the "Horace Mann charters" remain bound by school district collective bargaining agreements to the extent provided by the terms of their charters. "Commonwealth charters," another designation of charter schools are not bound by these agreements. Whereas in the state of Tennessee, a charter school's employees may form a bargaining unit, which may then elect to represent themselves in negotiations with the charter school's governing body. They may also elect to be represented by any qualified person or organization, including the local bargaining unit within the school district. Many of the above issues are being negotiated, and this picture of charter schools is constantly changing (Education Commission of the States).

Concerning the issue of teacher retirement, some states stipulate that teachers either must participate in or be eligible for the state retirement system, but as to the issue of who pays for that participation, many state laws remain silent. If charter school teachers continue to be school district employees, the district may share in the cost of the retirement benefits. But if the charter school is the employer, that school may have to use its own funds to contribute to the retirement system.

As one example of state law in this area, Minnesota allows teachers to continue to accrue district retirement credits while at a charter school, but they must pay both employer and employee contributions. In Utah teachers do not have equal access to the public school retirement system. While on leave in Utah, a teacher may retain seniority accrued in the school district and may continue to be covered by the benefit program of the school district if the charter school and the school district mutually agree. In Florida, teachers in each of a state's charter schools do not have equal access to the public school teachers' retirement system unless the charter school is organized as a public employer.

The issue of conversion charter schools versus start-up charter schools is of legal importance as well. In New York, conversion charter schools are bound by existing school district collective bargaining agreements. Start-up charter schools enrolling up to 250 students in the first year are not deemed members of any existing collective bargaining unit representing employees of the school district in which the charter school is located, and the charter school and its employees are not subject to any existing collective bargaining agreement between the school districts and its employees. Start-up charter schools with enrollment larger than

250 are deemed to be represented in a separate negotiating unit at the charter school by the same employee organization, if any, that represents like employees in the school district in which such charter school is located; however, this provision may be waived if up to 10 charters issued by the State University of New York, is not applicable to the renewal or extension of a charter and does not subject such a charter school to any collective bargaining agreement between any school district and its employees, or does not make such a charter school part of any negotiating unit at such school district. The charter school may, in its sole discretion, choose whether or not to offer the terms of any existing collective bargaining to school employees (Ibid.).

Other states, like Colorado and Minnesota, provide protected leaves of absence so teachers can leave their public school posts and teach in charter schools; evidently, the intent is to encourage excellence in both teachers and teaching in charter school recruitment. Other states, however, like Georgia and New Mexico, do not even include or mention a leave for teachers in their state laws.

When addressing issues of employment and collective bargaining with classified and certified staff, some states allow their charter schools to bargain independently and directly with staff while others do not. In Arkansas, for example, charter schools bound by school district collective bargaining agreements and teachers in each of a state's charter schools have equal access to the public school teachers' retirement system. In Minnesota, on the other hand, charter schools are not bound by district collective bargaining agreements. Minnesota charter school's teachers may negotiate as a separate unit with the charter school governing body or work independently. A charter school's bargaining unit may remain part of the school district unit if teachers, the charter school governing board, the local school board and the teachers' union in the school district agree. In Oregon, a charter school's teacher may participate in existing collective bargaining units or may form collective bargaining units that are separate from existing ones. Also, if a school board is not the sponsor of the charter school, the school board is not the employer of the employees of the charter school and the school board cannot collectively bargain with the employees of the charter school (Ibid.).

Similarly, many states allow the charter schools to operate as independent legal entities while some states do not. In Minnesota a charter school is its own local education agency (LEA). In Georgia, a charter school that is approved by both a local school board and the state board of education is part of the LEA that is the school district. A charter school that is approved on appeal by the state board of education is treated as its own LEA. In New York a charter school is its own LEA, except that for special education purposes it is part of the LEA that is the school district. Whereas in California, a charter school chooses to be part of the LEA that is the school district or it can be its own LEA. In Idaho, the charter school staff is considered a separate unit for purposes of collective bargaining.

However, according to a study done by the Western Michigan University Evaluation Center, from 1997-2006 as many as 40 percent of newer charter school teachers ended up leaving for other jobs. Attrition among new teachers in charter schools is close to 40 percent annually, according to the study. The authors of the study, Gary Miron and Brooks Applegate, note that this is particularly critical for charter schools because the percentage of charter school teachers under 30 (37 percent) is more than three times that of traditional public schools (11 percent). According to Miron and Applegate:

High attrition consumes resources of schools that must regularly provide pre- and in-service training to new teachers; it impedes schools' efforts to build professional learning communities and positive and stable school cultures; and it is likely to undermine the legitimacy of the schools in the eyes of parents. (Great Lakes Center for Education, Research and Practice)

The researchers found that teachers more likely to leave were those who reported less satisfaction with their charter school's mission, its ability to achieve that mission, or its administration and governance. Also more likely to leave, according to the recent study, were noncertified teachers and those who taught in upper grades. Based on their findings, Miron and Applegate recommend that supporters of charter schools: would be well-advised to focus on reducing high turnover, especially for new teachers in charter schools (Ibid.). They go on to conclude: The high attrition rates for teachers in charter schools constitute one of the greatest obstacles that will need to be overcome if the charter school reform is to deliver as promised (Ibid.). Teacher unions and their role in the charter school movement is discussed in detail in chapter 7.

CHARTER SCHOOL FINANCING AND THE LAW

The funding of American public schools is historically based on local property taxes. Notwithstanding subventions from the state to local school districts, spending per pupil has long varied from district to district. More specifically, ever since the nineteenth century, spending on public education has importantly been a function of the per-pupil wealth of the local district, with low wealth districts the most disadvantaged.

Because of more than thirty years of litigation that began in the late 1960s, this problem has now been substantially ameliorated in some states—states like Kentucky, New Jersey, Texas, Wyoming, and California—although, even today in California, for example, some wealthy communities like Beverly Hills continue to outspend most other districts. Overall, however, interdistrict spending inequalities remain significant in most states and very large in some states. Interdistrict spending inequalities also create a dilemma for charter school funding. Either, charter schools will be funded (typically by their local sponsoring districts) at a level that relates to the spending level per pupil in the districts that charter them—this is the most typical solution around the country. Or, they will be funded (perhaps directly by the state) at some state average level of funding per pupil—this, for example, is increasingly the California solution (*Serrano v. Priest* ("Serrano II"), 557 P.2d 929 (Cal. 1976); *Serrano v. Priest* ("Serrano I"), 487 P.2d 1241 (Cal. 1971); *Abbott v. Burke* ("Abbott II"), 575 A.D.2d 359 (N.J. 1990); *Abbott v. Burke* ("Abbott I"), 495 A.D.2d 396 (N.J. 1990); *Edgewood Indep. Sch. Dist. v. Kirby* ("Edgewood "III"), 826 S.W.2d 489 (Tex. 1992); *Edgewood Indep. Sch. Dist. v. Kirby* ("Edgewood "II"), 804 S.W.2d 491 (Tex. 1991); *Edgewood Indep. Sch. Dist. v. Kirby* ("Edgewood "I"), 777 S.W.2d 391 (Tex. 1989); *Lincoln County Sch. Dist. No. 1 v. State,* 985 P.2d 964 (Wyo. 1999); *Campbell County Sch. Dist. v. State,* 907 P.2d 1238 (Wyo. 1995); *Washakie County Sch. Dist. No. 1 v. Herchler,* 606 P.2d 310 (Wyo. 1980)).

CHARTER SCHOOL COSTS

The costs associated with charter schools can be separated into start-up costs and ongoing expenses. For new charter schools, start-up costs can be quite high—especially during the initial year—and charter schools that convert existing public or private schools to charter schools must bear the cost of conversion; by far the most significant cost is the cost of the facility. Building codes, insurance concerns, and local regulations often require renovation of existing buildings for charter school use. The cost of readying a facility for use as a charter school and assuring that construction complies with local regulations can be both costly and bureaucratic.

Staffing can be an expensive cost as well. The staff must have orientation and be prepared for the opening of the school. Schools also need equipment and resources, and these costs must be funded initially by the school through private or nonprofit sources. Accounting systems, security systems, and the like all work together to create significant costs, especially initially.

Once the schools are open, the ongoing expenses begin to resemble those of a regular public school. The only difference between the two is the charter school's ability to control and maintain its own budget and financial identity in accordance with its specific needs. Salaries and benefits make up the lion's share of the ongoing costs, but the day-to-day operation of the school must also be factored into ongoing costs.

FUNDING CHARTER SCHOOLS

Because charter schools control their own budgets, their spending is not monitored or handled by the local school district through the central office. Charter schools have the flexibility to spend their money any way their governing bodies see fit. Their autonomy provides them more flexibility and freedom than the conventional schools have. For example, charter schools can usually design salary schedules and systems of compensation to meet their particular needs.

If charter funding is tied to district spending per pupil, then charter schools may be very differently funded based on who they can get to charter them. This sort of inequality among charter schools surely must seem unfair to many charter school operators, and especially so as charter schools begin to lose their connection to families living in a particular district and begin to serve children from a metropolitan area. Moreover, this arrangement gives those seeking charters special incentives to seek charters from some, but not other, districts. This can be particularly true in the case of "virtual charters," a form of homeschooling which we will look at in subsequent chapters. The disincentive applies most strongly with respect to low wealth/low spending districts, and these are the very districts that charter school supports typically argue have the most to gain from charter schools (Sugarman 1999, 121-123).

On the other hand, if charter school funding is provided based on the state average per pupil spending level in public schools, then this discourages the conversion of existing public schools to charter schools in high spending districts, and it also makes it hard for new charter schools to compete in districts that have high-spending. State average spending also artificially encourages conversions to charter schools in low-spending districts. At the same time, regular public schools in those low-spending districts would understandably feel unfairly disadvantaged as compared with charter schools with which they compete.

In their analysis of charter school funding, The Thomas B. Fordham Institute, in its 2005 study argues that charter schools are being starved for needed funds in almost every community and state. Drawing on a study of Dayton, Ohio schools the report found that district schools in Dayton received an average of $10,802 per pupil from all sources while charter schools were funded at $7,510 per pupil, in essence thirty percent lower than the monies flowing into district schools. They argue that the funding gap for charter schools is in the millions, threatening the charter school movement (Charter School Funding 2005).

Similar arguments have been made by many other charter advocacy organizations. According to the National Alliance for Public Charter Schools:

What is consistent across the country—and most problematic—is that public charter schools receive significantly lower funding than non-charter public schools. According to a recent study, the average public charter school receives $1,800 per pupil, or 27.1 percent, less than what the average non-charter public school receives. For an average-sized charter of 250 students, the total funding difference is $450,000. (National Alliance for Public Charter Schools)

In New Hampshire, The Academy of Science and Design, which opened its doors in Merrimack in September of 2007, is one of several charter schools in the state that could be in danger of closing because of a lack of state funding. Currently in New Hampshire, charter schools receive $3,709 per pupil to cover their annual operating costs, in addition to a one-time federal start-up grant. But Bill Wilmot, head of the recently formed New Hampshire Public Charter School Association, said that isn't nearly enough. According to Wilmot, there are 10 charter schools operating in the state, including the Academy for Science and Design. As of this writing, Wilmot and other charter school supporters are hoping that a bill being considered to increase the per-pupil funding for charter schools will solve that problem. The bill, H.B. 1639, would increase annual funding to $7,000 per pupil. The bill would also allow charter schools to be eligible for receiving state building aid (Nashua Telegraph 2008).

In Utah, a bill that would have placed some of the burden of funding charter schools back on the school districts failed the clear the legislature in early 2008. H.B. 278 would have required school districts to provide an allocation of property-tax revenues for each resident student attending a charter school, so a student's home-district funding would follow him to whatever school he chose to attend. The failure could mean that local replacement funding could once again be appropriated to fund charters next year (Deseret News 2008).

As New Hampshire and Utah indicate, seemingly the primary source of revenues for charter schools is the public coffer. Although state funding formulas vary, they all attempt to provide a fair share of public funds for each student who wishes to attend a charter school. Because the needs of the students vary widely, from special education needs to socioeconomic ones, funding can be a complicated issue. And because charter school funding comes from public districts, as we shall see when we turn our eye to the politics of charter schools, revenues and funding are two of the chief political issues facing the charter movement as public funds find their way into the financial coffers of private interests.

Funding formulas vary from state to state and can be quite complicated. In Oregon, for locally approved charter schools, at least 80 percent of the amount of the school district's general purpose grant per weighted average daily membership for K-8 and at least 95 percent of the amount of the school district's general purpose grant per weighted average daily membership for 9-12 can follow the student. For state approved charter schools, at least 90 percent of the amount of the school district's general purpose grant per weighted average daily membership for K-8 and at least 95 percent for 9-12 of the amount of the school district's general purpose grant per weighted average daily membership follows the student (U.S. Charter Schools, under "Funding Formulas").

In New York, school districts are required to provide 100 percent of a state-specified per-pupil funding calculation to charter schools, although this amount may be reduced pursuant to an agreement between the school and the charter authorizer set forth in the charter; whereas in Pennsylvania, relevant funding follows students based on average school district per-pupil budgeted expenditure of the previous year. For regional charter schools and nonresident students, funds come from the school district of a student's residence. Charter schools receive additional funding for special needs students, or may request the intermediate unit to assist in providing special needs services at the same cost as provided to a school district's schools (U.S. Charter Schools).

Funding is quite simply the key critical issue for charter schools, and it affects them in a myriad of ways. States set their own formulas and establish their own funding mechanisms, and the mechanisms differ from state to state. For example, some states, such as Michigan, Massachusetts, and Hawaii, have established clear funding levels in their charter school legislation. In other states, such as Colorado, the funding levels are set on a school-by-school basis. Colorado funding levels start at 80 percent of the district per-pupil operating costs and then go up based on negotiations. Revenues that go to charter schools reduce a district's overall available funds, and this has led to a source of tension and debate among school boards, parents, legislators, and governors. In fact, it is one the major points of contention between advocates of charter school proposals and people who are opposed to the charter idea (Ibid.).

Take Minnesota, for example. One of the biggest problems for Minnesota charter schools is financing. In order to reduce class size and implement other reforms, these schools relied on asking experienced teachers to accept low salaries and take on administrative and other responsibilities at no cost. Basic equipment and facility financing were also problems for many charter schools in Minnesota, and private sources had to be sought to continue long-term support (Molnar 1996, 4). As a result, many of the teachers at charter schools find they do more for less salary.

Financing problems are not unique to Minnesota but seem to be universal around the country. In a University of Minnesota study of charter schools throughout the United States, the authors found that financial support and a lack of start-up funds were the most frequently mentioned problems charter schools face (University of Minnesota Humphrey Institute 1996). The new costs associated with charter schools have not been adequately addressed in many, if not most states and the public remains unaware of how the financing is received or spent.

Current levels of per-pupil funding may not meet the need of many charter schools (Hassel 1999, 106). First, the start-up costs associated with charter schools for the first year of operation generally must be funded separately because the schools do not receive public funds until the fall. Second, many charters must pay the cost of their facilities separately from the operating costs, which are covered by the per-pupil funds. As a result, many charter schools must scramble to obtain funds from sources other than public revenues. And this situation, argue those people who are less than enamored with the charter school idea, allows private companies to influence the governing and curriculum at many charter schools because the companies offer prepackaged managerial solutions to public financial problems. For example, an American Federation of Teachers (AFT) study shows:

> **Arizona** charters receive overfunding in the amount of $1,000 per pupil;
> **Minnesota's** charter school overfunding is about $200 per pupil for elementary students and $1,000 per pupil for high school students;
> **Colorado's** charter school overfunding is $1,200 per pupil;
> **California's** charter school overfunding is about $500 per pupil;
> **Massachusetts** charter school overfunding is so large it was not measurable; and
> **Michigan's** charter school overfunding is about $600. (Nelson 1997, 5)

The AFT has argued that charter schools impose new costs on districts and that they are not necessarily underfunded when all public revenue sources are matched to the specific kinds of students educated in charter schools. In fact, the AFT argues that unless a charter school primarily serves at-risk children, it is probably *overfunded*. The AFT also found that charter schools add new fixed costs, new facility costs, new start-up costs, new costs associated with private school to charter school enrollment shifts, and, in fact, are not only not underfunded, as charter school advocates claim, but actually receive excess funding (Ibid.). Per pupil spending, as of 2007, on education for all states in the union can be found in Appendix B.

Leveraging charter schools with public and private funds

The issue of charter school funding can be deceptive. The Education Policy Studies Laboratory notes that for charter schools, there is a much greater concern that no charter school will have much of a chance to succeed unless it has substantial extra outside funding from either for-profit or non-profit sources; funding that goes beyond per-pupil state financial limits. This, in turn, means that certain sorts of charter school initiators are far more likely to survive than others, with local grassroots groups most likely to be in the "worse off" category. Why is this? Simple, competition creates winners and losers and any economist will be quick to report. (*Education Policy Analysis* Archives)

In light of the new experiment in charters the funding for facilities for charter schools by profit, nonprofit, and public sectors has grown exponentially with the surge in the growth and development of charter schools. In the 2007 edition of the *Landscape,* in their study entitled "2007 Charter School Facility Finance, Landscape," the Local Initiatives Support Corporation, a national nonprofit dedicated to helping nonprofit community development organizations transform distressed neighborhoods noted:

> *Due in part to support from the U.S. Department of Education (ED), the facility-financing sector for charter schools has grown rapidly over the last few years. Today,*

25 private, nonprofit organizations provide financing to charter schools for their facilities, collectively providing over $600 million in direct financial support to date. In addition, although not within the scope of this study, private capital from traditional lenders and the tax-exempt bond market is also becoming increasingly available. Several national financial institutions, including Bank of America, Citigroup and Prudential Financial, have each invested between $100 million and $150 million in charter school facilities, and other regional commercial lenders have participated on a smaller scale to finance schools in their geographic markets. The tax-exempt bond market has grown similarly. In addition to unrated charter school facility debt, there are now roughly 70 rated charter school bond issuances totaling over $1 billion. See Appendix A for Standard & Poor's and Moody's Investors Service ratings on 67 of these issuances. While the financing opportunities available to charter schools for their facilities are increasing, the sector remains fragmented, with individual providers having different eligibility requirements, financial products and geographic markets. Obtaining access to financing is still difficult for smaller schools and those earlier in the charter school life cycle, with start-up schools facing the greatest challenges. This fragmentation stems from the state-specific nature of charter law and the limited public funding available. Only 11 jurisdictions provide a "per pupil" funding stream specifically for charter school facilities. Of those 11, only eight provide such funding at a level of $500 or more, and only three provide $1,000 or more on a per pupil basis. Recognizing these obstacles, the federal government has sought to stimulate private sector investment and increase state per pupil funding for facilities through two U.S. Department of Education programs: the Credit Enhancement for Charter School Facilities Program and the State Charter School Facilities Incentive Grants Program. However, while receiving appropriations over the past several years, both programs have faced challenges garnering congressional support for funding at levels requested by the Administration. (Local Initiatives Support Corporation 2008)

As the study notes, in the private sector there are 25 nonprofit organizations that provide significant facilities assistance to charter schools in the form of grants, loans, guarantees, real estate development, and technical assistance. There are currently two public-private partnerships that help provide facilities financing for charter schools, the Indianapolis Charter Schools Facilities Fund and the Massachusetts Charter School Loan Guarantee Fund. Six federal programs provide varying types of assistance to, or on behalf of, charter schools for their facilities. The U.S. Department of Education provides grant funds through two programs administered by the Office of Innovation and Improvement: the Credit Enhancement for Charter School Facilities Program and the State Charter School Facilities Incentive Grants Program. The Department of Education has made credit enhancement grant awards totaling $160 million that have helped attract private capital to the sector and state incentive grant awards totaling $50 million to spur states to share in the public funding of charter school facilities. In addition, there are four other federal programs administered by diverse federal agencies that charter schools can access for their facilities needs, including the Public

Assistance Grant Program administered by the Federal Emergency Management Agency, the New Markets Tax Credit Program and the Qualified Zone Academy Bond (QZAB) Program administered by the Department of the Treasury, and Community Programs administered by the Department of Agriculture. Descriptions of these six programs are provided in "Public Initiatives—Federal Programs" (Ibid.).

Private philanthropy has been aggressively recruited in the struggle to fund charters. For example in New Orleans where charters are becoming a national experiment, three philanthropic groups plan to give $17.5 million for public schools in New Orleans. It is the largest donation by private groups since the system was reorganized after Hurricane Katrina. The grants, from the Bill and Melinda Gates Foundation, the Doris and Donald Fisher Fund and the Broad Foundation, will be given over three years. They will go to three non-profits, New Schools for New Orleans, New Leaders for New Schools and Teach for America-Greater New Orleans. New Schools for New Orleans will get $10 million, mainly to support and bolster charter schools. New Leaders for New Schools will get $1 million to train and support 40 principals. Teach for America, which pairs recent college graduates and professionals to urban or rural schools in need for two years, will get $6.5 million to attract teachers for the city (*New York Times* 2007).

Or, take for example, the issue of long waiting lists for charter school students who wish to enroll in successful charter schools. In Texas, Knowledge is Power Program (KIPP) co-founder Mike Feinberg lamented when he found out that KIPP run charter schools in Houston, Texas had long waiting lists for its charter schools. A group of philanthropists decided a superexpansion of both the Houston-based KIPP schools and another charter group, the YES Prep Public Schools was in order. In two years these philanthropists raised more than $90 million for a supercharged expansion of KIPP and YES in Houston.

According to the Philanthropy Roundtable:

> *Within a decade, the two programs expect to use that money to create a school district within the school district. By 2017, they intend to be serving a total of more than 30,000 students annually—roughly 15 percent of all public school students in the Houston Independent School District (HISD). It will require a massive expansion effort. In ten short years, KIPP and YES plan to build, staff, and launch a total of 55 new schools—42 KIPP schools, 13 YES schools-all without diminishing the quality of the education provided. It is a philanthropic initiative never before witnessed in the realm of charter schools, with implications for the growth of charter schools nationwide— and for large urban school districts everywhere. (Philanthropy Roundtable 2008)*

The magazine goes on to note that:

> *A project of this scale has attracted Texas-sized contributions. So far, five donors have made eight-figure grants to the effort. Houston Endowment Inc. has given $20*

million, split evenly between KIPP and YES. From Austin, the Michael and Susan Dell Foundation has donated a total of $10.9 million to the two charter school networks. Three more philanthropists have each given $10 million to KIPP. Two are prominent Houston couples: Jeff and Wendy Hines, as well as John and Laura Arnold. The third is the Seattle-based Bill and Melinda Gates Foundation. In every case, the donors say they decided to make major gifts to KIPP and YES not only because of the schools' success at raising the academic achievement of inner-city students, but also because the expansion plans present an opportunity to revolutionize urban public education.

The group is not alone. John Arnold and Jeff Hines, both of whom serve on the KIPP: Houston board, were among the first to respond to the call for philanthropy; each gave $10 million to the expansion effort. At age 33, John Arnold was the youngest member of the Forbes 400 in 2007. He was formerly an oil trader at Enron, he now runs the hedge fund Centaurus Energy. (Ibid.)

But as board members with governing responsibilities, including financial decision making, was the philanthropic giving a conflict of interest?

The Walton Family Foundation through its Public Charter School Initiative aims to increase the number of children who have access to high-quality public charter schools by making grants available. For many who envisioned that charter schools would be a kind of democratic, local community response to regular public schools, this is likely to be disheartening (*Education Policy Analysis Archives* 2008).

And these private entrepreneurial fund-centers are just the tip of the iceberg. New Schools Venture Fund, created by venture capitalists and in existence since 1998, "is a national nonprofit venture philanthropy firm that seeks to transform public education—particularly for underserved students—by supporting education entrepreneurs and connecting their work to systems change." (New Schools Venture Fund, under "Private Funds").

The goal of such venture capitalists is to create and increase the number of charter schools in low-income communities and because traditional funding will not cover the myriad costs associated with establishing and maintaining a charter school this requires private funds. The New Schools Venture Fund hosts funding by mega-charities such as the Bill & Melinda Gates Foundation, Eli and Edythe Broad Foundation, Robertson Foundation, Irvine Foundation and Walton Family Foundation and the Walton Family. In their first phase funding, from 1998-2002, New Schools:

. . . supported nine entrepreneurial nonprofit and for-profit ventures. These organizations addressed key leverage areas within the context of standards, accountability and choice. Some of these organizations started systems of public charter schools, while others focused on preparing and supporting teachers and leaders, developing research-based curricula, or providing school performance information that parents and community members need to make effective decisions about education. (Ibid.)

In the second phase funding, from 2002-2006, New Schools:

. . . raised a second fund, which totaled nearly $50 million. The goal of the fund was ambitious: to help create dozens of new public charter schools and to develop organizations with the capacity to provide thousands of underserved students with an excellent education. Toward this end, the fund supported more than a dozen charter management organizations (CMOs) that today collectively manage more than 100 schools that serve close to 30,000 students. These organizations are tightly managed nonprofit systems of charter schools that bring more consistent quality and greater scale to the growing charter school movement. In addition, the fund invested in a variety of charter school support organizations. These organizations provide charter school operators with the critical infrastructure they need to continue growing with quality, such as facilities development, administrative services and academic support. (New Schools Venture Fund, under "Second Phase Funding")

Unquestionably, the huge increase in charters has included a massive growth in private and philanthropic start-up monies to support them, as well as the growth of a burgeoning educational industry to distribute the grants and sell "educational products and services." This is true all over the nation. But is the purpose to provide charter school innovation as a competitive model that can raise the standards and levels of education at all public schools, the stated purpose of charter school supporters? According to Don Gaetz, a Florida Republican freshman senator and former Okaloosa school superintendent:

Charter schools were a movement, but now charter schools are an industry. They have lobbyists—they walk around in thousand-dollar suits, some of them. (St. Petersburg Times 2007)

The *St. Petersburg Times* of Florida noted that in the state of Florida:

Those lobbyists, and an embarrassingly compliant state Department of Education, have turned charter education into a $560-million-a-year enterprise that is so immune to oversight that an Escambia school convicted of fraudulently using its students to work on road crews is still receiving tax money. A Pensacola school where not a single student has passed the state's standardized reading and math tests in four years is still receiving tax money. A Vero Beach school investigated twice for suspicion of cheating on standardized tests is still receiving tax money. (Ibid.)

Charter benefactors have a vested economic and social interest in seeing the charter experiment work and for this they will donate tremendous amounts of capital to help establish new charters in their attempt to dismantle traditional public schools. They understand that charters provide a unique business opportunity for many players in the educational entrepreneurial industry and they also know that left by itself the charter movement would not be able to come up with the start-up costs needed due to the way public funding for schools is presently confabulated. Yet ironically, as we will see when we look at New Orleans, much of the "success" of the charter movement is economic and comes from both the government as well as the private sector.

CHARTER ADMISSION POLICIES AND THE LAW

By federal law, charter schools must have a fair and open admissions process; yet again, this varies from state to state. Some states require that charter schools admit students through a lottery system while others require schools to give preference to those students who live in geographic proximity to the school. In a few states, the law allows charter schools to limit admission based on the subject area focus of the school. So just how do parents get their child admitted to a charter school? This can vary from state to state, district to district, and school to school.

In a non-regulatory guidance statement the Department of Education put out in 2004 under Title V part B of the Charter School statute, the U.S. Department of Education lays out the federal provisions directly related to charter school admissions, the use of lotteries, and religion affiliation and admission policies. These federal non-regulatory guidance provisions provide in part:

A charter school that receives funds under the CSP program may weight its lottery in favor of students seeking to change schools under the Title I public school choice provisions. Item C-3 clarifies that this is permitted.

Item C-3 through C-5 state:

A lottery is a random selection process by which applicants are admitted to the charter school.

A charter school receiving CSP funds must use a lottery if more students apply for admission to the charter school than can be admitted. A charter school with fewer applicants than spaces available does not need to conduct a lottery.

Weighted Lotteries

Weighted lotteries (lotteries that give preference to one set of students over another) are permitted only when they are necessary to comply with Title VI of the Civil Rights Act of 1964, Title IX of the Education Amendments of 1972, Section 504 of the Rehabilitation Act of 1973, the Equal Protection Clause of the Constitution, or applicable State law.

In addition, a charter school may weight its lottery in favor of students seeking to change schools under the public school choice provisions of ESEA Title I, for the limited purpose of providing greater choice to students covered by those provisions. For example, a charter school could provide each student seeking a transfer under Title I with two or more chances to win the lottery, while all other students would have only one chance to win.

Exemptions from the Lottery?

A charter school that is oversubscribed and, consequently, must use a lottery, generally must include in that lottery all eligible applicants for admission. A charter school may exempt from the lottery only those students who are deemed to have been admitted to the charter school already and, therefore, do not need to reapply.

Specifically, the following categories of applicants may be exempted from the lottery on this basis: (a) students who are enrolled in a public school at the time it is converted into a public charter school; (b) siblings of students already admitted to or attending the same charter school; (c) children of a charter school's founders (so long as the total number of students allowed under this exemption constitutes only a small percentage of the school's total enrollment); and (d) children of employees in a work-site charter school (so long as the total number of students allowed under this exemption constitutes only a small percentage of the school's total enrollment). When recruiting students, charter schools should target all segments of the parent community. The charter school must recruit in a manner that does not discriminate against students of a particular race, color, national origin, religion, or sex, or against students with disabilities; but the charter school may target additional recruitment efforts toward groups that might otherwise have limited opportunities to participate in the charter school's programs. Once a student has been admitted to the charter school through an appropriate process, he or she may remain in attendance through subsequent grades. A new applicant for admission to the charter school, however, would be subject to the lottery if, as of the application closing date, the total number of applicants exceeds the number of spaces available at the charter school.

A charter school may create separate lottery pools for girls and boys, in order to ensure that it has a reasonably equal gender balance. Item C-5 clarifies that such an action is not permitted. A school seeking to achieve greater gender balance should do so by targeting additional recruitment efforts toward male or female students.

A tuition-based private preschool that becomes a public charter school at the kindergarten level may permit children enrolled in the preschool program to continue in the elementary school program without going through a lottery process. Item I-6 clarifies that this action is not permitted. However, a school in this situation might hold its lottery a few years early, giving students who will enroll in the preschool program and those who will not an equal chance of receiving the opportunity to enroll in the charter school (elementary) program.

A charter school receiving its final year of CSP funds may select students for the next school year (when the school will not be receiving program funds) without using a lottery. Item C-7 describes the circumstances in which this action is permitted.

Item C-7 states:

A charter school receiving its final year of CSP funds may select students for the up-coming school year without using a lottery, provided that the school obligates all funds under its CSP grant before those students actually enroll in the school. If the school has carryover funds or extends its grant period, then it must continue to meet all pro-gram requirements, including the requirement to hold a lottery if it receives more ap-plications for enrollment than it can accommodate for the upcoming school year.

Section C-10 of the nonregulatory provision provides in part:

The Elementary Secondary Education Act (ESEA) does not specifically prohibit charter schools from setting minimum qualifications for determining who is eligible to enroll in a charter school and, thus, to be included in the lottery. As stated above, however, charter schools receiving CSP funds must inform students in the commu-nity about the charter school and give them an "equal opportunity to attend the charter school."

Thus, a charter school funded under the CSP may set minimum qualifica-tions for charter only to the extent that such qualifications are: (a) consistent with the statutory purposes of the CSP; (b) reasonably necessary to achieve the educa-tional mission of the charter school; and (c) consistent with civil rights laws and Part B of the Individuals with Disabilities Education Act. CSP grantees should consider using program funds to assist "educationally disadvantaged" and other students to achieve to challenging State content and performance standards.

Finally, section D of the guidelines addressing religion and admissions states that:

As public schools, charter schools must be nonreligious in their programs, admis-sions policies, governance, employment practices and all other operations, and the charter school's curriculum must be completely secular. As with other public schools, charter schools may not provide religious instruction, but they may teach about religion from a secular perspective. And though charter schools must be neu-tral with respect to religion, they may play an active role in teaching civic values. The fact that some of these values are also held by religions does not make it unlaw-ful to teach them in a charter school. Furthermore, as discussed below, faith-based and religious organizations can be involved with charter schools in many ways, and religious expression by students is allowed in charter schools to the same extent as in other public schools. See also the Department's guidance on Constitutionally pro-tected prayer in public elementary and secondary schools of ESEA. (U.S. Depart-ment of Education)

Let us shift our attention to some examples of how charter schools in vari-ous states attempt to comply with both federal and state statutes regarding char-ter school admissions.

The Westlake Academy Charter School in Westlake, Texas is a typical "open enrollment" charter school that spells out its admission's policy on its Web site:

The Westlake Academy is an open-enrollment Charter School operating under a Charter awarded to the Town of Westlake by the Texas State Board of Education, with oversight by the Texas Education Agency (TEA), Charter School Division. An open-enrollment Charter School may not deny admission to a student based on sex, national origin, ethnicity, religion, disability, academic ability, artistic ability, athletic ability, or based on the school district that the child would otherwise attend.

Definitions

Primary Geographic Boundary Student: *a child of school age: (a) living with his/her parent or legal guardian who is a resident of Westlake, or (b) whose parent or grandparent is employed by, or is an officer of, the Town of Westlake or the Westlake Academy.*

Secondary Boundary Student: *a child of school age that does not meet the definition of Primary Geographic Boundary Student.*

Application Deadline: *January 31st of each year.*

Lottery: *publicly posted and publicly conducted random drawing from names of Secondary Boundary Student applicants desiring admission to the Westlake Academy. The date, time and location of the lottery will be posted on the front page of the Westlake Academy Website by February 1 of each year. All applicants in the lottery will be notified by mail.*

Waiting List: *a list of applicants desiring admission when space becomes available.*

Late Application: *an application received after the Application Deadline but before the beginning of school.*

Application Procedures

All parents wishing to enroll their students in the Westlake Academy must complete an Application for Enrollment. Applications are available at the Westlake Academy Offices, 2600 Ottinger Road, Westlake, Texas, between the hours of 9 am and 5 pm, Monday through Friday. Applications should be picked up in person. Applications must be received by 5 pm, January 31st of each year for that year's lottery.

Admission Order

All Primary Geographic Boundary Students will be admitted to the Academy provided the Academy has received a completed application.

The admission of Secondary Boundary Students is contingent upon available space. If, after February 28 of each year, there remain vacancies in any grade, Secondary Boundary Students will be admitted until all available vacancies are filled. Names drawn after available vacancies have been filled will be placed on a Secondary Boundary Student waiting list and will be enrolled as vacancies occur.

Any Secondary Boundary Student application received after the Application Deadline will be placed at the end of the waiting list and will be admitted in the order that vacancies occur.

Siblings

It is the intent of Westlake Academy that siblings desiring enrollment will be afforded that opportunity. Therefore, if one Secondary Boundary Student sibling is admitted to the school then the other siblings will be moved to the Sibling Waiting List and have priority over other Secondary Boundary Students.

Year-to-Year Admission

It is the current policy of the Board that, once admitted to the school, an eligible student would automatically qualify for enrollment in subsequent years without being subject to lottery. If, however, a student leaves the school, then that student will be considered a new student for admission purposes (Westlake Charter Academy 2008).

But not all charter schools are, nor do they wish to be, "open enrollment" schools. Some schools seek "admission preferences." In San Diego, for example, the Albert Einstein Academy Charter School in San Diego offers a German-English language immersion program that is unique in the region. Starting in kindergarten, students are taught part time in German and part time in English. Albert Einstein Academy Charter has about 300 students in its elementary grades. Its middle school grades, which were recently added under a separate charter, serve 120 students. The tuition-free, dual-language immersion program has attracted students from throughout the county since it began in 2002. It has operated under what is called an "admission preference" policy—basically a form of selective admission. The San Diego Unified School District says the school's admission policy of giving "admission preference" to German speakers may violate equal protection clauses in state and federal law (Gao 2007).

On the other hand, in the state of Arizona, a well-known bastion of charter school experimentation, the Arizona legislature added section 15-184 to their charter school law in 2000. The added section on admissions provides:

A. A charter school shall enroll all eligible pupils who submit a timely application, unless the number of applications exceeds the capacity of a program, class, grade level or building. A charter school shall give enrollment preference to pupils returning to the charter school in the second or any subsequent year of its operation and to siblings of pupils already enrolled in the charter school. A charter school that is sponsored by a school district governing board shall give enrollment preference to eligible pupils who reside within the boundaries of the school district where the charter school is physically located. If capacity is insufficient to enroll all pupils who submit a timely application, the charter school shall select pupils through an equitable selection process such as a lottery except that preference shall be given to siblings of a pupil selected through an equitable selection process such as a lottery.

B. Except as provided in subsection C, a charter school shall not limit admission based on ethnicity, national origin, gender, income level, disabling condition, proficiency in the English language or athletic ability.

C. A charter school may limit admission to pupils within a given age group or grade level.

D. A charter school shall admit pupils who reside in the attendance area of a school or who reside in a school district that is under a court order of desegregation or that is a party to an agreement with the United States department of education office for civil rights directed toward remediating alleged or proven racial discrimination unless notice is received from the resident school that the admission would violate the court order or agreement. If a charter school admits a pupil after notice is received that the admission would constitute such a violation, the charter school is not allowed to include in its student count the pupils wrongfully admitted.

E. A charter school may refuse to admit any pupil who has been expelled from another educational institution or who is in the process of being expelled from another educational institution. (Charter School Law, Ariz. Rev. Statutes Education Codes. 15-184)

Like most school districts and states, in Wake Forest, North Carolina there is a "cap" on the number of charter school students admitted each year. Currently, charter schools are capped at 100 and as of February 2007 there were 94 operating in North Carolina. According to Wake Forest resident and parent, Juliet Connoll, who will be playing a lottery to assure her children get into the Franklin Academy Charter in Wake Forest:

I've got my fingers crossed—I've got everyone that I know crossing their fingers. We're hoping for entry . . . into Franklin Academy. (Bowens 2007)

But is "crossing fingers" an adequate public policy designed to properly guarantee an education to all American citizens? Reporter Dan Bowens who covers issues for the Wake Forest school district for WRAL-TV in Raleigh, North Carolina writes that Connoll's daughters are two of a record 1,520 students applying for acceptance at the Franklin Academy Charter School in Wake Forest for the 2007-2008 school year and only 101 new students will be accepted to Franklin Academy for this school year (Ibid.).

Because most charter schools are oversubscribed, meaning they have more people wishing to enroll than they have actual space for, they are allowed to select students randomly, or, on a first-come first-serve basis, keeping with federal laws, of course. What is currently known is that in 2001 at least one in four charter schools admitted to imposing admission requirements, which in many cases ranged from including academic records, test scores, aptitudes, and criminal records of expulsion or suspension records (Anderson et. al 2002, 18). Educational academics and researchers, Ronald Corwin and Joseph Schneider, found that:

They [charter schools] also use a variety of informal techniques to select particular students, for example, by targeting recruiting practices to preferred types of families, by counseling our un-preferred individuals, and by expelling difficult students.

Most schools deny having any special admission requirements. At the same time, as just noted, many do require applications and interviews, and some admit to considering factors such as academic records, admission tests, recommendations, and other personal criteria. Moreover a large percentage of charters require or expect parents to work on behalf of the school, including fund raising activities—which conveniently excludes families who choose not to participate. (Corwin and Schneider 2007, 4)

We will look closely at the arguments by both backers of charter schools and their opponents as they relate to student admission policies in a later chapter.

A Tale of One City: New Orleans

In late August 2005, Hurricane Katrina pummeled the Gulf Coast and pulverized New Orleans' increasingly dysfunctional public school system. Over half of the city's school buildings were destroyed and tens of thousands of students and teachers were scattered across the country. Prior to Hurricane Katrina, the New Orleans Public Schools (NOPS) served 63,000 students, mostly low income and almost entirely African American. Like many other urban districts, the district was faced with a declining tax base and a dwindling student enrollment. It was also widely assailed for corruption and academic failure.

According to a long-time union activist in the city, Jordan Flaherty:

Post-Katrina New Orleans has become a battleground in the national fight over competing visions for the future of urban education. In September of 2005, with the city evacuated and all the schools closed, with no parents or students or teachers around, suddenly anything became possible. Instead of making gradual changes to an existing system, there was no system, and virtually no rules or limits on what could be changed. "The framework has been exploded since the storm," confirms New Orleans-based education reform advocate Aesha Rasheed. "It's almost a blank slate for whatever agenda people want to bring." (Flaherty, 2006)

Nearly half of the 30,000 children in the New Orleans public school system that were expected to enroll in the fall of 2007 in New Orleans public schools were enrolled in charter schools. These schools have been given tens of millions of dollars by the federal government in extra money, over and above their regular state and local money, to set up and operate, not to mention the private funds they have managed to cobble together. They have also enjoyed the largess of many philanthropic organizations. Yet the newly formed charter schools are not open to every child and do not allow every student who wants to attend to enroll. Some charter schools have special selective academic criteria, or selective admission policies, which allow them to exclude children in need of special academic help. Other charter schools, as we will discuss, have special admission policies and student and parental requirements that effectively screen out many children. While still others have long enrollment lists and "caps" on admission; the waiting lists are generally handled by lotteries. Children in the newly formed charter schools also have better facilities than those children not enrolled in charters. They are equipped with low teacher-to-student ratios as well. Post-Katrina public education in New Orleans has now morphed into an "educational experiment," or what human rights lawyer and law professor at Loyola University in New Orleans, Bill Quigley, labels: "experimenting on other people's children" (Quigley 2007). However, what about the other half of the New Orleans public school students, where did they end up after Katrina?

According to Quigley:

The other half of public school students, over ten thousand children, have been assigned to a one year old experiment in public education run by the State of Louisiana called the "Recovery School District" (RSD) program. The education these children receive will be compared to the education received by the first half in the charter schools. These children are effectively what is called the "control group" of an experiment—those against whom the others will be evaluated.

The RSD schools have not been given millions of extra federal dollars to operate. The new RSD has inexperienced leadership. Many critical vacancies exist in their already insufficient district-wide staff. Many of the teachers are uncertified. In fact, the RSD schools do not yet have enough teachers, even counting the uncertified, to start school in the fall of 2007. Some of the RSD school buildings scheduled to be used for the fall of 2007 have not yet been built.

In the first year of this experiment, the RSD had one security guard for every 37 students. Students at John McDonough High said their RSD school, which employed more guards than teachers, had a "prison atmosphere." In some schools, children spent long stretches of their school days in the gymnasium waiting for teachers to show up to teach them.

There is little academic or emotional counseling in the RSD schools. Children with special needs suffer from lack of qualified staff. College prep math and science classes and language immersion are rarely offered. Class rooms keep filling up as new children return back to New Orleans and are assigned to RSD schools.

Many of the RSD schools do not have working kitchens or water fountains. Bathroom facilities are scandalous—teachers at one school report there are two bathrooms for the entire school, one for all the male students, faculty and staff and another for all the females in the building.

Danatus King, of the NAACP in New Orleans, said "What happened last year was a tragedy. Many of the city's children were denied an education last year because of a failure to plan on the part of the RSD."

Hardly any white children attend this half of the school experiment. (Ibid.)

After Katrina hit the city, groups, including but not limited to the nonpartisan Urban Institute, and former Housing and Urban Development secretary

Henry Cisneros (now chair of City-View, a private venture dedicated to urban housing development) in New Orleans, Baton Rouge and Washington D.C. saw a unique opportunity to put forth ideas to radically restructure public education in New Orleans and turn many public schools into publicly funded charter schools. Within days of Katrina, then Gov. Kathleen Blanco (D) convened a special meeting of the state legislature to talk about a takeover of the Orleans Parish Public School District, a district with a half-billion dollar budget serving New Orleans students. According to Nat LaCour, secretary treasurer of the American Federation of Teachers:

> This meeting took place while there were still people on roofs and at the Superdome waiting to be rescued." (Davis)

The rapidity with which politicians and special interests leaped into action to virtually dismantle the then current system and reconfigure the New Orleans public school district is quite astonishing. Within two weeks of the hurricane U.S. Secretary of Education Margaret Spellings set public policy for education in the city referring to charter schools as "uniquely equipped" to serve students displaced by Katrina. Two weeks later, Spellings announced the first of two $20 million federal grants to Louisiana, solely for the establishment and opening of charter schools; there would purposely be no monies forthcoming for traditional New Orleans Public Schools. Leigh Dingerson, from the Center for Community Change, notes:

> Many of those who saw green in New Orleans were members of the Education Industry Association—the trade organization representing corporations that market services to schools and school districts. Others included conservative think tanks like the Center for Education Reform, the Thomas B. Fordham Foundation, the Heritage Foundation, and the University of Washington's Center for Reinventing Education. For years, these well-funded and well-connected institutions and interests have argued that public schools and school districts ought to join the free market economy. In the emergence of charter schools in the early 1990s, these reformers saw their opportunity: charter schools present the vehicle for outsourcing. "Choice" and "competition" could become the new clarion call. Conveniently, such a model also created a multi-billion dollar market for the services some of them sell. (Dingerson Summer 2007)

In October 2005, Louisiana Gov. Kathleen Babineaux Blanco issued an executive order waiving key portions of the state's charter school law. The executive order, which remains in effect today, allows public schools to be converted to charters without the input—or even the knowledge—of the school's parents and teachers. This is precisely what happened directly after the hurricane. A month after Katrina, the state legislature voted to take over 107 New Orleans Public Schools, and place them in the state-controlled "Recovery School District." Finally, in February 2006 all 7,500 teachers, custodians, cafeteria workers, and other unionized employees of the devastated district were fired (Ibid.).

In Washington and Baton Rouge conservative education policy groups and the education industry lobbyists (the Education Industry Association represents corporations that market goods to school systems—textbooks, assessments, tutoring services—and also includes major corporate operators of public schools) are ready with a unified message regarding education in New Orleans: This is a unique and once in a lifetime opportunity to create a new paradigm of publicly funded, market-based schools that provide flexibility and free market choice for individual families. They collectively and individually begin lobbying heavily in Baton Rouge and holding private meetings in Washington with U.S. Secretary of Education, Margaret Spellings.

This influential interest group is also quick to dominate the media. Their message is simple: Those who call for rebuilding the old centralized public school infrastructure are defenders of the status quo and obstacles to reforms. Either you think the schools are working for everyone or you agree that the whole system, and the people who work in it, must be scrapped in favor of new innovative reforms—the new innovative reform, of course, is the charter school policy. The following is a brief overview of the changes accomplished directly after Hurricane Katrina and is compiled with the partial assistance of the excellent research work of the Center for Community Change in Washington, D.C. and specifically their publication, Dismantling a Community.

The following is a month-by-month look at the rebuilding of New Orlean's school system.

September 2005

In September the Orleans Parish School Board, convening (in Baton Rouge) for the first time since the storm, votes to place the district's 7,500 school employees, including 4,500 teachers along with cafeteria workers, custodians, and school nurses on "disaster leave" without pay; the move is unilateral. Also at this meeting, the board quickly approves an application to establish the Lusher Charter School. Lusher is an existing K-5 public school that largely serves students of professors at nearby Tulane University. Charter status allows Lusher parents to establish admissions criteria for their school and do away with collective bargaining and the teacher's union as well as direct the school's curriculum and finances independent of the city school system.

Secretary Spellings announces a U.S. Department of Education grant of $20.9 million to Louisiana for the establishment and opening of charter schools.

Mayor Ray Nagin creates the *Bring New Orleans Back Commission* to guide redevelopment and rebuilding of the city. The commission's education committee is heavily populated by charter school proponents and national education activists that have converged on the city. There are no seats on the committee designated for representatives of parents or teachers from the New Orleans Public Schools. During the post-Katrina period, Tulane University President Scott S. Cowen, chairman of the Educational Task Force of Mayor Ray Nagin's *Bring New Orleans Back Commission,* is empowered to shape the redevelopment of K-12 public education in New Orleans.

Over the next three months the committee holds a series of public hearings, including hearings in cities like Atlanta and Houston where thousands of evacuees have landed. The commission also consults with other school districts around the country and looks at what's working and what isn't in public education, especially as it pertains to the charter school movement. But while this deliberative process is underway, other interests are moving swiftly ahead with rapid speed. The Bring New Orleans Back education committee's final report will not be released until January 2006.

October 2005

The near total evacuation of New Orleans, and the storm damage that makes much of the city uninhabitable at this time, decimates the already inadequate primary source of funding for the New Orleans public schools—the local property tax.

Meanwhile, low-income African Americans from the Ninth Ward see little hope of being able to return to their homes for months—if ever. But middle-class and upper-class neighborhoods are largely intact, and so the early faces returning to New Orleans are largely white and middle-class, as our their concerns. A debate opens up around how, or even *whether,* to rebuild all of New Orleans. Some citizens are quite blunt in their promotion of a plan that would restore only the middle class, or predominantly white neighborhoods.

Proposals of all sorts emerge, but no one proposal gathers enough support to move forward. In the void created by indecisiveness, the free-market "reformers" continue to move rapidly and decisively, at least when it comes to the public schools.

For example, the Orleans Parish School Board (OPSB) votes 4-2 to convert all 13 schools in the Algiers community on the west bank of the Mississippi River to newly formed charter schools. These are to be open admission schools (with no academic criteria, selective admissions or neighborhood boundaries guiding enrollment). However, because they are charter schools, they are permitted to establish a limit on the size of their student body virtually guaranteeing waiting lists for students wanting to attend them. Unlike regular public schools, they are not legally required to admit anyone once they reach their stated capacity; this is the beauty of deregulation. Furthermore, the application for the newly formed charter schools specifically states that employees of the Algiers Charter School District cannot be members of the teachers union or considered employees of the New Orleans Public Schools.

The Algiers Charter Schools Association (ACSA) was created in 2005 to provide New Orleans students, mainly on the West Bank, with public education. ACSA is now a charter school network that currently operates nine charter schools—two authorized by the OPSB and seven authorized by the RSD. All of the schools were previous OPSB schools converted into charter schools. All ACSA schools have open enrollment policies, with long waiting lists. For most operational issues, ACSA operates largely as a school district would. It has centralized funding and purchasing, teacher recruitment, and shared services; all ACSA schools use the Louisiana Comprehensive Curriculum as their academic focus. However, unlike a traditional school district, each ACSA school and principal is empowered to select the instruction style and academic and developmental services that best suit the needs of their student populations. Principals are also allowed to manage their staffing decisions and all ACSA schools are nonunion. This means they are semiprivatized.

During this time, Gov. Kathleen Babineaux Blanco issues an executive order waiving key portions of the state's charter school law to make conversion and creation of charters easier. One of the provisions waived is a requirement that the conversion of a traditional public school to a charter be conditioned on the approval of a school's faculty and parents (Saulny 2006).

Following the board vote, an African American pastor in Algiers files a lawsuit against the new charter district demanding a public and transparent debate over whether the proposal is necessary and in the best interests of the community.

A civil court judge in New Orleans orders the school board to stop its plans for a charter district in Algiers, agreeing that the board acted without providing the opportunity for public comment, as required.

The Orleans Parish School Board meets again and takes several steps:

1. Having complied with the requirements for public comment, they revote to create the Algiers Charter School District, converting all 13 schools on the West Bank to charter schools. Eight are slated to open in November of 2005, with five additional schools opening at a later date.
2. The new district has no board of directors, so the Orleans Parish School Board names itself as the founding board.
3. The board also grants charters to seven east-bank schools. One of those is for the establishment of Lusher Middle and High School. The board agrees to turn over the Alcee Fortier High School building for Lusher's expansion into a K-12 charter with two campuses. Fortier was a virtually all-black, low-performing high school with just over 900 students before the storm. Most of these families are still outside the city and are not aware that their school is being closed and the building handed over to Lusher. The new Lusher charter school will be a selective-

admissions school, with first preference given to the children of professional staff at Tulane, Loyola, Dillard, and Xavier Universities. (When registration at Lusher begins, the school reaches capacity so quickly that even some former Lusher Elementary students are denied access to the middle school). In the months after the takeover of Fortier, Tulane University helps raise more than $15 million in private and public funds to renovate the Fortier building. In the face of concern that the growing number of charter schools in the city might attempt to "cream" their student bodies, the school board passes a resolution requiring each charter approved by the board to accept a minimum of 10 percent students with disabilities and a minimum of 20 percent low-income students (prior to Katrina, 20 percent of New Orleans public school students were in special education, and 75 percent were eligible for free and reduced meals). Yet, conceding that it would be unrealistic to expect compliance with these requirements given the uncertain and still-chaotic situation in the city, the resolution allows schools to waive them until New Orleans is "fully repopulated."

November 2005

The first public school in the city—Benjamin Franklin Elementary Math and Science School—reopens its doors to students. Ben Franklin was a selective admissions school before Katrina, but opens now an open enrollment school without restriction for any elementary students who are back in the city.

The state legislature votes to take over the 107 New Orleans Public Schools that performed at or below the state average in 2004-2005. The legislation, known as Act 35, creates the Recovery School District (RSD) as the operating entity for these schools. According to the report:

Originally, the RSD envisioned a district composed primarily of charter schools with a lean central administrative staff . By early 2006, however, it had become apparent that there were not enough high-quality charter operators for the number of schools that needed to open, and the RSD was forced to transform itself into a district able to operate schools. With little time and a lack of experienced leaders, the RSD had to rely heavily on outside contractors and staff from the Louisiana Department of Education to bridge its staffing gap in order to open schools quickly. Thus, the RSD began the 2006–07 school year at a severe disadvantage and continued to struggle throughout the year. (Cowen 2008)

The legislature leaves only four schools under the control of the Orleans Parish School Board (OPSB). Ironically, these are the formerly high-performing selective-admission schools in the city. All but three of 15 Orleans Parish legislators vote against the takeover.

As 2006 approaches, an increasing number of African Americans are beginning to migrate back to New Orleans. Although returning to the Ninth Ward is impossible (armed military personnel continue to bar access to the neighborhood and no demolition or rebuilding is allowed), returning families are finding temporary or permanent shelter elsewhere in the city.

December 2005

The Orleans Parish School Board votes to fire all teachers and other employees of the New Orleans Public Schools, effective January 31, 2006. A lawsuit filed by several employees succeeds in winning a temporary restraining order, putting the official firings on hold for two months.

Many returning teachers have no input into the reconfiguration of the school system and express anger at the rapidly proliferating charter schools, which are requiring teachers to take written tests as part of the application process and to work on year-to-year contracts. Many teachers opt to take early retirement, which gives them access to union health insurance and pension plans they otherwise fear losing; hundreds find teaching positions outside of New Orleans.

Five Algiers schools open their doors as newly formed public charter schools.

January 2006

The mayor's Bring New Orleans Back Commission finally releases its education committee report. Among other things, the committee recommends establishing a "single aligned governing body" to provide a unified vision and stronger accountability for public schools in New Orleans. Even the procharter chairman of the committee expresses concern that without some central oversight it will be difficult to guarantee or even adequately monitor the schools' academic and administrative quality. The recommendation seems to call for a 'school system', something antithetical to the charter school movement's supporters. State Superintendent of Education Cecil J. Picard rejects the idea of any centralized oversight. (Nossiter 2006)

Civil rights attorney Tracie Washington files a lawsuit in New Orleans. The suit presents the names of 13 students, including one with autism, who have been denied seats in some of the city's public schools.

The same day, Orleans Parish officials present state officials with a list of 170 students who have been turned away from New Orleans schools. There is emerging concern that the city's charter schools are filled to capacity and not enough guaranteed-access schools are available for the increasing number of returning students. The state's Recovery School District—which will offer universal access—is not scheduled to operate at scale until the 2006-2007 school year.

Seemingly, what is needed is more open admission, universal access public schools; but there is no money for the Orleans Parish School Board to repair and staff additional buildings. The money is going to the newly formed charter schools. Groups wanting to open charter schools can receive as much as $2,000 per student as seed money to get up and running as schools. And although federal and foundation funding is beginning to flow into New Orleans, the money is going to newly formed charters—the traditional public school system is seeing none of this cash.

By the end of January there are 17 schools open in New Orleans:

Three are Orleans Parish public schools.
Three are charters authorized by the Recovery School District.
Five are charters operated by the Algiers Charter School District.
Six are charters operated by other entities.

All of the Algiers charter elementary schools are reported to be at full capacity and are turning children away.

February 2006

The Orleans Parish School Board again votes 4-1 to fire 7,500 teachers and other school employees. Attorneys representing some of these workers argue that if the teachers are furloughed, rather than fired, they would be entitled by law to first consideration for teaching and other positions in the Recovery School District once the city began operating and functioning. But the vote proceeds anyway with everyone knowing that one of the agendas being played out in the historic vote is the planned elimination of collective bargaining for the school district's workforce. The vote is taken and effectively ends the district collective bargaining agreement with the teacher's union of New Orleans (Cowen 2008).

Charges continue to surface that hundreds of children have been turned away from the city's newly formed public charter schools. Many charter schools are full and at capacity and thus need not accept additional students. In the midst of the lack of guaranteed access to public schools for New Orleans' children there is also anecdotal evidence as well as rumors that the schools are turning away and/or failing to provide services for children with disabilities, in violation of federal law. What is obvious is that without a centralized administration and centralized planning, the charter schools lack the shared infrastructure to offer the expensive, specialized, and multifaceted services required under law. Without any regulations, there is not even a functioning enforcement mechanism to assure children with disabilities get a public education.

What is slowly emerging in New Orleans is a patchwork of independently operated charter schools, each with its own admissions procedures and policies and educational strategies. There is no central public school system nor are there schools that guarantee access to students living within defined neighborhood boundaries. Furthermore, there is no transportation provided to children who enroll in schools that are outside of walking distance from their shelters, trailers, or homes. Parents returning to the city and seeking a desk for their children must navigate this "new paradigm" alone, and on their own.

May 2006

The Orleans Parish School Board announces its plan to re-establish academic admissions criteria at the four schools they are operating.

As new charter schools continue to open and establish their own admissions and enrollment rules across the city, a battle is brewing over high-performing and low-performing students—no one really wants the latter. Each school operator—the Orleans Parish School Board and the independent charter boards—knows that its school's performance will be evaluated based on the academic achievement of its students on standardized tests. This fact creates a school's incentive to limit the number of students likely to be underachievers or those students requiring expensive special education services. Not surprisingly amidst all of the competition for access to public schools, schools are quickly filled to capacity by students whose savvy parents have registered them early and efficiently at some of the most promising charter schools. Other schools seem to turn away students with special needs, claiming that they are unable to provide the necessary support.

As more and more New Orleans residents return to the city, there is an indisputable shortage of seats for a large block of children whose parents were late in returning, have been unable to navigate the completely decentralized system of patchwork schools, or have no transportation to access the process, which virtually requires school-by-school registration. These students, clearly left behind, are disproportionately the poor and as well as students with special needs.

The varied independent school administrators and boards are astutely aware that the higher the number of selective-admission charter schools that open, there will be a corresponding larger pool of low-performing students that will be looking for seats in these schools. When the Orleans Parish School Board announces that it will seek selective-admission status for all four of its schools, the director of the Algiers Charter District threatens to establish similar admissions policies for all the Algiers schools. The competition is now developing over who can refuse students.

Only the state-run Recovery School District (RSD)—which is not scheduled to open until August—is required to guarantee a public seat in a classroom for all New Orleans children. This is the only universal access to public schools that the New Orleans City has available.

By June, 25 public schools are operating in New Orleans:

Four are run by the Orleans Parish public schools.
Seven are charters authorized by the Recovery School District.
Six are charters affiliated with the Algiers Charter School District.
Eight are charters authorized and run independently.

According to Leigh Dingerson:

By spring 2006, 25 public schools had opened in New Orleans. Eighteen (72 percent) of those were charter schools, and 14 (56 percent) had established "selective" admissions policies. In addition to the charter schools, the Orleans Parish School Board opened five schools in the city. In summer 2006, as families began to flood back into the city, the state conceded that it, too, would need to open and operate some schools. The Recovery School District opened 17 state-run schools that fall. (Dingerson 2007)

June 2006

The Recovery School District (RSD) announces that it must postpone the opening of RSD schools for the 2006-2007 school year. Seven months after it is established by legislative mandate, the district has yet to hire a *single* teacher for its schools, although they are poised to dismiss the entire unionized teaching staff.

The chief of staff for the Recovery School District acknowledges that the district has only a paltry 10 people on its administrative staff. *One* of these employees is tasked with coordinating special education programs, which require students to be individually assessed and placed. Some estimates are that as many as 2,000 special education students have failed to find seats in the city's public charter schools.

The operating plan for the Recovery School District is released. Like the Orleans Parish resolution, it requires that schools chartered by the state admit a minimum of 10 percent of their student body with students with disabilities.

Also in June of this year, U.S. Education Secretary Margaret Spellings announces an additional $24 million grant to Louisiana for the development of charter schools; not one cent is allocated for the traditional public schools that must operate in the city (Saulny 2006).

July 2006

The existing collective bargaining agreement between the United Teachers of New Orleans and the New Orleans Public Schools finally expires. Now, even those teachers working in Orleans Parish-run public schools are working without a contract. The Orleans Parish School Board makes no move to renew the agreement, preferring instead to see the union disappear.

The Algiers Charter School Association, which plans to have a total of eight schools open in 2006-2007, passes a fiscal year budget that includes a $12 million *reserve* fund. The State Department of Education issues a list of New Orleans public schools that will be opening for the 2006-07 school year. Of these schools:

> *Thirteen* are charters authorized by the Recovery School District and operated by independent charter associations, for-profit entities, national charter school operators, or others.
> *Six* are charters operated by the Algiers Charter School Association.
> *Two* are charters authorized directly by the State Board of Elementary and Secondary Education and operated by separate entities.
> *Five* are operated directly by the Orleans Parish School Board. Four of those are "selective admission" schools.
> *Ten* are charters approved by the Orleans Parish School Board and operated by a range of groups.
> *Seventeen* are operated directly by the Recovery School District. They are all open admission schools and must guarantee seats for all students who enroll. (Center for Community Change)

August 2006

Just three weeks before opening day, the Louisiana State Board of Elementary and Secondary Education (BESE) revokes the charters of three schools in the Tremé neighborhood of New Orleans. The schools' partnership with a San Diego-based corporation that helps operate charter schools in several states has fallen apart over disagreements between the corporation and the local association board on issues including hiring and curriculum. More than 500 students enrolled at the three schools must now find alternative placements.

March 2007

The Scott S. Cowen Institute for Public Education Initiatives at Tulane University, Louisiana, is founded. The Institute states as its mission:

> *The Scott S. Cowen Institute for Public Education Initiatives at Tulane University, founded in March 2007, operates as an action oriented think tank that actively addresses the issues impeding student achievement by designing and advancing innovative, high impact policies and programs. It also serves as a clearinghouse for charter and traditional public schools in Orleans Parish to directly access the myriad of experts and resources available at Tulane.*

May 2007

Paul G. Vallas is picked as the new superintendent to run the school district of New Orleans.

June 2007

Because the city school district is now essentially three separate systems—public charter schools, the Recovery District schools, and city-run schools—each is now doing its own teacher recruiting. Recovery District officials have recruited in New York and Detroit, with trips planned to Atlanta, Houston and Dallas, says coordinator Wade Bailey. After a standard background check, new teachers can expect to begin on-the-job coursework this summer. Once school begins in September, the teachers are told they can expect to earn as much as $36,900 working in a Recovery District school—about $5,000 more than the national average for a new teacher. Though teachers in public charter schools could earn less, the state promises a $10,000 bonus to those who stay for two years, as well as up to $2,500 in moving expenses and a one-year, $400-a-month housing allowance. Local teachers are eligible for a $5,000 bonus and experienced principals can make as much as $40,000 in bonuses on top of an average $77,000 salary (Toppo 2007). The incentive and reward system is obviously geared towards the newly formed charter school experiment.

February 2008

Two for-profit companies, Abraxas and Camelot Schools, are given the green light to run "alternative" educational programs in New Orleans. Under a contract approved by the state board in January after a bidding process, Camelot won the contract to handle management tasks at Schwartz Alternative High School and Washington High School for a period of seven months, earning as much as $467,500 in profits. Through a separate contract, Abraxas Education Group gets the go-ahead to create a pilot program for elementary school-age students throughout the district that will likely result in self-contained classrooms for students with behavioral issues. The contract for the pilot, covering a seven-month period, is for $270,000. The proliferation of outside educational service providers begins to be felt more heavily now in New Orleans and reflects a nationwide shift at work, with such for profit corporations taking on unprecedented roles in shaping educational policy and managing publicly funded schools and even whole districts. That shift came more radically and abruptly in New Orleans, where the number of groups, nonprofit and for-profit alike—offering everything from school security to principal training—continues to grow, is something we will discuss in a subsequent chapter (Carr 2008).

April 2008

The Cowen Report from Tulane University, *entitled The State of Public Education in New Orleans* is released. The report notes that:

> *Eighty public schools in New Orleans are run by 29 different operators, including the OPSB, the RSD, and 27 charter school operators.*
>
> *Fifty-seven percent of public school students now attend charter schools, more than any other urban school district in the country.*
>
> *The newly created New Orleans School plan also differs from a traditional school district plans in its staffing flexibility—the Recovery School District teaching staff, for example, is not unionized. Salaries are based on a common salary schedule and performance incentives are currently being considered. The district is able to hire, fire, and promote based on policies other than seniority. Furthermore, with the formation of the RSD, the OPSB was left to run or oversee only those schools that had traditionally been the board's highest-performing public schools, many of which have some form of selective admissions criteria.*
>
> *In most cases, parents now have the choice to send their children to any public school in New Orleans where they can gain admission, regardless of where they live. (Cowen 2008)*
>
> *Currently, the Board of Elementary and Secondary Education (BESE) and the Louisiana Department of Education, under the direction of State Superintendent, Paul Pastorek, run the New Orleans Public Schools. As of February 2008, 80 schools in New Orleans educated 32,900 students in total. Under the umbrella of BESE and the Louisiana Department of Education the new public school plan called for trifurcating the school district and its services and then contracting out the services to charters. So, the Recovery School District (RSD) was created and under the direction of Superintendent Paul Vallas it is responsible for running 59 schools. Thirty-three of the RSD run-schools educate 12,300 students while 26 RSD charters educate 10,000 students. The second arm of the newly trifurcated district, BESE, runs two charters that educates 800 students and the third branch of the new school system, Orleans Parish School Board (OPSB), under the direction of Superintendent Darryl Kilbert, runs 19 schools. Of the 19 schools there are seven OPSB run schools that educate 2,700 students and 12 OPSB charters that educate another 7,100 students. (Cowen Report 2008)*

The Cowen report goes on to identify the following five successes achieved since the end of previous school year:

1. Strong new leadership has emerged at the state and local levels;
2. School buildings have been brought up to basic standards and have significantly more supplies;
3. A sufficient number of teachers were hired for the 2007-08 school year;
4. The community is much more involved in schools than before Hurricane Katrina;

5. Overall, there is a sense among students, teachers, school leaders and community members that there has been a significant improvement in most schools since the last school year. (Ibid.)

July 2008

On July 9, Louisiana Governor Bobby Jindal puts his signature on 11 education bills, including several boosts for public charter schools. According to the Governor:

For charter schools, we increased the cap on charter schools from 42 to 70, provided for for-profit charter school operators to operate public schools, extended leaves of absence for teachers who are temporarily employed in charter schools from three to five years, and BESE has been given greater flexibility to renew charter schools for shorter periods of time.

Representative Don Trahan added:

As we work to improve low-performing schools with the public domain, we must open the door to innovative practices that will help our students succeed. Charter schools offer many proven educational models that can help turn around failing schools and teach us how to improve other traditional public schools around the state. While I have always said that the state taking over public schools should be a last resort, we cannot stand by and watch our children fall further and further behind. We owe it to our students to commit to pursuing every opportunity that might bring them success. These bills will enable Louisiana to deliver on that promise. (U.S. Charter Schools, under "Louisiana Charter Schools")

December 2008

The New Orleans' Recovery School District announces plans to convert four low-performing traditional public schools to public charter schools in 2009, ending the current even split between 33 charter and 33 non-charter schools (Simon 2008).

DIRECTIONS IN THE LAW

Charter Laws State by State

The following is a brief look at the adoption of charter school laws state-by-state as of the end of 2007. Changes in state laws nationwide continue. For this reason, it is important for the reader to update and revise this list on a consistent basis. As of this writing, the state of Washington, Montana, North Dakota, South Dakota, Nebraska, Wet Virginia, Kentucky, Alabama, and the state of Maine had no charter school legislation. This review of charter school laws was aided by research from the Education Commission of the States, the National Charter Research Project, and U.S. Charter Schools, respectively. See Appendix E for state comparisons.

Alaska 1995

Adopted in 1995, Alaska's charter school legislation permits up to 60 charter schools. All charter schools in the state must be approved by both the local school board where the charter school operates as well as the state board of education. There is no appeal from a local board's denial of a charter. Charter schools in Alaska may not employ or bargain with staff independently; charters are bound by the school district's collective bargaining agreement and the schools operate under a limited term of ten years with a performance-based contract. Alaska's legislation does not exempt charter schools from most state rules and regulations; charter initiators may apply for a waiver of local policies only. Charter schools have full responsibility for special education evaluation and services; some negotiate an insurance arrangement with their LEA. As of December 19, 2006 Alaska had opened twenty-three charter schools with an enrollment of 4,700. Operational funding is equivalent to "the amount generated by the students enrolled minus a portion for administrative costs." The local school board is responsible for setting the charter school's budget based on student enrollment (U.S. Charter Schools, under "Alaska Charter Schools").

Arizona 1994

Arizona's charter law, passed in 1994, permits three different organizations to sponsor charter schools within the state: local districts, the state board of education, and any new state-chartering agency may charter a school. Currently, local school boards or state boards for charter schools approve new charters (the department of education is under a self-imposed moratorium). There is no appeal process from the denial of a charter; however, the initiator may apply to multiple grantors. There are no caps on the number of charter schools the state may charter. Charter schools receive an automatic waiver from most state education laws and regulations, and they may employ and/or bargain with staff independent of local bargaining units. Charter schools are independent legal entities in Arizona, and they receive a fifteen-year charter term. Arizona is considered to be a beacon, by those bent on market reforms in education, for charter school experimentation and legislation, and approximately 348 charter schools were operating in Arizona during the 1997-1998 school year. If sponsored by a local district, a charter school receives per-pupil funding equal to at least the average cost per pupil for the district as a whole. If a charter is state approved, the charter school is funded directly by the state based on the state funding formula for all schools.

Arkansas 1995

According to a 1995 Arkansas law, for nonprofits, government entities, and colleges; the district must create conversions. No private or parochial elementary school in existence on or before July 30, 1999 shall be eligible for open enrollment charter school status. The state board of education is the eligible chartering authority. The number of charter schools allowed is limited to 24 new unlimited conversions; Knowledge Is Power Program (KIPP) charter schools and schools that have demonstrated success in student achievement gains are exempt from the cap and may apply for licenses for additional open enrollment charter schools, and the state board of education can waive rules and regulations. There is no appeal of a charter denial in Arkansas, nor is there any automatic waiver of state education laws and regulations, although waivers may be applied for and granted. Charter schools do not get an automatic waiver from most state and district education laws, regulations, and/or policies. Any exemptions from particular laws, regulations, and policies must be specified in charter. Arkansas charter schools are not independent entities; they cannot bargain with or employ staff independently. Teachers in conversions remain covered by a district bargaining agreement, but may request a waiver from certain provisions; teachers in open enrollment schools and charters can negotiate as a separate bargaining unit, or work independently. All Arkansas charter schools operate under a five-year contract that is renewable. All charter schoolteachers are bound by the school district collective bargaining agreement. There is state and district funding. For conversion charter schools, it is the school district that is the source of funding. For open enrollment charter schools, it is the state (Education Commission of the States).

California 1992

California legislation permitted up to 100 charters in 1992. The state board of education decided that it had the power to waive the law, and by 1998, there were 130 charter schools operating in the state. California has raised the number of charter schools that can be opened in California to 1,050 with 100 new charters permitted each year. Charter schools must be approved by the local school board and by a county school district or by a county panel on appeal from a local district. Charter schools in California receive an automatic waiver from state education laws and regulations, and they are independent legal entities that can employ and/or bargain independently with their staffs. All charter schools are operated under a five-year, limited-term, performance-based contract. There are 710 open and operating charter schools operating in the state as of the 2007. Charter schools are not bound by school district collective bargaining agreements. A charter school's teachers have the same option to form a union as other school district employees. The drafters of the school's charter decide whether they will remain covered by the school district's collective bargaining agreement or have the right to organize independently. If they are independent, they are generally subject to the state's education collective bargaining laws. General purpose and categorical funding for charter schools is comparable with other public schools, and charter schools may receive funds directly from the state (Ibid.).

Colorado 1993

Anyone requesting charter status in Colorado must specify which state rules and regulations they wish to have waived. It is then up to the state board of education to determine which rules and regulations it will waive. Colorado legislation of 1993 requires that people who wish to start a charter school seek approval from local school boards; state Charter School Institutes in districts that have not retained exclusive authority to grant charters; or the state board may recommend conversion of "failing" schools. Waivers from state, district, and local laws are limited; exemptions from district policies must be negotiated with a sponsor district and specified in charter, and waivers from state statutes must be granted by the state board of education; in practice, however, waivers from state statutes are invariably granted upon request, and many districts grant charter schools wholesale waivers from district policy as well. Charter schools are not bound by school district collective bargaining agreements. A charter school's teachers may remain covered by the school district's collective bargaining agreement, negotiate as a separate unit with the charter school governing body, or work independently. If the local board rejects the proposal, it can be appealed to the state board of education, which can approve or turn the appeal down. The number of charter schools allowed is unlimited and there were 144 charters operating in the state as of 2007. As to funding, 95 percent of the district per-pupil revenues come from the state and this varies widely from district to district (Ibid.).

Connecticut 1996

A 1996 Connecticut law permits up to 24 charter schools; of those schools, up to 12 must be authorized by local school boards and up to 12 may be authorized by the state board of education. Schools authorized by local school boards must conform to the local collective bargaining agreements. Charter denials may be appealed to the state board, which may order the local board to grant a charter. There is no automatic waiver of state education laws and regulations, but charter schools, like other public schools, may seek waivers on a case-by-case basis from the state board of education. Charter schools are independent legal entities in the state of Connecticut, and a local charter school's teachers are covered by the school district collective bargaining agreement, but such agreement may be modified by a majority of a charter school's teachers and the charter school's governing council. A state charter school's teachers may negotiate as a separate unit with the charter school governing council or work independently. They operate under a limited-term, performance-based contract. As of the 2006 school year, Connecticut had twenty charter schools operating. Local charter schools receive funding from the school district. State charter schools receive funding from the state. For local charter schools, the amount of funding is specified in the charter. For state charter schools, 110 percent of state and school district operations funding follows students, based on average school district per-pupil revenue. Special education in charter schools is funded by the state (Ibid.).

Delaware 1995

In Delaware, 1995 legislation allowed for the creation of an unlimited number of charter schools. Charter schools may be approved by either a local school board or the state board of education. There is no appeal process for the denial of a charter. Charter schools in the state are automatically granted waivers from state education laws and regulations. Delaware charters are independent entities that can employ and negotiate directly and independently with their staffs. A charter school's teachers are not covered by school district collective bargaining agreements. They may negotiate as a separate unit with the charter school governing body or work independently. Charter schools are given a four to five year charter. As of 2004, there were 19 charter schools operating in the state. Funding of charters is based on 100 percent of computed state funding based on a state unit funding formula and 100 percent of local funding based on previous year per-pupil expenditure in a student's school district of residence follows students (Ibid.).

District of Columbia 1996

The U.S. Congress authorized charter schools to operate in the District of Columbia in 1996. The eligible charter authority is the D.C. Public Charter School Board (DCPCSB); the D.C. City Council may designate an additional entity by enactment of a bill. (The D.C. Board of Education transferred all their authorized schools to the DCPCSB and is no longer an authorizer). District of Columbia law allows for 20 charters per year. There is no appeals process. There is an automatic waiver from state education laws and regulations. The charter schools in the District of Columbia are not bound by the school district bargaining agreement. Charter schools operate under performance-based contracts of fifteen years, with at least one review every five years. As of 2005, there were 72 charter schools operating in D.C. Charter Schools receive public funds based on the number of students they enroll, as do all D.C. public schools (Ibid.).

Florida 1996

A 1996 Florida law allowed for local school boards to charter schools and the district school board may sponsor a charter school in the county over which the board has jurisdiction; Florida Schools of Excellence Commission has been established to authorize schools in districts that have not been granted exclusive authority over charters and may also approve cities and universities as co-sponsors of charters. There are an unlimited number of charter schools that may be authorized to operate within the state. The term of the initial charter is 4 or 5 years with renewal after 5 years. Nonprofits are eligible for up to a 15-year charter, and charters operating for 3 years that have demonstrated success can renew for a 15-year term to facilitate financing. Florida charter schools receive a limited waiver from most state and district education laws and regulations. Specific statutes apply to charters (including class size) but charter schools are exempt from local school board policies. Charter schools are not bound by district collective bargaining agreements and charter school employees shall have the option to bargain collectively. Employees may collectively bargain as a separate unit or as part of the existing district collective bargaining unit as determined by the structure of the charter school. As of 2006-2007 school year, there were 379 charter schools operating in the state. Funding of charters is comparable with all other schools (Ibid.).

Georgia 1993

In 1993, Georgia initially permitted the conversion of existing public schools into charter schools, and the law was changed in 1998 to permit the creation of an unlimited amount of entirely new charter schools. The local school board in a particular town within which the charter school will operate must approve either a conversion or a new school. Charters that are denied cannot be appealed in Georgia. The state board of education has the power to grant appeals and become the sponsor of a state charter provided a majority of teachers and of parents from the appealing school support the application and it meets a set of state rules and regulations that the board has set and are not specified in law. Charter schools receive a blanket waiver from state and local rules and regulations reinstated in 2005. Charter schools are not bound by the school district's collective bargaining agreements. As of 2007, there were 66 charter schools operating in the state. The Georgia Charter Schools Act of 1998 states that a charter school shall be included in the allotment of funds to the local school system in which the charter school is located (Ibid.).

Hawaii 1994

The entire state of Hawaii is a single school district. The eligible chartering authority is the state board of education, upon recommendation of the New Century Charter Schools Review Panel. The state allows for 23 new starts, one new school may be authorized for every new start that either has its charter revoked or has been accredited for 3 years or longer by an education accreditation authority; and 25 for conversions. As of February 1, 2008, the state had also reached its cap of 23 new charter schools, and continues to limit conversions to charter schools to 25; as of 2007 there were 27 charters operating in the state. According to 1994 legislation, charter schools are exempt from most school code regulations but must adhere to collective bargaining agreements, civil rights legislation, health and safety regulations, and performance standards. Applications denied by the Charter School Review Panel may be appealed to the state board of education. Funding is determined annually, based on per-pupil funding but all federal and other financial support for charter schools shall be no less than for all other public schools (Ibid.).

Idaho 1998

In 1998, the Idaho legislature authorized the creation of up to 6 new charters per year statewide, and only one per school district each year not including virtual charter schools. No whole school district may be converted to a charter district. Schools can either be converted or new. Charters are granted to local school boards for conversions and for approval of new charter schools. Public Charter School Commission (PCSC) for virtual charters or for schools not acted upon by school boards or referred by school boards. Applications denied by the local school board or the PCSC may be appealed to a hearing officer selected by the state superintendent of public instruction. The hearing officer can make recommendations, but they are nonbinding. Upon further disapproval by the local board or the PCSC, an applicant may appeal to the state board of education. Decisions by the state board of education are subject to judicial review. An automatic waiver from most state and district education laws, regulations, and policies are limited from state laws, exempt from most local laws. Charter schools are not bound by school district collective bargaining agreements and staff of the charter school is considered a separate unit for purposes of collective bargaining. As of the 2006-2007 school year, there were 28 charter schools operating in the state. Funding is based on the same schedule of payments as other public schools (Ibid.).

Illinois 1996

Illinois legislation of 1996 permitted up to 60 charter schools: 30 in Chicago, 15 in Chicago suburbs, and 15 in the rest of the state. Local school boards that are the eligible chartering authorities and the state have an appeal process if a local board denies a charter. Illinois has a limited appeals process that involves one review. Charter schools are given an automatic waiver from most state and district education laws, regulations, and policies. Charter schools are not bound by school district collective bargaining agreements, however, any bargaining unit of charter school employees that is formed shall be separate and distinct from any bargaining units formed from employees of a school district in which the charter school is located. As of 2006-2007 school year, there were 34 charter schools operating in Illinois. Funding is negotiated with sponsor school districts and specified in each charter, but not less than 75 percent or more than 125 percent of per-capita student tuition of school district in which the charter school is located (Ibid.).

Kansas 1994

Kansas legislation passed in 1994 permitted up to 15 charter schools. They had to be approved by both the local and the state board of education, and there is no appeals process in the event that a local board turns down a charter application. Kansas does not grant automatic waivers from state education laws and regulations; the waivers must be applied for individually. Kansas charters are granted for specific terms under performance-based contracts. As of the 2006-2007 school year, Kansas had 27 charter schools operating in the state. A charter school's teachers remain covered by the school district collective bargaining agreement, although a waiver may be granted if specified in the charter. Funding for charter schools is at the discretion of the school district. Funding, is and has been, as follows: 2003-2004 = $2.5 million; 2004-2005 = $2.5 million; and 2005-2006 = $3 million (Ibid.).

Louisiana 1995

Charter schools in Louisiana are governed by the provisions of the Charter School Law and changes to the Charter School Law were made by bills passed during the 1999, 2001, 2003, 2004, 2005, and 2006 in both regular and/or extraordinary legislative sessions. Much of the revisions were due to the redesign of education and the unleashing of the charter school movement as a result of Hurricane Katrina. The local school board or the Louisiana Board of Elementary and Secondary Education (BESE) can act as authorizers for charter schools, but with the law changing so rapidly, keeping up with current events regarding charter laws in Louisiana can be difficult. Charters are granted for five years and at this point, U.S. Charter Schools, an organization devoted to expanding charter access, states on their Web site the cap is 42 statewide (U.S. Charter Schools). Funding for charter schools comes from two governmental sources; one, the local school board and the other, the State Department of Education and the Louisiana Board of Elementary and Secondary Education. This can be misleading due to the fact that much of the monies fueling charter schools in New Orleans, as we will see in chapter seven, comes from philanthropic organizations such as the Walton Family and the Bill and Melinda Gates Foundation. According to U.S. Charter Schools, as of September 9, 2008 there were 66 charter schools in the state enrolling 25,000 students. However this figure changes monthly if not weekly.

Maryland 2003

Under certain conditions specified in the state's charter school law, local boards of education can approve the restructuring of a public school as a charter school. The local board of education determines the length of the charter. In terms of appeals processes, there is a non-binding review; the state board can provide guidance to local boards. For restructured schools, the state board may become the authorizer if the proposal is rejected or ignored at the local level. There are no caps on the number of charters and the Maryland public charter schools authorized by local education authorities receive a fair per-pupil foundation grant that is at least equal to the calculated operating costs for educating the like kind of students in existing public schools within that jurisdiction. As of the 2006-2007 school year there were 23 charters operating in the state. Charter schools are bound by the district collective bargaining agreement although a charter school and a local teachers' union may mutually agree to negotiate amendments to the existing agreement to address the needs of the particular public charter school. As of the writing of this book it is expected that Maryland public charter schools authorized by local education authorities will receive a fair per-pupil foundation grant that is at least equal to the calculated operating costs for educating the like kind of students in existing public schools within that jurisdiction (Ibid.).

Massachusetts 1994

Originally authorizing up to 25 charter schools, the Massachusetts legislature has changed the law to permit an additional 12 state-authorized charter schools, and 13 new "Horace Mann" charter schools. For Commonwealth charter schools, the state board of education is the authorizer. For Horace Mann charter schools, the local school board, local teachers' union, and state board of education can fulfill the role of authorizer. The latter are schools authorized by a local school board using a contract approved by the local teachers' union. Massachusetts has no appeals process for denied charters, it does not grant automatic waivers from state education laws and regulations, and it does not provide for a process to obtain waivers. Horace Mann charters remain bound by school district collective bargaining agreements to the extent provided by the terms of their charters. Commonwealth charters are not bound by these agreements. The charter schools are legal entities that can contract and negotiate directly with staffs. As of the 2006-2007 school year, Massachusetts had 59 charter schools in operation. In terms of funding charter schools, the Commonwealth charters receive funding from each student's sending district. Horace Mann charters receive an agreed-upon budget allocation from their school board (Ibid.).

Michigan 1993

In 1993, the Michigan legislature made it possible for individual local districts, regional district cooperatives, and public universities to sponsor charter schools—the public universities may sponsor a total of 75 charter schools. Charter schools are under the supervision of the Michigan State Board of Education. Any group that wishes to start a charter school must ask the local community for permission and a public vote decides whether a charter proposal will be considered. If the vote is no, the idea cannot go forward. If the vote is yes, the idea must be submitted to the local school board in the district in which the school wishes to operate. In Michigan, there is no appeals process for denied charters, but when a charter is denied, the initiator may petition to have the issue placed on the next election ballot. There are no automatic waivers from state education laws and regulations. Michigan charters are contracted for a term based on performance. There is no current legal limit on the length of the authorizing charter for most charter schools. There is a cap on the number of charter schools that may be authorized by public state universities. That cap of 150 remains in effect, and the maximum number of schools that may be chartered by state public universities was reached several years ago (U.S. Charter Schools, under "Michigan Charter Schools").

There is no cap on the number of charter schools that may be authorized by local education agencies (LEAs), community colleges, or intermediate school districts. Recent legislation provides for the authorization of up to 15 "urban high school academies" that may be authorized and located in the City of Detroit. Under that legislation, Public Act 179 of 2003, those "urban high school academies" would be authorized for initial terms of 10 years with subsequent renewal terms of 10 years. That law is being challenged in the Michigan courts. Teachers in charter schools authorized by local school boards are covered by school district collective bargaining agreements. Other charter school teachers are not, and may negotiate as a separate unit with a charter school governing body or work independently. As of the 2006-2007 school year, Michigan had 229 charter schools. Charter funding is capped at the statewide average (Education Commission of the States).

Minnesota 1991

In Minnesota, local school boards, intermediate school boards, cooperatives, non-profit organizations, public postsecondary institutions, and private colleges may approve charter schools, all subject to approval by the state commissioner of education. Also, the state commissioner of education may approve charter schools on appeal. When a charter is denied, the state board of education handles the appeal. Minnesota charter schools are not covered by local district collective bargaining agreements and charter schoolteachers may negotiate as a separate unit with the charter school governing body or work independently. There is an automatic waiver from most state, district education laws, and state requirements. A charter school's bargaining unit may remain part of the school district unit if teachers, the charter school governing board, the local school board, and the teachers' union in the school district agree. Schools are chartered for a specific term, and the contracts are based on performance. As of the 2006-2007 school year, Minnesota had 131 charter schools operating in the state. Charter schools are publicly funded. General purpose funding for charter schools may be less than funding for other public schools because charters do not have bonding authority and do not receive excess local levy aid. They do, however, receive funds to partially defray the cost of leasing school space. Special education for charter students is funded by the state (Ibid.).

Nevada 1997

A charter school application must be approved by the state department of education and a local school board. A charter school that is formed exclusively to serve special education students must be approved by the state board of education. The length of the charter is six years. There is a cap on the number of "non-at-risk" charter schools that may be formed: 21 throughout the state, with some geographic restrictions. If the local school board takes no action or denies an application, it can be appealed back to the state committee on charter schools, which will recommend sponsorship to the state board of education. If the state approves the charter, it will be the sponsor. If the state denies the application, the decision can be appealed to the district county court in which the proposed charter will be located. There can be an unlimited number for charter schools serving at-risk students. Nevada has limited waivers from most state, district education laws, regulations and policies. As of the 2006-2007 school year, Nevada had 17 charter schools operating within the state. Charter schools receive the same per-pupil funding that local districts receive and special education is funded by the state (Ibid.).

New Hampshire 1995

New Hampshire passed charter legislation in 1995. Both the local school board and the state department of education must approve applications in the state. If a charter is denied, an appeal can be taken to the state board of education. New Hampshire grants automatic waivers to charter schools, and the schools are considered legal independent entities. They are contracted for a term based on performance. The length of charters in the state is five years. There is no cap on charters. Teachers are not covered by local school district collective bargaining agreements; any teacher may choose to be an employee of a charter school, in which case such teacher shall have the rights of a teacher in public education to join or organize collective bargaining units. As of the 2006-2007 school year, New Hampshire had 8 charter schools in operation. When it comes to funding charter schools a minimum of 80 percent of the school district's prior year average cost per pupil, as determined by the state department of education, follows students to school. Special education funding also follows students and is provided by the state (Ibid.).

New Jersey 1995

The Commissioner, with the authority of the Charter School Program Act of 1995, may approve or deny an application for a charter after review of the application. Newly created charter schools do not have to follow local labor-management agreements, but charters converted from existing public schools must do so. Regulations may be waived only by petition. The length of a charter is four years. Applications denied may be appealed to the state board of education. There is no cap on the number of charter schools that can be open in the state. New Jersey charter schools are independent legal entities that are contracted for a term based on performance. Teachers in converted public schools are covered by a school district collective bargaining agreement. Teachers in start-ups may remain covered by a school district collective bargaining agreement, negotiate as a separate unit with a charter school governing board or work independently. As of the 2006-2007 school year, New Jersey had 53 charter schools operating in the state. Funding for the charter school comes from the state and local taxpayers through the district board of education (Ibid.).

New Mexico 1993

All school districts in New Mexico are charter school authorizers. Parent involvement in the discussion and adoption of the charter school plan must be documented. A charter is granted for 5 years, and then can be renewed for term of up to 5 years. There are caps on charter schools, 75 start-ups and 25 conversions in a five-year period. Teachers are not covered by local school district collective bargaining agreement. As of the 2006-2007 school year, New Mexico had 62 charter schools. For funding, a minimum of 98 percent of state and school district operations funding follows students, based on average school district per-pupil revenue (Ibid.).

New York 1998

As of 1998, the state of New York was still debating its charter school legislation. Still, there were 3 charter schools operating in the state in 1998. As of the 2006-2007 school year, 94 charter schools were operating in the state. The charter school authorizers for the state are, for conversions, local school boards; for start-ups, the State University of New York Board of Trustees (up to 50 start-ups) and the New York State Board of Regents (up to 50 start-ups). For the New York City Public Schools, the local chancellor charters conversions and start-ups. The law sets a limit of 100 charter schools. However, public schools that elect to convert to become charter schools are not included in the count. Conversion charter schools are bound by existing school district collective bargaining agreements. Applications denied by the local school board may be appealed to the state board of education. If the local school board does not act on an application within 60 days, it will automatically be reviewed by the secretary of education. Waivers from state laws are not automatic but certain exemptions from particular laws, regulations, and policies may be negotiated and specified in the charter or requested through a waiver process from different parties. Start-up charter schools enrolling up to 250 students in the first year are not deemed members of any existing collective bargaining unit representing employees of the school district in which the charter school is located, and the charter school and its employees are not subject to any existing collective bargaining agreement between the school districts and its employees. Start-up charter schools with an enrollment of more than 250 are deemed to be represented in a separate negotiating unit at the charter school by the same employee organization, if any, that represents like employees in the school district in which such charter school is located; however, this provision may be waived in up to 10 charters issued by the State University of New York, is not applicable to the renewal or extension of a charter, and does not subject such a charter school to any collective bargaining agreement between any school district and its employees or does not make such a charter school part of any negotiating unit at such school district. The charter school may, in its sole discretion, choose whether or not to offer the terms of any existing collective bargaining to school employees (Ibid.).

North Carolina 1996

In North Carolina, the legislation of 1996 permitted local school boards, the University of North Carolina, or the state board of education to authorize charter schools. Charter schools approved by local school boards and the University of North Carolina must also be approved by the state board of education. The law caps charter schools to no more than 100 charter schools statewide, with a maximum of 5 per school district per year. The charter legislation allows for both the creation of new schools and the conversion of existing ones. Applications denied by the local school board or UNC institution may be appealed to the state board of education. An automatic waiver of most state education laws and regulations is granted, and charter schools may negotiate directly with their staffs regarding employment and salaries. For charter schools sponsored by local school boards, teachers remain subject to school district work rules unless they negotiate to work independently. For all other charter schools, teachers are not subject to school district work rules. As of the 2006-2007 school year, North Carolina had 93 charter schools in operation. Special education is funded by the state (Ibid.).

Ohio 1997

The Ohio 1997 charter law allows for both new schools and conversions. Major sponsors include the State Board of Education, the Lucas County Educational Service Center, and the Ohio Council of Community Schools (who serve as charter authorizers). In terms of caps on charter schools, through July 1, 2005, there is a cap of 225 schools. After that time, the cap expires and an unlimited number of schools may open. There is no appeals process for the denial of a charter. There are no automatic waivers from the state, district regulations, requirements, or policies except for a few non-education regulations identified in the charter law. For start-ups, teachers may work independently or form a collective bargaining unit. Conversions are subject to a school district's collective bargaining agreement, unless a majority of the charter school's teachers petition to work independently or form their own unit. As of the 2006-2007 school year, Ohio had 315 charter schools operating within the state. As to funding, a community school is funded by the state through per-pupil foundation payments; by additional funds from grants, government and private services; by state start-up grants for developers with preliminary agreements; and by the Public Charter Schools Grant Program through the U.S. Department of Education (Ibid.).

Oklahoma 1999

Local school boards or vocational-technical school districts are charter authorizers in the state. There are caps on the number of charter schools allowed. Charter schools may open only in school districts with 5,000 or more students and a population of at least 500,000 or in vocational-technical school districts that serve such school districts. There is no appeals process, only binding arbitration and mediation paid for by the school district. Only limited waivers from most state and district education rules and regulations are available. Teachers in charter schools are not covered by local district collective bargaining agreements, however, a charter school may choose to be a part of the collective bargaining agreement. As of the 2006-2007 school year, Oklahoma had 15 charters in operation. Like any public school, charter schools receive state funding through the state aid funding formula, set by law. Up to 5 percent of a school's allocation may be retained by its sponsor for administrative costs. Charter schools may receive additional funding through public aid, grants, and other revenue as well as private sources, but the schools must be nonprofit. The Charter Schools Incentive Fund (70 O.S. §§ 3-144) assists those interested in establishing charter schools. Applicants are eligible for up to $50,000 for start-up costs and renovation efforts (Ibid.).

Oregon 1999

Charter schools can only be authorized by the local education agency (LEA). The state board of education may sponsor a charter school if the decision to deny by the LEA is appealed to the state and the state approves the application. The length of a charter is five years. Applications denied by the local school board may be appealed to the state board of education. Decisions by the state board of education may be appealed to the circuit court. There are automatic waivers from most state and district education laws but local school boards have limited discretion over applicable rules and statutes. There are no caps on the number of charters. As of the 2006-2007 school year, the state had 70 charter schools. Teachers are not covered by local district collective bargaining agreements. However, charter schoolteachers may participate in existing collective bargaining units or may form collective bargaining units that are separate from existing ones. Also, if a school board is not the sponsor of the charter school, the school board is not the employer of the employees of the charter school and the school board cannot collectively bargain with the employees of the charter school. Charter schools are funded through the State School Fund. They receive 80 percent of the ADMw (Average daily membership, weighted) if they are a K-8 and 95 percent of the ADMw if they are a 9-12 (Ibid.).

Pennsylvania 1997

The Pennsylvania legislature actually authorized funds to help individuals and groups plan charter schools, and in 1997, it then authorized an unlimited number of charter schools. Act 88 of 2002 established the Department of Education as the authorizer for cyber charter schools. Cyber charter schools can be identified as schools that provide a significant portion of instruction online. Individuals or groups seeking to establish a charter public school must apply to the local school board of the district in which the school will be located. School boards are the entities that can sponsor charter schools, and advocates have the right to appeal to the state if a local board turns them down. Any appeal to the state requires the gathering of at least 1,000 signatures of district residents—or 2 percent of the district's residents, whichever is fewer. The length of a charter is three to five years. There are automatic waivers available from most state and district education rules and regulations. There is no cap on the number of charters. Teachers are not covered by local school district collective bargaining agreements, however, a charter school's staff may bargain collectively, but not as part of the school district's collective bargaining unit. As of the 2006-2007 school year, there were 119 charter schools operating in the state. Charter schools are funded through partial grants and special education is provided by the state (Ibid.).

Rhode Island 1995

Rhode Island's 1995 approach to charter school law gives groups of public personnel the opportunity to create new schools and enables existing public schools to convert to charter status. The commissioner of education and/or the school committee where the charter public school is to be located are authorized to recommend to the Board of Regents the granting of the charter. Charter applicants must ask for waivers of local and state regulations in their proposal, and charter school employees remain part of the collective bargaining unit for all teachers in the district. There is no appeal process in the event a charter is denied. Rhode Island charters are granted for five years under a performance-based contract. A charter school's teachers are covered by school district collective bargaining agreements. In the 2006-2007 school year there were 11 charters operating in, Rhode Island—100 percent of state and school district operations funding follows students, based on average school district per-pupil revenue minus 5 percent of the state share, which the school district retains for administration and impact. The charter school and school district negotiates the cost of services that the charter school wants the school district to provide (Ibid.).

South Carolina 1996

According to 1996 legislation, only local school boards can authorize charter schools in the state of South Carolina. Both new schools and converted public school plans are permitted. Applications denied by the local school board may be appealed to the state board of education. The state board may listen to an appeal but may not actually grant a charter. The length of a charter is five years. There are limitations on automatic waivers from state and district education rules, laws, and regulations. There is no cap on the number of charter schools. Charter schools are contracted on term-based performance contracts and are considered to be independent entities. For conversions, a charter school's teachers remain covered by school district employment policy. For start-ups, a charter school's teacher may remain covered by a school district employment policy, negotiated as a separate unit with a charter school's governing body, or work independently. In 2006-2007 South Carolina had 31 charter schools. A charter school is entitled to receive local, state, and federal funds based on its student population. The district distributes local and state funds to the charter school (Ibid.).

Tennessee 2002

Local school boards can authorize charter schools and the state board of education can also authorize if appealed by a charter sponsor and warranted in a charter application. There is a cap of 50 charter schools. The length of a charter is five years. Applications denied by the local board may be appealed to the state board of education. The state board's decision is binding. There are no waivers from any state or district education rules, laws, or policies. As of the 2006-2007 school year, there were 12 charter schools operating in the state. When it comes to funding charters, the local school board allocates 100 percent of the state and local education funds to a charter school based on the per-pupil expenditures of the school district, which are based on the prior year's average daily membership for the school district (Ibid.).

Texas 1995

Texas legislative action in 1995 allowed the state to charter up to 120 schools. The legal authorizers of charters are: open enrollment charters—granted by the state; campus program charters—granted by a school district; and home-rule school district charters—granted by a school district. Called campus or program charters, district-sponsored schools are operating throughout the state. There are no appeals when a charter is denied. Charter schools are contracted under performance-based contracts for a specific term and presumably are considered to be independent legal entities. Automatic waivers from state and district education rules, laws, and regulations are limited and exemptions determined by commissioner. The length of a charter is not set by statute. There are caps on the number of charter schools and are: open enrollment charters—cap of 215 schools unless the school serves at least 75 percent "at-risk" or drop-out students; campus program charters—no cap; and home-rule school district charters—no cap. Teachers at school-district approved charter schools are school district employees. Teachers at open enrollment charter schools work independently. As of the 2006-2007 school year, Texas had 207 charter schools. Funding for district-approved charters is negotiated with the sponsor district and specified in the charter. Open enrollment charters receive 100 percent of the state and district operations and maintenance funding that follows students based on average district per-pupil revenue (Ibid.).

Utah 1998

In 1998, Utah legislators authorized the creation of up to eight charter schools, which can be either new schools or conversions. LEAs and the state board of education are the authorizing bodies with responsibility for chartering schools. Charters are valid until revoked. Applications denied by the local school board or the state charter school board may be appealed to the state board of education. The state board's decision is final. There is no automatic waiver from any state or district education rules, regulations, or policies. Charters may seek waivers on a case-by-case basis from the state board of education. The state board is authorized to have 24 charters in 2003 and 8 additional in subsequent years. LEAs have no caps on their numbers. Charter school teachers are not covered by local school district collective bargaining agreements. As of the 2006-2007 school year, Utah had 51 charter schools operating in the state. When it comes to funding, on average, 75 percent of per-pupil funding follows the child. The school district in which a charter school student resides shall pay to the host school district one-half of the amount by which the resident school district's per-student expenditure exceeds the value of the state funding (Ibid.).

Virginia 1998

Charter legislation, adopted by the state in 1998, stated that until June 2000 no more than two charters may be granted per district. Beginning June 1, 2000, the number of charter schools shall not exceed 10 percent of the total number of schools in a district or two schools, whichever is greater. The initial charter school legislation was enacted in 1998. The session of the 2002 Virginia General Assembly resulted in amendments to previous statutes governing public charter schools. Senate Bill 625 required all local school boards to review and act on applications for public charter schools. (Legislation passed in 2000 allowed local school boards the option to review or not to review charter school applications.) House Bill 734 required local school boards to report the number of public charter school applications that were approved and denied to the Virginia Board of Education on an annual basis. The new legislation maintained the requirement that local school boards submit annual evaluations of any public charter school to the state board of education. The local school district where the charter school is located authorizes the school. There is no appeals process. However, applications may be submitted to the state board of education for examination; but the state board is prohibited from making any recommendation. Local boards retain sole chartering authority. There are no automatic waivers from any state or district education laws, rules, or regulations and any exemptions are made at the discretion of the school board. There is a cap on the number of charter schools in each school district. By law, the total number of charter schools shall not exceed ten percent of the school division's total number of schools, or 2 public charter schools, whichever is greater. The length of a charter is five years. Charter school teachers are covered by local collective bargaining agreements. As of the 2006-2007 school year, Virginia had 3 charter schools operating in the state. Charter schools negotiate with the local school district for funds to operate the schools. The current 8 charter schools received funding from the federal charter school start-up grants that Virginia received during the past three years. That grant expired in September 2003 (Ibid.).

Wisconsin 1993

In Milwaukee, the Milwaukee City Council, the University of Wisconsin-Milwaukee, the Milwaukee Area Technical College Board, the Milwaukee School Board, and local school boards outside of Milwaukee can serve as charter authorizers. Charters are given for five years. There are no caps on the number of charter schools allowed, however the University of Wisconsin-Parkside, however, may only sponsor one charter school. There is no appeals process. Automatic waivers from regulations, laws, and rules are granted but the waiver can only be granted from the state, not from the district (except in Milwaukee). In charter schools that are part of a school district charter schools may negotiate directly with employees regarding wages and conditions, and it is only there that charter schools are considered to be independent legal entities. As of the 2006-2007 school year, Wisconsin had 190 charter schools operating in the state. As to funding charters, the contract between the school board and charter school specifies the amount of funding for the school, which may be more, less, or the same as spending for noncharter school pupils. Funding for the Milwaukee City Council, the University of Wisconsin-Milwaukee, and the Milwaukee Area Technical College Board-authorized charter schools, in an amount prescribed by state statute, is paid by the state directly to the charter school (Ibid.).

Wyoming 1995

According to 1995 legislation, only local school boards may sponsor charter schools in Wyoming. There is no appeals process in Wyoming. The length of a charter is five years and there are no caps on charter schools. Teachers are not covered by local school district collective bargaining agreements. As of the 2006-2007 school year, Wyoming had 3 charter schools. New law requires that the charter school receive at least 95 percent of the money generated by its students (the district may keep up to 5 percent for administrative costs) (Ibid.).

Nationwide, in the 2006-07 school year, there are 3,940 charter schools serving over 1.16 million students in 40 states and Washington, D.C. Charter schools have experienced an annual double-digit growth since the mid-1990's, shortly after the first charter school law. In 2007, there was an 11 percent increase in the number of charter schools across the country (Center for Education Reform) and with the advent of virtual charter schools, this number may literally explode in future years.

STARTING A CHARTER SCHOOL

Even though laws regarding charter school laws differ from state-to-state, charter school developers usually proceed through the same rudimentary steps when looking to create a charter school. Starting such a school is relatively easy, but there are some things that should be kept in mind when thinking about starting one.

Doing a Situational Analysis

The first thing charter school developers must do is think about the reasons they and others wish to start a charter school—what their goals, missions, and objectives are and how they plan to accomplish them. It is important to have clear and precise reasons as to why one is even contemplating the idea. From there, one should begin to gather the necessary background information to help in the design process. For example, one needs to review the state law, assemble a team that can share the responsibilities for beginning the school, look at some other charter schools in the state, and design a framework for how to proceed. Because the charter school laws are mercurial and change considerably over small amounts of time, it is advisable to investigate how the laws in the state might have changed.

A state's charter law defines who may grant a charter, and it is important to look at the granting agency to determine if certain rules and guidelines must be followed in the submission of the charter proposal. The guidelines can help make thoughts regarding the charter school more specific as well as help prepare one for the necessary legal work and other paperwork involved.

An informal plan can be put together, one that is not specifically detailed but provides a general direction, or one can proceed with a more complicated and detailed strategic plan. It is important to think about funding at this point and perhaps even look for some start-up funds from either public or private sources. Looking at foundations that provide grants could be a useful way to proceed.

Assembling a Core Group of True Believers

It is necessary to put together an organizing group, the group that will move the idea from imagination to actual reality. This group will write the charter, and some of the members might even operate the school. Careful thought should go into thinking about whom to include in the organizing group. The organizing group will need expertise in at least the following areas:

- Curriculum and instruction
- Community relations and marketing
- Finance and fund-raising
- Governance and management
- Legal issues and school law
- Real estate issues of where to locate
- Student assessment
- Writing charter and grant documents

The key to putting together a core or organizing group is to draw together diverse people from various walks of life. It might be useful to include community leaders, professional workers, blue-collar workers, parents, educators, entrepreneurs, and people with vision and imagination, and it is necessary to identify key people who might serve as a resource such as parents, business people, community leaders, and management experts.

Designing the Plan

Once the organizing group has been assembled, it is time to think in terms of designing a plan for realization. The original idea may be a good one, but until it is fleshed out and implemented, it will remain a dream. Some of the issues that must be considered in the start-up design or plan are:

- A mission and vision statement
- An overview of curricular goals
- A description of the day-to-day operation of the school and its governance
- A statement of facility needs
- A preliminary budget

In reviewing the mission statement of a number of charters, the Consortium for Policy Research in Education at Pennsylvania State University found that although the charter schools it studied varied in terms of student population, level of schooling, and whether they were new schools or conversions, the school missions were similar. Wording such as "preparing students for the twenty-first century" or "what it means to be an educated person in the twenty-first century" was common in the mission statements (Wohlstetter and Griffin 1997, 11). Technology preparedness and consideration of students' emotional needs were also found to be themes in the mission statements of the schools studied.

The study also found that although a broad and general mission statement may be helpful when seeking approval for the charter, broadly defined, generalized missions are not helpful in providing specific directions regarding teaching and learning. In one start-up middle school studied, the consortium found that the school's mission was so vague that approaches to math instruction were being used differently by different teachers (Ibid.). Thus, the mission statement that is drafted should be broad enough to gain wide appeal and allow for diversity in style yet specific enough to allow the statement to serve as a guide for specific teaching principles and methods of learning.

No school can become a charter school until its charter is approved. In order to gain approval, the charter must be written and the charter-granting agency applied to. When writing the charter, it is a good idea to procure a charter for a similar school in the area that has already been approved (see also Appendix A). Other applications can act as benchmarks and allow the people writing the charter to see what is necessary and important to highlight or emphasize. Some key components of solid charter applications are:

- Clear mission and vision statement
- Statement of why such a school is needed
- Description of the educational program to be used and the curricular approaches
- Descriptive methods of assessment
- Personnel policies
- Student policies, including discipline
- Financial plan for the school
- Learning objectives and connection with state standards
- Governance of the school

Having a well-articulated and integrated instructional program is key for successful charter applications, and having a consistent and content-based professional development program for staff members is crucial for implementation. In its study of start-up and conversion charters, the Consortium for Policy Research in Education at Pennsylvania State University found that buying or adopting an educational instruction system was not enough for the charter schools studied. What was needed, the study concluded, was an ongoing, school-wide professional development program that encouraged development and dialogue around curricular issues and concerns (Ibid.). Quick-fix, formula-based approaches to learning and teaching are too simplistic and divorce the conception of teaching from its practice. In writing the charter, it is necessary to consider how the school will provide professional development time, funding, and formal structures for teacher collaboration and personal growth.

One should also make sure that there are formal accountability systems and standards in place for assessing student achievement. These should include multiple assessments. It is also important to make sure one fully understands the state assessment requirements. The Consortium for Policy Research in Education also found in its study of numerous charter schools not only that formal systems of accountability were lacking at most of the schools they studied but that without clear directions from the state, most of the charter schools had to draw on their own organizational capacities to generate accountability plans, and few of the schools had a strong enough capacity to do so. Accountability problems can be avoided by ensuring that that are clear and definitive structures set up to measure student performance, which means that everyone involved will need a clear and accurate understanding of the state standards and the curriculum goals that will be used to meet them.

Gaining Approval for the Charter

After the charter has been drafted and key components have been addressed, it is time to get the charter approved. It is important to first pass the draft of the charter around to community leaders and any other interested parties that have been identified. Their feedback should be elicited, and changes in the draft should be made if it is felt such changes are warranted. It is also important to get information about the charter-granting agency (authorizer) in order to know what the agency is looking for and what it has done in the past in terms of granting or denying charters. Look at other charters they have approved and be prepared to show how the school being applied for will meet the specifically detailed needs that have been identified.

After Approval: Opening the School

After the charter is approved, it is time to actually begin to set up the school, and it is important to pay particular attention to some of the basic navigating issues for this phase of the school. At a minimum, pay attention to:

- Developing a detailed plan for all the tasks that need to be done once the school opens its doors. Tasks and responsibilities should be delegated and understood by the core organizing group and others who will be involved in the daily operation of the school.
- Developing some agreements with the sponsoring district, its servers and providers, to assure that they will provide needed services.
- Formalizing the instructional program. Get the needed materials and resources, discuss them, and have them available the first day the school opens.

- If a nonprofit status is being considered, procure the materials or legal advice needed to begin and legalize the nonprofit organization with the government.
- Make sure the facility services, such as food, transportation if provided, and other services, are in place.

Once issues involving the school have been thought about and the inevitable first day of opening has been planned for, the school's doors are ready to be opened. Everyone involved must work hard to establish a culture for the school, set up lines of communication, assure that student performance issues and reporting requirements are met, collect information and data to justify the school's continued existence, and begin troubleshooting—especially looking for ways to improve the school. Some areas of concern:

- Have an opening date for the school and work to establish and maintain a culture
- Implement the designs and procedures and consistently review them for monitoring purposes
- Look for gaps and unforeseen problems in the operation procedure
- Monitor and refine the curriculum and instruction
- Develop good problem-solving procedures and identify problems and subproblems that may arise
- Make sure data on the school are constantly collected in order to support rationales and to plan for the future.

If good planning and effective organization are emphasized in the early stages, the success of the charter school will be far more secure. Good planning, competent teamwork, and effective delegation of authority and tasks can assure that the charter school operates effectively and competently.

Developing, Enabling, and Sustaining a Learning Community

Developing, enabling, and sustaining the learning community are all crucial, for charter schools are successes or failures depending on the learning environment. Some issues to consider when making sure that the school environment is one of learning and development are:

- Autonomy—The amount of autonomy a charter school has seems to have a great deal to do with its ability to sustain a learning community (Wohlstetter and Griffin 1997, 34). Whether or not a school can avail itself of community resources; maintain control of budgetary issues; develop autonomy from the district office; and be able to set its own agenda, craft its own curricular approaches, and select and adopt curriculum programs has a lot to do with sustaining a learning community.

- Having the organizational capacity to develop programs.
- Networking—Organizations that support charter schools have begun all over the United States. Linking up with these organizations can be crucial to a charter school's ability to sustain its learning community. Networking with state, local, and regional organizations can help a charter school develop and sustain a learning environment. These organizations can offer anything from curriculum ideas to funding conduits.
- Parental involvement—Supportive parents who are actively engaged in the mission and vision of the charter school can make the difference between success and failure. Setting up focus groups, governing mechanisms, and structural approaches to elicit and maintain parental involvement is crucial. Parental involvement can make many different things happen, from financial support to providing food at staff meetings. Knowing that parents are involved and can be counted on for support can set staff members at ease and allow them to form collaborative partnerships with students, the administration, and parents.
- Continually revisiting and reflecting on the performance of the school with all stakeholders. Such action is necessary to craft and sustain a learning community at a charter school. Dialogue and communication in an atmosphere of civility and inquiry can assure a charter school's success even in the face of some difficult problems.

Building support with the community and working well with all participants at the school will help assure the school's success and development. Continually identifying problems and working toward common solutions will ensure that the school is engaged in self-assessment for continual improvement. For those who start community charter schools, like the Neighborhood Charter School or the Freire School, both which we will discuss in chapter 4, these issues are of the utmost importance. But is this the case for charter schools that operate as educational retail chains, in essence, those schools opened purely for profit throughout a particular state or nationwide? This is discussed in detail in chapters 5 and 6.

REFERENCES

Anderson, L., K. Adelman, L. Finnigan, et al. *A Decade of Public Charter Schools: Evaluation of the Public Charter School Program, 2000-2001.* Stanford, CA: SRI International, 2002, 18.

Berger, J. "A Post-Katrina Charter School in New Orleans Gets a Second Chance." *New York Times.* 7 October 2007. http://www.nytimes.com/2007/10/17/education/17education.html?_r=2&oref=slogin&pagewanted=print&oref=slogin.

Bowens, D. WRAL.com Charter School Admission Becoming a Matter of Luck. 12 February 2007. http://www.wral.com/news/local/story/1201464/.

Carr, S. "N.O. Schools Enlist Outside Help." *Times-Picayune,* 7 Feburary 2008. http://www.nola.com/news/index.ssf/2008/02/no_schools_enlist_outside_help.html.

Center for Community Change. http://www.communitychange.org.

Center on Reinventing Public Education. National Charter School Research Project, University of Washington. http://www.crpe.org/cs/crpe/view/projects/1?page=yes&id=5&parent=1&question=1.

Chubb, J.E., and T. Moe. *Politics, Markets, and American Schools.* Washington, DC: Brookings Institution, 1990.

Channel Five WLWT.com. http://www.wlwt.com/education/16293555/detail.html.

Charter School Funding: Inequities Next Frontier, August 2005, Thomas B. Fordham Institute. http://www.edexcellence.net/doc/Charter%20School%20Funding%202005%20FINAL.pdf.

Charter School Law, Arizona Revised Statutes Education Codes. http://www.azed.gov/charterschools/info/districtinfo/CSLawALIS.pdf.

Corwin, R., and J. Schneider. *The School Choice Hoax: Fixing America's Schools.* Lanham, MD: Rowman and Littlefield Education, 2007.

Cowen, S. *The State of Public Education in New Orleans.* A Report Prepared by The Scott S. Cowen Institute for Public Education Initiatives at Tulane University, 2008. http://education.tulane.edu/documents/2008Report_000.pdf.

Davis, L. "Privatizing New Orleans' Schools" *Counterpunch,* 30 August 2006. http://www.counterpunch.org/davis08302006.html.

The Denver Post, 7 May 2008.

Deseret News, 26 February 2008, Salt Lake City, UT. http://www.deseretnews.com/article/1,5143,695256342,00.html.

Dillon, S. *The New York Times,* 17 September 2004. http://query.nytimes.com/gst/fullpage.html?res=9901E5D61639F934A2575AC0A9629C8B63&sec=&spon=&pagewanted=print.

Dingerson, L. ReThinking Schools, Summer 2007, Narrow and Unlovely, ReThinking Schools Online. http://www.rethinkingschools.org/archive/21_04/narr214.shtml.

Education Commission of the States. Collective Bargaining Agreements, Denver CO, 2008: http://mb2.ecs.org/reports/Report.aspx?id=98.

Education Policy Analysis Archives, 10 No. 34, 9 August 2002. ISSN 1068-2341. http://epaa.asu.edu/epaa/v10n34.html.

Finn, C. http://www.hoover.org/bios/Finn.html.

Flaherty, J. *Left Turn Magazine,* New Orleans, no. 22 (Fall, 2006). http://www.leftturn.org/Articles/Viewer.aspx?id=975&type=M.

Gao, H. "District Disputes Charter School's Admission Policy." *San Diego Union Tribune,* 27 February 2007. http://www.signonsandiego.com/uniontrib/20070227/news_1m27einstein.html.

Great Lakes Center for Education Research and Practice. Miron, G. and B. Applegate. Teacher Attrition in Charter Schools. http://www.greatlakescenter.org.

Hassel, B. *The Charter School Challenge: Avoiding the Pitfalls, Fulfilling the Promise.* Washington, DC: Brookings Institute, 1995.

———. *The Charter School Challenge.* Washington, DC: Brookings Institute, 1999.

Hoxby, C.M. "Does Competition among Public Schools Benefit Students and Taxpayers? Evidence from Natural Variation in School Districting." *American Economic Review,* 2000.

Local Initiatives Support Corporation. New York, NY, 2008. www.lisc.org/effc.

Miron, G., and C. Nelson. *What's Public about Charter Schools?* Thousand Oaks, CA: Corwin Press, Inc., 2002.

Molnar, A. "Charter Schools: The Smiling Face of Disinvestment." *Educational Leadership* 54, no. 2 (October 1996): 1-9.

Myers, B. *The Examiner*, 30 March 2007. http://www.examiner.com/a-647263~Charter_funding_system_invites_fraud_and_abuse.html.

Nashua Telegraph, 29 January 2008. http://www.nashuatelegraph.com/apps/pbcs.dll/article?AID=/20080129/NEWS01/516023267&template=printart.

Nathan, J. *Charter Schools: Creating Hope and Opportunity for American Education.* San Francisco: Jossey-Bass, 1996.

National Alliance for Public Charter Schools. http://www.publiccharters.org/section/issues/stateleg/funding1

Nelson, E.H. "How Much Thirty Thousand Charter Schools Cost." Paper presented on behalf of the American Federation of Teachers at the annual meeting of the American Education Finance Association, Jacksonville, FL, March 1997.

New Schools Venture Fund. Private Funds. http://www.newschools.org/about/history.

———. Second-phase Funding. http://www.newschools.org/about/history#fund1.

Nossiter, A., "Plan Shifts Power to New Orleans Schools;" NY Times, January 18, 2006. http://www.nytimes.com/2006/01/18/national/nationalspecial/18orleans.html?sq=New%20Orleans%20Schools&st=nyt&scp=11&pagewanted=print

Philanthropy Roundtable. 5 May 2008. http://www.philanthropyroundtable.org/article.asp?article=1530&cat=147.

Quigley, B. Experimenting on Someone Else's Children 6 August 2007. http://www.counterpunch.org/quigley08062007.html.

Saulny, S. "Students Return to Big Changes in New Orleans." *New York Times*, 4 January 2006. http://www.nytimes.com/2006/01/04/national/nationalspecial/04schools.html?_r=1&sq=New%20Orleans%20Schools&st=nyt&oref=login&scp=12&pagewanted=print.

———."U.S. Gives Charter Schools a Big Push in New Orleans." *New York Times,* 13 June 2006. http://www.nytimes.com/2006/06/13/us/13charter.html?sq=New%20Orleans%20Schools&st=nyt&scp=9&pagewanted=print.

Simon, D. "More New Orleans Schools to Convert to Charter Status." *Times-Picayune,* 22 December 2008. http://www.nola.com/news/index.ssf/2008/12/more_schools_to_join_new_orleans.html.

Smith, K. "Charter Schools Owe Texas $26M for Overstated Admissions Numbers." *Dallas Morning News* 5 April 2008. 2008http://www.dallasnews.com/sharedcontent/dws/dn/latestnews/stories/040608dnmetCharterMain.3a5ff8c.html.

Solomon, L., M. K. Block, and M. Gifford. *A Market-based Education System in the Making: Charter Schools.* Phoenix, AZ: The Goldwater Institute, 1999.

St. Petersburg Times, 1 April 2007. http://www.sptimes.com/2007/04/01/Opinion/Charter_schools_run_w.shtml.

Sugarman, S. "School Choice and Public Funding" in *School Choice and Social Controversy* Sugarman, S. and Kemerer, F. eds., Washington, DC: Brookings Institution Press, 1999.

Toppo, G. "In New Orleans Schools, It's Like Starting Over." *USA Today* 7 June 2007. http://www.usatoday.com/news/education/2007-06-06-new-orleans-schools_N.htm.

University of Minnesota Humphrey Institute of Public Affairs and Education Commission of the States. *Charter Schools: What Are They Up To? A 1995 Survey.* Denver: Education Commission of the States, 1996.

U.S. Charter Schools. Charter School Basics. http://www.uscharterschools.org/pub/uscs_docs/o/charterlaws.htm.

———. Charter School Caps. http://www.uscharterschools.org/cs/sp/view/sp/7.

———. Consultant Organization. http://www.qualitycharters.org/i4a/pages/index.cfm?pageid=3278.

————. Accountability Plans. http://www.uscharterschools.org/gb/account_auth/terms.htm.

————. Funding Formulas. http://www.uscharterschools.org/cs/sp/view/sp/3).

————. Louisiana Charter Schools. http://www.uscharterschools.org/cs/n/view/uscs_news/1750.

————. Alaska Charter Schools. http://www.uscharterschools.org/cs/sp/view/sp/7.

————. Michigan Charter Schools. http://www.uscharterschools.org/cs/sp/view/sp/11.

U.S. Department of Education. http://www.ed.gov/policy/gen/guid/religionandschools/index.html; U.S. Department of Education Charter Schools Program Title V, part B Nonregulatory Guidance, July 2004, Washington D.C. http://209.85.215.104/search?q=cache:pmY_8anlaBEJ:www.ed.gov/policy/elsec/guid/cspguidance03.doc+Charter+admission+policies&hl=en&ct=clnk&cd=7&gl=us&ie=UTF-8.

Westlake Academy Charter School, Westlake Texas 2008. http://www.westlakeacademy.org/visitors/foundation.html.

Wohlstetter, P., and N. Griffin. *Creating and Sustaining Learning Communities: Early Lessons from Charter Schools.* Philadelphia: Consortium for Policy Research in Education, 1997.

Chapter Four

Curriculum and Instructional Approaches

Because there are so many questions regarding the efficacy of charter schools, this chapter explores the diverse curriculum and varied instructional, managerial, and philosophical approaches that some charter schools are pursuing. These curriculum and instructional approaches vary from school to school—reflecting the diverse educational philosophies that underlie the curriculum approaches and management and governance of the various schools. A brief and general overview of the curriculum approaches and instructional and managerial philosophies of some these schools will provide an insight into how many of them construct their educational designs, manage their institutions, and develop and apply their curricula. Both urban and rural charter schools in various states will be briefly discussed.

WHAT SOME CHARTER SCHOOLS ARE DOING

The Mater Academy Schools, Florida

Founded in 1998, the Mater Academy, Inc. opened one of the first charter schools in Miami-Dade, Florida to 75 students in grades K-2. It is now called the Mater Academy. Today, Mater Academy, Inc. can be called in marketplace parlance a "retail educational charter chain," operating 10 franchise schools in Florida that serve over 3,000 students in grades K-12. The list includes:

Mater Academy Elementary School—Hialeah Gardens
Mater Academy Charter Middle School—Hialeah Gardens
Mater Academy Charter High School—Hialeah Gardens
Mater Performing Arts Academy—Hialeah Gardens
Mater Academy East Charter School—Miami
Mater Academy East Middle School—Miami
Mater Academy Gardens Elementary School—Miami Gardens
Mater Academy Gardens Middle School—Miami Gardens
Mater Academy Lakes Middle School—Miami Gardens
Mater Academy Lakes High School—Miami Gardens

Mater Academies are run by their parent company Academica, Inc. Academica, Inc., a corporate for-profit charter school service founded in 1999, boasts on its Web site that the company:

> *has put together an experienced team to provide services and solutions for every aspect of charter school establishment and operation. The company ensures the school's Governing Body has complete autonomy and control over its school academic program, staffing needs, and curriculum.*
> *and, its (Academica, Inc.) services include assistance with facilities design, staffing recommendations and human resource coordination, as well as bookkeeping, budgeting, and financial forecasting that is provided to the Governing Board for its oversight and approval. (Academica)*

A list of services provided to charter schools and their sponsors on Academica's Web site include a myriad of before, during, and after charter school establishment services. For example:

Prior to Charter Approval
Completing the Charter Application
Training and assistance through the Application Process
Corporate establishment and administration
Budget forecasting
Financial reporting
Bookkeeping and records management

Facilities
Site selection and school design
Land use approvals
Site acquisition and development
Construction contractor selection and supervision

School Operations
Recruiting of Staff
Human Resource Management
Payroll
Bookkeeping and accounting services
Grant Writing
Capital Outlay plans
Setting up a Lunch Program

Government Compliance (including, but not limited to)
Financial Reporting
End of Year Accountability Report
Report Submission
(Ibid.)

We will look more critically at Academica, Inc. in chapter 5 when our focus shifts specifically to the nonprofit and for-profit management of charter schools. However, suffice it to say that Academica, Inc.'s Mater Academies are simply part of what is now Academica, Inc.'s thirty five school retail charter chains operating in three states—Florida, Utah, and Texas with a business eye for eventually expanding its presence into every state in the country.

In an attempt to appeal to an educational constituency, i.e., parents and their potential students, Academica, Inc.'s Mater Academy Charter Schools have marketed three basic concepts to parents and their children: (1) a multi-age learning environment that in the words of Mater "allows children to learn and progress at their individual pace," (2) small classroom sizes, and (3) "a parental involvement program which Mater claims ensures an active role in a child's education." These concepts are present at all Mater schools.

The educational retail chain stresses the importance of parental involvement in the school and all Mater schools have very specific institutional measures, such as parental involvement agreements, which encourage parents to become involved in the educational process for their children. Parents actively participate in meetings and volunteer activities at the schools and as a result, Mater claims the schools enjoy a level of parental involvement and satisfaction that is extraordinary among public schools.

Educational Focus

According to the schools' philosophy, the key to the success of the school is the belief that "each child learns differently" (Academica).

In the words of Mater Academies Web site:

Our program is designed to meet your child's individual needs. The staff will expose every child to a variety of learning experiences to foster intellectual, social, and emotional growth. Our professional staff is highly qualified and trained to educate your child, and to work closely with you the parent, according to the guidelines by the National Association if the Education of Young Children (NAEYC). (Mater Academy Charter School, under "Before Care and After Care")

Therefore, Mater Academy schools pride themselves on constantly striving to take the best from a variety of educational approaches and match them to the learning style of each child for maximum success. The efficacy of this technique, the schools' Web site notes, is evident from the schools' report card grades.

The Mater Academy Web site also states that Mater Academy charter schools:

- are one of Miami-Dade County's first Charter Schools;
- are Federal "Title I" schools serving low income Hispanic immigrant families;
- offer Complete Pre-K through High School System in four South Florida campuses;
- are the 2nd highest performing Elementary and 4th highest performing Middle school in Miami-Dade County, FL;
- have graduation rates that exceed the average for Hispanics in the nation;
- are accredited by the Southern Association for Colleges and Schools SACS/CASI;
- are recognized for financial and academic excellence;
- have been awarded a school grade of "A" by the State of Florida, and;
- are a Federal 21st Century, State Charter School Dissemination, and Walton Family Foundation Grants Recipient (Mater Academy Charter School, under "Charter Schools").

Organizational Management and Educational Accountability

The Mater Academy High school is one of the ten Academica, Inc. run Mater Academy schools operating in Florida today. The high school serves grades 9-12. According to School Matters, an online Web service of Standard and Poor's designed for parents researching for educational information about public schools, the overall quality of Mater Academy Charter High School located in Hialeah, Gardens, Florida was three out of five stars for overall quality, two out of five stars for teacher quality, three out of five stars for extracurricular activities, three out of five stars for school safety, three out of five stars for after school programs, and two out of five stars for educational service for special needs students. At the School Matters Web site, one parent who has a child attending the Mater Academy High school noted:

This school is said to be the nation's top 500 hundred schools!!! Forgeeetttt about it! My son attends this school and he has the most unorganized teachers who slack off and never even teach. My son has been in this school for two years. He has already had about 19 different teachers and only about four of them were good or actually taught the class. For the first two weeks of his second school year he didn't even have a geometry teacher! So basically he would sit around and do nothing for about two hours. Then this school pops out with some sort of b.s that "it is imperative that everyone passes the FCAT." How do you really expect to have these children pass these types of tests with a mediocre or should I just say crappy school system like this. So for other deeply concerned parents out there you have the option to do some more research on this top "500" best school if you don't believe me.

Another parent posted the following regarding the Mater Academy Charter High School:

The school overall is very good. Very involved administration, and strict rules and discipline. My kid luckily has had excellent teachers, but there has been on occasion some teachers of his friends that are not good at all and speak very little English, I feel the school needs to quickly get rid of these teachers because they are a sore spot on a group of excellent teachers and administration. There's basically anything a kid could want to as far as extracurricular activities go and they are quite good and successful. The school is pretty overcrowded but the school is expanding at the same time building new buildings. The school is very safe, at every point of entry in the building and grounds there is security and the kids at this school are mostly good kids. A friend of mine was a teacher at other schools that were not even that bad but there was just kids that were scary, but from what I've seen and been told the crowd here is mostly cheerful, good kids, but there's always the bad crowd at every school, but again the school is very safe and full of good kids. (Mater Academy Charter School, under "Parental Opinions")

Some statistics made available by School Matters are revealing. In terms of state testing, the school-wide reading proficiency for the Mater Academy Charter High school for 2007 was 38.5 percent and the schoolwide math proficiency was 69 percent. The student population has risen dramatically from 85 students in 2003 to 1,165 in 2006. In 2006, economically disadvantaged students comprised 73 percent of the student body while 92.4 percent of the students were Hispanic, with whites comprising 4.6 percent of the student population and Blacks 2.6 percent. While School Matters notes that in 2007 the Dade County Public School System had 9.4 percent of the total district teachers that are considered "not highly qualified," Mater Academy Charter High School had nearly three times as many, or 27.8 percent of their teachers in the category of "not highly qualified teachers." In 2007 only 15.9 percent of the teachers at the charter high school had master degrees and only 4.8 percent had doctoral degrees (Mater Academy Charter School, under "Classroom Profile").

At another Mater Academy School, the Mater Academy Charter School, K-5th grade, students are eligible for before and after-school child care. Centro Mater West II Child Care Center provides the after care and morning care. Centro Mater West is a nonprofit organization operated by Catholic Charities of the Archdiocese of Miami, Inc. and services children from the ages of 3 to 12 years, and from over 20 different countries. The Center's Day Care program operates Monday through Friday between 7:00 am and 6:00 pm. The after-school program operates between 1:00 pm and 6:00 pm during the 42-week school year, and from 7:00 am through 6:00 pm during the 10 weeks of summer camp. According to the philosophy of the child care center, posted at the Web site for the school:

Teaching staff will implement developmentally appropriate practices. Learning occurs through explain exploratory play activities; all children grow and change in a predictable sequence during the first years of life. Teachers recognize and respect the social and cultural context in which the child lives. Each child has a unique pattern of growth, strengths, interests, experiences and background. The curriculum and adults interactions should be responsive to these individual differences.

As to class size at the Mater Academy Charter High School, in the 2006 school year the Dade County Public School System's district average for students per teacher was 17.6 students per teacher. In Florida, statewide, the ratio averaged a little lower, on average 16.8 students per teacher. At Mater Academy Charter High School the average student per teacher ratio was 25.9 percent or roughly one hundred and fifty percent more than the statewide average (Mater Academy Charter School, under "Before Care and After Care").

Lusher Charter School, Louisiana

Located at two sites, the Lusher Charter School is a prestigious charter school located in New Orleans, Louisiana at their Willow Street campus, which houses the elementary school (K-5), and the Fortier campus on Freret Street, where the middle and high schools (6-12) have been located since August 2006. The total number of students in 2007 was 1,435 with 50 percent of all students being minority students—African American (41 percent), "other minorities," (9 percent) and Caucasian students (50 percent). Currently, Lusher consistently ranks within the top 10 performing schools in Louisiana.

According to its Web site:

Lusher Charter School is a Kindergarten through 12th grade New Orleans Public School located in Uptown New Orleans and operated by the nonprofit, Advocates for Arts-Based Education Corporation. Lusher focuses on a high-academic college-preparatory curriculum, with early college credit classes through Tulane University, gifted/talented programs, Advanced Placement courses, and academic challenges in every classroom.

Additionally, the school incorporates the arts throughout the curriculum with comprehensive arts education (CAE) and an award-winning performing arts program in creative writing, dance, drama, music, and visual arts. Lusher offers a strong athletic program and numerous other extracurricular opportunities. These programs combine with a philosophy of decision-making that places student well-being as a top priority of all school staff. The unique educational experiences and proven results of Lusher Charter School make it a leader among schools in the city, state, and nation. (Lusher Charter School)

The school became a charter school in January of 2005 but the idea was in an embryonic stage long before Hurricane Katrina. According to Tulanelink, as far back as 2003 Tulane University's ambition was to create an exclusive high school that would employ its own personnel and be financed by the state. Despite employment practices by Tulane that would conflict with policies negotiated between the Orleans Parish School Board and the American Federation of Teachers for school employees, some school board members endorsed Tulane's participation in establishing a new high school in 2004, directly after Katrina. And according to Tulanelink, the history unfolded like this:

With the prospect of further access to public funding, Tulane began to insinuate itself into the New Orleans Public Schools (NOPS) with devices such as a new Internet library resource "offered only to educators in the New Orleans Public School District. . . ." Although Tulane does not have a school of education, it began "testing the waters" by sending student observers into various public schools and by enlisting the cooperation of Kathy Riedlinger, principal of Lusher Extension School. It also installed a business program into the John McDonogh High School curriculum.

Exercising powers newly afforded him by Senate Act 193, Superintendent of Schools Anthony Amato quietly negotiated with Tulane to make it a "partner" in a new Lusher High School that would be housed in an uptown school building (Sophie B. Wright Middle School), whose current students would be displaced. Public outrage following disclosure of this "under-the-radar" scheme was a factor that contributed to Amato's abrupt resignation.

Well-organized Lusher parents, determined to sever the school's relationship with a dysfunctional central administration now in crisis, drafted a proposal to convert Lusher into a publicly-supported charter school administered by a private board selected by the school's parents. In a move toward self-imposed privatization, Lusher teachers overwhelmingly agreed to give up their representation by the teachers' union in exchange for a system of accountability to an untried administrative board with which they will now have to negotiate salaries, working conditions and benefits and depend upon to resolve disputes and grievances. (Tulanelink, under "The Louisiana Decision")

Due to Hurricane Katrina, the middle and high schools moved into the historic Alcee Fortier High School building directly after Fortier's closing in 2005. In June 2007, the American Federation of Teachers revealed that of the $52 million that FEMA had allocated for all New Orleans schools, $16 million had been used to renovate Alcee Fortier High School building for use by the upper grades of the Tulane-affiliated Lusher Charter School (Tulanelink, under "Saving Public Schools, Tulane Style").

According to Leigh Dingerson of the Center for Community Change, in Washington D.C.:

When Lusher Charter School was handed the Alcee Fortier High School for the expansion of their program, the building, like many other New Orleans public school buildings, was in disrepair. But as a charter, Fortier was able to access $14 million in state dollars, as well as over $1 million from Tulane University to complete a top-to-bottom renovation. Across the river, the Algiers Charter School Association initiative is heavily underwritten by Baptist Community Ministries, the state's largest private foundation. On the strength of private support like this, Algiers reported in July 2006 that it had a $12 million reserve fund. (Dingerson 2007)

The school is a favorite of philanthropists, grant foundations, and other such benevolent institutions and has received huge private and public grants and funds since its inception in 2005, including special grants from Tulane University, FEMA, the State of Louisiana, a German Foundation which gave $1.1 million to renovate the gymnasium, and other foundations (Schools Matter).

Both campuses were also the beneficiaries of the Laura Bush Foundation, which gave one million dollars to Gulf coast school libraries (The Laura Bush Foundation). The National Automobile Dealers Charitable Foundation of New Orleans also donated $400,000 to restore the athletic fields at Lusher High School (Reuters).

Lusher is an Orleans Parish School Board (OPSB) charter school and as a result, the students and their parents or guardians must live in the Orleans Parish school district in order to be able to attend the Lusher charter school. Lusher is bounded by what is called an "Attendance District." The way it works is that all elementary grade students who live in the Lusher Elementary attendance district are automatically admitted if their registration is completed by March 14 of any given year. After March 14, acceptance is based on the availability of seats. All students wishing to apply after the March date must apply and qualify to be admitted. Qualification for admission is based on standardized test scores and grade point average. Based on the elements noted above, a student is assigned a score based on their test result and grade point average. There is a cutoff score; those students with a score above the cutoff are "qualified" and thus admitted to the school. Once an application is completed, the office then contacts parents to set up a testing date for the elementary school. Middle and high school applicants are asked to choose a testing date when completing the application. In an arrangement made for Tulane employees and their children, as a result of a partnership between Tulane University and Lusher Charter School, a certain number of seats are set aside for children of Tulane full-time employees, guardians of students who work at the university, and full-time graduate or professional program students at Tulane (Tulane University, under "Tulane University Partnership").

Lusher Charter School is a "selective-admissions school," and the admission selective admission criteria and policies are multifaceted and complex. According to the University of Tulane:

> *At each grade level, the slots set aside for Tulane will be allocated in the following manner: 75% of the available Tulane slots will be allocated to students in the rank order of their level of qualification. The remaining 25% of the slots are allocated based on a lottery of all remaining qualified students. (For example, if there are 12 slots available and more than 12 qualified students seeking slots, the first 9 slots would go to the students with the highest qualifying score in rank order of their score. The other 3 slots would be assigned by a lottery to the remaining qualified students seeking a slot. (Tulane University, under "Selective Admission Criteria")*

And what happens if a child is not admitted through the regular admission process? If a child is not admitted through the regular Lusher admission process, that child is placed on the waiting list based on an assigned lottery number. If a seat in the charter school opens up, the parent will be notified that a seat is available and enrollment proceeds. Another admission practice utilized by the school involves a procedure whereby community applicants fill seats that are not set aside for Tulane University. The allocation process for the community seats is the same as for the Tulane seats—the first 75 percent of the available community slots are allocated in the rank order of their level of qualification. The remaining 25 percent of community slots are allocated based on a lottery of all remaining qualified students. A child is added to the community pool and will be eligible for a lottery of the 25 percent of the community seats (Ibid.).

Educational Focus

According to the school's Web site:

> *The centerpiece of the Lusher experience is a rigorous college-preparatory academic curriculum. The pursuit of academic excellence is combined with Lusher's renowned student-centered approach in which students are supported and encouraged to meet high expectations. Teachers tailor assessments and instruction to meet the academic needs of individual students, differentiating the curriculum to insure that all students are challenged and engaged. The Lusher faculty takes pride in knowing their students —their interests and abilities, their struggles, their learning*

profiles and personal histories. Students are further engaged in learning because of the connections they feel to their teachers, from kindergarten to high school.

Throughout the K-12 curriculum, teachers are constantly improving their craft through school-wide and individual professional development in the best research-based strategies for elevating student performance. Teachers integrate this knowledge of brain science, child and adolescent development, positive discipline strategies, and curricular expertise into weekly and annual lesson plans closely monitored by the administration to create a cutting-edge 13-year educational program for a diverse student body. In the past few years, professional development has focused on reading intervention strategies, arts integration, curriculum design, learner profiles, and collaborative leadership. Lusher Charter School closely monitors and charts student growth through comprehensive data, observing trends that inform instructional practices and further professional development and responding to individual student needs. (Lusher Charter School)

Neighborhood House Charter School, Massachusetts

Set in Dorchester, Massachussets, the Neighborhood House Charter School (NHCS) promises to offer Boston parents and their children a quality education within a diverse community-elementary and middle school. Through a neighborhood-based school that combines educational services with social services and health care programs for the benefit of students and their families that otherwise have limited public educational and health opportunities, the Neighborhood House Charter School has as its fundamental philosophy:

"Succeed Anywhere" is the school's educational philosophy—that every student at the school will have the necessary knowledge and skills to attend a high quality high school, whether that school be public or private, focused on college preparation, the technical trades, or the creative arts. To achieve this goal, NHCS offers individualized learning programs for each student—including students where "special effort" is needed to overcome learning, physical, social, or emotional challenges. The school is committed to developing the interests and talents of all of its students. (The Neighborhood House Charter School, under "Succeed Anywhere")

The school was founded out of long-standing struggles of local settlement-house networks, which have for some time offered services to ease the transition of new immigrants in the area (Schorr 2000).

It was legally awarded its charter in 1994 and the Neighborhood House Charter School is a publicly funded, independently managed elementary and middle school. The school houses 400 students aged four to fourteen. NHCS has become very popular and is one of the most parent sought after prekindergarten through 8th grade public schools in Boston.

Educational Focus

The school's academic philosophy could best be described as developmental; this is especially true in both the reading and writing program even though students in grades 3-8 must take the Massachusetts Comprehensive Assessment System (MCAS) exam every year (The Neighborhood House Charter School, under "Academic Philosophy").

As an example, strong computational skills along with developmentally appropriate conceptual introduction form the cornerstone of the mathematics program at the school. The kindergarten math program utilizes the Big Math for Little Kids series, while students in grades 1-5 study math using the TERC curriculum, Investigations in Number, Data, and Space, and Math Trailblazers. Science is taught using hands-on educational science kits that allow for experimentation and hands-on kinesthetic learning. In KidLab (a science program), students engage in experiments designed to build their skills in four areas: critical thinking, inquisitiveness, academic persistence and creative doing. Research and information skills, map and globe skills, as well as time and chronology skills form the backbone of the social studies curriculum. The following five strands: geography, history, economics, civics and government, and ethics and beliefs systems comprise the subjects of study. The school boasts a strong visual arts and music program and the school begins their Spanish instruction in grades 5-8. Technology accompanies all learning at the Neighborhood Charter School (Ibid.).

KidLab is a novel approach to assuring a rigorous and comprehensive science education. Touted on the school's Web site, the impressive lab:

is an inventive, project-based science program that presents students with an opportunity to experience science and the arts in a risk-free, highly engaging environment. With a unique classroom environment that is akin to a science lab, art studio and a hands-on museum, KidLab gets students excited about and involved in learning by integrating science with art, imagination, and real-world problems.

In KidLab, art is used as a tool to facilitate experimentation, communication and learning. The scientific focus of KidLab provides students with a way to link theoretical concepts to concrete experiences. For example, students use the scientific method to discover how circuits work and the difference between bug and bird wings.

KidLab topics range from the human body, to space and everything in between. In investigating electricity, students take apart and rebuild radios, build robots with blinking eyes and wire model houses with light switches and rheostats. KidLab challenges high-achieving students by giving them alternate ways to approach a problem, and it provides an alternative learning environment for students who struggle in a traditional academic classroom.

KidLab is in full compliance with the Massachusetts Science Frameworks, and the KidLab teacher collaborates with classroom teachers to build on the class-

room curricula. NHCS disseminates the KidLab program in a partnership with the Project for School Innovation (PSI), which supports grassroots networks for educators. (Ibid.)

Organizational Management and Educational Accountability

The school is unique in that it has a school parent center where new families and their children are welcomed by a welcoming coordinator. The welcoming coordinator also makes home visits and helps to form networks with parents for any health and educational services they or their children might need. The welcome coordinator also oversees the "family learning contracts"—contracts parents are required to sign with the school when they enroll their children. The contract is designed in order to assist with their child's studies and assure their children attend school regularly and on time, aid and abet the child's "Individual Learning Plan," as well as work to build an educational and community center at the school site.

There is a parent council at the school and the role of the council is not simply to welcome all parents and their children and to orient them to the school and its procedures and policies. The Parent Council also meets once a month to recommend school programs, sponsor events, and fund-raise. From this council, a variety of school committees are formed, giving parents many avenues for involvement. Meetings are held in the evening and dinner and childcare are provided. Along with the parent council, some of the school's organizations and committees include a School Site Council, Parent Advisory Council, Parent Transition Committee, New Parent Welcoming Committee, Parent Fundraising Committee, Political Action Committee and Eighth Grade Graduation Committee (The Neighborhood House Charter School, under "Parent Involvement"; Schorr 2000).

In order to truly grasp and understand just how unique the Neighborhood Charter School is, one must become familiar with their organizational structure and vision. To begin with, the Neighborhood House Charter School is a community made up of a variety of members. Each member plays a specific role in the functioning of the school. The actual school organizational plan consists of a Board of Trustees, school site council, management team, teachers and specialists, student support staff, parents, and students. According to the school Web site:

The Management Team is composed of the Headmaster, Assistant Headmaster, the Director of Development, the Chief Financial Officer, the Dean of the Middle School, the Dean of the Lower School, and the Dean of Special Education and Student Support. Together, they are responsible for overseeing the day-to-day academic and social support services at NHCS.

The teachers and specialists are responsible for the educational program at NHCS. The school believes that open communication is the key to the school's success and parents are encouraged to raise concerns with individual teachers or specialists as soon as they arise. Parents are also encouraged to participate in the classroom by attending the beginning of the year orientation session for each classroom and by asking the teacher what they can do to help. Parents who want to discuss ideas or offer comments should schedule an appointment through the teacher, specialist, or Dean so that the continuity of the day is not interrupted.

The Student Support team works to identify students and families in need and to provide individualized supports and services, as needed. The staff is made up of the Dean of Special Education and Student Support, the Director of Student Affairs, a social worker, a school nurse, a pediatrician from Boston Medical Center, the Headmaster, and the deans of the lower and middle school.

The school not only welcomes but also requires a high level of family and parental involvement. Parents and guardians are encouraged to support and advise in the administration of the school functions, work closely with teachers to provide the best educational experience possible for all students, work directly with students, including with their own children at home, and build positive parent-to-parent relationships to foster the development of a caring community both at and outside of the school. The Family Learning Contract is a vital element of parental involvement at NHCS. For the charter school, learning is not an easy process; it requires hard work. The NHCS staff and parents are constantly encouraged to work together to support students in their learning and students are expected to care for and help each other in this growing and learning process (The Neighborhood House Charter School, under "Community Support").

The school is also governed by a set of eight values that include caring cooperation, courage, trustworthiness, effort, justice, respect, and responsibility (Ibid.). These values are reinforced through frequent conversations and discussions between students, parents and values throughout the school year both within class and informally.

The Board of Trustees functions similarly to a school board. The role of the Board is to ensure that the school is an academic success, and a viable organization, as well as faithful to the terms of its charter and parents have the right to attend all Board of Trustees' meetings.

There is also a School Site Council that consists of a Headmaster, two NHCS staff members, and three parents. This group meets regularly throughout the school year and serves the school community by listening to parent, teacher, and student concerns and then giving recommendations to the Trustees about the school's charter as well as approving specific operating and policy decisions (Ibid.).

What is especially unique about the school is not only its commitment to educational excellence but also its service as a center for health care, social services, after-school activities and adult education. What is known as the "Full-Service Program," is an integral part of what makes Neighborhood Charter School successful. The program's mission is to ensure that students have the support they need to learn, grow and be successful in school, and this means being healthy. It also means partnering with community health organizations.

The school offers an after school program, a summer program, consisting summer school and a recreation program, and a high school placement support program. At the high school placement program, 7th and 8th graders are provided individual support and mentoring to gain acceptance at a good high school. The school also has a special education program, which covers a wide range of services.

The charter school touts an impressive Health Initiative as part of the full service program it offers and the initiative is spearheaded by NHCS trustee Dr. De-Wayne Pursley, a pediatrician and Chief of Neonatology at Beth Israel Deaconess Medical Center in Boston. NHCS also partners with Dr. Barry Zuckerman, Chairman of the Department of Pediatrics at Boston Medical Center; Betsy Groves, Director of the Child Witness to Violence Project at Boston Medical Center; and, Dr. Patricia Kavanaugh, a pediatrician and Fellow at Boston Medical Center. Dr. Kavanaugh visits NHCS one day a week to act as a liaison between staff and the health care system to better care for our students' physical and mental health.

In addition, NHCS offers the following services:

- A school-based health center with a full-time nurse
- Mental health services for our students
- Health care referrals for families
- Regular vision and hearing screenings through our partnership with the Massachusetts Eye and Ear Infirmary
- An annual Health and Wellness Fair
- Regular dental services through our partnership with Smile Massachusetts
- Regular health education and resource updates for parents
- The school's community partners include, but are not limited to:
  - Beth Israel Deaconess Medical Center
  - Boston Medical Center
  - Boston Police Department
  - Boston Public Health Commission
  - Boston Urban Asthma Coalition
  - Boys and Girls Club
  - Child Witness to Violence Program
  - Codman Square Health Center
  - DotWell
  - Family Services of Greater Boston
  - Federation of Children with Special Needs
  - Good Grief Program
  - Kids Can Cook
  - Massachusetts Eye and Ear Infirmary

- Medical-Legal Partnership for Children
- Operation Frontline—Share Our Strength
- Smile Massachusetts
- Tufts-New England Medical Center
- Ultimate Boot Camp
- Youth Services Provider Network

NHCS also employs a part-time registered nurse. The nurse's office is open Monday through Friday and the nurse provides in-school care for students, implements required screenings while managing health records and forms for all students, and contacts parents regarding health problems (The Neighborhood House Charter School, under "Succeed Anywhere").

Other than private transportation, such as cars and bicycles, K1- 5 students are eligible for transportation to and from school by school bus if they live more than one mile from school (Ibid.).

According to the Web site for the school:

Volunteering is a mandatory part of parents' commitment to sending their child to NHCS. According to the Family Learning Contract, parents are required to volunteer five hours of their time per year. There are many different ways that parents can volunteer their time to NHCS.

Parents are free to participate in one of the schoolwide councils listed above or in one of the myriad of ways found below. It is possible for committees and volunteering opportunities to change over the course of the year. There is a broad range of volunteer activities at NHCS so that every parent can find an opportunity that fits their schedule and interests. Parents can volunteer at different times during the day, at school or from home, with a group or independently, and on a regular basis or for a special event.

Some opportunities include the following:

Administrative Support
Book Fair Helper
Chaperone
Classroom Fundraising
Classroom Help
Classroom Volunteer
Front Desk Coverage
High School Placement Volunteer
Library Helper
Parent Liaison
Planning Schoolwide Events
(The Neighborhood House Charter School, under "Volunteering")

The school also has a student code of conduct whereby students are held to precise criteria for their behavior while at the school.

In terms of enrollment, the Web site for the school offers parents, families, and their students a breakdown by ethnicity and gender. There is a lottery for admission and the lottery is for children who will be four years old on September 1 of the year the lottery is held (The Neighborhood House Charter School, under "Lottery Admission").

Ben Gamla Charter School, Florida

Try to fathom a charter school that was, until recently, run by an orthodox Rabbi (Rabbi Siegel was originally the school's principal, but he hired someone else after people said it was inappropriate for a rabbi to oversee instruction) and that serves kosher lunches and concentrates on teaching Hebrew to students. Ben Gamla Charter school in Hollywood, Florida is such a school. About 400 students started classes at Ben Gamla in August of 2007 amidst caustic debates over whether a public school would be able to teach Hebrew without touching Judaism and thus cross the unconstitutional side of the church-state divide. According to Peter Deutsch, a former Democratic member of Congress from Florida who started Ben Gamla and hopes to replicate it in Los Angeles, Miami, and New York:

South Florida is one of the largest Hebrew-speaking communities in the world outside Israel, so there are lots of really good reasons to try to create a program like this here. I just didn't appreciate the demand at all. If I had 5,000, maybe 10,000 desks available in South Florida today, I think I could fill them. (Goodnough 2007)

The school is also is managed by Academica, the private company that also runs the Mater Academy schools and on whose board Mr. Deutsch has served. As noted, Academica, Inc. manages 35 of Florida's roughly 350 charter schools.

Named after a Jewish high priest who established free universal schooling in ancient Israel, Ben Gamla Charter School (BGCS) received 800 applications in just one week in the summer of 2007. And about half of the applications were from adjacent Miami-Dade County, but the school admitted only Broward County residents, ensuring that almost everyone from the county who wanted to attend could do so. The school does have a handful of black students, including members of a Baptist church that provides their transportation to and from the school (Goodnough 2007).

Students at Ben Gamla are in kindergarten through eighth grade. About 80 percent transferred from other public schools and many, if not most of the rest of the students came from private Jewish day schools.

Ben Gamla is a uniform school. Boys must wear a baby blue, royal blue, or white polo shirt with an embroidered Ben Gamla logo and beige or navy khakis or shorts with BGCS appropriately monogrammed on the pants. Girls must wear a baby blue, royal blue, or white polo shirt with an embroidered Ben Gamla logo and a beige or navy blue skort with BGCS appropriately monogrammed as well (Ben Gamla).

Educational Focus

According to their Web site:

> The mission of the Ben Gamla Charter School is to deliver a first-class academic program that offers a unique bilingual, bi-literate, and bi-cultural curriculum, which prepares students to have an edge in global competition through the study of Hebrew as a second language. Graduates will leave the charter school with a sense of purpose, a belief in their own efficacy, a commitment to the common good, and a zest for learning. (Ibid.)

The Web site goes on to note that:

> The Ben Gamla Charter School provides an enriching educational program for students in kindergarten through eighth grade. The Ben Gamla Charter School has its own curriculum, though it is based on Florida's Sunshine State Standards and encompasses the core subject areas of math, science, reading/language arts, and social studies through a dual language of English and Hebrew.
>
> Our school is a place where children will enjoy learning, teachers will enjoy teaching, and parents will be expected to be a key part of the educational process. The school's mission is to provide a loving, caring, and supportive educational environment that furthers a philosophy of respect and high expectations for all students, parents, teachers, and staff. The key to the success of this program is flexibility and a willingness to work with interested and concerned parents and public officials in designing and implementing the school facility and program. (Ibid.)

What this means is that under the school's charter agreement, students are to spend one period a day learning Hebrew. They will then have a second daily class—math or science, for example—conducted in a mix of Hebrew and English. Ben Gamla's roughly 400 students in kindergarten through eighth grades follow the state curriculum but they also are take a Hebrew language course. One of their core subjects—math or physical education, for example—is to be taught bilingually as well. There are no separate classes on Jewish culture, but Rabbi Adam Siegel, the school's former director, said the issue would come up during Hebrew instruction. Teachers might also do special units on aspects of Jewish culture, like Israeli folk dancing.

The local school board rejected Ben Gamla's first two Hebrew curriculum proposals after finding they included religious references. The second, which relied on a textbook titled *"Ha-Yesod,"* asked students to translate phrases like "Our Holy Torah is dear to us" and "Man is redeemed from his sins through repentance" (Goodnough 2007).

In fact, the first three weeks at Ben Gamla at the end of 2007 were spent without any Hebrew language instruction whatsoever. On September 11, 2007 the Broward County school board eventually verified that the curriculum was, in fact, cleansed of any possible reference to religion.

The school district agreed to work with Ben Gamla Charter School in Hollywood, Florida, to create training programs for teachers and board members to ensure the separation of church and state, Superintendent James Notter said. Lesson plans will be submitted monthly for district review.

As of this writing Ben Gamla is now on its third rendition of a Hebrew curriculum: the first, NETA (created by Hebrew University in Jerusalem), was summarily ruled out, as was the second. Based on a compromise hammered out by Ben Gamla and the school board, the school board hired Nathan Katz, a religious studies professor at Florida International University, to vet the latest curriculum proposal back in September of 2007. The school could not teach Hebrew before then, a school board spokesman said.

For Eleanor Sobel, a school board member and vocal critic of the school, the decision is troubling:

> I don't know how to monitor this, and that's why I have great concern. Accountability is real important when you're dealing with taxpayers' money. (Goodnough 2007)

According to Mr. Simon of the ACLU, who has been monitoring the school closely:

> Whether this is going to cross the line or not will depend on what goes on in the classroom. Will they neutrally and academically address religious topics, or will there be more preaching than teaching going on in the classroom? It is too early to tell. (Ibid.)

Freire Charter School, Philadelphia

The Freire Charter School in Philadelphia opened on 7 September 1999. The school's physical space, equipment, cleaning, and security service are provided by Temple University in Philadelphia. The school's students are 95 percent African American, and the remaining 2 percent Hispanic, and 3 percent non-Hispanic whites. According to the school's 2008-2009 Executive Summary,

> To serve all of our students we have a faculty of 44 staff members. 20% of these staffers are African American. 35% of our total staff is male and the other 65% female. 59% of our staff currently holds a master's degree or is currently pursuing one. In addition, 3 of our staff members currently hold a doctorate degree or is currently pursuing one. Many of our administrators also work as teachers and many of our teachers also hold some administrative responsibility. Also remarkably, Freire has a

97% retention rate of staff from 2007-2008 into this next academic school year.
(Pennsylvania Department of Education)

Of the thirty teachers at Freire, 60 percent are certified. With only 440 students, this means Freire can boast of one teacher for every fifteen students. Yet the success of the school over the years has increased its reputation; the school now has a waiting list of over five hundred students.

The Freire Charter School attempts to offer a blend of academic and experiential learning. In an interview with Jay Guben in 2000, the school's founder, he indicated to me that the school uses experiential learning mixed with the philosophy of the Brazilian educator Paolo Freire. Emphasizing individualized, self-directed learning, the school requires individualized learning plans from its students. These plans are designed to offer a focus and unite students with the resources they will need to complete their learning, such as teachers, mentors, parents, community members, and employers.

Educational Focus

Freire's curriculum and programming, which are notable for their extraordinary quality and depth, include features such as:

- A small learning community
- A student-teacher ratio of 18 to 1
- A mentor for every student
- Community service, work experience, and entrepreneurial training
- Research and evaluation combined with student reflection and analysis
- Individual learning plans
- Structured, ongoing parental involvement and learning programs for parents
- A computer in every student's home
- A core commitment to making Freire's learning program work, based upon the considered choice of its students, parents, faculty, and administration that Freire is where they want to be.

The school envisions a progressive education for young people. Its vision is comprehensive and speaks to what the school is trying to accomplish and what it sees as education for democracy. Further, the vision statement provides a theoretical understanding of the school's day-to-day practice—why the school is structured as it is, why the curriculum is constructed as it is, the role of learner and teacher, and the collaborative nature of learning. Many schools have mission statements that accompany their charter, usually four or five sentences about what the school seeks to accomplish, but the Freire Charter School goes further to actually envision the educational climate and reality it seeks for students and educational workers. According to Guben, the school is attempting to put forth a philosophy of learning to change the mind-set regarding what schools should be, how they should function, and what should go on within them. In this respect, the Freire Charter School is unique.

The following is the vision statement in its entirety, as first introduced on the school's Web site:

> *What makes Freire Charter School special? Freire Charter School brings to life concepts that everyone agrees are sound. It puts the student at the center of a rich and interconnected set of learning experiences. It structures a range of multi-disciplinary experiential learning in community workplaces and other settings. It makes multiculturalism a living part of the curriculum and communal life. It cares for students through small classes, advisory relationships, and formal mentoring. It governs itself democratically, nurturing and honoring student participation in governance as well as in instruction. It values consensus and accountability. It infuses technology and will provide every student and family with a computer on loan and Internet access at home. It involves families directly in learning—their children's and their own. It partners with successful people and organizations, it aspires to be a joyful community of empowered people.*

Critical thinking is at the heart of what the Freire School is all about and this is reflected in the school's eight core values:

1. *The classroom extends beyond school walls. We utilize the city of Philadelphia as much as possible.*
2. *Reading is the most important part of the learning process. Our younger students focus on reading first and foremost.*
3. *We insist that all Freire seniors complete a rigorous, intensive year long senior project that holds social change at its core.*
4. *Student voice is essential to making a school work successfully. So are the voices of parents, teachers, and community members.*
5. *We are a learning to learn organization, ensuring that learning and excellence happen at all levels and everywhere.*
6. *Freire is a completely nonviolent school—we are not just free from physical violence, but also from emotional and mental violence. Our peer mediator program makes this possible.*
7. *Freire students are exposed to many extracurriculars such as: basketball, book club, video production, music and musical writing, drama, art, chess club, dance group, soccer, track, and football.*
8. *Relationships between teachers and students are at the heart of every decision we make. These relationships need to be of mutual respect, love, and friendship between the student and the teacher. (Freire Charter School)*

Learning experiences at Freire are designed by the students, their teachers and their families to address current and future learning needs. Teachers will guide students as they embark on their own search for knowledge. That search focuses students on developing the skills to acquire, assess, and produce knowledge. Freire equips them to grow into strong family members, good neighbors, responsible citizens, lifelong learners, and productive adults.

> *The student test scores at Freire have been steadily climbing as well. In 2003, 6.3% of 8th graders scored proficient or above in math and 9.45 in reading. In 2004, 12.5% scored proficient or above in math and 35.4% in reading. In 2005, test scores revealed that 20.6% scored proficient or above in math and 34.9% in reading. Similarly, in 2003 2.8% of 11th graders scored proficient or above in math while 19.5% in reading. In 2004 8.4% scored proficient or above in Math and 21.6% scored above proficiency in reading. In 2005, 25.5% scored proficient or above in math and 27.5% in reading. (Ibid.)*

At Freire, the learning process is part of the outcome. Students engage in real-world activities that make knowledge coherent, connected, memorable, and useful. Coursework at Freire is crafted around problematizing curriculum that emphasizes exploration into "meaningful" issues and problems. Academic courses are challenging. A longer school day and year enable students to engage in hands-on study in a variety of community and workplace settings. Mistakes are valued for their learning potential.

Freire has designed the five-year high school program to begin with 8th grade. This configuration capitalizes on the energy and intellectual curiosity of these young people as it initiates them into a systematic process for maximizing the development of their interests and capabilities. The five-year program also allows ample time for students to discover and explore diverse options and set priorities, and to take full advantage of the multiplicity of community partnerships that are available to them. For example, at Freire, each student receives a mentor. The mentorship program is sponsored with the school in conjunction with Big Brothers and Big Sisters of America. The mentorship calls for personal contact once per week between mentor and mentoree. The five-year program also eases the transition from elementary to high school.

The five-year curriculum includes a graduated program of applied community experiences with emphasis on team skills and workplace readiness. The first three years involve students in community service and the exploration of careers in commercial institutions and entrepreneurial ventures. The last two years are focused on more intensive research and extended internship in students' given fields. Academic coursework, especially in the last year, is explicitly geared to support and connect to students' emerging career and life goals.

Relationships are paramount at Freire. Freire seeks to be inclusive of cultures and conditions among students and staff. Differences are expected to be acknowledged and respected. Awareness of, and sensitivity to, multiple perspectives infuse relationships and the actual school curriculum.

Organizational Management and Educational Accountability

The school boasts that Freire students will never doubt that they are part of a community of students and at the center of a circle of adults who care about them and their development. The adults include their families, their teachers, and community partners, the last including job-site associates and mentors. These adults are highly accessible to the students in person, by telephone, and online.

At the Freire Charter School, internal evaluations are used to measure the school's success, and there are also outside consultants who comment on the school's progress. The school uses authentic assessment, i.e., performance assessment, peer review, and portfolios, to test and develop student performance, and the school also is subject to state standardized testing mechanisms.

In the mentoring program, the mentors are more than just role models. They help provide students with real-life experiences and a hands-on approach in dealing with the experiences. National research by Public/Private Ventures, a national nonprofit organization, has shown that mentoring by Big Brother and Big Sister programs makes it significantly less likely that young people will start using illegal drugs or alcohol, skip a class or a day of school, hit someone, or lie to their parents, and participation in mentoring relationships makes young people more trusting of their parents or guardians and allows them to feel more supported by their peers and friends.

According to discussions with Jay Guben as well as the school's Web site, Freire also pursues democratic ideals. Students and adults alike have rights and responsibilities. Students have a voice in designing their studies and demonstrate what they have learned, are active constructors of knowledge and makers of meaning, and participate in evaluating their learning throughout their years at the school. Students are expected to play multiple roles in governance. They not only develop and run a representative student council but they also have seats on the school's board of directors and the school's management team. Students are also invited to join various advisory and decision-making task forces, focus groups, or committees. Staff, families, and community partners also have roles in management and governance.

Professional growth among teachers is also important. Like the students, the teachers must develop an individualized professional growth plan that they will pursue, and the school pays the costs of professional development for the staff. The school does not have a collective bargaining unit, that is, it is not a union school. Teachers have the option to join the state and national teachers' unions, but so far, they have not done so.

Freire is considered by students and their parents, as well as those who labor at the school very special for the following reasons: the students get to make many choices about their own education; they are encouraged to articulate, pursue, and expand their interests; they learn to control powerful technological tools; they develop interpersonal skills they can use in daily life; they work with other students; they share learning with their families; they are equipped to encounter new people and new situations; they make a difference in their communities; and they dream about what they want to become while they actively work toward bringing their dreams to fruition (Freire Charter School).

In my interview with Jay Guben, he mentioned that the greatest barrier to achieving success is implementing the dream. From his point of view, living up to the promises made to the students, parents, staff, and community remains the biggest challenge. Much like in other public schools, the tension between the students who are at Freire to learn and those who are merely there to escape traditional public schooling remains high. However, for Guben and the Freire Charter School's staff, parents, and students, the promises are great, the hope and optimism are encouraging, and the possibility for success is high.

Urban Prep Charter Academy for Young Men, Illinois

In the city of Chicago, on any given weekday, 300 boys might gather in a gym on Chicago's South Side. What all of these boys have in common is that they are all black and an excess of 80% of them are poor. While Chicago has been plagued for years with gang violence and poverty at the Urban Prep School boys can be found standing in straight lines, each student wearing a blazer and a red tie. In unison they shout their creed, the creed of the school:

We believe. We are the young men of Urban Prep. We are college-bound. (The Economist)

The Urban Prep Charter Academy for Young Men is located in the Englewood community on Chicago's South Side, and it is Chicago's first and only secondary charter public school for boys. In fact, it is the city's first all-boys public high school in decades. The school was founded by a group of African American education, business, and civic leaders and eventually approved under Chicago Public Schools' Renaissance 2010 program. According to the school's Web site:

The Urban Prep Charter Academy is part of Chicago's groundbreaking effort to support innovative new schools that better meet the diverse needs of our city's youth. Urban Prep's mission is to provide a high-quality and comprehensive college-preparatory educational experience to young men that results in graduates succeeding in college. It is a direct response to the urgent need to reverse abysmal graduation and college completion rates among young men in urban centers, particularly African American males. Urban Prep's tailored curriculum is based on the developmental stages and learning styles of boys as well as the unique challenges facing urban youth. The Urban Prep motto is "We Believe." We believe that our students will shatter negative stereotypes and defy low expectations. We believe that our students can be prepared for and will succeed in college. We believe in the long-lasting impact community support and positive role models can have on our students' lives. In short, we believe in our students' futures.

One of the features of the school is longer school days that teachers say give them more time to help boys catch up. (Ibid.)

Growing up in Englewood, one of the city's toughest neighborhoods, the statistics for young black men are not very good. Only one in 40 African American males in Chicago is expected to finish college and 50 percent are expected to drop out of high school (Dugandzic 2008).

According to the Web site for the school:

The Englewood Community has a rich and storied history dating back to before it was annexed to the City of Chicago in 1889. Its prominence within the city was due in part to the extensive array of transportation routes that terminated in or passed through the area. Of particular note was a terminal for the Underground Railroad at 67th and Racine Avenue. Englewood was an early beacon of hope for African Americans escaping slavery and this identity provides an important link to the neighborhood's present. Englewood is on track to shine again with opportunity and Urban Prep Charter Academy for Young Men - Englewood Campus is one of the lights in this rekindling.

Seeing the declining national achievement at its lowest point in decades among African American males, proponents of the school say single-gender schools are slowly once again being embraced in some urban education circles with the assumption that they provide African American boys with more structured, supportive environments of smaller class sizes, less distractions and more African American male role models. "To give these boys a chance, we have to catch them earlier and earlier if we don't want to lose them forever," says David Arnold, head of George Jackson Academy in the East Village of New York City, an all-boys independent school. In 2003 the school opened with 52 boys in the 4th and 5th grades. In 2008 there were 120 boys in grades 4 through 8 (Urban Prep Charter Academy for Young Men, under "African American Males").

According to Tracy Robinson-English:

What's happening in Chicago is part of a nationwide movement to create predominantly African American, all-male academies in urban school districts across the country. Providing nurturing alternatives to traditional schools, these public and private academies hope to offer Black boys a better chance to succeed in their lives. (Ibid.)

From the point of view of David Arnold, head of George Jackson Academy in the East Village of New York City, an all-boys independent school:

Black male students who thrive in these single-gender academic settings often have demonstrated higher test scores, graduation rates and acceptance into college than their public school counterparts. The leadership of this country is going to come from this population when you look at the demographics. It's becoming more and more diverse. We have to provide more places like these to validate these young men.

Dr. Pedro Noguera, of New York University, notes:

As late as 1998, only 4 public schools in the United States offered single-sex educational opportunities. By April, 2006, this number rose to 223 U.S. public schools and 44 of these schools are completely single-sex. A significant policy change in ESEA 2002 reauthorization (also known as NCLB) paved the way for such single-sex classroom environments to be permissible. Simultaneously, schools and districts throughout the country are searching for understanding and interventions for addressing the persisting limited academic success of Black and Latino male students. The nature of these compounding academic outcomes raises substantive questions as to the schooling and social contexts Black and Latino males are experiencing, and more importantly how do we intervene? The prevalence of single-sex schools as an intervention to ameliorate the academic and social difficulties this population is experiencing begs for further examination. (Noguera)

The National Association of Single-Sex Schools estimates that about a dozen single-sex, predominantly African American schools exist around the country. Supporters of these schools will also point to the nation's historically Black colleges and universities, which still produces the majority of the nation's Black degree-holders, educators and physicians, among other leaders (Urban Prep Charter Academy for Young Men, under "African American Males").

Educational Focus

At the school's Web site, the approach to education is described as:

The Urban Prep approach to education is to encircle the student with four connecting arcs that provide a comprehensive educational experience. The Academic Arc promotes a rigorous college-prep curriculum that focuses on Reading, Writing, and Public Speaking. In the Service Arc, students' sense of responsibility is deepened by identifying community needs and completing volunteer programs to address those needs. The Activity Arc requires students to participate in two school-sponsored activities per year (sports teams, clubs, etc.) in order to more fully develop their confidence, interpersonal skills, leadership qualities and respect for others. The Professional Arc provides opportunities for students to spend one day per week in a professional setting to increase their understanding of the business world, reinforce character and leadership development, and serve as a means for students to gain valuable work experience. (Urban Prep Charter Academy for Young Men Web, under "Approach to Education")

Urban Prep bases its educational approach on the following *curricular* and *extracurricular* "arcs":

- The Academic Arc: a focus on reading, writing, and public speaking skills.
- The Service Arc: a focus on deepening the students' sense of responsibility and identification of community needs by completing volunteer programs throughout the area.
- The Activity Arc: a focus on increasing students' confidence, interpersonal skills, and leadership qualities by participating in at least two school-sponsored activities per year (sports, clubs, etc.).
- The Professional Arc: a focus on providing students with valuable experience in a professional setting by requiring them to spend one day a week within such a setting. This serves to reinforce character and leadership development in students, as well as providing for them a means of work experience. Each student has access to a laptop computer during the school-year. Use of these computers will be an integral part of student's fulfillment of the Urban Prep Arc requirements.

Organizational Management and Educational Accountability

What makes the school unique is not just its all-male African American student body—the majority of whom are from single-parent, low-income families. What also makes the school a unique and different place for students and parents is its emphasis on discipline. All students are referred to formally by last names. There is a daily "community meeting" in the auditorium where Urban Prep students stand in straight rows according to their respective "pride" or group to listen to acknowledgments and to address concerns. The atmosphere can be said to be militaristic.

As Tracy Robinson-English writes:

Students who arrive late must also acknowledge themselves, report to the front of the stage, and apologize to the entire class. Before attending an eight-hour day of English, math, science, and school activities, students stand in straight rows to shout the school creed: "We are college bound. We are exceptional—not just because we say it, but because we work hard at it. We will not falter in the face of any obstacle placed before us . . . We never fail because we never give up. We make no excuses."

We will examine more carefully the arguments for and against single sex charter schools when we explore the multitude of points of view surrounding charter school issues.

The Virtual Charter Movement: Connections Academy and the Wisconsin Virtual Academy (WIVA) Charter School

Young Jaime, Tori and Hope Leonard wake up at 6:30 a.m. and by 7:30 they are dressed and—virtually—in school, without ever leaving home. Like all children who are home-schooled, the three sisters don't even have to leave their house. But unlike home-schooled children, the Leonards are actually enrolled in a public school—a virtual charter school that is part of the Wisconsin, Appleton Area School District about 100 miles away. Because her children are enrolled in Wisconsin Connections Academy, Leonard pays nothing, the school is public. State taxpayers provide about $5,745 to the Appleton School District for each of her daughters. That's the amount all school districts receive for students who live in another district and register through the state's open enrollment option.

According to Principal Nicole Schweitzer about $3,600 of the money the school receives for each student goes to Connections Academy, a for-profit company under contract with the district (Wisconsin Charter Schools Association).

Connections Academy, which has virtual for-profit charter schools in 15 states, also provides the curriculum it adapts to meet standards, along with computers, technical support, textbooks, and related materials for the 465 kindergarten through eighth- grade students enrolled in the Wisconsin school (Ibid.). Connections Academy also provides professional development for their teachers as well as other support services—the other $2,145 remains with the district, and is used to pay the salaries of the school's state-licensed teachers and other services provided to students, she said (Ibid.). However, unlike home-schooled students, those enrolled in the state's virtual charter schools must meet curriculum standards established by the Department of Public Instruction (DPI) and take its Wisconsin State Knowledge and Concepts exams. And as we shall explore in a subsequent chapter, this represents a problem for many homeschool parents.

Connections Academy is careful to point out that it is not a homeschooling program nor does it provide online learning or training. However, the distinction is without difference. According to Connections Academy, they provide virtual schools. At their brochure site for the Academy, Connections Academy defines a virtual school as:

> *The simplest way to describe a virtual school is that it is a school that doesn't exist in a traditional building. Instead, the classes, instruction, interactions, and feedback all occur outside of the traditional classroom setting—often at the student's home.*
>
> *Connections Academy is a complete public school, accredited with a full time staff of teachers and counselors, often working together, whose job it is to focus on teaching and supporting each student individually. (Connections Academy, under "Brochure Site")*

The history of Connections Academy "virtual charter" plan is relatively new to the homeschooling movement as well as something virtually unheard of in the public school system, of which it claims it is not a part. In the spring of 2001, Sylvan Ventures started a separate business unit of their corporation to create a "turnkey" virtual school program. The result was Connections Academy and the company began operations of its first schools in the fall of 2002. In September of 2004, Connections Academy was sold to an investor group led by Apollo Management, L.P. The for-profit company now operates schools under management contracts from charter schools or school districts in Arizona, California, Colorado, Florida, Idaho, Maryland, Minnesota, Mississippi, Missouri, Nevada, Ohio, Oregon, Pennsylvania, South Carolina, and Wisconsin. They also are currently developing charter schools in Washington State, Utah, New Mexico, Mississippi, Georgia, and South Carolina where the company boasts that it uses all certified teachers in its academic programs (Connections Academy, under "Virtual School Program").

In another part of Wisconsin, parent Julie Thompson of Cross Plains, exclaims with enthusiasm:

"My daughter has the most wonderful, hardest-working teachers in the world working for her," says Thompson. "My seventh-grader logs on with software made for virtual schooling. She goes to a virtual class with a live teacher. She has lessons assigned for her by a teacher. She does one-on-one work with a teacher. She gets her homework evaluated by a teacher, or she talks on a phone or meets face to face with a teacher." (McIlheran 2007)

What Julie Thompson is so excited about is the Wisconsin Virtual Academy (WIVA), an organization offering a program similar to the Connections Academy. According to the WIVA Web site:

Based out of the Northern Ozaukee School District, the Wisconsin Virtual Academy is a public virtual school program that blends innovative new instructional technology with a traditional curriculum for students in grades K-8 all across Wisconsin.

Currently, the Academy is serving approximately 850 K-8 students throughout the state of Wisconsin. Students living anywhere in Wisconsin may be eligible to attend the Wisconsin Virtual Academy. They offer another program entitled Honors High Online of Wisconsin for grades 9-11 based out of the Northern Ozaukee School District. The Wisconsin Virtual Academy is a public charter school program and there is no tuition for enrollment. WIVA loans students a computer system and provides all instructional materials for the program. However, students and families are responsible for providing some consumable materials (such as printer ink and paper), and a district student fee ($30 per child in the 2005-2006 school year).

Educational Focus

At Connections Academy the teacher works directly with both the student and "Learning Coach" to develop an individual learning plan, provide instruction, and evaluate assignments. Instruction and administration is conducted through the Internet, by telephone, fax, and by mail. The teachers work together from centralized offices, providing coordinated support and accountability that often can not be achieved with teachers working on their own.

The Connections Academy has a "regulatory program description" that sets forth what regulations apply to virtual students and their parents or guardians. These regulations spell out attendance, how it is compiled by the Connections Academy, the role of parents in guidance and learning, as well as the day-to-day activities the student is responsible for completing. To accomplish their education, students use print textbooks, lesson plans, workbooks and, for schools where it is offered, a desktop computer.

The curriculum at Connections Academy is grounded in mathematics, language arts, science, and social studies. Electives are offered in foreign language from kindergarten on. A Learning Management system aids and abets both the parent and student in recording the children's lessons and online activities. Parents and guardians are trained in the technology needed to guide their children and manage their grades and lessons.

At the Wisconsin Virtual Academy, the curriculum is purchased from K12 Inc. According to K12 Inc.'s Web site, the for-profit curriculum company:

> *offers outstanding, highly effective curriculum that enables mastery of core concepts and skills for all kinds of minds. The minds that are superbly gifted—or that are gifted in some areas and struggling in others. The minds that need to use hands to learn on some days, and eyes or ears on others. The minds that move faster or slower than average. The minds that are connected to bodies that need to run off steam periodically, or that are medically unable to attend a physical school. All kinds of minds, not just the best and brightest—not just the ones that are easy to teach in a classroom. (K12 Inc.)*

The curriculum is developed by K12 Inc. and then administered by the WIVA with the promise that students meet or exceed Wisconsin state standards of education.

Organizational Management and Educational Accountability

At the Connections Academy, the Learning coach plays an active and visible role. The Learning Coach plays a key role in developing study skills and implementing the learning. As students become more independent as they enter into middle school and high school, the Learning Coach typically spends less time on daily oversight and guidance and more of a counselor role.

To help parents understand the challenges and responsibilities of the Learning Coach role, Connections Academy provides tutorials; an orientation program; and a community of parents who can provide first-hand advice (K12 Inc.).

Another important role in the educational charter plan for the Connections Academy is the "local community coordinator." The Connections Academy encourages events, trips, study sessions, and other activities that promote educational and social benefits for students and their families and each Connections Academy school designates parents or teachers to serve as community coordinators. The community coordinators organize these local events and field trips and publicize them to families in the school. Parents may also serve as local community coordinators.

SUMMARY

Thousands of charter schools across the country are designing and pursuing diverse curriculums and educational approaches to learning; they are also reconstituting public education in myriad ways. From virtual charter schools to for-profit charter schools, from community-based charter schools, to parent-led charter schools, as this book is written, charter schools are springing up throughout the United States and plan to offer varied educational roads and organizational challenges to student learning and organizational management. How these schools will fare and how they will affect the future of public education is and will be the subject of much debate and inquiry as the charter idea now has taken a firm hold in communities throughout the country.

REFERENCES

Academica. http://www.academicaschools.com/schools.html.
Ben Gamla Charter School. Hollywood, FL. www.bengamlacharter.com/.
Connections Academy. Brochure Site. http://www.connectionsacademy.com/.
———. Virtual School Program. http://www.connectionsacademy.com/ourschool/find_a_school.asp.
Dingerson, L. "Narrow and Unlovely." *ReThinking Schools,* 21 no. 4, Summer 2007. http://www.re-thinkingschools.org/archive/21_04/narr214.shtml.
Dugandzic, M. "Against All Odds: School Offers Hope, Opportunity for Young Men." CNN. 25 June 2008. http://www.cnn.com/2008/US/06/25/bia.urban.prep/.
The Economist. "Red Ties and Boy's Pride." 10-16 May 2008, Chicago, IL http://www.urbanprep.org/file.asp?F=economist%5Fmay%5F08%2Epdf&N=economist%5Fmay%5F08%2Epdf&C=news.

Freire Charter School. http://www.freirecharterschool.org/.

Goodnough, A. "Hebrew Charter School Spurs Dispute in Florida." *The New York Times,* 24 August 2007. http://www.nytimes.com/2007/08/24/education/24charter.html?_r=1&fta=y&oref=slogin.

K12 Inc. http://www.k12.com/about_k12/.

The Laura Bush Foundation. http://209.85.173.104/search?q=cache:bXR9XtYJ6CsJ:www.laurabushfoundation.org/release_11292006.pdf+Lusher+Charter+School&hl=en&ct=clnk&cd=90&gl=us.

Lusher Charter School. http://lusherschool.org/.

Mater Academy Charter School. Before Care and After Care. http://materacademy.dadeschools.net/BEFORE%20CARE%20%26%20AFTER%20CARE.html.

———. Classroom Profile. http://www.schoolmatters.com/schools.aspx/q/page=s1/sid=55395/midx=classroomprofile.

———. Charter Schools. http://www.materacademyschools.com/our_schools.php.

———. Parental Opinions. http://www.schoolmatters.com/schools.aspx/q/page=pr/sid=55395.

McIlheran, P. "It's Virtual War." *The New York Sun*, 14 December 2007. http://www.nysun.com/opinion/its-virtual-war/68078/.

The Neighborhood House. 2008: Succeed Anywhere. http://www.neighborhoodhousecharterschool.org/about.asp.

———. Academic Philosophy. http://www.neighborhoodhousecharterschool.org/academic.asp.

———. Community Support. http://www.neighborhoodhousecharterschool.org/about_community.asp.

———. Lottery Admission. http://www.neighborhoodhousecharterschool.org/parent_learning.asp.

———. Parent Involvement. http://www.neighborhoodhousecharterschool.org/parent_involvement.asp.

———. Volunteering. http://www.neighborhoodhousecharterschool.org/parent_volunteer.asp.

Noguera, P. "Is All Male Alright?" An Intervention Study of Schools for Black and Latino Males. New York University. http://www.urbanprep.org/userfiles/file/docs/Gates Study Executive Summary.pdf.

Pennsylvania Department of Education. Freire Charter School, 11 August 2008. http://charter schools\CharterAnnualReport[1]FINAL.htm.

Reuters. National Auto Dealers' Charitable Foundation Donates $400,000 to Restore Athletic Fields in New Orleans, 14 May 2008. http://www.reuters.com/article/pressRelease/idUS43478+15-May-2008+PRN20080515.

Schools Matter. http://schoolsmatter.blogspot.com/2007/08/pre-determined-success-of-new-orleans.html.

Schorr, J. "Giving Charter Schools a Chance." *The Nation*, 18 May 2000. http://www.thenation.com/doc/20000605/schorr).

Tulane University. Tulane University Partnership. http://www.Tulane.edu.

———. Selective Admission Criteria. http://www.Tulane.edu/Lusher.

Tulanelink. The Louisiana Decision. http://www.tulanelink.com/tulanelink/decision_03d.htm.

———. Saving Public Schools, Tulane Style. http://www.tulanelink.com/tulanelink/saveourschools_07a.htm.

Urban Prep Charter Academy for Young Men. Approach to Education. http://www.urbanprep.org/arcs/.

———. African American Males. http://www.urbanprep.org/file.asp?F=urban%5Fprep%5Febony%5Farticle@2Epdf&N=urban%5Fprep%5Febony%5Farticle%2Epdff&c=news.

Wisconsin Charter Schools Association. http://www.wicharterschools.org/news.main.cfm?id=75.

Chapter Five

The Political Economy of Charter Schools

INTRODUCTION

Your traditional public schools are failing and your children aren't learning. The management and day-to-day operations of the school system is being choked by an inefficient bureaucracy and overregulation and is held hostage to resistant teacher unions and incompetent management bureaucracies that won't respond to parents' concerns nor adopt meaningful educational reforms. Principals who run the traditional public schools are weak, ineffectual, and their hands are tied by overly bureaucratic boards and powerful unions; they refuse, or simply cannot, fire teachers who underperform. The public schools are overcrowded, class sizes are maximized and many of the schools linger in unconscionable disrepair while the state and local municipalities and boards, which run them, are financially insolvent and cannot afford the cost of curriculum, books, and repairs to the infrastructure of schools, not to mention the personnel, supplies and technology needed to educate students; nor can they even manage the day-to-day organizational duties of the schools, from cafeteria needs to janitorial functions to clerical duties. The whole traditional public school system seems to be collapsing or on the precipice of collapse. What can be done? The only answer is to privatize schools, says the collective voice of the burgeoning entrepreneurial educational industry and their public advocates and think tanks; for it is only a huge, vibrant, and creative private sector that can, by providing parental "choice," fix what is ailing public schools for the betterment of parents, their children, and society.

The clarion call is concise, the call to arms for a paradigm shift resonant and clear: reform education through market-based competition and privatization and in the case of public schools, most notably charter schools, allow private, for-profit management companies or private and nonprofit independent operators to run charter schools for the maximum profit of shareholders or investors who invest in these companies. In return, all that is asked by the for-profit management companies or independent operators, or EMOs (educational management organizations) that increasingly operate many traditional public and increasingly charter schools throughout the nation, is a chance to make a decent taxpayer-subsidized profit—a chance to bring in a profitable return for their investors by encouraging the start-up of more and more charter schools and their eventual creation and management for-profit. The perpetrators of this "market-based solution" claim that this is the only public policy reform that will succeed in educating our children for the twenty-first century—the privatization of the nation's public schools, their services, and even the day-to-day management of these schools with an eye on giving parents and their children a "choice" as to what schools they may attend.

From the perspective of the private sector and those in the public sector that champion private, market-driven reforms, any success in education is based not on mere compliance with government regulations or mandates; nor, they argue, should success be measured by public bureaucrats seeking inefficient reforms. The only "true" reform available to public education, claim many, if not the majority that support charter schools and most specifically the private sector, will come by developing the best "educational product" and attracting the most "customers" through the provision of "consumer choice."

HISTORICAL, ECONOMIC AND SOCIAL BACKGROUND

Any understanding of the politics of the charter school reform movement, its recent emergence, challenges, and promises, must be understood within the socio-economic and historical context that spawned it. Charter schools are a unique and historical educational reform concept with deep roots in important historical controversies over the purposes of education, educational funding, what role education is to have in market societies, morality, cultural hegemony, race, gender, and social class. Unfortunately, as educational author and reformer, Herbert Kliebard has lamented, movements for school change generally fail to understand the history of educational reform in the United States. According to Kliebard:

New breakthroughs are solemnly proclaimed when in fact they represent minor modifications of early proposals, and, conversely, anachronistic dogmas and doc-

trines maintain a currency and uncritical acceptance far beyond their present merit. (Kliebard 1970, 259)

Kliebard calls upon educators to examine new and popular school reform proposals from a historical perspective. For our purposes, this historical examination will specifically focus on the historical development of education as it affected and still affects the growth and maturation of charter schools as a reform movement.

We begin our understanding of the politics of charter schools by briefly exploring the socioeconomic historical origins that frame some of the controversies popular in educational discourses today. We also look at the rise of public schooling in the United States from the late nineteenth century up to, and including, the present. This period of time includes the industrial revolution, the urbanization of the United States, the development of modernism, and the current situation in postindustrial United States—all historical developments and issues that affect the development, popularity, and growth of charter schools.

The historical treatment of these epochs in the United States is not intended to be exhaustive but is designed instead to be illustrative of the forces that have given rise to the current political climate, terms, and level of debate regarding charter school reform in education in the United States today. By placing the charter school concept under the critical lens of historical scrutiny, we can better understand charter schools as a contemporary educational reform movement: a movement born as the result of specific, cultural, economic, and historical relations and forces. With this understanding, we will be in a better position to acquire a deeper and richer comprehension of the contemporary politics that configure the current controversy over charter schools and therefore in a better position to assess their strengths and merits.

AMERICAN INDUSTRIALISM AND THE FACTORY SCHOOL

The end of the American Civil War in 1865 and the immediate years that followed brought unbridled economic growth and development to the country. New scientific and technological developments fueled the expansion of markets and shaped a deeply changing country. More and more Americans began to live in large urban centers, which led to the increased development and expansion of cities. Coupled with immigration, the increased urbanization and industrialization of the late nineteenth and early twentieth centuries led to a rapid growth of U.S. industry and a new concentration of economic power in the hands of emerging industrialists and corporations.

Immigration helped the political and cultural landscape of the country in the late 1800s as larger urban centers were not only growing but for the first time were growing with people other than white Anglos (Kincheloe 2000, 151). Along with this rapid growth there was a need to assimilate the new immigrants into the melting pot of "mainstream" American life. An obvious and logical forum for this assimilation was the public school. Work in urban centers during this time in history was largely relegated to factory work, so the first public schools in the United States resembled the factory as well. There were bells to sound the beginning of classes, desks were bolted to the floor in regimented rows, strict discipline was maintained, and there was a rigidly imposed social order (Kincheloe 2000, 152).

The costs of building these new factory-type schools were justified in the minds of the public by appeals to the "national interest." The argument was simple: immigrant children were in the United States because the United States needed the labor of their parents to become rich and prosperous. The market rational at the time also argued that educating these children would lead to a positive return on investment, that is, a more productive workforce and a more competitive country. One leading educational reformer at the time, Ellwood Cubberley, wrote: "Our schools are, in a sense, factories in which the raw products (children) are to be shaped and fashioned into products to meet the demands of life. The specifications for manufacturing come from the demands of twentieth century civilization, and it is the business of the school to build its pupils according to the specifications laid down" (Cubberley 1916, 338).

If the public school represented the factory, the students themselves were little more than the raw material or objects of production; they were products to be fashioned by the public school system. In the emerging modern public schools of the United States, children, especially immigrant children, were to be trained to follow directions and routines, learn proper English, and develop rudimentary "basic skills" such as reading, mathematics, and writing. Schooling, in a sense, developed as a center for socialization and indoctrination as the United States entered the industrial era.

In the post-Civil War United States, market interests and business concerns rapidly permeated public schools. Not only was the curriculum of the public schools immersed in the growth, regulation, and maintenance of urbanization and the rise of industrialization and factory existence, the schools were also implicated in the development of a modernist conception of knowledge and intelligence. When we examine charter school politics in depth, we will see that this marriage, the marriage between market interests and public education, is one of the most controversial aspects of charter school reform.

Between 1880 and 1920, as the factory-style public school system emerged, so, too, did the philosophy which specified that the reality and life of both students and teachers needed to be scientifically oriented and regulated (Kincheloe 2000, 153). Standardized tests began during this period, and emphasis in the tests was on sorting and categorizing mechanisms that would place students on specific curricular tracks. Modern rationalism and specific, linear ways of knowing emerged as the measure of intelligence, and the new standardized tests, such as the Stanford Benet Test, were designed to calibrate and classify students based on emerging modernist notions of intellectual behavior. These instruments of assessment also gave specific direction to teachers as to what they should be doing in their classrooms, how they should organize their time and priorities, and what subjects should be emphasized.

The burgeoning industrial capitalism of the late 1800s and early 1900s needed schools to preserve, extend, and legitimize the economic relations of production and the arrival of new forms of unprecedented consumption. Consequently, during this period, there was the rise and development of an educational philosophy called *social functionalism:* education organized, implemented, and controlled to meet the functional needs of society's business and economic interests. These functional needs became increasingly identified with what was necessary in the workplace, and as we shall see, controversies regarding social functionalism were one of the impetuses that encouraged the growth of charter schools.

Directly associated with the social functionalism of schools was an excessive preoccupation with the values of productivity, efficiency, and thrift (Goodman 1995, 6). With the development of the assembly line and specifically the contributions of Frederick Taylor to the new science of business management that was being realized on assembly lines, efficiency, productivity, and speed began to capture the imagination of the American public. Factory work relied on workers who could follow instructions, understand simple directions, and work swiftly to increase production with maximum efficiency. With the small shopkeeper disappearing and corporate power beginning to emerge, the industrialist and the industrial tycoon now became the cultural model for a successful person (Huber 1971). Industrial production proceeded at levels unheard of before, and the power and ideology of industrialized production became the infatuation and ideology of the United States during this period.

It is hard not to see the parallel between that historical time period and today. Although contemporary production has shifted to technological and service work as the United States enters into the "third wave" or postindustrialism, infatuation with technological tycoons, cybernet billionaires and the ideology of efficiency and "lean production" now dominates the country's culture. School-to-work programs are important aspects of many public schools, and charter schools have arisen partly in response to the demands of the new social functionalism and the proclaimed need to prepare students for the exigencies of production in the twenty-first century. However, as we will see this is not always the case, as some charter schools have also arisen as a result of general opposition to this idea of superfunctionalism.

The social functionalism prevalent in the philosophy of early-twentieth-century educational discourse, along with a preoccupation for speed and efficiency, was described by the then-leading reformer Franklin Bobbitt, one of the key social functionalists for the school restructuring movement during the industrial age. Bobbitt claimed as early as 1924:

> *It is helpful to begin with the simple assumption to be accepted literally, that education is to prepare men and women for the activities of adult life; and that nothing should be included which does not serve this purpose. . . . The first task is to discover the activities which ought to make up the lives of men and women; and along with these, the abilities and personal qualities necessary for proper performance. These are educational objectives. When we know what men and women ought to do then we shall have before us the things for which they should be trained. (Bobbitt 1912, 259-271)*

The activities to which Bobbitt referred were tied to necessities that resulted from changes in the relations of production and consumption that were exploding at the time.

Not only did the industrial age have an impact on the purposes and goals of education, but the social functionalism of the time also affected staffing patterns, curriculum construction, and instructional design (Goodman 1995, 6). What Raymond Callahan referred to as the "cult" of efficiency and productivity had an effect on every aspect of schooling (Callahan 1962). Taylorism, (named for Frederick Taylor, the father of the assembly line) the modern science of business management, was rapidly being implemented in school production. With educational goals being restructured and defined as increasing productivity in schools, in essence the quantity rather than the quality of what students learn, the factory school began to predetermine outcomes and then plan backward to restructure education so that those outcomes could be reached. Bobbitt described this process as early as 1913:

> *The third grade teacher should bring her pupils up to an average of 26 correct combinations in addition per minute. The fourth grade teacher has the task, during the year that the same pupils are under her care, of increasing their addition speed from an average of 26 combinations per minute to an average of 34 combinations per minute. If she does not bring them up to the standard 34, she has failed to perform her duty in proportion to the deficit; and there is no responsibility beyond the standard. (Bobbitt 1913, 21-22)*

Specifically stated learning objectives that could be measured, controlled, and regulated became the language of the modernist's educational discourse, much like the No Child Left Behind standards of current times. These objectives were tied to what was needed or what was divined to be functional in the new industrial society that was emerging. With an "objectives first" approach to education and schooling, curricula underwent unique changes. Not only were educators at the time concerned with efficiency and production, they also believed strongly in the practice of differentiated staffing (Goodman 1995, 10). Knowledge acquisition was fragmented into disciplines and subjects much like the work on the assembly lines in the industrial factories. The conception of education was divorced from its execution. Thus, a fragmented curriculum and "teacher specialists" developed.

The important goal for the social functionalists and efficiency educators of the day was to reduce the number of educational workers by maximizing their instructional efficiency. Thus, not unlike what Taylor advocated for the factory, no one person was to ever be responsible for too many different tasks. Scientism and the instrumentalist approaches of the functionalist educators divided teaching up into distinct and differentiated tasks staffed by distinct individuals.

The reconfiguration of the school day and the redesign of curriculum during the industrial revolution in the early part of the twentieth century helped shape what we now know as the large, factory-style urban public school and the public school curriculum. As we shall see, Bobbitt's appeal to link school to work was not much different than positions taken by certain educational policymakers and business leaders today. And in the same way that Taylorism and the new science of business administration influenced the conception and organization of schooling during the early twentieth century, contemporary changes in production, consumption, and business management theory continue to exert a tremendous influence on the public school debate today. This, in turn, is reflected in the debate regarding school choice and the charter school reform movement.

AFRICAN AMERICANS AND THE FACTORY SCHOOL

With the emergence of the factory school, educating children for the responsibilities associated with public citizenship was increasingly sacrificed for the quantitative imperatives of the newly emerging industrial society and capitalist market. The purposes of education were deeply connected to the necessities of efficiency and productivity. School administrators at the time even began to think of themselves as "school executives" rather than as educators of children (Callahan 1962). One can liken this to the newly named CEOs of education as opposed to principals. Educational language changed, just as it is now, as the vocabulary of business was adopted to describe education and schools. Another leading reformer and educational functionalist at the time, Ellwood Cubberley, asserted a vocabulary of business when expressing the need for educational efficiency and production:

> *Every manufacturing establishment that turns out a standard product . . . Maintains a force of efficiency experts to study methods of procedure to measure and test the*

output of its workers. Such men ultimately bring the manufacturing establishment large returns, by introducing improvements in processes and procedure, and in training the workmen to produce larger and better output . . . In time, it will be possible for any school system to maintain a continuous survey of all of the different phases of its work, through tests made by its corps of efficiency experts, and to detect weak points in its work almost as soon as they appear. (Cubberley 1916, 338)

Yet the historical reality of the emerging factory school, with its social functionalism and cult of efficiency, produced a quandary for many African American children. The questions at issue that both the black community and the white Anglo community were to wrestle with during this period involved the purposes of education, whom it should serve, who should have access to it, and why. This debate was most evident in the African American community in the decades that followed Reconstruction.

Two powerful and contrasting African American leaders at the time expressed profoundly different ideas as to the purposes for educating black children. Booker T. Washington stressed the necessity of agrarian and vocational education for African American children. In the spirit of social functionalism, he felt the role of schools was to teach children a trade or useful skill they might use in the larger white-controlled society. An ex-slave, Washington, much like the social functionalists Bobbitt and Cubberley, felt that education should be prepare one for future work. His prescription to blacks in the South is useful to consider for it summed up succinctly his view on education and educational purpose: "Make yourself useful to the south; be honest, be thrifty; cultivate the white man's friendliness; above all, educate your children and prepare them for the future" (Perkinson 1989, 49).

W.E.B. DuBois, unlike Washington and his social functionalist contemporaries, felt that the overriding purpose and goal behind the education of African American children was to educate them for full citizenship in American society, not simply for the needs of a segregated and white market civilization. Although Washington stressed economic pragmatism as the chief consideration in defining educational purpose, DuBois argued that African American children should be educated in the tradition of the liberal arts, the necessities of responsible and moral leadership, and participation in democracy. He felt that the role of education "is not to make carpenters out of men, but men out of carpenters" (DuBois 1973, 52). And while Washington believed that African Americans could not achieve full citizenship until they were economically self-sufficient, DuBois believed that education itself was the key to full citizenship, not simply a means to economic self-sufficiency. DuBois declared in 1906: "We claim for ourselves every single right that belongs to a freeborn American, political, civil, and social; and until we get these rights we will never cease to protest and assail the ears of America" (DuBois 1924, 53).

Controversies in the black community over the purposes of education, social functionalism, and the role of culture in schooling are arguably more complex issues today than they were during the time of Washington and DuBois. The Washington-DuBois debates, although heated and controversial at the time, were concerned with the goals of education for African Americans during a time when education was adapting to an emerging industrial society. Similarly, today we see these controversies reflected in the emerging cybernetic revolution as educational goals are debated in a rapidly changing technological and social environment. Similar struggles for access to educational excellence and equal opportunity emerge now, as they did during the Washington-DuBois debates.

Washington's vision of schooling prevailed over that of the more visionary DuBois. Yet it is important to note that the discussion concerning educational purpose continues unabated in the black community with many if not all the same issues at the center of concern. However, with the advent of charter schools, this debate now takes on different proportions and levels of complexity as charters have the ability to serve various philosophical tenets.

PROGRESSIVE RESPONSES TO THE FACTORY SCHOOL

Although the factory style of education during the latter part of the nineteenth century and the early part of the twentieth imposed a functionalistic, industrial education on all U.S. citizens—African American, Native American, newly arriving immigrants, and Anglos—it was not without its critics and staunch opponents. Even though the prevailing wisdom at the time argued for impersonal factory schools grounded on modernist approaches to curriculum and teaching, many educators protested. They not only saw the factory school as an impersonal social arrangement, they saw industrial society and the factory life that was emerging as an impediment to human development. Margaret Haley, a union organizer and teacher-activist at the time, expressed the following:

> *Two ideals are struggling for supremacy in American life today; one the industrial ideal, dominating through the supremacy of commercialism, which subordinates the worker to the product, and the machine; the other ideal of democracy, the ideal of educators, which places humanity above all machines, and demands that all activity shall be the expression of life. (Tyack 1974, 257)*

Educators like Haley opposed what they viewed as the rigid and impersonal social order imposed by the capitalist relations of factory life. She, like many of her contemporaries, felt that the rise of corporations and corporate power were far more menacing to life in the United States than was the role of government (Kincheloe 2000, 159). These educational progressives wanted schools to provide educational experiences for children that expanded their involvement in citizenship activities and civic responsibility, and to this end they argued that public education must construct its own mission and purpose. They viewed education as a vehicle for human freedom, emancipation, and democratic citizenship—not simply a means to an economic end. Nowhere could this controversy be better exhibited than in the John Dewey-Walter Lippmann debates of the 1920s that captivated the American public both then and now.

THE DEWEY-LIPPMANN DEBATES

Besides DuBois and Haley, another prominent progressive educator and philosopher during the early part of the twentieth century was John Dewey. Like Haley and other opponents of social functionalism, Dewey argued against reducing schooling to mere functionalism—boring and repetitive tasks designed to prepare students for future work under capitalist relations. Dewey's argument against social functionalism maintained that the role and purpose behind education should be to prepare students to live fully in the present, not simply to prepare them for the future. Like Boyd Bode, another progressive educator of the time, Dewey argued that for schooling to be merely a preparatory institution for future market needs was dehumanizing and denied children the opportunity to find relevancy, identity, and meaning in their lives. Dewey commented:

> *The ideal of using the present simply to get ready for the future contradicts itself. It omits, and even shuts out, the very conditions by which a person can be prepared for his future. We always live at the time we live and not at some other time, and only by extracting at each present time the full meaning of each present experience are we prepared for doing the same thing in the future. This is the only preparation which in the long run amounts to anything. (Dewey 1976, 49)*

Walter Lippmann was a journalist and contemporary of John Dewey, as well as a speech writer for presidents. In the 1920s, Lippmann was in his mere 20s while Dewey was much older, in his 60s. Dewey was a philosopher at Columbia University at the time while Lippmann remained a distinctive journalist and essayist. Much like today, as Susan Jacoby argues in her book, *The Age of American Unreason,* this brief period of time was one in which there was growing belief in human irrationality and unreasonableness (Jacoby 2008); this could be summed up as the belief that people can and could not govern themselves, that participatory democracy was simply an illusion born out of appearances, not whole cloth, and that if left to his own devices, "man" would simply slide towards demagoguery or mob rule or perhaps even worse, barbarism. Many public debates, not simply here in America, but abroad as well as to whether people could govern themselves or if they would need to be governed by managerial elites, in the case of Germany, Italy and Japan, fascists, was in full force.

For Lippmann the answer was clear: it was a false notion of "public opinion" that was the culprit in modern society and offered an explanation of why people could not possibly hope to manage or govern their own affairs. In his book of that name, he argued that public opinion is really "manufactured consent" due to the effects of propaganda and mediated reality on the psychological minds of people. He argued, like many of his contemporaries do today, for the imposition of social governance by intellectual managerial elites, a form of enlightened expertise, whereby there would be those who would manage the governance of a democracy through "objective" thinking and the rational imposition of principles of science. These autocratic elites would administer or govern society by applying scientific management to democracy in an effort to maintain orderly control, something Lippmann was thoroughly convinced the public could not achieve. Of course in such a society there would be little need for citizenship education. In fact, Lippmann is adamant in his contempt, if not disdain, for what he labels the "unattainable ideal"—a self-governing citizenry. With suspicion for anything democratic and the view that the average citizen was incapable of governance let alone democratic governance, Lippmann's view of education can be summed up in his book *The Phantom Public* where he declares:

> *The usual appeal to education can bring only disappointment. For the problems of the modern world appear and change faster than any set of teachers can grasp them, much faster than they can convey their substance to a population of children. If the schools attempt to teach children how to solve the problems of the day, they are bound always to be in arrears. The most they can conceivably attempt is a teaching of a pattern of thought and feeling which will enable the citizen to approach a new problem in some useful fashion. But that pattern cannot be invented by the pedagogue. It is the political theorist's business to trace out that pattern. In that task he must not assume that the mass has political genius, but that men, even if they had genius, would give only a little time to public affairs. (Lippmann 2009, 17)*

Disillusioned with democracy, reform, and populism, from Lippmann's perspective:

> *The people are fundamentally selfish, interested in themselves, and the press simply feeds to this selfishness and self-interest. Furthermore, the people are not interested enough in being informed that they are prepared to pay the true price for reliable information, so they are content to purchase papers at very low cost, increasing newspapers' dependence on advertising which, in its turn, further subverts the independence and reliability of the news that is provided. The press sees the reader as more a target for advertising than as a citizen in a democracy. To be sure of gathering together a sufficient number of people to be of interest to advertisers,*

the newspapers serve up a news diet that fits within the existing range of expectations and stereotypes of the reader, emphasizing, for example, local news over national, and national over international and so on. In any case there is also a problem with news, which simply signals events but does not explain them in their full complexity and context. What news the newspapers choose to select is as much based on convenience (time and effort required) as on the public importance of events. Convenience leads the press to undue dependence on "press agents" (i.e., lobbyists, public relations people etc.). We should therefore not confuse "news" with "truth." The power of symbols rest, says Lippmann on the irrational character of human emotions, coupled with the ambiguity of symbols themselves. Symbols can be pictures, representations, words or slogans. (Bybee)

Arguably Lippmann's argument is more compelling now and embraced even tighter by many neoconservatives than they were when he wrote them in 1927. The "public interest" versus what Lippmann called "disinterestedness" still remain central topics in discussions of governance, power and reform and no more noticeably than within the realm of "public interest" and education. This is important, for many who advocate "reform" of the public educational system through the development of charter contract schools, are also some of the same voices whom echo both the ideological sentiments and despairing rhetoric of Lippmann's 1927 prognosis as it pertains to a democratic citizenry. Many of the charter schools are back-to-basic charters, designed in the carpeted offices of air-conditioned buildings in major cities by entrepreneurs and their subordinates who often have little or no understanding of education, curriculum, or the controversies that surround it.

Dewey responded to Lippmann's book in the magazine, *The New Republic,* shortly after its publication. According to Dewey, while agreeing with Lippmann that people's perceptions could be and are managed by propaganda and demagoguery, especially in an era of mass communications and advertising, Dewey remained more of an optimist when it came to human rationality, democracy, education, and self-governance.

Disagreeing vehemently with Lippmann, Dewey argued that class divisions in society were really the culprit and by implication contrary to an ethics of rationality; an ethic he felt so necessary to carry out the public interest. For Dewey, democracy was a system designed for people to develop their maximum potential and this meant that they would need to be educated as a democratic citizenry capable of the management of their affairs. Citizen education for participatory democracy became the themes that Dewey would echo all his life and throughout his writings and activism, while Lippmann would go on to argue that the public's role in citizen life was to vote for whatever candidate was put forward by the ruling elite and then allow the "elected" official to manage the economy, social institutions, and conditions of human life for the betterment, if not to outright prevent, the rebellion of the masses. For Lippmann, people were to be spectators of their own lives, not active participants, for according to his thinking due to the totalizing effects of cultural deception, advertising, and propaganda they could not possibly acquire the rationality necessary to conduct human affairs.

The implications of the Dewey-Lippmann debate of the 1920s were to have a large effect on theories of education and institutions of learning for years. John Dewey would go on to argue against Walter Lippmann's managerial elitism and liberal authoritarian posturing on issues regarding public affairs, human governance, the role of education, and human nature. For Dewey, democracy was to be discovered through an educated public that had been severely compromised by the advent of historical forces of capitalism and technology that served to restructure both the social reality of life and the psychological dimension of life through mass technology. Education for liberation would be the theme for Dewey's position on the role of education, for he himself was very clear regarding what he and other progressives conceived of as the purpose and objective of education:

> *The problem of education in its relation to the direction of social change is all one with the problem of finding out what democracy means in total range of concrete applications; domestic, international, religious, cultural, economic, and political . . . The trouble . . . is that we have taken democracy for granted; we have thought and acted as if our forefathers had founded it once and for all. We have forgotten that it has to be enacted anew with every generation, in every year, in every day, in the living relations of person to person, in all social forms and institutions. Forgetting this . . . We have been negligent in creating a school that should be the constant nurse of democracy. (Dewey 1940, 357–358)*

Dewey was convinced that democracy was not a "thing" that is found, but an idea that is perpetually created and that if given the correct social relations, citizen education and access to basic needs people not only could but would learn to govern and manage their affairs in the interest of democracy. His notion of education rested upon a citizenry concerned with developing the ability to visualize the type of society its members wished to live in and then working collaboratively to create it. Lippmann, on the other hand, disagreed, notably arguing that the forces of technology along with censorship and social segregation and social isolation as a result of the industrialized capitalism of his time had so summarily distorted the perceptions of what is deemed "the public," that to allow such an unbridled herd to participate in democracy would be tragic if not farcical.

Although the debates between progressive educators like Dewey, Bode, DuBois, and Haley on the one hand and functionalists and managerial elitists like Bobbitt and Cubberley and Lippmann on the other were intense and controversial, in the end, functionalism triumphed over progressivism. There are many reasons for the triumph of social functionalism in the educational debates in the United States during the early part of the twentieth century, not the least being the cost of subsidizing and operating public education as an enterprise. Progres-

sive educational ideas arguably would have required new structural configurations of schools, an emphasis on quality education as opposed to educating quan-
tities of students, new assessments, and more creative and innovative curricula.
Social functionalist approaches to education, on the other hand, were less expensive precisely because within the factory style of school, students could be "produced" through educational "formulas" on an educational assembly line in much
larger numbers than the painstaking craftsmanship required by progressive education (Wirt and Kirst 1992). Education was far more efficient, it was argued,
when it was reduced to an ecumenical formula. The importance of this history
cannot go unnoticed when we examine the charter school movement for so much
of the innovation charters claim to be breeding and that is uncritically touted by
the media is really a hyper or superfunctionalist approach to education, for the
charter schools themselves are wedded to legal state-mandated tests that give
them little wiggle room for a curriculum that is not geared towards the needs of
standardized testing. Couple this with the for-profit management of many of
these charter schools and we can see how the ideological underpinnings of an education tied to superfunctionalism also translates neatly into business plans of
for-profit charter schools. Basically said, superfunctionalism is cheaper, less expensive to develop, can be commodified easily into standardized approaches and
practices, and it then can be taught for delivery purpose to teacher-managers responsible for its execution. Done well, charter schools can then be set up as franchises, accounting procedures developed, and profits made for investors through
the standardization of the whole "school package."

Perhaps even more important, the progressive agenda for education at the
time of the Dewey-Lippmann debates was highly controversial and threatened
the managerial elite agenda of control and power that, as Lippmann noted and
helped advance ideologically, was beginning to take shape in an industrialized,
modern America. With the emergence of union activism, independent socialist
movements—coupled with the creation of the former Soviet Union in 1917 and
the so-called Red scare and the Sacco and Vanzetti trial—the last thing that policymakers in education, business, or politics wanted was education for social liberation and individual realization. Business interests, policymakers, and
politicians were worried that opening up education to such things as personal
awareness, democracy, social exploration and personal development, along with
critical analysis might compel the public to examine the social, cultural, and economic relations that governed their lives. Such a result had the possibility of pos-
ing a considerable threat to power, authority, and elite control of social affairs and
was of little interest to the captains of a industry and a market society undergoing a huge economic expansion, technological revolution, rising industrialization, and an unprecedented creation and concentration of wealth and industry.
Their notion of education for social function and control was far more pragmatic
in an emerging industrial world in which commercialism relied on disciplined

workers and irresponsible consumers subject to the perception management and "manufactured consent" admonished, yet implicitly advocated, by Lippmann. As a result, Dewey's progressive ideas had little support from administrators and other educational policymakers, unlike Lippmann's liberal elitism of the times which was heartily embraced by the aristocracy, the business class and the then contemporary elite managerial class.

Nevertheless, the debates between and among progressives, social functionalists, and scientific management elitists had a large practical effect on the growth, design, and development of traditional public education during the early part of the twentieth century; schools would be now increasingly organized along the lines of factory models and their curricula were increasingly wedded to organizational and intellectual endeavors that promoted education as preparation for work and obedience, not education dedicated to personal and social development, the citizenship education Dewey had longed for.

Today, admittedly many progressive educators and parents who find Dewey's notion of educational purpose of utmost importance have begun to open charter schools with instructional methodologies and curricula based on progressive educational concerns. The Freire School and the Neighborhood Charter School, both highlighted in chapter 4, are simply two examples of the many charter schools begun with "education for liberation" as their theme and sole intent. For many of these progressive educators, parents, students, and community stakeholders the charter school reform effort has meant freedom from the anachronistic factory style of education still so prevalent today. It also means these constituencies can now organize, orient, and construct their school vision formulated and based on interdisciplinary and progressive ideals and their own brand of philosophy, and not be held hostage to the rigors and formulas of traditional public schools.

The arguments between Washington and DuBois, Dewey and Lippmann, and a host of educational functionalists, elitists, and educational progressives is as heated today as it was in the beginning of the twentieth century, perhaps even more so. The issues that confronted educators in the early twentieth century—curriculum construction, access to quality education, the education of minority children and newly arriving immigrants, race, gender equity, social class, market capitalism, technological innovation, work, efficiency and production, and the purpose and goals of education—represent similar but different challenges, much as they did close to 100 years ago. However, now with the rise of new technologies like television, radio, and the Internet (to name a few), Lippmann's ideas of an irrational public not only resonate loudly, but arguably serve as even a greater warning regarding the power of a small corporate elite to control or "manufacture the consent" of the public. If Lippmann was alive today, he would most likely argue that the opportunities for elite control of the public mind are more prevalent in our contemporary society as they ever were, and thus the role of education should be one of domestication, because for Lippmann people are simply incapable of carrying out the civic duties required by democratic life.

The idea of the charter school, or the notion of public school choice, has its roots in the controversies that Washington, DuBois, Haley, Dewey, and their functionalist and elitist contemporaries—Bobbitt, Cubberley, and Lippmann—engaged in more than 85 years ago. These issues help explain, to some extent, the outgrowth and development and demands of charter schools among specific segments and constituencies of the population. Without this historical examination and analysis the notion of "charter schools" and "public choice" remains, as Kliebard acknowledged decades ago, a fragment of history divorced from the whole.

POST-WORLD WAR II POLITICS OF PUBLIC EDUCATION

Public education in post-World War II United States involved some of the most dramatic transformations and challenges in the context of the cold war: McCarthyism, economic prosperity, suburban development, technological innovations in consumer goods, the advent of television and advertising, the growth of the civil rights movement, and the rapid development of scientific innovation and discovery. During this time, controversial and rancorous debates arose over the role of education and universal access to school facilities, especially among minority constituencies.

Perhaps the most important event that marked post–World War II social, racial, and educational politics was the 1954 Supreme Court decision *Brown v. Board of Education.* (*Brown v. Board of Education* 1954). Up to that time, what was referred to as "the separate-but-equal doctrine," upheld in *Plessy v. Ferguson,* had governed relations between blacks and whites. The *Brown* decision overturned *Plessy,* declaring the separate-but-equal doctrine "inherently unequal." In a 1955 follow-up decision, the Court further clarified its position on the matter by stating that public school systems that had been segregated until that time now had to become desegregated (*Brown v. Board of Education II* 1955).

The Supreme Court decisions also brought up the heated issue of "states rights" versus federal control—an issue as old as the Civil War itself. Many conservative southerners felt that decisions regarding local issues should be left to the states and local government bodies, not be mandated by the federal government. Many conservatives at the time saw the Supreme Court's decision in *Brown v. Board of Education* as a federal invasion of states' rights. But it was more than that: the issues revolved around integration into a post-war industrial society based on capitalist relations of power and authority. Integration was seen as a panacea for educational equity. Much of this ideology is currently being challenged and discussed by charter school proponents who, if not advocating "separate but equal" as their mantra, certainly have posed many controversial questions and challenges to the wisdom of attempting to homogenize education. This is perhaps why we see the rise of what might be termed "charter school identity politics," as various ethnic, religious, gender, and faith-based groups and their members clamor for culturally specific, if not race specific or religious specific education via charter schools.

Another important post-World War II event that was to have a massive impact on the nation's school systems and the continued public debate over education was the 1957 advance of the Soviet Union into space with the launching of *Sputnik*. U.S. leaders reacted to that Soviet success with shock and disbelief, arguing that the Soviet Union now had a military advantage over the United States. Business leaders, military leaders, and educational policymakers scrambled to assign the blame to the public schools. Given the permissiveness of the 1950s, in everything from music to new conventions regarding sexuality and conformity, blaming public education for not preparing the United States for global and economic competitiveness was convenient, and attacks on public education intensified with increasing regularity (Kincheloe 2000, 164). Evidently, the functionalists had let down their educational guard. The reaction by the government and business elites was quick and forthcoming.

After the launching of *Sputnik* and given the perceived Soviet superiority in matters of technology and military development, the federal government began to become more involved in the legal and economic realities of public education. The National Defense and Education Act was passed, and the educational emphasis now focused primarily on science, mathematics, foreign languages, guidance, career counseling, and vocational endeavors in an effort to compete more effectively with the Soviet Union. The federal government also appropriated and spent massive sums for capital improvements and the construction of schools and buildings. Competition in education was now being ushered into the debate over educational improvement as world dominance and the United States supposed failings in the education for supremacy was wholly seen as lacking.

Worried that the Soviet Union was achieving technological and military dominance over the United States, educational policymakers believed they were the custodians of a public educational system designed to prepare U.S. citizens for the rigorous necessities of economic and military dominance. Education was now to be perceived as a vehicle for gaining the necessary skills for the promotion of "the national interest" and was directly linked to defeating communism at any cost. For the first time in its history, the U.S. government declared education a national preoccupation and a national interest, and linking U.S. readiness to educational standards became the talk of the day. The public schools were still organized like large factories, but they were now factories that were more preoccupied with the regulation of the curriculum in the interests of national sovereignty and economic readiness to meet the challenges of securing world dominance. In this atmosphere of political fear and a worldwide competitive stated educational purpose tied to military and technological preparedness, the voices of educational progressives, like Dewey and DuBois, were not merely muted, they seemed to have been silenced—at least for a time.

It is not surprising that amidst the historical shifts in American power and its conception the efforts to promote an educational marketplace through privatized school choice could be traced directly to the work of the conservative economist Milton Friedman in the 1950s. Unlike proponents of public education who sought restructuring and reform of factory-style public schools, Friedman, keeping with the competitive spirit of capitalism and the domestic debate over foreign affairs and public education at the time, proposed in 1955 that every family be given a federal "voucher" to be used for each child attending any school—public or private. Under the proposed plan, the voucher would be paid for by public funds and would allow families to select a school of their choice that met minimal governmental oversight. Parents could also add their own resources to the value of the voucher, and each school would operate like a business, setting its own tuition and admission requirements (Friedman 1955).

At the time Friedman's argument for market-driven education was not historically situated to win over much of the public. Not only did Friedman's proposal fail to attract public interest at the time, the prevailing ideology argued that a simple retooling of the curriculum and the addition of advanced placement classes would remedy whatever problems were associated with public education. However, the ideology was that "public schools" would remain "public schools." Furthermore, after the *Brown* decision, any primacy of states' rights over federal law in the form of state-imposed desegregation was illegal. Although Friedman voiced his support for integration by asserting the primacy of freedom to choose over equality, Friedman's proposal would have directly or indirectly furthered segregation (Lowe and Miner 1996). Why? Simple, the economics of voucher-driven education further stratifies existing society resulting in higher percentages of inequality, class stratification, and racial and social segregation (Weil 1998).

Even though Friedman's proposal was rejected by the public in a time of increased government spending following Roosevelt's reforms, it would return with a vengeance in the late 1980s and early 1990s when the ideology of privatization and its private and public think tanks and advocates convinced Americans to define less government with economic and social superiority. The conservative proposal for educational reform would find currency and expression in these later decades and directly give rise to the development of privatization, public choice, and charter schools as educational reform movements. The proposal would prove to be one of the biggest and most controversial issues in U.S. politics at the beginning of the twenty-first century and the beginning of what can only be described as an "educational industry."

The importance of the post–World War II era in education is significant for any understanding of the current debates regarding public schools and, specifically, charter schools. Issues regarding states' rights, race, market initiatives, the role of government, and "failing U.S. schools," so predominant in the educational discourse of the 1950s, encompassed some of the identical topics and questions that the educational community has to deal with today. The development of the charter school reform movement must be understood as a direct outgrowth of the issues that faced the United States as a nation in the 1950s and those that continue to haunt and spawn educational debate today. It is not some historical aberration but in the alternative, must be seen as an extension of historical debates and current historical reality.

THE 1960s AND THE POLITICS OF EDUCATION

If the United States experienced conformity in the 1950s, the 1960s were anything but conventional. Changes in educational policy during the 1960s and issues that composed the debate over educational purpose and access must be situated and understood within the context of the political activism and resistance that marked the decade. Antiwar demonstrations, the civil rights movement, boycotts, the emergence of the gay movement in 1969, multiculturalism, feminism, assassinations of political leaders, and multiple marches on Washington, D.C., all worked directly to change the conception of the United States and the consciousness of its citizens. The decade of the 1960s was also to have a dramatic and far-reaching impact on educational issues and schooling.

Probably the most important political event of the 1960s was the passage of the Civil Rights Act in 1964. Not only did passage of the act guarantee African Americans access to all public facilities, it empowered the U.S. government to assure compliance with the act by authorizing it to bring suit against any institution or local government body that discriminated. According to estimates, almost 99 percent of black students in the eleven southern states were in segregated schools at the time the act was passed (Orfield 1969, 45), and schools that remained segregated were now to be stripped of any federal aid. The government played a direct and active role in the reconstitution of educational opportunity and access.

Another legislative enactment of consequence in the 1960s was the passage of the Elementary and Secondary Education Act in 1965. Signed into law by President Lyndon Johnson as part of the war on poverty, the act provided another nail in the coffin for segregated schools by bringing even more African Americans into the mainstream of public schooling. This act, as we saw in chapter 3 was amended, or in the eyes of many decimated, to create the No Child Left Behind Act.

With the fight over desegregation often being a violent one, the Supreme Court was once again forced to act when it decided in the case of *Green v. City School Board* in 1968. The issue involved so-called freedom-of-choice plans that had been adopted in some southern areas as a way of avoiding desegregation. The *Green* decision outlawed these schemes as barriers to desegregation, further assuring that schools would be desegregated in accordance with the *Brown* decision. Once again, the notion of choice was to become a major factor in the educational and political arenas. The historical times were controversial to say the least, and the rise of the moral majority would have long-standing implications.

In the late 1950s and the decade of the 1960s, there was an increasingly desegregated school system in the United States and immense changes in public education, especially in the South. For the first time, African Americans were allowed to attend public schools with whites, albeit at times under the protection of National Guard troops. Universal access to education was hatched from the struggle for equality and justice on behalf of African Americans, white anti-apartheid activists, members of labor unions, students, feminists, and other groups.

There were also intense debates over school curriculum in the 1960s, the subjects of which could never be covered here. Yet the roots of what is currently termed as "the multicultural movement" in education lie in the radical challenges put forth by progressive educational forces in the DuBois-Washington debates in the early century, Dewey-Lippmann debates of the 1920s, and the racial struggles of the 1960s and early 1970s. The movement toward a multicultural curriculum originated largely from the country's culturally subjugated and marginalized citizens, such as African Americans, Mexican Americans, Native Americans, and women. Multicultural proponents criticized the schools for practices of discrimination in the admission of people of color; they condemned the academic establishment for its subservience to business interests at the expense of an informed citizenry; they reprimanded the schools for their racist, sexist, and culturally biased curricula; they objected to the hiring practices for women and minorities; and they exposed and condemned the practice of tracking, placing students on hierarchical tracks or levels of learning and opportunity, usually in accordance with social class and race or ethnicity. They lambasted the curriculum for its claim of neutrality and "objectivity," and they labored assiduously for the passage of beneficial entitlement programs such as bilingual education and Title VII–mandated educational programs.

Multiculturalists argued that a lack of understanding and an acceptance of racial differences were recognized problems for both teachers and students (Stent, Hazard, and Rivlin 1973, 73). From within the multicultural educational community there were calls to directly address issues of prejudice and discrimination in the classroom curricula. Multicultural theorists posited that schools should not seek to do away with cultural differences within our pluralistic society but instead should celebrate those differences in an atmosphere of educational inquiry. Therefore, they pointed out, schools should be oriented toward the cultural enrichment of all students though programs aimed at the preservation and extension of cultural pluralism. They put forth the idea that cultural diversity was a valuable resource that should be recognized, preserved, and extended, and they argued that only by directly confronting racism and prejudice could society ensure an understanding and appreciation for human dignity. Dewey's progressivism and DuBois's vision of education for liberation reached their apexes in the 1960s and early 1970s and threatened to reopen the debate over education and educational priorities; threatening the elite notion of education and reclaiming public responsibility, racial equality, gender equality, class equality, and an informed participatory citizenry as the goal of education.

The movements and educational struggles of the 1960s and early 1970s produced a new vocabulary of educational critique, one at odds with the managerial elite rhetoric of the twentieth century. "Democracy," "education for citizenship," "plurality," "equal access regardless of class or race" replaced the market managerial doublespeak of "efficiency, conformity and obedience." There was no talk of "CEOs" as protagonists of reform and in fact the notion was disdained as an intrusion by business elites into the ideology of educational purpose. Coupled with the critiques of schooling clothed in newly coined "vocabularies of liberation," were calls for the "abolition of inequality" in school financing and for a commitment to "federal funding" for educational programs for and to the benefit of all. The struggle for universal access, changes in the curriculum, and the passage of social legislation in the 1960s profoundly changed public education in the United States and gave new currency to progressive calls for a democratic educational purpose that had started with DuBois and Dewey. Old progressive arguments and positions regarding the role and purposes of education that had been silenced by the cold war of the 1950s began to reemerge in the national controversy regarding education. Democracy in learning was now on the rise and the role of "education" and "schooling" in America was subject to constructive critique.

It must be understood that all these phenomenal social and personal changes evident in the late 1900s produced a formidable American public seeking a national identity, which itself was under reconsideration, as diversity and an understanding and appreciation of differences became intense objects of controversy and debate, especially in universities, which at the time were sites of militancy and resistance. During the controversial years of the 1960s and early 1970s, the seeds that would eventually develop into the charter school reform movement were sown. Postmodernism, with its emphasis on difference, decentralization, devolution, and identity politics, would begin to affect the way Americans thought about education, what they expected from it, and how they would choose to organize, fund, and support it. But these philosophies and subsequently communicated ideologies were not existent in isolation: Capturing the public sentiment in regards to "competition" and education was the agenda of powerful business interests intent on commodifying education, turning it into a product, for eventual "sale" to the American public.

PRIVATIZATION, MARKETS, CONSERVATISM, AND POLITICS OF EDUCATION

In the 1970s, the National Education Association (NEA), the nation's largest teachers' union, endorsed a candidate for president of the United States for the first time. Jimmy Carter received the endorsement of this union in his bid for presidency in 1976 mainly because of his expressed intent to establish a cabinet-level Department of Education. The NEA had lobbied for such a national cabinet position since World War I, and with the union's endorsement, Carter was finally able to raise education to the cabinet level in 1979.

Although Carter proved to be more conservative than many observers had expected from an "education president," there is little doubt that Ronald Reagan, Carter's successor, left a lasting conservative ideological stamp on public education in the United States, far more thought out and understood than the complacent Carter administration. Considering the Department of Education an unnecessary expense and perceiving of it as opposed to states' rights, Reagan sought to radically propose the abolishment of the Department of Education directly after he took office in 1981. Invoking the rhetoric of free-market enterprise and the logic of market-driven forces as the panacea to the country's social and economic troubles and blaming public education for its lackluster role, Reagan and his administration embarked on restructuring social policy, including education, to reflect the primacy of market solutions to public problems (Lugg 1996). Education became part and parcel of a larger debate over the role of government, privatization, government regulations and oversight, and the promises of "free market" capitalism.

All of this was part and parcel of new economic configurations that were changing the world as of the late 1970s. These new economic programs of deregulation, privatization, and the withdrawal of the government from many areas of social provision that had been gained during the Roosevelt era and the Great Society of the 1960s could be felt not just here at home, but in Thatcher's Britain, Chile's "liberalization of markets" and in the new emerging China. This particular doctrine which goes under the name "privatization" reigned, and has now firmly placed itself within the economic, cultural, and social framework of our times. Charter schools must be understood within this new public privatization policy paradigm shift from traditional public education toward private choice within the economic market.

Privatization and the Rise of "Choice"

In the first instance, privatization of education through choice postulates that human well-being can best be achieved allowing citizen choices within an economic system based on entrepreneurial freedoms and skills articulated within an institutional framework based on strong private property rights, free markets, and open trade. The role of the government is to assure the stable institutional framework appropriate to such practices. Furthermore, the role of the government, or what is called "the state" in economic parlance, is to assure that the legal structures and clerical and day-to-day functions required by such a societal commitment to property rights and market freedom based on the entrepreneurial spirit are guaranteed. If the markets that are required under the theory of economic privatization do not exist then it is the role of the state to assure they do, by privatizing key industries and services such as health care, land rights, water rights and yes, the privatization of education through market "choices" and deregulation and economic and political legislation. Thus, any argument conservative or otherwise regarding the abolition of "state or government power" or the "role of government" is plainly contradictory for what a private economic market needs is a strong state to assure the supremacy of its economic ideology and practices. So when critics argue public schools are bureaucratically wasteful and that charter schools, especially those run by for-profit companies, can come in and cut the waste, the claim must be subjected to rigorous questioning and scrutiny. Quite frankly, the growth of charter schools has meant more bureaucracy, not less.

Ron Corwin, professor emeritus in sociology at Ohio State University and Joseph Schneider, senior fellow at the National Policy Board for Educational Administration in Washington, D.C. sum up the reasons why charter schools are and will inevitably require more bureaucracy: the demand for more oversight regarding admission policies, funding, information, transportation, and daily requirements of running schools will require bureaucracy; the introduction and recruitment of new clientele will require more rules and administrators to enforce them as many charters try to reach a broader market than they currently have; program expansion will require more bureaucracy as parents demand more educational offerings at the charter schools their children currently attend, more specialization as parents demand specialty subjects and specialty charter schools which is what is happening now, as well as more additional costs for everything from school materials to teacher salaries. All of this will require clerical work, staff, and a coordinated center or bureaucracy. And this will become more and truer as many charter school companies either merge or acquire new localities and thus new students and parents they must serve. The issue is not "bureaucracy versus no bureaucracy," the question at issue is more basic: who will control the bureaucracy, for what purposes, and who is it designed to serve?

Privatization advances market exchanges as a theory for the smooth and efficient running of society and as such, it also provides an overreaching ethic or morality that claims that market solutions to social problems will maximize the public good and thus it seeks to bring all institutions and indeed, all actors within the reach if not under the control of market transactions. Therefore, the role of the state under these stated specific economic policies is to produce legislative and regulatory frameworks that advantage private corporations, wealthy individuals, and the property class. There can be no argument that the government does not play a role in educational policy and subsequent services; the only issue is "why and how." And as one can see, this is done in myriad ways that currently advantage the privatization agenda.

Nowhere can the claims and assumptions of those advancing the privatization of schools be seen more dramatically than in the calls for the elimination of the Department of Education throughout the 1980s, which was met with severe resistance by progressive and liberal educators. The vocal opposition and activism on behalf of many teachers, their unions, and parents and students made it virtually impossible for certain conservatives to abolish the department in entirety, which was their hope. As a result, the Reagan administration sought to use state regulatory and legislative power, the government, to reconstitute the Department of Education, transforming it into a vocal advocate for controversial policies like organized prayer, public and private school choice, charter schools, and private school vouchers. Privatization and deregulation combined with competition and "choice," so the claim went, would eliminate bureaucratic red tape, eliminate inefficiency in services, increase productivity (in this case student standardized test scores), and reduce costs (wages and benefits paid to teachers).

As a result, blistering attacks and recriminations were increasingly leveled by proponents of the market-based privatization theory against public education, teachers' school management, unions, and nonstandardized curriculum. The Department of Education actually began in this period to actively work against the interests of the educational stakeholders in the public schools by promoting a new economic agenda for schools. The battle between the ideas of competition—competition between individuals, schools, teachers, firms, entities, and in fact in all areas of economic and social life within the market-place—and those of progressive ideas that valued cooperation and education for citizenship was now in full formation; but the institutional voice box had changed. Now the Department of Education, which was set up to assure education to all citizens, was quietly and slowly being transformed, though public policy changes and changes in personnel, in ways that would serve in effect to undermine the goals and aspirations of public education in the United States.

In 1983, the best-publicized educational achievement of the Reagan administration was issued in the form of a book-length report entitled *A Nation at Risk.* Issued by the National Commission on Excellence in Education (NCEE), the report provided a scathing critique of the public education system, arguing that U.S. education had become a bastion of mediocrity. The report concluded that the state of education in the United States was actually threatening the nation's future economic growth. With its dire predictions and warnings, *A Nation at Risk* once again focused public attention on the issue of education as an economic issue, and as educational urgency took on market proportions, progressive educational concerns were not considered a priority. The controversy regarding improvement in U.S. education was now firmly attached to the perceived need to link the country's readiness to educational standards and school performance based on privatization theories of the role of the government or state, and the economy and its competitive actors. This aim was to be best accomplished, in the eyes of conservative politicians and their constituencies, in a free and unbridled marketplace. The failure of public education and "government schools" became favorite topics for those who now proposed market solutions to educational problems and educational institutions and management arrangements. The language had shifted from one of "public interest," so important for Dewey, to one of "managerial excellence through market forces," a notion close to the heart of Lippmann.

After *A Nation at Risk* was released in 1983, scores of magazines and news reports jumped on the supercharged privatization bandwagon and concentrated their stories on the supposed "failure of public education." For instance, *Newsweek* rushed a scathing story to press asking if the schools could be saved, and the sum of the report was that progress from generation to generation was being "shattered" by the mediocre condition of the U.S. schools ("Saving Our Schools," 1983). Responsibility for the economic recession that plagued the United States during the early 1980s was placed squarely on the public educational system. Public education was no longer cast as an expression and vehicle for economic excellence, citizenship requirements, and national security but instead was now looked at as an actual inhibiter of economic growth (Shor 1986, 108). Like the *Sputnik* scare decades earlier, *A Nation at Risk* sounded a wake-up call to educators and policymakers, but this time the call was not for an improved public educational system, but for a private one. This time, instead of Soviet superiority in outer space, it was the influx of quality goods from Japan that was to be considered the threat to national security. It was argued that the ability of the United States to compete globally was being jeopardized by a public educational system that simply did not work and leashed markets instead of allowing them to operate relatively free from regulation by the state. Proponents of privatization and free-market solutions to educational crises began to emerge almost overnight, with conservative think tanks and entrepreneurial largess and funding that had not existed before. The media, the government, educational policymakers, and conservative think tanks all joined forces in portraying education in America as a looming failure that needed to undergo market-based surgery.

To build the case for a mediocre school system, the NCEE turned to an analysis of Scholastic Aptitude Test (SAT) scores to make its point. The NCEE pointed to the long SAT score decline from 1963 to 1980, and it also began to publicly compare U.S. education to other Western school systems. Playing to a sense of political patriotism and economic nationalism, *A Nation at Risk* pointed out that the United States would continue to be a preeminent country only so long as material benefits and great ideas remained a part of the country's legacy and argued that the nation's national security was in jeopardy as long as public schools threatened this legacy.

In June 1983, another report, entitled *Action for Excellence: A Comprehensive Plan to Improve our Nation's Schools,* was published by a state governors' group called the Education Commission of the States (ECS). Often referred to as the Hunt Report, after Governor James B. Hunt of North Carolina, this report continued to echo the notion that U.S. schools were failing (Education Commission of the States 1983, 3).

The alarms did not stop with the Hunt Report. The next major statement regarding the state of public education was issued in September 1983 in a National Science Board (NSB) report. In its dramatic work *Educating Americans for the 21st Century,* the NSB warned that

> . . . the nation that dramatically and boldly led the world into the age of technology is failing to provide its own children with the intellectual tools needed for the 21st century . . . Already the quality of our manufactured products, the viability of our trade, our leadership in research and development, our standard of living, are strongly challenged. Our children could be stragglers in a world of technology. We must not let this happen; America must not become an industrial dinosaur. We must not provide our children a 1960's education for the 21st century world. (National Science Board 1983, 9)

The exigencies of education were once again being linked to the nation's competitive economic readiness, or lack of it. And this fit nicely with the new economic privatization, now firmly entering the public stage.

In the 1980s, not only was the public's obsession with everything private fueled but the case for a super-functionalism was built. Instead of the rudimentary skills required by the social functionalism that arose during the time of industrialization, the new information and technological revolution that was taking place needed a different type of worker with different kinds of skills. Preparing students for the twenty-first century's technological and cybernetic revolution, or "the third wave," became the mantra of reports similar to *A Nation at Risk.* Calls to focus education on "back to basics" became the antidote for the economic crisis, similar to the "objectives first" clamor in the early 1900s. The NSB defined the new cognitive-economic relationship between school and work as follows:

Alarming numbers of young Americans are ill-equipped to work in, to contribute to, profit from and enjoy our increasingly technological society. Far too many emerge from the nation's elementary and secondary schools with an inadequate grounding in mathematics, science, and technology. This situation must not continue . . . We must return to the basics, but the "basics" of the 21st century are not only reading, writing, and arithmetic. They include communication, and higher problem-solving skills, and scientific and technological literacy. (National Science Board 1983, 12)

The superfunctionalism and new basics, now defined as "ultrabasics," included science, computers, higher-order reasoning, social studies, foreign languages, and correct use of the English language. What were once thought to be basic skills were now obsolete, and schools were now to place the ultrabasics at the core of their curriculum. While "the second wave" of educational restructuring was established for the industrial age of the 1900s, "the third wave" restructuring movement of the 1980s focused on preparing students for the information/technology age.

The educator Larry Hutchins expressed the new third-wave superfunctionalist restructuring argument like this:

The old design [schools] worked relatively well for the society it served; it brought schooling to millions of immigrants [who] . . . were needed to stoke the engines of the industrial society. Today's society no longer requires such a work force. We need people who can think and solve problems using information and technology. (Hutchins 1990, 1)

Maintaining the U.S. "empire," creating better goods and services to do so, dominating world markets under the guise of competition, and creating the new workforce of the future were all interwoven into the calls for a new and radical restructuring of schools. Any discussions as to what type of society Americans wished to create or the relationships among school, democracy, culture, and the emerging cybernetic society were conspicuously absent from these discussions and, if it was discussed, conservative think tanks quickly mobilized the media in an attempt to convince the public of the superefficiency of the privatization model. Furthermore, much like the efficiency-of-production arguments of the industrial age, teachers were encouraged to develop curricular goals based on step-by-step procedures and time schedules that corresponded to "the schools of tomorrow" (Goodman 1995, 10). The superfunctionalism was now itself a business, offering schools and teachers corporate educational solutions in the form of kits, packages, services, and products. As we shall see, this entrepreneurialism was to later be codified in the repeal of the Elementary and Secondary Education Act in favor of a new national policy, No Child Left Behind.

With the advent of free-market theory in cultural and public life, during the 1980s the educational reform movement once again increasingly found expression in a language of business efficiency, productivity, and the application of management theories to the educational enterprise. More than at any other time, test scores became the products of the schools. Students became the workers who created this product using instructional programs given to them by "the educational organization." Teachers were transformed into shop managers who presided over the students' production within the confines of the "new curriculum"; school principals became the plant managers or "CEOs" who managed the school personnel and assured the functioning of the clerical aspect of education; and specialists, such as social workers or school counselors, were employed to handle the students' emotional needs (Goodman 1995, 11).

Transformed into being classroom managers overseeing the student-workers, teachers became further disengaged and divorced from the nature of teaching as they were galvanized to follow prescribed "teaching recipes" in the form of corporate produced, preformulated lesson plans. With the increasing rise of prepackaged instructional materials in the 1980s, intellectual engagement with the curriculum had now become for many teachers a luxury, as they were transformed into mere managers of learning in service to the state tests. For many of these teachers, charter schools offered an attractive way to escape these educational prescriptions for learning and to re-conceive of education as an act of creativity rather than one of constraint. For many teachers, charter schools offered a way out of a depersonalized system and convened a semblance of hope in the prospects of developing personalized learning, innovative teaching, and deeper and more meaningful associations.

SCHOOL CHOICE AND THE POLITICS OF THE CHARTER MOVEMENT

The development of a new educational discourse of business productivity and efficiency in the 1980s set the stage for the current educational controversies that would mark the beginning of the twenty-first century. As the United States exited the 1980s, unregulated capitalist markets and corporate globalization monopolized mainstream thinking and created a psychology of privatization that determined that market-driven solutions offered the remedy to all social problems, private or public, economists and pundits warned that the United States should concentrate on market solutions to human problems if it were to compete vigorously in the global arena. Unregulated educational markets and the privatization of education were seen by a vocal group of economists and social planners as an advantage for all those interested in the notion of American progress and institutional reform.

With the fall of the Soviet Union in 1991, this vision of the United States, a country with unregulated markets and a capitalist hegemony, became the primary vision for education as well. Not only were public schools continually perceived as failing and mediocre, the argument now began to pose the possibility that these public schools would better serve the country's citizens if they were forced to compete with schools that were privatized. As the argument went, schools need to develop students the way corporations develop products. School choice proponents now claimed that the government should provide vouchers to pay for the schooling students or their parents wished them to have. The idea, claimed voucher adherents, was that private and public schools could then compete for the most academically able students. The schools that did not prepare students for the emerging information/technology-driven market in an efficient manner would lose out to a "natural selection" imposed by privatized economic policies (Kincheloe 2000, 171). Friedman's forty-year-old proposal for privatized education had now found a suitable political environment within which to stew and it eventually developed into a fait accompli.

For the first time, in a real way, the notion of public education itself was being questioned by a new generation of super, social functionalists and free-market economists. And while the majority of educational discussions and debates in the past had focused on how to bring the country's public school system up to speed, the new superfunctionalist arguments actually questioned the very efficacy, existence, and necessity of public schools. Education was now being conceived of as an "educational marketplace" and a new language of "choice" began to emerge to define the terms of the debate. Progressive educational concerns regarding the role of democracy, equity, and social justice were purged from educational discourse in favor, once more, of competitiveness, efficiency, and productivity needs. The new rhetoric of privatized schooling and "choice" defined the terms of the debate and Americans, in a very real way, were now embroiled in a controversy over the continued existence of public education itself.

The charter school proposal in many ways is a turning point in educational discourse. Charter schools bring up issues of individual choice and actually question whether the nation can really hope to achieve, or any longer even want, a common public school experience. Yet, just as charter schools offer new challenges and possibilities, they reflect the evolutionary compilation of historical arguments and disagreements over not simply the economic life of a country, but the nature of American schools, what they are supposed to accomplish, how they will be organized, who they will serve, and what they will teach. The entire notion of modernism and the factory school is now being called into question. The current reality seems to favor some form of decentralization and looks to challenging large public institutions that claim to universally serve all citizens. Lippmann, if he were alive today would be both amused and more adamant, for once again he would mostly likely cling to the claim that there is no real "public interest or public opinion" that education can serve.

MARKET-BASED SOLUTIONS AND THE POLITICS OF SCHOOL CHOICE

The market-based social and economic policies begun in the 1970s and which found their nesting ground during the 1980s, postulated that the whole idea of school choice in the United States was associated with free markets, choice, competition, and individualism. Many political and educational policymakers insisted that the government should exist only to guarantee and preserve individual liberty, and of course free up regulation for private profit. Motivated by the belief that public education was antithetical to the public interest and a free market was the best way to organize education for all the nation's citizens, many conservatives embraced private choice as a way of dismantling public education in its entirety (Rinehart and Lee 1991). The private choice argument that had not caught the public's attention in the 1950s now found a willing audience in a shifting political environment in which many people had lost confidence in anything public, including public education. Private and public choice was now a major policy issue for schools.

The strongest academic voices for private choice in education have been John Chubb and Terry Moe. In their book *Politics, Markets, and American Schools,* Chubb and Moe devoted their analysis to demonstrating that private choice would enhance student achievement. Published by the Brookings Institute in 1990, their book helped to move the argument for private choice and educational vouchers out of the conservative camp and into the mainstream. More important, the book was the first attempt to ground support for privatized choice in scholarly terms (Chubb and Moe 1990).

Chubb's and Moe's analysis went so far as to argue that private choice itself "has the capacity all by itself to bring about the kind of transformation that, for years, reforms have been seeking to engineer in a myriad of ways" (Chubb and Moe 1990, 217). According to these two authors, allowing parents and educational consumers to have a "choice" in the kind of school they want their children to attend would fix what is wrong with U.S. education by providing competition. It would also give those parents better resources to find an educational marketplace in which "the human capital" of their children could be developed at higher levels. Chubb and Moe's argument, then, reasoned that public schools should be forced to compete with private schools for tax dollars. Not only should parents have the right to choose, they argued, it was choice itself that would fix the schools. The answer was the Friedman proposal of 1955: allow parents to receive a voucher they could use to buy a quality education for their children. For Chubb and Moe, the argument was simple: students, not schools, should receive public funds in the form of vouchers.

The underlying assumption behind the private voucher proposal is the claim that allowing parents the freedom to act as rational educational consumers with the ability to take their business elsewhere if dissatisfied with the level of education their children are receiving will force all schools to increase their efficiency. Schools that do not, private choice claimants argue, will risk extinction.

Market advocates for school reform maintain that students are consumers of education as a product, much like they are of athletic shoes or designer clothing. According to voucher advocates, education needs to be treated as a purchase that parents and their children make in the educational marketplace. Only by reducing education to individual choice, maintain private choice advocates, can meaningful educational reform take place. But do these forces really wish to "reform" public education through "choice" or is their goal more ambitious, to wage a bidding war for our kids and in the process replace public education with charter contract chains, privatization schemes, prepackaged curriculum, vouchers and other measures aimed at undermining public education? In the 1930s when similar but different public policy economic battles were engaged in by the American people, Walton Hale Hamilton perhaps summed it best:

> *Business succeeds rather better than the state in imposing restraints upon individuals, because its imperatives are disguised as 'choices.'* (Hamilton 1934, 10)

Is "choice" the answer to what ails American schools?

THE EMERGENCE OF PUBLIC CHOICE IN THE 1990s

The controversy over choice took distinct and particular forms as the 1990s progressed. In many ways, public choice was embraced by many liberals as a concept to head off the movement for the complete privatization of schools through private vouchers. But in a more significant way, the call for public choice also reflected changing global political and socioeconomic realities.

Public choice is part of a historical evolution: an evolution from modernism, characterized in the United States by the rise of industrialism, to postmodernism, or the developing cybernetic revolution in information and technology. As production and consumption are being redefined with the advent of the computer and post-assembly-line approaches to work, the notion of a national identity as one single identity is currently being questioned. Diversity is now a secure part of the country's ideological character, and cultural differences; class differences; ethnic differences; and ideological, religious, and philosophical differences are now leading many people to question the entire notion of a universal system of public education. And with rapid changes in consumption and production, the factory-school model of education is being called into question as it pertains to its ability to serve new levels of human development—both technological and social.

The modern epoch of education, the historical period between the Renaissance and the late twentieth century, occurred during a shifting emphasis from an agrarian society to an industrial society. Although modernity was synonymous with industrialization and the shift from the first wave (agrarian production) to the second wave (industrial production), the current socioeconomic and political global reality is characterized by rapid cybernetic changes in the way Americans and the people in other societies now produce and consume. Postmodernism, and the actual existing state of capitalism, now represent a shift from the second wave (industrialism) to the third wave (cybernetic/technological revolution). Throughout the world, these changes have sparked what appear to be new controversies over the challenges that face schools, and the result has been an emphasis on school choice in hundreds of countries throughout the world, not just the United States (Whitty, Power, and Halpin 1998).

Public school choice promises to be many things to many different people, and it therefore represents a very complex and unique educational reform movement—one that must be analyzed and understood as a "moving mosaic" (Hargreaves 1994). Even though different groups that support charter schools may experience intense dissatisfaction with the state-run educational process, they also have very different reasons for their frustration and dissatisfaction. For many diverse groups and for many different reasons, the charter school idea, or public school choice, offers distinct advantages. Furthermore, many parents, teachers, students, and educational policymakers who support public school choice and the charter movement do so with a heavy commitment to public schools in general. They look at public school choice, and specifically charter schools, as a way to strengthen the nation's commitment to public education. They are against privatized choice, which they believe is an attack on public schools, but are in favor of public choice as a reform measure for restructuring schools.

Deborah Meier, educational reformer and founder of the Central Park East Elementary School in New York City, explained the important distinction between privatized choice and public choice this way:

There are two unrelated perspectives, and they both use the word choice. When many conservatives talk about choice, they mean that private enterprise and the marketplace are better and that public institutions are, by their very nature, inferior. We need to dismiss the idea that the concept of choice has anything to do with such proposals. They are not about choice at all. They are about privatization and a means to get rid of public education. . . . When I have argued for choice, it has had nothing to do with abandoning public education. It has been a way to argue against the factory model of education. (Meier 1996, 101)

For many public choice advocates, charter schools can be enthusiastically welcomed precisely because they appear to promise to protect public education as an institution while at the same time provide opportunities for fundamental restructuring and reform. Arguably this was the position taken by California, Senator Gary Hart when in the 1990s at the time of the great emergence of charter schools he sponsored the California Charter schools project, putting it this way:

. . . the tradeoff has always been outcomes versus deregulation. And if we can't demonstrate the outcomes, we're not entitled to the deregulation. (Hart 2004)

And because the vast majority of U.S. students will continue to attend public schools, the argument continues, they should have the same kind of choice that students in private schools enjoy (Young and Clinchy 1992).

COMPETITION AND SCHOOL CHOICE: RISING TIDE LIFTS ALL BOATS?

Whether choice is looked at as an opportunity or as a disaster, the most commonly held rationale behind the choice argument, public or private, is that competition provides the best or most efficient motor for change and reform. The premise of the contention is similar to the private voucher argument, that traditional public schools (TPSs) can be best improved by competitive market mechanisms. Like private choice, the public choice rationale maintains that all public schools as well as all student-learning improve when the public schools have to compete for students and students and their parents have the right to choose. Historically, according to its staunchest advocates, public school choice is not simply about one particular charter school or another as much as it is about raising the educational standards of all public schools. However, as we shall see this is rarely the argument given for charter schools today. Today the large players in the charter school movement have little or no interest in competition as they seek to suck up the charter market in as many states as possible. However at one time this was the argument mouthed by advocates.

Ted Kolderie, a leading charter school adherent, stated the goals of competition this way more than a decade ago:

For those who enact the laws it is to create dynamics that will cause the mainline district system (school) to change and to improve. The charter schools, helpful as they may be to the students who enroll in them, are instrumental. (Kolderie 1998, 4)

The Hudson Institute agreed around that time, noting that "the whole point of charter schools is to answer today's call for bold school reform by injecting freedom, choice and accountability into school systems and thereby providing a better education for America's children" (Vanourek et al. 1997, 23). Joe Nathan, a charter school advocate and organizer, echoes similar sentiments:

> *The charter idea is not just about the creation of new, more accountable public schools or the conversion of existing public schools. The charter idea also introduces fair, thoughtful competition into public education. Strong charter laws allow these schools to be sponsored by more than one type of public organization, for example, a local school board, a state school board, or a public university. Evidence shared later shows that when school districts know families can get a public education from more than one source, that competition helps produce improvements. (Nathan 1999, xxviii)*

Yet not all public policymakers and educational theoreticians would agree. Some educational policymakers argue that competition through choice, whether it is public or private, undermines a shared citizenship in U.S. society and is little more than a cleverly designed slippery slope to individualized, privatized education. The lack of a common educational leadership, opponents maintain, helps ensure that the argument for charter schools is dominated, not by educational ideas, but by economic necessity (Molnar 1996, 5). Protesting against competition and in favor of cooperation, these educators claim that the concept of choice threatens the community and shared citizenship necessary for the realization of democracy and democratic citizenship, ideas that go back to John Dewey. Asserting that competitive, individual choice supplants shared decision making, educational policy groups such as the *Carnegie Foundation for the Advancement of Teaching* reason that the Darwinian market mechanism of choice used to weed out the weakest schools in fact exacerbates inequities among districts (Carnegie Foundation for the Advancement of Teaching 1992). It does so, claim opponents, because when students move out of their district to one charter school or another, they take the funding from their own district with them. If the new district has a higher per-pupil cost, the move means that the home district, which is often already suffering from low funding, pays far more to educate the transfer students, which leaves even less for those that remain behind. The districts that begin with fewer resources are left with even fewer with which to educate their own students.

As far back as 2000, Howard Koenig, a former superintendent of schools in Roosevelt, New York, expressed the concern that charter schools in the State of New York would drain off millions from their districts and will lead to tax hikes and program cost increases. He and other superintendents joined with some parents and unions to oppose charter school legislation. Les Black, superintendent of Brentwood schools in New York State estimated his district had lost $1 million as a result of New York charter schools that have recently been approved. According to Black, "There's precious little research on charter schools" (Pratt 2000). Thus, the Carnegie Foundation argues, "If fair competition is to occur, all states with 'choice' programs must first resolve the financial disparities that exist from district to district" (Pratt 2000, 20). If Koenig was right then and correct now, this leaves problems for charter school advocates for as we will see, financial disparities abound and are even worse than at the time Koenig was superintendent.

And of course the argument brings up the question of school funding in its entirety: how schools are subsidized and whether we want to continue the practice of funding our public schools mainly through local property taxes as an expression of our commitment as a nation to the education of our children. Many politicians and educational policymakers argue that the chances that the market and competition will create educational opportunities and options for all parents are limited by the current financing mechanisms employed to subsidize the public schools, not to mention the growing inequality and class stratification in American society. And, they maintain, without equity in funding, charter schools will do little to correct the state of education in the United States, in fact as we will examine, they may make the situation worse. They also claim that if freeing the charter schools from burdensome regulation and reams of legal considerations works, then why are these same freedoms not offered to the traditional public schools? How can public schools compete, they ask, if they must continue to operate under regulations and restrictions that the charter schools can simply avoid?

The issue of educational equity is paramount to numerous educational interests and certain policymakers see public school choice as a way to accelerate what is already an inequitable situation. In a study of small, private Catholic schools, Anthony Bryk and Valerie Lee noted:

> *Market forces, for example, cannot explain the broadly shared institutional purpose of advancing social equity. Nor can they account for the efforts of Catholic educators to maintain inner-city schools (with large non-Catholic enrollments) while facing mounting fiscal woes. Likewise, market forces cannot easily explain why resources are allocated within schools in a compensatory fashion in order to provide an academic education for every student. Nor can they explain the norms of community that infuse daily life in these schools. (Bryk and Lee 1993, 11)*

For educators like Bryk and Lee, the answer to providing quality education lies with developing a higher notion of community, not simply pursuing naked self-interests through competitive choice. They also argue that the communal effects they noted in the Catholic schools they used as the object of their study were the result of face-to-face contacts and a sense of sharing and caring between teachers and students. They also claim that this communal experience is a result of a moral authority that results in a "set of shared beliefs about what students should learn, the development of proper norms of instruction, and how people should relate to one another" (Bryk and Lee 1993, 7).

Bryk and Lee's admonitions regarding the market's claim to provide quality community education through choice strike a chord with many other educational policymakers who are opposed to charter schools. The claim that the notion of public choice is built on the idea that society can be held together solely by the self-interested pursuits of individual actors in the educational arena is not palatable to many educational interests. In fact, many would argue charter schools themselves are Trojan horses for the real agenda of free-market economic policymakers—the creation of educational retail chains that can be run as "franchises" or charter schools by contract and serve to target students caught in the crosshairs of racial, gender and economic inequality, and discrimination. They dispute conservative claims, that they are interested in innovation for the purposes of strengthening public education in our nation and would instead argue that these market forces that have been unleashed seek to create markets and capital formation opportunities and are thus driven by profit and maximizing capital, not the needs of American children.

One leading opponent of charter schools and privatization, Jonathan Kozol, a Pulitzer Prize–winning educational author, argues that charter schools only isolate the privileged elite (Manetto 1999). For opponents like Kozol, the charter school idea, and public choice itself, represent a contemporary, postmodern rejection of the possibility of a common school for all citizens. As a result, he and many others argue, the idea threatens to turn the relationship between society and its educational needs, into little more than a commercial transaction based on individual self-interests and competitive self-advantage.

CHARTER SCHOOL SUPPORTERS

According to the U.S. Department of Education's Office of Innovation and Improvement:

> *The promise charter schools hold for public school innovation and reform lies in an unprecedented combination of freedom and accountability. Underwritten with public funds but run independently, charter schools are free from a range of state laws and district policies stipulating what and how they teach, where they can spend their money, and who they can hire and fire. In return, they are held strictly accountable for their academic and financial performance. (U.S. Department of Education, under "Office of Innovation and Improvement")*

The Office of Innovation and Improvement goes even further, claiming:

> *charter schools are free to: lengthen the school day, mix grades, require dress codes, put teachers on their school boards, double up instruction in core subject areas like math or reading, make parents genuine partners in family-style school cultures,*

adopt any instructional practice that will help achieve their missions—free, in short, to do whatever it takes to build the skills, knowledge, and character traits their students need to succeed in today's world.

By allowing citizens to start new public schools with this kind of autonomy, making them available tuition-free to any student, and holding them accountable for results and family satisfaction, proponents hope that this new mix of choice and accountability will not only provide students stronger learning programs than local alternatives, but will also stimulate improvement of the existing public education system. With charter schools, it is accountability that makes freedom promising. No charter is permanent; it must be renewed—or revoked—at regular intervals. Continued funding, which is tied to student enrollment, also depends on educational results. (Ibid.)

An interesting aspect of the current debate regarding charter schools is the variety of philosophies and positions that support the concept. The contemporary discussion about charter schools is unlike the earlier educational debates that marked the beginning of the twentieth century, debates in which progressive educators and social functionalists found themselves on distinct opposing sides of the controversy. With charter schools, the issue is far more complex, and its acceptance as an idea among a wide range of educational interests and communities is far more diverse, often creating unusual bedfellows.

The authorization of charter schools is different in each state where legislation has approved them and thus, some charters permit and even welcome an enormous variety of innovative educational approaches, though they support very traditional approaches as well. Some of the charter founders are idealistic education leaders with great new ideas, strong imaginations, and inexhaustible energy. Other charter founders are committed community activists who have struggled for decades to operate their own schools, or to serve only one group in a community. However, as we will see many are managed by private corporations that hope to reap a tidy profit from their educational operation. Finally, for many charter school founders, there is an implicit assumption that less government control and oversight will produce positive educational benefits.

Many progressive educators, in the tradition of Dewey, DuBois, and others, support charter schools, and they do so for several reasons. The Neighborhood House Charter School or the Freire School, two charter schools we examined in chapter 4, all try to work on a curriculum and environment that offers not just simple functional teaching, but also citizenship development and critical thinking both in how and what students are taught, to how parents can participate in the management and organizational decisions within the school and they challenge traditional assessment techniques. Although these schools are held hostage to state standardized tests by the No Child Left Behind Act, they work assiduously to create memorable and innovative curricula and strive to create a community of caring, a community of inquiry, and a community of civility.

These progressive educators, to begin with, question modernity itself, especially its emphasis on scientific and technical bureaucratic rationality at the expense of personal and social development. This questioning translates into curricular concerns about such issues as student-centered classrooms and logistical concerns such as length of the school day and how students learn and study. And as previously mentioned some people look to public choice and charter schools as a method of discouraging total privatization of schools—reasoning that allowing public choice will prevent the wholesale loss of public schools (Young and Clinchy 1992). Others, such as the educator Deborah Meier, look to the charter idea as a method of creating community schools that can experiment with creativity and innovation.

For many progressive educators, like Meier, charter schools offer an opportunity to break down factory schools and the factory style of education. The postmodern situation in this country's society provides an opportunity to create small, intimate schools and communities that organize their philosophies around curricula and teaching methods that encourage self-reflection and democratic citizenship. Breaking with the factory model of education completely, something that was never realized during the modernism of Dewey's period can now become a postmodern reality, and this fact, educators like Meier argue, will serve to raise the educational efficacy of all public schools.

Meier, like other progressives who support charter schools, make the assumption that public schools can be strengthened, not weakened, with the option of public choice. In her book The Power of Their Ideas, Meier makes a passionate plea for preserving and strengthening public education. She is also critical of many progressive educators who have dismissed public school choice:

> *Progressive policymakers and legislators have on the whole allowed their concern with equity to lead them to reflexively attack choice as inherently elitist (naturally, choice doesn't tend to make friends among educational bureaucrats either). This is, I believe, a grave mistake. The argument over choice, unlike the one over private school vouchers, offers progressives an opportunity. After all, it wasn't so long ago that progressive educators were enthusiastically supporting schools of choice, usually called alternative schools. These alternatives were always on the fringe, as though the vast majority of schools were doing just fine. We now have a chance to make such alternatives the mainstream, not just for avant-garde "misfits" or "nerds" or "those more at risk." (Meier 1995, 92–93)*

Meier and her supporters insist that successful experiments in public education—innovation and creativity—are the result of expanded choices and the diversity in experimentation that public choice brings. The factory-style school that dominates U.S. education, they argue, is not inevitable but historical, and public choice allows for new and innovative challenges to this concept. Further, Meier displays her exasperation with people who dismiss public choice by noting that many concerned policymakers and progressives who are dead set against choice because of its impact on equity are already exercising choice for their own children. While arguing against public choice, these progressives are either sending their children to private schools, moving to more-affluent communities where the schools tend to be better, taking whatever necessary means they need to take to make sure that their children qualify for gifted programs, or selecting specialized schools (Meier 1995, 99). According to Meier, "What we must do is shape the concept of choice into a consciously equitable instrument for restructuring public education so that over time all parents can have the kinds of choices the favored few now have, but in ways that serve rather than undercut public goals" (Meier 1995, 99).

Deborah Meier is not alone in embracing public school choice. Many other progressive educational policymakers find that public school choice offers the educational community, parents, teachers, administrators, students, and community members the chance to achieve greater parental and community control over schools. In some inner cities, charter schools have had tremendous neighborhood involvement and appear to have been a source of revitalized community participation in local schools (Rofes 1996, 50–51).

Also, many parents and teachers support charter schools because of curriculum concerns. Some members of minority communities as well as many women argue that traditional schools are focused on narrow conceptions of valued knowledge based on Eurocentric and patriarchal notions of intelligence, and certain educators claim that teachers fail to match their instruction to the cultural backgrounds of their students. They criticize a litany of educational practices for failing to offer multicultural experiences to students, and, as a result, they argue, marginalized groups, such as African Americans, often must work with a curriculum that fails to reflect their lives, values, needs, and cultural distinctions (Tyack 1993). For many low-income and minority families, charter schools offer a way to legitimize their knowledge and celebrate their cultural backgrounds by developing curricula around cultural and/or ethnic identity. The Urban Prep Charter Academy for Young Men, the charter school we looked at in chapter 4, certainly can be said to be concerned with such issues. And the rise of single gender charter schools is a response to curriculum concerns as well.

Many charter school advocates promote centricity in their curriculum goals, such as Afro-centricity or Mexican-centricity. They want their students to have a greater knowledge and appreciation of their cultural history. The movement to begin charter schools is a uniquely postmodern movement and involves fighting for independence from what they believe to be a state-controlled system of oppression (Wells et al. 1999).

And then there are millions of homeschooling advocates of all persuasions who also favor the notion of public choice and charter schools because charter schools actually enable them to withdraw from the public school "community of attendance," while at the same time allowing them a public school umbrella and eventual diploma for the curriculum they implement in their homes. Virtual charter schools are literally exploding, both as a business opportunity as well as a vehicle for re-segregation. These constituencies now find that they can educate their children in the privacy of their own home according to whatever philosophical, pedagogical, or religious orientation they wish and still receive public funding, without ever having to send their child to a "public school." They are not asked to adopt one method of instruction and therefore each family can make its own pedagogical decisions as to what is valued knowledge and what culture it wishes to reflect in the home curriculum. This means that although homeschooling families are held accountable to state educational standards, they can emphasize particular philosophies within a like-minded community (Wells et al. 1999, 13). Thus, homeschooling charters and virtual charters can range from fundamental Christian families to secular humanistic families. Charters also allow older students, who for whatever reason have dropped out of regular public schools, to finish their schooling at home through independent study programs. These students can earn true public high school degrees as opposed to general equivalency diplomas.

THE VIRTUAL CHARTER SCHOOL

One of the most recent developments within the charter school movement, as we briefly discussed in chapter four when we looked at the Wisconsin Virtual Academy, is the growth of the *virtual charter school,* a new but rapidly growing idea and educational reality that seeks to capitalize on state charter school legislation for purposes of obtaining charter school funding at public expense, while offering education online at home, at the office, or in the gym. This notion of the virtual charter finds a large and enthusiastic audience within the burgeoning homeschooling community as well as the business community. So just what is a "virtual school," let alone a "virtual charter school"? According to a new report released by Gene Glass, noted educational scholar and professor at Arizona State University, "virtual schooling":

> . . . can be taken to mean "acts, affordances, and relationships that simulate real schooling," where "real schooling" is taken to be teachers and students interacting in the same place and at the same time for the purpose of learning things. (Glass)

In the past decade this form of computer-based mediated activity between teachers and students exploded on the public scene. With the growth in what is often referred to as "online education," the entire enterprise of education now has become a thriving multimillion-dollar business. In fact, according to Professor Gene Glass, virtual education:

has grown from a novelty to an established mode of education that may provide all or part of formal schooling for nearly one in every 50 students in the U.S. In a non-random 2007 survey of school districts, as many as three out of every four public K-12 school districts responding reported offering full or partial online courses. (Ibid.)

In reality, the statistics for online learning, or virtual school growth, are surprisingly dramatic. According to an article in Technology and Learning, a publication funded by The American Council of Online Learning, as early as 2006:

38 states have now established state-led online learning programs, policies regulating online learning or both. Enrollments in online courses have increased as much as 50% in some states. 25 states have established state-wide or state-led virtual schools. Michigan now requires high school students to take at least one online course before they graduate. The Connections Academy—a pioneering virtual school that began serving K-8 students in 2002 and has now expanded to K-11 in 12 states—"combines strong parental involvement of learning at home, the expertise and accountability of public education, and the flexibility of online classes." Teachers work with their students using a variety of methods including Web-based exchanges, phone conversations, and videoconferencing. Students work on collaborative projects, and the schools even facilitate face-to-face field trips and gatherings for students in the same area—or beyond. (Armstrong)

Former Education Secretary William Bennett, under George Bush, Sr., created K12, Inc. backed by the education firm Knowledge Universe, the brainchild of former convicted felon and junk bond seller, Michael Milkin. Milkin partnered with Bennett to financially start up Bennett's virtual learning, for-profit school business plan which has been quite successful and seems to be growing across the United States by leaps and bounds. After the creation of his company in 1999, Bennett managed to cut a deal with then-Governor Tom Ridge of Pennsylvania to be allowed into the state as an "educational business," winning approval for the company's first virtual charter school in Norristown, Pennsylvania. This served to establish Bennett's political connections and subsequent business connections, assuring his ability to manage to secure business relationships with several other states for the idea of virtual learning and virtual charter schools. He also has his own radio show where he can be heard lambasting public education throughout the week. And Bennett's company is not alone. Literally dozens of such companies have blossomed seemingly overnight.

So then if a virtual school is an online learning school, just what is a virtual *charter school* and how does charter law come into play when offering distant learning education or virtual school education to the nation's children? The answer lies not simply with understanding the legal process of chartering the school and thus the virtual schools designation as a charter, but understanding must also lie in examining the direct economic subsidies from the public coffers that accrue to a virtual charter schools and their "owners," or as they would prefer to be called, "providers" (much like employees at Wal-Mart can be considered "associates"), as a result of being legally chartered.

An example of the controversy over virtual charter schools can be seen in Pennsylvania. Here the state has debated the financing of virtual charter schools for years. Concluding that such schools were draining them financially, many school districts in the state filed suit in 2001, portraying online schools as little more than home-schooling at taxpayer expense. The districts lost in court, but the debate continues (Dillon).

Professor Glass's study adds to the Pennsylvania controversy:

> *In some instances, virtual schools that have taken advantage of the charter school legislation in a state are funded exactly as if they were "brick-and-mortar" charter schools. In other places, state support to virtual schools is reduced from that of other types of school (conventional schools or charter schools). (Ibid.)*

With financial funding the central issue and charter legality simply the codifier and "legal cover" for what is arguably privatization, Glass goes on to show how the cost of providing virtual education at the K-12 level differs substantially from locality to locality. Furthermore, he specifies there has been great difficulty in assessing the cost of virtual education for purposes of reimbursing "providers." According to Glass, legislatures often embarked on virtual school creation with the uncritical assumption the virtual "model" would substantially reduce public educational costs. Yet as Glass's report testifies, virtual education providers adamantly insist, and for a reason, that their costs remain at levels near that of expenditures for conventional schools and they vigorously lobby politicians for what they regard as "adequate funding," which in the end really translates into taxpayer subsidies for higher profits.

What is most compelling and worthy of examination is the overwhelming evidence that clearly points to the fact that these "provider" financial claims seem grossly overstated. Glass continues:

> *In 2003, Florida funded two pilot virtual schools—one operated by Connections Academy, a private company headquartered in Baltimore, Maryland, and the other by K12, Inc., the McLean, Virginia company, (mentioned above)—at $4,800 per student, only about $700 less than the standard per-pupil expenditure in the state at that time. In 2004, the Pennsylvania Auditor General conducted an audit of each of the state's virtual charter schools; as a result, virtual schools' reimbursement was lowered to $7,200 for each full-time student, approximately 75% of the conventional per pupil expenditure. Wisconsin reimburses virtual charter schools at approximately half the rate of conventional brick-and-mortar schools. Recent legislation ensuring the existence of virtual schools in Wisconsin requires an audit of such schools to be completed by December 2009. In 2004, the Idaho Legislature*

funded the Idaho Virtual Academy, a public virtual school run by K12, Inc., at approximately half the per-pupil expenditure of conventional public schools in the state. However, principals for the K12, Inc. corporation have accused the Idaho legislature of deliberately under funding the Academy due to ". . . opposition from the establishment." (Ibid.)

The *New York Times* article referred to above goes on to observe that in 2007, the Pennsylvania state auditor found several online charters had received reimbursements from students' home districts that surpassed actual education costs by more than $1 million dollars. Now legislators in the state are considering a bill that would in part standardize the payments at about $5,900 per child, according to Michael Race, a spokesman for the State Department of Education. California, for example, specifically guards against privateers like K12, Inc. from taking public taxpayer money in the form of profits from charter and virtual schools. By passing oversight legislation the state has enacted a statute that specifically requires that online charter schools be audited to insure that no funds are taken as profits by the providers. The statute also provides that the state has the discretion to adjust the allocation based on the results of such audits (Green, Preston, and Mead 2004).

The opportunity to make huge financial profits off of the growing emergence of virtual charter schools cannot be understated and thus also serves as one argument as to why we see the growth of these for-profit providers. The fact is, these companies and their investors shrewdly see tremendous financial gains in further disabling public education in favor of "choice" and the virtual charter school is surely the latest vehicle for this political and economic convergence of forces demanding privatization. Furthermore, with many homeschoolers wanting the imprimatur of graduating from a public school without the "public," the virtual charter school offers the convenience of disassociation from having to physically attend public schools while fostering claims the virtual charter schools provide a "public education" as well as innovation to improve TPSs. Caught in a tight embrace with political allies, for-profit companies (like K12, Inc. and many, many others) work assiduously with their political constituencies in the home school community to garner political, community, and parental support for their business plans. This is really their base.

Yet not all homeschoolers and their parents are enthralled with the idea of a virtual charter school. Why? The reason lies in the fact that once the virtual charter actually becomes a "charter," it by definition becomes "public," thus not only eligible for public subsidies but also the object of public regulation, even if such regulations might be minimal. And this means that students of virtual charter schools must pass state standardized tests that meet federal requirements and adopt a publicly approved curriculum. Many conservative homeschoolers would then need to meet public school standards and requirements which is an anathema to many in the home schooling community and is precisely the reason many decided to home school in the first place.

Take for example a not-so-distant article published in the *Home Education Magazine,* the voice of a large segment of the national home school community, entitled "How William Bennett's Public E-Schools Affect Homeschooling." In the article, the authors, Larry and Susan Kaseman, are critical of Bennett and his plans, arguing:

> *Bennett is acting in ways that disregard our interests as homeschoolers and undermine our homeschooling freedoms.*
>
> *It is important to see Bennett's actions in the context of the Knowledge Universe (KU), a huge educational enterprise. KU is the brainchild of Michael Milken, the former "junk bond king" who made as much as $500 million annually while dealing in junk bonds. He then served time as a convicted felon in connection with his financial dealings.*
>
> *According to an article from Forbes.com, September, 2001, KU is designed to make money by selling information over the Internet to people from cradle to grave. It is a network of nearly 50 companies (as of September, 2001), many of them interlocking. It includes a number of companies that provide online curriculums, tutoring, test preparation, testing, and school management for preschoolers through middle schoolers. These companies are amassing a huge data base that includes the names and skill levels of people using their products or services and that can be used by other KU companies. (Kaseman and Kaseman)*

The authors go on to point to K12's president, William Bennett's comments regarding virtual charter schools during an interview by Mark Standriff on WSPD radio in Toledo, Ohio, August 16, 2002:

> *Standriff: What kind of opposition have you folks found?*
> *Bennett: We found opposition from both sides of the political spectrum. Some of the homeschooling people have opposed us.*
> *Standriff: Oh really, I would think this would be right in line with their thinking.*
> *Bennett: Well it should be. Frankly, I'm disappointed. I've been defending homeschoolers for twenty years. But the principle I'm defending, Mark, is school choice, parental choice. The objection they have is that it shouldn't be involved in public funding, at all. It shouldn't be involved with government schools, as they say. But, I'm not prepared to relinquish $400 billion and just say, well never mind, this is not money that I'm entitled to. Parents are paying that money in taxes, they should have an option within the public school system that gives them a chance to educate their children at home, but be publicly accountable as all public schools should be. (Ibid.)*

Disgruntled with what they see as the outright exploitation of the homeschooling community for-profit and personal gain, authors Larry and Susan Kaseman go on to cogently point out that:

Homeschoolers are a key to the K12, Inc. enterprise. Milken and Bennett are build-ing on the success of homeschooling. Parents who are not certified teachers have been very successful in educating their children. Homeschooled children are well socialized. Thousands of grown homeschoolers are now successful adults, employ-ees, and college students. Without evidence provided by the success of the modern homeschooling movement, Milken, Bennett, and others would be having a much more difficult time launching their enterprise and recruiting investors and potential participants. (Ibid.)

In fact, conservative opposition to virtual charter schools and companies like K12, Inc. that use them to make a quick buck have also been expressed by the Christian Home Educators of Ohio, Christian Parents Education Fellowship (Findlay, OH), Wisconsin Parents Association, Illinois Christian Home Educa-tors, and the Christian Home Education Association of California, to name a few (Ibid.)

OPPOSITION TO PUBLIC CHOICE AND CHARTER SCHOOLS

Many educators of varied political persuasions are adamantly against any consid-eration of public school choice, be it for a charter school or otherwise, arguing that charter schools represent a slippery slope to the eventual disinvestment of public schools and the destruction of the idea of a common school (Molnar 1996, 5). These educators also worry that public choice is really a step toward privatiz-ing education through vouchers, not a way of preventing it by creating alterna-tives in "public choice" and charter schools. They also point to the increasing commercialization of "public choice" through laws such as No Child Left Behind that allows for SEMs (supplemental educational materials) to be sold directly to schools if schools fail and also allow for the for-profit management of schools be they charter or traditional public schools (TPSs).

They concede that the charter movement may free some marginalized groups and citizens to start their own schools based on new and innovative cur-ricula and ideas, but they contend that charters will do little or nothing at all to address the material inequalities that are expanding throughout the world and within American society and education. For these educators, charter schools are simply educational enclaves for those lucky enough to get their child enrolled through a "lottery" or through a "sibling" clause, but they argue these schools cannot hope to accomplish what is needed in terms of social and economic jus-tice and equality in the provision of education. What is needed, many of these ed-ucators argue is a institutional revolutionary change in cultural, economic, and social life. They contend that charter schools will simply create exceptional en-claves, not exceptional educational systems. By failing to consider larger post-modern socioeconomic issues implicated in the institutional life of societies, many educators argue that genuinely concerned charter school promoters fail to see that charter schools cannot deliver the emancipation they offer and in fact, will end up simply reproducing the inequalities that are expanding in what they see as a new postindustrial, global society (Whitty, Power, and Halpin 1998). Within the context of inequitable and institutionalized sociopolitical relations, the claim goes, charter schools can do little to offer real educational reform, all they can hope to accomplish for the most disadvantaged students and progressive minded parents and their students is offer an "island" within a turbulent sea. An example of such a school, many would argue, would be the Lusher charter school, which we examined in chapter 4, which caters to the mainly upper and middle classes.

For commercial interests bent on creating an educational industry subsidized by working people's taxes, the movement towards charters is more easily understood: charter schools can offer private owners, corporations, entrepreneurs, and Wall Street investors a financial goldmine and with the shift in public educational law and legislation from state to state, that is precisely what is taking place. Understanding all this it is still important to realize that when making their general arguments against "choice" within the educational marketplace, those opposed to charter schools or those who are at the very least hesitant or tepid in their accord with the idea, concentrate their questions on particular issues they find troubling in the movement. Let us begin by examining some of these specific issues and questions directed towards charter schools as an educational reform movement.

CONCERNS FACING CHARTER SCHOOLS

Do Charter Schools Increase Racial, Class, and Gender Segregation in Education?

In a study of ethnic and class stratification in fifty-five urban and fifty-seven rural charter schools in Arizona done for Education Policy Analysis, a nonprofit think tank some ten years ago, researchers noted that nearly half the charter schools studied exhibited evidence of substantial ethnic separation (Cobb and Glass 1999, 1). They concluded that subtle exclusionary practices among charter schools, including initial parent contacts and the provision of transportation, had an appreciable affect on ethnic and racial segregation in charter schools:

> *The ethnic separation on the part of Arizona's charter schools, though de facto, is an insidious by-product of unregulated school choice. If parents can choose where to send their children to school, they are likely to choose schools with students of similar orientations to their own. Moreover, it is well documented that choices (in this case, charter students and parents) differ from non-choices in several meaning-*

ful ways, which further contributes to the stratification of students along ethnic and
socioeconomic lines. (Ibid.)

In North Carolina, when the state legislators years ago were debating charter schools it was feared there would be a recurrence of the flight of white academies that had been a historical part of the South a generation earlier in the
aftermath of the *Brown* decision. In approving the charter idea, the legislators put
a clause in the legislation that required the schools to reasonably reflect the demographics of the school districts they serve. Yet two years after passage of the
legislation, twenty-two of the state's charter schools appeared to violate the diversity clause (Dent 1998). The irony lies in the fact that the law is being violated by
charter schools that are 85 percent black and populated by children whose parents sought to flee the failing public schools.

The charter school movement is having the effect of re-segregating schools
in North Carolina, and thus they pose a legal and social dilemma. Many policymakers are asking how, if the charter school movement is really going to be a public choice reform, can that be accomplished without re-segregating schools? Or
can it? And where charter schools are located in predominantly black neighborhoods, how can they be centers for diversity if few white parents want to send
their children to schools located in those neighborhoods?

Racial and ethnic segregation and stratification can happen subtly: in the
way the schools are organized, how they state their mission, and the symbols and
signifiers they use to attract students. For example, in a suburban charter school in
California, the founders created a high-tech image and orientation for the school.
This emphasis permitted marketing strategies to attract students whose parents
worked in the technology industry, which, in turn, resulted in the procurement of
more computers and software for the school through grants and donations. Creating an ideological mission for the school along with the symbols of technology and
computer literacy meant that this charter school could subtly give the message of
who belongs at the school—who will fit in and who will not (Wells et al. 1999, 22).

In a recent report entitled *False Promises,* published by The Institute on
Race and Poverty at the University of Minnesota (ironically the state where the
charter school movement was first launched), the study found through an exhaustive examination and thorough study that charters in the Twin Cities not
only continue to perform worse than traditional public schools, but that they are
more segregated than traditional public schools and are forcing those traditional
public schools themselves to become more segregated. Why? A purview of the report, released in November of 2008, is enthusiastically unhesitant in its portrayal
of the growing problem of increased segregation and the assumed accompanying
issues of underachievement:

Charter school proponents promoted charter schools as a means to improve the per-
formance of students who would otherwise have no choice but to attend failing tra-

ditional public schools. They claimed that families of means always had school choice—they had the financial resources to either send their children to private schools or to move to better neighborhoods with higher quality public schools. Advocates of charter schools promised that charter schools would extend the same school choice to low-income parents and parents of color, who were stranded in low-performing traditional public schools. They further pledged that by severing the link between segregated neighborhoods and segregated schools, charter schools would liberate low-income parents of color from the racially segregated traditional public schools they attended. Overall, they claimed that charters would promote a race to the top for all parties that were involved.

This study finds that in Minnesota charter schools failed to deliver the promises made by charter school proponents. Despite nearly two decades of experience, charter schools in Minnesota still perform worse on average than comparable traditional public schools. Although a few charter schools perform well, most offer low-income parents and parents of color an inferior choice—a choice between low-performing traditional public schools and charter schools that perform even worse. The study finds that other public school choice programs such as The Choice is Yours Program offer access to much better schools than the charter schools in Minnesota.

The analysis also shows that charter schools have intensified racial and economic segregation in Twin Cities schools. A geographical analysis shows that the racial makeups of charter schools mimic the racial composition of the neighborhoods where they are located. This contrasts sharply with the claim that charter schools would sever the link between segregated neighborhoods and schools. On the contrary, the data show that charter schools are segregating students of color in nonwhite segregated schools that are even more segregated than the already highly-segregated traditional public schools. In some predominantly white urban and suburban neighborhoods, charter schools also serve as outlets for white flight from traditional public schools that are racially more diverse than their feeder neighborhoods. (False Promises)

The report also looked at Twin Cities school racial make-ups, and it includes a map that plots out all the metro area charter schools. It clearly shows demographically that segregated schools far outnumber integrated schools and in some cases, predominately white schools are surrounded by a moat of predominately nonwhite schools (Ibid.).

Unfortunately, this empirical evidence of segregation is more norm than aberration. In their comprehensive study, "Charter Schools and Race: A Lost Opportunity for Integrated Education," Erica Frankenberg and Chungmei Lee, both of Harvard University, evidenced the same troubling patterns found by The Institute on Race and Poverty report:

Segregation is worse for African American than for Latino students, but is very high for both. In some states, white student isolation in charter schools is as high as that of African Americans. The problems reported here may not be due either to the in-

tent or the desires and values of charter school leaders. They may reflect flaws in state policies, in enforcement, in methods of approving schools for charters, or the location where charter schools are set up. (Frankenberg and Lee 2003)

In 2003, the Delaware State Board of Education and Delaware Department of Education hired an Evaluation Center from Arizona State University to assess the state's charter schools and charter school reform efforts from 2003 to 2006. The report was presented to the Delaware State Board of Education by Dr. Gary Miron, the Evaluation Center's chief of staff and the study's project director at Arizona State University. In addition to Miron, Anne Cullen and Patricia Farrell, also of the Evaluation Center, and Dr. Brooks Applegate, West Michigan University's professor of educational leadership, collaborated on the project and jointly authored the 226-page report. The final report, issued after a three-year, $150,000 evaluation of Delaware's charter school movement, summarizes findings across the Delaware charter schools. The report concludes that the charter schools have resulted in resegregation and disparities between mostly white and mostly minority charter schools. The study goes even further, stating it:

found "substantial differences in student demographics," both among charter schools and also between charter schools and surrounding traditional public schools. On the whole, the study finds that traditional public schools have higher percentages of low-income students, students with special education needs and students who have limited English proficiency. (WMN)

Even more recently, in a report in the Educational Resource Information Center (ERIC) entitled *Are Charter Schools More Racially Segregated Than Traditional Public Schools?*, published in 2007, author Yongmei Ni made several key findings from her analysis of the Michigan charter school experiment. She summarizes her findings:

(1) Although charter school students were more racially diverse at the state level than those in Michigan's traditional public schools, not all charter schools are more diverse; (2) Depending on where their students come from, charter schools had very different effects on racial segregation. Charter schools drawing students mainly from the districts in which they are located tended to be more racially segregated than their host districts, while charter schools drawing students from outside the host districts show some positive evidence toward racial integration; and (3) The effects of charter schools on racial segregation vary across districts depending upon their degree of racial segregation. While charter schools drawing students from segregated districts show no further racial segregation, charter schools drawing students from racially diverse districts are more segregated than these districts. (Ni [ERIC])

She concludes that if diversity in charter schools is an important goal for policymakers, the state legislature and charter school authorizers could encourage charter schools to adopt racial integration as a major goal of their recruitment process.

In their 2007 granular examination of segregation and the impact of charter schools, Suzanne Eckes and Kelly Rapp, in a report entitled "Dispelling the Myth of 'White Flight': An Examination of Minority Enrollment in Charter Schools," examined data of reported student body diversity in the 32 states that enroll more than 1,000 students in charter schools (as of 2002-2003). They came up with the following finding:

> at the outset of the charter school movement, some opponents feared that charter schools would become havens for White students wishing to flee the traditional public school system, resulting in publicly funded segregation. However, studies suggest that this has not occurred. In fact, charter schools on average remain slightly racially segregated, enrolling more minority students than traditional public schools. (Eckes and Rapp 2007)

The authors continue, arguing:

> Segregation in charter schools is not unavoidable considering that they often can exercise more control of student body composition through recruitment measures. (Ibid.)

The article details a disappointing set of findings regarding its central question—namely, that charter schools are largely more segregated than public schools and segregation is much worse for African American than for Latino students. According to the study, in some states white student isolation in charter schools is as high as that of African Americans. Going on, the authors note:

> The justification for segregated schools as places of opportunity is basically a "separate but equal" justification, an argument that there is something about the schools that can and does overcome the normal pattern of educational inequality that afflicts many of these schools. Charter school advocates continually assert such advantages and often point to the strong demand for the schools by minority parents in minority communities, including schools that are designed specifically to serve a minority population. It is certainly true that minority parents are actively seeking alternatives to segregated, concentrated poverty, and low-achieving public schools. White parents have also shown strong interest in educational alternatives as evidenced by the strong demand for magnet schools. (Ibid.)

Yet as Chungmei Lee and Erica Frankenberg argue, the high level of racial segregation in charter schools is really not a big surprise when viewed in light of the existing segregation in many aspects of American life. Nor is their argument regarding resegregation something to be taken lightly. They go on to claim that those who think that charter schools are inherently likely to be free of racial inequality need to reflect on the racial consequences of other market-based approaches to life operating in such areas as housing, employment, health care, the provision of public transportation, opportunity and availability of health care, climbing prison populations, percentage of foreclosures and home ownership, and the list could go on. Here, it can be argued, as both Harvard professors do, that markets have worked more to perpetuate and spread racial inequality rather than to confront it and cure it. From the authors' point of view:

> *One could accurately say that the normal outcome of markets when applied to a racially stratified society is a perpetuation of racial stratification. This is why early educational choice programs were often found to produce white flight from integrated schools and to contribute to segregation in many school desegregation trials. Those experiences were apparently unknown or overlooked by designers and supporters of many charter school policies. (Frankenburg and Lee 2003)*

Many parents and their political constituencies, from homeschoolers preferring to segregate from the public forum altogether, to religious and ethnic advocates for charter schools there is an increased mobilization to use charter schools and charter school legislation as a means to actually voluntarily segregate from others in the public realm, either by gender, race, religion, cultural, or ethnic focus.

Take for example, the passage of a bill in January of 2008 changing Delaware's charter school law to allow single-gender schools. The bill was passed in the state House, with legislators reaching a compromise to assure it provides equal protection and would not be vulnerable to constitutional challenge. The bill sailed on through the legislature to eventually achieve passage in the senate, despite some opposition. Delaware Rep. Diana McWilliams, D-Fox Point, questioned: "I am very concerned that this will be a very slippery slope back to segregated schools." She wondered aloud why "segregation of a gender" is a good thing. The bill's passage clears the path for a middle school targeting at-risk boys (Kenney and Miller 2008).

Tarek ibn Ziyad Academy charter school is located in Minnesota and has mostly Muslim students. In fact, Minnesota has many ethnically focused or culturally focused charter schools, servicing not just Muslim students but also Christians and Hmong students. The rational for such segregated schools can be best summed up by the director of the Hmong charter school in Minnesota, who commented:

> *Yes, with our focus on culture, language and achievement, we create an environment with a sense of community, of trust, of respect, of valuing education. I've worked in the big traditional schools, and that same sense is not there for many of our families. Our kids and parents feel welcome because they see the displays of their culture and values of respect, responsibility. They see staff people who look like them. I'm Hmong; they can relate to me. It makes a huge difference. In this environment, give them time and kids achieve. Our school is making AYP [annual*

yearly progress, a reporting measure required by federal No Child Left Behind rules],
and we had no discipline problems at all last year. How many schools can say that?
Yes, with our focus on culture, language and achievement, we create an environ-
ment with a sense of community, of trust, of respect, of valuing education. I've
worked in the big traditional schools, and that same sense is not there for many of
our families. Our kids and parents feel welcome because they see the displays of
their culture and values of respect, responsibility. They see staff people who look
like them. I'm Hmong; they can relate to me. It makes a huge difference. In this en-
vironment, give them time and kids achieve. (False Promises)

Re-segregation or voluntary segregation within and by charter schools continues to grow, as can be seen by an examination of the the Urban Prep Charter
Academy for Young Men, located in Chicago and Ben Gamla Charter in New
York, as discussed in chapter 4. Now, with the controversial opening of the Ben
Gamla Charter School, by its parent company, Academica, Inc., the trend currently seems to be the exercise of legislative leniency on behalf of lawmakers,
politicians, and charter school authorizers to the idea of religiously oriented charter schools, gender oriented charter schools, "class oriented" charter schools, and
ethnically or culturally focused charter schools.

Take for example the state of Rhode Island. Pressed by the Governor, education officials agreed in early 2009 to change the way they approve applications
to open public charter schools, giving a higher priority to proposals that serve
low-income and disadvantaged students in low-performing school districts. By
"courting" charter schools as an answer to low-income student achievement
rather than working to strengthen existing TPSs isn't the Governor of the state
further stratifying the school system by social class? In other words, wouldn't this
be the same thing as having one side of a traditional public school classroom set
up for one social class, divided by a large panel and another side set up for mid-
dle- and upper-social classes? Not according to officials from Rhode Island who
agreed to change the way they approve applications to open public charter
schools, giving a higher priority to proposals that serve low-income and disadvantaged students in low-performing school districts. To do this the Governor of
the state proposed a budget that sets aside $1.5 million for new charter schools
in the 2009-10 school year. Yet, argue opponents of the idea, isn't this an example of the state subsidizing class stratification? (Jordan 2009)

In fact, serving low-income students is now one of the growing missions
and reflects the realities of many charter schools set up for specifically this purpose. Where once the practice of "creaming" the best students concerned those
opposed to the development of charter schools—"creaming" meaning charters
would take only the best academically qualified or prepared students—the continued development of the charter school concept has now extended to serving
particularly "low-income and low performing" students. One can argue, and
many proponents of the idea like the Governor of Rhode Island do, that this ef-

fort is a worthwhile attempt to reach students who are low-income and low-performing academically in traditional public schools. The notion of a charter school actually saving struggling groups of low-income students has become an all-too-familiar theme among politicians, as evidenced by Rhode Island's recent decision and the explosion of hundreds of charter schools seeking to serve low-income students; and this has become especially alluring to low-income parents who argue their children are caught in a vicious cycle in TPSs.

But opponents to such an idea would argue that politicians, business interests, and Departments of Education throughout the states that have legislated charter schools are really playing a shell game with the American people and not broaching the real problem that plagues society and schools. They argue that not only will charter schools not solve the problem of failing schools, but that they serve to stratify citizens along racial, ethnic, and social class. The real answer, echo these opponents, is full funding for all public schools for the decades of proven methods of educational reform: smaller class size, smaller schools, comprehensive preschool for three- and four-year-olds, after-school and in-school tutoring and enrichment programs and mentoring for those who need them, state-of-the-art school buildings equipped with updated books, materials, equipment, technology and caring, well-trained educators who have the needed experience for the job are also needed. Furthermore societal poverty, not to mention the fact that one out of every fifty children in the United States is homeless, simply does not support the academic development of children and thus issues of economic equity and economic policies that encourage the eradication of social poverty must be faced when confronting public education reform (Kozol, 2006).

What does support academic development of children, argue opponents to the idea of class or race-based segregated charter schools, are decent living wage jobs, available health care, senior care, day care, and affordable housing along with full access to public transportation. These are all part of the kind of sustainable environment that would support a positive family life and the cognitive development of all children. Arguing that public schools need to transform into charter schools that target low-income students (usually of color) to be innovative and creative, is a red herring. After all, doesn't public education work in many suburbs throughout the nation without any problems? And if it does, then it begs the question as to why we need special segregated enclaves for less fortunate students, again usually students of color. Why can't a decent, quality public education be the right of every citizen regardless of socioeconomic class, race, gender, or ethnicity and not simply the privilege of the wealthy? One cannot help but see the similarities behind calls to help "low-income" students through charter schools and the subprime housing loans directed at the "low-income" wage earners. Eyeing the "low charter school income market" or subprime loan market seems to have paid out handsomely for the many investors and business interests involved. But what about students and their parents?

The notion of segregation by class, race, ethnicity, or gender is all very disturbing to many progressive educators who argue that religious, gender, and racial segregation (not to mention virtual segregation by "virtual charters") can only serve to damage pluralism and diversity in education. This, they say, not only flies in face of the *Brown v. Board of Education* court decision but vitiates the hundred of millions, if not billions of dollars and hard work spent by the states historically to desegregate schools and depressingly harkens back to an ideology of "separate but equal." Perhaps Erica Frankenberg and Chungmei Lee, both from Harvard University, put their finger on the problem when they write:

> *The justification for segregated schools as places of opportunity is basically a "separate but equal" justification, an argument that there is something about the schools that can and does overcome the normal pattern of educational inequality that afflicts many of these schools. Charter school advocates continually assert such advantages and often point to the strong demand for the schools by minority parents in minority communities, including schools that are designed specifically to serve a minority population. It is certainly true that minority parents are actively seeking alternatives to segregated, concentrated poverty, and low-achieving public schools. White parents have also shown strong interest in educational alternatives as evidenced by the strong demand for magnet schools. (Frankenberg and Lee 2003)*

Lee and Frankenberg make the point that one might think that charter schools would have a better chance to be integrated than public schools. They argue that like magnet schools a generation earlier, charter schools can offer distinctive curricula and the opportunity to create and manage schools with freedom from many normal constraints in large districts. Yet, as they state, unlike magnet schools, charter schools have the added advantages of even greater freedom to innovate and for the most part, are not tied to geographically fixed attendance boundaries in residentially segregated communities as are neighborhood public schools but can draw from wherever interested students can be found (though it must be mentioned that in some places where school districts grant charters, they are limited to the school district boundaries) (Ibid.).

Performance in Charter Schools vs. TPS: Charters as Reform Mechanism for Public Schools?

As to achievement or student performance, unfortunately, despite claims by charter school advocates there is no systematic research or data they can point to that shows that charter schools outperform traditional public schools. Since charter schools embody wildly different educational approaches, curriculum, teaching styles, and the like and since charter and public schools obtain their enrollment in very different ways, evaluation and comparisons between the two require very careful analysis, an analysis that is still lacking, close to 20 years after the first state introduced legislation for charter schools. It is certainly safe to say that there is little convincing evidence for the superiority of charter schools over public schools in the same geographical areas within which they are located. In fact, some of the studies suggest that charter schools are, on average, even weaker in terms of increasing student performance.

One of the problems in evaluating the academic effectiveness of charter schools is that their effect is normally examined by comparing them to regular public schools, but their student body and parent groups are not the same, which makes the comparison of academic achievement inaccurate. Even if one were able to control for income, parent education, and other relevant, easily measurable family resources, there are several kinds of selection bias that make such comparisons virtually impossible. First, the families who are informed enough to choose a school and make the effort to get their child to a more distant school every day are not the same as the families who do not. Second, charter schools commonly lack the expertise and programs to serve students who are English Language Learners or severely disadvantaged children such as those in Special Education. As these students tend to score lower on standardized tests, if students from lower achieving groups do not enroll, the school's average scores will tend to rise. Third, many charters seek applications from students they believe would succeed, or who would respond to their approach, while not recruiting others. Some schools have screening procedures that public schools are prohibited from using because the public schools are required to serve all students. These biases mean that even if there were higher test scores or lower dropout rates for charter schools it might well be because of selective recruitment—students from families with more resources and/or fewer students with special needs—than because of the school's superior educational approach. Yongmei Lee's study is appropriate to cite here:

> *Curiously, in an era in which tests and accountability have been the hallmark of education policy, there has been little serious accountability for charter schools. Theoretically charter schools must meet the terms of their charter or they will be terminated. In most states, however, there are few resources for oversight of schools and revocations of charters for educational failure, as opposed to financial problems, are rare. Often their impact on racial segregation is ignored by the policymakers, despite the growing body of research evidence that has documented a trend of segregation in charter schools. If there is no real evidence linking superior performance to educational program rather than admissions selectivity, looking at general characteristics of the student body that are usually linked to educational inequality, such as levels of segregation, certainly deserves attention. On this front, there is little positive to say about these schools. (Lee)*

The evidence that traditional public schools (TPSs) are improving as a result of the advent of charter schools is contradictory, unreliable and scant, for many reasons. Early on in the charter school controversy educator and charter school expert Eric Rofes, in congressional testimony before the U.S. Senate Committee on Labor and Human Resources, presented his research and findings regarding the impact of charter schools on school districts. His findings suggested that charter schools' impact on traditional school districts in that district experienced:

- A loss of students and often an accompanying loss of financing;
- The loss of a particular kind of student to niche-focused charter schools;
- The departure of significant numbers of disgruntled parents;
- Shifts in staff morale; and
- The redistribution of some central office administrators' time and increased challenges to predicting student enrollment and planning grade levels (U.S. Senate 1998, 7).

Rofe's study, at the time, also concluded that of the twenty-five schools examined throughout the United States, in terms of responding to the advent of a charter in their district, school districts typically did not respond quickly with any dramatic improvements. His study concluded that the majority of districts that were impacted by the beginning of a charter school went about their business as usual and responded to the charter initiatives slowly, if at all. Only one-quarter of the districts responded to the charter schools with new educational programs (Ibid.). Rofe concluded with a recommendation to the Senate committee that policymakers actually create charter laws with the intent of having districts transfer new and innovative pedagogical practices to the schools in the district so that these schools do not simply become innovative havens for a select few (Ibid.).

Moving the clock eleven years forward to 2009, to a Rand Corporation commissioned study on the achievement of students in charter schools, we find any evidence for achievement claims made by proponents of charter schools simply illusory. Funded by the Bill and Melinda Gates Foundation, the Joyce Foundation, and the William Penn Foundation, among the report's goals was to assess charter school student test score gains as a gauge for assessing student achievement and performance. While the study was quick to emphasize that even though the charter school movement has grown to forty states with over one million children enrolled within just a period of 17 years, the report reiterated what most studies attempting to assess student achievement at these schools have concluded that since the conception and implementation of charter school legislation and subsequent charter schools throughout the United States:

With this growth has also come a contentious debate about the effects of the schools on their own students and on students in nearby traditional public schools (TPSs). In recent years, research has begun to inform this debate, but many of the key out-

comes have not been adequately examined, or have been examined in only a few states. We do not know whether the conflicting conclusions of different studies reflect real differences in effects driven by variation in charter laws and policies or, instead, reflect differences in research approaches—some of which may be biased. (Zimmer et al.)

Interestingly, more than eleven years after Rolfe's testimony the report greeted the reader with the same tired appeals to guarded optimism when it comes to charter school student achievement, claims that it is too premature to assess performance of charters, and a host of other excuses as to why results might be "mixed" or nonascertainable. Quoting the report:

The average effect that charter schools are having on their students across grades K-12 is difficult to estimate, largely because prekindergarten baseline test scores are unavailable to assess the achievement gains of students in elementary charters (as well as K-8 and K-12 charters). For charter schools with entry grades at the middle- and high school levels (plus a handful of schools that begin in grades 3 and 4), for which we have baseline scores, we have greater confidence in the impact estimates. In five out of seven locales, these nonprimary charter schools are producing achievement gains that are, on average, neither substantially better nor substantially worse than those of local TPSs. In Chicago (in reading) and in Texas (in both reading and math), charter middle schools appear to be falling short of traditional public middle schools. Results that include charter schools at every tested grade level (i.e., those that start in kindergarten as well as those that serve exclusively middle- and high-school grades) are, in most cases, similar to the results that are limited to nonprimary charter schools, providing xiv Charter Schools in Eight States no evidence that charter-school performance varies systematically by grade level. (Ibid.)

Not only did the Rand report find that student performance in charter schools were not substantially worse nor substantially better than traditional public schools (TPSs), what they did find when examining the world of virtual charter schools in Ohio was even more surprising and disturbing:

The inclusion of kindergarten-entry charter schools in the analysis makes a substantial difference to our estimate of their achievement impacts in only one location. In Ohio, as in most of the other sites, the average performance of nonprimary charter schools is indistinguishable from that of nonprimary TPSs. But when the K-entry charter schools are included in the analysis, the estimated impact of Ohio's charter schools is significantly and substantially negative. The dramatically lower estimated performance of Ohio's K-entry charter schools appears to be attributable not to grade level per se but to virtual charter schools that use technology to deliver education to students in their homes. Virtual schools constitute a large part of the enrollment of K-entry charter schools in Ohio, and students have significantly and substantially lower achievement gains while attending virtual charter schools than they experience in TPSs. This result should be interpreted cautiously, because students who enroll in virtual charter schools may be quite unusual, and their prior achievement trajectories may not be good predictors of their future achievement trajectories. In most locations, charter schools have difficulty raising student achievement in their first year of operation, typically producing achievement results that fall short of those of local TPSs. This is consistent with prior research and common sense and may not be a charter specific phenomenon: Opening a new school is challenging, regardless of whether the school is a charter school. Across locations, we see a general pattern of improved performance as schools age. Finally, charter schools in most locales have marginally greater variation in performance than TPSs, as measured by the achievement impact estimate for each school, and, in some locations, this may simply reflect greater measurement error associated with the smaller average size of charter schools. Ohio is a notable exception: Its charter schools have a much wider range of variation in performance than its TPSs have. (Ibid.)

The Brookings Institute was no less critical in regards to the claimed efficacy of charter schools and their effect on student achievement. In a study of Milwaukee charter schools, conducted by the Brookings Institute in 2009, the authors' state:

We conclude that while charter schools overall may help the education of urban youth, our study of Milwaukee indicates that they should not be expected to be the silver bullet that some reformers seek. We also suggest that it is important to better understand and deal with instability in school attendance in urban school districts, as it proves to be the most significant determinant of student achievement in all of our statistical models. (Witte and Lavertu)

One of the most important studies regarding charter schools was launched by the U.S. Department of Education, Institute of Education Sciences. Entitled, *America's Charter Schools: Results From the NAEP 2003 Pilot Study.* The report's findings, based on an extensive investigation of 150 charter schools nationwide, found that:

For example, in mathematics, fourth-grade charter school students as a whole did not perform as well as their public school counterparts. However, the mathematics performance of White, Black, and Hispanic fourth-graders in charter schools was not measurably different from the performance of fourth-graders with similar racial/ethnic backgrounds in other public schools.

In reading, there was no measurable difference in performance between charter school students in the fourth grade and their public school counterparts as a whole. This was true, even though, on average, charter schools have higher proportions of students from groups that typically perform lower on NAEP than other public schools have. In reading, as in mathematics, the performance of fourth-grade students with similar racial/ethnic backgrounds in charter schools and other public schools was not measurably different.

There are also instances where the performance of students with shared characteristics differed. For example, among students eligible for free or reduced-price lunch, fourth-graders in charter schools did not score as high in reading or mathematics, on average, as fourth-graders in other public schools.

When considering these data, it should be noted that the charter school population is rapidly changing and growing. Future NAEP assessments may reveal different patterns of performance. Further, NAEP does not collect information about students' prior educational experience, which contributes to present performance. Nonetheless, the data in this report do provide a snapshot of charter school students' current performance. (U.S. Department of Education. Institute of Education Sciences. National Center for Education Statistics. America's Charter Schools: Results From the NAEP 2003 Pilot Study, NCES 2005-456, by National Center for Education Statistics. Washington, DC: 2004)

Yet not all pundits and educational policy makers agree with the findings of the 2004 report. Jennifer A. Marshall and Kirk A. Johnson, Ph.D. from the conservative Heritage Foundation argued in a Web memo for the foundation, entitled, *Why the NCES Study Is Not the Only—Or Best—Word on Charter School Evaluation,* which they released December 17, 2004 directly after the report's findings:

The NCES study relies on averages of student's academic achievement as a sample of charter schools from across the country. It compares these averages with averages of academic achievement among traditional public school students, also from across the country.

This methodology effectively neglects the major ways in which charter schools and public schools differ. For example, some charter schools cater to low-performing students who have languished in traditional public schools. Additionally, many charter schools locate in low-income and minority communities. As Manhattan Institute Senior Fellow Jay P. Greene notes, "Because so many charter schools are specifically targeted to struggling students, a large percentage of their minority and poor students face obstacles greater than students of similar demographics in regular public schools." Thus, charter schools and traditional public schools often serve very different student bodies, and comparing them using blanket averages is problematic at best. (Marshal and Johnson, 2004)

Move the clock forward to June of 2009 when an exhaustive study by the *Center for Research on Education Outcomes* (CREDO), at Stanford University was released. The scope of the study entitled, *Multiple Choice: Charter School Performance in 16 States,* released in June 2009, is a meticulous and comprehensive study of charter schools, the first national assessment of charter school impact of its kind. The findings from the Stanford researchers must be disheartening to charter school advocates like Marshall and Johnson for the report concludes that:

The Quality Curve results are sobering:

Of the 2,403 charter schools reflected on the curve, 46 percent of charter schools have math gains that are statistically indistinguishable from the average growth among their TPS comparisons. Charters whose math growth exceeded their TPS equivalent growth by a significant amount account for 17 percent of the total. The remaining group, 37 percent of charter schools, posted math gains that were significantly below what their students would have seen if they enrolled in local traditional public schools instead.

The national pooled analysis of charter school impacts showed the following results:

- *Charter school students on average see a decrease in their academic growth in reading of .01 standard deviations compared to their traditional school peers. In math, their learning lags by .03 standard deviations on average. While the magnitude of these effects is small, they are both statistically significant.*
- *The effects for charter school students are consistent across the spectrum of starting positions. In reading, charter school learning gains are smaller for all students except those whose starting scores are in the lowest or highest deciles. For math, the effect is consistent across the entire range.*
- *Charter students in elementary and middle school grades have significantly higher rates of learning than their peers in traditional public schools, but students in charter high schools and charter multi-level schools have significantly worse results.*
- *Charter schools have different impacts on students based on their family backgrounds. For Blacks and Hispanics, their learning gains are significantly worse than that of their traditional school twins. However, charter schools are found to have better academic growth results for students in poverty. English Language Learners realize significantly better learning gains in charter schools. Students in Special Education programs have about the same outcomes.*
- *Students do better in charter schools over time. First year charter students, on average, experience a decline in learning, which may reflect a combination of mobility effects and the experience of a charter school in its early years. Second and third years in charter schools see a significant reversal. (CREDO, 2009)*

These findings, where only 17% of all the charter schools studied by Stanford report superior achievement over traditional public schools is hardly anything to get excited about, especially after close to 20 years of experimenting with charter schools and the report in tandem with NAEP act both as an indictment of charter schools and NCLB, as well as evidence against their hollow claims.

Not so, says Nelson Smith, president of the National Alliance for Public Charter Schools, when commenting on the CREDO study. He was quick to add that the results should be considered in light of chronically inadequate funding for charter schools:

In most states, public charter schools get sharply lower per-pupil funding than their traditional public school peers, on average about 78 cents on the dollar. In seven of the 16 states surveyed, charters also do not receive facilities aid—which means that they must take money needed for teaching and learning, and apply it to leasing and renovations. (National Alliance for Public Charter Schools, 2008)

The National Alliance for Public Charter Schools also goes on to argue that the report found:

Students in poverty attending public charter schools have better academic growth results than similar students in traditional public schools, according to Multiple Choice: Charter School Performance in 16 States, *a new report released today from the Center for Research on Education Outcomes (CREDO). In addition, the report finds that English Language learners realize significantly better learning gains in public charter schools than their peers in traditional public schools, and charter students in elementary and middle school grades have significantly higher rates of learning than similar traditional public school students. (Ibid.)*

Yet no matter how the NAEP and CREDO reports are repeatedly interpreted, they certainly both raise significant contemporary doubts over the claims made by privatization fans and market based fundamentalists regarding the efficacy of charter schools. The best that Smith could add upon the reports release, other than the same arguments regarding methodology for the study that was aimed at the NAEP report, was a feeble:

We are encouraged by the ground-breaking results being achieved by many public charter schools across the country. However, if high-quality performance is to become the norm for public charter schools, we need to ramp up our efforts to replicate what's working as well as enhance our work to "remove the barriers to exit" and make it easier to close chronically low-performing charters. (Ibid.)

Once again, after close to twenty years of "experimentation" with choice and charter schools, one wonders what it means to "remove the barriers to exit"—for it is clear from the evidence that charter schools are not performing any better than traditional public schools and in some cases are doing even worse.

This book cannot attempt to go state by state in analyzing student achievement claims and studies; that is beyond the dimensions or the goals of the book. However, a cursory look from state to state provides no evidence of increased student achievement at charter schools. Sure, studies and reports will always display conflicts in conclusions, but the mere fact that those favoring charter schools cannot point to any direct, let alone circumstantial, evidence of increased student performance on what are questionable standardized tests is telling, if not troubling. However, it is also important to confront the argument, put forth by almost all charter proponents that charter schools create and promote innovation at TPSs through their competitive performance. In fact, this is one of the fundamental theories put forth in support of the charter school movement: that charter schools, by introducing competition into the traditional public school system, will provide new innovation, new curriculum approaches, and critically acclaimed "good" practices for educators along with new forms of managerial design and institutions. This was the impetus, we were told, for charter school legislation: that charter schools would act as centers of innovation that would then breathe change and creativity within a decaying public school system; yet there is no statewide or local system in place in any of the states to catalogue the supposed influential changes and innovations that charters assume to bring to the forefront and then disseminate this information to TPSs. More importantly, not only is there no convincing proof that charter schools increase student achievement, any claims to such achievement is based on student performance on standardized test.

Relying on studies regarding student achievement in charter schools and their comparison to traditional public schools can be an exercise in frustration and a bit maddening. The problem is the myriad of studies and pervasive problems inherent in their research. Furthermore, a problem is that studies that purport to make claims regarding charter school efficiency and student achievement rates consider only average differences and do not account for variations in the schools studied. Many of the pressures facing schools are variegated and have disparate impacts on students and their teachers. Speculation, pieces of information, assumptions, unwarranted correlations, and inferential leaps in logic serve to pave the path to claims made on both sides of the aisle when it comes to the effect of charter schools on student achievement.

Do Charter Schools Encourage Innovation in TPSs?

The argument that charters will oxygenate the practices of TPSs with new and promising educational innovations and practices thereby raising all boats has been more propaganda than fact. Take the study done by Good and Braden in 2000 that found that public school officials did not believe that charter schools were providing new models and programs for best practices to be highlighted; nor did they see anything being done within the charter schools that they and their schools wished to emulate (Good and Braden 2000). And in Arizona, a state where charter schools have witnessed enormous growth and support, over half the administrators polled said their districts had not been affected by charter schools nor did they believe charter schools would improve education (Ibid.). As Corwin and Schneider consider, charters are really not doing many things that have not been done somewhere else at one time or another and frankly, many public school teachers find little in common with experimental charters nor do they have any form of institutional support or mechanisms in place for learning about what they might be doing (Corwin and Schneider 2005).

Currently, when one looks at contemporary arguments for charter schools we find strikingly little talk anymore of innovation and best practices raising the efficacy for all TPSs; the opposite seems to be true. On close scrutiny the real issue can arguably be said to be about going about the business of eliminating TPSs in totality and replacing them with large corporate educational retail chains the provide educational franchises as "charter schools."

While old arguments advancing innovation and best practices in charter schools might have once been the sales pitch employed by many of the early charter advocates, the game plan has shifted as far as the conservative Hoover Institute is concerned. The Winter 2008 issue of *Education Next,* a publication put out by the Hoover Institute was straightforward in rejecting any of the theoretical arguments regarding innovation, raising "all boats for TPSs" and providing best practices to create innovation in TPSs. In fact, innovation in TPSs is the last thing these outspoken conservative charter advocates want. The publication is straightforward as to the "game plan" charter advocates must employ to create greater and greater number of new charter schools, nationwide:

> *Here, in short, is one roadmap for chartering's way forward: First, commit to drastically increasing the charter market share in a few select communities until it is the dominant system and the district is reduced to a secondary provider. The target should be 75%. Second, choose the target communities wisely. Each should begin with a solid charter base (at least 5 percent market share), a policy environment that will enable growth (fair funding, non-district authorizers, and no legislated caps), and a favorable political climate (friendly elected officials and editorial boards, a positive experience with charters to date, and unorganized opposition). . . . The solution is not an improved traditional district; it's an entirely different delivery system. . . . Charter advocates should strive to have every urban public school be a charter. (Smarick 2008)*

The Hoover Institute's article went on to identify Washington D.C. as such a location where a "corporate takeover" of charters could proceed. With 27 percent of public school enrollment now in the hands of charter schools, D.C. was labeled a "potential fertile district" for an all-out attack on TPSs with the intent of replacing them with charter schools. The market-based conservatives are outspoken in their aspirations: they want to completely replace TPSs with charter schools. Nowhere can this best be seen than in the recent move by the Los Angeles School Board on August 25, 2009, when they voted six to one to turn 250 public schools over to what the *Los Angeles Times* called "outside operators" (Blume and Song, 2009). Fifty of the 250 schools have not even been built, but they are scheduled to be built over the next four years with taxpayer money through bonds the voters were told would vitiate overcrowding in schools. Los Angeles, too, is becoming a potential fertile district for charterization.

Michelle Rhee, the school chancellor of D.C. openly commented in 2007, when she was asked about the future of charter schools: "The corporate world will be our model" (Jaffe 2007).

Jack Buckley and Mark Schneider, notable researchers in the area of charter schools concur in their book, *Charter Schools: Hope or Hype*, published in 2007, that charter schools offer little in the ways of laboratories for reform:

> *Additionally, even if we assume that one of the prime justifications for charter schools is their role as "laboratories of reform," that are free from the bureaucratic restrictions placed on traditional public schools by teacher unions and administrators (Nathan 1998; Kolderie, 1998), empirical research has found little evidence of this (Rofes, 1996; Teske et al. 2001) and the structure of real charter-school markets may actually act to inhibit programmatic competition (Lubienski, 2003). Ironically, it may be that parents are risk-averse when it comes to their children's education—they may choose schools that emphasize traditional values and educational approaches rather than "buy" innovative programs with a high degree of risk. This is quite reasonable from a parent perspective, but may create systemic problems in a system of schools that is designed both to innovate and to respond to parental preferences. (Buckley and Schneider 2007)*

When no actual systems exist to encourage, catalogue, or share "innovative practices" between charters and TPSs, the movement towards charters can be seen not as a mechanism by which to inform and improve public education and educational curriculum, but as a vehicle for various constituencies to escape the traditional public school system and therefore the entirety of the public realm itself. This, perhaps, is the greatest tragedy of the charter school experiment; how many charter schools have been commodified as islands of specialties for purposes of segregation and sabotaged from their stated public mission—to improve traditional public education through better practices.

The Rand Report also directly confronts any claims to charter school innovation:

> *There is no evidence in any of the locations that charter schools are negatively affecting the achievement of students in nearby TPSs. But there is also little evidence of a positive competitive impact on nearby TPSs. (Gill et al. 2001)*

Again, not all, but an increasing number of conservative charter school proponents have become very clear as the charter school movement has matured: they are not interested in raising student test scores at TPSs, instead they want to replace TPSs with a new educational retail chain of for-profit charter schools that would operate as educational franchises, and they need the help of elected officials and closely connected politicians to do just that.

Take Arizona for example, one of the beacon states that offers a "favorable political climate" for conservative charter advocates to initiate a 'takeover' of public schools; this is a state where there has been a phenomenal surge in charter schools and charter school legislation within the last seventeen years. El Dorado High School, a charter school operated by one of the largest for-profit Charter School groups in Arizona, The Leona Group of Arizona, an LLC (limited liability company) that is part of the national Leona Group, an educational management organization (EMO) that operates private schools across the nation was scheduled to receive about $1,151,743.82 from the Arizona Department of Education for fiscal year 2006-2007. El Dorado is listed on publicschoolsreview.com as one of the Top 20 Schools in Arizona (listed in 9th place) with the highest expenditure of money per student of $16,644. Yet according to a 2006 article in the *American Chronicle*, whose source contributors include The Arizona Department of Education, the U.S. Department of Education and the Arizona Charter School Board:

> *Despite the enormous expenditure of taxpayer dollars at El Dorado High School their performance rate indicates nothing but problems. For school year ending June 2006 the promotion rate at El Dorado High School was only 48%, as opposed to 82% for the entire state. They retained 10% of all students at the same grade, as opposed to only 3% in the state pubic schools. They had a high school drop out rate of 32% as opposed to 6% on a statewide level, and they only graduated 43% of their senior high school senior class as opposed to 79% in the states public schools. (Harrington)*

And according to the in-depth investigation of El Dorado:

> *El Dorado's performance on the AIMS Test—required to test proficiency of school students—was even more frightening. Only 10% of El Dorado High School Students met state proficiency standards in mathematics, as opposed to 49% of all high school students in the State of Arizona. 35% of El Dorado's students met state standards in reading compared to 63% of all Arizona high school students, and 39% met state standards in writing, compared to 63% of all Arizona High School students. (Ibid.)*

SchoolsMatter, a public policy watchdog and think tank that investigated Ohio charter schools in 2007, agreed that the school's record has been more than a little spotty. In 2007, the Ohio state's school report card gave more than half of

Ohio's 328 charter schools a D or an F. According to the group, with wide-open authorization and an explosive gallop towards the charter school concept, they found:

> some charters are mediocre, and Ohio has a far higher failure rate than most states. Fifty-seven percent of its charter schools, most of which are in cities, are in academic watch or emergency, compared with 43 percent of traditional public schools in Ohio's big cities.

Part of the problem, SchoolsMatter noted, was that behind the Ohio charter failures are systemic weaknesses that include loopholes in oversight, a law allowing 70 government and private agencies to authorize new charters, and financial incentives that encourage sponsors to let schools stay open regardless of performance (Ibid.). Governor Ted Strickland of Ohio, commenting on the charter school experiment in his state in 2007, was succinct and clear:

> Perhaps somewhere, charter schools have been implemented in a defensible manner, where they have provided quality. But the way they've been implemented in Ohio has been shameful. I think charter schools have been harmful, very harmful, to Ohio students. (Ibid.)

Strickland went even further, telling *Time* Magazine in 2006:

> About $500 million, I believe, was taken out of our (Ohio's) public system to fund underperforming charter schools last year. I think that's a waste of resources—for-profit charter schools trouble me greatly. (Pitluk 2006)

Texas, another bellwether state for charter schools, is faring no better according to SchoolsMatter. According to the Texas Education Agency, one out of every six charter schools in the state is a failure (SchoolsMatter).

But opposing points of view regarding charter schools achievements abound, as testified to by the Center for Education Reform, a firm charter advocacy organization and distinct and early player in the charter school movement. According to their 2009 report:

> Performance-based accountability is the hallmark of charter schools. Unlike conventional public schools that remain open year after year despite their inability to manage a school or raise student achievement, charter schools close if they fail to perform according to their charter. And while opponents claim that charter schools are not being held accountable or that only "responsible" charters should remain open, the data on closed charter schools across the states proves that the performance-based accountability inherent in the charter school concept is working—especially in states with strong and clear charter laws. (Center for Education Reform, under "The Accountability Report: 2009 Charter Schools")

As of 2008 the Center for Educational Reform cited the fact that Charter schools are providing high-quality education options for Massachusetts families. Using data from the 2006-2007 Massachusetts Comprehensive Assessment System (MCAS), the report documents the achievement of students in conventional public, pilot schools, and charter schools in the Boston area. Among the reports key findings:

- Charter school students in Boston outpace students in pilot schools and conventional public schools on the MCAS. In eighth grade math alone, charter school students outperformed their district peers by as much as 50 percentage points.
- There are no more seats available in these successful charter schools due to the cap established by the legislature. In 2007, there were 5,649 applications for 1,249 spots in Boston charter schools.
- While pilot school programs, which operate similarly but not as independently as charters do, are better than other public schools, the report shows that charter schools are outperforming both pilot schools and conventional schools on eighth and 10th grade MCAS tests.
- Boston charter schools enroll a higher percentage of African American students than the district as a whole (61 percent versus 43 percent, respectively). According to *Education Week,* pilot high schools enroll fewer struggling students, fewer students with severe special needs, and fewer students with limited English skills than charters. These data mirror the data nationally.

The report goes on to observe that charter schools in Boston receive approximately $5,000 less per pupil than their peers in conventional public schools. Additionally, districts are compensated with "impact" funds for students who move to charter schools. Nevertheless, cites the report, Boston public schools still fall, on average, 37 percentage points below charter students on statewide assessments (Center for Education Reform, under "Student Achievement Higher at Boston Charter Schools") Yet in the past decade, according to a Nightly Business Report interview conducted in 2008, about five percent of the nation's charter schools have been closed for poor performance. This is a troubling statistic for a movement that stated its goals were to raise educational performance for all students, not just those in charter schools (Eastabrook 2008).

The fact is, not only do many charter schools nationwide not only close they do so far more rapidly than the public is aware of. On examination, the reasons why they close seems to have to do with fraud, abuse of taxpayer's funds, illegitimate business practices, legislative collusion, insufficient oversight, lack of financial transparency, lack of managerial responsibility, and a failure of public disclosure. This certainly is troubling even to the most ardent supporters of charter schools.

In their book, *Charter Schools: Hope or Hype,* authors Jack Buckley and Mark Schneider confront the issue of the actual failure rates of charter schools throughout the nation. They document that:

> *While data calculating actual closure rates are hard to find, Hassel and Batdorff (2004) studied decisions to renew school charters throughout the nation. They looked at all 506 nationwide renewal cases through 2001, and then focusing on fifty randomly selected cases they found that 16 percent of charter schools up for renewal were terminated (conversely, 84 percent of the charter schools were renewed). The Center for Education Reform reports that 429 charter schools have closed from the inception of charter schools through 2003. If we set the number of remaining charter schools in the nation at around three thousand, we can estimate a closure rate of approximately 13 percent, not much different than the Hassel and Batdorff finding of 16 percent (also see Teske, Schneider, and Cassese 2005, who look at the politics involved in authorizing and renewing charter schools). (Buckley and Schneider 2007)*

It is hard to see from the myriad research and conclusions conducted by some of the most prestigious think tanks and educational policy experts, how an argument can be made or sustained that charter schools have raised student achievement at their schools or that they have served as a catalyst for higher student achievement and innovation at traditional public schools. The notion of competition between schools raising innovative levels of instruction, management, student performance, teacher morale and commitment and the host of claims made by charter advocates under the rubric of competition and public choice simply have not been born out by the evidence. And as the Hudson Institute so laconically stated, the real, rarely spoken of goal is the replacement of all traditional public schools, at least in urban areas, with charter schools.

Charter School Admission Practices and Discrimination

One main issue facing progressive educators is the concern that charter schools, or public choice, could lead to the re-segregation of schools through unfair and discriminatory admission policies (Cobb and Glass 1999), as was noted in our discussion above. These educators shoulder the claim that charter schools further stratify schools on the basis of race, class, gender, and socioeconomic status (Corwin and Flaherty 1995). For example, in one urban district in California, educators and Latino parents struggled successfully to form a school that catered to the Latino students' cultural history and origins. In doing so, they ended up separating themselves politically and socially from African Americans and other racial groups in the school district (Wells et al. 1999, 20).

One of the hallmarks of American public education has been the fact that admission to public schools was and is open to all students. American schooling has prided itself since the industrial revolution for not turning away students due to socioeconomic class, race, religion, sexual orientation, special education needs, and the like. Although this noble experiment has been short on practice and long on theory, generally, it is agreed that our nations' children have a human right to equitable education and equity, beginning with admission to schools. As researcher, author, and public school policy expert, Ted Sizer argues:

> *Children should never be turned away from their public school of choice. Doing so violates a public system of education. (Sizer 2008, 13)*

The problem that researchers who study charter schools encounter when looking at admission practices, race, unemployment, discrimination, special needs students, social class disparities, and the host of issues surrounding admissions to charter schools, is that the level of social inequality in the United States has skyrocketed within the last thirty years, leaving myriad roles for public schools to play—from educating students, to providing meals, to counseling, providing after school programs, day care, special educational services, and so on. This spiraling inequality coupled with conservative Supreme Court decisions, disparate economic and political legislation by the states, taxation policies that redistribute income upwards, housing and neighborhood segregation, and low wages not keeping up with inflation, all of this serves to undermine public education and thus the equity required for admissions of all students to institutions of learning. Arguably the same market-based proposals pushed for by charter proponents have, when applied to the social and common good, undermined and further stratified admission to quality schools as well as quality schools themselves. And when applied to the economy as a whole they have been devastating as the present economic crisis testifies. Charter schools certainly cannot be argued to be an antidote for an economy and social system that serves to increase inequality in all aspects of daily life through the imposition of unregulated market reforms, can they? And the market itself, what are we to make of the idea that the market holds the promise for future educational reforms? In these grueling times who really believes that leaving education to unregulated entrepreneurs and Wall Street financiers is the answer to what ails public education in our nation?

All of this seems to imply that if charters are to be a part of the educational stew then they need to remain accessible and open to all students. Yet the history of public schools and charter schools has shown a pattern of exclusion not keeping with the provisions of equity or educational opportunity. For example, charter schools can cleverly use "screening mechanisms" and admission tests to decide who is admitted to a charter school. Schools like the KIPP-managed charter schools (which we look at more closely in chapter 6) require that parents sign, as a testimony to their commitment to their children's education, a contract or commitment form with the charter school stating that they will "commit" or donate either time, resources, or both to the charter school they wish their child to attend. Although the intent behind the theory and practice is laudable—the idea that parents should commit to spending time involved in the education of their children—tying parents hands with such commitment forms or contracts is unfair to many working class families who often work two jobs to survive and simply do not have the time, resources, or often the transportation to travel to school functions and events. These practices, argue opponents to such charter school admission practices, are not equitable and constitute a form of screening for selective admission purposes. Who would argue that parental involvement in education is not important? The question at issue is if the larger societal commitments that parents have to meet allow them to actually devote time to their child's personal or social development and whether this class disparity should deny their children's admittance to charter schools based on the fact they can't.

Many opponents of charter schools are also concerned about admission practices that exclude "undesirable" or "special education" students and parents through "creaming" (Lopez, Wells, and Holme 1998). Charter schools, they argue, should admit special needs students and these students must have access to programs that will help them learn while students who are able to go beyond the standard curriculum should be encouraged to maximize their learning. However, as early as a 1999 Michigan State University study regarding charter schools in that state found that Michigan charter schools were taking students who comprised the cream of the crop financially. The report also stated that the charter schools were generally taking the students who were the cheapest to educate and leaving behind the students who were more costly to educate. For example, because junior high and high school students cost more to educate owing to the need for athletic equipment, laboratories, extensive libraries, and specialized teachers, most of the groups who have opened charter schools in Michigan have elected to open elementary schools ("Michigan Charter Schools," 1999–2000).

The study also disturbingly found that three-quarters of the charter schools in the state had no special education services, and even the few that did enroll special needs students provided them with fewer and less costly services than the nearby public schools did. Several early studies of charter schools have identified special education as one of the key challenges facing charter schools in the future (Urahn and Stewart 1994).

In 1995, the U.S. General Accounting Office studied charter schools in eleven states and identified a number of challenges charter schools encountered in implementing federal programs such as the Individuals with Disabilities Education Act of 1990. This study found, in particular, that because the local school district is the usual point of federal program administration, the lack of connection between some charter schools and a local district raises concern about the flow of federal money and oversight and accountability (U.S. General Accounting Office 1995).

A ten-year-old Michigan State University study points out that when charter schools enroll low-cost students and exclude high-cost students, they increase the average costs for the public school districts that must provide the more expensive services (Lewin 1999). This situation threatens to impact greatly on public schools in states such as California where charter schools are allowed to select their students and can require parents to contribute resources, fill out applications, and go through lengthy interviews. In such states, most charter schools are located in suburbs or small towns and enroll fewer poor and minority students than do neighboring districts. Yet a December 1999 report issued from the U.S. Department of Education rebuts this criticism and contention. The report concluded that no "creaming" had occurred (U.S. Department of Education, under "Joint Committee of Public Schools").

The evidence gleaned from charter schools themselves show that at least one in four charter schools admit to imposing admission requirements in the form of records, tests, or aptitudes (Anderson et al. 2002). And of course some states and districts legally mandate and limit enrollment to low-income or low-achieving students, the subprime market, under the notion that charters can "fix underachieving kids."

Finally, there is the issue of admission by lottery, which is the favored practice for charter schools who have more applicants for their school than seats in the classroom. Take the following scenario found in a *New York Sun* article and described by Jonathan Dolle, of Stanford University and Anne Newman, from Washington University. In their 2008 study, "Luck of the Draw: On the Fairness of Charter School Admission Policies," they describe a typical lottery scene from New York:

> *"Would scholar Bobby Bowman come on up," the head of the school, Eva Moskowitz, boomed into a microphone after Bobby's name was the first to be plucked from the box. A few parents did a little dance as they were handed a yellow piece of paper with instruction about how to officially enroll their child.*
> *"It's like 'American Idol.' I got my gold ticket to Hollywood," Nigel White beamed after his daughter's name was pulled from the box. (Dolle and Newman 2009)*

For a charter school to receive state and federal financial support, they are required by law to use an admissions lottery when the number of applicants exceeds available seats in the classroom. The notion of utilizing lotteries has been argued to be effective for admissions as these lotteries vitiate any "creaming" potential on behalf of charter schools by not relying on market mechanisms or merit-based testing to target their admission of students. At first blush, the lottery admission system seems appropriate and fair; using lotteries, argue policymakers, is a provision to assure that admission to the schools not be reliant on merit-based admissions and acts, that it is necessary to give all students an equal chance to attend a charter school of their choice. But does it? Not according to the 2008 study conducted by Dolle and Newman. They note:

> a closer examination of charter admissions lotteries is warranted for three important reasons. First, charter schools often incorporate preferences into their lottery procedures, increasing the chances that certain types of students get admitted. The fairness of these preferences deserves closer examination. Second, because the outcomes of lotteries are random, the fairness of results cannot be checked in the same way market- or merit-based distributions can be checked. In the case of market distribution, fairness can be defended after the fact by gathering evidence that demonstrates an absence of coercion, truth in advertising, or other common legal requirements. In the case of merit- based admission, fairness can be defended after the fact on substantive grounds: does the distribution respect the relative strength of individuals' claims? But lotteries have no ex post check on the fairness of outcomes. The only way to know a lottery was fair is to know a fair procedure was used—that is, one resulting in genuinely random outcomes. We argue that confirming the fairness of a lottery procedure ex post is more difficult in the case of charter admissions than is typically understood. A third reason admissions lotteries warrant more attention is because the integrity of findings about charter schools' outcomes is contingent upon the integrity of their admissions processes. This is especially true as a growing number of educational researchers use school admissions lotteries as proxies for random assignment: those admitted are the treatment group and those denied admission (presumably because they lost the admissions lottery), are the control group. If, as we argue, there are reasons to question the transparency and accountability of charter admissions lotteries, this may have implications for the trust we put in comparisons of charter schools and regular public schools. (Ibid.)

The potential danger described by Dolle and Newman in their report is that charter school admission policies, such as the lottery mechanism, can actually serve to discriminate against specific families, students or groups that a charter school might not like; thus the concern with transparency and accountability on behalf of those constructing the lottery. Finally, one cannot help from noticing just how insidious "public choice" or competition can be when it operates to induce parents to compare their child's admission in a charter school with a privileged contestant in a "game show" or "winning" in "American Idol." Of course for the disillusioned and frustrated parents that don't succeed in "winning the lottery" they become transformed into mere "spectators" of the auctioning process. The scarcity model offered by lotteries and the individualistic competition between parents for adequate public education for their children cannot, arguably, be healthy for building strong community ties and relationships built on collaboration and equity. It certainly cannot be said to constitute a legitimate "public choice."

Financial Transparency in Charter Schools

Ted Sizer, in his study entitled *Charter Schools and The Value of Public Education* argues that because charter schools are publicly owned they must have a level of adequate transparency in their day-to-day operations. Quoting Sizer:

> *A public school is a public trust, and that trust must be validated by openness (except of course where students' right to privacy must be protected). Information on finances, curriculum, assessment, teacher qualifications, program, student demographics, and other operational issues must be widely and publicly available. This information about any school that receives public funds must not only be shared with the school community, but also with the public at large, and must always be subject to commentary. (Sizer 2008, 13)*

Unfortunately, transparency and full disclosure eludes many charter schools and their operators. When the *New York Times* reported in 2002 that according to the Center for Education Reform, 4.5 percent of charter schools nationwide had folded or had their charters revoked and that in Arizona, which had 422 charters at the time—more than any other state—nearly 10 percent of the charter schools had failed, no one expected that these failures would compound and skyrocket throughout the 40 states that now have charter school legislation (Egan 2002).

Yet sadly this has proven to be the case as national cases of charter school fraud, financial abuse, financial accounting schemes, and a host of other deliberate and intentional criminal practices have been employed at literally hundreds of charter schools throughout the United States. Texas, California, and Arizona account for 40 percent of the nation's charter schools but the movement and the accompanying fraud and abuse, is growing in all states. In fact, the apparent fraud and abuse seen in the growing charter movement over the last 18 years has truly been remarkable and usually unreported nationally; but the facts on the ground can be seen as testimony as to the effects of deregulation, the subsequent lack of transparency, and wholesale forfeiture of disclosure.

Charter school proponents and defenders like to argue that any charter schools on the "fraud and abuse" chopping block, are just "bad apples" in an otherwise fully transparent, innovative charter system; however the evidence wholly disagrees, pointing to mounting evidence of widespread systematic and institutional abuse from the failure of oversight and full disclosure of business practices, to fraudulent accounting procedures reminiscent of Enron. What are some of the factors that contribute to abuse and fraud within the charter school movement? They can be summarized as:

- Accounting schemes that base payments to charter schools on "projected" student enrollment figures;
- A lack of oversight by regulatory agencies in assuring that public monies be spent responsibly by charter authorizers and/or legislative bodies;
- Favorable legislation that encourages privatization, conflict of interests, and lax regulation of charter schools;
- Nepotism, self-dealing, and cozy financial and political relationships between charter school operators and financial speculators, relatives, and friends; and
- A lack of transparency in public oversight of charter school finances and expenditures.

ACCOUNTING SCHEMES AND PROJECTED ENROLLMENT

One such factor that fuels much of the fraud and abuse within and among many charter schools is the way in which funding is handed out to charter schools based on "projected" enrollments. Charter advocates, The *Center for Education Reform* reported that between 1999 and 2002, 194 charter schools closed. This amounted to about 7 percent of all the charter schools in existence at the time. The Center then went on to publish the reasons given for the closings. Corwin and Schneider tabulated these findings in their book, *The Charter School Hoax*. What the Center found and what Corwin and Schneider tabulated was that the number of schools closed for corruption and mismanagement outnumbered the number of schools closed for academic reasons by three to one; and this tabulation does not even include the charter schools that closed voluntarily, nor does it include schools that districts closed in an effort to consolidate school sites. The categories that Corwin and Schneider developed to tabulate the *Center's* findings included ineffective planning, which then was broken down into three categories, low enrollment, indebtedness, and administrative conflicts—(28 charter schools closed for low enrollment, 27 due to indebtedness, and 6 due to administrative conflicts); corruption and mismanagement, such as fiscal mismanagement, falsifying enrollment, keeping inadequate records, violating legal codes, administrative mismanagement, and violating special education codes—67 schools fell into these categories and were forced to close; administrative problems, such as lack of faculty or staff instability along with lack of innovation—the total number of charters closed for these reason were 19. Finally, Corwin and Schneider looked at academic deficiencies forcing charter school closures, such as low student achievement and curriculum deficiencies—19 charters were shuttered for falling into this category (Corwin and Schneider 2005). Much like what happened on Wall Street in the financial crisis that hit the nation in 2008 where oversight committees and bodies were relegated to a bad joke, there is virtually no oversight of educational programs or how they operate. States are the responsible parties in monitoring school performance, but with their cash-strapped status they can hardly afford to keep schools open, let alone monitor new charter schools. We cannot be sure, due to the lack of oversight by agencies and public bodies along with insufficient and inadequate reporting on the issue by the news media, but there must be a plethora of hidden, yet unethical practices going on in charter schools throughout the nation and if you are a parent, this can be frightening news. As Corwin and Schneider note, the controversy over the oversight of charter schools has reached unacceptable levels:

> *After nearly fifteen years, the risk associated with malfeasance can be no longer passed off as growing pains. (Ibid.)*

CHARTERS IN WASHINGTON D.C.

In a 2007 *Washington Examiner* investigative article that exhaustively looked at the District of Columbia's charter funding mechanism in some detail, it was documented that the District of Columbia's $300 million-a-year charter school funding formula has been a dangerous enticement to fraud and waste for years. Gina Arlotto, of the Save our Schools Coalition, a nonprofit group that advocates for traditional public schools in the D.C. area stated firmly:

> *I'm not totally opposed to all charter schools. But the reality is that some of these charter school operators are hustlers, quite a few of them are outright criminals and a lot of them are doing a big bait-and-switch. (Myers 2007)*

According to the *Examiner* investigation, there are some 55 charter schools in D.C.—more than in any other city in the nation. The Board of Education governs 18 of those schools; the D.C. Public Charter School Board governs the rest. And according to the article, the charter schools are given four financial payments a year—in July, October, January and April. What the schools do is to estimate their attendance in July and then they are paid at the public rate until financial audits based on enrollment are finally conducted. The problem arises in that the enrollment audits aren't finished until late January or early February, so the charter schools are paid based on their "projected" enrollment up and until the last payment. This gives unscrupulous operators quite a bit of wiggle room in projection estimates. The Washington D.C. Education Office conducts the enrollment audits every year but officials in the Education Office acknowledged privately, according to the *Examiner* article, that there are gaps in the system.

The problem, according to Arlotto, is:

> *There's anecdotal evidence that some of these guys are loading up on students until they pass the audit. Once they pass, they make it clear that some of the kids aren't welcome and send them back to the neighborhood schools. (Ibid.)*

She goes on to wryly note that:

> *The charter schools are popping up on every corner. They're like liquor stores. (Ibid.)*

Projected enrollment and the system of finance by which charters are funded is the culprit in many fraudulent practices among charter school operators and these practices have caused problems in other places in D.C. as well. For example, the Jos-Arz Therapeutic Public Charter School, a District of Columbia Charter school, was shut down in 2006 after spending nearly $40 million per year in public dollars. Its projected attendance was 190 students, but it never enrolled more than 50. The school was being probed by a grand jury at the time the article in the *Examiner* was published. Another D.C. federal grand jury was exploring allegations that officials at the New School for Enterprise and Development in D.C. inflated the school's enrollment figures as well (Ibid.).

Texas, home of a great many charter schools, is also the subject of recent widespread abuse and fraud. In April 2008 the *Dallas Morning News* reported the stunning figure that Texas had 206 charter schools, and 93 of them were bilking the state out of millions of dollars by overcounting their enrollment. According to the newspaper report:

> *The Texas Education Agency, which oversees public education in the state, is working to recover $17 million of the $26 million from nearly half of the charters now operating in Texas. TEA records show that 20 schools went out of business before the state could recover its money, leaving taxpayers holding a $9 million bag of debt. (Smith 2008)*

It seems the situation is similar to what occurred in the District of Columbia, the charter schools collected state funds either by inflating the number of students in their classrooms or by making so called "accounting mistakes." The $26 million debt, owed as of 2008 to the state, comes from 93 of the 211 charter operators in Texas, according to the report. The amount equals the average state funding for about 4,800 students at roughly $5,400 per student. Texas state funding for charter schools has grown from just under $10 million to more than $646 million in 11 years. Problems with charter attendance reports run the gamut. Some fail to report absences throughout the year, so, the state gives them money as if every student showed up each day. Others count students long after they dropped out, and of course others "project enrollment" to receive funding. And as the extensive investigative report in the *Dallas Morning News* found, some schools report too many students in special education and other programs that generate extra state funding. In reality, the report notes, no one knows for sure if the charter school debt is really $26 million dollars, as indicated by the auditors due to the lack of full disclosure and transparency. The sum owed, in fact, could be more.

According to the *Dallas Morning News,* which printed a full map with all the names of the charter schools that owe the millions of taxpayer dollars to the state (those operating and those closed), Texas Education Agency officials stated that Texas law makes it hard to close a charter school except for health and safety violations. The law provides that the state can revoke a charter for academic or financial problems, but it requires a lengthy history of documentation to support any decision to do so. This prompted Jack Ammons, a former school superinten-dent who works with troubled charter schools on behalf of TEA, to say he believes charters can succeed—but only with strong supervision and oversight. Noting the growing problem of fraud and abuse and suggesting the need for disclosure, transparency, and legislative oversight, Ammons acidly commented:

> *If taxpayers knew how much of their tax money was going to charter schools and what the actual return on their tax money was in some charter schools, they would see that the Legislature address the whole charter school concept. (Ibid.)*

Are these simply the good intentions of the many overcome by the financial greed of a few? Although certainly not all charter schools are run by "hucksters" and financial swindlers, the problem is so rampant that more and more states are looking at legislation to reign in many charter abuses. When government bodies offer free public money to charter school operators with no oversight, no necessity for disclosure, no transparency, and no regulations we have a recipe for disaster.

NEPOTISM, SELF-SERVING LEGISLATION AND DEAL MAKING

On April 29, 2009, the Pennsylvania Department of Education filed suit against Agora Cyber Charter School (a virtual charter school) in Devon, alleging fraud and breach of fiduciary responsibility by its board of trustees. By state law, the education department has oversight responsibility for the 11 cyber charter schools that provide online instruction to students in their homes. The civil complaint maintained that the cyber charter's board entered into improper contracts with the Cynwyd Group LLC, a management company that was co-created by Agora's founder

Dorothy June Brown, "for the purpose of making money from managing and operating the school." Brown's Cynwyd Group not only has a management contract with Agora but owns the school's administrative offices on Chestnut Street in Devon. The school pays $25,000 per month in rent to Brown and Brown, who initially was Agora's chief executive officer, is Cynwyd Group's senior consultant to the cyber charter school and an ex-officio member of the charter board. Brown founded three traditional charter schools in Philadelphia and was the CEO of two of them until the summer of 2008 (Woodall 2009).

According to documents filed in Commonwealth Court, the state Department of Education has concluded that Agora "is operating in such a grossly unlawful and improper manner" that if the department continued making payments of taxpayer funds, it would be "facilitating and enabling Agora in the perpetration of ongoing and pervasive unlawful and improper conduct" (Ibid.).

The suit goes on to contend that Agora's board of trustees "participated in a scheme to defraud" the department and had "defrauded Agora students by entering into a lease that was far above fair market value" and paying Cynwyd Group a management fee when "little was done by Cynwyd . . ." (Ibid.).

Based on current enrollment, Agora officials projected that the charter's revenues will total about $41 million in taxpayer funds for the 2008 school year. The management contract calls for Brown's company to be paid 7 percent of gross revenues. The fee could be as much as $2.8 million this school year, according to officials (Ibid.).

Florida, another bellwether state when it comes to charter school legislation, has nearly half of its state charter schools operating at a deficit. Mary Shanklin and Vicki McClure, investigative reporters for the *Orlando Sentinel* poured copiously through property records, federal tax reports, school district records, and literally hundreds of state-required financial audits filed by Florida charters. The findings of the two reporters is distressing, with the investigation yielding evidence that nearly half of the audited charters in the entire state of Florida had operating deficits in 2005, the latest year of audits released by the state. Total operating losses for these schools exceeded $37 million to the taxpayer. Nearly 100 met one of the criteria for being declared in a state of financial emergency under a law passed last year. Furthermore, the two investigative reporters found that more than 140 schools had intertwined business relationships that would raise questions at traditional schools or at charters in several other states. Most were disclosed by charter auditors, who reviewed each school's finances and reported them as "related-party transactions." Finally, the report noted that nearly one in 10 charters spent more on administration than on the classroom (Shanklin and McClure 2009).

The investigative team also found that that the same time the schools suffered deficits, more than $200 million of the $492 million Florida spent on these privately operated schools in 2005 alone went to charters that had business relationships with school officials: renting buildings to the charters, selling services to them, hiring relatives as employees, and the like (Ibid.).

Yet in light of the facts released by the *Sentinel* reporters, former education commissioner, John Winn seemed to excuse the problem, commenting that although charters need to follow ethical business practices it can be hard to find committed volunteers for the charters and that many times this means that there will be business ties to the schools. Winn went on to say he saw no need for any state oversight and called the majority of the failing charter school financial problems "benign," apparently not concerned with the failed schools and costs to taxpayers (Ibid.).

In light of the disturbing statistics and analysis revealed by the investigative reporting work of the *Orlando Sentinel* these financial problems can hardly be said to be "benign" to the taxpayers who must fund them. And certainly the issue of nepotism and business wheeling and dealing on the backs of public charter schools and the students and parents who attend and support them is certainly not benign; in fact, as is shown year after year it is often criminal.

Another big issue facing charter schools that do not confront traditional public schools is actually finding a school building, and this can open powerful potential loopholes for fraud and abuse. Public schools are required to go through a bidding process to construct schools. For charters, the common scenario is for a charter applicant to enter a prelease agreement with a contractor, without bidding. Then the contractor builds the school if the charter is granted. The lease on the school is then paid for with public funds. In many ways, real estate management/development companies appear to be driving the charter process in all forty states, advising the charter groups on construction and gaining zoning clearance, handling legal issues with planning departments and city councils regarding land use, and so on.

In a 2005 report entitled *Debunking the Real Estate Risk of Charter Schools,* the Ewing Marion Kauffman Foundation looked at risk factors for landlords who might wish to lease buildings to charter schools. They argue that entrepreneurs might not be seeing the inherent financial advantage in leasing to charter schools do to perceived risks that do not exist. In fact, they go on to state that charter schools:

> *represent a growth market for lenders, developers, and the like, affordable deals are often hard to come by—in part because this is a fairly new and unusual kind of market, and the risks of a school failing or defaulting are not well understood. (Ewing Marion Kauffman Foundation 2005)*

The Department of Education (DOE) has established a "Credit Enhancement for Charter School Facilities Program" that channels funds, on a competitive basis, to organizations in order to "credit enhance" charter loans or leases.

As of 2005, Congress had appropriated approximately $125 million for this program. According to the U.S. Department of Education:

> The Credit Enhancement for Charter School Facilities program provides assistance to help charter schools meet their facility needs. Under this program, funds are provided on a competitive basis to public and nonprofit entities, and consortia of those entities, to leverage other funds and help charter schools obtain school facilities through such means as purchase, lease, and donation. Grantees may also use grants to leverage funds to help charter schools construct and renovate school facilities.
>
> To help leverage funds for charter school facilities, grant recipients may, among other things, guarantee and insure debt to finance charter school facilities; guarantee and insure leases for personal and real property; facilitate a charter school's facilities financing by identifying potential lending sources, encouraging private lending, and other similar activities; and establish charter school facility "incubator" housing that new charter schools may use until they can acquire a facility on their own. (U.S. Department of Education, under "Credit Enhancement for Charter School Facilities")

Of course from a market-based, entrepreneurial point of view the key advantage of the credit enhancement program is that it legalizes the transfer of federal taxpayer money to private corporations and private charter school operators and thus leverages private entrepreneurial capital with federal tax dollars. The Kauffman report found that in 2005, conservatively, one dollar of federal monies were being used for each five dollars of private capital invested. This means a 20 percent taxpayer subsidy to private sector actors willing to lease private property to charter schools (Ewing Marion Kauffman Foundation 2005). Not a bad deal.

Charter schools, of course, must also acquire start-up funding from investors because money from the government is allocated according to grant specifications that usually deal with the day-to-day operations of schools, such as paying for utilities and buying textbooks. This need for real estate and "seed" money has paid off handsomely for some unscrupulous charter operators and real estate entrepreneurs that either charge excessive rent, loan money at usurious rates, or actually sell real estate for school buildings to charter schools at tremendous profits. Take the case of the Mater Academy charter we previewed in chapter 4.

Miami-Dade County school-district auditors estimated that officers of the company that manages the Mater Academy charters, Academica, Inc., overcharged the schools about $1.3 million in rent at the warehouse where classes were held. Ignacio Zulueta was the manager of the company that bought the school building and charges the charters more than $3 million a year in rent. His brother, Fernando, was president of Mater Academies and is on the board of Academica, Inc. Both have been officers of Academica Corp. for years, and Academica manages more than 25 South Florida charters, including Mater Academy schools and the company has growing interests, as we mentioned, in Utah and Arizona (Shanklin and McClure 2009).

Yet even more incredulous is that the employees of the Mater schools also served on the Academica board of directors. District auditors for the state called it "an interwoven web of governance" that operated with few checks and balances. The auditors wrote that:

> *These relationships in turn create weak boards because board members are depen-*
> *dent on Academica for their continued livelihood. (Ibid.)*

However, in an interview given to the *Orlando Sentinel,* Academica's chief financial officer characterized the district allegations as baseless and biased, saying there was no evidence that Mater's rents were high. He stated that the Mater board could not afford to buy the building and thus they exercised good judgment when they agreed to the lease (Ibid.).

Auditors also found that elsewhere in South Florida, at the Somerset Academy Charter Middle and High schools, Pinecrest Preparatory Academy and the Archimedean Academy, also managed by Academica, pay rent to their own charter trustees, managers, or directors (Ibid.).

In Utah, where Academica, Inc. has made a notable presence, around a third of the state's 52 charter schools contract with companies like Academica, Inc. In fact, as of 2006 Sen. Sheldon Killpack, R-Syracuse, helped run Academica West, a situation begging questions of propriety and conflict of interest. The issue raises troubling questions precisely because it seems that lawmakers can simply pass laws that actually will allow them to benefit financially off the public trough. The issue prompted Utah in 2006 to have its legislative auditors try to determine whether charter development companies and charter schools were in compliance with the state procurement code. The audit and subsequent report was intended to address a number of unanswered questions about the roles of charter management and development companies—some of which are run by legislators—and whether the public money that goes into them is appropriate (Erickson 2006).

Loans are another business relationship prominent between some charter directors and the schools they run. Florida audits showed six charters in Florida collectively owed their board members more than a half-million dollars in 2005 (Shanklin and McClure 2009). Nearly half of Florida's charters had operating deficits, but that's not all. The loans were not born out of altruism, nor did they meet the spirit of the stated goals of the charter school movement. In fact, the "hard money" loaned was found often to be a usurious lending racket.

Take the Language Academy in Pasco County, which auditors claimed spent less than half of the monies it received on instruction. According to the *Orlando Sentinel* investigation of the state's charter schools, an unnamed school official at the charter was charging the school as much as 21 percent interest for private loans—more than double the lending rate available from banks at the time. Academy Administrator Joyce Nunn stated the loan had been repaid. Yet although charter schools are subject to the public-records law, she refused requests for information about who made the loan. The issues of transparency and public disclosure seemed to be nonexistent in the minds of many policymakers. When questioned about the identity of the school official who made the loan, Nunn replied:

I'm not telling you who it was. I am tired of newspapers dredging up the past instead of focusing on the future. (Ibid.)

Isn't transparency and disclosure a necessary prerequisite to "focus on the future"?

The 2005 Florida state auditor general's report made it clear that charters that go into debt either have to cut services, such as teacher pay and instructional materials, or they have to shift funds from education of children to interest payments on the debt. This means less instruction, certainly less innovation, and inevitably, less quality education; hardly a recipe for spreading "best practices" and innovating traditional public schools.

The Charter School Institute, another Florida-based charter school, caters mainly to students who come from Haiti. Four fifths of the students cannot read at grade level and despite all this, the school is so deeply in debt that it spends only 13 percent of its state dollars on instruction. Cutting back on instruction or actually purchasing standardized lesson plans from many of the same companies that manage or run charter schools is one way of keeping costs down and profits high for investors and operators. It is also another way many charters shortchange our nation's children and taxpaying public under the rubric of market-driven educational reform.

Joseph Littles-Nguzo Saba Charter School, in Florida, knows this scenario all too well. The school has been short on cash since it opened in 1999; it has one-hundred thirty students sharing seven computers. The "science-lab equipment" consists of two microscopes and a set of scales. The school does not let children take home books and the "D-rated school" spends less than half the money it gets from taxpayers on instruction. However, it does have the money to pay a $2,000-a-month pension and provide several life insurance policies for the school's founder, who no longer even works at the school. Although traditional public schools could never legally borrow money from individuals, the struggling charter school is, as of this writing, $120,000 debt to the same founder who is receiving the $2,000 monthly pension (Ibid.).

And then there was the reported case of the Palm Beach County's Survivors Charter School, where $100,000 was spent by the public for eight season's worth of tickets to see the Miami Dolphins games. According to audits conducted by the Palm Beach County School District, the principal of the charter school and his cronies received the sport tickets while the principal of one of the other Survivors' campuses also received $600 per month in taxpayer money to lease a BMW while pulling in $163,412 per year in salary (Ibid.).

Supporters say failures among the country's charter schools are to be expected as the schools try to find their footing 18 years after they began to take hold, but the lack of transparency and accountability is notoriously lacking and the length of time to get "footing" for a movement more than 18 years old is troubling. In Washington D.C., for example, every charter school is a private nonprofit corporation. These nonprofit corporations operate with public funds but are accountable only to their board of trustees. Furthermore, the executive director of the D.C. Association of Chartered Public Schools has declared that charter schools are not government bodies and therefore are not held accountable to the Freedom of Information Act or any public records acts. In fact, in 2006 the D.C. City Council exempted all D.C. charter schools from the city's open meetings law (El-Amine and Glazer 2008). Why?

The District of Columbia is an exemplar of non-accountability and a purposeful failure to provide the public with charter school transparency, from exempting charters from Freedom of Information Act requests and public records act requests, to refusing to hold open public meetings, to refusing citizen access to information and plans regarding charters school finance and development. Part of the problem is that many of the charters in D.C. are controlled not by community groups, although certainly some charters are community-based, but rather by large corporations and distinct business interests. Joseph E. Robert Jr. provides such an example of how corporate interests have served to ride the vehicle of charter schools, profiting handsomely off the idea of "public choice," while remaining unaccountable to the public through the use of intensive business and political ties.

As the founder of an educational group, Fight for Children, Robert is also the chair and CEO of a real estate development company. He is on the board of the Real Estate Roundtable, a private interest group that works to lobby congress for favorable legislation. He is also a principal investor in what is known as Venture Philanthropy Partners that seeks to expand charters throughout D.C. and beyond. Robert is not alone; along with his corporate efforts to expand charter schools and thus profits for his firms, he is joined by Walton Family Foundation, the Kimsey Foundation, the Pisces Foundation, AOL, the GAP, and Wal-Mart. Of course these groups are private and thus operate outside any public oversight or accountability; they are subject to no transparency. Their operations in the charter school arena only serve to complicate the notion of "public choice," for if their records are not available to the public in regards to their plans for charter schools then oversight, transparency, and accountability fall into the hands of corporate CEOs and their managerial teams; the fox then guards the hen house (Sen 2006).

RELIGION AND CHARTER SCHOOLS

History of Religion and Public Schools

Religion has long played a divisive role in American education. Ever since the founding of the country, U.S. political leaders have been concerned as to if and how to create an American educational system not chained to sectarian rivalry and strife. As we noted in our discussion of the history of public schooling in the United States, the system of sectarian schools that existed at the beginning of the country was, by the mid-nineteenth century, supplanted with publicly funded "common schools." These schools were described and designed to offer children a public secular education free from the pressures of religious conflicts. Yet as Benjamin Hillman notes in a 2008 article in the *Yale Law Review Journal,* from the start, common schools drew their ideology from the teachings of mainline Protestantism. The creation of the common school, according to Hillman, did not lead to the disappearance of religious schools nor did it erase the conflict over the role of religion in education. During this time Catholics perceived a heavy-handed Protestant influence within the public schools and this prompted them to create their own school system in the late nineteenth century. In response, Protestants successfully advocated for "Blaine Amendments" to state constitutions that prevented any state funding of religious schools (Hillman 2008). Hillman goes on to explicate that:

> In the second half of the twentieth century, advocates of secular education and religious traditionalists alike turned to the courts to arbitrate their disputes over the proper role of religion in public education. Although a legacy of Protestant influence remains, these Supreme Court decisions have helped to secularize American public education. By the end of the twentieth century, a robust constitutional regime governing religious expression in public schools appeared to be in place.
>
> Over the past several decades, however, school choice has significantly changed the structure of American schooling. In particular, publicly funded, privately managed charter schools have made the school offerings of many urban districts unprecedentedly diverse. No longer must those attending urban public schools go to a neighborhood school or choose only between undifferentiated generalist schools; today, a menu of specialized offerings exists, from Afro-centric schools to those with a focus on art or social change. (Ibid.)

Contemporary Charter Schools and the Establishment Clause

By virtue of the fact that charter schools are part of the public educational system in the United States, charter schools are legally bound by the First Amendment of the Constitution of the United States. This means charter schools are subject to what is called the "Establishment Clause" of the U.S. Constitution, also often referred to as the notion of the "separation of church and state." When applying the Establishment Clause to public schools, the Courts have often emphasized the importance of maintaining "neutrality" on behalf of public school officials toward religion What this means is that legally public schools may neither inculcate nor may they inhibit religion. They also may not prefer or privilege one religion over another—or even religion over nonreligious beliefs. This means that charter schools, since they are pubic schools, should not do anything that promotes a particular religion or faith. But is this the case? Are charter schools being utilized by religious communities to establish their own religious schools? The ACLU thinks so.

In 2008, after concerns were leveled at the Tarek ibn Ziyad Academy charter school (TiZA) located in Minnesota briefly mentioned early in this chapter, the Minnesota Department of Education proceeded to investigate the school and they eventually found the school was mostly in compliance with state and federal law. The school was told to take corrective actions regarding prayer services held each Friday at the school and the officials of the school were ordered to make bus rides home available right after school ends, instead of after a "voluntary" after-school religious program that the school held. Yet on January 20, 2009, the ACLU filed charges against the Minnesota Department of Education alleging that the charter school, which caters to Muslim students, is using taxpayer money to illegally promote religion in violation of the First Amendment. According to the lawsuit the TiZA has violated the First Amendment by preferring the Muslim religion over others. For example, the ACLU cites the fact that the school allows prayer sessions during school hours. They also allege that the charter school prefers Muslim dietary practices by serving certain foods and endorses Muslim clothing rules. This they allege is a violation of the Establishment Clause. The school said in a written statement that though officials haven't yet seen the ACLU's complaint, they believe the lawsuit is without merit; however the deputy education commissioner for the state said in a written statement that the department is reviewing the ACLU lawsuit and will continue to monitor operations at TiZA. He also said the department is drafting legislation to address some of the concerns (Dunbar 2009).

On the other hand, Lawrence Weinberg and Bruce Cooper, writing for *Education Week,* imply that the U.S. Supreme Court's 2002 decision in *Zelman v. Simmons-Harris,* which said that public vouchers could be used for students' tuition at religious K-12 schools, opened the door for religiously based charter schools, or at least the authors and their supporters seem to believe this to be the case. The issue of mandatory school attendance at a public school within a state was presented to the State Supreme Court of Oregon in 1925 for adjudication. In the case of *Pierce v. Society of Sisters,* the Supreme Court noted that an earlier 1922 Oregon state law requiring that all school-aged children attend a public school in their community cannot outlaw attendance at private or religious schools; that to do so was unconstitutional and a violation of parents' rights to direct the upbringing and education of their children. However, it is important to note that the court in no way allowed for the public financing of such schools. It simply stated that a private religious education met the requirements of mandatory attendance in school for Oregon students. As a result of the Oregon state court decision as well as federal decisions that have held the same, the issue of religious charter schools and public funding should be an open and shut issue, right?

Authors Weinberg and Cooper claim that TiZA offers an example to citizens as to how to tailor such "religious theme" schools to meet the exigencies of the Establishment Clause while still allowing for a religiously or ethnically based "theme" charter school. Take their commentary published in *Education Week* in 2007, whereby they counsel those interested in opening such "theme" schools could follow Ziyad Academy's example. They offer the following tips, and others, for religious groups that may be interested:

create a separate, secular foundation to support the school; adopt a mission statement that includes specific educational goals unrelated to the religious or cultural purposes; and develop a curriculum that meets the school's religious, cultural, and educational needs. In short, the school should be designed "to teach the ethics and history of the faith, but not to practice it." (Weinberg and Cooper 2007)

But is this simply a political game plan for a runaround the separation of church and state in an attempt to get public funding for religious schools? Is the so-called "religious camel's nose" under the tent? Opponents say it is and that we can expect more debates as the charter school movement grows and as cash-strapped public schools turn to outside groups for programming.

Yale Law Review Journal author Benjamin Siracusa Hillman argues that:

Given that charter schools provide private groups the chance to get involved in public education, it was only a matter of time before religious groups sought to provide educational services—whether to their own adherents or to others—at public expense. In recent years, charter schools that are self-consciously centered around Muslim, Jewish, and Christian values have sprung up. These "religious charter schools" differ significantly from private religious schools in that they purport to comply with the Establishment Clause's requirements for public schools, while simultaneously reflecting the values and culture of a particular religious group. Religious charter schools raise difficult constitutional, social, and political questions, which courts and the legal academic literature have only begun to explore. (Hillman 2008)

And here lies the contentious debate: the notion that these specific charter schools "purport to comply with the Establishment Clauses's requirement for public schools. . . ." But do they?

TiZA is not the only charter school that has raised eyebrows among civil libertarians bent on assuring the "separation of church and state." The Hebrew Language Academy Charter School, located in New York has also seen their share of controversy. The school is scheduled to open in the fall of 2009 and will focus on Arabic language and culture. But should public schools celebrate a particular culture? The question is being asked in many circles as the controversy heats up. According to civil rights advocates and progressive educators the role of public schools is not to celebrate one culture but to celebrate the pluralism of cultures in a public setting. Michael Meyers, executive director of the New York Civil Rights Coalition doesn't think so. In statement published in the Associated Press he stated, "They're trying to transmit cultural values and identity, and that's not the purpose of a public school" (Associated Press 2009).

Public schools are supposed to be for all ethnicities, cultures, and races aren't they? And is this really a thinly veiled attempt to wrap the idea of an ethnic or religious charter school within calls for an "opportunity to become bilingual"?

According to an Associated Press report published 3 February 2009 in the U.S. education section of the MSNBC news site, the Hebrew charter school, which still remains without a location or site for instruction, is due to open with 150 students in kindergarten and first grade and will grow to 450 in grades K-5. Like other charter schools, it will be taxpayer-funded but the report indicates that the school is expected to raise additional money from private donors and has commitments of $500,000 a year from philanthropist Michael Steinhardt and $250,000 a year from the Charles and Lynn Schusterman Family Foundation. Even though Steinhardt, the father of Berman, the school's chairwoman, founded the Steinhardt Foundation for Jewish Life in 1994 with the goal of revitalizing Jewish identity he told reporters the charter school will not promote the Jewish religion but will instead be using secular texts to teach modern Hebrew (Ibid.).

The Brooklyn Hebrew school is not the nation's first Hebrew charter school, either. The Ben Gamla Hebrew Charter School which we covered in chapter 4, located in Hollywood, Florida, also sparked controversy when it opened in 2007. It serves kosher meals and its director is a rabbi, but an expert hired by the district deemed Ben Gamla's lesson plans "entirely appropriate for a publicly funded charter school." Diane Ravitch, a professor of education at New York University and a senior fellow at the Brookings Institute, said in an op-ed piece in the *New York Daily News* that she objected to the Hebrew school because a public school should not be "centered on the teaching of a single non-American culture." According to Ravitch:

> We don't send children to public schools to learn to be Chinese or Russian or Greek or Korean. We send them to learn to be American. (Ibid.)

The controversy is heating up as "religious" charter schools or "ethnically or culturally based" charter schools begin to proliferate over the national educational landscape. Take the latest controversy over charter schools and religion in New Jersey, for example. If allowed by the New Jersey state Department of Education to open, Hatikvah International Academy Charter School could be the first charter in New Jersey with a mission statement centered on a foreign country. Founders say it would seek to "build partnerships for future cultural and economic opportunities" with Israel. The school would provide "in-depth study of Hebrew and Hebrew culture," and would open in the fall of 2010 with 108 students from kindergarten through third grade, according to its application. The founders argue their school would steer clear of religion while teaching a vital twenty-first century skill—a second language that would prepare students for the global economy. But critics say the school represents a thinly veiled and unfairly competitive substitute for a local private Jewish school in town that teaches religion and charges up to $13,000 a year in tuition. There is no charge for students to attend a charter school, which is funded by taxpayers (Keller 2009).

While opponents argue the proposed New Jersey charter school violates separation of church and state, the school stressed it would abide by requirements separating church and state. The schools Web site indicated that the school would observe the same holidays as local public schools and the cafeteria would not serve kosher food, although students would not be discouraged from bringing kosher food to school, said co-founder Michelle Ann Wilson (Ibid.). Yet from the point of view of many residents in New Jersey the new proposed charter represents a problem. Liti Haramaty, a woman born in Israel whose two children attend a traditional public school sees the newly proposed charter school as a violation of the spirit of public education by allocating taxpayer monies for identity groups and perhaps subtle religious anchoring. She was one of many New Jersey residents who signed a petition to oppose the new school. Speaking for herself, but also for many who felt a petition to oppose the school was necessary, Ms. Haramaty stated:

> I don't think it's fair. If people want a specific education for their kids, they should be willing to pay for it. (Ibid.)

But is religion the actual issue when it comes to the proliferation of "Hebrew" charter schools or "Muslim" charter schools or any ethnic charter school? Or is the sole and real issue about providing educational havens based on culture, identity politics, and the chance to become bilingual, as the schools advertise for students?

The answer perhaps can be found by looking at the newly proposed New York Brooklyn Preparatory Charter School, being discussed as this book is written and scheduled to submit its application in 2009 for a 2010 opening. According to an article in the *New York Post* in May of 2009, an e-mail circulated by the charter schools proponents clearly stated:

For those parents that are unhappy with the secular education that their children are receiving or feel that their children are not getting the proper academic skills necessary to succeed in the global 21st century, the charter school option is a viable one. For those parents that feel that the dual curriculum offered by our yeshivas stresses too heavily on religious training rather than on secular studies, a charter school may be a desired alternative. (De Meglio 2009)

The newly proposed school also noted in its e-mail:

. . . that when the official school day ends, an independent Talmud Torah organization would lead an after-school program teaching Judaism. (Ibid.)

The charter school, if approved, would charge an annual tuition of $3,000 per student but the school would receive another $12,000 per student per year of taxpayer monies. This would put it in an economic position to compete with private Yeshivas that charge outlandish admission fees unaffordable to many religious communities. And this, say opponents, is really the issue. Subsidizing religious schools under the auspices of religious studies, bilingual education, religious history, and ethnic identity with culture is already available to those parents seeking to send their children to private, religious based or ethnically based schools. Why then, argue opponents to the idea, should taxpayers subsidize parental choices around charter schools that really advocate one religion while masquerading as ethnic studies, comparative religious education, and bilingual education? Isn't this specifically what the founding fathers sought to prevent with the codification into law of the separation of church and state?

Church-Based Facilities and Charter Schools

Finally, there is the controversial issue of churches that host charter schools at church locations, usually for a fee. Is this considered legal? Many charter schools have turned to local churches in their states for space or a location to hold the school. This "partnership" between a religious entity in this case the church, and a charter school means that the state can pump public monies into churches under the auspices of paying for renovations, expansions and new buildings. A Harlem church that wants to run a charter school has sued New York State officials, in a challenge to a law preventing religious entities from operating such institutions. In 2007, the New Horizon Church Ministry filed suit against the state of New York claiming that a New York law prohibiting charter schools from operating under the direction of a religious denomination violated the church's rights of free religious exercise, free speech, and equal protection under the law (Hughes 2007).

They claim the New York Cities Charter School Act denies those who wish to express their religious beliefs from receiving public funds or access to public resources.

The St. Peters Missionary Baptist Church in Indian River County, Florida received a new multipurpose room thanks to a $364,875 school-construction grant made on behalf of St. Peter's Academy, a public charter school. Several of the charter board members are associated with the church and the church leases space and a bus to the school (Shanklin and McClure 2009). The Rio Grande Charter School of Excellence, another Florida charter school, pays $96,000 of state tax monies to the New Covenant Baptist Church to lease land and ten portable classrooms on church grounds. Rio Grande also borrowed money from the church to stay in operation for the 2005 school year. Isn't this indicative of an incestuous relationship between church and state? Not so fast, says Florida Education Commissioner Jeanine Bloomberg:

> When done appropriately, the combined use of space is helpful to both the church and school. (Ibid.)

Sure it is. The school gets the space and the church receives income from taxpayers. Isn't the real issue not how helpful the relationship between church and state might be, but if the relationship itself is legal? According to the *Nonregulatory Guidance Title V part B, Charter Schools Program* issued by the U.S. Department of Education:

> Like other public schools, charter schools may enter into partnerships with community groups for secular purposes, such as tutoring or recreational activities. Religious groups may be partners for these types of activities so long as charter schools select partners without regard to their religious affiliation, ensure that no public funds are used for religious purposes, and do not engage in or encourage religious activity. Charter schools may not limit participation in the partnership to religious groups or certain religious groups, and they may not select students to encourage or discourage student participation with particular partners based on the religious or secular nature of the organization. (U.S. Department of Education, under "Charter Schools Program")

The Guidelines go even further, spelling out legal charter school affiliate and business relationships and duties with regards to creation or use of facilities and religious organizations:

> A charter school may use the facilities of a religious organization to the same extent that other public schools may use these facilities. Generally, this means that charter school may lease space from a religious organization so long as the charter school remains nonreligious in all its programs and operations. Most importantly, a land-

lord affiliated with a religion may not exercise any control over what is taught in the charter school. (Ibid.)

The controversy over church-charter partnerships and the founding of national, ethnic charter schools that operate under the rubric of "cultural studies" and "ethnic identity" and language acquisition promises to remain heated and cacophonous as the interpretations of these guidelines and the current movement in "religious theme" charter schools is both disconcerting and unacceptable to those who advocate the separation of church and state. Florida psychology professor, Ira Fischler, is troubled by what he sees as the move towards religiously based charter schools. According to Fischler the constitution is clear and no monies may be spent, either indirectly or directly, to support religious organizations (Shankler and McClure 2009). Spending public monies to "partner" with churches whereby these religious institutions receive public monies for renovation of buildings they can then lease to charter schools at a profit or even at cost seems to both violate the U.S. Department of Education Guidelines as well as the Establishment Clause. One can be certain that these issues will remain contentious in the future and the subject of much legal and public debate.

DISASTER CAPITALISM: CHARTER SCHOOLS IN NEW ORLEANS

In 2005, after the devastation wrought in New Orleans by Hurricane Katrina, the atmosphere among many politicians and those in the business sector was jubilant. Commenting on the devastation wrought by tumultuous events before, during, and especially after the hurricane, Richard Baker, a prominent Republican congressman from the city spoke to a group of lobbyists telling them:

We finally cleaned up public housing in New Orleans. We couldn't do it, but God did. (Harwood 2005)

What Baker was referring to were plans to level the existing public housing projects that had been in the city for years and ironically survived the hurricane. In a similar vein, Joseph Canizaro, a New Orleans developer expressed similar sentiments acknowledging:

I think we have a clean sheet to start again. And with that clean sheet we have some very big opportunities. (Rivlin 2005)

The plan was to replace the leveled public housing units with private condos. And that's what happened. But this was not and is not part of just a "housing plan" for urban New Orleans. No, the hurricane offered successive opportunities for politicians and businessmen alike. Lower taxes, fewer regulations, cheaper workers, gentrification, an opportunity for development of urban centers, and yes, the replacement of the traditional public school system with a system of charter schools.

We spoke in chapter 4 of the New Orleans debacle and its experimentation with "public charter education." In chapter 7 we will look specifically and in more detail at the actual governance and restructuring of the educational system in New Orleans. But why did it take a hurricane to reverse the ravages of an ailing traditional public school system in favor of a new "charterized" version of public choice? Why didn't privatization advocates like Baker and Canizaro jump on the New Orleans privatization bandwagon before the hurricane?

The answer to these questions lies with the ideology of privatization, as expressed by its main proponent, Milton Friedman, who ironically died less than a year after his economic philosophy was put into effect and became "the charter experiment in New Orleans." In Friedman's 1962 book entitled *Capitalism and Freedom,* Friedman was clear:

> *Only a crisis, actual or perceived, produces real change. When that crisis occurs, the actions that are taken depend on the ideas that are around. That, I believe, is our basic function: to develop alternatives to existing policies, to keep them alive and available until the politically impossible becomes politically inevitable. (Friedman 1962, 2)*

Hurricane Katrina provided the impetus that Friedman counseled would be needed. With the city devastated and much of its population forced from the state, policy wonks, economists, developers, businessmen, corporations, and politicians seized the hurricane as an opportunity for radical privatization, not much unlike that which Friedman had helped engineer in Chile decades prior. In Chile, after Friedman's counsel and ideas came to hold sway under Augusto Pinochet's dictatorship, Chile saw its entire public school system replaced through privatization in the form of "vouchers," long ago advocated by Friedman. Now, with New Orleans devastated the opportunity to privatize or at least reconfigure education presented itself as a gift horse opportunity.

The American Enterprise Institute, a conservative think tank that embraces most if not all of the Friedman ideology, expressed its enthusiasm for the opportunity to implement Friedman's economic and public policy program this way:

> *Katrina accomplished in a day . . . what Louisiana school reformers couldn't do after years of trying. (Saulny 2006)*

Whether public housing or public education, the race was on; no longer would New Orleans public schools be held hostage to teacher's unions, government bureaucrats, or regulation, oversight and transparency. Now, as Friedman himself noted in the *Wall Street Journal* shortly before his death:

> *Most New Orleans schools are in ruins. As are the homes of the children who have attended them. The children are now scattered all over the country. This is a tragedy. It is also an opportunity to radically reform the educational system. (Freidman 2005)*

Within months, if not weeks, well-heeled businessmen and lobbyists converged on New Orleans with well-orchestrated and copious reorganization and restructuring plans to convert traditional public schools into charter schools. These, they hoped, would be then run by educational maintenance organizations (EMOs) for a profit. Friedman's plans would be one step closer to reality and the millions to be made in "charterizing" public schools and then contracting them out to private EMOs would be enormously attractive and lucrative. As we discussed in chapter 4, within less than 19 months most of the traditional public schools in New Orleans had been "charterized" and not only were all public school teachers fired with lightening speed, but their collective bargaining gains were torn to shreds, along with any existing contracts. The charter movement exploded with a radical "takeover" of public education. Naomi Klein, in her book *The Shock Doctrine,* succinctly sums up the obvious:

> *I call these orchestrated raids on the public sphere in the wake of catastrophic events, combined with the treatment of disasters as "exciting market opportunities," "disaster capitalism." (Klein 2007)*

Rapid and irreversible change of the New Orleans public educational system was the objective of the market-based economists advising the state after the hurricane, mostly from the "Chicago School of Economics" located at the University of Chicago where Friedman had left his guru-like mark and a well-clad and well-heeled group of admirers and supporters. Conservative think tanks were at the beck and call of the new economics of charter schools in New Orleans, quickly advocating for-profit run charter schools, for-profit educational curriculum, for-profit services, curriculum, and the like. They understood that the "charter experiment" in New Orleans could spread to other states if they acted swiftly enough to put their new plans for New Orleans education into immediate play. The movement had to be done with immediacy, and it was.

As Sarah Carr, a long-time follower of the burgeoning charter school movement in New Orleans and staff writer for the Times-Picayune, noted in 2007:

> *Throughout the city, various organizations have stepped in to perform the functions no longer handled by a traditional central office. In effect, the role of the Orleans*

Parish schools administration—which previously oversaw more than 120 schools and now oversees five traditional ones—has been outsourced. (Carr 2007)

And the outsourcing has been a boon for executive salaries, according to an article in the *New Orleans Metro Real Time News:*

Now in control of their own budgets, many New Orleans charter school boards have invested heavily in school leaders, with a few paying well into the six-figure range, doubling or tripling the salaries that principals earned under the old regime.

Atop the pay range sits veteran Kathy Riedlinger, head of Lusher Charter School, who earns $203,556, including a $5,000 yearly car allowance. Lafayette Charter School's Mickey Landry, recruited from a prep school in a national search, is No. 2 at $186,000.

At Ben Franklin High School, Principal Timothy Rusnak, also recruited nationally, earns $150,000 annually. And Jay Altman, chief executive of FirstLine Schools, earns $132,000 to oversee both S.J. Green and Arthur Ashe charter schools.

Those salaries are the city's highest, but they reflect a broader trend of sizable increases for nearly all city school principals, charter and traditional. Nonprofit charter boards have generally led the way in boosting pay. But the market pressure has caused the Recovery School District and the Orleans Parish School Board to set more competitive salaries for their centrally managed schools.

State data show most New Orleans charter principals now earn between $80,000 and $110,000 annually, in line with national averages. Principals at RSD-operated schools make between $83,173 and $101,803. The Orleans Parish School Board pays base salaries between $82,330 and $92,054. Both agencies also pay stipends for additional work.

That's a big jump. Before Hurricane Katrina, which led to widespread chartering, base salaries for principals ranged from about $55,000 to about $70,000. (Theveno, 2009)

Louella Givens, New Orleans' only representative on the state board of education stated, when she asked about the exorbitant salaries:

I was essentially told that, because charters are independent, they have freedom to set salaries however they want. When I find out that some of these places are operating like little kingdoms, I think this kind of information should be readily available to the public. You assume there's oversight, but apparently there isn't. (Ibid.)

It seems that salaries at the more affluent charters are much higher than those serving the neediest students. The myth that the New Orleans' educational market naturally works in the favor of the neediest students under the novel New Orleans charter experience is contradicted by the evidence. This is troubling to many residents and those interested in public education for it seems illogical that those working with the most advantaged students would be rewarded greater than those who must work with students with greater educational needs.

In fact, after the hurricane and in the clamor to charterize as many schools as possible, an entire new educational system has emerged that is not only top heavy in "executive salaries" but, according to Carr, outsourcing is the rule of thumb and:

> . . . . the outsourcing is not to a single company or group. Instead, the job has gone to a complicated array of school administrations, nonprofit groups, foundations and charter school cooperatives, such as the Algiers Charter Schools Association.
>
> Some charters have formed cooperatives, like the Algiers Charter School Association or the East Bank Charter School Cooperative, to bolster their economic might. For a fee of either $8,000 or $18,000 per year—depending on the number of hours requested—charter schools in the East Bank group can access joint legal services, communication, financial accounting, grant writing, public relations and local teacher recruitment, among other things. Baptist Community Ministries significantly subsidizes the cost to schools. (Carr 2007)

New Orleans now boasts the largest number of charter schools serving the largest population of students in any state, with 55 percent of all public schools students in New Orleans now attending charter schools. And many of the charter schools are run by EMOs.

According to the Center for Educational Reform:

> Louisiana's 66 charter schools serve a total of 23,600 students statewide, many of whom come from low-income families that are eligible for free or reduced-price lunch programs (Center for Education Reform, under "Louisiana Charter Schools")

What happened in New Orleans, is happening in other places as well, most notably Washington D.C., where charters account for 27 percent of all public student enrollment (El-Amine and Glazer 2008) and in Los Angeles where 250 public schools are being handed over to the new "charter school turnaround artists" as they euphemistically refer to themselves (Blume and Song, 2009).

In fact, such rapid and irreversible changes have been suggested by billionaire Bill Gates in a recent publication entitled *Tough Choices or Tough Times,* put out by The National Center on Education and the Economy in 2007. The report harkens back to the early debates between DuBois and Washington, Cubberly, Bobbitt, Lippman, and Dewey. Much like the revered report, *A Nation at Risk,* published under the Reagan administration in the 1980s as a call for privatization and tougher educational standards, one finds in the new report a corporate wish list of sorts—and the similarities to what the report promotes in theory and what is actually happening in New Orleans, the charter capital of the nation, can't help but be noticed.

Tough Choices or Tough Times represents a firm radical privatization approach to education that would entail the construction of completely new private institutions and systems to replace traditional public institutions. Some of the talking points in the report include moving beyond charter schools to privatized contract schools. No longer are charter schools even discussed as engines of innovation to raise educational standards and practices in traditional public schools. On the contrary, agreeing with the *Education Next* report put out by the Hudson Institute, *Tough Choices or Tough Times* implicitly concurs that charter schools are simply Trojan horses for what entrepreneurs and investors really want, which is the privatization of all public schools for lucrative profits and standardization of both curriculum and its delivery. This of course will require the elimination of all school board powers and all regulations in favor of empowering private companies to create a new "school system," both in governance and oversight. What will be the role of the state? The answer is simple, to assure that all laws, regulations, and oversight remain within the new private system—to assure a "free market" for educational goods and services and unfettered opportunities for continued capital formation. In the words of the report:

> *First, the role of school boards would change. Schools would no longer be owned by local school districts. Instead, schools would be operated by independent contractors, many of them limited-liability corporations owned and run by teachers. The primary role of school district central offices would be to write performance contracts with the operators of these schools, monitor their operations, cancel or decide not to renew the contracts of those providers that did not perform well, and find others that could do better. The local boards would also be responsible for collecting a wide range of data from the operators specified by the state, verifying these data, forwarding them to the state, and sharing them with the public and with parents of children in the schools. They would also be responsible for connecting the schools to a wide range of social services in the community, a function made easier in those cases in which the mayor is responsible for both those services and the schools. The contract schools would be public schools, subject to all of the safety, curriculum, testing, and other accountability requirements of public schools. The teachers in these schools would be employees of the state, as previously noted.*
>
> *The schools would be funded directly by the state, according to a pupil-weighting formula as described below. The schools would have complete discretion over the way their funds are spent, the staffing schedule, their organization an management, their schedule, and their program, as long as they provided the curriculum and met the testing and other accountability requirements imposed by the state.*
>
> *Both the state and the district could create a wide range of performance incentives for the schools to improve the performance of their students. Schools would be encouraged to reach out to the community and parents and would have strong incentives to do so. Districts could provide support services to the schools, but the schools would be free to obtain the services they needed wherever they wished.*

No organization could operate a school that was not affiliated with a helping organization approved by the state, unless the school was itself such an organization. These helping organizations—which could range from schools of education to teachers' collaboratives to for-profit and nonprofit organizations—would have to have the capacity to provide technical assistance and training to the schools in their network on a wide range of matters ranging from management and accounting to curriculum and pedagogy.

Parents and students could choose among all the available contract schools, taking advantage of the performance data these schools would be obligated to produce. Oversubscribed schools would not be permitted to discriminate in admissions. Districts would be obligated to make sure that there were sufficient places for all the students who needed places. The competitive, data-based market, combined with the performance contracts themselves, would create schools that were constantly seeking to improve their performance year in and year out. (Tough Choices or Tough Times 2007)

Tough Choices or Tough Times even goes so far as to recommend ending high school for many poor and minority students after the 10th grade, such as those who score poorly on standardized tests intended for high school seniors. Students testing poorly on the mandated tests could go on to "vocational" schools, while those who did well would be channeled into the corridors of power through the colleges or universities:

Our first step is creating a set of Board Examinations. States will have their own Board Examinations, and some national and even international organizations will offer their own. A Board Exam is an exam in a set of core subjects that is based on a syllabus provided by the Board. So the point of the exam is to find out whether the student has learned from the course what he or she was supposed to learn. For most students, the first Board Exam will come at the end of 10th grade. A few might take it earlier—some might not succeed on their first try, so they might take another year to two to succeed. The standards will be set at the expectations incorporated in the exams given by the countries that do the best job educating their students. But it will in any case be set no lower than the standard for entering community colleges in the state without remediation.

We believe that when all of our recommendations are implemented, 95 percent of our students will meet this standard. Students who score well enough will be guaranteed the right to go to their community college to begin a program leading to a two-year technical degree or a two-year program designed to enable the student to transfer later into a four-year state college. The students who get a good enough score can stay in high school to prepare for a second Board Exam, like the ones given by the International Baccalaureate program, or the Advanced Placement exams, or another state or private equivalent. When those students are finished with their program, assuming they do well enough on their second set of Board Exams, they can go off to a selective college or university and might or might not be given college credit for the courses they took in high school. These students and the ones who went the community college route will have the option when they finish their programs of taking a second set of state Board Exams, and if they hit certain scores, they will be guaranteed the right to go to their state colleges and some state universities as juniors. (Ibid.)

Also suggested in the report, is ending remediation and special education aid for low-performance students in an effort to cut costs. Furthermore, the report is clear on the need for ending teacher pensions and reducing their health and other benefits. The idea is not to motivate teachers to create innovation; on the contrary, teachers are now to be "trained" to deliver a predetermined curriculum and held to "standards" the new system would impose. This is hauntingly familiar to demands currently made on students—to be "trained" to meet what many teachers feel are inauthentic state mandatory standards, ill-designed to motivate or create innovation among students. According to the Gate's funded report, the conception of curriculum on the part of teachers is to be divorced from the actual implementation:

When we have the right assessments, and they are connected to the right syllabi, then the task will be to create instructional materials fashioned in the same spirit and train our teachers to use the standards, assessments, syllabi, and materials as well as possible, just as we train our physicians to use the techniques, tools, and pharmaceuticals at their command as well as possible. But it all starts with the standards and assessments. (Ibid.)

And like the charter experiment in New Orleans, *Tough Choices or Tough Times* points the accusatory finger of blame for educational malaise at teachers recommending that unions be reduced and/or eliminated. The report also urges ending teacher seniority and introducing competition among teachers through devices such as merit pay and other teacher differentials based on student performance on standardized tests.

Tough Choices or Tough Times is a summary or playbook for what actually is going on in New Orleans since hurricane Katrina devastated the city and what could be a theory and practice foisted on other states. The message seems to be clear: create a system like the New Orleans model to show other states that what is happening in New Orleans could happen to them, as has happened in Los Angeles. The transformation of public schools into private entities is gradually being accomplished as the privatization agenda makes its ascendancy in economically strapped and often bankrupt urban centers throughout the nation. This is why Naomi Klein and others critical of the privatization schemes posed by charter schools as Trojan horses for a larger privatization agenda compare the structural adjustment programs taking place in New Orleans, Ohio, Washington D.C., and elsewhere to the global structural adjustment made by the world bank and the IMF. Certainly they represent a step ever closer to the privatization of education advocated for years by conservative free-market advocates and market-based reformers. As Zein El-Amine, a longtime D.C. community activist and writer and founding member of the Save our Schools Coalition astutely noted, what the public is witnessing is:

> The purposeful neglect of public entities, the siphoning of public resources, the attack on public sector workers, and a false promise that a market solution is less bureaucratic, less costly and more effective (El-Amine and Glazer 2008).

Tough Choices or Tough Times is a throwback to Cubberly, Bobbitt, Lippman, DuBois, and the educational debates of the past. Echoing the calls of the superfunctionalists who bemoan America's "competition" in the world and the entrepreneurial class that stands to make billions off any transformation to a market-driven approach to education where education is seen as a product or commodity to be delivered, the report claims:

> *The governance, organizational, and management scheme of American schools was created in the early years of the 20th century to match the industrial organization of the time. It was no doubt appropriate for an era when most work required relatively low literacy levels, most teachers had little more education than their students, and efficiency of a rather mechanical sort was the highest value of the system.*
>
> *In recent years, American industry has shed this management model in favor of high performance management models designed to produce high-quality products and services with highly educated workers. Some school districts are moving in this direction. That movement needs to be accelerated, formalized, and brought to scale. We share here one way to make that work. No doubt there are others that would work as well. (Ibid.)*

The report is certainly correct as to one issue: there absolutely are other approaches to providing a decent and sound education to our nation's children; the issue is whether we as citizens wish education to remain public, accompanied with full disclosure, transparency, equitable and decent funding, authentic standards for educational student achievement, excellence in teacher recruitment, pay, and training; or if we, as citizens, prefer to have a privatized system of education operated by for-profit entrepreneurs and corporations, accompanied by commodified and standardized curriculums, "class" and "race" based educational opportunities, and for-profit management of schools subsidized by tax dollars. This too is a "public choice," and that choice, as citizens, is ours. If we are not educated as to the circumstances within which we make these choices and well informed as to the implications for our society and our children that each educational choice brings, we may awaken to find a system not of our own making, one instead that is constructed to do the bidding for those who conceive, control, and otherwise make the educational "choices" as to how we are going to live.

REFERENCES

Alliance for Public Charter Schools. *Report Finds Public Charter Schools Helping Students In Several Areas. But Study Shows Critical Need for Strengthening School Accountability and Authorizer Accountability.* 15 June 2009. http://www.publiccharters.org/node/964.

Anderson, N., K. Adelman, L. Finnigan, M.B. Cotton, Donnelly and T. Price. *A Decade of Public Charter Schools: Education of the Public Charter Schools Program 2000-2001.* Stanford, CA: SRI International, 2002, p. 18.

Armstrong, S. Virtual Learning 2.0, Tech and Learning. http://www.techlearning.com/article/8090.

Associated Press. "Debate Rages over NYC Hebrew Charter School." 3 February 2009. http://www.msnbc.msn.com/id/28992198/.

Blume, H. and J. Song. "Vote could open 250 L.A. Schools to Outside Operators." *Los Angeles Times,* 25 August 2009. http://www.latimes.com/news/local/la-me-lausd-schools26-2009 aug26,0,4203620.story.

Bobbitt, F. "The Elimination of Waste in Education." *Elementary School Teacher* 12 (1912): 259-271.

———. "Some General Principles of Management Applied to the Problems of City School Systems." In *Twelfth Yearbook of the National Society for the Study of Education.* Ed. S.C. Parker. Chicago: University of Chicago Press, 1913.

Brown v. Board of Education. 347 U.S. 483, 74 S. Ct. 686. 1954.

Brown v. Board of Education II. 349, U.S. 294, 75, S. Ct. 753. 1955.

Bryk, A., and V. Lee. *Catholic Schools and the Common Good.* Cambridge, MA: Harvard University Press, 1993.

Buckley, J., and M. Schneider. *Charter Schools: Hope or Hype.* Princeton, NJ: Princeton University Press, 2007.

Bybee, C. Walter Lippmann and John Dewey. http://www.infoamerica.org/teoria_articulos/lippmann_dewey.htm.

Callahan, R.E. *Education and the Cult of Efficiency.* Chicago: University of Chicago Press, 1962.

Carnegie Foundation for the Advancement of Teaching. *School Choice.* Princeton, NJ: Carnegie Foundation, 1992.

Carr, S. "Schools Rely More on Outside Help. *The Times-Picayune* 28 November 2007. http://blog.nola.com/times-picayune/2007/11/school_rely_on_more_on_outside.html.

Center for Education Reform. The Accountability Report: 2009 Charter Schools. http://edreform.com/accountability/.

———. Student Achievement Higher at Boston Charter Schools. March 2008. http://www.edreform.com/index.cfm?fuseAction=document&documentID=2818&sectionID=140&NEWSYEAR=2 009 1998): 1.

———. Louisiana Charter Schools. http://edreform.com/accountability/states/CER_2009_AR_Louisiana.pdf).

Center for Research on Education Outcomes (CREDO). *Multiple Choice: Charter School Performance in 16 states.* Stanford University: Stanford, CA. June 2009. http://credo.stanford.edu.

Chubb, J., and T. Moe. *Politics, Markets, and American Schools.* Washington, DC: Brookings Institute, 1990.

Cobb, C., and G. Glass. *Ethnic Segregation in Arizona Charter Schools.* Tempe, AZ: Education Policy Analysis, January 1999.

Corwin, R. G., and J.F. Flaherty, eds. *Freedom and Innovation in California's Charter Schools.* Los Alamitos, CA: Southwest Regional Laboratory, November 1995.

Corwin, R. and Schneider, J. *The Charter School Hoax.* MD: Rowman and Littlefield Publishers.

Cubberley, E. *Public School Administration: A Statement of the Fundamental Principle Underlying the Organization and Administration of Public Education.* Boston: Houghton Mifflin, 1916.

De Meglio, M. "Charter School Wants to Make Room for Religion." *New York Post* 4 May 2009. http://www.nypost.com/seven/05042009/news/regionalnews/brooklyn/charter_school_wants_to_make_room_for_re_256440956.htm.

Dent, D. "Diversity Rules Threaten North Carolina Charter Schools that Aid Blacks." *New York Times,* 23 December 1998.

Dewey, J. *Education Today.* New York: Greenwood Press, 1940.

———. *Experience and Education.* New York: Collier Books, 1976; first published in 1938.

Dillon, S. "Online Schooling Grows, Setting Off a Debate" *New York Times,* February 2008. http://www.nytimes.com/2008/02/01/education/01virtual.html?pagewanted=2&_r=1&sq=Online%20schools%20setting%20off%20debates&st=cse&scp=1.

Dolle, J., and A. Newman. "Luck of the Draw: On the Fairness of Charter School Admission Policies." Midwest Political Science Association Annual Conference, Chicago, 2 April 2009. 364353/364353-2. http://www.allacademic.com//meta/p_mla_apa_research_citation/.

DuBois, W.E.B. *The Education of Black People: Ten Critiques, 1906-1960.* Ed. H. Aptheker. New York: Monthly Review Press, 1973.

Dunbar, E. "ACLU Sues Charter School Over Religion." The Associated Press, 21 January 2009. http://www.bemidjipioneer.com/ap/index.cfm?page=view&id=D95RPLBO0.

Eastabrook, D. "The New Business of Education—Charter Schools." 18 February 2008. http://www.pbs.org/nbr/site/onair/transcripts/080218e/.

Eckes, S., and K. Rapp. "Dispelling the Myth of 'White Flight': An Examination of Minority Enrollment in Charter Schools." *Educational Policy* 21 no. 4 (2007): 615-661.

Education Commission of the States. *Action for Excellence: A Comprehensive Plan to Improve Our Nation's Schools.* Washington, DC: Task Force on Education for Economic Growth, 1983.

Egan, T. "Failures Raise Questions for Charter Schools." *New York Times,* 5 April 2002. http://www.nytimes.com/2002/04/05/us/failures-raise-questions-for-charter-schools.html.

El-Amine, Z., and L. Glazer. "'Evolution' or destruction? A look at Washington, D.C." in *Keeping the Promise? The Debate over Charter Schools.* Milwaukee: Rethinking Schools in Conjunction with Center for Community Change, 2008.

Erickson, T. "Auditors eyeing charter schools." *Desert Morning News.* Salt Lake City: 5 June 2006. http://www.deseretnews.com/article/1,5143,635213116,00.html.

Ewing Marion Kauffman Foundation. *Debunking the Real Estate Risk of Charter Schools.* http://74.125.47.132/search?q=cache:ezt9y9BbKWQJ:www.edreform.com/_upload/kaufmann_study.pdf+Debunking+the+Real+Estate+Risk+of+Charter+Schools&cd=1&hl=en&ct=clnk&gl=us&ie=UTF-8.

False Promises: Assessing Charter Schools in Twin Cities Institute on Race and Policy. http://minnesota.publicradio.org/features/2008/11/26_charter_school/charterreport.pdf.

"For-profit Schools." *Business Week,* 7 February 2000.

Friedman, M. "The Role of Government in Education." In *Economics and the Public Interest.* Ed. Robert A. Solow. New Brunswick, NJ: Rutgers University Press, 1955.

———. *Capitalism and Freedom*, Chicago: University of Chicago Press, 1982.

———. "The Promise of Vouchers." *Wall Street Journal*, 5 December 2005.

Frankenberg, E. and C. Lee. "Charter Schools and Race: A Lost Opportunity for Integrated Education." *Education Policy Analysis Archives,* 11(32), 2003; see also http://epaa.asu.edu/epaa/v11n32/.

Gill, B., P.M. Timpane, K.E. Ross and D.J. Brewer. *Rhetoric v. Reality: What We Know and What We Need to Know about Vouchers and Charter Schools.* Santa Monica, CA.: Rand Education, 2001.

Glass, G. http://epicpolicy.org/files/PB-Glass-VIRTUAL.pdf.

Good, T.L., and J.S. Braden. *The Great School Debate: Choice, Vouchers, and Charters.* Mahwah, NJ: Lawrence Erlbaum Associates, 2000.

Goodman, J. "Change without Difference." *Harvard Educational Review* 65, no. 1 (1995): 1–29.

Green v. School Board. 391 U.S. 430 (1968).

Green, Preston, and Mead. *Charter Schools and the Law: Chartering New Legal Relationships.* Norwood, MA: Christopher-Gorden Publishers, Inc, 2004.

Hamilton, W.H. cited in James Rorty, *Order on the Air!* New York: The John Day Company, 1934, P. 10.

Hargreaves, A. *Changing Teachers, Changing Times: Teachers' Work and Culture in the Postmodern Age.* New York: Teachers College Press, 1994.

Harrington, R. "Arizona's Charter Schools Are an Abysmal Failure that Should Be an Example to the Nation." *American Chronicle,* 20 August 2006. http://www.americanchronicle.com/articles/view/12648.

Hart, G.K., and S. Burr. "The Story of California's Charter School Legislation Journal." *Phi Delta Kappan* 78 (1996).

Harwood, J. "Washington Wire: A Special Weekly Report from the Wall Street Journal's Capital Bureau." *Wall Street Journal,* 9 September 2005.

Hillman, B.S. "Is There a Place for Religious Charter Schools?" *Yale Law Review Journal* (December, 2008.)

Huber, R. *The American Idea of Success.* New York: McGraw-Hill, 1971.

Hughes, C. "Church Challenges New York Law Banning Religious Charter School Operators." *The Roundtable on Religion and Social Welfare Policy.* 30 October 2007. http://www.religionandsocialpolicy.org/news/article.cfm?id=7247.

Hunt Report. *See* Education Commission of the States.

Hutchins, L. *Achieving Excellence.* Aurora, CO: Mid Continent Regional Laboratory, 1990.

Jacoby, S. *The Age of American Unreason.* New York: Pantheon Books, 2008.

Jaffe, H. "Can Michelle Rhee save D.C. Schools." *Washingtonian,* 1 September 2007. www.washingtonian.com/articles/people/5222.html.

Jordan, J. "State Wants New Charter School To Serve Low-income." April 2009. http://www.projo.com/news/content/charter_school_criteria_change_04-30-09_LPE78_v20.36ab0dc.html.

Kaseman, L. and S. Kaseman. "How William Bennett's Public E-Schools Affect Homeschooling" *Home Education Magazine* (November-December 2002). http://www.homeedmag.com/HEM/196/ndtch.html.

Keller, K. "Critics Question Taxpayer Funding for Proposed Hebrew Charter School in East Brunswick." *The Star-Ledger.* 10 May 2009. http://www.nj.com/news/mustsee/index.ssf/2009/05/critics_question_taxpayer_fund.html.

Kenney, E., and J.L. Miller. "Charter Gender Bill OK'D in House Legislation Would Allow All-Boys, All-Girls Options." *The News Journal,* 23 January 2008. http://www.delawareonline.com/apps/pbcs.dll/article?AID=/20080123/NEWS/801230363/1006/NEWS.

Kincheloe, J. *Contextualizing Teaching.* New York: Longman, 2000.

Klein, N. *The Shock Doctrine,* New York: Metropolitan Books, 2007.

Kliebard, H. "The Tyler Rationale." *School Review* 78 (1970): 259-262.

Kolderie, T. *What Does It Mean to Ask: Is "Charter Schools" Working?* St. Paul: Charter Friends National Network, 1998.

Kozol, J. *The Shame of the Nation: The Restoration of Apartheid Schooling in America.* New York, NY: Three Rivers Press, 2006.

Lee, Y. "Are Charter Schools More Racially Segregated Than Traditional Public Schools?" Policy Report 30. 2007-03-00 ERIC. http://www.eric.ed.gov/ERICWebPortal/Home.portal?_nfpb=true&ERICExtSearch_SearchValue_0=ED430323&ERICExtSearch_SearchType_0=no&_pageLabel=RecordDetails&accno=ED498628&_nfls=false&objectId=0900019b80201c86.

Lewin, Tamar. "In Michigan, School Choice Weeds out Costlier Students." *New York Times,* 26 October 1999.

Lewis, D. L. *W. E. B. DuBois: A Biography of a Race, 1868–1919.* New York: Henry Holt, 1993.

Lippmann, W. *The Phantom Pubic.* New Brunswick: Transaction Publishers, 2009.

Lopez, A., A.S. Wells, and J.J. Holme. "Bounds for Diversity: Structuring Charter School Communities." Paper presented at the annual meeting of the American Education Research Association, San Diego, April 1998.

Lowe, R., and B. Miner, eds. *Selling Out Our Schools: Vouchers, Markets, and the Future of Public Education.* Milwaukee, WI: ReThinking Schools, 1996.

Lubienski, C. "Innovation in Education Markets: Theory and Evidence on the Impact of Competition and Choice in Charter Schools." *American Educational Research Journal*: 40 (2), (2003): 395-443.

Lugg, C.A. *For God and Country: Conservatism and American School Policy.* New York: Peter Lang, 1996.

Manetto, N. "Public Schools Touted." *Times* (Trenton, NJ), 4 November 1999.

Meier, D. "The Debate Is about Privatization, Not 'Choice.'" In *Selling Out Our Schools: Vouchers, Markets, and the Future of Public Education.* Eds. R. Lowe and B. Miner. Milwaukee: ReThinking Schools, 1996.

————. *The Power of Their Ideas.* Boston: Beacon Press, 1995.

"Michigan Charter Schools." *ReThinking Schools* (Winter 1999-2000).

Molnar, A. "Charter Schools: The Smiling Face of Disinvestment." *Educational Leadership* 54 (1996): 5.

Myers, B. "Charter Funding System Invites Fraud and Abuse." *The Examiner*, 30 March 2007. http://www.examiner.com/printa-647263~Charter_funding_system_invites_fraud_and_abuse.html.

Nathan, J. *Charter Schools: Creating Hope and Opportunity for American Education.* San Francisco: Jossey-Bass, 1998.

National Commission on Excellence in Education. *A Nation at Risk.* A Report to the Nation and the Secretary of Education United States Department of Education (April 1983).

National Science Board. *Educating Americans for the 21st Century.* Washington, DC: Commission on Pre-College Education in Mathematics, Science, and Technology, 1983.

Ni, Y. (ERIC). *Are Charter Schools More Racially Segregated Than Traditional Public Schools?* Policy Report 30. (March 2007). http://www.eric.ed.gov/ERICWebPortal/Home.portal?_nfpb=true&ERICExtSearch_SearchValue_0=ED430323&ERICExtSearch_SearchType_0=no&_pageLabel=RecordDetails&accno=ED498628&_nfls=false&objectId=0900019b80201c86.

Orfield, G. *The Reconstruction of Southern Education: The Schools and the 1964 Civil Rights Act.* New York: Wiley Interscience, 1969.

Perkinson, L.M. "The History of Blacks in Teaching: Growth and Decline within the Profession." In *American Teachers: Histories of a Profession at Work.* Ed. D. Warren. New York: Macmillan, 1989.

Pitluk, A. "Rethinking Charter Schools in Texas." *Time,* 4 October 2006. http://www.time.com/time/printout/0,8816,1542554,00.html.

Pratt, C. "Rallying the Troops: Public School Outcry over Charter Plans." *Newsday,* 17 January 2000.

Rinehart, J., and J. Lee. *American Education and the Dynamics of Choice.* New York: Praeger, 1991.

Rivlin, G. "A Mogul Who Would Rebuild New Orleans." *New York Times*, 29 September 2005.

Rofes, E. "Charters: Finding the Courage to Face Our Contradictions." In *Selling Out Our Schools: Vouchers, Markets, and the Future of Public Education.* Eds. R. Lowe and B. Miner. Milwaukee: ReThinking Schools, 1996.

Saulny, S. "US Gives Charter Schools a Big Push in New Orleans" *New York Times*, 13 June 2006.

"Saving Our Schools." *Newsweek,* 9 May 1983, 50-58.

Schoolmatters. Charter School Crackdown. 8 November 2007. http://schoolmatters.blogspot.com/2007/11/charter-school-crackdown-in-ohio.html.

Sen, B. "Corporate Puppeteers: A Look at Who's Behind the Charter School Movement." Left Turn Magazine October/November 2006, 50-54.

Shor, I. *Culture Wars: School and Society in the Conservative Restoration.* Chicago: University of Chicago Press, 1986.

Sizer, T., and G. Wood. "Charter Schools and The Values of Public Education." *In Keeping the Promise? The Debate over Charter Schools.* Milwaukee: ReThinking Schools in Conjunction with The Center for Community Change, 2008.

Shanklin, M., and V. McClure. "Deals and Debts: Nearly Half of Florida's Charters Had Operating Deficits." *Orlando Sentinel.* 17 May 2009.

Smarick, A. "Wave of the Future: Why Charter Schools Should Replace Failing Urban Schools." *Education Next* (Winter 2008). www.hoover.org/publications/ednext/11130241.html.

Smith, K.A. "Charter Schools Owe Texas $26M for Overstated Admissions Numbers." *The Dallas Morning News,* 5 April 2008. http://www.dallasnews.com/sharedcontent/dws/dn/latestnews/stories/040608dnmetCharterMain.3a5ff8c.html.

Stent, M., W. Hazard, and H. Rivlin, eds. *Cultural Pluralism in Education: A Mandate for Change.* New York: Appleton-Century Crofts, 1973.

Thevenot B. "Local School Principals' Pay Reaches New Heights." *The Times-Picayune,* Sunday 17 May 2009. http://www.nola.com/news/index.ssf/2009/05/local_school_principals_pay_re.html.

Tough Choices or Tough Times. The Report of the New Commission on the Skills of the American Workforce 2007 National Center on Education and the Economy. http://www.skillscommission.org/pdf/exec_sum/ToughChoices_EXECSUM.pdf.

Tyack, D.B. *Constructing Difference: Historical Reflections on Schooling and Social Diversity.* N.p.: Teachers College Record, 1993.

———. *The One Best System: A History of American Urban Education.* Cambridge, MA: Harvard University Press, 1974.

Urahn, S., and D. Stewart. *Minnesota Charter Schools: A Research Report.* Minneapolis: House Research Department, December 1994.

U.S. Department of Education. Institute of Education Sciences. National Center for Education Statistics. *America's Charter Schools: Results From the NAEP 2003 Pilot Study,* NCES 2005-456, by National Center for Education Statistics. Washington, DC: 2004.

U.S. Department of Education. Joint Committee on Public Schools. Report. December 1999.

———. Office of Innovation and Improvement: U. S. Department of Education 2004, 1

———. Credit Enhancement for Charter School Facilities. Number: 84.354A. http://www.ed.gov/programs/charterfacilities/index.html.

———. Charter Schools Program, July 2004. Nonregulatory Guidance Title V part B, Charter Schools Program D-3. http://209.85.173.132/search?q=cache:MWArrVv1ygIJ:www.ed.gov/policy/elsec/guid/cspguidance03.pdf+religion+and+charter+schools&cd=4&hl=en&ct=clnk&gl=us&ie=UTF.

U.S. General Accounting Office. *Charter Schools: New Model for Public Schools Provides Opportunities and Challenges.* HEHS-95-42. Washington, DC, January 1995.

U.S. Senate. Committee on Labor and Human Resources. *Congressional Testimony of Eric Rofes in a Hearing on the Overview of Charter Schools.* Washington, DC, 31 March 1998.

Vanourek, G., B. Manno, C. Finn, and L. Bierlein. *Charter Schools as Seen by Those Who Know Them Best: Students, Teachers, and Parents.* Charter School in Action Project. Final report, pt. 1. June 1997.

Weil, D. *Towards a Critical Multicultural Literacy: Theory and Practice for Education for Liberation.* New York: Peter Lang Publishing, 1998.

Weinberg, L., and B. Cooper. "What about Religious Charter Schools?" *Education Week.* 20 June 2007. http://www.edweek.org/login.html?source=http://www.edweek.org/ew/articles/2007/06/20/42cooper.h26.html&destination=http://www.edweek.org/ew/articles/2007/06/20/42cooper.h26.html&levelId=2100

Wells, A., A. Lopez, J. Scott, and J. Holme. "Charter Schools as Postmodern Paradox: Rethinking Social Stratification in an Age of Deregulated School Choice." *Harvard Educational Review* 69, no. 2 (Summer 1999).

Whitty, G., S. Power, and D. Halpin. *Devolution and Choice in Education: The School, the State, and the Market.* Birmingham, Eng.: Open University Press, 1998.

Wirt, F.M., and M.W. Kirst. *Schools in Conflict: The Politics of Education.* 3d ed. Berkeley, CA: McCutchan, 1992.

Witte, J. and S. Lavertu. "The Impact of Milwaukee Charter Schools on Student Achievement." The Brookings Institute. http://www.brookings.edu/papers/2009/03_charter_lavertu_witte.aspx.

WMN. Some Delaware Charter Schools Segregated Unequal. 4 April 2007. http://www.wmich.edu/wmu/news/2007/04/014.html.

Woodall, M. "PA Lawsuit Charges Agora Cyber with Fraud." *Inquirer,* 30 April 2009. http://www.philly.com/philly/news/breaking/20090430_Pa_lawsuit_charges_Agora_Cyber_with_fraud.html.

Young, T., and E. Clinchy. *Choice in Public Education.* New York: Teachers College Press, 1992.

Zimmer, R., B. Gill, K. Booker, S. Lavertu, T. R. Sass, and J. Witte. "Charter Schools in Eight States Effects on Achievement, Attainment, Integration, and Competition."

2009 RAND Corporation, Rand Education. http://www.rand.org/pubs/monographs/2009/RAND_MG869.pdf.

Chapter Six

Educational Maintenance Organizations (EMOs)

For-Profit and Nonprofit Management of Charter Schools

Reading the educational public policy literature of the late 1990s, when the neo-liberal agenda for the for-profit management of schools was becoming a formal reality in American consciousness and public education, one might conclude from media reports that a new, burgeoning market stood on the horizon of educational reform dramatically poised to fix what ails the nation's public schools; or at least that is what much of the literature was enthusiastically reporting at the time. Take for example the Mackinac Center for Public Policy, a notable conservative think tank. In August of 1999, they reported with sheer exuberance that:

Michigan is home to the nation's third-largest number of charter schools, many of which rely on private, for-profit companies for administration and management. The companies, commonly known as education management organizations (EMOs), manage approximately 70% of the state's 144 charters. But some EMOs are not content to simply manage charter schools for others; in some cases they are starting up their own schools, creating greater educational choice and competition for Michigan families. One such company is National Heritage Academies (NHA), a Grand

Rapids-based EMO. Founded by J. C. Huizenga in 1995, NHA is rapidly achieving its goal, which is to create and manage a strong network of K-8 charter school academies. Huizenga operated just one charter school in NHA's first year. Three years later, the company is managing 13 schools in western Michigan and plans to open nine more schools this fall. Like other EMOs, NHA has sought private, outside investors. To date, it has raised $100 million in investor capital in addition to millions of dollars provided by Huizenga from his own personal finances. Yet, even with this level of funding, the risk is great, and there are no guarantees of success. Charter schools cannot sell bonds for buildings and equipment like traditional public schools. First-year charters must be fully staffed and teaching students long before any money comes from Lansing. The high up-front costs for starting charter schools cause a negative cash flow for many months and also keep many "mom and pop" charter schools from entering the market. On the plus side, the high up-front costs may also lead charters to use more cost-saving measures such as contracting out school support services. NHA, for example, contracts out 100% of its food and custodial services to other private firms. (Education Management Organizations)

The Educational Policy Studies Laboratory at Arizona State University has been reporting extensively on for-profit management of public schools, including charter schools, for more than ten years. Each year they issue a *Profiles of For-Profit Education Management Organizations* in which they look at data that documents the number of for-profit firms (EMOs) involved in the management of publicly funded schools. They include data that identifies the schools these firms manage, the number of schools they manage, and the number of students they serve and other sundry disclosure data. In 2008 they released their first study of nonprofit educational management of schools, which we will look at later in the chapter.

First, turning our attention to the 2007-2008 *Profiles of For-Profit Education Management Organizations Tenth Annual Report,* authors of the report, Alex Molnar, Gary Miron, and Jessica Urschel, sum up the argument conservatives use to garner public support for the for-profit EMOs this way:

While faith in market competition as an effective engine of reform provides a general theoretical basis for both EMO-run district and charter public schools, the specifics of the competition are somewhat different in each instance. Adherents of market-based school reform favor charter schools in the belief that they provide competition that will force existing public schools to improve their outcomes or be put out of operation. Support for for-profit management of district schools, meanwhile, arises essentially from a belief that private business models are more efficient and effective than nonprofit, government operated institutions. A for-profit company contracted to manage district public schools, it is reasoned, will have incentives (making a profit in the short term and retaining a profitable contract in the long term) to seek efficiencies and improve student outcomes and achievement. The competition, in this context, takes place not among schools or districts themselves, but among current or potential managers of schools. (Molnar, Miron, and Urschel)

So the assumptions, at least by some, behind the educational and economic theory supporting the for-profit EMO is clear, according to Molnar. EMO advocates believe that competition in the management of public schools will raise all boats. This is important, because the argument is not simply that competition in the *types* of schools students may go to (though that too is part of the educational privatization agenda) is essential to improve public schools; free-market ideologues go even further, arguing that if schools compete effectively in *how* they manage a school, be it a charter or district school, student performance will rise and efficiency will increase. But is this really true and is it really the true underlying ideology of conservative forces that support charter schools and EMOs? In other words, is the real goal of these companies to improve traditional public school performance across the national educational line through competition, as they claim, which would include both charter schools and traditional public schools? Or is the real unstated purpose and rarely spoken objective to actually replace traditional public schools with a business form of "privately run educational retail franchises," in the form of charter schools?

For-profit EMOs are now big players in the rocketing charter school movement that has swept the country and their relationships, agendas, and claims must be critically examined and thoroughly scrutinized. We will attempt to do this in this chapter. First, however, it is important to define and understand a for-profit educational management organization (EMO), what they propose to do, have done, or haven't done in the name of improving public schools.

WHAT IS A FOR-PROFIT EMO?

Just what is a for-profit educational management organization (EMO)? The answer is ascertained by first defining the notion of the "privatization" of "public services," in general. As we noted in chapter 5, the transfer of public duties traditionally performed by government actors and/or agencies to privately held or publicly traded companies for-profit who assume complete responsibility for the public assets and answer only to their shareholders or owners, can be called "privatization" (also referred to abstractly as *neoliberal economic policy*). When public educational duties are "privatized," thereby transferred from the public to the private sector (in this case comprising the "management" of schools with all the myriad of responsibilities this entails), and subsequently this private management is contracted for with a public school entity, be it a public educational district or simply a public school (charter or otherwise), we can say that this private company is or will be a "for-profit management" company or what is now called in contemporary educational jargon, an Educational Management Organization (EMO). The Education Policy Studies Laboratory at the College of Education at

Arizona State University is more thorough and specific in its definition of an EMO:

> *We define an education management organization, or EMO, as an organization or firm that manages schools that receive public funds, including district and charter public schools. A contract details the terms under which executive authority to run one or more schools is given to an EMO in return for a commitment to produce measurable outcomes within a given time frame. The EMOs profiled in this report operate under the same admissions rules as regular public schools and are operated for-profit. The term "education management organization" and the acronym "EMO" are most commonly used to describe these private organizations that manage public schools under contract. However, other names or labels such as "education service providers" are sometimes used to describe these companies. An important distinction should be made between EMOs that have executive authority over a school and service contractors that are often referred to as "vendors." Vendors provide specific services for a fee, such as accounting, payroll and benefits, transportation, financial and legal advice, personnel recruitment, professional development, and special education. EMOs vary on a number of dimensions, such as whether they have for-profit or nonprofit status, whether they work with charter schools or district schools or both, or whether they are a large regional or national franchise or a single-site operator. Historically, only a small portion of EMOs have been nonprofits. In recent years, however, nonprofit EMOs (sometimes referred to as CMOs, charter management organizations) have expanded rapidly. (Ibid.)*

Gary Miron, Alex Molnar, and Jessica Urschel, authors of the report, note that EMOs vary on a number of legal standards, such as whether they have for-profit or nonprofit status or whether they contract with charter schools or district schools or both. They even differentiate EMOs as to whether they are large regional businesses with "national educational retail franchises," or simply single-site operators.

A PUBLIC-PRIVATE PARTNERSHIP?

To reiterate, the transfer of public duties traditionally performed by government actors to private companies who assume complete responsibility for the public assets and answer only to their shareholders is "privatization"; yet the argument often made by both the private and public sectors who support the EMO idea is that state takeovers of school districts or other forced transfers of school management to for-profit school management corporations (EMOs) are not strictly speaking, privatizations, but rather represent a "private-public partnership." You might ask how this could be called a private-public partnership when public taxpayer monies are transferred directly into the coffers of for-profit management companies for the services they are contracted to render. The reasoning set forth for the public-private partnership claim rests on the assumption that because the private EMOs (under a contractual relationship with individual charter schools, the districts, or the state) remain accountable to governmental entities, the conclusion is that this relationship is therefore really a form of a "private-public partnership," not an outright privatization. But as the *Profiles* report noted, "A contract details the terms under which executive authority to run one or more schools is given to an EMO in return for a commitment to produce measurable outcomes within a given time frame" (Ibid.). Thus, the relationship is not a "partnership," but a contractual relationship subject to legal terms and outcomes.

Adherents to the "public-private partnership" argument claim that schools remain open to the public while taxpayers continue to finance education by subsidizing the private management of schools, therefore forming the "partnership." Furthermore, they argue, the public school administration or the state bureaucracy can always terminate the for-profit management company's contract if they are dissatisfied with their performance and resume school operations as they had in the past or in the alternative produce new institutional arrangements that they deem more favorable. But what makes this any different than a mere contractual relationship for services entered into for-profit between a public entity (in this case say a charter school or school districts) and a private for-profit firm like an EMO? How can this contractual arrangement and the institutional, economic, and legal consequences that follow from the agreement between the two parties be categorized as a "public-private partnership" when profits and returns not only drive the EMO business model but are expropriated by the EMO as a result of the fiduciary responsibilities an EMO has to their shareholders or partners? In fact, the use of the term "partnership," is the real key to understanding the way EMOs have framed the issue for the public, insofar as the term implies a mutual playing ground between parties in the contract. According to Jonathan Kozol, educational writer and best selling author:

> One of the early strategies employed by private corporations to soften resistance to their presence in our public schools was the creation of so-called business partnerships between the poorest inner-city schools and large companies. The financial side of the partnership usually turned out to be inconsequential. Kerr-McGee, the multinational petrochemical giant, gave one impoverished public school in Oklahoma City the trivial annual sum of $36 for each pupil. In return, one of the company's executives was appointed to direct a "governance committee" to oversee the school operations, and the school consented to be known not simply as a public elementary school but as an "Enterprise School." Throughout the 1990s, many inner-city schools underwent the same accommodation to the goals and even to the lexicon of their benefactors in the private sector. "Academy of Enterprise" became a common term adopted by such schools in genuflection to their corporate patrons.

Principals I met in schools like these would tell me they wished no longer to be known as "principals" but preferred to be known as "Building CEOs" or "Building Managers," in which cases their teachers frequently would be described as "classroom managers." Mission statements heralding the need for children to be trained to serve our nation's interests in "the global marketplace" were posted on the walls of many schools I visited. In practice, however, students were more often being trained for careers at supermarket checkout counters or for the bottom level "service jobs" at nursing homes. (Kozol 2007)

From the point of view of author and attorney Kathleen Conn, she agrees with the implications we can draw from Kozol's observation: there simply are no private-public partnerships with EMOs nor can there ever be; the whole notion is woven out of uncritically accepted ideological cloth. And this might go a long way to explain the eagerness to embrace the language of corporations when referring to principals as "CEOs" and teachers as "managers."

According to an article written by Conn in the *Journal of Law and Education* that specifically looks at the legal and economic responsibilities of EMOs and concludes the idea behind the EMO economic model is simple legality:

In the euphoria of "solving" America's educational woes, a basic inconsistency in the notion of private, for-profit corporations controlling public education escaped serious consideration. Private corporations are legal entities established within a paradigm of maximization of profits for those who provide the working capital of the organization, the shareholders. The directors of such corporations owe fiduciary duties of care and loyalty to the shareholders. They owe, under the law, no concomitant duties to other constituencies. (Conn 2002)

It is clear to any beginning business student that any director or directors of corporations have a fiduciary duty of loyalty that requires that all profits of the corporation accrue to shareholders; this is the simple logic of the economics of corporations and the fundamentals of the capitalist system. As Conn noted, the Michigan Supreme Court, addressing the demands of shareholders in the early twentieth century, stated the principle succinctly:

A business corporation is organized and carried on primarily for the profit of the stockholders. The powers of the directors are to be employed for that end. The discretion of directors is to be exercised in the choice of means to attain that end, and does not extend to a change in the end itself, to the reduction of profits, or to the non-distribution of profits among stockholders in order to devote them to other purposes. (Ibid.)

So in the case of corporate EMOs, just like any other business, the corporate EMO is organized and day-to-day practices of the organization carried on primarily for the profit of the stockholders, or in the case of single operators the private venture capitalists looking for a return on their investment; and this means the powers and actions of the directors of these corporation are to be employed exclusively to that end. The directors of these companies really have no other legal choice, for they have accepted the fundamental economic and legal fiduciary duties in the corporate context that comprise the twin sisters of loyalty and care in the running of their organizations with the sole intent of maximizing profits for shareholders. The only discretion that directors have in assuring profit maximization is in the choice of means they choose to attain this end, nothing more. Nonshareholders, or what are often referred to as "constituencies," simply have no property interest in the corporation and thus few rights in terms of power, decision making, and control. Due to the lack of constituency property interests in an EMO, the issue of public-private partnership is not only moot but in fact a complete misrepresentation of real legal relationships due to the reality that the public at large, the district, or charter school, the students and parents being served by the EMO corporation within the public arena would be considered "constituencies" under the law and constituencies do not have the power, authority, and control over the fiduciary duties necessary for shareholder wealth maximization. In corporate terms they are "second class citizens."

So what does all this mean? The answer is simple: when a for-profit EMO takes over the functions of traditional public education or the day-to-day operations of a charter school the companies' nonshareholding "constituencies," in this case the students, parents, teachers, and workers at the school, have little or no bargaining power with the corporate directors due to the directors' fiduciary duties to shareholders; they in fact may be at the mercy of the companies in the absence of adequate regulatory safeguards or union contracts and collective bargaining agreements, all of which are of course an absolute anathema to the ideological interests of privatization supporters. And because dollars spent on education are not available as dollars for shareholder dividends, in order to realize profits for investors in these for-profit educational management organizations, the bottom line is that EMOs must seek to increase their share of the educational pie through the "volume" business of attracting increasing numbers of students, as well as spend less than they collect; the scramble to keep costs down becomes part and parcel of the profit seeking as they seek simultaneously to expand market share. And these entities do this in myriad ways.

According to Conn, companies like EdisonLearning and other EMO corporations actually accomplish cost cutting in two ways.

> *First, and perhaps least importantly, school management companies contract with vendors of non-educational supplies and services, trying to get volume discounts on everything from tissues to floor strippers. These strategies, while they may save money, have limited, if any, real educational significance. (Ibid.)*

This of course resembles the Wal-Mart business model of bargaining and contracting with suppliers. But as Conn astutely realizes, the second way companies and private operators or EMOs keep costs down is through corporate bottom-line choices that can have immediate and outright devastating effects on practical issues of educational significance, such as choices related to cutting or increasing class sizes, the type, pay and quality of the teachers, and the quality and quantity of educational resources and instructional materials provided to students. So it seems the real "choice" is buried within a particular EMO's plans for-profit maximization.

Take the notion of charter schools: here, for-profit school management companies (EMOs) are free to hire noncertified teachers who then legally become employees for the EMOs, not the public schools they manage. This is an important distinction, because EMO-hired teachers do not work for the districts or charter schools they may labor in; they have virtually been "contracted out" to EMOs. The EMOs often hire noncertified teachers in an effort to keep labor costs (and the cost of benefits) low. This also allows their management to control the daily routines of work. They also employ certified teachers who cannot obtain jobs in the public sector, at salaries far lower than those in comparable publicly run schools, again for the same reason. This is all part and parcel of an effort to reduce labor costs and to assure nonunionization and thereby avoid the need to collectively bargain for the distribution of shareholder or privately held profits. But if this is good for the bottom line, for capital and its owners, is it really good for teachers, educational workers, parents, students, or even education in general, as the public has been continually told over the years by the companies and their media counterparts and think tanks? It would help to take a look at some facts.

EMO-run charter schools, for example, have higher rates of teacher turnover than other entities. Edison Schools, Inc., admitted in 2005 to a teacher turnover rate of 23 percent, twice the national average for urban public schools (Molnar, Miron, and Urschel 2008). Is this cost effective, or a waste of valuable resources needed to train new teachers as the attrition rate rises? Is this fiscally and educationally responsible to the public the EMO proclaims to serve, especially when public funds are deployed?

EMOs also experience significant cost savings in the area of the educational resources they choose to utilize. Most EMOs come equipped with their own "model curriculum" as part of their contract with charter schools and/or districts; this is usually part of their management "packet" to be used at each school, or franchise, the EMO manages. Easily produced "cookie cutter" or "one size fits all" curriculum, realizes significant savings. This kind of spending is far less than what public schools spend for creative, nonstandardized diversified curricula. Teacher-conceived curriculum takes time, patience, and a commitment on behalf of the school management and staff for more allocated preparation time for the construction of meaningful curricula and educational activities for students. It involves working with other teachers in mentoring relationships in order to formulate ideas and best practices; this is a collaborative activity done by teachers with and for students. Creative and innovative curriculum construction is often individually geared to specific students and themes and rebels against prepackaging or standardization.

Yet from the point of view of the for-profit EMO this is a problem for at least two reasons: one, collaboration among teachers is problematic for the EMO business plan that seeks only profits, for it often leads to teacher organized off-site meetings to talk about the conditions of work, the possibilities for unionization, and a discussion of collective interests. Second, what these companies wish to do is create large ready-made curricula that can be used with a high volume of students with a onetime up-front financial investment in both the curriculum and the teacher "training" necessary to implement the curriculum. As author and educational researcher David Plank noted back in 2000, a way for EMOs to profit is to scale down their economies and they do this by reducing pupil costs. He goes on to explain:

> *Scale economies rely on the possibility of lowering per-pupil costs by spreading them over larger numbers of students. For example, a national firm offering a standardized curriculum for hundreds or even thousands of schools may significantly reduce the per-pupil cost of curriculum development and instructional materials in the schools they manage. Similarly, it may be possible to standardize financial and other administrative services for large numbers of schools, reducing the per-pupil cost of providing these services. When economies of scale are present, firms can profit by increasing the number of students they serve. (Plank et al. 2000)*

So, for example, teachers are often given a preconceived and ready-made curriculum and then are trained as "managers" to implement it throughout the educational retail chains owned and operated by the EMOs. In sum, it's obviously cheaper for the EMOs as well as private charter school operators to encourage the adoption of one-size fits all curriculum than it is to provide paid time for teachers to collectively conceive of their own curriculum which could then also lead to the teachers identifying their class interests with each other, not management.

Once again, we are left with the question of how any of this can possibly serve to create "innovation" in instruction and "empowerment" for teachers and students, two arguments we find repeated in the soaring rhetoric supporting the idea of the charter school movement. If the lesson plans come equipped with the "school management package," then once again, as we saw in the last chapter in the historical development of education, teachers are divorced from curriculum conception and reduced to mere "managers" of packaged student "delivery systems," not the chief architectures of cooperative educational excellence and curriculum development. Nor can educational innovation be highlighted, shared, and modeled for the benefit of introducing creativity at either traditional public schools or charter schools. Instead, teachers in many EMO-run schools are "tethered to the carpet loom," required to teach to the prepackaged curriculum that is largely wedded to inauthentic standardized testing and an environment of competition. This "commodification" of educational curriculum and teaching runs not only counter to the arguments historically made by charter school advocates regarding innovation and best practices, but is problematic for teaching and learning. It can also open the door to unscrupulous business entities who seek to introduce their "educational products" into charter schools without any regard to innovation, best practices or educational values.

EMOs AND EDUCATIONAL PRODUCTS

There are many private companies that work hand-in-hand with EMOs to provide educational products as part of a "school management package," which EMOs offer to their districts and charter schools.

The Curriculum on Wheels (COWS) "product" is sold by Ignite!Learning, which is owned and operated by former President George W. Bush's brother, Neil Bush. It was founded in 1999, just one year before the passage of No Child Left Behind. The company's Web site talks about Ignite!Learning's "educational products" but not about teaching. Instead "easy to use delivery" are the words used to describe the prepackaged curriculum. While President Bush formulated and successfully passed No Child Left Behind to promote "teaching to the tests," brother Neil is busy "selling to the tests," with a curriculum that promises higher test scores.

What Ignite!Learning does is sell a "computerized learning center" to school districts, charter schools, and any EMO company or school wishing to add to their "management package" or curriculum. Made to look like a purple cow, the assemblage is a self-contained software projector that is wheeled into classrooms and uses electronically made jingles and cartoon videos to "deliver instruction" to students. Each COW costs $3,800 and at least 13 school districts in 22 states have used No Child Left Behind monies to purchase them. The money allocated is said to be primarily intended to help disadvantaged kids learn reading and math—yet surprisingly, Neil's COWs don't teach either of these subjects (Hightower 2006).

Business Week noted in 2006:

> *Now, after five years of development and backing by investors like Saudi Prince Alwaleed Bin Talal and onetime junk-bond king Michael R. Milken, Neil Bush aims to roll his high-tech teacher's helpers into classrooms nationwide. He calls them*

"curriculum on wheels," or COWs. The $3,800 purple plug-and-play computer/ projectors display lively videos and cartoons: the XYZ Affair of the late 1790s as operetta, the 1828 Tariff of Abominations as horror flick. The device plays songs that are supposed to aid the memorization of the 22 rivers of Texas or other facts that might crop up in state tests of "essential knowledge." (Epstein, 2006)

An article reviewing the company, noted there were problems:

The inspector general of the Department of Education, John P. Higgins Jr., said he would review the matter after a group, Citizens for Responsibility and Ethics in Washington, detailed at least $1 million in spending from the No Child Left Behind program by school districts in Texas, Florida and Nevada to buy products made by Mr. Bush's company, Ignite!Learning of Austin, Texas. Members of the group and other critics in Texas contend that school districts are buying Ignite's signature product, the Curriculum on Wheels, because of political considerations. The product, they said, does not meet standards for financing under the No Child Left Behind Act, which allocates federal money to help students raise their achievement levels, particularly in elementary school reading.

Much of the product's success in Texas dates from a March 2006 donation by Barbara Bush, who gave eight units to schools attended by large numbers of hurricane evacuees. (Citizens for Responsibility and Ethics in Washington 2007)

And so, as we saw when we looked at the No Child Left Behind Act, passed in 2001 by the George W. Bush administration, in addition to emphasizing "public" choice as an alternative to students in "failing" Title 1 schools, the federal budget for fiscal year 2002 allocated $200 million in grants for "expanding the number of high-quality charter schools available to students across the Nation" (No Child Left Behind Act of 2001 § 5201(3)). This provided the opportunity for "market penetration" on behalf of many of the privatized companies offering "teach to the test" curricula like those of Ignite!Learning. Now, with education reduced more and more to a business model, "delivery systems" replaced teaching, "delivery platforms" replaced classroom instruction, "prepackaged curriculum" replaced "teacher led conception and innovation" and "students" came to be looked at as "products" to be produced. With classrooms, many of them charter schools, thanks to No Child Left Behind, now full of COWs and similar "educational products," teachers no longer have to know *how,* let alone *what,* to teach. They become mere instrumentals in the commodification of education for-profit. This, claim opponents, is hardly curriculum innovation and excellence, but instead resembles more of a well-coordinated division of labor that is designed to further a business model, not the education of children. More discouraging is the fact that it is being marketed in low-income communities. This should be of no surprise, for as we will see, it is this burgeoning "subprime" market of children that seems to appeal to the new

EMO entrepreneurs and many charter school advocates looking to make hefty profits.

So, in summary, if the fiduciary duty of a director of a corporate EMO is to maximize shareholder profit and do so by putting profits first, then how are non-shareholder "constituencies," otherwise known as "our nation's children and their parents," not to mention the general public at large, to be protected under an EMO agreement? Conn answers only by noting that this protection could be afforded by explicit side contracts or regulatory schemes:

> Some commentators argue that, if nonshareholder constituencies need protection, explicit contracts and regulatory statutes, rather than fiduciary duties, should determine management's obligations. (Conn 2002)

But the last thing that free-market advocates of deregulation and charter schools want is more regulation and contractual side agreements that would legally hold them responsible to government agencies. This, say opponents of the idea, is the problem.

WHO PROTECTS EDUCATIONAL "CONSTITUENCIES"?

The answer is found in legal cases and constituency laws that support the notion that the nature of the corporation itself can impose upon its directors fiduciary duties of loyalty that flow to the public, for the public good, not just to the shareholders.

Let's look first at a decision by the courts in this matter, discussed by Conn in her article in the law journal. The case involved the responsibilities of the directors and owners of a professional baseball club to their "constituencies," in this case the fans. The court held that the directors of the corporation, in deciding whether to install lights for night baseball games, had a duty to consider the safety of the patrons attending night games in a deteriorating neighborhood. The court also asserted that the directors had an interest in the long-term health of the neighborhood in which their stadium was located. However, the court explicitly stated that deciding the correctness of the directors' decision whether or not to consider these nonshareholder interests was "beyond [the court's] jurisdiction and ability" (Ibid.).

In light of the court's seeming unwillingness to grant fiduciary responsibilities to directors of corporations that would protect the public, some cities and states have passed "constituency statutes" that expressly spell out the fiduciary duties corporations owe to the public. The legislatures of approximately thirty states have enacted "other constituency" statutes allowing corporate directors to consider nonshareholder interests in corporate decision making. Yet unfortunately, these statutes are merely permissive, they carry no real legal weight. Again, Conn is salient here:

> *Pennsylvania, one of the first states to enact an "other constituency" statute, has experienced several challenges to the statute's constitutionality. The first occurred in a derivative action to enjoin Strawbridge and Clothier, the department store giant, from presenting to shareholders a stock reclassification plan that would have defeated a raider's tender offer. The court refused to grant the injunction, holding that Strawbridge directors rightly considered the potential effect a successful tender offer would have had on the company's employees, customers, and community. More recently, application of the Pennsylvania statute was upheld in a 1996 court decision in which Conrail sought a friendly merger with CSX Corporation, rejecting a more lucrative Norfolk Southern bid that cost shareholders $1.5 billion. Conrail argued, and the court accepted, that, under the Pennsylvania statute, corporations have the right to consider constituencies other than shareholders and shareholders' financial interests in making business decisions. (Ibid.)*

Connecticut enacted what can be called a mandatory "other-constituency statute" that attempts to compel directors to consider stakeholder or "constituency" interests in decision making, but this statute has also failed to make an impact, precisely because it lacks any enforcement mechanism (Ibid.). So can charter schools that contract with EMOs pass constituency statutes? The answer, legally, is "no" and this then begs the question of not only how the schools will be run, but who will make decisions in the interest of students, teachers, and their parents?

In sum, case law and statutes, and other-constituency statutes make it clear that a director's duties of loyalty, in regards to a corporate entity, flows exclusively to shareholders for the express purpose of maximization of profits. In the context of public education, the primacy of *shareholder wealth maximization* legally means the directors of a for-profit school-management corporation (EMO) owe fiduciary duties of loyalty to one constituency only: their shareholders. And if this is the case, which the courts have ruled it is, then students' educational needs can simply never be legally on par with shareholder needs and this means that EMOs will seek to replace public governance with corporate governance, public decision making with corporate decision making. The corporate or independently owned business model must, by the very nature of the laws governing it as an economic and legal entity, put profits before kids. At the present time, the only response a traditional public school, charter school, or a state can make in response to a nonperforming for-profit EMO or single operator is to cancel its contract for malfeasance or close its charter school completely. The former requires time, hefty legal fees, and devotion of staff. The latter, besides leaving students in the lurch and resulting in unplanned-for overcrowding in the traditional public school districts, is simply insufficient to recover the public costs of the educational losses experienced by the students, the state, and the management nightmares that entail when contracts are vitiated or cancelled.

Let's now look at the other side, and assume that advocates of corporate EMOs are right. If the concept of a "public-private partnership" position with EMOs is really a boon for both "partners," a number of questions need to be answered regarding governance, accountability, student performance, financial transfer of public funds, transparency, and ultimately decision making.

THEN WHY EMOs?

Later in this chapter we will look at the questions and claims made by EMOs and their supporters that the for-profit management of schools, notably charter schools, leads to higher performance by students, more efficient operations of schools, and the various and sundry counterarguments to the entire notion of for-profit management of schools. However, suffice it to say that part of the reason EMOs have gained in popularity is that school boards and superintendents often see the idea of for-profit management of schools as an economic plus in times of financial turbulence amid a shortage of public funds. It is tempting for school boards and superintendents to see for-profit management firms as a quick, painless panacea for educational ills. But many educators argue that there is no such corporate-driven panacea—that good schools, well-designed curriculum, and excellent teaching practices have to be painstakingly built on the local level by staff and students with the support of parents and school administrators. In the end, these educators argue that the improvement of schools is the result of the hard work of school staff with administrative and parental support. Everything these EMOs say they can do, claim opponents of the idea, has already been done in publicly run public schools; every curriculum and program these EMOs use, the argument goes, is also available for every public school in America to implement on its own without adding corporate managers and subsidizing for-profit EMOs.

Couple this with the often heated corporate and think tank rhetoric eschewing the public management of schools and pushing for the wholesale privatization of every aspect of education, and it is easy to see how a perfect storm created EMOs development and growth in the last few decades. The media did not critically and thoroughly cover the issue of EMOs and charter schools, promoting the notion of "public choice." "Choice" means many things to many different constituencies, but this was hardly noted by an eager media seeking to promote privatization. The public was greeted, as they have been in the private health care industry, with the idea that the more "choices" they have within an unregulated, market-driven economic system the better off they'll be. However, as one philosopher once said, "We all make choices but we do not all choose the circumstances under which we make them" (Marx 1978).

There are many definitions of "public choice," and the voices for the idea are diverse, as noted in chapter 5. As researchers and authors, Ron Corwin and Joseph Schneider recently wrote in their book, *The Charter School Hoax:*

> When we see the implausible claims and boasts asserted by rabid choice proponents, we always wonder who is speaking, and who is listening. We know there is more than one voice, more than one audience. Some of the fans of choice are idealistic educational reformers who honestly believe that choice will improve public education and are eagerly searching for ways to prove it. Others are cunning disciples of free markets who, under the guise of bogus pledges and unfounded allegations, have succeeded in creating publicly funded safe havens. Their rants against bureaucracy and their impossible promises were from the start devious plots to justify what amounts to a special status for select groups. (Corwin and Schneider 2007, 13)

Take a recent report entitled, *NCLB's Ultimate Restructuring Alternatives: Do They Improve the Quality of Education?* Author of the report, William J. Mathis, Associate Professor at the University of Vermont, found that:

> EMOs appeal to politicians and to some parents for many of the same reasons as state takeovers. Center city urban blight, poor building maintenance, disruption, poorly qualified teachers, safety, high dropouts, and poor test scores sound a siren call. When EMO managers say they will come in and sort out corruption, throw out bad teachers, impose curricular reforms, break the union strangle-hold, dismiss the bureaucrats and save money in the process, the promise makes for a potent political message. (Mathis 2009)

Although EMOs present themselves as "turnaround artists" or "takeover artists" whose mission is to boost test-standardized scores and revolutionize the delivery of instruction by running schools for-profit, critics shake their heads in disagreement arguing that too many public servants are being beguiled by these same corporations or privately owned for-profit businesses into believing the argument of market efficiency through deregulated educational competition masquerading as "public choice." This is true, they say, when it comes to everything from raising test scores, organizing the workplace, hiring and firing teachers, and reforming the day-to-day operations of education in general.

EMOs AND THE RISE OF CHARTER SCHOOLS

In search of for-profit management opportunities, EMOs have been drawn like a magnet to the charter school movement. Guilbert Hentschke, Scott Oschman, and

Lisa Snell, writing on the parallel growth of charters and EMOs for the libertarian Cato Institute's May 2002 *Reason Foundation* publication states:

> The growth of EMOs has paralleled the growth of charter schools. By 1999, EMOs were operating about 10 percent of all charter schools. According to data compiled by the Education Policy Studies Laboratory at Arizona State University, the number of for-profit companies managing public schools in the United States soared 70 percent in 2001. The fourth annual Profiles of For-Profit Education Management Companies found that 36 companies now operate 368 schools in 24 states and the District of Columbia. Reliable data on the exact number are unavailable, and anecdotal reports of numerous one-school firms operating in some states, such as Michigan, would probably increase these estimates. EMOs have become part of a long-standing political contest between professional reformers (largely educationists) and radical reformers (largely business leaders and community activists) over what is wrong with public schooling and how to improve it. As a relatively new service option available to local education agencies, EMOs have been adopted so far in relatively few settings, rejected in a few others, and not yet even considered in many others. (Hentschke et al.)

These companies have found a tremendous financial opening as it is estimated that new charter schools receive only 60 percent of their funding from public sources; this means the need for private funding sources has been, and continues to be, dramatic and enormous, as has the need for management of the schools. But in order to understand the parallel development and penetration of EMOs into the charter school movement, it is important to first understand some facts and history about these EMOs, their geographical location, size, potential market share, investor agendas, and their revenues streams and business models.

MODERN HISTORY OF EMOs

In August 2007, Miron and Berry found that for-profit EMOs operated in 31 states, two states more than the previous year's study in 2006. In their most recent report published in July of 2008, entitled *Profiles of For-Profit Educational Management Organizations Tenth Annual Report,* the authors found that:

> In 2007-2008 the for-profit education management industry continued to grow slowly. The number of schools managed by for-profit Education Management Organizations (EMOs) remains relatively constant. Some large and medium-size EMOs are expanding their businesses to include, in addition to school management, other education-related products, and services.
>
> The number of states in which for-profit EMOs operated declined from 31 in 2006- 2007 to 28 in 2007-2008 (Molnar, Garcia, Miron, and Berry 2008).

Since the first Profiles report was produced for the 1997-1998 school year, the number of for-profit EMOs profiled has increased from 14 to 50, and the number of states in which EMOs are operating increased from 16 to 28. In the past year, however, the number of EMOs profiled has a net increase of only 2 companies. While the number of companies has remained relatively stable over the past few years, many of the large and medium size EMOs are expanding into new service areas, such as supplemental education services. Edison Schools experienced the largest net decrease in the number of schools it reported to managed, from 97 to 80 schools. It should be noted that in July 2008, Edison announced a name change. The new company is called EdisonLearning, Inc. *At the time of publication, the company's new Web site did not mention the management of public schools. Ohio-based White Hat Management experienced the largest net increase in the number of schools managed, from 38 to 54 schools. (Molnar, Miron, and Urschel)*

In 2004, only 14 states had laws specifically authorizing EMOs, although such privately run schools were operating in 28 states in 2008. The Center on Educational Policy recently studied restructuring schools in five of these EMO states. Except for California (where 10 percent of restructuring schools chose the EMO option), no more than 2 percent of restructured schools chose the for-profit EMO model; the General Accounting Office (GAO) national estimate for EMO market share is 9 percent of the five percent of Title I schools in restructuring. When the rate of EMO implementation is considered as a percentage of all of a state's schools, or as a percentage of Title I schools, the rate drops below one percent (Mathis 2009).

The *Profile* report produced by Miron and Berry in 2007 categorized 23 private EMO companies as large, medium-sized, or small operators. For purposes of their report, those EMOs categorized as large signifies that they operate more than ten schools; those categorized as medium indicates they manage four to nine schools, and small EMOs are restricted to three or fewer schools. The report also noted that although the number of states within which the EMOs operated was up by 2 states in the 2007 report, the actual number of schools managed by the medium and large sized EMOs was 457, down from 480 in the previous year's study. Among all the EMOs profiled in the 2006-2007 report, Edison Schools, now EdisonLearning, lost the greatest net number of school contracts in 2007, a total of four (Ibid.) In fact, the *2008 Profiles Report* found that the number of states in which for-profit EMOs operated declined from 31 in 2006-2007 to 28 in 2007-2008. The report finds:

In the past few years the number of schools operated by EMOs has leveled off. Eighty-four percent of the 533 schools profiled are operated by large EMOs. Eighty-five percent of EMO-managed schools are charter schools, and 15 percent are district schools. The number of district schools operated by EMOs declined slightly between 2006-2007 and 2007-2008. The majority (60%) of EMO-managed schools profiled are primary schools. The number of virtual schools operated by EMOs in-

creased to 40 in 2007-2008, which is equivalent to 8 percent of all EMO-managed
schools. (Molnar, Miron, and Urschel 2008)

With 85 percent of EMO-managed schools in the nation being charter schools, this is quite rational from a business standpoint, for it seems the for-profit EMOs are also now currently following and paralleling the growth of virtual charter schools throughout the nation. As time goes on it will be interesting to see how this relationship develops, for it promises to offer tremendous financial opportunities for private companies who gain contracts to manage the growing virtual charter school market.

In light of the findings indicated above, the report did go on to articulate that although EMOs have slightly declined in the schools they operate, they continue to serve a larger and larger student population:

The number of students in EMO-managed schools increased by 16,444 over the last
2 years (i.e., since the 2005-2006 school year). This means that even while the num-
bers of companies and the numbers of schools they operate has been leveling off, the
number of students in their schools continue to grow as the average school size con-
tinues to grow. (Ibid.)

Mathis comes to the same conclusion, claiming in his study:

The majority of the EMO schools are primary schools. Both the number of schools
and the number of companies has leveled off in the past two years, even as the to-
tal number of children they enroll has increased. Of these students, 88% are in
schools operated by 15 major corporations, with Edison being the largest (48,000
students). During the first decade of the 21st century, EMOs began shifting their fo-
cus away from operating schools and toward supplemental services (such as tutor-
ing, summer schools, and consulting) catering to the requirements of the NCLB
legislation. (Mathis 2009)

So as we can see, Miron and Berry arrive at the same conclusions as Mathis, indicating that in 2007-2008, medium- and large-size EMOs managed a total of 494 schools, up from 465 in 2006-2007. However, if an estimate of the EMO Imagine Co., managed schools (38) is added to the 2006-2007, the total the number of schools managed by large- and medium-size EMOs has actually decreased from 503 in 2006-2007 to 494 in 2007-2008. Miron and Berry conclude as well that Edison Schools is largely responsible for this change, experiencing a 17 school net decrease in schools under management from 97 to 80. The biggest net increase in managed schools from 2006-2007 was for Ohio's "White Hat Management," which managed 38 schools in 2006-2007 and reported managing 54 schools in 2007-2008 (Molnar, Miron, and Urschel).

Specifically looking at charter schools, a similar study done by Miron and Urschel found in 2007 that:

> *Large-size EMOs enroll 131,379 charter school students. 91,794 are primary, 2,316 are middle, 21,277, are high, and 15,992 are other. These numbers are driven by a relatively few large-size EMOs. Also, larger than average enrollments in large-size EMO-run charter schools are concentrated in the primary grades. Eighty-nine percent of primary students in schools run by large-size EMOs are in schools with enrollments above the national charter school average enrollment at the primary level. It appears that the business model suggested in the 2005-2006 Profiles report seems to be holding: large-size EMOs are focused on relatively high enrollments at the primary level in order to deliver profits. (Molnar, Garcia, Miron, and Berry 2007)*

Among EMOs whose business largely or exclusively focuses on managing charter schools, the largest is National Heritage Academies, which enrolls more than 30,000 students in 53 schools throughout the United States. Founded in 1995, it is a privately held company based in Michigan and now operates schools in five states.

In the 2007 *Profiles for For-Profit Management Organizations*, Miron and Berry found:

> *Other large-size EMOs, in order of the number of charter schools they manage, are The Leona Group (45); Edison (3710); White Hat Management (3611); and Mosaica Education with 3412 charter schools. Together these five firms manage 205 charter schools—more than two-thirds of the 296 charter schools operated by the 12 large-size (10 or more schools) EMOs and more than half of the 352 charter schools managed by all 21 firms in this edition of the Profiles. These five firms enroll a total of 97,286 charter school students, almost two-thirds of the 151,471 students in all charter schools operated by the 21 large- and medium-size EMOs. (Ibid.)*

The most recent 2007-2008 data from the *Profiles Report*, the study came to the conclusion that relative to all schools:

> *Large EMOs (i.e., those that manage 10 or more schools) now account for 84.4 percent of all EMO-managed schools, medium-size EMOs account for 8.3 percent of all EMO-operated schools and small EMOs account for an additional 7.3 percent. (Molnar, Miron, and Urschel)*

It is hard to see how the market consolidation of EMO schools in the hands of a few large companies has anything to do with bureaucratic decentralization and local control of community schools along with effective and efficient school management, which is what charter school advocates continually say they aspire for; instead, it seems clear the consolidation of large EMO firms represent the building blocks of a new centralized for-profit educational retail chain model, similar to that of major department stores or fast food chains with educational franchises in primarily low-income urban neighborhoods serving predominantly low-income, minority-primary students, utilizing the same products and "ingredients" from one school site to another. As Alex Molnar, then an education professor at the University of Wisconsin-Milwaukee, commented as early as 2000:

> *You have an industry with a lot of Wall Street sharpies and insider wheeler-dealers and a gaggle of marketing executives trying to convince the public that they can reform education and turn a profit and everybody wins. (Greenberger 2001)*

The evidence suggests according to opponents of for-profit EMOs, that far from improving education and providing a win-win situation, the records of for-profit EMOs have been more discouraging than encouraging, with what can only be seen as drastic implications for our nation's children, the direction of our public expenditures, and the future of public education.

PRIVATIZATION OF SCHOOL SERVICES AND THE EMO CONCEPT

Educational entrepreneurs, notably EMOs, and their think tank counterparts arose during the heady time of free-market ideology, often referring to themselves as the new "turnaround artists," arguing that they would be able to beat back educational stagnancy in the public sector by unleashing the forces of the private sector and the "free market" on the educational landscape, deregulating educational policy, and thereby cutting and slashing bureaucratic waste while at the same time delivering better results in the classroom and on standardized tests. All of this while making a tidy profit for their owners, shareholders, and their Wall Street backers. As we saw in chapter 3, the growing charter school movement and changes in federal educational policy, notably No Child Left Behind (NCLB), launched many of these entrepreneurs into very viable and profitable financial positions while also giving them huge sway over both the private management of public charter schools and the debate over educational reform. Plus, they were given the economic purse strings by the public or, better yet, by their elected representatives in state houses and school districts throughout much of the nation.

You might be thinking: "A public policy that relies on private stock in companies to further our children's education?" The answer is yes. From for-profit management of traditional public schools to for-profit charter school management, the public policy privatization efforts of the educational industry continues to proceed virtually unbridled, and as we shall see too often outside the regular channels of public purview. Why the rush to privatize the management of public charter schools? The answer is simple. Education is now big business where more and more investors seek penetration into the newly created market for educational goods and services where they are promised a hefty return on private investment. And charter schools aid and abet this effort quite nicely.

For-profit EMOs find the charter school formula attractive for many reasons. First, a steady flow of public money combined with exemptions from costly government regulations and school board requirements such as collective bargaining are attractive to capital formation and this is what the charter school concept offers. In exchange for this funding and freedom, charter schools are expected to fulfill the terms of their charters, which usually have to do with improving standardized student test scores over a fixed number of years. Second, as we noted above, the EMOs find ready private partners in the creation of "educational products" that can then be marketed to public schools in exchange for public funds.

In 2007, noted prize-winning author, Jonathan Kozol, writing in *Harper's Magazine,* anecdotally summed it up best:

Some years ago, a friend who works on Wall Street handed me a stock-market prospectus in which a group of analysts at an investment-banking firm known as Montgomery Securities described the financial benefits to be derived from privatizing our public schools. "The education industry," according to these analysts, "represents, in our opinion, the final frontier of a number of sectors once under public control" that "have either voluntarily opened" or, they note in pointed terms, have "been forced" to open up to private enterprise. Indeed, they write, "the education industry represents the largest market opportunity" since health-care services were privatized during the 1970s. Referring to private education companies as "EMOs" ("Education Management Organizations"), they note that college education also offers some "attractive investment returns" for corporations, but then come back to what they see as the much greater profits to be gained by moving into public elementary and secondary schools. "The larger developing opportunity is in the K-12 EMO market, led by private elementary school providers," which, they emphasize, "are well positioned to exploit potential political reforms such as school vouchers." From the point of view of private profit, one of these analysts enthusiastically observes, "the K-12 market is the Big Enchilada." (Kozol 2007)

As Kozol noted, the trend towards for-profit management of public schools has been growing across the country with many communities considering or actually in the process of turning over their public schools to private business. Businesses, always ready to seize a financial opportunity, especially in a market as potentially lucrative as public education, have been quick to respond.

Take for example, the former Education Secretary under George Bush Sr., William Bennett's company, K12, Inc. This for-profit charter school company, based in Virginia, operates, among other things, the Ohio Virtual Academy (OVA) in the state of Ohio. The Ohio Virtual Academy is a virtual, online charter school that enrolled 3,408 students in the 2006-2007 school year. In early December of 2007, K12, Inc. held an initial public offering of its stock. Even though only 63% of its hoped for $172.5 million was raised, the *Washington Post* reported K12's share price rose 36%. The company has operated the Ohio Virtual Academy since the 2002-2003 school year and currently not only enrolls 3,408 students in Ohio, but over 27,000 in its combined national schools for-profit operation (Columbus Educational Association 2007).

According to the Columbus Educational Association, out of the 3,408 students OVA enrolled in the 2006-2007 school year, 88% of its students were white (versus 28.4% for CCS), 8.0% were African American (versus 62% for CCS), 42.7% were economically disadvantaged (versus 73.3% for CCS), no students were listed as Limited English Proficient (versus 7.7% for CCS), and 6.7% of students were classified as having disabilities (versus 15.6% for CCS). Yet state data gathered on the school indicates that the school spends 33% less per student than the state average. Furthermore, records show that although the company made about $108 million from the initial public offering (IPO), it continues to pay its 91 nonunionized teachers an average of $32,341 per year (Ibid.).

This is all part and parcel of the cost cutting and reduction of labor costs we spoke of earlier, which is so necessary to the real intent and goal of these corporations—capital formation, increased shareholder values, and further capital expansion. But is this policy good for the students who attend these for-profit, EMO-managed charter schools? What about the teachers who labor in them?

As we've seen, Ohio is hardly the only state that allows for the for-profit management of charter schools. More and more cash-strapped states and municipalities are bending over backwards to usher in an era of for-profit charter schools. Many of these government agencies simply cannot keep pace with rising economic costs for school infrastructure and falling tax revenues to pay for them.

Imagine International Academy and McKinney Charter School

In November of 2008, the Texas Education Agency approved the opening of a McKinney Charter School, run by a company that other states rejected over concerns about its tax status; the company was the for-profit educational management organization, Imagine International Academy. The Texas Board of Education allowed the for-profit EMO, Imagine International Academy of North Texas (the headquarters of the company are located in Arlington, Virginia) to run the school even though state law allows only nonprofit organizations to open state-funded charter schools. Imagine argued that it would use the nonprofit status of an affiliate charter school in Indiana as an umbrella for its profit-making venture, a clever idea and one that works its way around state law.

According to the *Dallas Morning News,* Imagine also intended to open 15 schools in Florida, but there the company met heavy resistance from local and state education officials and in the end withdrew its applications. The problem: Florida education leaders questioned whether Imagine was a certified nonprofit, as it attempted to disguise itself as, or a business attempting to profit from public education money *under the cover of nonprofit status.* Whatever the case, it didn't seem to matter to Texas or officials in other states; the company has opened dozens of schools in 13 states (Hagg 2008).

School officials in Florida and Nevada also raised questions about other Imagine schools, saying they have not proven they are nonprofit and that public money should not flow into for-profit hands through "straw nonprofits." According to Tina Pinkoson, chairwoman of Florida's Alachua County Public schools:

> *They do not have a 501c3. They say they can prove it, but we won't believe it until they show us. (Ibid.)*

"Nonprofit *as* for-profit" is Imagine's business plan and what all this means is that Imagine Schools, Inc. would receive 12.5 percent of the Texas per-pupil state public funding, which is about $750,000 from each of its Texas schools, according to the Texas Education Association, if its plans go through (Ibid.). But that's not all. The Texas charters, which Imagine would manage and then operate, would also pay Imagine Schools, Inc. a "vigorish," or small fee, in the form of monthly "allowances." Although the amount of the "monthly allowances" has not yet been determined in Texas, a cursory glance at the educational system in Alachua, Fla. has Imagine Schools, Inc. proposing that they receive a $3,000 a month "vig" for 20 years, plus, on top of all this, one percent to three percent of the charter's revenue for the same time period. According to the charter application that Imagine filled out, in return for the fees, Imagine Schools, Inc. has promised to provide the two Texas charters everything from teachers to budgeting to human resources. Is this a public-private partnership or an economic scheme wrapped up in a policy proposal designed to simply transfer public monies to private corporations under the auspice of "public charter schools"? Why are for-profit EMOs using nonprofit status illegally to circumvent regulations and state law and then being allowed to open and run charter schools?

Perhaps the real issue was best summed up by Ms. Brady, a founding parent of the McKinney campus who was later hired as school development director of Imagine International Academy of North Texas:

> *It's hard to find a vendor to lease something or provide loans to a new charter school. It's (the deal with Imagine) essentially a way for schools to tap into an existing company with a strong credit background. (Ibid.)*

Distilled down to basic and simple economics, cities and states simply do not have the revenues to provide capital improvements, buildings, management, and a public education for an increasingly growing national student body. Companies like Imagine, Inc. and others promise the government entities they contract with "economic prosperity" and "higher student achievement" in the form of shared costs and services, all for a hefty public fee. But is this really the case; do they really bring economic prosperity or darkening economic and educational clouds?

Advantage, Inc. and Golden Door Charter School

Golden Door Charter School in Jersey City, N.J., with the help of Mayor Bret Schundler, took advantage of the state's charter-school legislation and worked to establish five charter schools in one of the nation's most ethnically diverse cities. In collaboration with the mayor, EMO Advantage Schools, Inc. implemented every detail of Golden Door's curriculum and staffing in a record six-month period of time. Golden Door, at the time, was one of eight charter schools Advantage had established in the late 1990s and early 2000 across the country, serving a total of 4,500 students.

Advantage stated that their goal was twofold: to improve student performance and at the same time make education a profitable venture. According to Theodore Rebarber, co-founder of the for-profit management company, at the time:

> *We thought the for-profit culture would create the kind of discipline and focus on execution that nonprofit environments sometimes lack. It also works well with our commitment to expand. We want to have an impact on education, not just one or two schools. (McCloskey 1999)*

In September of 1999, Golden Door moved into a new $8.75 million structure that Mayor Schundler financed with public municipal-bond money. The public bond deal underwrote the cost of construction for the school and obviously saved Advantage millions on start-up costs, costs they would otherwise have had to bear as a private company. To buttress his decision to ally with for-profit EMO Advantage, the mayor pointed to a $30 million dollar public elementary school the city was currently building, evidently implying he was both investing in public education and privately run corporations. The public elementary school would serve the same number of students in the same square footage as the new Golden Door Charter School, the mayor argued. And it came as no surprise nor did it seem to bother many residents of New Jersey that the city's mayor sat on Golden Door's board when he made the financial deal; certainly a conflict of interest by any stretch of the imagination. The press even went so far as to applaud the move. According to *Business Week,* Mayor Schundler made what the publication called "a shrewd deal for the city." Schundler even went on to try to rationalize the decision to publicly underwrite Advantage's costs by claiming the public investment in the EMO charter really needed to be seen as an investment in a New Jersey community center. Why? According to the mayor:

> *The building is a community center with a daytime tenant, Golden Door. In the evenings and on weekends, local groups use the facility. Golden Door pays the principal and interest. We end up having a community center for free, as far as the local taxpayer is concerned. (Ibid.)*

But that was not the whole deal: By state law, Golden Door got only 90 percent of the $9,200 allocated per public-school pupil in Jersey City. Out of that amount, Advantage paid $1,500 per student in rent, which went back to the municipality, and then paid salaries, benefits, and operating expenses for the school. According to the mayor's office, this translated into a 40 percent reduction in the per-pupil cost to the taxpayer (Ibid.). In 2000, Schundler, writing in a publication produced for the conservative Heartland Institute, noted:

> *The Golden Door Charter School educates children for approximately $8,000 per child per year, including operating costs, space rental costs, and staff pensions. By contrast, the Jersey City School District will spend between $13,000 to $15,000 per child per year, including capital and pension costs, for children attending any of the new school facilities being planned by the district to decrease class overcrowding.*
>
> *Approximately 90 percent of the Golden Door charter school's students are from low-income families and are eligible for the federal school lunch program. Most are considered "at risk" by the state. Yet 100 percent of the students who have attended Golden Door for a full year have progressed at least a full year in learning, and many have progressed by almost two full years in learning. Kindergartners who on average performed at the 24th percentile nationally on their Iowa Reading Tests in September of 1998, tested at the 39th percentile nationally this past spring—a remarkable 15 percentile point increase in just one year. (Schundler 2000)*

Yet in spite of its claims, the New Jersey charter school and its EMO, Advantage, found themselves in trouble soon after the conception of Schundler's financial business deal with the company. In March 2000, New Jersey's education department put Golden Door on ninety-day probation, ordering it to fix more than a half-dozen accounting and other fiscal problems, including running a $600,000 deficit on a $4.4 million budget the previous year (Greenberger 2001). This can hardly be touted as the "schrewd deal" for the public interest that *Business Week* would have liked the public to believe, nor could it be seen as a "budget saving opportunity," as Schundler and his corporate partners promised. So not only did the New Jersey City's Golden Door Charter School end up with a $600,000 deficit in 2000 due to the management by EMO Advantage Schools, Inc., but class sizes were a third larger than advertised (Ibid.) and the amount spent on students went down.

THE RISE OF FOR-PROFIT EMOs

The rise of the educational industry and Educational Maintenance Organizations (EMO)s began in the 1990s, long before the No Child Left Behind Act served as an impetus for the growth of the industry. It is important to look at the for-profit management of charter schools and other public school issues from an historical perspective, as the for-profit school management, or EMO model, although a relatively new concept is now yielding much available evidence and information to draw upon in rendering a judgment as to the efficacy of such a public policy approach to managing public schools, be they charter or district schools.

The Early Years: Wall Street and Lobbying Efforts

In the 1990s, what appeared to be a grand opportunity for privatization efforts through for-profit management companies was also catching the eyes of some mega-investors on Wall Street, including J.P. Morgan and Fidelity Ventures. And why not? In 1992, the United States devoted approximately 5 percent of its GDP to public spending on education (National Center for Educational Statistics 2003).

At the time, Paul Allen's Vulcan Ventures was just one financial entity poised to seize the for-profit opportunity that EMOs offered by rounding up significant public funds for the creation and sale of private educational management services. Lamar Alexander, a former U.S. education secretary and Republican presidential candidate who sat on the board of Leeds Equity Partners III, an investment firm specializing in the up-and-coming educational industrial complex, commented during what seemed the heady times of the 1990s, "We're on the brink of fundamental change" (Slowey 2000).

As the decade progressed, Wall Street began penetrating the educational market: In 1999 Chase Capital Partners of New York led the initial financing of Advantage Schools, the for-profit EMO; Nassau Capital of Princeton, New Jersey was investing in private equity and real estate exclusively on behalf of Princeton University; Salomon Smith Barney acted as a placement agent for the financing in the case of the new EMO, Advantage Schools. Steven F. Wilson, former president and chief executive officer of the Boston-based Advantage Schools, was ecstatic at the time. In the minds of educational entrepreneurs like Wilson, the growth of charter schools was the key to assuring an educational market for EMOs and promised to be an enormous and profitable fount for the profit-driven companies seeking to manage these charter schools. Wall Street and the new companies that sprung up virtually overnight to meet the new "demand" were excited at the chance to capture public funds and get their nose under the educational tent, a goal they had been pursuing for decades.

Indeed, an article that appeared in the *New York Times* in 1999 profiled the galloping speed on behalf of Wall Street to profit from the management of public schools and the virtual sprint on the part of the corporate media to uncritically sell the public on the virtues of investment driven privately, for-profit managed schools as a panacea for "failing government schools" (Wyatt 1999).

The financial sector (the same financial sector responsible for the 2008 Wall Street debacle) claimed they could invest in the for-profit management of schools for the express purpose of making money and yet still have the best interests of our children at heart. EMOs embraced a model of trickle-down economics as applied to the nation's public schools, especially the burgeoning charter schools and the "underperforming school market," which was, and is sure to continue to grow, under NCLB.

So we see that at the EMO's initial conception, the investor class was dizzy with huge visions and expectations of larger profits and a proportionally bigger market share of the public educational system. Running schools for-profit was seen in the late 1990s and early 2000 as a virtual gold mine for Wall Street and venture capitalists and the surge was in full force. But would they do a better job than their public counterparts? Henry M. Levin, a professor of economics and education who headed the National Center for the Study of Privatization in Education at Teachers College, was quick to comment at the time:

> *It's difficult to impossible to determine if a for-profit school is doing a better job than a comparable public school. Private schools and those public schools that are run by for-profit management typically seek students that are not costly to educate. That's not cheating. They are playing by the rules of the game. They want to do a good job, but they also want to make a profit. But the result is that you can't really compare them with public schools. (Ibid.)*

The *New York Times* went on to suggest:

> *The opportunity to make money in education certainly looks good. The education and training industry accounts for 10 percent of the United States economy, as measured by gross domestic product, according to "The Book of Knowledge," a report issued last spring by Michael T. Moe, director of global growth research at Merrill Lynch. But education and training account for less than two-tenths of 1% of the*

value of the domestic stock market—$16 billion out of $10 trillion, so there is plenty of room for growth and for companies to find profits in the education sector. Health care, by comparison, represents 14 percent of GDP and a similar percentage of the value of the United States stock market.

Scott L. Soffen, a financial analyst at Legg Mason Wood Walker, an investment firm in Baltimore, echoed the same sentiment, regarding the financial opportunities and interest inherent in the EMO model:

Nothing attracts interest more than an industry group with momentum on Wall Street. (Ibid.)

In fact, the success of some of the early players in the for-profit entry into education—Apollo, DeVry, the Learning Company—was so exceptional that Wall Street was captivated (Ibid.)—and so were the business press, their think tank and media counterparts. For example, in a 7 February 2000 *Business Week* cover story entitled, "For-Profit Schools: They're Spreading Fast. Can Private Companies Do a Better Job of Educating America's Kids?," the authors detailed a virtual stampede of private investors and their firms on Wall Street who sought to profit from the up and coming EMO model (Symonds et. al. 2000).

Michael R. Sandler, one such investor and chief executive of *EduVentures,* a private investment and consulting firm in Boston, noted:

There are plenty of private companies ready to soak up investors' dollars. Roughly $6 billion has been invested in private education companies by venture capital firms and other investors, an enormous amount of untapped market value. (Ibid.)

Steve Wilson and his company Advantage Schools was one of the first to jump on the EMO bandwagon during this time of venture capitalist formations of the EMO. The idea from his point of view was simple: to create charter schools and then have private companies brought in to manage the public charter schools. Wilson, now with the Kennedy Business School at Harvard, summed up his thinking at the time:

In the early 1990s, state legislators, business leaders, and the nation's governors were radicalized by the failure of repeated efforts to reform the public schools from within. American schools were, on the whole, failing to equip students with the skills they needed. Many inner-city schools were entirely dysfunctional. As spending on public education had climbed sharply over the preceding decades, and the United States outspent almost every other nation on its schools, some reformers began to question the conventional wisdom: Were inadequate resources really to blame for poor performance? And was still-greater spending the solution?

Supporters of charter schools reasoned that the system's structure was itself an impediment to reform. It was time to launch new public schools that were inde-

pendent of the school districts, free of collective bargaining agreements, and out from under the bureaucracy of the district office. New charter schools would bene- fit from driven leaders, innovative academic designs, and high expectations for their students. Maybe they would demonstrate what public schools could achieve—and point the way for the majority system. (Stark 2006)

Given Wilson's claims, where is the evidence behind the argument proponents of such models make when they claim they want to create charter schools with driven leaders, innovative academic designs, and high expectations for their students all in the name of demonstrating what traditional public schools can and should achieve? The "majority system" that Wilson speaks of is the traditional public school system and it is precisely this system that has been targeted not for improvement through EMO run charter schools, but for replacement with a new system of charterized for-profit schools. This can be gleaned directly from the report issued from the National Center on Education and the Economy 2007, *Tough Choices or Tough Times,* as well as from think tanks like the Hudson Institute, which we examined in the last chapter.

Another key to understanding the enormous growth in the privatization of education and the for-profit management of schools is the multibillion dollar lobbying campaign on behalf of all private industry and the private sector in general. According to the *Boston Herald,* the financial sector spent $5.1 billion in political influence-peddling in all areas of public concern over the past decade as lobbyists won deregulation efforts that led to the nation's wholesale financial collapse. The *Herald* goes on to describe in their report entitled, "Wall Street Spent Billions Lobbying," that over the past decade Wall Street investment firms, commercial banks, hedge funds, real estate companies, and insurance firms made $1.7 billion in political contributions and spent another $3.4 billion on lobbyists to undercut federal regulation (Grillo 2009).

Much of this money went into lobbying for changes in the regulation of education, especially, as we have seen in the No Child Left Behind Act passed in 2001 by President George W. Bush, shortly after taking office. The following is a sampling of just some of the campaign contributions made by EMO interests in the last few years, in the state of Philadelphia alone:

From 2002-2006, Chris Whittle, CEO of Edison Schools, contributed $15,500.00 to the campaign of Representative Dwight Evans.

From 2002-2006, Rhonda Lauer, CEO of Foundations Inc. and her Chief of Staff, Emilio Matticoli, contributed $13,203.00 and $6,100.00, respectively, to the campaign of Representative Dwight Evans.

Overall, from 2001-2006, Representative Dwight Evans received a total of $66,103.00 in campaign contributions from Victory Schools, Foundations, Inc., Chancellor- Beacon, and Edison Schools. Edison Schools and Foundations, Inc. contributed the largest amounts, $21,500.00 and $43,853.00 respectively.

From 2001-2005, Representative John Perzel received a total of $19,400.00 from Foundations Inc., Edison Schools, and Universal Companies. $12,900 of this sum came from Foundations, Inc.

From 2001-2006, Representative Vincent Fumo received $9,000.00 in campaign contributions from Foundations, Inc.

From 2001-2004, former Mayor John Street received $41,750.00 from Universal Companies and Victory Schools.

Between 2001 and 2006, Governor Ed Rendell received $28,250.00 in campaign contributions from Universal Companies and Foundations, Inc. (Nijmie 2008)

By 1999, for-profit schools taught 100,000 students at about 200 schools out of America's 53 million children in kindergarten through 12th grade. In two years, the Boston-based Advantage Schools saw their profits skyrocket from $4 million in revenues to $60 million. Similarly, in the five years since it opened its first four schools, publicly traded Edison Schools Inc. (EDSN) saw its revenue jump from $12 million to $217 million. In 1999 it ran 79 schools in 16 states (Stark 2006).

In spite of their rhetoric regarding "raising all boats" within traditional public schools, private companies really had little or no interest in traditional public schools other than capturing them as a "market" thereby eliminating them, as Michael T. Moe, analyst at Merrill Lynch & Co., which helped Edison Schools raise $122 million in an initial public offering on the stock exchange in November, 1998 declared. He predicted that by 2005 New York-based Edison Schools alone would be managing 423 schools with 260,000 students, thereby giving it revenues of $1.8 billion. And he went even further, confidently predicting that by 2009 EMOs could capture as much as 10 percent of the $360 billion the United States now shells out annually on K-12 schooling. At the time, CEO H. Christopher Whittle and founder of Edison Schools proclaimed, "In 20 years, 20% to 30% of U.S. public schools will be run by for-profits" (Symonds 2000).

Yet, the picture became more complex than anyone could have anticipated. While entrepreneurs were stating they wanted to help create and run outstanding public schools through for-profit management arrangements, the only thing that was to really remain public were the taxpayer subsidies that would go to the companies themselves. All the decision making, all the management of the schools, all the curriculum and in fact, all the day-to-day organizational procedures and rules would be the providence of the for-profit EMO. As Wilson bemoans in his book, *Learning on the Job:*

The business plan for Advantage Schools . . . promised investors we would "create a new generation of outstanding public schools that would enable students—regardless of their socioeconomic background—to reach the heights of academic achievement." I admit I'm uneasy reading these words today. (Stark 2006)

He may be even more uneasy now that the economy has been severely devastated by the economic collapse of Wall Street in 2008, as capital investment and credit dried up and the educational standards and performance of the United States has declined rapidly.

Even now, EduVentures' Michael Sandler, once so optimistic regarding what he saw as a mushrooming market for taxpayer monies to provide for the for-profit management of schools is now a bit more reticent and sanguine. On February 9, 2008, EduVentures' support for K-12 firms coalesced into its Business Research Division, a syndicated research service with fees in the several tens of thousands of dollars per year and on January 22, 2008 the firm announced the sale of its K-12 research business to Outsell, a syndicated research and advisory services firm headquartered in London and San Francisco (Millot 2008).

It seems that some investors are simply finding that getting their hands on public funds is not as easy, and the profits to be made not as lucrative, as they had once thought.

A LOOK AT FOR-PROFIT EMOs

In a recent interview, Steven Wilson, now at the Harvard Business School and author of the book, *Learning on the Job: When Business Takes on Public Schools,* summed up some of the history of EMOs this way:

> The first education management organization was Education Alternatives, Inc. (EAI), which attracted national attention when it won ill-fated contracts to manage the Baltimore and Hartford school systems in the early 1990s. The company went public and later collapsed when both contracts were cancelled. The next wave of private managers learned some lessons from EAI—simply taking over the central office of existing school districts and ousting superintendents in favor of private-sector managers was not enough to effect decisive improvement.
>
> Edison Schools, the first of the second wave of managers, focused on implementing a comprehensive "school design" at each client school and began modestly, opening just four schools in 1992. Most organizations focused on opening only de novo charter schools, built from the ground up. But like EAI, other EMOs continued to over-promise and under-deliver. They were thwarted by contractual arrangements that, while superior to EAI's, fell far short of providing them the authority they needed to implement their models exactingly. And political resistance from the education establishment remained fierce.
>
> A third wave, first appearing in 2000, employed a different strategy—they would organize as nonprofits, build a base of schools in just one region, and eschew publicity. (Stark 2006)

With this history in mind, let us look briefly at some of the EMOs currently operating both charter schools and traditional district schools.

Edison Schools

With opportunities for the development of the "educational entrepreneur" escalating in the 1980s, responding to widespread calls in the late 1980s for broad educational reforms in face of deteriorating urban school systems, media entrepreneur Christopher Whittle and businessman John Golle offered for-profit school plans to redesign U.S. schools. Edison Schools was founded by Christopher Whittle, a publishing and media entrepreneur who earlier created Channel One, which broadcasted news and advertising in schools under an arrangement that gives schools television equipment in return for required viewing of its broadcast material. However, in its initial advertising, Edison Project's proposal regarding the for-profit management of schools to potential investors emphasized the bottom line rather than the quality of its educational product. And why shouldn't it? After all, the investors were investing to make a profit and paying attention to the bottom line certainly meant a higher return on investment.

In his solicitation for investment funds, Chris Whittle, founder of the Edison Project (now EdisonLearning), suggested that investors compare the company to Home Depot, McDonalds or Wal-Mart—companies that are not top-end companies but mass marketers that have become leaders in retail and profitable investments—not a bad comparison it turns out. Fast-food enterprises and box stores were now idealized as the metaphor for public education (Light 2000). The comparison certainly might be in order for as we shall see many of the EMOs are little more than private entities running what can be called "national or regional educational retail chains" with for-profit managed school franchises often occupying unlikely geographical locales such as strip malls, box stores, or sharing buildings with businesses, churches, or private and public entities.

It was in May 1991 that Whittle announced the formation of the Edison Project, a plan for a multibillion-dollar educational retail chain of 150 to 200 private "franchise" schools, which, he declared, would provide better instruction at lower per-pupil cost than public schools. The idea was to replace the public school management of schools with private sector management. A year later, Whittle hired Benno C. Schmidt, Jr., president of Yale University, to head the Edison Project. After initially failing to raise sufficient capital, the project was scaled back, focusing instead on obtaining management contracts with existing schools or winning public funds to establish new schools.

In March 1994 Massachusetts became the first state to award charters for a project to operate schools for-profit. In the not too recent past, Golle had started Education Alternatives, Inc. (EAI), in 1986. His first schools, which opened in 1987, did not turn a profit so he too turned his attention to managing public schools for-profit. Following mixed results in Miami, Florida, and Duluth, Minnesota, EAI went on to obtain a $133 million contract to operate nine public inner-city schools in Baltimore. EAI had finally penetrated the "underperforming" or "subprime educational market," which as we will see is currently now the most explosive "niche" market for EMOs.

Meanwhile, Edison Schools, Inc., now flushed with new capital, opened four schools in August of 1995. By 2000 the company could boast that they taught 38,000 enrolled students and ran seventy-nine schools in sixteen states and the District of Columbia. Edison's contracts, which paid the company approximately $5,500 per student for their educational management services, were paid by diverting public money previously earmarked for the school districts or for charter schools to the coffers of Edison. And although the company boasted improved standardized test scores, it was losing tens of millions of dollars, not a good prospect for its investors. Some analysts estimated it would reach profitability if it grew to three-hundred schools and so the race was on to expand market share. On September 12, 2003 Edison Schools, Inc. reported its first quarterly profit in its 11-year history of managing public schools.

As we noted earlier, The Edison Project was and still is one of the main EMOs in the for-profit management of schools. After it opened its first four schools in 1995, its revenues rose from $12 million to $227 million. (Symonds 2000). At that time, Edison projected it would manage 423 schools in the future with 26,000 students, giving it revenues of $1.8 million. By 2009, they predicted that they would take over as much as ten percent of the $360 billion the United States currently pays annually for K-12 schools. According to Chris Whittle, "in twenty years 20 percent to 30 percent of U.S. public schools will be run by for-profit." (Ibid.).

As of this date however, profits continue to remain illusory for the company and their forecasts remain largely rhetorical, intangible, and basically unmet. The answer to improving profits, according to Whittle, was to cut administrative costs at EMO-run schools. He figured that 27 cents of every dollar was spent on the central office of most public schools. Whittle promised to bring this amount down by a massive 19 percent, to just 8 cents. The savings, he claimed, would be put right back into the classroom, with a slight 7 percent profit for the company (Ibid.). In light of the need for cost-cutting measures, the companies' claim that they could improve student learning and simultaneously make a profit seemed unsubstantiated; the current evidence, in fact, seems to point to the contrary. At the time of their inception, little formal research had been done on the effectiveness of these for-profits EMOs that operate charter schools, but even in a 1998 report by the NEA, it found that these companies fell through on their promises (Corporate Watch 1998).

As of 2008, Edison Schools, as we noted, changed its name to EdisonLearning. The company's current Web site now states that:

> *In the 2008-2009 school year, EdisonLearning will serve over 350,000 students in 24 states and the United Kingdom, through 120 school partnerships and in programs that are provided in hundreds of additional buildings. (EdisonLearning)*

A recent report from *Hoovers,* a company that offers proprietary business information through the Internet, data feeds, wireless devices, and co-branding agreements with other online services, states that EdisonLearning's revenues have gone down from 69.4 million dollars in 1998 to 8.7 million dollars in 2007, hardly the massive increase forecasted by Whittle and his entrepreneur friendly investors in the formative years of EMOs (Hoovers).

The new EdisonLearning, according to the Web site for the company, now offers what it calls a plethora of educational "products and features" which include professional development, national and regional training, top talent, benchmark assessment, operational services, enrollment services, quality tools and metrics, achievement-driven management, academic programs, and demanding content and customized instruction (EdisonLearning).

These "products and services" all comprise the "supplemental educational services (SES)" now allowed under No Child Left Behind and seem to offer a more promising future for EdisonLearning than expanding its share of the retail education market.

Currently, Edison manages more district public schools than they do charter schools. By the 2006-2007 school year Edison Schools managed 60 district schools and 37 charter schools for a total of 97 public schools nationwide, located in 18 states with a total enrollment of 56,383 students. As of July of 2008 this amount went down to 49 public district schools and 31 charter schools. Edison, with its focus now more keenly set on the variety of privatized educational products and services it offers to schools may not remain a large player in the for-profit management industry as it pertains to charters, but instead may seek to diversify its educational profit market and scope through supplemental educational services, which can be purchased by other for-profit EMOs for use in the schools they manage and run. New private partnerships may be on the horizon as companies seek to revamp and set their sights on myriad privatization efforts.

Advantage Schools

Although the struggle of Edison is one of economic miscalculation to some extent, in some cases EMOs were a tremendously lucrative investment, at least initially. Advantage Schools was a for-profit management corporation based in Boston that went from $4 million in revenues to $60 million in just a few years after its founding in 1996. The company opened and operated new urban charter public schools throughout the country. They began with K-5 charter schools and then added a grade each year until there were K-12 programs. Advantage Schools opened its first two charter schools in 1997. By the year 2000 it had schools in nine states serving more than 9,000 students (Advantage Schools) and it clearly intended to keep growing. On February 22, 2000, Advantage Schools Incorporated announced that is had secured $28 million in additional private equity capital. The earnings were to be used to open new urban charter schools in cities nationwide by the fall of 2000 and to develop the fourteen Advantage schools already in operation. Wall Street-based Credit Suisse First Boston Equity and Partners, L.P., of New York happily secured the financing, and the affiliates that led the financing were a large conglomerate of private venture capitalists.

To give some idea of the business model, in his book Steven Wilson detailed his experience with the EMO business plan:

> *The business plan for Advantage Schools, the for-profit management company my colleagues and I started in 1996, promised investors we would "create a new generation of outstanding public schools that would enable students—regardless of their socioeconomic background—to reach the heights of academic achievement."*
>
> *I admit I am uneasy reading these words today. But at the time we were thrilled with the company's plan. Charter school legislation was sweeping the states, and with it the opportunity to build a network of new schools that would serve students from the most troubled urban neighborhoods. Open to all students, publicly funded and tuition free, and accountable for meeting new state education standards, our charter schools would truly be public institutions. Yet Advantage, the company that ran them, would be fueled by not only private capital but also the entrepreneurial desire to succeed. (Wilson 2006)*

Here we get a further glimpse into the need to capitalize on what Wilson refers to as the "most troubled urban neighborhoods" or what I refer to as "subprime kids." With class stratification growing along with economic inequality throughout the 1980s and 1990s, targeting "subprime students," or the often disenfranchised, low-income urban minority community through the development of charter schools became an early big business and a strongly spoken selling point for the new EMOs. They claimed their efforts in these communities would raise test scores, settle troubled school financing, and produce effective management and decision-making in underachieving urban areas. As early as 2000, pundits and educators were claiming that:

> *By specializing in the education of low-cost students, charter schools are able to reduce the average cost of educating the students in their schools. The margin between the subsidy provided by the state and the average cost of education is available for other uses, including profits for EMOs. (Plank et al. 2000)*

However, the report also went on to presciently point out that the social costs for such charter school business plans are:

> *When charter schools reduce the average cost of educating students in their schools, however, they raise the average cost of educating students in nearby public schools,*

which must continue to offer high-cost programs, including secondary education and special education services. If low-cost students leave to take advantage of opportunities elsewhere, then the subsidy provided by the state will begin to fall short of the average cost of educating students in the traditional public school system. (Ibid.)

But getting back to the notion of profit and cost savings, the EMO business plans that emerged were to serve the most "disadvantaged students"; the "at-risk students," as they had been labeled, or what policymakers refer to as "low-income urban" students. Although no longer involved with EMOs, Wilson still sees a bright future for the educational industry in tandem with the charter school movement and he is banking on companies getting their hands on a portion of the $400 billion in public monies spent on public education. He admits, quite laconically:

Soon enough, an education entrepreneur will devise a scaleable business model for opening high-achieving schools. I predict a fourth generation of education management organizations will appear, with retooled designs from the EMOs. We will see much more disciplined management by entrepreneurs, careful growth plans, refined academic designs, and much stronger academic and financial results. The country currently spends $400 billion annually on K-12 public education and posts chronically mediocre results in international comparisons of student attainment. The first company to demonstrate consistent academic success at scale will not only be in enormous demand, but will have made an extraordinary contribution to society. (Stark 2006)

It is plain to see from Wilson's comments that the game plan is not fixing what ails traditional public schools through the creation of exemplary charter schools and publicly available and widely shared innovative practices, but instead the plan is for opening up new charter schools that are then privatized through EMO contracts, creating a new school system harnessed to subsidizing corporate businesses and private venture capitalists while keeping the "appearance" of a public school system. This then is a system where the "public" turns over not just their taxpayer monies to these corporations and private operators, but also the control, decision making, oversight, transparency, and regulation of their schools to private entities solely seeking to financialize education and expand capital, market share, and maximize profits.

White Hat Management

When Ohio authorized a pilot project for charter schools in 1997, the result was a virtual dream-come-true for privatization forces and particularly for a company called "White Hat Management," the EMO brainchild of Akron, Ohio businessman,

David Brennan. By 2007 the Ohio charter school reform movement had blossomed from a pilot of 20 schools statewide, to an educational retail industry of over 313 privately run franchise charter schools receiving more than six-hundred million annually in both state and federal funds (*Keeping the Promise*). Amy Hanauer, the founding executive director of Policy Matters, a nonprofit in Ohio that looks at charter school reform measures, points out that currently:

> *More than half of the state's charter money goes to for-profit companies whose bottom line is sometimes less the well-being of the children than the balance of their bank accounts. White Hat made 4.16 million in profit during 2004-2005. (Hanauer 2009)*

White Hat Management is named after Brennan who prides himself on sporting a white hat, a publicly created metaphor for good guy, superhero-like qualities he seeks to project. Brennan interestingly got his start as an educational entrepreneur by launching publicly funded, private voucher schools and of course he was and is a big political player in the privatization and anti-public school charter reform movement. He first became a financial investor in the bourgeoning charter school movement in Ohio in 1998, at which time he founded White Hat Management. At its Web site, White Hat boasts that it is the third largest for-profit operator of K-12 charter schools in the country (White Hat Management).

Like most for-profit EMOs, White Hat claims it is a problem-solving company with student interests at heart:

> *Think of us as a company dedicated to students reaching their full potential. White Hat looks at problems, comes up with solutions and provides proven results. (Ibid.)*

In 2007 in Ohio alone, White Hat Management earned more than $79 million dollars in the transfer of state, federal, and local funds to its company and affiliates and in 2008 White Hat Management received more than $400 million in public funds, courtesy of philanthropic Ohio taxpayers (Ohio Department of Education).

It seems that much of Brennan's success can be owed to his political ties and gratuitous tax-campaign contributions. For example, in 2005 he personally gave more than $120,000 to former Ohio Governor George Voinovich, as well as helped the former governor raise $500,000 for his political campaign (Hanauer 2009). According to the newspaper, the *Columbus Dispatch* of 23 October 2005, Brennan at one time also held a backyard fundraiser for the governor charging $25,000 per person to attend. The "backyard fund-raiser" allowed Governor Voinovitch and other well-healed attendees the opportunity to rub shoulders with then President George W. Bush. Not surprisingly, Voinovitch was instrumental in the privatization of Ohio schools. Brennan has also given hundreds of thousands of dollars to the Ohio Republican Party throughout the years (Hallett 2005).

In April of 2008, the *Ohio Plain Dealer,* a newspaper that can be found online and in print, reported that David Brennan may have violated state law by directing political contributions through two political action committees in addition to his own generous bout with giving, according to state campaign finance officials. The report goes on to note that coincidently Brennan and his wife, Ann have been major political contributors precisely at the same time the Ohio legislature had dealt with charter school issues in recent years. In 2007 for example, they couple gave a combined $733,300 to state candidates and Republican organizations, including $400,000 to the Ohio Republican Party, according to state records. The Brennans also each gave $10,000 contributions—the maximum allowed at the time—to the 2006 campaign of unsuccessful gubernatorial candidate Ken Blackwell (Rollenhagen 2008).

Brennan's White Hat Management also has managed to build an economic business model that can only be conceived of as comprising elaborate "economic feeder trays" that seem to flow directly to the mother corporation, White Hat, itself. These feeder trays, such as its Hope Academies, currently with only one Cleveland High School and its Life Skills Centers, primarily aimed at "at risk-students," operate under the White Hat corporate umbrella with undisclosed accounting techniques. White Hat also owns Alternative Education Academy (AEA), an online K-12 that operates throughout Ohio (Ibid.). Although the relationship between the "mother company," White Hat Management and its various subsidiaries is murky at best, it is known that The Hope Academy Schools cedes 96 percent of the public dollars they receive to White Hat directly (Livingston et. al. 2006).

In a report, entitled *A Comprehensive Report on the Origins, Evolution and Business Model of Ohios Largest Charter School Company*, prepared by the Food and Allied Service Trades Division of the AFL-CIO in cooperation with the Ohio Federation of Teachers was published in 2007. The report not only found that White Hat Management, Inc., not the actual charter schools themselves that White Hat manages, owns the names of the charter schools it operates. White Hat legally incorporated a limited liability company in the name of each of the schools it operates and has also registered each school's name as a Trade Name, owned by none other than White Hat. But that's not all. The extensive report uncovered details of the business model employed by Brennan and White Hat. The report documents:

> *A trail of financial statements showing that the charter schools are indebted to the management company, and that Brennan used some school buildings as collateral to secure a $5 million loan;*

Brennan's use of campaign contributions to influence charter school legislation and how that legislation enabled White Hat to avoid accountability and public scrutiny; Brennan's conversion of private schools to charters, which is barred by state law; Wal-Mart's early involvement in bankrolling David Brennan's ventures. (Ohio Federation of Teachers 2006)

In previous years, studies by the Ohio Federation of Teachers have also uncovered:

The academic performance of White Hat-managed charters is far below achievement in Ohio's traditional public schools. If White Hat schools were a school district, it would be the ninth largest in Ohio and would be rated in Academic Emergency. In 2005, 79 percent of White Hat charter schools that received state report cards were rated in Academic Emergency or Academic Watch, the lowest categories.

The Ohio Department of Education confirmed an October 2005 OFT analysis that found White Hat's charter high schools failed to administer state-required tests to the vast majority of students for which they received state tax dollars. ODE data showed that White Hat's Life Skills charter schools tested only 15 percent of students in reading and only 16 percent of students in math.

Brennan and his family (wife Ann and daughter Nancy) gave $3.8 million to Republican lawmakers between 1990 and 2005, based on analysis of campaign finance reports. (Ibid.)

Although White Hat remains the nation's third-largest player in the educational national retail charter school business chains, the company's ambitions and dreams of a profitable future hardly stop there. A cursory look at its Web site uncovers the fact that White Hat Management also operates charter schools in Arizona, Colorado, Florida, Michigan, Ohio and Pennsylvania and has plans for future educational franchises that include Texas, New Mexico, Indiana, and New York; they also have high hopes of spreading to as many other states as they can throughout the United States (Ibid.).

Unfortunately, White Hat has run into some stiff opposition at home and could be poised to lose market share if Governor Strickland's 2009 educational bill passes. White Hat Management almost found itself relegated to states other than Ohio, for the governor's initial proposed budget for fiscal year 2009 would have prohibited for-profit management companies, like White Hat, from providing services to charter schools and the bill would have forced charter schools to meet the same standards of quality a traditional public school is forced to confront (Ohio Educational Association 2009).

In spring of 2009 this portion of Strickland's bill was voted down by the Ohio Legislature, but had it passed, it would have represented a severe blow to Brennan's corporate educational empire, at least in Ohio, and would have sent a direct and unwelcome message for those who support the privatization of public school management and to legislatures and governors in others states regarding regulating or the outright banning of for-profit EMO services at state expense. The fight over charter schools in Ohio is hardly over, as the Center for Education Reform reported in May 2009:

> *The Governor's proposed budget cuts charter funding by another 20 percent (fully 50 percent less than conventional public schools) and virtual schools by 70 percent. In its April 28, 2009 version of the budget, the Ohio House eliminated Strickland's probation of education management companies but added more anti-charter provisions. The Senate is reviewing the proposed budget as of this writing and a heated conference session is expected between the anti-charter school House and pro-charter school Senate. (Center for Education Reform 2006)*

Mosaica

According to claims made by representatives of Mosaica Education in the early 1990s, the concerns driving educational reform challenge public remedies. They, like their privatization counterparts, also echoed the mantra of growing dissatisfaction among voters and employers with the quality of public education and put forth the remedy of profit oriented education to assure competition. They also continue to claim, as do all privatization advocates and EMOs, that existing educational resources are simply insufficient to meet the future needs of a competitive workforce. In fact, they argue, that with student enrollment scheduled to mushroom in the future, U.S. public schools are simply not equipped to meet the challenge of providing a quality education.

Mosaica, like other EMOs, claims that its graduates are prepared to make immediate contributions to the workplace. They achieve this result, they argue by investing private capital in each school they manage. They also upgrade buildings, assure that modern technology is available to both students and teachers, and take pride in offering a safe and appealing learning environment. This can be very tempting to charter school start-ups and especially for the traditional public school districts facing loss of revenue.

The history of Mosaica Education, one of the largest EMOs on the educational horizon, was begun in 1997. It was with "seed money" from the sale of Prodigy Consulting that Dawn and Gene Eidelman spawned Mosaica Education, Inc. Dawn Eidelman had sometime earlier founded the successful company, Prodigy Consulting, which operated day care centers for corporations in seven states before she turned her attention, together with her husband, to founding Mosaica Education, Inc.

Mosaica's business plan was quite simple on the surface: they would offer and sell "blueprints" for how to run schools, in essence how to manage them, as well as a "set of curriculum" to go with the "school package," which Mosaica claimed would provide students with a "world class education"; or, as some progressive educators would argue, an educational "happy meal," depending on how one looks at it (Wilson 2006).

Steve Wilson is quick to note that the dramatic rise in Mosaica's business profitability was owed not to the excellence of its educational products and services, but to its rigorous public relations campaigns:

> *Mosaica wooed parents and charter (school) boards with promises of abundant technology (one computer for every three children), limited class size (no more than 25 students), and extended day and year (7.5 hours of instruction a day for two hundred days), and a personalized learning plan for each child. (Ibid.)*

But there were other reasons the company became successful: the seed money provided by the sale of Prodigy Consulting by Dawn Eidelman creator of Mosaica at the time (the proceeds of which were then used to start Mosaica), as well as securing venture capital and a keen interest in an investment in the "education industry" on behalf of Wall Street. For example, the New York investment firm, Lepercq Capital Management, helped out the Eidelman's by acquiring a majority stake in the Mosaica in 1998. Following suit, in 1999 another Wall Street firm, Murphy and Partners, bought into the company as well for an additional $10 million. This allowed Mosaica, during these formative years, the capital to market its services and continue to double its enrollment in the charter schools it managed.

At its Web site, the company writes with pride about its relationship with charter schools, noting the company:

> *is a leader in the operation of innovative charter schools which emphasize strong basic skills, an inter-disciplinary curriculum and extensive use of technology. Mosaica currently operates 77 charter school programs in seven states, the District of Columbia, and the Middle East serving over 16,000 students. (Mosaica Education 2009)*

In 2001 Mosaica Education, Inc. acquired the fledgling Advantage Schools, Inc. and has now become one of the largest K-12 for-profit EMOs in the nation. In fact, the company has gone from managing just 2 schools in 1998 to managing 36 charter schools in the 2007-2008 school year, a whopping eighteenfold increase with a total enrollment of 12,505 students in 8 states (Molnar, Miron, and Urschel). The company is a privately held corporation and thus little information is available on its profitability or economic outlook. In fact as we will see, companies like Mosaica have no duty to disclose anything to their "constituencies," the public, another troubling aspect of for-profit EMOs. However, according to Hoovers, the online service that provides economic profiles on companies throughout the world, Mosaica Education, Inc. had "sales" of $61.1 million dollars in 2007 (Mosaica Education 2009).

Recently not all has gone well for the corporation. The board of the Lafayette Academy Charter School located in New Orleans, where the nation's largest charter school "experiment" is now underway, recently fired Mosaica Education, Inc. in 2007 after a bitter dispute over the EMOs performance. During the year that Mosaica ran Lafayette, more than half the staff quit and textbooks and supplies were scant, according to teacher and administrator accounts. An executive at Mosaica disputed those claims but evidently not to the satisfaction of the board (Carr 2009).

Academica, Inc.

The first Florida charter school statute was approved in 1996, opening the door for the creation of charter schools as part of the state's public education system, where they would operate independently. Since that time the race has been on, with Florida, along with other states such as Arizona, Louisiana and Texas, becoming the fasting growing charter school environments in the United States (Florida Consortium of Public Charter Schools).

One of the first players to jump into the foray of for-profit EMOs in the quickly transforming charter school climate in Florida, was Academica, Inc., a private corporation founded by entrepreneur and attorney, Fernando Zulueta. Originated in 1999, Academica's Web site describes itself as:

> *Academica is one of the nation's longest-serving and most successful charter school service and support organizations. The company was founded in 1999 on the principle that each charter school is a unique educational environment governed by an independent Board of Directors that best knows the right path for its school, and Academica's mission is to facilitate that governing board's vision. Academica has a proven track-record developing growing networks of high performing charter schools. (Academica Schools)*

In speaking about its business plan, the Web site goes on to claim:

> *Academica's winning business formula has played a major role in the success of Mater Academy and all charter schools under their management. Academica takes care of administrative duties such as payroll, budgeting, accounting and facility maintenance, which allow school principals and teachers to focus on providing top-notch education for their students. Academica is a charter school service and support organization that works with schools in Florida, Utah and Texas. It was founded in 1999 on the principle that each charter school is a unique educational environment governed by an independent board of directors that best knows the right path for its school. Academica's goal is to facilitate the governing board's vision. (Ibid.)*

So, with this in mind Academica's philosophy, like most for-profit EMOs, was geared to the notion that independent boards of directors would now decide school policy—forget about school boards, public hearings, and community input. This is due to the fact that charter schools, managed by their own governing and oversight boards, are legally independent entities. Eleven states grant them outright independence, according to educational researchers Corwin and Schneider, while eight others permit them to be independent. Corwin and Schneider report that:

> *The thirteen states that curiously require their charters to operate as part of a school district account for only 12% of the nation's 3,400 charter schools. Their legal status not withstanding, charter schools as conceived, are supposed to operate autonomously, although their actual freedom varies widely in practice. (Corwin and Schneider 2007)*

Much like the changes in the Ohio law that allowed David Brennan to cash in on the EMO wave that hit the state, Fernando Zulueta the owner of Academica, Inc. himself got started early in the movement around 1996 with the initial passage of the Florida charter school law. At the time, Zulueta was a Miami-based Excel Development Corporation president. By 1996, according to the National Center for Policy Analysis, Zulueta had managed to have the biggest influence on charter school development in the state of Florida. Today, nearly 300 charter schools are open in Florida.

Zulueta was an innovative if not a clever businessman. In 1997 for example, seeing the tremendous opportunities in the charter school "business," Zulueta was the first Florida builder to put a charter school in a housing development. He then went on to build two 50-student facilities, each costing $300,000. And as The National Center for Policy Analysis noted, he now he owns a retail chain of charter schools across the state (Georgiou 2005).

At the time his plan was certainly pioneering in using housing developers and community-based organizations to assist charter schools by leasing, renovating, or building new facilities for a profit. Zulueta understood that charter schools contained within housing subdivisions would make the housing developments more appealing to prospective buyers and lenders, thereby increasing housing sales, revenues, and profits to his company. Instead of offering a "club house" or golf course, why not offer a charter school? And if a management company could be established or found that could manage the day-to-day operations of the housing subdivision charter school, well that would represent another golden opportunity for business. Now, thanks to the politicians in Florida and the first steps made by Zulueta, the recent passage of a new Florida law in 2004 allows housing developers to steer impact fees that would otherwise have gone to school districts to charter schools in their own housing developments. Supporters of the idea claimed at the time of passage that this would encourage developers to build new schools by donating land or money for construction (Ibid.).

However, many would ague that this is just an example of how privatization disinvests in the public sector, steering public funds to private interests through legislation favorable to capital, leaving decaying infrastructure in its stead as public financing dries up for traditional public schools.

Similar to David Brennan, Fernando Zulueta established his political connections the old-fashioned way, with large campaign contributions to primarily Republicans on both the state and federal level. For example, in the first quarter of 2004 Zulueta gave $2,000 to the campaign of George W. Bush for president, as did Zulueta's wife. In the first quarter of 2008, according to the *Huffington Post*, Zulueta gave $2,300 to the campaign of Lincoln Diaz Balart for Congress, and the same amount to the campaign of Rudy Giuliani (*Huffington Post* 2008).

It is no coincidence that these politicians also happen to support the privatization of education. Zulueta has also been quick to ingratiate himself and rub shoulders with influential people in the conservative Florida political establishment and immerse himself into charter school "oversight" committees and charter school "fraternities and organizations," in general. This too represents no surprise as the marketing of charter schools, Mosaica comes to mind, is a necessity if the schools are to exist and then be managed for a profit—the more charter schools, the more for-profit opportunities for EMOs like Academica, Inc. Also serving on public boards and organizations allows Academica to monitor its business opportunities as well as steer politicians to legislation favorable to their business plans.

The National Alliance for Public Charter Schools sketches a brief biography of Fernando Zulueta:

> *Fernando Zulueta is the president of Academica Corporation, a successful charter school service and support organization founded in 1999. He is Chairman of the Florida Charter School Review Panel and founding Board Member of the Florida Consortium of Charter Schools. Zulueta has helped establish numerous high performing charter schools that have been recognized on local, state, and national levels for their achievements. In 2005, Zulueta received the "Cervantes Award" sponsored by Nova Southeastern University for his contributions toward excellence in the education of Hispanic students. (The National Alliance of Public Charter Schools)*

As early as 1996, Governor of Florida Jeb Bush signed House Bill 135 into law, a bill that created the Florida Schools of Excellence Commission, a state-level charter school authorizer that the governor said would improve school quality and accountability in the state. Not surprisingly, Zulueta was appointed to the commission by the governor.

The Commission, according to the pro-charter Center for Education Reform:

allows municipalities and universities to share in the chartering responsibility to help bring into existence new, quality charter schools. Legislators in Florida told CER "we couldn't have done it without you," when they successfully passed legislation, and CER has been called on to continue that leading role in working with legislators and charter leaders in the ongoing development of the Commission. (Center for Education Reform 2006)

As noted on their Web site, Academica, Inc. has schools in three states: Florida, Utah and Texas. In Florida, it operates ten schools, among them the Mater Academy we looked at in chapter 4. Academica also operates seven schools in Miami-Dade County and three schools in Broward County. Calling itself, Academica West, the company also operates The Brooks Academy of Science and Engineering, a college preparatory school in Texas, as well as schools in Utah (Brooks Academy 2009).

At their Academica West Web site, the company describes in detail the stages, products, and services they offer charter schools (all at a profit):

Prior to Charter School Approval
- *Completing the charter application*
- *Training and assistance through the application process*
- *Corporate establishment and administration*
- *Budget forecasting*
- *Financial reporting*
- *Bookkeeping and records management*

Construction Management
- *Site selection and school design*
- *Land use approvals*
- *Site acquisition and development*
- *Construction contractor selection and supervision*

School Set-up
- *Setting up a lunch program*
- *Setting up a student information system*
- *Student Registration Assistance*
- *Recruiting of Staff*
- *Human Resource Management*
- *Payroll*
- *Governmental Compliance*

Training
- *Computer training*
- *Board training*
- *Teacher and staff training*
- *Special education compliance*

Report Submission (including, but not limited to)
- *Financial reporting*
- *October 1 count assistance*
- *Economically disadvantaged report assistance*
- *CACTUS report submission*
- *Immunization report assistance*
- *December 1 count assistance*
- *End-of-year report*
- *Grant writing (Academica West)*

With the recent 2007 expansion of Academica in Utah, according to the Enterprise Business Newspaper, Inc. of Utah, Academica West, as it is called, now has its fingers in four different charter schools along the Wasatch Front, a large region in the state. Academica West also provides "business services" to the North Star Academy in Bluffdale, Utah (Moon 2005).

Quoting Academica West's Vice President for the company, Sheldon Killpack:

> *The main goal is to make sure the principal is freed up do what he does best, which is work with teachers to make sure effective instruction is taking place. (Ibid.)*

What Utah found is what many charter schools are finding across the nation, which is why they are calling in firms like Academica West: that they must also acquire start-up funding from investors because money from the government is allocated according to specific grant specifications that usually deal with the day-to-day operations of the school, such as paving for utilities and buying textbooks.

Whether it is Academica, Inc. in Florida or its offshoot, Academica West in Utah and Arizona, the market decision of the company is to expand their EMO services and charter schools to as many states as they possibly can. In fact, one of their company public relations strategies is to attend "town hall" like meetings with parents, community leaders, and businesses to speak up about charter schools and what they might be able to offer any organization, individuals or groups seeking charter status.

In Magic Valley, Utah for example, where Academica West has been expanding and is now managing ten schools, such a public session was held in September of 2007 at the Twin Falls Board of Realtors and featured speaker Jed Stevensen, head of Academica West. Although Stevensen said he was visiting as only an "adviser" and that he was "also eager to meet those who show up to the meeting and see what the odds are of a school starting up in the Magic Valley," the real odds are that his presence at the meeting was more than a simple display of altruism, but rather part of a well-heeled and cleverly designed public relations campaign to gain charter school contracts. Again, one thinks of the shoulder rubbing and "networking" done by Mosaica that Wilson alluded to in the company's launching its successful endeavors (Poppino 2007).

The fact that Academica West, as well as other EMOs, work with local groups and help sponsor meetings by organizations and individuals seeking to open charter schools is simply because it is part of their marketing campaign—for without charter schools there is no outlet for their "products and services." Every charter school that opens is another invitation to Academica, or to be fair to any other EMO to manage the school's business for-profit and sell them instructional "kits" and "educational materials," which is why Academica has been a strong player in encouraging the opening of charter school after charter school in such town hall meetings or quasi-public events. What is not known is if at these public sessions Academica West, or other educational sales entities for EMOs for that matter, tout these companies' ability to add innovation through competition to the traditional public schools to improve their services, for after all traditional public schools were supposed to be the beneficiaries of new and exciting practices and curriculum development created by the charter school movement and its for-profit managers, the EMOs. The answer to the question is doubtful, it is simply not part of these companies' business plans, plans which are clearly built on the creation of ever more independent public charter schools as eventual sites for contractual relationships involving the for-profit management of their day-to-day operations.

FOR-PROFIT EMOs: PRO AND CON

The key mainstream arguments critics of EMOs put forth when disputing the EMO model for public education generally fall into four categories:

1. Transfer of public funds to for-profit EMOs
2. Financial and educational accountability
3. Financial and educational transparency
4. Governance of public schools and decision making

Below are examinations of the first three points. Point 4 is covered in chapter 5, and again in chapter 7.

Transfer of Public Funds to For-Profit EMOs

Advocates of for-profit EMOs claim that they will bring entrepreneurial spirit and a competitive ethos to the problems that plague public education all to the betterment of the nation's educational system. Opponents of the idea have two major concerns:

1. Outsourcing public educational management to EMOs will result in already limited school resources being redirected for service fees and/or profits to simply another administration, this time a for-profit EMO.
2. Ceding sovereignty over decision making processes at school sites to privately held companies or single operators who have no duty to disclose their decision making or financial plans will create a new system of privatized schools and privatized decision making without full disclosure and transparency, even though they are subsidized by public funds.

Relinquishing public control or ownership of public schools to Wall Street corporations or privately held educational management companies in order to create a new system of "privateers," instead of public workers, begs the question: Why replace a public school system, that although might have problems but which has operated for more than a century to educate generations of successful citizens, with a corporate run school model of educational retail chains and franchises?

Specifically at issue:

- Can for-profit management companies solve the problems associated with public education?
- Do Wall Street investors and entrepreneurs hold the answers as to student learning and organizational management of schools?
- Does the rise of EMOs lead to the development of schools as mere educational retail chains and franchises for learning and thus transfer huge public sums to private coffers in return for little accountability and prepackaged curriculum and instructional "delivery methods and platforms?"

As we can see, for the champions of privatized educational policy the answer is a resounding call for the complete privatization of educational services and schools, contrary to the rhetoric often reported about improving traditional public schools through "choice" and competition. For those who believe public education should remain publicly run and managed with full oversight and disclosure to the public, the response is that privatization certainly offers opportunities to investors but not to public schools, parents, and students they purport to serve and thus to transfer such public funds to the coffers of these privately owned firms deepens educational problems, it doesn't resolve them; it instead centralizes control and decision making in favor of capital, putting profits first, not the interests of the public and their children, as EMO charter advocates have zealously argued.

All of this raises the serious question: Does putting the profit needs of investors and private venture capitalists before the needs of the students they are designed to serve make the best public policy sense? Remember the discussion regarding the fiduciary duties of corporations and corporate officers to their shareholders? If the real fiduciary duties and responsibilities of a for-profit EMO is to their shareholders or private capital, then the stakeholders, like parents and their children, will at best be considered marginal, if not simply another commodity. To create a school system or charter schools based on for-profit needs of private EMOs can also lead to abandonment of entire school systems when these companies fail to come through for their investors, in essence maximize profits.

Take for example the thousands of California students who were left to look for new schools after one of the nation's largest charter school operators shut its doors in 2004. The closure of the 5-year-old EMO, California Charter Academy (CCA), which ran about 60 schools under four charters in California and enrolled some 10,000 students, represented at the time one of the largest charter school failures since the nation's first such independent public school opened in 1991. The closure left the state and the districts that had issued the charters scrambling to find attendance records for students and get in touch with the students who had attended the CCA schools so they might give them information about other charter and regular public schools in their neighborhoods they might attend. The age of the students was unclear, but a significant number of the students were believed to be over age 19 and might not be eligible to enroll in regular schools (Sack 2004).

Advocates of charter schools admit to charter failures but point to a "few bad apples" to explain the phenomenon. They also place the blame on governmental agencies designed to oversee the responsible management of these charters. For example, when commenting on the abject failure of the California Charter Academy in 2004 that left students stranded, without attendance records and for many, with no place to go, Gary L. Larson, the spokesman for the Los Angeles-based California Charter Schools Association stated:

> *There's a sigh of relief from within the charter school community because this one bad apple has been held accountable. (Ibid.)*

Chester E. Finn, Jr., the president of the Thomas B. Fordham Foundation in Washington, which vehemently supports charter schools, simply commented that:

> This is just another wake-up call. It's another symptom of things that can go wrong if people aren't careful. (Ibid.)

Yet according to the Center for Education Reform, a strong backer of the charter school movement, there seem to be a lot of "bad apples" in the charter school experiment, for they report that the percentage of charter schools that have closed due to failure as of 2006 was 11 percent. The failure of eleven percent of charter schools nationwide reeks of more than a few "bad apples" but of a system that is not working. Is this acceptable?

In their February 2006 report entitled "Charter School Closures: The opportunity for Accountability," the Center seemed jubilant at the news:

Business analysts offer that of all small businesses that open, nearly half close within the first year. After 16 years, only eleven percent of the nation's public charter schools have closed. This is a testament to the power of the idea, the demand, and the concept of quality control that is alive and well throughout the charter school arena. (Allen, Beaman, and Hornung 2006)

From the point of view of these charter advocates there seems to be nothing wrong with the "system." The problem resides with a few bad apples or an inability to compete in the market, as we saw in chapter 5. Opponents would argue the contrary, stressing that of those eleven percent of charters that failed, countless students were effected, facing not just loss of time in the classroom, but the disappearance of valuable personal school records and disruption in their lives and the lives of their families. The problem, opponents argue, is the lack of accountability, oversight, and limited regulation that allows these EMOs to operate their businesses with little transparency or disclosure. And this lack of accountability, oversight, and limited regulation is part and parcel of the for-profit business model calling into question the entire notion itself.

This of course brings up another issue for those who argue against the concept. Assuring the education of all students regardless of race, social class, gender, and special education needs must be the mission of education; putting profits before kids means that if these corporations wish to expand, and expand they must simply to meet the profit expectations of their shareholders and the Wall Street investment firms that often bankroll much of their operations, the for-profit schools will have to engage in volume increases in the students they serve, thereby targeting less capable students and serving as profitable dumping grounds for many "at risk students," special needs students and "subprime kids," all to be warehoused and managed by an emerging for-profit school system armed with a standardized curriculum wedded to the needs of inauthentic state mandated tests. This has the eerie aroma of the subprime loan business model where "at-risk lenders," or subprime lenders, became victims of predatory lending schemes and usurious interest rates. Creating a "subprime" educational business market serving low-income, mostly minority urban students can't really be the answer to what ails public education, can it? According to the EMOs who target such markets, it certainly can.

Is the shift from public management of public schools to private management of public schools a profound and troubling movement away from public education and public schools to increasingly private education and for-profit managed schools with class stratification built in the business models designed to serve "at-risk" and "minority-low income" students? If so, can parents, their children, and educational stakeholders really rely on a theory that advances bottom-line profits, returns on investment for company shareholders, and profitable investment venture capital as the way to go about "fixing schools"? Or is the increasing shift from public management of public schools to the for-profit management of public schools a worthy, imaginative, and long-awaited reform? Again, ask privateers like Steve Wilson and they will tell you the time for radical reform through the privatization of public schools is at hand and that publicly run schools are anachronistic and ineffective. The problem, he tells us, is more than just the public schools; it also involves the institutional structure of the "public mind" and the unions and bureaucrats who bar the doorway to entrepreneurial friendly educational reform:

> The "common school" is a cornerstone of the American ideology: Public schools afford every child, regardless of circumstance, a chance to realize the American dream. Because this ideal of public education is inseparable in the American public's mind from the school's longstanding institutional structure—of local school boards, school districts, and unionized public employees—private managers of public schools encounter a deeply felt, if unexamined, resistance in the public at large. Opponents, chiefly the teachers' unions, successfully portray private management as an assault on public education itself—and the democratic ideals for which it stands. Never mind that for many students, especially the urban poor, the neighborhood public school is an utterly failed institution. (Ibid.)

Yet as Corwin and Schneider write, this is more mythology than reality:

> Specialized schools are polar opposites of the common school, which has dominated the history of education in this country and continues to strangle broad scale reforms. The typical public school system offers a common curriculum for diverse students from all backgrounds. In the ideal common school, students are assigned randomly to schools and to teachers under principles of equitable treatment, rather than on consideration of distinctive needs. Though bent out of shape by segregated housing patterns and tracking practices, the common school prevails in popular mythology as the perfect public school. Even the reality that suburban schools, safely walled off from the inner cities, cater to a homogenous middle class pursuing a single, college oriented goal has not tarnished the nation's belief that the common school is the most appropriate for a democratic society. (Corwin and Schneider 2007)

For Wilson the need is to shift the ideological terrain omnipresent in the public mind, as much as it is to continue the effort to privatize education. Wilson argues that unions and bureaucrats have served to brainwash an unwitting public into believing that the current institutional structure of schools is what serves the nation best. It is this type of rhetoric that has been greatly responsible for the success of many EMOs as privatization looks to manage the perceptions of the public.

The American Enterprise Institute, a leading conservative think tank for the promotion of entrepreneurship, counsels and offers suggestions on how to encourage more capital investment in the for-profit ventures in educational management:

> *For-profit investment has been rare because capital typically flows to ventures that offer an attractive, risk-adjusted return, which has generally not existed in schooling. But there are steps that would help the sector attract more private funding to support research, development, and creative problem solving. For instance, clear standards for judging effectiveness can reassure investors that ventures will be less subject to political influence and better positioned to succeed if demonstrably effective. Entrepreneur-friendly reform is also undermined directly by statutes that restrict the involvement of for-profit firms in school management. (Hess 2007)*

The favored economic analogy that drives home this arguably contentious issue and raises concerns is the comparison between EMOs and HMOs. Health Maintenance Organizations (HMOs) initially marketed their goods and services to those whom were relatively healthy, such as say pools or groups of employees from large corporations. As these HMOs began expanding their economic growth by accepting less healthy individuals into their plans, their costs inevitably rose and their profitability inevitably sank and their investors faced huge losses. And here lies the point. Investors want to make a profit and thus will work at almost any cost to serve the bottom line that profit engenders, even if it means denying or cutting back on services. Nowhere can this be seen so strikingly as in the health care industry that excludes over 49 million people from coverage and the direct comparison to EMOs is strikingly analogous and clear.

However, it seems that plans have shifted and what is quite striking is that instead of taking all students, as the HMOs initially decided to do in their business plan, many EMOs are finding it far more profitable to niche-serve the low-income, minority, and inner-urban youth. This is why many of the EMOs have shifted their interests to "subprime kids" or "at-risk students," attempting to carve out an economic niche for their services, much like Pay Day Loans, Rent to Own, and other subprime schemes that cater to low-income citizens. They, like their counterpart HMOs, also found that the inclusion of "all students" in their business plans was problematic especially when it came to special education students and thus rather than "creaming," as was the concern many years ago when the charter school movement started and certainly still is, the business plan is now aimed at "targeting" the less fortunate students and their parents and communities. The business format is built on a high student volume model accompanied by assuring low costs and services. With millions and millions of students to educate across the nation, EMOs can look on the horizon at a multibillion-dollar industry that they are helping to forge as a numbers game. But will they too find that profitability inevitably forces cuts in student services, just as the large HMOs have found in the health care industry? And will they find that less and less students are "covered" under their educational plans due to enrollment caps at most charter schools?

"Entrepreneur friendly" reform represents a dramatic paradigm shift—away from administration of public schools by the public to the wholesale for-profit control of the management operations of schools by EMOs, big, medium, and small. This includes, but is not limited to, the development and control of the curriculum to be used, the private management of daily activities between students and educational stakeholders, the creation of standardized instructional materials, the hiring of teachers, and the actual running of the day-to-day operations of public schools; and accompanying the rise of the for-profit management company the consequence has also meant the proliferation of educational "niche" services, like privatized landscape services, privatized cafeteria, transportation and janitorial services, to name just a few. But is it really educational reform? Researchers and authors Corwin and Schneider think not, arguing:

> *If choice schools were leading reform, they either would be producing breakthrough inventions that regular schools are rushing to adopt, or serving as models to them. They are doing neither. (Corwin and Schneider 2007)*

For Mallory Stark of Harvard Business School, the salient question really is the following:

> *Can professional business management practices improve the performance of troubled public schools? (Stark 2006)*

Take Fordham Foundation, one of the leading think tank advocacy groups in favor of the private management of public schools. According to a report put out for the foundation by economists Michael Podgursky and Dale Ballou:

> *When schools are held accountable for results and freed from red tape governing personnel decisions, they take advantage of their freedom by adopting innovative strategies for hiring and rewarding teachers. This study is based on a survey administered to a random sample of 132 public charter schools that have been operating for at least three years. (Ballou and Podgursky 2001)*

It is important to note that "freed from red tape" also means free from accountability and oversight by governmental agencies and the public at large. It means no necessity to disclose information to a demanding public.

The Friedman Foundation, another big player and supporter of privatization efforts in public schools on all levels, even goes so far as to argue that in countries such as Scandinavia not only is privatization improving Scandinavian schools, but they also claim that one of the reasons for such improvements in Scandinavian education is allegedly:

> *Most of the independent schools are run by for-profit educational management companies, with no negative effect on the quality of education. (Darden 2008)*

A close examination of the for-profit business EMOs and their charter school counterparts reveals there is a plan in place to radically alter the entire way education is conceived and run in the nation; the idea is to develop networks of "contract schools," which can mean only one thing—the overhaul and disintegration of current institutional public education in favor of an eventual shift to a for-profit system.

Financial and Educational Accountability

One of the biggest controversies over the EMO model is the issue of accountability to the public for student achievement. One can go to the Internet, read countless magazines, books, research articles, reports, and otherwise busy themselves with the dizzying array of research claims and methodological descriptions as to the efficacy of EMOs. The amount of studies and claims are numerically too much to digest and the average member of the public who simply wants to be assured of a good education for their children cannot hope to read, let alone seek to validate, the subjective claims the studies make. Yet at the same time the question certainly must be asked: "If EMOs promise higher student achievement through for-profit management then student performance on standardized tests, themselves a questionable measure of student progress, should go up, right?" But is this the case? It really depends on whom one asks and the studies relied on, the assumptions inherent in the studies one looks at, and the agenda or source of the studies themselves. The studies that make claims as to the achievement of students in for-profit managed schools can be maddening for the researcher. Research methodologies, political agendas, purposes and objectives of the studies, researchers involved, sources for the studies, samples used to arrive at findings, and the list could go on and on all render the reported claims and statistics over the years little more than a cacophony of think tank claims, pro and con. One thing we do know, say Corwin and Schneider, at best the evidence is mixed on student achievement and at worst it is negative (Corwin and Schneider, 2007).

Claims on all sides of the issue abound. Take, for example, respected educational theorist Barbara Miner writing about Edison Schools in *ReThinking Schools,* an educational journal steadfastly opposed to EMOs:

One of the biggest controversies in all of the districts where it operates involves whether Edison's schools actually perform better than public schools. Edison says yes, but the company's performance indicates otherwise. And not just in San Francisco.

Dallas Superintendent Mike Moses told the American School Board Journal *this December that "we looked at their seven schools against seven comparable schools, and truthfully, Edison's performance was not superior."*

Bracey, author of The War Against America's Public Schools, *issued a report in early February on Edison's claims of improved academic achievement, and said that Edison makes "hyperbolic conclusions, using data that can only be described as questionable." (Miner 2002)*

A recent study of 10 Edison schools by the National Education Association, done by the Evaluation Center at Western Michigan University, researcher Gary Miron found that Edison schools are performing the same as or slightly worse overall than comparable public schools. "Our findings suggest that Edison students do not perform as well as Edison claims in its annual reports," the report said. An earlier report by the American Federation of Teachers reached similar conclusions:

U.S. Rep. Chaka Fattah (D-PA) reviewed Edison's claims of improved achievement this fall and found that "the overwhelming majority of Edison schools perform poorly, and in many cases are fairing worst than some Philadelphia schools."

Edison disputes such reports as political sniping. The RAND Corp., a respected independent research group, has been hired by Edison to analyze the company's academic achievement, but the report will not be completed until 2003 or 2004. (Ibid.)

Yet in an article in *EdNews* in 2008 the opposite was reported; that school test scores recently released by the Pennsylvania System of School Assessment revealed that schools partnering with private education management organizations (EMOs)—including EdisonLearning—showed greater gains in student achievement than the schools operated by the Philadelphia School District. The article noted that the 2008 PSSA test results (the Philadelphia standardized tests given to students each year) revealed that:

In Philadelphia schools, all private providers, including EdisonLearning, improved student performance by nearly twice the amount as the schools operated by the school district. (EducationNews.org, under "Philadelphia Standardized Tests")

This, according to Dr. John Chubb, Managing Director of The EdisonLearning Institute and Senior Executive Vice President of New Product Development for EdisonLearning is good news. Chubb is a long-time supporter of EMOs and privatization, having written extensively on the issue for some years. According to the report, the number of students performing at grade level and above in reading at the EMO schools increased by 6.1 percent, and in the EdisonLearning schools by 6.5 percent, as compared to 3.3 percent in the district schools; and students performing at grade level and above in math at the EMO schools rose by 6.0 percent, and in the EdisonLearning schools by 4.6 percent, as compared to 3.1 percent in the district-managed schools (*EducationNews.org*, under "Student Gains in Privately Managed Philadelphia Schools").

Chubb went on to comment:

The state's results clearly confirm that the outside providers are meeting and ex-ceeding expectations in Philadelphia, and they validate the work and highlight the success of all the private providers in Philadelphia. More importantly, this is a pure and objective measurement of student performance in the Philadelphia's schools—the Pennsylvania System of School Assessment. (Ibid.)

Affirming the study and the report, Dr. Martin West of Brown University concurred:

Student achievement in Philadelphia as a whole, after years of stagnation, has im-proved markedly since the implementation of the Diverse Provider Model. Competi-tion and expanded capacity created by having multiple providers operating in the district is playing a role in the district's success. (Ibid.)

However in the newspaper just two years earlier, *Education Week* reported that:

Philadelphia students who attend public middle schools managed by outside groups are making learning gains that generally are no greater than those of their counter-parts at regular district-run middle schools, according to results from a study of that school system's improvement efforts. The study, which was conducted by a pair of researchers from Johns Hopkins University in Baltimore, was released here this week at the annual meeting of the American Educational Research Association, a Washington-based group representing 25,000 scholars. (Viadero 2006)

So then which is it, do students outperform in EMO-managed schools or underperform? And if they do outperform, as Chubb would like us to believe, then is the "dramatic increase" in achievement of one to three percent really that significant? Is it significant enough to overhaul the entire public school system in favor of a for-profit model with such penurious achievements?

In May 2009, the *American Journal of Education* reported that the:

large-scale experiment in Philadelphia represents an important opportunity to re-search and evaluate the effectiveness of privatization in education. The need to do so is made even more important by the lack of conclusive research presented on the matter to date despite its high publicity level. While conservative proponents of the policy have founded their arguments on the strong rhetoric of classical economic theory, they have offered little in the way of empirical evidence to ground and support their theories (CER 2007; Finn 1993; Hill 1997a, 1997b, 1997c, 1998; Peterson 2007). This lack of scientific evidence is due in large part to few opportunities, with there being just over 400 privately managed schools across the country at the time of privatization in Philadelphia (GAO 2003). Where empirical studies have been done on different privatization models, the research has been quite mixed, with positive results for privatization in some cases and negative results in others (Ascher 1996; GAO 1996, 2003; Boyles 2000). John Chubb (chief education officer of Edison, Inc.) and Terry Moe's 1990 study is often considered a hallmark case linking higher student achievement to lower levels of bureaucratic organization, but the study's methods and validity have been brought into question (Fruchter 2007). Similar to past research on privatization in general, the early studies on Philadelphia data have also been mixed, with studies by Johns Hopkins University (MacIver and MacIver 2006) and the RAND Corporation and Research for Action (Gill et al. 2007) both finding EMO schools to have achieved less than the other district schools but not significantly so in statistical terms, while Peterson and Chingos (2009) found statistically positive results among for-profit EMOs when compared to the rest of the school district but no differences among nonprofit EMOs. (Byrnes, 2009)

But don't tell that to Paul Peterson, the Henry Lee Shattuck Professor of Government and the Director of the Program on Education Policy and Governance at Harvard. In 2007 Peterson published a do-over—another study of Philadelphia schools, one of many, alleging improvement in the Philadelphia School District's for-profit model. Interestingly, the study was partially underwritten by Edison Schools, Inc. (the District's largest for-profit manager) and makes claims that there have been substantial gains in math for Edison and other EMOs in the schools they operate. In 2005, Peterson, who heads Harvard's Program on Education Policy and Governance, released a controversial study which attempted to refute a RAND/Research for Action study, that showed that privatized schools in the Philadelphia district did not academically outperform comparable district schools despite receiving over $100 million in additional public funding. Peterson's 2005 study, also partially funded by the then Edison Schools, used a smaller sample size and reached different conclusions. It showed math gains in middle schools among a number of privatized schools including Edison Schools, Inc. (now EdisonLearning) (Philadelphia Public School: The Notebook 2009).

The Southwest Educational Development Laboratory, in a study of the EMO business model and school restructuring options under NCLB, concluded in light of all the studies and their proponents that:

Comparable data about our experience with educational contracting thus far is not similarly available. Although there are more than 500 schools in districts across the country run by EMOs, there is little research about the success of their experience. (Southwest Educational Development Laboratory)

In 2007 the Rand Corporation, a nonprofit research group, looked at achievement in Philadelphia schools as a result of state-takeover, restructuring, and private EMOs. Their study concluded that:

Different interpretations of the results of this study may lead to different judgments about whether Philadelphia's experiment in the private management of public schools has succeeded and whether it should be continued. On the negative side of the ledger, despite additional per-pupil resources, privately operated schools did not produce average increases in student achievement that were any larger than those seen in the rest of the district. Meanwhile, district managed restructured schools outpaced the gains of the rest of the district in math.

. . . . although it is theoretically possible that the introduction of the providers increased district wide capacity for improvement and that the schools they managed would have done worse without them, we find no evidence supporting this view. If the privately managed schools had remained under district management instead, it seems likely that the district could have replicated the gains of other schools that received no special interventions—getting results similar to those actually achieved by the private providers without expending additional resources. In sum, with four years of experience, we find no evidence of differential academic benefits that would support the additional expenditures on private managers [Roman au]. Philadelphia provides no evidence to support private management as an especially effective method of promoting student achievement, but it does not represent a clear test of full private management in a competitive market. Whether a model of private management that involves more autonomy to managers, parental choice, and competition for students would produce better results remains an open question. (Gill et al.)

The inconsistency in charter school research methodologies, too extensive to cover here, are based on standardized tests as a model for statistical research and the argument throughout the nation is that these tests cannot possibly measure the state of education or learning (FairTest; Weil, and Kincheloe 2001). And given the promise that educational choice exercised in the form of selecting charter schools increases student performance, one would think there would be significant comprehensive "data banks" within the states that legally authorize charter schools for public preview and examination. In fact, there are no mechanisms state by state to evaluate the claims made by EMOs or any other charter school proponents nor are there any data banks that the public can rely on when making choices as to what schools their children should attend. This job seems to have fallen to the multitude of political think tanks that weigh in pro or con on the debate and then appropriately issue studies, based on questionable methodologies, purportedly supporting their claims.

All this seems troubling, for if for-profit management has produced low or no gains in student achievement for more money, why is it still considered an option? The answer is simple and straightforward: because there are profits to be made—if not in managing schools, then in taking the company public, trading its stock, and investing its assets into more stocks. Add to this the fact it is tempting for school boards and superintendents to see for-profit management firms as a quick, painless panacea for educational ills and you have a perfect climate for these firms to operate in. But many educators argue that this model offers no real panacea—they argue that good schools have to be painstakingly built on the local level by staff and students with the support of parents and school administrators, not corporate executives, corporate, middle management, and teams of hired consultants. In the end, improvement of schools is the result of the hard work of school staff with administrative, community, and parental support. Everything the for-profit companies say they can do has already been done in publicly run public schools and every curriculum and program they use is available for every school in America to implement on its own—without adding corporate managers and without deducting corporate profits and paying EMOs hefty fees.

So why change the system from a for-public model to a for-profit model and is this really being put forth as a reform or can it be seen as more of an opportunity to disinvest in public education? Are charter schools and the for-profit EMOs that manage many of them really a Trojan horse for the incremental privatization of education many said they would be? Not according to Steven Wilson. Investors, according to Wilson, share the company's commitment to "offering urban families new choices in public education" and creating new environments where teachers can succeed. And Advantage claimed at the time Wilson ran it, before it went under and was bought out, that it had already achieved spectacular academic improvements in the schools it operated (Slowey 2000). The rhetoric and the reality are truly incredible.

Financial and Educational Transparency

One of the most difficult problems in researching the current financial status or academic status of for-profit management companies is their lack of disclosure and transparency, and their refusal for public requests for information. Miron and Berry noted in their 2007 *Profiles* report:

> *This year (2006-2007) the following firms failed to respond to repeated requests for enrollment and other information.*
>
> **Charter School Administrative Services**
> *Charter School Administrative Services did not provide information about itself or its schools. The company was contacted on 1/3/07, 1/9/07, and 2/20/07. Previous profile data was compiled from the Texas Education Agency and the Michigan Department of Education Web sites on 7/26/05.*

Educational Services of America, Inc.

Educational Services of America did not provide information about itself or its schools. The company was contacted twice on 2/22/07. Educational Services of America, Inc. was previously tracked under Ombudsman Educational Services, Ltd. Educational Services of America, Inc., acquired Ombudsman Educational Services, Ltd. on 9/16/05.

Excel Education Centers, Inc.

Excel Education Centers Inc. did not provide information about itself or its schools. The company was contacted on 2/22/07. Previous profile data was compiled from the Great Schools Web site on 10/25/06.

Helicon Associates

Helicon did not provide information about itself or its schools. The company was contacted on 1/3/07 and 2/20/07. Previous profile data was verified by Helicon, except for-profitability status, on 12/7/05.

Mosaica Education, Inc.

Mosaica did not provide information about itself or its schools. The company was contacted on 1/25/07 and 2/21/07. Previous profile data was verified by Mosaica, except for-profitability status, on 12/23/05.

Nobel Learning Communities, Inc.

Nobel did not provide information about itself or its schools. The company was contacted twice on 2/22/07. Previous profile data was compiled from the School District of Philadelphia Web site on 10/17/05, Great Schools Web site on 10/17/05, and the National Center for Education Statistics (Common Core of Data) Web site on 11/3/05.

The Planagement Group, LP

Planagement did not provide information about itself or its schools. The company was contacted on 1/25/07 and 2/20/07. Previous profile data was verified by Planagement on 12/19/05.

Victory Schools, Inc.

Victory Schools did not provide information about itself or its schools. The company was contacted on 1/25/07 and 2/20/07. Previous profile data was verified by Victory Schools on 12/21/05.

White Hat Management

White Hat Management did not provide information about itself or its schools. The company was contacted on 1/25/07 and 2/20/07. Previous profile data was verified by White Hat Management, except for-profitability status, on 1/13/06. (Miron and Berry 2007)

The study went on to find that:

Some EMO founders have operated in relative obscurity, but others have had relatively high profiles over the years. National Heritage Academies was founded by J.C. Huizenga, owner of a half-dozen manufacturing companies. White Hat Management was founded and is run by David Brennan, an Ohio industrialist. Edison Schools was founded by Christopher Whittle, a publishing and media entrepreneur who earlier created Channel One, which broadcasts news and advertising in schools under an arrangement that gives schools television equipment in return for required viewing of its broadcast material. Whittle later sold Channel One; its current owners, Primedia, announced the sale of the business in April of 2007. Whittle originally founded Edison to operate private schools, and after the failure of private school voucher plans to achieve significant traction nationally, redirected Edison to the management of public district schools and public charter schools. All five firms are privately held and, therefore, as already noted, are largely free of any requirement to provide the public with financial or other information. Additionally, the companies' practices vary with regard to outside scrutiny. National Heritage, Leona, and Edison all responded to the authors of this report by providing updated information on the names, locations, and enrollments of the schools they operate, listing both new schools and schools they no longer operated. Mosaica and White Hat did not respond to repeated telephone and email inquiries. (Ibid.)

Unlike days gone by when one could simply go to their local school or district and request and be dutifully given the information they needed regarding test scores, financial issues, student performance, and the day-to-day operations of their local schools, the new paradigm of for-profit EMOs is assuring that much of this information is now proprietary and many if not most states now have Freedom of Information Act or Public Disclosure Act requests that must be mandatorily filled out and submitted before anything is revealed to those wishing information about a charter school or its management. Even then, due to the private nature of the corporations or operators of EMOs, much of the financial information is never fully disclosed. And if it is, it can be costly to acquire.

How then are parents and their students supposed to make informed decisions as to what school to attend if they are not given full disclosure regarding the schools operating procedures, finances, and solvency? And more importantly, how can the government accomplish legal oversight if a tug of war over full disclosure exists between for-profit EMOs and the states and municipalities they operate in?

THE RISE OF THE NONPROFIT EMO

Not all EMOs are for-profit organizations looking to receive a return on investment. In their 2008 report entitled *Profiles of Nonprofit Education Management Organizations: 2007-2008,* Gary Miron and Jessica Urschel, both of Western Michigan University, put out the first-of-its-kind comprehensive report regarding nonprofit EMOs.

To begin with, the authors state that while the number of for-profit EMOs has grown rapidly in the 1990s and is now leveling off, in their stead the number of nonprofit EMOs has been growing more steadily over the last few years. These findings reveal that the number of nonprofit EMOs grew consistently, up to its current total of 83 organizations, nationwide in 2008. The number of states in which EMOs operate has grown from 6 in 1995 to 24 in 2007-2008. In total, there were 488 public charter schools managed by nonprofit EMOs during 2007-2008. KIPP (Knowledge is Power Program) schools account for a very large proportion of the schools operated by nonprofit EMOs. KIPP was operating 57 schools in 2007-2008, almost 3 times the size of the next largest nonprofit EMO, Summit Academy Schools. The report went on to contrast the market share of nonprofit EMOs with the market share of for-profit EMO run schools:

Large (nonprofit) EMOs account for 44.5% of all EMO-managed schools, medium-sized (nonprofit) EMOs account for 38.1% of all EMO-operated schools and small (nonprofit) EMOs account for 17.4%. This pattern contrasts sharply from that of for-profit EMOs. In the for-profit sector, large companies manage the lion's share of the schools (88.4%), while the medium-sized companies account for only 8.3% and small firms 7.3%. (Miron and Urschel)

Historically, as the report illuminates, a smaller portion of EMOs has been nonprofits. In recent years, however, nonprofit EMOs (sometimes referred to as Charter Management Organizations (CMOs), have expanded phenomenally. But what is a nonprofit EMO? The answer is found in the definition of an EMO given earlier in the chapter by Molnar et al. In essence, they serve the same function as for-profit EMOs except for one important and compelling factor: they are run under a "nonprofit" status and thus cannot derive a profit from their management of charter schools or any other schools for that matter. So, the legal issue becomes to whom do they owe their fiduciary duties and responsibilities? The answer is found in their mission statements and their IRS classifications, where they legally define their purpose and the constituencies they purport to serve. Nonprofit EMO "constituencies," unlike those of a for-profit EMO, have the power, authority, and control over the fiduciary duties of the nonprofit through elected boards that govern them. Yet Miron and Urschel found in their findings that the boundaries that separate nonprofit EMOs from simple networks or community partnerships are confusing and ambiguous. This is due to nondisclosure by many nonprofit EMOs, which can lead to ambiguity over their actual classification. The authors note, for example that:

During the course of our research for this report, we encountered a number of difficult examples that were not easy to classify. KIPP, for example, indicates that it is a network and not an EMO. At the same time, the New Schools Venture Fund identifies KIPP as a charter management organization since it was providing funds to two of KIPPs clusters of schools in order to help the organization expand the number of charter schools. For the purpose of this report, we have included KIPP as a nonprofit EMO, given that the organization plays a strong role in establishing and operating new schools. (Ibid.)

The report went on to find that twenty-nine percent of all nonprofit EMO-managed schools were at the primary level in 2007-2008. By contrast, the report noted, 60 percent of the schools managed by for-profit EMOs were primary schools in 2007-2008. The nonprofit EMOs studied by Miron and Urschel reported they not only managed 83 schools across the nation, but they enrolled 129,836 within 24 states in the 2007-2008 school year (Ibid.). Thirteen of the nonprofit EMOs operated 10 charter schools or more and were considered for the purpose of the report, large nonprofit EMOs; 34 of the nonprofit EMOs were considered middle-size EMOs, operating 4 to 9 charter schools, and for the report's sake, the small nonprofit EMO organizations ran 3 or fewer charter schools.

The extensive report contains charts for all the nonprofit EMOs that currently run charter schools in the 24 states. The various charts show significant spikes in the projected future enrollment in all of the nonprofit EMOs studied. In terms of disclosure, the *Profiles Report,* through their research, creates "individual profiles" of each nonprofit EMO and then sends the profile to the various EMOs for analysis and response for eventual dissemination to the public. Miron and Urschel received an overall response rate of 69 percent from all the nonprofit EMOs they sent complete profiles to for the years 2007-2008. This discouraging response shows that for nonprofit EMOs, the failure of full disclosure is as disappointing as it is for-profit EMOs.

Charter Management Organizations

Recently the nation has witnessed the rise of what is called the Charter Management Organization (CMO). Just what is a charter management organization and how does it differ from a nonprofit EMO? The answer is difficult and often confusing but can be found in the fact that CMOs are deemed nonprofit *networks* of schools that serve a specific geographical area. Their goals seem to be different, concentrating their efforts in one area for purposes of solidification, experimentation and yes, centralization, and accompanying bureaucratic growth. Mathematica Public Research, Inc., an online public policy research lab that works with the Center for Reinventing Public Education at the University of Washington defines CMOs as:

> *Charter management organizations (CMOs) are nonprofit entities that start and manage new charter schools. By centralizing and sharing certain functions and resources across schools, CMOs aim to enhance school performance and student outcomes, achieve greater efficiency, and expand and sustain schools. Over the last several years, the number and reach of CMOs has increased dramatically, leading to a diverse array of organizational models and school designs. In the 2007-2008 school year, there were at least 33 CMOs operating more than 189 schools that enrolled over 57,000 students. (Mathematica Policy Research, Inc. 2009)*

In the spring of 2008 NewSchools Venture Fund, teaming with The Bill & Melinda Gates Foundation, announced the launch of what they referred to as an ambitious new longitudinal research study to measure the impact of nonprofit charter school management organizations (CMOs). Mathematica Policy Research, Inc., and the Center on Reinventing Public Education at the University at Washington (CRPE) currently serve as lead research partners for this National Study of CMO Effectiveness, which will purportedly examine the impact that CMOs are having on student achievement, as well as the internal structures, practices, and policy contexts that influence these outcomes. No doubt the report will offer recommendations as well.

According to Joanne Weiss, Partner and Chief Operating Officer at NewSchools Venture Fund and a leading spokesperson for the fund:

> *Across the country, charter management organizations are serving an increasing number of our nation's public school students—including many low-income and minority students who deserve access to a high-quality education. This study will answer a number of important questions about whether and how these organizations are improving academic outcomes for the students they serve, and will contribute to our understanding of how to structure public school systems so that they serve all children well. (Bill and Melinda Gates Foundation 2008)*

NewSchool Ventures Fund describes itself:

> *As a nonprofit venture philanthropy firm, we raise capital from both individual and institutional investors; we then use those funds to support promising education entrepreneurs, help them grow their organizations to scale, and connect their work with public school systems particularly within targeted urban areas. We analyze the national education landscape and the ecosystem for this type of dramatic change in each our key urban areas to determine how education entrepreneurs are poised to make a difference.*
>
> *Once potential ventures are identified, our team engages in a rigorous investment process that includes due diligence on the organization, its management team, its model, product, and results, as well as the market it seeks to address. When we invest in an organization, we serve as active partners by taking a seat on the board of directors and by providing ongoing management assistance to the leadership team as the venture grows to scale. (Ibid.)*

Joining both NewSchools Venture Fund and the Center for Reinventing Education in the creation of the CMO research report is Mathematica Public Research Inc. Mathematica is a research organization whose clients include the David and Lucile Packard Foundation, the Ford Foundation, the Henry J. Kaiser Family Foundation, the Rockefeller Foundation, the Smith Richardson Foundation, the Spencer Foundation, and the U.S. Department of Education, just to name a few.

KIPP: The Knowledge is Power Program

Of the 83 nonprofit EMOs identified by Miron and Urschel, many could serve as the object of study and inquiry. For purposes of providing the reader with a look at a nonprofit EMO, and analysis and discussion of the implications of such public policy development, we will concentrate on the largest and most rapidly growing nonprofit entity of its kind, the *Knowledge Is Power Program* or *KIPP*. Due to the fact no understanding of nonprofit EMOs can be attained without understanding the philanthropic funds that fuel the rise of such organizations, we will also look at the use of philanthropy to spur the development and institutionalization of nonprofit EMOs as an infrequently reported cornerstone of an all-out effort to eventually replace the traditional public school system.

KIPP or the *Knowledge Is Power Program,* was born from the minds of two then aspiring teachers, Michael Feinberg and David Levine when they met as Teach for Education recruits in 1992. Convinced that high expectations, excellence in teaching and hard work would create the perfect storm for the creation of the ideal school, both Feinberg and Levine went on to enlist in Teach for America and then continued to spend their first year teaching in the classroom. At their Web site, KIPP proudly proclaims the history of the school and their founders:

> KIPP (Knowledge Is Power Program) began in 1994 when Teach For America alumni Dave Levine and Mike Feinberg piloted a fifth grade public school program in inner-city Houston. In 1995, Levine moved to New York to found KIPP Academy in the South Bronx, while Feinberg founded KIPP Academy, Houston.
>
> With a staff of three teachers, KIPP Academy in the South Bronx opened its doors to 50 fifth graders from the surrounding neighborhoods. By the 1998-1999 school year, the school had grown to serve 200 fifth through eighth graders, and in 2000 KIPP Academy became a New York City Department of Education Charter School. (KIPP Academy)

KIPP is operated as a nonprofit EMO, the first in what is becoming a rapidly growing enterprise.

Following their one-year experience in the classroom, Feinberg and Levine opened the first KIPP classroom in Houston, Texas in 1994. The idea was that they would initially co-teach fifty fifth graders, nearly all low income and with limited English proficiency skills. They did not begin with the idea of expanding the notion of nonprofit charters in their initial conceptions.

The environment and teaching worked and with amazing results, at least as measured by standardized tests; by the end of the first year, nearly 98 percent of the students passed the Texas state standardized test and the following year, 1995, Feinberg opened the KIPP Academy in Houston and Levine opened a KIPP

Academy in New York City's South Bronx. Both schools admitted students by lottery and both began initially with only fifth graders. The first two KIPP classrooms in Houston and the Bronx were also deemed successes when measured by standardized test results. In Houston, on grade-level proficiency students progressed over four years on average 7.3 grade levels in each subject area. The scores were so impressive in mathematics that the school's students gained ten grade levels and left eighth grade performing in math better than the average American high school graduate (Wilson 2006).

But the real economic story and the success of KIPP really began in January 2000, when Feinberg and Levin met with Scott Hamilton, then the managing director of the philanthropic Pisces Foundation, to discuss the possible national replication of the KIPP school model. Hamilton was no stranger to the charter school idea, having worked in Massachusetts as an associate commissioner of education. He also served for two U.S. Secretaries of Treasury (Ibid.). Hamilton wanted to create new national school networks; he had no interest in throwing money at traditional public schools for reform or innovation purposes, nor was he interested in raising their achievement levels. The goal was to design and develop a new national educational system that would eventually replace the traditional system of public education.

Donald and Doris Fisher, founders of the Gap retail clothing chain liked the idea, too. As the founders of the philanthropic Pisces Foundation in 1997, which Hamilton headed, they decided to enter into the school "reform" fray and donated $15 million to replicate the success of KIPP in San Francisco. The idea was not simply to open a charter school based on KIPP principles and commitments, but also to provide a national office where KIPP "Fisher fellows," as they are called, could be trained and a curriculum could be developed and used to eventually roll out hundreds of KIPP schools throughout the nation. In fact, in its first three years KIPP selected forty out of eight hundred applicants to run KIPP educational franchises. The candidates had rigorous preparation, including a yearlong fellowship that included six weeks at the University California at Berkeley—the Haas School of Business, and residencies (much like doctors at a hospital) at existing KIPP schools. They studied organizational leadership, business leadership, academic leadership and culture, management, and community development. According to Steven Wilson:

> At a start up "Boot Camp," they (Fellows) prepare a detailed school implementation plan for turning their "original vision" into a "viable, thriving school. In the final seven months of the fellowship, the fellows return to their communities to execute their plans, including hiring school staff, recruiting students, building a board of directors, fundraising, and developing the school's curriculum. The fellows reconvene twice during the period and receive assistance and guidance from KIPP staff and their peers. KIPP bears the full cost of the program. (Ibid., 72)

KIPP now has 66 academies in 19 states and, although KIPP does not like to think of itself as an educational management organization, they license their schools under an agreement similar to that used by national retail and restaurant chains when they contract with their independently owned franchises (Ibid.).

EDUCATIONAL PHILANTHROPY AND A NEW EDUCATIONAL SYSTEM

The entire growing philanthropic movement in education is spurring the growth of KIPP and other nonprofit EMOs, and this, many would say, is really a philanthropic undermining of the whole notion of public schools. As we discussed in the last chapter, many charters cannot get start-up funds without appealing to "turnover" artists and "hard money" for beginning costs. When this start-up money is not available through private channels, many charters increasingly turn to philanthropic organizations for capital. The lack of financial support for charter schools coupled with the 2007 recommendations contained in *Tough Choices or Tough Times,* released by the National Center for Educational Excellence (NCEE) (which we might remember put out *A Nation at Risk* in the 1980s with a similar impetus for privatization reforms), provided a new impetus for leveraging philanthropic funds towards the vision of a newly conceived public policy of a "reformed education," favoring the eventual corporate governance of schools through charter schools. *Tough Choices or Tough Times* is quite forthright in what they see as a new national educational system:

> *The schools would be funded directly by the state, according to a pupil-weighting formula as described below. The schools would have complete discretion over the way their funds are spent, the staffing schedule, their organization and management, their schedule, and their program, as long as they provided the curriculum and met the testing and other accountability requirements imposed by the state.*
>
> *No organization could operate a school that was not affiliated with a helping organization approved by the state, unless the school was itself such an organization. These helping organizations—which could range from schools of education to teachers' collaboratives to for-profit and nonprofit organizations—would have to have the capacity to provide technical assistance and training to the schools in their network on a wide range of matters ranging from management and accounting to curriculum and pedagogy.*
>
> *The competitive, data-based market, combined with the performance contracts themselves, would create schools that were constantly seeking to improve their performance year in and year out.*
>
> *Executive Summary: students from low-income families and other categories of disadvantaged students would get substantially more money than schools with more advantaged student bodies and this would ensure that these students would*

be served by high quality school operators. It would be very hard for low-quality school operators to survive in this environment. (National Center on Education and the Economy 2007)

The nonprofit EMO movement clearly is geared towards the vision put forth by the NCEE Report, *Tough Choices or Tough Times*—the creation of a network of contract schools that would replace the current public school system and charter schools are to serve as the vehicle for the research, development, and realization of this vision with for-profit, nonprofit, and other organizations running the schools.

Interestingly, according to MediaTransparency, an organization designed to trace financial interests in foundations and the media, the Fishers, The Bill and Melinda Gates Foundation, and Wal-Mart are just a few of the large philanthropic players that subsidize KIPP; interestingly, they also were part and parcel of the NCEE's, *Tough Choices or Tough Times*. According to a source in their 2005 report entitled *Philanthropy the Wal-Mart Way,* Wal-Mart graciously:

". . . gave a string of grants totaling nearly $3 million to the national Knowledge Is Power Program, which recruits teachers to create public college prep charter schools in underserved communities. The gifts included donations to 21 such schools around the country." Steve Mancini, a spokesperson for the Knowledge Is Power Program said that "The Walton family, and particularly John Walton, is building a kind of quiet revolution in public education." (Berkowitz 2005)

And quiet it certainly is, for there is virtually no media coverage of any critical proportion on the issue. The public seems unaware of the enormous changes and transformations in public education that is underway and the efforts towards new ends that are being leveraged and realized on the part of a few wealthy actors with philanthropic funds through the subsidization of "public" charter schools. Thanks to the Internet, more information is being made available but news in the mainstream media is still almost invisible. For example, a list of philanthropic contributors for all KIPP schools can be found online (Coleman and Pearlstein 2008).

Not surprisingly, the Walton Foundation emerges time after time as a philanthropic knight in shining armor when it comes to subsidizing KIPP schools. But they are by no means alone. Philanthropic funds given to KIPP from wealthy foundations are coming in almost faster than can be counted. KIPP has captured a spirit that combines American individualism with corporate entrepreneurial values that are part and parcel of privatization as a practical ideology that appeals to many of the philanthropic interests that are silently financing KIPP schools.

Exactly who funds KIPP schools and why? The answer might be found in a subtle perusal of an article in April of 2009 published in the *L.A. Now* Web site.

This is an online site specifically created and written by *L.A. Times* staff writers. They report that:

> *Local KIPP leaders are relying on philanthropy to pay for their extras and also to help front the start-up costs charter schools face. Charters are independently run public schools that are exempt from some provisions of the Education Code. (Blume 2009)*
>
> *L.A. residents Bruce and Martha Karsh have pledged $3 million to help KIPP LA reach its goal of expanding to seven elementary schools and seven middle schools over the next five years, the organization announced today.*
>
> *The Karsh gift comes a year after a $12-million pledge from the Eli and Edythe Broad Foundation. Bruce Karsh heads Oaktree Capital Management, an international investment firm. Martha Karsh is an attorney with extensive experience in nonprofits. Their family foundation has made gifts and pledges totaling more than $50 million to support education. (Ibid.)*

Philanthropists like the idea of replacing public education with contract schools. For the majority of KIPP's philanthropic donors (who many all say are Republicans who embrace free-market "values") this is a chance to enhance their reputations; they appear to be concerned about and engaged in reforming public education while slowly and silently replacing what they refer to as failed public bureaucracies—public schools—with a new public educational model beholden to philanthropy and eventually increasing privatization. At the same time, they receive large donor tax breaks from the IRS.

The Pisces Foundation's point of view is somewhat different. They and the Fishers who founded it, say, "The Foundation seeks to leverage change in public education—especially in schools serving disadvantaged students—through large, strategic investments in a small number of initiatives focused on bolstering student academic achievement. Pisces focuses its education giving on efforts to promote high-quality charter schools" (Pacific Charter School Development).

Either way, one thing is for sure: without philanthropic funds KIPP would not be able to compete with traditional public schools in the areas it serves.

BLUEPRINT FOR SCHOOL SYSTEM TRANSFORMATION

As we mentioned earlier, KIPP initially sought to expand nationwide after proving its success in Houston and the South Bronx. Yet at the same time, KIPP founders were slowly being convinced by powerful elite forces interested in replacing the traditional public school system that instead of a heady national expansion, focusing on one demographic area would give KIPP longevity, credibility, and eventual permanence and growth while serving as a model to compete with public education. According to a report published by *Philanthropy Roundtable Magazine* entitled "Growing Up Fast; Will Houston's Charter School Expansion Revolutionize Urban Education?" authored by Jay Mathews and found at KIPP's Web site, the national expansionary plans adopted by KIPP came under critical scrutiny when:

> *Shawn Hurwitz, a friend of Feinberg's, proposed an alternate idea. Hurwitz, the president of Maxxam, a real estate development company, thought it would make sense to focus much of KIPP's growth in one place-and Houston presented an attractive opportunity. HISD is the largest public school system in Texas, and the seventh-largest in the country, with bellwether demographics that make it a leading indicator for national trends 20 years from now. Moreover, the city has long been friendly to reform. Before he was named Secretary of Education, Rod Paige was superintendent of HISD; the current superintendent, Abelardo Saavedra, was a fellow at the Broad Superintendents Academy*
>
> *Linbeck, Hurwitz, and Feinberg took their findings to the KIPP: Houston board. They all agreed. Expansion was necessary. The board members began to think seriously about how to expand the charter network. Once again, they relied on the advice of Leo Linbeck.*
>
> *Linbeck . . . holds two undergraduate degrees from Notre Dame, a master's degree in structural engineering from the University of Texas, and an MBA from Stanford. Today, Linbeck is the CEO of Aquinas Companies, LLC, the parent company of eight values-driven enterprises; under his leadership, the family-owned business grew from annual revenues of $40 million in 1994 to $550 million in 2007. Linbeck also teaches in the business schools at Rice and Stanford. His specialty: managing rapid growth in small businesses. (Mathews 2008)*

The plan that the powerful forces concocted was plain and simple: build a blueprint for the future growth and expansion of KIPP schools right in Houston, Texas that would serve as an educational beacon and bellwether to highlight exceptional educational excellence and thereby serve as an empirical argument against traditional public schools in favor of eventual privatized, retail contract chains. The philanthropic money would be looked at as "seed money" to develop the idea on the ground and ideologically in the public's mind, all in favor of privatized radical reform. As the article goes on to recall:

> *Linbeck first met Feinberg and Hurwitz when they asked him to build an elementary school for $5.5 million. He told them he didn't think they needed one. "You're building this elementary school, but you have no idea what goes into an elementary school because you haven't run one yet," Linbeck told them. "And yet you have this middle school and its doing great, but it's in trailers. Why don't we build you a middle school, and put the elementary school in trailers until you've figured out exactly what you want?" What they really needed, Linbeck concluded, was to build a middle school for $2.5 million.*

Start with what you know, Linbeck explained. That way, the elementary school could experiment with different class sizes, different schedules, and different teaching styles, just as they had done with the middle school. Linbeck encouraged them to take advantage of their flexibility before locking themselves into an expensive building that would limit further experiments. Feinberg and Hurwitz thought about it, and agreed that Linbeck's idea made a lot of sense.

Ultimately, they did exactly as Linbeck advised—not least because, as Linbeck later discovered, "they didn't have $5.5 million." KIPP would start with what it knew (middle schools), and then, as KIPP gained experience, build up (high schools) and build down (elementary schools). Barbic was likewise impressed with Linbeck, and asked him to begin building schools for YES as well. (Ibid.)

The article in the *Roundtable* goes on to detail just how much KIPP was able to tap into financially:

KIPP: Houston has also secured commitments of $10 million from both Houston Endowment and the Gates Foundation. George Grainger, a senior grant officer at Houston Endowment, points out that while the Endowment has been funding K-12 projects for many years, it has only recently come to see that it needed to reconsider its education funding strategy. Its new approach involves investing in a small number of large-scale efforts. Only then, Grainger believes, will the Endowment significantly increase the number of low-income and minority students from Houston who go on to college.

The Michael and Susan Dell Foundation has been among the most active and engaged of the donors to both expansion programs, particularly under the leadership of its Texas program officer Lori Fey (rhymes with "high"). The foundation has long supported national school leadership programs like New Leaders for New Schools and teacher programs like Teach For America. When Dell began to consider supporting charter schools in Texas, KIPP and YES were among the four charter school networks that received its first grants. Those grants have continued, and are now directed towards the expansion efforts. To date, the Dell Foundation has given $7.1 million to YES, as well as $3.8 million to KIPP: Houston.

One of the newest contributors to the expansion program is the El Paso Corporation, which plans to contribute $400,000 in 2008 to support KIPP's expansion. According to Bruce Connery, vice president for investor and media relations, the company's involvement began when a former El Paso executive served on the KIPP board and suggested the schools might be worth the company's support. El Paso CEO Doug Foshee (pronounced "Fo-shay") toured KIPP and agreed. (Ibid.)

According to the *Roundtable* report, in the city of Houston alone, between 2006-2008, private donors have given more than $90 million dollars for a supercharged expansion of KIPP and YES (another KIPP educational program) in the city. And that's just in Houston! Within a decade, the two programs expect to use that money to create a school district *within* the current public school district and by 2017, they intend to be serving a total of more than 30,000 students annually—

roughly 15 percent of all public school students in the Houston Independent School District (HISD). This is the "takeover" plan that has been conceived in coordination with many interests and it will require a massive expansion effort and huge sums of money; that's where the philanthropy comes in. In ten short years, KIPP and YES plan to build, staff, and launch a total of 55 new charter schools—42 KIPP schools, 13 YES schools all, they say, without diminishing the quality of the education provided. It is a philanthropic initiative never before witnessed in the realm of charter schools with implications for the growth of both charter schools nationwide—and for large urban school districts everywhere (Ibid.).

KIPP ACADEMIC SUCCESS: HOW DO THEY DO IT?

The academic success of KIPP is often attributed to its virtual fanaticism as an organization dedicated to kids and its mandatory parental involvement, among other things. But it is important to understand that when assessing any claims KIPP makes as to academic performance that these claims are tied to how well students score on state-mandated standardized tests. This is important, for these tests are the subject of much educational, political, and social controversy and debate over their adequacy as adequate assessment measures insofar as many say they fail to test little but rote memorization and regurgitation (FairTest; Weil and Kincheloe 2001). Once again one is reminded of John Dewey and debates that raged in the 1920s and 30s over the role of education. As Dewey noted:

> *no one thing, probably, works so fatally against focusing the attention of teachers upon training of mind as the domination of their minds by the idea that the chief thing is to get pupils to recite their lessons correctly. (Dewey 1933)*

Therefore, it seems that basing any assessment as to quality education and educational tactics and strategies on an outdated factory-style test model is wrongheaded for the simple reason the tests do not test problem solving and critical thinking skills (Weil and Kincheloe 2001). Given this, any analysis of student achievement can only point to these state-standardized test scores as academic achievement indicators, for this is all that is available. This is saddening but true not just for KIPP's claims, but for all educational achievement claims, as noted.

One thing is known for sure about the KIPP success story is that the academic program at KIPP is relentless in its back-to-basics focus. Called a boot camp, the program runs nearly 10 hours a day, from 7:30 am until 5 pm, not including transportation and homework, and half a day every other Saturday. This means, potentially, a lot of rote learning and test prep, day in and day out to meet the state standardized test requirements. Furthermore, teachers, parents and students have to commit in writing to certain pre-ordained "decisions" about the aspects of the KIPP program. In fact, all KIPP schools require a Commitment Form be signed by teachers, parents or guardians and students. The form includes a "teacher's commitment," a "parent or guardian commitment" and a "student commitment." According to one such KIPP school commitment form, the teacher's commitment requires:

We will arrive every day by 7:15 am (Monday—Friday)

We will remain at KIPP until 5:00 pm (Monday—Thursday) and 4:00 pm on Friday

We will come to KIPP on appropriate Saturdays at 9:00 am and remain until 1:05 pm

We will teach at KIPP during the summer.

We will always teach in the best way we know how, and we will do whatever it takes for our students to learn.

We will always make ourselves available to address the concerns of students, parents, and colleagues.

We will always protect the safety, interests and rights of all individuals in the classroom.

Failure to adhere to these commitments can lead to our removal from KIPP.

The parent commitment requires:

We will make sure our child arrives every day by 7:30 am (Mon.—Fri.), or boards a bus at the scheduled time.

We will make arrangements for our child to remain at KIPP until 5:00 pm (Monday—Thursday) and 4:00 pm on Friday.

We will make arrangements for our child to come to KIPP on appropriate Saturdays at 9:00 am and remain until 1:05 pm.

We will ensure that our child attends KIPP summer school.

We will always help our child in the best way we know how, and we will do whatever it takes for him/her to learn. This also means that we will check our child's homework every night, let him/her call the teacher if there is a problem with homework, and try to read with him/her every night.

*We will always make ourselves available to support our child's education at **KIPP TECH VALLEY**. This also means that if our child is going to miss school, we will notify the teacher as soon as possible, and we will read carefully all the papers that the school sends home to us.*

We will allow our child to go on KIPP field trips.

We will make sure our child follows the KIPP dress code.

We understand that our child must follow the KIPP rules in order to protect the safety, interests, and rights of all individuals in the classroom.

We, not the school, are responsible for the behavior and actions of our child.

We will always protect the safety, interests and rights of all individuals in the classroom.

Failure to adhere to these commitments can cause my child to lose various KIPP privileges.

The student commitment requires:

I will arrive at school every day by 7:30 am and remain at KIPP until 5:00 pm (Monday—Thursday) and 4:00 pm on Friday.

I will come to KIPP on appropriate Saturdays at 9:00 am and remain until 1:05 pm.

I will attend KIPP during the summer.

I will always work, think, and behave in the best way I know how, and I will do whatever it takes for me and my fellow students to learn. This also means that I will complete all my homework every night; I will call my teachers if I have a problem with the homework and I will raise my hand and ask questions in class if I do not understand something.

I will always make myself available to parents, teachers, and any concerns they might have. If I make a bad choice, this means I will tell the truth to my teachers and accept responsibility for my actions.

I will always choose to behave in order to protect the safety, interests and rights of all individuals in the classroom. This also means that I will always listen to all my KIPP teammates and give everyone my respect and support.

I will follow the KIPP dress code.

I am responsible for my own choices and behavior, and I will follow the teachers' directions.

Failure to adhere to these commitments can cause me to lose KIPP privileges.
(KIPP Commitment to Excellence)

There are penalties for violations of commitments. As Mosle observes:

Parents or guardians, too, must be hardy souls at KIPP. They have to sign a contract saying they agree to KIPP's exacting schedule, which serves, intentionally or not, to eliminate kids from less involved or determined families. While KIPP does have outreach efforts to broaden its applicant pool, only the most determined parents are likely to respond to such overtures and sign KIPP's demanding contract. This dedication suggests a higher value on education within these families, and thus kids better able or willing to learn. And the weakest students, not surprisingly, get disproportionately winnowed. In KIPP's schools in the San Francisco Bay Area, for example, the worst performing kids have dropped out (or been expelled) in greater numbers in the higher grades; the result has been to inflate the schools' grade-to-grade improvement. (Mosle 2009)

Steven Wilson describes it this way:

Teachers, who often began at seven in the morning and worked into the evening, carried cell phones and pagers to field questions from students about home work. Parents had to check homework every night, or they would see their child expelled from school. In Houston, students who misbehaved were "porched"—required to wear their uniforms inside and out for days or even weeks, not to speak with other students, and to study in separate areas under a banner that read, "If you can't run with the big dogs, stay on the porch." (Wilson 2006)

As to teachers who dedicate themselves to KIPP and the KIPP philosophy of excellence and hard work, Sara Mosle, writing in 2009 in *Slate* noted:

As a result, KIPP teachers typically work 65-hour weeks and a longer school year. Recognizing that students need more out-of-school aid to supplement their educations, the program also requires its staff to be available to students by phone after hours for homework help and moral support. For this overtime (which represents 60 percent more time in the classroom alone, on average, than in regular public schools), teachers receive just 20 percent more pay. Unsurprisingly, turnover is high. The program has relied heavily on the ever-renewing supply of very young (and thus less expensive) Teach for America alums, whose numbers, while growing, are decidedly finite. Indeed, it's unclear whether KIPP would exist were it not for TFA (and its own philanthropic investment in recruitment and training, which has not come cheap). (Mosle 2009)

In the most comprehensive look at KIPP schools to date, Richard Rothstein in his book co-written with Martin Carnoy of The Economic Policy Institute and professor at Stanford University *The Charter School Dust-Up*, raises some essential points for an analysis of KIPP schools and an evaluation of their claims to higher student achievement among the most disadvantaged of the disadvantaged.

To begin with, Rothstein acknowledges KIPP's claim to fame in the area of education is that it is able to boot test scores for the most disadvantaged of the urban students it serves. KIPP claims test scores for their students, typically black and Hispanic and from inner-urban cities, is remarkably higher than those of similar students in typical public schools. Rothstein argues that this claim by what he calls "charter zealots" is often exaggerated. To prove his hypothesis he conducted an examination of these claims. His findings were revealing. To begin with, he concluded that KIPP students are not representatives of students in regular public schools in disadvantaged communities as KIPP claims. Thus, the comparison is disanalogous. Take the case of Baltimore, where Rothstein reports that:

KIPP claims at its school in Baltimore, entering fifth graders in 2002-2003 had pre-KIPP (fourth grade) median national percentile ranks of 42 in reading and 48 in math. KIPP did not desegregate these scores by socioeconomic status, but the school is 100% black. The Baltimore City School System reports that, in the spring of 2002, its black fourth graders had a median national percentile rank of 36 in reading and 34 in math. Thus, entering students in the Baltimore KIPP school were more proficient in reading and math than typical black fourth graders in Baltimore. In this respect, students at KIPP-Baltimore are not typical of Baltimore's black students overall. (Carnoy et al. 2005, 53)

Rothstein found the same disparities when he looked at the widely touted success of the KIPP Charter School in South Bronx, New York. Here, KIPP students were found to be unusually high performing before they entered the school. Rothstein found that the reason might be owed to KIPP's reputation for academic success and the fact that this drew many higher performing students to its shores, where parents sought to enroll their children to escape failing public schools (Ibid.).

Rothstein also heard arguments that traditional public schools are more likely to recommend that their most troublesome students and underachievers attend KIPP schools, not necessarily because they could profit from the KIPP program, though this was often the case, but also that school test scores would rise if the most troublesome underachievers were taken out of the test sampling and placed in other schools. If true, this would go to the heart of KIPP's claim that it educates the most disadvantaged children. Yet Rothstein's study seemed to undermine the claims that schools were systematically referring their most troublesome students to KIPP in an effort to boost their own test scores. In fact, what he found was that teachers were suggesting to the most educated and sophisticated parents that they take their children out of traditional public schools and referred them to KIPP. He even found one fourth grade teacher who mistakenly thought KIPP was a "gifted" program and encouraged her most talented students and their parents to consider the KIPP school. He also found that principals encouraged the most motivated and involved parents of children to apply to KIPP schools. In Houston, the home of the first KIPP school that had celebrated success and the object of the NCEE's research study, the same themes were echoed by teachers in district schools who reported that they referred their students to KIPP who were above average (Ibid.). It is important to note that this did not lead Rothstein to conclude that KIPP was involved in actively recruiting a more advantaged student body from traditional public schools, but the inference that can be drawn by those that study such practices is that "creaming," as it is called in the educational world, is unconsciously built into the system of referral itself; this conclusion seems inescapable.

Therefore, as Rothstein suggests:

If KIPP Bronx (and other KIPP schools) truly do attract the most talented or advantaged fourth graders in their communities, KIPP resolves this policy dilemma no differently than New York city itself does by operating schools like Stuyvesant High School and the Bronx High School of science that admit only students with high test scores. Nor is the KIPP solution different from that of New York City and many other urban districts that create magnet schools to attract children with more motivation and parental support than typical children in disadvantaged communities. These magnet school serve the most motivated children well, while leaving zoned public schools with a more difficult job because their enrollment concentrates disadvantage more intensively. (Ibid.)

Assuming that Rothstein's analysis is correct, the consequences and implications of the study on public policy are inescapable: KIPP schools, rather than serving the "most disadvantaged" of the "disadvantaged," serve the top end of the "disadvantaged." Perhaps this is part of KIPP's national and regional educational plan—to serve the most highly motivated of the "subprime kids" by creating a national retail chain of KIPP schools that target the "best of the worst." The problem, as Rothstein notes, is the lack of data and this lack of data, as indicated earlier, is due to a lack of transparency, reliance on inauthentic testing measurements, and a failure to disclose vital information to the public.

Given all this, it is not hard to understand how this effort to start up KIPP-type schools would certainly mirror the recommendations made by the Bill and Melinda Gates Foundation-supported report, *Tough Choices or Tough Times,* published by the NCEE. KIPP now remains the beneficiary of philanthropic funds not made available to for-profit EMOs; and the philanthropic foundations that have made hundreds of millions of dollars available to organizations like KIPP certainly have not done the same for traditional public schools. This fact alone should ignite a host of questions on behalf of the public and the understanding that philanthropy comes with a price and that price could be the complete transformation and transfiguration of the U.S. educational landscape not seen since the industrial revolution.

SUMMARY

In evaluating standards and the notion of what a public school should do, Kathy Hytten harkens back to John Dewey's debate with Walter Lippmann for suggestions and advice. She voices the need for sound critical thinking instruction in schools:

We must encourage students to develop questions that are individually and socially meaningful, and to take initiative in answering them fully. We also must help them to see the connections between classroom learning and a larger moral vision of social betterment. Dewey believes that the key to social progress is found in using our minds well. The only way we can do this as adults is if we practice thinking critically in schools. This necessarily involves conceptualizing educational practices that are premised upon social involvement, responsibility, engagement, critique, and an ethically committed sensitivity to others and to the world around us. Though we often say we value these ideas, what we do in schools, particularly in a climate of high stakes testing and accountability is not typically consistent. Consequently, student disengagement and passivity are all too prevalent. While Dewey's perspectives on the importance of thinking critically make practical sense, and resonate with contemporary calls for more engaged learning, we have yet to take seriously his passionate call for a change in how we think about thinking. His works thus still provide a valuable, largely untapped resource for rethinking how we educate democratic citizens in an ever-changing world. (Hytten 2002)

If she is right, will *charterizing* the public school system be the answer? One thing is sure. A new school system is quietly emerging in the United States and plans are underway to radically transform the nation's educational system, as was most notably done recently on a wholesale level in New Orleans. The real question in the debate over EMOs and charter schools, profit or nonprofit, boils down to whether the public will be involved in decision making over public policy, management of these charter schools, curriculum, testing, and financing when it comes to issues of the education for their children, or whether these decisions will rest in the hands of a few wealthy philanthropists, venture capitalists, entrepreneurs, politicians beholden to campaign contributions, politically charged think tanks, and Wall Street financiers. The answer to these, and other questions will be born from the struggle over our nation's educational agenda. These answers promise to open a new chapter in the long fought battle for the right of American citizens to demand a school system that give students time and resources to deeply explore ideas, to make meaningful connections, and to imagine possibilities, a school system that sees, as Dewey so ardently argued for, "knowledge operating in the direction of powers to the better living of life." (Dewey 1933) This, then is our challenge.

REFERENCES

Academica Schools. http://www.academicaschools.com/.

Academica West. http://www.academicawest.com/what-we-do.php.

Advantage Schools. http://www.advantageschools.com.

Allen, J., G. Beaman, and K. Hornung. "Charter School Closures: The Opportunity for Accountability." In *Charter Schools: Changing the Face of the Nation*, February 2006. Center for Education Reform. http://edreform.com/_upload/closures.pdf.

Ballou, D., and M. Podgursky. "Personnel Policy in Charter Schools." Fordham Foundation. 2001.

Berkowitz, B. *Philanthropy the Wal-Mart Way: Will the Walton Family Foundation become a $20 Billion Tax-Exempt Opponent of Public Education?* 1 August 2001. Thomas Fordham Institute. http://www.edexcellence.net/detail/news.cfm?news_id=19 and http://mediatransparency.org/story.php?storyID=88BillBerkowitz.

Bill and Melinda Gates Foundation. "National Research Study on Charter Management Organization Effectiveness to Be Led by Mathematica Policy Research and Center on Reinventing Public Education," 17 March 2008. http://www.gatesfoundation.org/press-releases/Pages/charter-school-management-research.aspx.

Blume, H. "Charter School Firm to Open More L.A. Campuses." *Los Angeles Times*, 29 April 2009. http://latimesblogs.latimes.com/lanow/2009/04/one-of-the-nations-most-highly-praised-charter-school-operators-has-landed-another-huge-donation-to-open-campuses-in-the-l.html.

Brooks Academy. http://www.brooksacademy.org/.

Byrnes, V. "Getting a Feel for the Market: The Use of Privatized School Management in Philadelphia." *American Journal of Education* 115 (May 2009).

Carnoy, M., R. Jacobsen, L. Mishel and R. Rothstein *The Charter School Dust—Up Examining the Evidence on Enrollment and Achievement* Washington D.C. and New York, New York: Economic Policy Institute and Teachers College Press, 2005.

Carr, S. "Some Charter Schools Cutting Ties with For-Profit Partners." *The Times-Picayune,* 24 April 2009. http://www.nola.com/news/index.ssf/2009/04/some_charter_schools_cutting_t.html.

Center for Education Reform. "Florida's Groundbreaking Charter Bill Creates New Authorizer." June 2006. http://www.edreform.com/index.cfm?fuseAction=document&documentID=2449.

Citizens for Responsibility and Ethics in Washington. "IG's Office to Study Complaint About Ignite!Learning." 13 November 2007, http://www.citizensforethics.org/node/30442.

Coleman, R., and M. Pearlstein. "Who Funds the KIPP Schools?" 2008. http://d2route.wordpress.com/2008/08/25/who-funds-the-kipp-schools/.

Columbus Educational Association. http://blog.ceaohio.org/wordpress/index.php/2007/12/17/ipo-for-ohio-virtual-charter-school-operator-falls-short/.

Conn, Kathleen. "For-profit School Management Corporations: Serving the Wrong Master."*Journal of Law and Education,* April 2002. http://findarticles.com/p/articles/mi_qa3994/is_200204/ai_n9079611/.

Corporate Watch. "Charter Schools Run by For-profit Companies." (1998). http://www.corpwatch.org.

Corwin, R.G., and E. J. Schneider. *The Charter School Hoax.* Lanham, MD: Rowman and Littlefield Education, 2007.

Darden S. "School Choice: Voucher Lessons from Sweden." 9 April 2008. http://www.friedman-foundation.org/friedman/newsroom/ShowNewsItem.do?id=802

Dewey, J. *How We Think.* NY: Houghton Mifflin Company, 1933. (Republished in 1998).

EdisonLearning. http://www.edisonlearning.com.

Education Management Organizations: *Managing Competition*. http://www.mackinac.org/article.aspx?ID=2140.

Education News.org. "Philadelphia Standardized Tests. (2009). http://ednews.org.

———. "Student Gains in Privately Managed Philadelphia Schools—Nearly-Double Those in District Schools." (2008). http://ednews.org/articles/27186/1/C/Page1.html.

Epstein, K. "No Bush Left Behind: The President's brother Neil is Making Hay from School Reform." *Business Week*, 16 October 2006. http://www.businessweek.com/magazine/content/06_42/b4005059.htm?chan=top+news_top+news+index_businessweek+exclusives.

FairTest. Boston, MA. http://www.fairtest.org.

Florida Consortium of Public Charter Schools. http://www.floridacharterschools.org/public/charter schoollawandcompliance.asp.

Georgiou, D. The National Center for Policy Analysis. No. 531, 5 October 2005. http://www.ncpa.org/pub/ba531.

Gill, B., R. Zimmer, J. Christman, and S. Blanc. "Education School Restructuring, Private Management, and Student Achievement in Philadelphia." The Rand Corporation, 2007. http://pdf.researchforaction.org/rfapdf/publication/pdf_file/262/Gill_B_State_Takeover.pdf.

Greenberger, S.S. "For-Profit School Firm Falls Short on Reforms." *Boston Globe,* 13 May 2001. http://www.commondreams.org/headlines01/0513-02.htm.

Grillo, T. "Wall Street Spent Billions Lobbying." *Boston Herald,* 5 March 2009. http://www.boston-herald.com.

Haag, M. "Texas Doesn't Heed Charter School Rule in McKinney." *Dallas Morning News,* 27 November 2008. http://www.dallasnews.com/sharedcontent/dws/news/localnews/stories/DN-imagine_27met.ART0.Central.Edition1.4a64ad0.html.

Hallett, J. "Self Appointed Superintendent Industrialist Builds Ninth Largest School District Using Political Clout." *Columbus Dispatch*, 23 October 2005. www.dispatch.com/dispatch/contentbe/dispatch/200.

Hanauer, A. "Profits and Privatization: The Ohio Experience. "In *Keeping the Promise: The Debate over Charter Schools."* Washington, DC: ReThinking Schools and the Center for Community Change 2009.

Hentschke, G., S. Oschman, and L. Snell. *Education Management Organizations: Growing a For-Profit Education Industry with Choice, Competition, and Innovation* P o l i c y B r i e f 2 1. http://www.reason.org/files/86f373eefe12bf11ff614e1305ff3362.pdf.

Hoovers. A D&B Company. http://www.hoovers.com.

Hess, F. "Reimagining American Schooling: The Case for Educational Entrepreneurship." *Education Outlook*, 27 October 2007.

Hightower, J. "Bush's Family Profits from 'No Child' Act." *Los Angeles Times,* 22 October 2006.

Huffington Post. "Fund Race." (2008). (http://fundrace.huffingtonpost.com/neighbors.php?type=name&lname=Zulueta.

Hytten, K. "Democracy and John Dewey," in *Standards and Schooling in the United States: An Encyclopedia,* by J.L. Kincheloe, and D.K. Weil. ABC-Clio. April 2002.

Ignite!Learning. http://www.ignitelearning.com/products/index.html.

KIPP Academy. http://www.kippny.org/kippacademy/history.asp.

KIPP Commitment to Excellence. http://www.kipptechvalley.com/commitment.pdf.

Kozol, J. "The Big Enchilada.." *Harper's Magazine Notebook*, 25 August 2007. http://www.harpers.org/archive/2007/08/page/0009?redirect=321247325.

Light, J. "A Local Battle Highlights the National Debate Over EMOs" Corporate Watch, (2000). http://www.corpwatch.org.

Livingston S., S. Stephens, and B. Paynter. "Who's Profiting from Ohio's Charter Schools." *Cleveland Plain Dealer* 19 March 2006.

Mathematica Policy Research, Inc. "Evaluating the Effectiveness of Charter School Management Organizations." (2009). http://www.mathematica-mpr.com/education/cmo.asp.

Mathews, J. "Growing Up Fast; Will Houston's Charter School Expansion Revolutionize Urban Education?" *Philanthropy Roundtable Magazine*, 5 May 2008. http://www.kipp.org/08/press detail.cfm?a=486.

Mathis, W. *NCLB's Ultimate Restructuring Alternatives: Do They Improve the Quality of Education?* Boulder and Tempe: Education and the Public Interest Center & Education Policy Research Unit. Accessed 2009. http://epicpolicy.org/publication/nclb-ultimate-restructuring.

McCloskey, P.J. " When the Profit Motive Goes to School." *Business Week*, 22 July 1999. http://www.businessweek.com/bwdaily/dnflash/july1999/nf90722b.htm.

Millot, D. "Eduventures' Sell Off Suggests the End of an Era." *Education Week*, 9 February 2008. http://blogs.edweek.org/edweek/edbizbuzz/2008/02/eduventures_sale_suggests_the.html.

Miner, B. "For-Profits Target Education." *ReThinking Schools*, 16 no. 3 (Spring 2002).

Miron, G., and J. Urschel. *Profiles of Nonprofit Education Management Organizations.* Boulder and Tempe: Education and the Public Interest Center & Education Policy Research Unit,

(2007-2008). http://epicpolicy.org/publication/profilesnonprofit-education-management-organizations-2007-2008.

Molnar, A., D. R. Garcia, G. Miron, and S. Berry. *Profiles of For-Profit Education Management Organizations Ninth Annual Report 2006-2007*. Commercialism in Education Research Unit (CERU) Education Policy Studies Laboratory College of Education Division of Educational Leadership and Policy Studies. Arizona State University. http://epicpolicy.org/files/EPSL-0708-239-CERU.pdf.

Molnar, A., G. Miron, and J. Urschel. *Profiles of For-Profit Educational Management Organizations Tenth Annual Report*, 2008. http://epicpolicy.org/files/EMO0708.pdf.

Moon, J. "Charter schools burgeoning along the Wasatch Front." *The Enterprise*, 27 June 2005. http://findarticles.com/p/articles/mi_qa5279/is_200506/ai_n24301391/.

Mosaica Education. http://www.mosaicaeducation.com/.

Molnar, A., G. Miron, and J. Urschel. *Profiles of For-Profit Educational Management Organizations Tenth Annual Report 2008*. http://epicpolicy.org/files/EMO0708.pdf.

Mosle, S. "The Educational Experiment We Really Need: What the Knowledge Is Power Program Has Yet To Prove," 23 March 2009. *Slate.com* Web site. http://www.slate.com/id/2214253/pagenum/all/.

The National Alliance of Public Charter Schools. http://www.publiccharters.org/node/265.

National Center on Education and the Economy. The Skills Commission. *Tough Choices or Tough Times*. 2007. http://www.skillscommission.org/pdf/exec_sum/ToughChoices_EXECSUM.pdf.

National Center for Educational Statistics. *Current Public Expenditure on Education as a Percentage of GDP*. (2003). http://nces.ed.gov/pubs/eiip/eiipid42.asp.

Nijmie, F.I. "Philadelphia Student Union Statement on EMO Contract Decisions." Young Philly Politics, 18 June 2008. http://youngphillypolitics.com/philadelphia_student_union_statement_emo_contract_decisions.

Ohio Department of Education. http://www.ode.state.oh.us/.

Ohio Educational Association. "Gov. Strickland's Efforts to Protect Education Funding and Improve Ohio Charter Schools." *Talking Points,* 9 February 2009. http://74.125.155.132/search?q=cache:iTSeEilKtJgJ:https://www.ohea.org/GD/DocumentManagement/DocumentDownload.aspx%3FDocumentID%3D13191+Governor+Strickland+and+charter+schools&cd=28&hl=en&ct=clnk&gl=us.

Ohio Federation of Teachers. "Education Empire: Report Unveils Corporate Control of 'Community' Schools." 7 March 2006. http://oh.aft.org/index.cfm?action=article&articleID=7b956e85-fda4-4cbe-aa9b-f0318b16dc03.

Pacific Charter School Development. http://www.pacificcharter.org/funders/Philanthropists.htm.

Philadelphia Public School: The Notebook. "Parents United for Public Education." 20 February 2009. http://www.thenotebook.org/print/1025?page=show.

Plank, D., D. Arsen, and G. Sykes. "Charter Schools and Private Profits—Educational Management Organizations." *School Administrator*, May 2000. http://findarticles.com/p/articles/mi_m0JSD/is_5_57/ai_77382336/pg_3/?tag=content;col1.

Poppino, N. "Uncharted Waters—Local Realtor Proposes More Magic Valley Charter Schools." *Times-News*, September 2007. Times News Magic Valley.com. http://www.magicvalley.com/articles/2007/09/25/news/local_state/121220.txt.

Rollenhagen, M. "Ohio Probes Campaign Giving by Charter School Operator David Brennan." *Ohio Plain* Dealer, 4 April 2008. http://blog.cleveland.com/openers/2008/04/give.html.

Sack, J. "Charter Failure Affects 10,000 Students." *EdWeek*, 1 September 2004. http://www.edweek.org/ew/articles/2004/09/01/01cca.h24.html.

Schundler, B. "The Face of Education Reform." *School Reform News*, February 2000. Heartland Institute. http://www.heartland.org/publications/school%20reform/article/11088/The_Face_of_Education_Reform.html.

Slowey, D. "Credit Suisse First Boston Equity Partners, L.P. Leads $28 Million Investment in Advantage Schools." *Boston Globe*, 22 February 2000.

Southwest Educational Developmental Laboratory. "School Restructuring Options under NCLB: What Works When? Contracting with External Education Management Providers." MONTH 2005. http://209.85.173.132/search?q=cache:3LsNTINnNYkJ:www.centerforcsri.org/pubs/restructuring/KnowledgeIssues3Contracting.pdf+EMo+and+student+achievement&cd=20&hl=en&ct=clnk&gl=us&ie=UTF-8.

Stark, M. "Lessons From Privately Managed Schools." Harvard Business School, 30 January 2006. http://hbswk.hbs.edu/archive/5189.htm.

Symonds, W.C., A.T. Palmer, D. Lindorff, and J. McCann. "For-Profit Schools, They're Spreading Fast. Can Private Companies Do a Better Job of Educating America's Kids?" *BuisnessWeek*, 7 February 2000. http://www.businessweek.com/2000/00_06/b3667001.htm.

Viadero, D. "EMO Schools Don't Outscore Other Philadelphia Schools." 19 April 2006. http://www.edweek.org/login.html?source=http://www.edweek.org/ew/articles/2006/04/19/32aera-philly.h25.html&destination=http://www.edweek.org/ew/articles/2006/04/19/32aera-philly.h25.html&levelId=2100.

Weil, D., and J. Kincheloe. *Standards and Schooling in The United States*: An Encyclopedia. Santa Barbara, CA: ABC-Clio, 2001.

White Hat Management. http://www.whitehatmanagement.com.

Wilson, S., *Learning on the Job: When Business Takes on Public Schools*. Cambridge, MA: Harvard University Press, 2006.

Wyatt, E. "Investors See Room for-profit In the Demand for Education." *New York Times*, 4 November 1999. http://query.nytimes.com/gst/fullpage.html?res=9B02E1D9113BF937A35752C1A96F958260&sec=&spon=&pagewanted=2.

Chapter Seven

Teachers' Unions and Charter Schools

BLUEPRINT FOR NEW ORLEANS

New Orleans provides a framework to understand the role of teacher unions, charter schools, and teachers themselves and how they operate and feel about the charter school movement; it also points directly to how public school systems in their entirety are being targeted for sweeping conservative change in the form of a contractualized charter school experiment that is the most radical of its kind in the nation. Currently, 54 percent of all schools in New Orleans are charter schools (Merrow, under "Charter Schools Exclude Special Education Students").

Yet the idea to "charterize" the schools in New Orleans directly after Hurricane Katrina in 2005 was not a new notion. It was, in fact, part of a well-orchestrated effort born out of conservative ideological think tanks and specifically the work of Paul T. Hill at the Center for Reinventing Public Education, at Washington University. Hill had been writing for years for the need to radically transform education through conservative market-based reforms and new public-private partnerships in education in order to cure what allegedly ails large urban school districts. In a publication for the Brookings Institute Press, in 2004 Hill and his colleague, James Harvey, wrote a small publication entitled: *Making School Reform Work*. In the book, the two authors write that the:

> *current system of education governance creates barriers that can make (educational) reform even harder. (Hill and Harvey 2004)*

The answer, they write, is the need for:

> *new institutions that can be created by foundations and civic groups to remedy deficiencies in local school governance, formulate bold reforms, and guarantee implementation. These institutions include incubators for starting new schools, independent data analysis centers, public-private partnerships for recruitment and training of school leaders, and new ways of funding and managing school facilities. (Ibid.)*

Hill and Harvey put forth these ideas in the year preceding Hurricane Katrina. In fact, Hill, Harvey, and scholar Christine Campbell had laid out this plan, entitled "Diverse Providers Strategy," in a 2000 book entitled, *It Takes a City*. The book was an audacious attempt at laying out a new architecture for school "reform," especially inner city, urban school reform. It was to be based on an ideology of market fundamentalism with the role of the government as an overseer of a network of privately run publicly funded schools, or in some cases schools operated by nonprofit EMOs.

What the book does is basically lay out two camps of what the authors refer to as "reformers"—those *inside* the educational community and those *outside* of it. The first group of reformers, according to Hill and his co-authors, want to concentrate on improving standards, better teacher development, and creating new school designs, and they tend to focus on decentralization and site-based management issues when it comes to school governance; in other words they wish to work within the current system of public education in hopes of improving it. It should also be noted that the first group of reformers favors collective bargaining and teacher unions in a social contract with schools and school management. The second group of educational reformers, according to Hill and his associates, include those bold and audacious voices for a wholesale sweeping change through the market reform of education, such as encouraging more charter schools, school contracting, and private school vouchers; it is firmly with this latter group that Hill and his colleagues are wedded.

What Hill, Harvey, and Campbell envisioned in their restructuring plans for inner-city urban schools was the construction of school reform strategies that they considered were more powerful than those anywhere in the United States, precisely because they would combine the quintessentially American "market" freedoms the authors believed were part and parcel of the American psyche, with the political and economic policies necessary for the wholesale reform of public schools in the direction of measurable outcomes based on standardized tests. The strategies to be employed, according to Hill and his co-authors, would:

> *introduce three features missing or barely evident in today's public education: choice, competition, and entrepreneurship. (Hill and Harvey 2004)*

The plan was a bold one and based on disturbing notions of individual freedoms and human nature; at least this was the concern voiced by many progressive educators. The notion of "measurable outcomes" based on competition among community members in an unregulated, unfettered economic market is and was part and parcel of the ideology that underlie Hill's calls for reform. The underlying assumption was that people are naturally calculating individuals, self-interested and self-motivated to pursue their own interests with little regard for the public good; indeed, really was no greater good, no public interest, only freedom of individual choice. This echoes some of the same historical sentiments voiced by Lippmann in the early twentieth century. This narrow view of human beings went further, arguing that that if people were given individual choices in the "free-market" where they would compete for goods and services, they not only would get what they wanted as "free" individuals, but the system as a whole would operate rationally. With this austere outlook of the human being operating solely as rational profit-maximizers, what then was needed were public policies that would work to free the competitive market from all government oversight, regulation, and control. Only an unfettered market of "public choice" would allow the rational pursuit of freedom for the individual by providing an economy based on a competitive maximum advantage. "Public choice" was a necessary ingredient for this view of personal freedom but it would be a "public choice" in a privately run market system, not a "private" choice in a publicly run system.

Hill's plan, which he presented to the American Youth Forum in 2001 and which is the subject of his writings and book, proposes three strategies that build on the principles of what he calls performance incentives, capacity investments, and school "choice" freedom:

The CEO-Strong Schools Strategy. *Under this plan, the superintendent would operate as the head of a decentralized district. As the chief executive officer, the superintendent would ensure that teachers and principals have everything they need to implement the reform effort. The superintendent would have the authority to issue rules or require schools to hire staff or use the services of the school system's central office if it would improve performance. This plan would require an annual performance agreement between the superintendent and the school. The CEO-superintendent could replace principals and teachers who fail to meet performance expectations. This scenario also gives the superintendent the power to move money and free up administrative staff and faculty.*

The Diverse Providers Strategy. *A local school board would aggressively use its state-delegated power to provide for publicly-managed schools and public schools run by independent providers. Each would have similar performance agreements and freedom of action. Schools would receive funding on a per pupil basis and have little restriction placed on spending discretion—except for contractual commitments. Small amounts would be held by the school board to support oversight of individual schools. Funds would be controlled by the schools. Parents could choose schools, and schools would admit students through a public lottery with no student exclusion. The school board would be obliged to shift contracts from low-performing school providers, encouraging better service.*

      The Community-Partnership Strategy. *The Community Partnership can be seen as a further development of the Diverse Providers approach. This strategy would also include multiple public and private partners and would be a genuine community-wide system in that all the community's resources, not simply its schools, would be available in an organized way to meet children's educational needs and their general well-being. It would license many entities to provide K-12 instruction, including conventional public school systems, contractors of the kind described under the Diverse Providers Strategy, unconventional educational and cultural options, including museums, libraries, arts agencies, church supported systems willing to operate under First Amendment constraints and dispersed "cyber schools." Community Partnerships would go beyond Diverse Providers in three ways. A community education board would (1) encourage non-school educational resources; (2) preserve a portfolio of education alternatives for the disadvantaged, and (3) broker health and social service resources to meet children's needs. (Hill 2001)*

For Hill and his colleagues to reconfigure the educational system based on "targets" and "incentives" in the marketplace much more had to happen; significant public policy changes had to be carried out and this, Hill noted, was the problem. The social engineering that Hill envisioned was necessary to improve the educational system called for the elimination of many public educational institutions and move decision making outside of traditional public school districts:

> *. . . we need to eliminate some institutions, change the missions and capabilities of others, and create new institutions. Some of the most important new institutional capabilities should exist outside what we now consider the central [district] office. (Hill and Harvey 2004)*

For Hill, this would mean that the management and day-to-day operations of these schools would no longer be driven by public regulations, collective bargaining agreements and bureaucratic oversight, but by "public choice" whereby the individual would pursue their self-seeking interest as consumers in the free-market, for only the free-market could offer any hope for democracy. In this new system of freedom through public choice performance targets could be locked into standards and incentives and efficiency targets would be the motivating features that would drive the system; there would be no need for what Hill and others see as burdensome governmental regulations and collective bargaining because the "free" market and the decisions made in that market by parents, would self-regulate the system. The whole notion of a publicly run educational system would be abandoned in favor of one based on privately run schools financed through public taxes or by elite philosophic interests and financiers. The role of the government would go from overseeing schools to overseeing and managing "providers," most of them for-profit ventures, as we have seen, to assure that they were meeting essential standards, targets, and performance objectives that would all be measured through standardized testing—this and the tax-collecting functions the government would need to engage in, in order to subsidize the new charterized, private system.

The authors go on to argue for subsidies for developers and construction concerns by advocating the development of public school real estate trusts to help new charter schools get off the ground by offering start-up costs for rent, purchases, or leases of school sites. These would be public funds we are talking about—subsidies—and they would eventually find their way into private sector pockets under the charter provider rubric presented by Hill and his cohorts, essentially providing for public financial support for future private profit accumulation. All this in the name of reforming education for our children.

The arguments embraced by Hill et al. basically harkens back to proschool choice advocacy arguments but with a new, perhaps fatal twist for public schools; for what Hill sees for urban education in particular and for education in general, is the development of a new governance structure as well as a new delivery system for schools—one that is firmly under private management and control while being quintessentially publicly financed. So, for example, while today many citizens are demanding a *public option* or "public choice," as it pertains to the provision of health care in an effort to compete with private health care providers to reduce costs and provide and maintain quality health care for all citizens, Hill and his colleagues reverse the paradigm and call for a *private option* in the public realm, which they claim will give parents a "public choice" (Hill et al. 2006). It would also equate freedom not with the public good, but with individual competition and individual choices. The wider concern for any social concerns would be provided for by the "free-market" as the arbitrator of democracy and liberty thereby at the same time, produce and provide quality education for all citizens. The political economic irony is compelling but the ideology is consistent; only private, individual choices within a capitalist market can provide real quality education and institutions need to be created that are privately run yet publicly funded. The market makes the rules, the market is the realm of freedom.

This ideology is the epitome of the economic model developed most notably by Milton Friedman and carried on by the Chicago School of Economics where he and his colleagues taught and developed their ideological experiments that were to take place in Chile, Argentina, Asia, and the former Soviet Union. They argued that that the speed, suddenness, and scope of large economic shifts, disasters, and transformations would provoke psychological reactions in the public mind that would serve to "facilitate the adjustment" in thought and reality on the part of the public in accepting new and severe economic policies—

what Naomi Klein called "the shock doctrine"(Klein, 2007). The "shock doctrine" would include rapid privatization, the imposition of tax cuts, free trade, privatized services, cuts to social spending, massive deregulation, selling off state assets and centralized control, all part of the economic policies put in place in Latin America, Asia, and the former Soviet Union by Friedman's "Chicago Boys." However, as Naomi Klein keenly observed in her bestselling book *The Shock Doctrine: The Rise of Disaster Capitalism*:

> *Friedman's Chicago School movement has been conquering territory around the world since the seventies, but until recently its vision had never been fully applied in the country of origin. Certainly Reagan had made headway, but the U.S. retained a welfare system, social security and public schools, where parents clung, in Friedman's words, to their irrational attachment to the socialist system. (Ibid.)*

That all changed in 1995 when the Republican Party gained control of the Congress. Now it was finally possible to consider the "shock doctrine" within the context of the American economic and political landscape. David Frum, a former speechwriter for George W. Bush, perhaps said it best when elaborating on the manner of rapidly and quickly transforming economic policies here at home:

> *Here's how I think we should do it. Instead of cutting incrementally—a little here, a little there—I would say that on a single day this summer we eliminate three hundred programs, each one costing a billion dollars or less. Maybe these cuts won't make a big deal of difference, but boy, do they make a point. And you can do them right away. (Ibid.)*

Little did Frum know that just a few years later his plan would be put in place in the new reconfiguration of New Orleans public schools. The disaster wrought by Hurricane Katrina meant that the political and social issues facing New Orleans schools could now fall under the counsel of the economic theories Friedman had devised for years and he cautioned, before he died, that policymakers in New Orleans must act quickly to impose rapid and irreversible changes in the educational institutions and systems before a crisis-ridden public became aware of the stark economic policy changes, in essence before they could organize and oppose these policies. A new language had to be invented to sell the idea to an unwitting public. "Clean sheets," "exciting opportunities for reform," and "new beginnings," "renaissance," and countless more were the common euphemisms found in the parlance of politicians, conservative think tank ideologues, and of course among the new business elite descending on the city directly after the disaster in an effort to topple the current educational system and replace it with one based on privatization theories of human economic and social life. As Naomi Klein notes:

Most people who survive a devastating disaster want the opposite of a clean slate: they want to salvage whatever they can and begin repairing what was not destroyed; they want to reaffirm their relatedness to the places that formed them. "When I re-build the city I feel like I am rebuilding myself," said Cassandra Andrews, a resident of New Orleans's heavily damaged Lower Ninth Ward, as she cleared away debris after the storm. But disaster capitalists have no interest in repairing what was. In Iraq, Sri Lanka and New Orleans, the process deceptively called "reconstruction" began with finishing the job of the original disaster by erasing what was left of the public sphere and rooted communities, then quickly moving to replace them with a kind of corporate New Jerusalem—all before the victims of war or natural disaster were able to regroup and stake their claims to what was theirs. (Ibid.)

Not so for the disaster capitalists, social engineers and think tank pundits who seek to replace public entities with privatized new ones in accordance with their theories that freedom can only be found in the marketplace. Orchestrated raids on the public sphere, whether they exist in Argentina or New Orleans, by capitalists seeking exciting new markets to exploit, can take place when disaster is viewed as an economic opportunity. Again, Klein is salient here:

I call these orchestrated raids on the public sphere in the wake of catastrophic events, combined with the treatment of disasters as exciting market opportunities, "disaster capitalism." (Ibid.)

And so it was to be, that a small cabal of conservative right-wing forces were able to capitalize on the disaster wrought by Hurricane Katrina in their heady efforts to overhaul one of the worst public educational systems in the country. A new educational system would be built practically overnight with new roles for the public and private sector, a new language of the marketplace, spoken by new social engineers and technocrats. The government or in this case the "public school management structure," would now "orchestrate" the new private stakeholders and nonprofit philanthropic "providers" that would emerge overnight to form a new charterized, contract school system inching ever closer and closer to privatization. At the time and continuing today, this was and is all being bundled up and reported in the press as "an experiment in choice" in schools for parents and students, when in fact it is and was an elaborate private takeover involving little public input or democratic decision making, let alone public disclosure, transparency or "choice." The irony, or perhaps the tragedy of it all, is that the people of New Orleans, those remaining at the time along with the 250,000 dispossessed, never "chose" this new system that was now being ideologically constructed, implemented and codified into law and sold as "public choice." Instead they saw, or perhaps missed due to both the disaster and displacement wrought by Katrina as well as the exuberant corporate media coverage that failed to critically examine the new plans for education, the fact that they, like increasingly most of the American economy, such as the military, the prison system, the health care industry, and the myriad of countless private contracting schemes were now caught up in the web of one of the most radical movements for wholesale privatization this country had ever seen.

IMPLEMENTING THE CHANGE

In his speech given to the American Youth Forum in 2001, years before Katrina, Hill was quick to point out that current city school systems are inflexible, troublesome political systems:

> *Central offices are full of warlords who are funded by federal funds and supported by federal policy. Unfortunately, cities lack a set of strategies to deal with these problems. The Federal government could be called upon to use its bully pulpit to intervene in city politics in order to give reform efforts a fighting chance. (Hill 2001)*

The "fighting chance" Hill spoke so eloquently about in 2001 presented itself as an immediate opportunity following the disaster that Katrina bestowed on the city and the federal government was indeed involved, as we noted in chapter 3, doling out millions for the effort after the hurricane. This was to be the opportunity to launch the strategy that Friedman and his powerful allies had long argued for: you simply wait for a powerful crisis (natural or economic) and then step in quickly to sell off state assets and implement radical privatization methods for economic "reform" while the public is still stumbling, disoriented, and confused from the shock; it's basically a form of "regime change," whether it takes place in ravaged New Orleans or abroad. As Klein notes, in this way the reforms become permanent, both on the ground and in public minds (Klein 2007).

As investigative reporter, Paul Tough writes in an exhaustive investigative piece in the *New York Times* regarding the newly birthed, New Orleans contract charter school system, this is precisely what transpired. Immediately after the hurricane powerful, elite social forces descended on the city to lubricate the way for "the shock doctrine," or what market fundamentalists euphemistically prefer to call "educational reform" or "reconstruction." The opportunity had finally arisen to inch towards the privatization of the whole school system and now newly anointed educational "reconstruction" czars for the city, Paul Vallas and Paul Pastorek, were poised to implement a new strategy for New Orleans Public schools; the ideology behind the new facts on the ground would be privatization, or the reliance on a new interlocking web of markets, both profit and nonprofit, to provide an educational system for New Orleans' children. According to Tough, Hill's model for the "Diverse Providers Strategy" would be what would be adapted for New Orleans:

It is this model (the "Diverse Providers Strategy") that Pastorek and Vallas have adapted for New Orleans. (Tough 2008)

With the takeover of the New Orleans educational system that ensued immediately after the hurricane, schools in New Orleans now would be charterized—this would necessitate that they be run as schools under contract, and this would mean they would receive money on a per-student basis which principals, now called "CEOs" could then use to staff their schools as they liked and pay for whatever instructional methods they chose. Each contract charter school would now have the power to negotiate salaries and work rules directly with their teachers and staff, there would no longer be any central union for collective bargaining purposes, in fact there would be no union at all. The system's small central office would operate and be responsible only for oversight of the contract charter schools and their providers in assuring they met the "targets" and "efficiency efficiency demands" demanded of the testing regime under No Child Left Behind, though the public office would also have considerable power to hold CEOs accountable and they would also have the power to hire and fire them. The narrow testing regiment under No Child Left Behind would actually serve to help the new "providers" of education to meet their "benchmarks" and "performance targets," thereby offering measurement guidelines to help the providers stay in business. The schools that didn't produce results in accordance with the standardized tests codified into law by NCLB would be deemed "failing schools" and they would be closed and successful schools would then be imitated and replicated, with new "providers," either profit or nonprofit. These new providers would then be awarded contracts to run schools based on their past performance in achieving the educational efficiency targets and performance demands set up by the system. The whole restructuring effort had the smell of a silent military coup; it was accomplished practically overnight and was quick, brutal, and done in a climate of secrecy with little public disclosure and insignificant media coverage.

Directly after the hurricane, it was obvious to those in power that new entrepreneurial leadership to implement the regime change was going to be needed immediately with "boots on the ground," to employ the "shock therapy." Enter Paul Pastorek, former president of the New Orleans state school and now the state superintendent of education. He was quickly ushered in to help run the new "reform" effort. Pastorek had come to believe, in concert with Hill and those who held the same conservative free-market ideology, that the problem with ailing school systems was their governance structure that hindered the freedom only found in the marketplace. Traditional schools, he argued, are run from the top down and this, according to Pastorek, is the problem. Or so he said:

The command and control structure can produce marginal improvements. But what's clear to me is that it can only get you so far. If you create a system where ini-

tiative and creativity is valued and rewarded, then you'll get change from the bottom up. If you create a system where people are told what to do and how to do it, then you will get change from the top down. We've been doing top down for many years in Louisiana. All we have is islands of excellence amidst a sea of failure. (Tough 2008)

A system that rewarded efficiency through incentives that encouraged meeting performance targets had to be established in order to create the new charterized network of schools. Pastorek needed assistance to swiftly carry out the lofty privatization ideals of Hill and the free-market reformers so he called his friend, the head of the Philadelphia public school system, Paul Vallas to come to work in New Orleans to help him manage the new reconstruction effort. Vallas, who was embroiled in a dispute over fiscal deficits in the Philadelphia school system he was running at the time, accepted the job to run the New Orleans Recovery School District, the government entity that controlled many of the public schools in New Orleans before and after the hurricane. Today, the two men run the New Orleans public school system, now an increasing patchwork of contract charter schools spurred on with public and, increasingly greater sums of, philanthropic funds. And, unlike the rhetoric they employ, they seem to run the system from the top down.

The educational system in New Orleans is now made up of interlocking organizational structures administering 86 public schools. There are basically three agencies: The Recovery School District, the Orleans Parish School Board, and state school board. The Recovery School District (RSD) had the power to take over any "failing" school in the city, which meant virtually every city school except for the selective-admission magnet schools the government agency Vallas was to run. The Orleans Parish School Board would have responsibility for select magnet schools, as well as the oversight and control of 5 schools; its oversight would be limited to 12 independently run charter schools. The Orleans Parish School Board was an elected group that, before the flood, controlled the entire educational system. Two charter schools that existed before Katrina are currently overseen by the state school board. There are now 33 charters under the supervision of the Recovery School District and there are 34 schools run directly by the RSD.

According to Tough's 2008 report in the *New York Times:*

Pastorek and Vallas are employing two parallel strategies for the Recovery School District. First, they're instituting a series of ambitious reforms in the district-run schools. They have expanded the school day by an hour and a half and are trying to extend the school year from 173 days to 193 days. This year teachers (who are working without a collective bargaining agreement) were each given a $3,000 raise. And in every school, principals and teachers are being trained in the "best practices" of the country's leading charter schools. (Ibid.)

In practice, Tough found that the new, charterized educational system in place in New Orleans continued to be vastly and inherently unequal and racially and class-stratified, with each network administered by different rules serving a different demographic and student population. So, for example, most of the Orleans Parish schools and charters construct the upper class of the new privatized network system; they are "selective" schools, admitting students on the basis of test scores and writing samples which, in some cases, give preferences to residents of the well-off neighborhood surrounding the school. As a consequence, they are the only public schools in the city with any significant population of middle-class white students. They are also the best performing schools when measured against standardized tests. The Lusher Charter School we looked at in chapter 4 would fall into this category; it is an elite educational enclave available only to a small, select group of students. On the other hand, the Recovery School District charters are *open enrollment schools,* which means they are required to accept students from anywhere in the city, regardless of academic performance. They have fewer white middle-class students with a lower socio-economic class of students; they service primarily the "sub prime" kids. In the Orleans Parish charters for example, 19 percent of students are deemed "talented and gifted," compared with just 1 percent of students in Recovery School District-run schools and charters. All around the country social inequality has been advancing for decades with more extreme consequences. The radical social engineers now at work in New Orleans with their ideological emphasis on freedom through economic markets is creating a new class-based school system masquerading under the auspices of reform; and it is being developed without hardly any oversight, public input, or public disclosure. As Tough cites:

> *The schools run directly by the Recovery district, as a result, are the schools of last resort, the schools required to admit every student: the kids who can't get into selective schools, the ones who get kicked out of charter schools, the ones who arrive in New Orleans in the middle of the school year, the ones whose parents couldn't get it together to find them anything better. (Ibid.)*

The New Orleans educational system, "free-market" rhetoric aside, is being designed by a few strong actors at a high cost to taxpayers. Vallas, for example, is well known nationally and in conservative circles as a "turnaround superintendent" for having "fixed" (led them toward privatization) the educational systems in Philadelphia and Chicago, while Pastorek served on the Louisiana State Board of Education from 1996 to 2004. Pastorek, also a partner with Adams & Reese law firm in Louisiana, took office in 2007 with a $227,249 yearly salary, a $48,000 annual housing allowance and a yearly car allowance of $24,000, bringing his total compensation package to $299,249. The state Board of Elementary and Secondary Education (BESE) voted 10-1 on February 21, 2008 to give Pastorek a 16.7 percent increase bringing his compensation to $349,249, or 32 percent higher than his predecessor (Maloney 2008).

Recovery School District Superintendent Paul Vallas draws a $238,386 yearly salary with a $4,000-per-year allowance for housing and travel (Ibid.). This, while teachers are expected to work ten-hour days, be available weekends and receive salaries lower than teachers in many, if not most, other states. High administrative salaries and low teacher costs are all part of the "reconstruction" efforts in the city of New Orleans.

Both men were responsible for implementing the new economic governance plan proposed by Hill, but it was not going to be easy, especially after the hurricane and they knew immediately they were going to need help from like-minded "reformers." So Vallas looked to Gary Robichaux, who only two weeks before Katrina hit the city, opened the first charter school in New Orleans associated with the Knowledge Is Power Program (KIPP). Quoting Tough:

> Last summer, Vallas persuaded Robichaux to leave his new KIPP school in the French Quarter to oversee the Recovery School District's elementary and middle schools and Robichaux is frank now about his intentions for his new job: he wants to apply as much of the KIPP model to the Recovery schools as he can. He has brought dozens of principals to visit the school he used to run, to observe the KIPP model up close, and this summer he conducted mandatory leadership training for the top administrators in each school.
>
> Although Vallas is a believer, in theory, in decentralization, he and Robichaux are providing a great deal of centralized support for the schools in the Recovery School District. They have created a "managed curriculum" for every school in the district to follow: detailed binders that each teacher can consult to see which skills and what knowledge they should be imparting each week and month in order to keep up with the state's standards. The RSD requires its schools to administer regular "benchmarking" assessments to each child in the district in each core subject, to monitor how much is being learned—and taught—in each classroom.
>
> But at the same time that Pastorek and Vallas and Robichaux are trying to improve the RSD's direct-run schools, they are also helping to create a competitive framework citywide that will most likely drive many of those schools out of existence. Part of the competition comes from a new voucher program, pushed through by Gov. Bobby Jindal, that will pay for nearly 900 New Orleans elementary-school students to attend private and parochial schools this year. But the more significant lever of change is charters—schools that get public money and are overseen by a government entity but are managed by an independent board. Pastorek, Vallas and Robichaux all say they expect charters to expand their presence in the district, to a point where 75 percent or even 90 percent of the city's schools are charters. (Tough 2008)

Implementing the new charterized contract schools in accordance with the "Diverse Providers Strategy," which implies that individual schools will be regulated only through their contracts and will operate as independent enterprises, is the primary goal of both Pastorek and Vallas. They are both intent on creating the "competitive framework" as part of the market-based, social engineering, and experimentation that they are conducting in New Orleans. They want to see the new "experiment" work so they can take it nationally, show it to other school districts in an effort to convince them that radical restructuring, favoring market principles, and reforms is the only way to organize education. Darran Simon, writing for the *Times-Picayune* reported in 2008:

> The Recovery School District is forging ahead with long-range plans to give charter status—and thus more independence—to many of the schools it still operates in New Orleans.
>
> As the first step, it plans to convert four low-performing schools to charters next year, ending the current even split between 33 charters and 33 non-charter schools, or those that the district operates directly. One of the goals is providing an infusion of help to schools that need it the most.
>
> The plan, backed by state Superintendent of Education, Paul Pastorek, reflects a desire by state education officials to charter most New Orleans schools operated by the Recovery District, which took over failing schools in New Orleans in 2005. (Simon 2008)

Tough goes further, exposing with particularity some aspects of the "plan":

> Their evolving plan would involve both the highest- and the lowest-performing schools in the Recovery School District becoming charters, though in different ways. Principals at high-performing Recovery District schools will be encouraged to apply for a charter that would let them run their schools independently—essentially, to "graduate" out of the control of the district. On the other end of the performance scale, schools that consistently fall short of state standards, even after all of the training and support that Vallas can muster, will be seized by the RSD, which will either hand the school over to a new or existing charter-school provider or shut it down and replace it with a new charter school. Failing charter schools will also be taken over or closed down, by having their charters revoked or transferred to another charter provider. (Tough 2008)

Under this plan, charter providers will be for-profit ventures. When they are not, such as the case with nonprofit charter school providers or EMOs, they will work to create an infrastructure that can one day easily be handed over to new, for-profit EMOs and private interest concerns, at little or no cost to them. In this case, the infrastructure involves developing a new model for institutionalized control of schools by private forces, as opposed to public control. This plan calls to create the economic conditions and institutions whereby the New Orleans educational system becomes tethered to a new educational model—publicly financed, privately run contracted charter schools with no messy teachers unions, no burdensome regulations and oversight and more importantly—no collective bargaining for teachers.

SOCIAL ENGINEERING FROM SCRATCH

In order to put the "Diverse Providers Strategy" in place, the 4,700 plus member teachers' union was dissolved and its teachers fired, almost overnight, directly after the hurricane. In the minds of the new reformers, teacher unions and collective bargaining would get in the way of implementing the new educational design for the city. Teacher unions impose the need for bargaining over shares of "profit," require accountability measures, public oversight, transparency, and public disclosure. Most disturbing to pro-market reformers, is that they operate to create a social contract with school management by encouraging active participation in decision making. Teacher unions stand for everything free-market fundamentalists do not.

In an article entitled, "Charter Schools' Big Experiment New Orleans's Post-Katrina Test May Offer Lessons for Ailing Systems," that appeared in the *Washington Post* in June of 2008, Jay Mathews a long-time follower of the charter school "experiment" in New Orleans, stated the new autocratic management plan quite succinctly:

> *For these new schools with taxpayer funding and independent management, old rules and habits are out. No more standard hours, seniority, union contracts, shared curriculum or common textbooks. In a crowd of newcomers—critics call them opportunists—seeking to lift standards and achievement. They compete for space, steal each other's top teachers and wonder how it is all going to work. (Mathews 2008)*

Mathews was right, this was to be a teachable moment for teachers as well as students and the public. For immediately after the hurricane, teachers who once held steady jobs, pension plans, health care benefits, paid vacations, sick leave, collective bargaining rights, collaborative curriculum construction with other teachers, and a modicum of decision-making power over the day-to-day operations of the public schools were no longer even players in the game. Their jobs, their livelihoods, and their positions had vanished overnight. Hill's plan was on its way to fruition—decisions now would be made in accordance with the radical autocratic restructuring of the New Orleans school system mired in collapse and struggling in the midst of disaster. There existed little public input in regards to the new plan. There were few public hearings regarding any of these decisions, and fewer opportunities in the future for such democratic policymaking. With the teachers union gone and the teachers with it, the system seemed to be now run by a secret parliament made up of business interests, lobbyists, think tank ideologues, conservative politicians, philanthropists, and media pundits rushing to sell the idea of a new "reconstructed" school system to a battered New Orleans public and a shaken nation.

Along with the firings of all the teachers, as author Kenneth Saltman writes in his book, *Capitalizing on Disaster: Taking and Breaking Public Schools:*

> *traditional modes of public administration and oversight, damaged though they were in New Orleans and elsewhere, have been jettisoned as a result of the voucher and charter schemes where corporate models dominate all aspects of school administration and process, resulting in authoritarian forms of management that, in addition to other things, have promoted "shoddy hiring practices" and intensified a pre-existing trend of putting squeezes on teachers to do "more with less." (Saltman 2007)*

Indeed, from the point of view of the new social engineers, it seems that one of the reasons that New Orleans offers promising opportunities for deeply institutionalized market-based reforms is precisely because there is little shared power or decision making, scant public oversight, and thus little need for public disclosure. Vallas is frank and a bit arrogant when he speaks of his new, autocratic power:

> *No one tells me how long my school day should be or my school year should be. Nobody tells me who to hire or who not to hire. I can hire the most talented people. I can promote people based on merit and performance. I can dismiss people if they are chronically non-attending or if they're simply not performing. (Tough 2008)*

Although this new control model appears on the surface to run counter to Paul Pastorek's enthusiastic support of a new model for school governance that avoids the top-down command style, Pastorek is counting on the combined components of nonprofit human-capital pipelines being set up by KIPP and others along with the philanthropic seed money of the Gates Foundation and Walton Foundation to make it much easier, in the coming years for him to accomplish the complete overhaul of the old system in favor of new contract charterized school system of made up of educational retail franchises.

According to Tough:

> *Each year he (Pastorek) hopes to have a handful of new schools ready to open, each one led by a Gates-financed, fully incubated, KIPP-marinated principal—the kind of academic superheroes who before the storm just didn't come to work in New Orleans in big numbers. Inevitably, he'll make space for them. And before long, that annual handful will add up. In a city like New York, with its 1,400 public schools, new-school innovations can seem like pebbles tossed into the ocean. But in a city with fewer than 100 schools, 5 or 6 new schools a year will have a big impact. (Ibid.)*

But who would pay for all the restructuring that was necessary for the free-market reformers eager to get their hands on the working machinery and levers of education in New Orleans? The answer was to be found in the elite philanthropic community and the closely knit group of financiers, entrepreneurs, and business interests that descended on the city directly after the tragedy. With shrinking revenues and cash-strapped counties and municipalities in fiscal agony, philanthropic charitable giving was, and is, essential to fund the thorough takeover of the system and the creation of the ideological framework and structure concocted by Hill and others. Added to this was federal government monies doled out after the hurricane, and financial backing by other entrepreneurs eager to get in the business of schools.

In 2007, Patrik Jonsson, writing an in-depth investigative piece on New Orleans and the rebuilding of the city for the *Christian Science Monitor,* commented on the enormous sums of private monies that were flowing into the city directly after the hurricane:

> *Billions of federal dollars have been allotted or spent in New Orleans since hurricane Katrina, so it may come as a surprise that the first public works project in the city's long-term recovery—the Rosa Keller Library in the middle-class Broadmoor neighborhood—was not paid for by American taxpayers but by the Carnegie Foundation in New York.*
>
> *Government money is still trickling through the pipeline: On Monday, Louisiana recovery officials approved $117 million for the first post-Katrina community development grants. But with the long wait for cash, private foundations, wealthy individuals, and philanthropies have stepped in, playing a bigger role in the city's rebuilding than ever expected.*
>
> *"The monies for rebuilding are coming first from private sources . . . and that is definitely what is leading the recovery effort," says Doug Ahlers, a fellow at the Kennedy School of Government at Harvard. "Government funding is slow to arrive and is . . . not playing a leadership role." (Jonsson 2007)*

As we noted in the discussion of New Orleans in chapter 3, much of the private and philanthropic funds were targeted at the New Orleans public school system to both dismantle the existing system and to be used as a fulcrum to leverage the building of the new, privatized contract charter system. Hill had been advocating philanthropic monies as a fulcrum of change for years. In fact, Tough notes in his piece that Hill even argued against giving any philanthropic funds to the old system of education in New Orleans after the hurricane—let it die of its own accord, seemed to be the prevalent philosophy.

To aid and abet the new radical restructuring of the New Orleans public schools, Pastorek and Vallas are counting on a powerful alliance of nonprofits supported by philanthropic money from the likes of The Bill and Melinda Gates Foundation, The Walton Foundation, and others. They want to use the funds they receive from these sources to recruit and train new charter school "operators" and to help provide them the support and the personnel they need to set up and run consistently high-quality charter schools with what they like to call "best practices." The role of the emerging alliance between nonprofit EMOs in tandem with the philanthropic funds is not only to cement the seed money needed for future charter start-ups, but also to function as a sort of Chamber of Commerce for the burgeoning charter school movement and growing network of increasingly private providers. The public school system, with the help of the new philanthropists, would now serve the private sector.

Yet according to proclamations in the media at the time, national charter school leaders claimed they had not planned a massive takeover of the public school district after Katrina. They said all they simply wanted to do was just help out. According to Jeanne Allen, president of the pro-charter Center for Education Reform, when speaking of New Orleans:

> *Charter educators and friends took games and books and organized dozens of small classrooms while the national government scratched its head over what to do. (Mathews 2008)*

The true story was to be entirely different. To begin with, the haste within which the dismantling of New Orleans public educational system was accomplished was breathtaking. According to Jay Matthews, writer for the *Washington Post* and a reporter who has covered much that has gone on in the New Orleans public education system since Katrina, radical educational reforms such as the ones proposed and eventually adopted in New Orleans were already in play in other parts of the nation. He writes of the difference in New Orleans:

> *Some cities are moving in this direction, but none has ever moved so far, so fast. Three in every 10 D.C. public school students are in charters, a much larger percentage than in most cities. The New Orleans charter school penetration rate is much greater: 53 percent of the post-Katrina enrollment of 33,200 students, according to school officials. Before the hurricane, charters had about 2 percent of the city's 67,000 public students. (Ibid.)*

New Orleans promised to be different. Philanthropic money, ideological high-spiritedness, NCLB, millions in federal funds for the new plan and the redefinition of charter school "providers" to include EMOs and independent operators, all worked in tandem after the disaster to make up the elements of a perfect storm. This translated into new liaisons and alliances necessary to carry out the "reconstruction" of the system, meaning new roles for teachers and new teachers with newly designed roles. As Tough writes in the *New York Times*:

> *At the center of this alliance is a well-financed organization called New Schools for New Orleans, run by a former KIPP executive and a former Teach for America administrator. This month, five schools incubated at New Schools for New Orleans will*

open their doors, including Miller-McCoy; next year there will most likely be four more. The New Orleans office of New Leaders for New Schools, meanwhile, will be training a new group of principals each year; five of the six members of this year's "class" are going into positions leading charters. Teach for America's regional operation in Greater New Orleans is growing quickly; its incoming class is the second-largest one in the country after New York City's. Each year, the group plans to send 50 or more teachers into charters in the Recovery district, where they will serve as a well-educated and highly motivated, if inexperienced, labor force for the start-ups. (At the same time, Teach for America is sending 75 teachers this year into direct-run Recovery schools, where it perceives a greater need.) Finally, a group called teach NOLA recruited about 100 new teachers this year, mostly career-changing professionals, and three-quarters of them will work in charters. (Tough 2008)

Training new teachers, instead of employing old ones, is part of an effort to avoid old practices by old teachers, instruct the new teachers in the "best practices" and the "managed curriculum" the new schools now offered, and assure that no former pro-union teacher be included in the new mix. Teachers would be given detailed binders that included which skills and what knowledge they would be imparting each week and month in order to keep up with the state's standards. This was the new accountability system: teachers would still "teach to the test" but under new guidelines, with new employers and laboring within a newly concocted system. Teachers were now to be considered as dispensaries of narrow facts to be tested, scored and monitored to assure the system was achieving the targeted outcomes.

The graduating class of Teach for America is usually young and inexperienced, with little historical or contemporary knowledge of the workings of an educational teacher's union. This is not their fault, nor surprising, for coverage of labor struggles are seldom found in the corporate media; when they are, unions and their members are often depicted as villains. In the United States in 1950, there were several hundred full-time labor reporters and editors at daily newspapers; fifty years later, there were barely any. Business news would be the rage of the day and it continues unabated (Foster et al. 2009). This is all fortuitous for the new reconstructionists, for the architects of the new school privatization restructuring effort are counting on a non-unionized workforce to make the whole plan work.

Let us take a cursory look at a study done by charter school researcher, Amy Wells, conducted in 2001. Wells studied eight unionized conversion charter schools in California and found that all but one charter school maintained their union affiliations. However, during the course of her study she also was able to discern that none of the start-up charter schools, those not converted, became unionized. Some teachers told her that new teachers should have similar benefits as those teachers in unions. But she also found that in one charter school in California, the Imperial Way Charter School, teachers opted out of the union bargaining unit when the union and sponsoring district required that the charter begin paying into the teachers' retirement fund. The principal or "CEO" of the school refused to do this and thus ended the relationship between union and charter. When the decision was made to abandon the bargaining unit, Wells found that many veteran teachers, although they professed a deep commitment to the charter school, simply quit. They were not ready to abandon the rights accorded to teachers in unions. As we will see, they are not alone (Wells 2002).

In the same study, Wells interviewed teachers in the new, start-up charter schools, many who had never been members of a teachers union. She found that teachers were either ambivalent about the union or they strongly rejected them. Many teachers were so ill-informed that they did not even know if they were members of a union, nor did they seem to care. Other teachers perceived that the union represented a roadblock to reform. These teachers identified their class interests with the management of the school, not with the workers, staff, and unions. According to one of the younger teachers at the Academic Charter School in California:

> *I don't see the (the union) as a need here, and if I ever got to the point where I saw it as a need, I probably wouldn't be here. (Ibid.)*

Wells also found that the administrators at the Academic Charter School seemed to create an anti-union environment which set an intimidating (or at least un-inviting) tone, for the young teachers who might be thinking of unionizing:

> *I mean in some districts you have a union for everything. It's like, how many contracts do you have before nobody is able to operate other than like in this square box?* (Ibid.)

Finally, at the Shoreline Charter School in California, Wells found that many teachers not only rejected representation by the union but in the words of one teacher she interviewed:

> *The community almost was unanimously opposed to (any) union activities (in the charter school) at all.* (Ibid.)

Wells discovered in her study and interviews that the founders of Shoreline had made significant efforts to head off any unionization by ensuring they offered salaries equivalent to the district-wide salaries, as well as the opportunity to receive performance bonuses and economic incentives. For many teachers, this bought off the need for any unionization. Wells again is salient here when talking about teaching staff at the charter schools she examined:

> *Yet younger teachers or those who were new to the profession generally lacked a vested interest in the union and any understanding of the benefits to be derived from union membership. These teachers were much more likely to be working in start-up*

charter schools and to express a desire to distance themselves from the status quo. Thus, for the most part, teacher's decisions about unions followed the lines of their status as working in either start-up or conversion charter schools. (Ibid.)

The non unionized, new graduates of the Teach for America program slated for New Orleans and the new charter start-ups have become the "reserve labor" force necessary to implement the takeover of New Orleans public schools. They are generally young, eager, innovative, and counted on to offer no resistance to the decision making plans of the new school czars. Working hand-in-hand with the KIPP organization the new teachers will be taught the "best practices" of KIPP. This, in part, will mean that they will be required to work far more than eight hours per day, for less pay, as well as more days per year (as mentioned earlier, the New Orlean's school year has been increased by 20 days) and as we saw when we looked at KIPP in our last chapter, they will now need to sign commitment forms, forcing them to be available on weekends and basically "on-call"; all of this without the benefits and working conditions associated with former unionized teachers—benefits such as health care, an eight-hour day, vacation pay, collective bargaining rights, grievance procedures, curriculum development, and power sharing in the affairs of the schools within which they work. This new generation of teachers that are currently working and will be working in the New Orleans' reconstructed educational system, are evidently expected to be part of the "new philanthropy" promoted by the architectures of the reforms, donating sixty or more hours per week of their lives for the benefit of the "kids." As teachers, it seems they are being asked to think of themselves as philanthropists, not as professional teachers with lives outside of the classroom and families to support. This is a very different message than the teacher's unions give teachers when they ask them to think of themselves as working professionals and to take pride and ownership in their profession. Even entrepreneur, Steve Wilson saw problems early on with the KIPP business plan. Commenting on KIPP's model in his book, Wilson brings up the point that the demands made on teachers and staff could be unsustainable as they are currently designed:

The first three replication schools posted strong gains on spring 2002 tests, and the KIPP brand remains strong. But the organization faces challenges. The extraordinary commitment KIPP demands of its school leaders and staff may not be sustainable. To sustain quality and preserve its brand, KIPP National may be forced to parachute in to rescue struggling schools. Can enough high quality fellows be identified to meet KIPP's ambitious agenda for expansion? If launching and supporting many small schools proves more costly than anticipated, will KIPP's backers be willing to foot the bill? (Wilson 2006)

The answer to Wilson's question was to be found in February 2009 when KIPP teachers in the South Bronx of New York decided it was about time they started a teachers' union to get some control over their working lives and the decision making at their schools, and this is precisely what they did.

UNIONIZING KIPP

In January of 2009 16 of the 20 teachers at KIPP AMP (Always Mentally Prepared) Charter School in Crown Heights Brooklyn, New York, informed their co-principals that they were organizing themselves into a union and seeking official recognition for their efforts from the Public Employees Relation Board in New York. The teachers signed a "card" in favor of a union at the school. Such a "card check" majority is all that's required under New York State law for public employees to unionize; some Democrats in Congress support passage of the Employee Free Choice Act (EFCA), which would make card-check, as opposed to the current system of secret-ballot elections, the law of the land for unionizing workplaces. In the interim, each state has their own legislation regarding bargaining unit formation and in New York only a majority of teachers are needed to sign union authorization cards in order to be identified as a bargaining unit.

In a letter delivered to co-principals Jeff Li and Melissa Perry the teachers said that they had decided to unionize in order to secure "teacher voices" and respect for the work of teachers in their school. They wanted:

> *"to ensure that the [KIPP] motto of "team and family" is realized in the form of mutual respect and validation for the work that is done [by teachers] each day."* (Casey, under "KIPP Teachers Organize")

KIPP AMP teachers also said they believe that the high staff turnover at the school had harmed their efforts to build a positive and consistent school culture for their students. According to teacher Luisa Bonifacio:

> *There is a need to make the teacher position more sustainable so that teachers don't burn out, but are able to make a long-term commitment to the students and the school.* (Ibid.)

KIPP AMP teacher Leila Chakravarty made a powerful argument that organizing a union is necessary for the well-being of the school, teachers, and students. The organizing effort, she said, was to:

> *"build a sustainable community in our school" and address the problem of teacher turnover. Because as KIPP teachers we are so invested in our kids and form such close bonds with them, because we are always available to our students by telephone and email and spend ten hours every day with them, it is so vital and important that they feel they can count on us, and we will continue to be there. When they*

become close to a teacher who is gone in three months because she has burnt out, it undermines the trust we are working so hard to build. (Ibid.)

Another teacher noted, in the *New York City Journal*:

It's a matter of sustainability for teachers. There's a heavy workload, and people have to balance their lives with their work. (Winters 2008)

The teachers went on to justify their decision to unionize:

Teachers and professionals must have a voice in the creation and implementation of school policy. We must have our concerns as professionals recognized and addressed. We must be evaluated in a clear and transparent manner and given support when we need it. We must feel secure in our employment so that concerns as well as ideas can be voiced in a trusting environment. (Ibid.)

Initially, KIPP's administration seemed to be caught off-guard. Ky Adderley, KIPP AMP's founding principal, met with seven of the teachers and told them that he was disappointed. Ms. Chakravarty stated:

He said he had founded the school as a nonunion school and he had done so for a reason and that he was not pleased. Forming a union, the teachers recalled Mr. Adderley saying, would mean staffing decisions would be out of his control, suggesting that state officials who approved the charter would be able to fire people at any time. (Ibid.)

However, American Federation of Teachers (AFT) president Randi Weingarten, concurred with the teacher's decision to join a union, commenting:

We know that teacher turnover is a major concern across the charter school movement. The unionization of KIPP's New York City schools provides a unique opportunity to create a model of sustainable teacher recruitment, development and retention. (Casey, under "KIPP Teachers Organize")

From a cursory glance at the teachers' comments it seems that the unsustainable "KIPP" educational model that Steve Wilson warned about years earlier was now beginning to fray. Saddled with long hours (often ten-hour days), little control over the day-to-day operations or decisions made at the school, a lack of a collective voice as professionals, and a high turnover of teachers due to "burnout," the 20 teachers at the Brooklyn KIPP were prompted by their daily working lives to sign authorization cards with the United Federation of Teachers (UFT) seeking certification. The support for the union organizing effort by KIPP teachers was shown by the supermajority of teachers who signed the authorization cards, 16 out of 20, a number well beyond the majority threshold necessary to certify the union. And they did not sign in isolation; they had the support of the majority of parents and families at the school.

What the KIPP teachers are demanding is not a traditional public school collective bargaining agreement, but one that is more in line with the EMO, Green Dot's collective bargaining agreements, another nonprofit EMO that has unionized employees. This is a basic contract that is tenureless (competency is based on performance reviews) that we will look at later in this chapter. However, under the tenureless contract sought by the teachers, administrators would have to prove "just cause" before firing a teacher as opposed to hiring and firing "at will" which had been the case. They are also demanding that the contract include discipline measures for teachers that would follow a graduated scale, including strategies to help struggling teachers.

But the KIPP teachers did not stop there. The union also announced in January of 2009 that teachers at a second KIPP charter school, KIPP Infinity, also wanted to enter into collective bargaining talks with KIPP. KIPP Infinity's teachers were already represented by the union in an agreement that guaranteed them health insurance and other benefits, but they now wanted to negotiate a job contract, i.e. a tenureless, collective bargaining agreement with 'just cause' firing provisions just like the Brooklyn KIPP.

The two organizing movements by the KIPP teachers represent an enormous victory for the UFT, which has been campaigning to bring charter school teachers into its union for at least the last year. If other charter school teachers in New York City follow suit, the unionization effort would also mark a significant turning point for the charter school movement, whose leaders—the EMOs and independent providers—scorned unions in their efforts to seize control of schools and implement their own new rules and regulations. In this particular case, the unionization of the teachers also means that since the original KIPP Academy Charter School is a conversion charter school with UFT representation, educators at three of the four KIPP schools in New York City will now also be members of the UFT. This is a staggering blow for the operators and providers of the charter schools for it means they must now engage in power sharing and negotiate salaries and benefits with teachers.

Under New York state law, if the majority of a charter school's teachers sign a petition supporting the union, as 16 of KIPP AMP's 20 teachers did, management has 30 days to recognize the union or the matter goes to arbitration with the state. Upon hearing the news Weingarten immediately reached out to co-founder of KIPP, David Levin, informing him of the developments at the school and asking for his cooperation with an understanding that the teachers wished to work with the KIPP "family" to assure a smooth union representation process and at the same time she informed him of the union's intention to enter into collective bargaining at the KIPP Infinity Charter School where the teachers are also members of the UFT. At the time, according to written reports, David Levin indicated he was open to working with the union.

KIPP MANAGEMENT FIGHTS BACK

Perhaps it was at the urging of his conservative colleagues or other charter schools and their providers who feared unionization, or maybe it was the various philanthropists who finance KIPP, but within one month of Levin announcing his openness to unionizing, the UFT was forced to complain to the state board that KIPP was not cooperating, not working to recognize the new union, and stifling and blocking the teachers' ability to organize. David Levin and KIPP was not willing to give up without a fight. Randi Weingarten, whose union represents teachers at more than 70 charter schools nationwide, suspects there was pressure on Levin from financial backers. KIPP presently has 66 charter schools in 19 states, with plans for more. A union precedent for their other schools would not be embraced. Weingarten expressed disappointment with KIPP and David Levin in a *New York Times* article:

> *We had talked in the abstract about doing great things together, about creating a laboratory for reform with teacher support. So I am deeply disappointed by these actions.* (Medina 2009)

The announcement that KIPP teachers were unionizing was to have other side effects as well. According to the *Times* article, teachers spoke of an environment at KIPP that had grown increasingly cold with suspicion, intimidation, and fear since the announcement of the union drive. Levin's initial offer to work with the union appeared to have deliquesced into anger and hostility. Covering the story for the *New York Times* when the initial controversy reared its head, reporter Jennifer Medina wrote:

> *. . . . several teachers said in interviews, the atmosphere at the school has grown increasingly tense, with administrators making veiled threats about the effect of creating a union. E-mail and text messages that would usually be returned at all hours have gone unanswered. And late last month, teachers said they were told by their students, school administrators pulled students into a private meeting and asked them to critique their teachers.* (Ibid.)

The teachers claimed the problem was even worse than reported to the public at the time. Complaints filed by the UFT with the Public Employees Relation Board accused human resource officials at the KIPP schools of spooking teachers, students and their parents by threatening that unionization might cause

KIPP to lose its affiliation with the whole KIPP network. The complaint filed with the board also alleges that the Brooklyn KIPP's AMA school's, founding principal, Ky Adderley, harassed teachers by sitting in the hallway of the school every day to monitor them and coming to a staff meeting to encourage teachers to give up their organizing drive. All and all the atmosphere painted in the complaints is one of a bone-chilling environment ratcheted up with threats and harassment to discourage teachers from organizing a union. In the *New York Times* article, two members of the KIPP AMA union organizing committee even quote a comment made by Adderley:

> *Have you ever gone sky diving? No? Its (sic) fun to watch the people's faces after they jump, they think they're flying but their (sic) really just falling.* (Ibid.)

Teachers go on to allege that:

> *Then during the last week in January, while teachers were at a faculty meeting, the principals met with seventh- and eighth-grade students alone, a move the teachers said was unprecedented. Several students told their teachers that they had been encouraged to talk about "negative feelings and interactions" with them, those teachers said.*
>
> *Mr. Adderley distributed notes on the meeting with the subject line "7th and 8th Grade feedback on Testing Environment." The comments included "Teachers are very disrespectful. They always tell us sarcasm and mean words and expect us to have respect for them," and "We need more reason to come to school, the classes are boring and there's nothing to do. I miss how it used to be," according to the memo.* (Ibid.)

If all of this is true, it is a direct violation of the New York "Taylor Act," which prohibits employers from such actions. KIPP management and their leaders have traditionally touted their freedom from teachers unions as a strength owed to the fact that it allows them to hire and fire teachers as they please. Whether the KIPP AMP teachers will force the KIPP "family" to step away from that position is up to the state labor relations board, which has to decide whether to grant their request to be represented by the UFT, a decision pending as of this writing.

Apparently, the openess promised by co-founder of KIPP, David Levin, promised to Randi Weingarten when the organizing effort began is no more. KIPP is now arguing that the union will hurt the teachers themselves. According to a complaint filed with the state relations board, by the KIPP teachers, Levin is accused of saying that if they organized they would "lose their staff's pensions, maternity leave, retirement etc. . . . all that goes away. All that is potentially in jeopardy" (Greene 2009).

Leila Chakravarty, a seventh-grade math teacher who helped collect signatures to form the KIPP teachers union noted:

The general tenor has been of increased distance, and administrators felt more in-accessible than they have ever been. (Medina 2009)

This is no surprise to anyone familiar with union organizing drives. In New York, 18 of the state's 115 charter schools are unionized, including two in Brooklyn operated by the teachers' union. There is no doubt that what is happening with the unionization effort at KIPP AMP is being closely watched nationally, especially by conservative market reformers who loathe unions and are now beginning to see their educational dreams targeted for organizing efforts by teachers. As Medina underscores in her article in the *Times*:

In the beginning, teachers' unions initially ignored charter schools or viewed them as the enemy, but as the charters grew in size and influence, the unions' feelings warmed somewhat. Green Dot, a Los Angeles-based charter network, has unions at each of its schools, including one that opened with the teachers' union's cooperation last fall in the Bronx. (Ibid.)

This situation has not been taken well by the conservative watchdogs and pundits for the privatized charter movement. Matthew Ladner's comments were typical of the conservative backlash against KIPP's teacher organizing efforts. Commenting on the conservative blog by Jay P. Greene, a long time conservative ideologue and proponent of complete school privatization, Ladner, now with the Manhattan Institute and formerly with the Goldwater Institute, commented:

The whole idea of running a KIPP academy along with a thousand page union contract is absurd. Half-days on Saturday? Not on your life. On call to help with homework? Are you kidding? KIPP has earned many donors, but can they afford a rubber room? Need to change a light bulb in your classroom? Page 844, paragraph 5 clearly states that you must call a union electrician. You kids sit quietly with your heads down in the dark until he arrives. It will be any day now.

KIPP has a methodology and a hard earned brand to protect, and there are plenty of other kids in other states to help. If Congress is misguided enough to pass a national card check, it will be up to individual states to ban the practice. Those that do, may find themselves rewarded by the opening of some very high quality schools. (Greene)

Marcus Winters, a writer for the *New York City Journal*, noted that if the teachers at KIPP became unionized, KIPP and other charter schools would collectively negotiate their own labor agreements. But he went on to argue that once the union succeeds, it would push charter schools toward the public agreements with teacher unions. The current nine to ten hour workdays and a longer work year would not survive many contract renegotiations, according to Winters. He claimed that it's equally unlikely that KIPP would retain its ability to fire ineffective teachers without having to go through what he called "an overly burdensome process." And like his ideological counterparts who are fiercely against unions of any kind, he quickly added:

> *If KIPP and other charter schools choose to unionize, they'll very probably come to resemble the failing urban public schools to which they currently provide such a hopeful alternative.* (Winters)

Winters went on to express his fondness for KIPP:

> *KIPP owes much of its success to the high standards it sets for both students and teachers. KIPP schools look past their students' backgrounds and simply demand that they do the work necessary for college admission. Teaching in a KIPP school entails a rigorous commitment, as the organization's Web site describes: "Teachers typically work a nine-hour work day during the week, half days on selected Saturdays, and three weeks in the summer. They also are available via cell phone for homework help in the evening." Compare that to the norm in public schools. For example, the New York City teachers' union contract stipulates: "The school day for teachers serving in the schools shall be six hours and 20 minutes." Like other such contracts across the country, it sets out the exact number of days per year that a teacher can be required to work and exactly which duties he or she can be asked to perform. Giving out cell-phone numbers to students is not among them. Teachers are well aware of the extra time and effort KIPP requires. Most KIPP students enter the classroom performing at low proficiency; their parents often lack the ability to help them with schoolwork. Teachers get compensated for these extra educational burdens, and usually make 15 to 20 percent more in salary than teachers in the surrounding school district. But the tougher demands in KIPP schools have reportedly led to high turnover rates. Some teachers burn out and leave; others that can't cut it are let go.* (Ibid.)

The intimidation efforts by KIPP management and the noticeable outcry from the conservative ideologues, conservative writers, privatization forces and philanthropic community just might have worked, because in March 2009, just weeks after the notification to KIPP of the teachers' desire to unionize, teachers at two other New York City KIPP charter schools requested, in petitions signed by every single teacher at the schools, that the state labor officials sever their ties from the city teachers union—in other words, that the union be decertified. The move is considered a powerful response to the organizing efforts by teachers at Brooklyn, KIPP AMP and puts out a formidable message to other charter schools and their teachers who wish to organize.

Teachers of Two KIPP Schools Speak Out

On Wednesday, March 18, 2009, the teaching staffs of KIPP Academy Charter School in the Bronx, New York, and KIPP Infinity Charter School in Manhattan, submitted to the Public Employment Relations Board (PERB) official petitions for decertifica-tion of the United Federation of Teachers (UFT) as our certified negotiating repre-

sentative. These petitions were signed and supported by every staff member at each school.

It is with great consideration that we take this next step in the life of our schools. We, the undersigned teaching staffs of KIPP Academy and KIPP: Infinity, feel the success we have attained to this point in our schools is largely because of the close relationship between all those interested in our students' well-being, from students to families to school staff. While we have nominally been unionized, the collective bargaining agreement has never been a prominent factor in deciding what is best for our students, our team, and our family. Rather, we solve problems using communication among staff members and working collaboratively with administration to best serve the needs of our students and families. We have found that this method of problem solving has fit our situations well, and we plan to continue following this model of open, positive communication among students, families, and staff in the future.

In recent months, the UFT has made clear its desire to play a more active part in the day-to-day operations of our schools. Two examples illustrate this point. In January, the UFT sent a letter to the KIPP: Infinity Board of Directors with the goal of beginning collective bargaining on teachers' behalf; the UFT neither consulted nor informed the staff of this request. In addition, a union-initiated grievance has been filed against KIPP Academy without solicitation or support of staff. It is our belief that the active presence of an external negotiating representative could compromise the strong environment of communication and collaboration that is integral to the success of our schools.

We recognize and respect the historical value of labor unions to protect the rights of workers and ensure quality working conditions, and our decision to decertify the union as our negotiating representative is not a reflection of our feelings either toward unions as a whole, or toward the UFT in particular. We also certainly understand the vital role labor unions have played, and continue to play, in supporting the interests of workers and facilitating communication between labor and management.

With that said, we do not believe that one size fits all. We firmly believe that the best way to move forward is to continue with what has made our schools great: parents, staff, and administration working cooperatively to teach character and academics in order to prepare our students for high school, college, and the world beyond. We look forward to continuing to serve the students and families of New York City to the very best of our ability.

Sincerely,

KIPP Academy Staff
KIPP Infinity Staff

TEACHER SUPPORT FOR UNIONS

The KIPP schools and their administrators and financial backers in New Orleans, with their "managed curriculums" and their "best practices" were no doubt looking at the union effort in New York with some consternation and hand-wringing. So were other charter school providers and EMOs, especially Washington D.C. where three out of every ten schools are charters and Chancellor Rhee has stated she wants a corporate model for the school system. The last thing Vallas, Pastorek, the philanthropists, and the business community want in New Orleans is the reemergence of teachers unions. But is teacher union organizing in New Orleans inevitable? With the long hours and dedicated commitment on the part of KIPP staff, teachers say they want a formal way to influence how schools are managed, how curricular concerns are dealt with, and how professional development is maintained. They are not alone.

In an *Education Sector Report,* put out in May 2008 by The Joyce Foundation, entitled "Waiting to be Won Over: Teachers Speak on the Profession, Unions, and Reform," Ann Duffett, Steve Farkas, Andrew J. Rotherham, and Elena Silva, authors of the report, surveyed 1,010 K-12 teachers about their views on the teaching profession, teachers unions, and a host of reforms aimed at improving teacher quality.

> *The survey revealed that it is hard to place teachers definitively in any one camp even though advocates on all sides of various issues do just that. As a whole, teachers today are what political analysts might describe as "in play" and waiting to be won over by one side or another. Despite frustrations with schools, school districts, their unions, and a number of aspects of the job in general, teachers are not sold on any one reform agenda. They want change but are a skeptical audience. For instance, nearly half of teachers surveyed say that they personally know a teacher who is ineffective and should not be in the classroom. But, although teachers want something done about low-performing colleagues, they are leery of proposals to substantially change how teachers can be dismissed.* (Duffett et al. 2008)

The report also found that:

> *Teachers see problems with their unions as well. For example, many say that the union sometimes fights to protect teachers who really should be out of the classroom. But teachers still see the union as essential, and they value the union's traditional role in safeguarding their jobs. New teachers are more likely today than they were in 2003 to call unions "absolutely essential." And many teachers would like to see their unions explore some new activities, especially some of the ideas associated with the "new unionism" agenda, and take the greater role in reform, but not if that comes at the expense of the union's core mission.* (Ibid.)

This should be enough for proprivatization charter supporters and their political and government allies to quake in their boots. Instead of the decades-long fighting the teacher unions eradicating their effectiveness, the report noted the contrary was true. An environment of distrust between administration and staff was the norm not an aberration, as the majority of the teachers reported in the survey. They did not trust the administrators of the schools they worked at nor did they think they had the best interests of teachers in mind. They cited weak evaluations, few rewards and lots of rules when they were surveyed. The report also noted:

> *Educators and policymakers frequently discuss ways to attract and retain high-quality teachers. One idea getting attention these days is to swap some of the benefits teachers enjoy later in their careers for more money in the early years. The survey finds teachers are protective of their pensions and the vast majority of teachers overall do not like the idea of raising starting salaries in exchange for fewer retirement benefits. But many teachers are open to other new ways of attracting and keeping good teachers. Generally speaking, teachers appear to be considerably more interested in recruitment and retention strategies that would improve the flexibility and conditions of their work. For example, most support making it easier to leave and return to the profession without losing benefits. A suburban teacher from California wrote, "As a mom of two kids under five, I'd like to see it more feasible to take a few years off and be able to go back without retirement being so negatively affected." And an overwhelming majority supports giving teachers more time for class planning and preparation. While this measure would come with a large price tag for public schools, it is notable that the measure teachers are most likely to favor does not come with any monetary gain for individual teachers. (Ibid.)*

CIVITAS SCHOOLS AND UNION ORGANIZING

KIPP teacher union organizing is only the tip of the iceberg. In Chicago, an overwhelming majority of teachers at three charter schools, joined by parents and community leaders, filed authorization cards April 3, 2009 with the Illinois Educational Labor Relations Board to be recognized as a bargaining unit. The teachers seek immediate recognition of their collective bargaining unit and for a commitment by school administrators to bargain in good faith and settle a contract with the newly recognized union immediately.

The teachers in question work at three of the Civitas Schools that are part of the Chicago International Charter Schools (CICS) under a charter held by the Chicago Charter School Foundation. Civitas Schools is a for-profit EMO and fully owned subsidiary of the charter holder, the Chicago Charter School Foundation. More than 1,500 students attend the three CICS campuses. If recognized as a union, teachers at the for-profit operated contract, charter schools would be the first unionized charter school teachers in the Chicago area. Three quarters of the total teaching staff at all three schools signed union authorization cards to be the first unit represented by the Chicago Alliance of Charter Teachers and Staff (Chicago ACTS), an affiliate of the Illinois Federation of Teachers (IFT). Since Illinois, like New York, allows union authorization by majority "card check," this exceeds the simple majority required by law. Brian Harris, a special education teacher at CICS/Civitas Northtown Academy and a member of Chicago ACTS, remarked when speaking about the organizing effort:

> *We continue to believe that these charter schools are public schools because they are funded with taxpayer dollars. We are prepared to proceed with an election as soon as possible and are confident that our union will prevail.* (Catalyst 2009)

The filing on behalf of the teachers at the three Civitas schools is a result of a two-year campaign by the American Federation of Teachers (AFT), headed by Randi Weingarten (Ibid.). According to Emily Mueller, a high school language arts teacher at CICS/Civitas Northtown Academy Charter School, the issue facing the Chicago charter teachers are the same as those faced in New York and in New Orleans and elsewhere:

> *We organized because a teacher's voice in a school's decision making process will help create the best work environment for teachers and the best learning environment for students. We love our work, and a union gives us security of being able to voice concerns and ideas without placing our jobs at risk.* (People's Weekly World *2009*)

Civitas didn't see it that way, arguing that its charter schools were essentially private schools not accountable to the public, despite the fact they receive taxpayer dollars. In a brief Civitas submitted to the NLRB arguing against recognition of the teachers' bargaining unit, it claimed that it was a for-profit company and therefore not required to provide any type of annual presentation to any government body or to justify its annual expenditures, and that it had no "direct personal accountability" to any government public officials.

On June 3, 2009, despite the brief by Civitas, which was rejected in principle, the teachers won their right to be recognized as a bargaining unit. The Board's decision made it clear that Civitas was correct that it was a private for-profit EMO and thus governed by the National Labor Relations Board and federal laws.

In a brief letter to the parents of students at the school, CEO, Simon Hess issued the following statement on the Civitas Web site after the ruling:

June 3, 2009
Greetings Civitas Teachers and Staff,

I have some very important news to share with you. We were informed today that the National Labor Relations Board ruled in favor of Civitas and our teachers.

The Board's decision makes clear that, as a private organization, Civitas is governed by the NLRB, and federal labor laws.

Accordingly, the NLRB affirmed our position that our teachers have a right to a secret ballot election, where teachers can make an informed, private decision about whether or not to have a union represent them.

We are gratified by the NLRB's decision. We have been adamant about fighting for the rights of our teachers to vote in a secret ballot setting.

We're very hopeful that this ruling will help us to promptly resolve this matter. As an organization, Civitas is committed to ensuring that our teachers have voice in the collaborative effort to provide an outstanding college preparatory education for our students.

This decision preserves your essential voice in shaping the future an vision of our Civitas campuses.

As always, many thanks to each of you for your hard work and dedication to our students.

Sincerely
Simon Hess, CEO Civitas Schools (Civitas 2009)

Through its affiliation with the American Federation of Teachers, the CICS/Civitas unit of Chicago ACTS now joins the nationwide Alliance of Charter Teachers and Staff, a community of educators and staff at more than 70 charter schools nationwide in ten states. All are AFT-affiliated unions. The card check authorization signed by teachers in Chicago poses a direct threat to the market-based, school "reform" effort in that city euphemistically known as "Renaissance 2010," the brainchild of Mayor Daley that seeks to open new schools under charter contract management while seeking to close current public schools in mostly African American and Latino communities. The organizing drive by the teachers at Civitas run charter schools is seen as another victory for the AFT and its affiliates and another challenge for the free-market fundamentalists.

Will the KIPP organizing effort and the Civitas teachers' unionization authorization reach New Orleans and Washington, D.C. where the corporate model of education is being fostered through charterized, contract schools? While it's probably too soon to tell, judging from the success of the union drive in New York and Chicago and with the growing focus on charter schools by the AFT and its affiliates, unions may well pose a threat to the Diverse Performance Strategies model Paul Hill and his conservative allies have put into play.

ANTI-TEACHER UNION SENTIMENT

The experience of teachers in New Orleans, Washington D.C. and New York are similar, and compelling in our understanding of teachers and their relationship to the charter school movement and the teacher unions. The experiment being conducted in New Orleans and Renaissance 2010 in Washington D.C. under Chancellor Rhee, exemplifies the ideology of conservative reformers in blaming teachers for the less than robust performance of public schools. As Tough noted in his article regarding the performance of New Orleans schools, New Orleans was a failed public educational system long before the hurricane hit the city. No one could rationally argue that the school system was serving the needs of students or their teachers, let alone the community:

> *In New Orleans, before the storm, the schools weren't succeeding even in an incremental way. In 2005, Louisiana's public schools ranked anywhere from 43rd to 46th in the federal government's various state-by-state rankings of student achievement, and the schools in Orleans Parish, which encompasses the city of New Orleans, ranked 67th out of the 68 parishes in the state. The school system was monochromatically black—white students made up just 3 percent of the public-school population, most of them attending one of a handful of selective-enrollment magnet schools—and overwhelmingly poor as well; more than 75 percent of students had family incomes low enough to make them eligible for a subsidized lunch from the federal government. The dysfunction in the city's school system extended well beyond the classroom: a revolving door for superintendents, whose average tenure lasted no more than a year; school officials indicted for bribery and theft; unexplained budget deficits; decaying buildings; almost three-quarters of the city's schools slapped with an "academically unacceptable" rating from the state.* (Tough 2008)

Yet the situation in New Orleans, as bad as it was, could be seen as a confluence of economic and social events. Poverty, drug-ridden neighborhoods, racism, class division and exploitation, broken families, and the lack of attention to infrastructure and the health care needs of children and their parents all played a part in the dysfunctional city school system. Conservative ideologues continue to argue, however, that the problem that plagues public schools is the fault of teacher's unions. As Steve Wilson noted in his book, *Learning on the Job*:

> *Organized interests have successfully resisted calls for radical change in the organization and delivery of public education, none more than the two national teachers' unions, the NEA and the American Federation of Teachers (AFT). Today the majority of K-12 public school teachers belong to a local union, nearly all of which are NEA and AFT affiliates. Together, the two unions count 3.5 million public school teachers, support staff, pre-school teachers, and college faculty among their members.*
>
> *The result is that the most prescriptive teacher contracts, which may run three hundred pages or more, dictate virtually every detail of what may and may not happen in schools. And the teachers contract is only one rule book governing the school. Where teachers are unionized, often every other employee group is unionized as well, including lunch room aides, the custodians, and the teaching assistants. Each arrives with a hefty union contract of its own.* (Wilson 2006)

The reasons why teacher unions run counter to market-based reform proposals are clear: the cost of union wages, health care benefits, protection from discrimination in hiring and firing, paid vacation, job security, and support for equity in decision making, curriculum development and the day-to-day operations. Wilson and Hill, who advocate for a radically new system of education based on market principles and privatization, have long been active in opposing unions precisely because of the costs involved in labor contracts. More importantly, they oppose the part unions play in democratic decision-making, public disclosure and transparency.

Diane Ravitch, an outspoken educational theorist disagrees with these free-market reformers, at least on this issue, and argues that teachers unions are both good for the public and the teachers who join them. In an article for *AFT Educator* in 2007, "Why Teacher Unions Are Good for Teachers and the Public," Ravitch reminds us:

> *It is worth recalling why teachers joined unions and why unions remain important today. Take tenure, for example. The teacher unions didn't invent tenure, despite widespread beliefs to the contrary. Tenure evolved in the 19th century as one of the few perks available to people who were paid low wages, had classes of 70 or 80 or more, and endured terrible working conditions. In late 19th century New York City, for example, there were no teacher unions, but there was already ironclad, de facto teacher tenure. Local school boards controlled the hiring of teachers, and the only way to get a job was to know someone on the local school board, preferably a relative. Once a teacher was hired, she had lifetime tenure in that school, but only in that school. In fact, she could teach in the same school until she retired—without a pension or health benefits—or died.*
>
> *One problem with this kind of tenure was that it was not portable. If a teacher changed schools, even in the same district, she would lose her tenure in the school where she was first hired, and she would have to go to the end of the line at her new school.*
>
> *Pay for teaching was meager, but it was one of the few professional jobs open to women, and most teachers were women. Pay scales were blatantly discriminatory. Teachers in the high schools were paid more than those in the elementary schools. Male teachers (regardless of where they taught, though almost all were in high schools) were paid more than female teachers, on the assumption that they had a family to support and women did not.* (Ravitch 2006-2007)

Unlike Ravitch and others who support teacher unions, conservatives like Wilson and Hill have bemoan the fact that NEA and AFT represent millions of struggling teachers throughout the nation, yet they have no problem when it comes to putting together their own "organized interests," "unions," or special interest organizations to promote their own private agendas. Whether it is the U.S. Chamber of Commerce or the National Association of Manufacturers or the AMA; from the Business Roundtable to Paul Hill's own think tank on education and school choice, conservative anti-union "reformers" have been busy promoting and organizing their own think tanks, unions, and organizations for more than three decades, if not longer. Public school principals have their own unions, as do many vice-principals. And what about the list of industry and trade associations who meet on a regular basis, have anti-union agendas, work to defeat unions? These include the Associated Builders and Contractors, the American Hotel and Lodging Association, the Alpine Group, Coalition for a Democratic Workplace (a front group for the U.S. Chamber of Commerce), the National Restaurant Association, the National Retail Federation Association, the Retail Industry Leaders Association, the Council of Shopping Centers, to name a few. All of these "trade organizations or associations," contrary to their worker friendly names, are vociferously aligned against unions and use their deep pockets to fight unionization, pass favorable legislation for their causes, and repeal favorable union legislation.

When working people, however, like teachers, want to organize around their social and self interests, it is viewed as partisan or destructive to students and parents. Teachers are labeled "special interests" while industry leaders, corporate captains, and CEOs are painted as reformers "held hostage" to irrational demands by teachers. It's interesting to note that Wal-Mart, through the Walton Foundation, funds many contract charter schools in dozens of states, while, at the same time, gives huge sums of money to fight unionization both on the national and state level.

Another example is the National Right to Work organization, a "union" of business interests working assiduously against other working peoples' unions throughout the nation. In October of 2007 they reported on the end of the "union monopoly bargaining" system, or what teachers call "collective bargaining," in New Orleans.

> *More than 30 states currently authorize and promote union monopoly bargaining over teachers and other public school employees. Though Louisiana law does not explicitly authorize monopoly bargaining, many school districts, especially in the state's larger jurisdictions, have long acquiesced to it. This abusive system grants the bosses of one teacher union monopoly power to negotiate over the pay, benefits, and working conditions of all teachers—including teachers who don't wish to join or have anything to do with a union.* (National Right to Work 2007)

They even went further complimenting the new privatized regime change in New Orleans on their dexterity and "nimbleness," as they put it, in scorching the old system and putting in place the infrastructure for a new, privatized, union hostile system:

> *Although charter schools may legally be unionized, up to now teacher union officials have secured monopoly bargaining power in only a handful of the 3500 char-*

ter schools, enrolling over a million students, nationwide. Because charter entrepreneurs were far more nimble in reestablishing schools after Katrina, and because Louisiana public officials generally didn't stand in the way, today 42 of New Orleans' 81 public schools are charters. (Ibid.)

Right to Work supporters have for decades argued that, in addition to violating teachers' freedom as individuals, monopoly bargaining undermines schools' ability to educate children. Right to Work supporters have also argued that eliminating monopoly bargaining paves the way for overall school reform. (Ibid.)

"Monopoly Dons," "union bosses," "special interest groups," "organized interests," "barriers to reform," "tyrannical organizations," "government workers," and other euphemisms have been leveled at teacher unions since their inception. Seeing behind the words and understanding the facts are often difficult for a public that receives media-generated sound bites and little or no news on educational events unfolding in the nation.

Another player in the anti-teacher union movement is Rick Berman, head of Center for Union Facts. He accuses teachers' unions of hindering the quality of public education by protecting bad educators and opposing school reform. The Center is currently soliciting nominations for the nation's 10 worst unionized teachers. Berman will give $10,000 to any of those names if they agree to stop teaching forever. He says the Center for Union Facts is funded by businesses, foundations, and members of the public, but he won't identify them (Masterson 2008). The Center's 2007 IRS tax return shows that it took in $2.5 million, almost entirely from unnamed donors including one who gave $1.2 million. Richard Berman is a food and restaurant lobbyist who started the Employee Freedom Action Committee. He runs at least ten interlocking corporate front groups in his fight against labor unions. He and his managers were paid $840,000, yet the Center is so concerned about highly paid union officials that they listed them by name and salary on its Web site (Silverstein 2009).

David Kirkpatrick, commenting in a 2006 essay written for the conservative think tank, the Buckeye Institute, summed up the anti-union teacher sentiment this way:

So teacher unions support charter school laws, right? Not quite!

Both major teacher unions, the National Education Association and the American Federation of Teachers view the charter school movement as a direct challenge, perhaps the greatest from any source. Thus they have opposed laws authorizing the establishment of charter schools, weakening charter school laws as much as possible and limiting the number of such schools that are authorized.

Even after all of this has failed, they continue to try to sweep back the sea. In Ohio where charter schools are called community schools, the Ohio Federation of Teachers wants the authorizing legislation to be found unconstitutional. Why is this so?

> *Primarily because of one thing that wasn't mentioned in the preceding positives about the charter school movement. That one thing is that charter school teachers, in overwhelming numbers, do not vote to affiliate with the teacher unions, nor do they tend to join the unions as individuals.*
>
> *More than anything else the charter school movement is illustrating that teacher union rhetoric about teacher autonomy, professionalism, and conducive working conditions are just that - rhetoric.*
>
> *The last thing the unions want - any unions, but especially teacher unions - is for the teachers to be able to function as independent professionals, like doctors, lawyers, etc. After all, if teachers can function independently, that will be true of their relationship to unions as well as traditional school boards. This presents the unions with an impossible, perhaps fatal, dilemma.* (Kirkpatrick 2006)

Attacks on unions of all stripes is certainly not new; they are part of the American experience. When companies like GM or Ford fail, the public is told it is the fault, in part, of the unionized workers. When school districts fail to function and underperform, we are told it must be the fault of the unionized teachers who only care about tenure and health care. Time and time again the managerial elite who run private and public organizations blame workers when things go wrong. The media has assisted union bashing by focusing on corrupt unions and painting a generalized picture of union forces set to destroy the nation's way of living when it was precisely the unions that fought for the wages and working conditions enjoyed by most of the middle class in the last century. Yet from Hollywood to the corporate media, the union "bosses" are portrayed as the harbingers of all that is wrong with American companies and public organizations. CEOs and upper management, who often have mismanaged for decades as we have seen in the Wall Street crisis, have been handsomely rewarded.

The controversy over unions is brought again to the attention of the public in a recent report entitled, "No Holds Barred: The Intensification of Employer Opposition to Organizing" by Kate Bronfrenbrenner of the Economic Policy Institute.

> *Overall, 12.4% of U.S. workers are represented by unions, a density far below what would be the case if all workers who wanted to belong to a union could freely do so. In fact, studies have shown that if workers' preferences were realized, as much as 58% of the workforce would have union representation. Yet, this low overall unionization rate obscures a striking imbalance—while almost 37% of public-sector workers belong to unions, less than 8% of private-sector workers do.* (Bronfrebrenner 2009)

Bronfrenbrenner goes on to indicate that it is the intensification of employer intimidation and opposition to union organizing that is responsible for the steady decline of unions throughout the United States, as we saw this in the KIPP and Civitas organizing efforts:

In the last two decades, private-sector employer opposition to workers seeking their legal right to union representation has intensified. Compared to the 1990s, employers are more than twice as likely to use 10 or more tactics in their antiunion campaigns, with a greater focus on more coercive and punitive tactics designed to intensely monitor and punish union activity. It has become standard practice for workers to be subjected by corporations to threats, interrogation, harassment, surveillance, and retaliation for supporting a union. An analysis of the 1999-2003 data on NLRB election campaigns finds that: 63% of employers interrogate workers in mandatory one-on-one meetings with their supervisors about support for the union; 54% of employers threaten workers in such meetings; 57% of employers threaten to close the worksite; 47% of employers threaten to cut wages and benefits; and 34% of employers fire workers. (Ibid.)

Intimidation can range from employer required "captive audience" meetings, which is employer run and anti-union and where union supporters cannot speak. Firing of union activists during organizing drives along with routine intimidation like we saw with KIPP or Civitas. According to the NLRB's most recent annual report it took an average of eighteen months to resolve charges of unfair practices, certainly long enough to harass and intimidate employees (Silverstein 2009).

The Employee Free Choice Act (EFCA) would allow for card-check authorization for union membership and collective bargaining when a majority of workers at an employment site sign authorization cards. This is the law that in New York and Washington allowed the teachers unions to unionize KIPP and Civitas. The Alliance for Worker's Freedom, an antiworker organization along with SOS BALLOT, another key industry group, seeks to amend state constitutions in New York, Chicago, and Washington D.C., which allow for simple majority card check by workers to form a union. SOS's sole officer is Charles Hurth, a noted conservative, who supports corporate efforts at stopping or breaking unions.

Opposition to the Employee Free Choice Act, or simple majority card check by employees, that is now before Congress can be compared with opposition to the Wagner Act during the 1930s, especially in the public prognostications of industry leaders. The Wagner Act gave workers the right to collective bargaining in the 1930s and if we look at the conservative politicians, business representatives, and other organizations that fought the Act at the time we see almost analogous arguments and rhetorical sophistry. Take the following examples of arguments posed during the Roosevelt era in opposition to the Wagner Act:

Specifically, the provisions of the bill will operate to provoke and encourage labor disputes, rather than diminish them . . . Its real effect will be to serve as a vehicle for the advancement of the selfish interests of minority labor organizations.—Walter Harnischfeger, National Association of Manufacturers, March 21, 1935

To support labor in this objective by enacting this bill would permanently close the door to recovery.—Guy Harrington, National Publishers Association, March 29, 1935

My general criticism of the . . . bill is not so much that it supports unionization as that it will in operation result in enforced unionization.—J.M. Larkin, Bethlehem Steel, April 5, 1935

The comparison of these comments made nearly 75 years ago with recent comments in opposition to the Employee Free Choice Act (EFCA) is strikingly similar:

Unions want it because it would make it easier to recruit dues-paying members, not because it would somehow defend workers' right to choose freely to unionize.—Heritage Foundation, April 23, 2007

The act is a poison pill for our ailing economy, which is why every major business organization from every industry sector has come out in strong opposition to it.—Brian Worth, Coalition for a Democratic Workplace, February 25, 2009

Labor unions are supposed to protect workers' rights, yet union bosses want Congress to pass a law that actually robs workers of their democratic right . . . through a forced unionization process.—Senator Orrin Hatch, June 26, 2007 (LaborNerd 2009)

Attacks on teachers unions are part and parcel of the attack on unions throughout the nation and have been historically. What is new, however, is that with the advent of charter, contract schools both in New Orleans and elsewhere, the controversies over teacher's unions and charter schools are heating up throughout the nation. While the attacks on teachers continue unabated, teacher union advocates argue that the role of unions in collective bargaining in any school reform effort holds great promise, and should potentially be enhanced and certainly maintained. They put forth the claim that a contract in a local district can provide a framework for improvement, and that teachers along with management and parents, should collaborate and guide any meaningful reform change. This, they argue, should be a cooperative effort among all educational stakeholders, parents, and students. The United Teachers of New Orleans (UTNO), or what is left of them, state the following when speaking of the charterized experiment conducted in their city schools. Asked if the union can improve the educational climate at a charter schools the union replied:

We firmly believe that it can. As three charter school advocates acknowledged in their book Charter Schools in Action, it is "difficult to launch successful charter schools." This is because it is a tremendous challenge to effectively fund, hire faculty and staff, develop curricula and programs, and carry out the other critical tasks that are involved in operating a good school.

Even more important is carrying out these tasks without losing focus on what matters most—the needs of students. The success of a charter school (or any school) depends on the ability of educators to come together, share their professional needs or concerns, and have a process for regularly communicating these needs on an open and ongoing basis with the administrators or management of charters.

Charter school teachers and many charter school leaders recognize that they can have both the freedom and reforms that charter schools foster, and the respect and fairness that teacher unions ensure. When educators have a voice, it translates into students who excel academically. (United Teachers of New Orleans)

Teacher union advocates agree that the role of unions and collective bargaining everywhere should be maintained and expanded, not vilified and decimated as opponents would like to see. They are beginning to come together to assure that they have the right to form unions and that these rights are not blocked by intimidation and harassment.

POWER OF TEACHER UNIONS

Whether one believes that teachers' unions are an obstacle to educational reform or that the unions are the driving force for reform, one thing is clear: teachers' unions are a powerful force in education. How these unions conduct themselves, the issues they embrace, the directions they take, and the challenges they face will help shape the future of education in the United States.

There are 2.8 million elementary and secondary teachers in the public schools, and more than 85 percent of them are organized into either the National Education Association (NEA) or the American Federation of Teachers (AFT) (Keller 2005).

In most states, like in New York and Washington D.C., teacher unions have collective bargaining agreements as formal processes to exert their power. These agreements are used as a way to ensure that working conditions and salary issues will be bargained for between the union and the local school district, but they are also a way of institutionalizing reforms that improve public education.

Many union opponents argue that institutionalizing reforms is not taking place, and claim that teachers' unions are really obstacles to reform. Owing to their assumed inflexibility surrounding staffing, evaluation, and teacher working conditions, many opponents of the teachers' unions argue that they are rigid and do not use their collective power to negotiate and foster school improvements. On the contrary, these opponents argue, the unions use their power to protect their self-interests and block significant school reform.

But the criticism of teachers' unions goes far beyond simply arguing that unions block significant reform. Anti-teachers' union advocates argue that union efforts to prevent the privatization of schools, from the cafeterias to the administration, clearly show that the unions do not have the best interests of the students at heart. Many anti-union reform advocates argue that unions such as the NEA and the AFT actually impede progress because they do not allow private management of schools.

What many anti-union activists have in common is their support for the privatization of schools—a position that the teachers' unions are clearly and adamantly against. In his book *Teacher Unions: How the NEA and AFT Sabotage Reform and Hold Parents, Students, Teachers, and Taxpayers Hostage to Bureaucracy,* Myron Lieberman argues the anti-union reform position quite eloquently. Opposing everything from collective bargaining agreements to contracts that spell out day-to-day school operations, Lieberman states that "the inevitable tendency is to consult the contract before taking action, a mindset that leads inevitably to union control" (Lieberman 1997). The same sentiments remain today and are, quite possibly, even stronger.

Besides opposition to teachers' unions over the issue of the privatization of schools, anti-union advocates also claim that teachers are being held hostage to unions and not getting their money's worth. By not supporting merit pay, for example, union opponents argue that the best teachers and best instructional strategies are being lost. The issue of merit pay remains a hot-button issue for teachers and their unions.

Merit pay assumes pay for performance, an assumption that argues teacher pay structures are not sufficiently guided by market mechanisms. The argument is that teachers who do a better job of teaching as reflected by higher standardized test scores, should receive higher pay. The belief is that extrinsic rewards, such as higher pay, will enhance school reform and increase the effectiveness of teachers in general even if it is wedded to inauthentic testing mechanisms.

Nowhere is the controversy between opponents and supporters of teachers' unions more evident than in the debate over public school choice and charter schools. In a postmodern society that has moved away from industrialism, many charter advocates argue that teachers' unions, as they currently operate, are barriers to innovation and change. Former public school teacher and chair of the California Senate Education Committee, Democrat Gary Hart, reports that "the California Teacher's Association (CTA) brought its immense power against efforts to create a charter law that gives teachers freedom to create the kind of school they thought made sense. The CTA would only support a law that retained union authority over charter schools." In his book *Charter Schools,* Joe Nathan makes the statement that:

> in most states, teachers unions have tried to prevent the charter school concept from getting a real test. The idea threatens their power and their concept of how public education ought to operate. However, because some legislators of both parties have stood up to this opposition, and because some charter schools are having real,

measurable success, some teacher union leaders and members are rethinking their opposition. (Nathan 1996)

Nathan is not alone in criticizing teachers' unions for standing in the way of charter school reform. Lieberman maintains that because these unions will be inextricably involved in the process of designing charter school legislation, they will make sure that the charter schools are not much different than the schools they replace. Arguing that the unions are incapable of promoting change, Lieberman goes on to argue that only entrepreneurial teachers freed from union constraints can accomplish true reform (Lieberman 1997). The attitude is that teachers should not have any decision making in the day-to-day operations of the schools.

Yet the unions would argue that Lieberman has ignored the success of over more than a 1,000 charter schools already operating with union collaboration, and they would claim that union opponents, like Lieberman, fail to address the differences within unions and how unions themselves are themselves in transition. Even Paul Hill wrote about the question being asked at a recent conference held in May 2006 at the Progressive Policy Institute:

So why did leaders from opposing camps agree to meet? One reason was that unions, particularly New York's United Federation of Teachers (UFT), are starting charter schools of their own, indicating that there may be some common ground between the two groups. Leaders also agreed to meet in part because chartering allows teachers to experiment and innovate in ways that are difficult in regular public schools, an opportunity that holds some attraction for progressive teachers union leaders. Another reason was that most charter school operators understand that their teachers have the right to form unions if they think it necessary; moreover, some charter leaders have found that organized teachers can make good partners. Both groups realize that they have to work together and need to figure out how best to co-exist while maintaining their most valued principles. (National Charter Research Project 2006)

Many union spokespeople and pro-union charter proponents would argue that their opposition to charter schools is not opposition to the idea but a fear of the loss of collective bargaining and strength among union members as the country embarks on market solutions to social problems in almost every area of life. In fact, union supporters point out that it was the AFT, through its then leader, Albert Shanker, that introduced the notion of charter schools to the public in a 1988 speech given to the National Press Club in Washington, D.C. And although the AFT supports the idea of charter schools, the organization would probably assert that conservatives support charter schools not as an educational reform measure that preserves public schools but because: charters will hasten the advent of vouchers; a charter school policy will undermine the teacher's unions;

and charter schools can advance conservative support for deregulation and for allowing the market to reign. Both the NEA and the AFT oppose vouchers and believe that many supporters of educational reforms such as charter schools are disingenuous and really simply wish to abolish the idea of teachers' organizations in favor of market solutions to educational problems. But many like Randi Weingarten, head of the United Federation of Teachers are now arguing:

> *To get better schools we have to learn how to merge teachers' commitments to their daily work with the spirit of entrepreneurship. Today there is too little entrepreneurship within the school district structure and too little [teacher] professionalism in charter schools.* (Ibid.)

However, many teacher union leaders disagree with Weingarten, arguing:

> *We will never believe [that charter leaders] are concerned about children as long as [they] include people who want to run schools for profit. This led to an equal and nearly opposite reaction from a charter leader, who said, Unions' day-to-day business is defending bad teachers. Unions refocus everyone's energies away from serving kids.* (Ibid.)

The opposition to teachers' unions by anti-union charter school advocates is a reflection of the changing historical nature of the educational debate. And while the media attempts to cast the debate over unions as pro-union or anti-union, the debate is far more complex than that and many pro-union proponents of charter schools also argue that unions need to change, as we will look at when we discuss tenureless collective bargaining. However, again, as Hill was quick to note:

> *Not all disagreements are about history and ideology. The most heated exchange about the details of schooling focused on the respective roles of "teacher voice" and school leadership. One union leader described chartering as a way to put managers totally in charge and deny teachers any voice in their work or professional life.* (Ibid.)

There are other voices in the union controversy as well; the issue is not limited to two camps. In their book *Taking Charge of Quality*, Charles Kerchner, Julia Koppich, and Joseph Weeres argue that teachers' unions, as they are presently constructed, are antithetical to educational reform. Insisting that we no longer live and work in an industrial society, the authors claim the agendas of the unions must change. They say that "until recently, teacher unions have focused almost exclusively on conventional job rights and protection issues—ensuring job security and adequate wages, benefits, and working conditions. They have excelled in that arena. As industrial style unions, they have provided teachers with the kinds of benefits they have needed as workers" (Kerchner, Koppich, and Weeres 1998, 11). Although a staunch defender of teachers' unions, Robert Lowe has expressed similar complaints in his study of the Chicago Teacher Federation (CFT) led by Margaret Haley in the early part of the twentieth century:

> *Yet despite its [CTF] support for a number of good causes beyond the schools and its opposition to some deleterious reforms within the schools, it [the CTF] prefigured the limitations of contemporary teacher organizations by developing a trade-union mentality that focused too narrowly on protecting jobs, raising wages, and limiting effort. In keeping with that mentality it adopted an oppositional stance to virtually all educational reforms, regardless of merit—a hallmark of teacher unions since. While this resistance has typically has been directed against reform initiatives from the top down, in the collective bargaining era it also has meant resistance to efforts to achieve equality of educational opportunity through school desegregation and community control.* (Lowe 1999)

TEACHER UNIONS: FOR AND AGAINST

The debate over school reform and the role of the teachers' unions bring up complex and controversial issues, often not covered by the simplistic characterization in news reporting. The following section explores the ways free-market advocates of public choice and charter schools oppose teacher unions, responses from teacher union advocates and, finally, discusses how thinking among teachers unions is changing.

Teacher Unions and Merit Pay

Advocates of privatization argue that teachers block educational reform in myriad ways. One is by refusing to accept a system of merit pay. Anti-union advocates argue that without competitive incentives to improve, teachers will continue to fail their students educationally as they have been doing for decades. "Why not tie teacher's pay to the performance of their students on standardized tests," ask conservative ideologues? Merit pay proposals have been at the heart of the debate over school performance for years, they are part and parcel of the "target incentives" of privatization economic theory. The assumption is that teachers are failing American public school students due to the lack of competition among them. Merit pay, they say, would provide incentives for performance benchmarks; with competition for bonuses, the "quality of the product" would increase, in this case the education teachers would dispense.

In March 2009, even newly elected President Obama came out for the merit pay reform for teachers:

Too many supporters of my party have resisted the idea of rewarding excellence in teaching with extra pay, even though we know it can make a difference in the classroom. Too many in the Republican Party have opposed new investments in early education, despite compelling evidence of its importance. Despite resources that are unmatched anywhere in the world, we have let our grades slip, our schools crumble, our teacher quality fall short, and other nations outpace us. The relative decline of American education is untenable for our economy, unsustainable for our democracy, and unacceptable for our children. We cannot afford to let it continue. What is at stake is nothing less than the American dream. (Washington Post *2009*)

In fact, Obama's proposed fiscal 2010 budget for education calls for boosting spending on the Teacher Incentive Fund, a program that awards grants to school districts to devise performance-pay programs, to $517.3 million, up from $97.3 million in the current year (Viadero 2009).

The principal of Hazel Park/Hilda Knoff Elementary School in River Ridge, Louisiana has been running a "pay for performance" program for six years and she credits it for helping make Hazel Park the top-rated campus among all non-magnet elementary schools in Jefferson Parish. According to an article in the *Times-Picayune* in New Orleans:

Performance pay, also known as merit pay, remains a controversial topic in United States' public schools 10 years after it was introduced on a large scale in Denver. Since then it has gained some traction, and Louisiana now has 28 schools participating in the national Teacher Advancement Program including two in Jefferson Parish, two in St. Bernard Parish, six in the Recovery School District in New Orleans and all nine in the Algiers Charter School Association. Fourteen more Louisiana schools are considering it. St. Tammany Parish school officials are looking into starting an incentive pay program, and St. John the Baptist Parish school officials said they would consider the idea. There are no such plans in St. Charles Parish, where public schools are among the highest performers in Louisiana and teachers among the highest paid. (Bronston 2009)

Despite some initial trepidation, the merit program seems to be working at the school, at least according to Joe Potts, the president of the Jefferson Federation of Teachers, in New Orleans. That's partly because bonuses for teachers, which range from $1,000 to $3,300, are based on how much students grow academically from year to year, as opposed to how high they score on standardized tests in a single year. The way the program is supposed to work, according to the *Times* article, is that Louisiana schools in the Teacher Advancement Program (TAP) use a model designed by the Milken Family Foundation of Santa Monica, California to set pay-raise criteria. The aim of the program is to boost student achievement through professional development, teacher assessments and cash rewards. Each teacher is now eligible for a bonus based on a formula: 30 percent coming from the school's overall performance score growth, 20 percent from score growth of students in the individual teacher's classroom, and 50 percent from observations of the classroom by the teacher's peers four times each year (Ibid.).

The Teacher Advancement Program has been embraced under the new school restructuring plan now in place in New Orleans. Now that the New Orleans public school teacher union is basically decimated, Pastorek and Vallas can work quickly and privately to institute new forms of teacher compensation and incentives, for they are no longer tied to collective bargaining agreements; not yet anyway. Many of their incentive plans are being welcomed by some teachers. Nicole Jackson, master teacher at O. Perry Walker Charter College and Career Preparatory High School and Community Center, in New Orleans said recently:

> TAP gives teachers the ability to evolve, advance professionally and earn higher salaries, just as in other careers. And we are able to do so by creating a student-centric environment where our focus is on helping the students learn and helping each other be better teachers. (Ibid.)

Yet while merit-pay plans for teachers may be growing more popular with politicians and some educators like Jackson, a report by the Economic Policy Institute released in May 2009 entitled, "Teachers, Performance Pay, and Accountability" argues that such compensation plans are rarely used in the private sector, as Nicole Jackson has been led to believe; furthermore, the report argues that the practice can sometimes in fact bring about unintended negative consequences.

According to John S. Heywood, of the University of Wisconsin-Milwaukee, an economist who co-wrote part of the study along with Scott J. Adams, an associate professor of economics at UW-Milwaukee, and Richard Rothstein of the Economic Policy Institute, compensation plans that use formulas or indicators to reward private employees on the basis of their productivity—which are among the kinds of programs that growing numbers of policymakers have in mind for teachers—are less common, and may even be declining (Adams et al. 2009).

Michael J. Podgursky, an economics professor from the University of Missouri, Columbia, who has studied teacher pay-for-performance plans, noted that lessons for education from such efforts in the private sector may be limited, because most workers in the private sector do not have tenure, as teachers do. Private-sector employers, particularly those whose workers are not members of unions, may not need to spur motivation when employees know they can be fired at will (Ibid.).

The United Teachers of Los Angeles, representing the second largest school district in the country, expressed their opposition to merit pay for the following reason:

> Teacher unions have historically resisted merit pay proposals because they undermine one of the core principles of teaching and learning: collaboration. Whether it

*is the informal discussion that takes place in the lunchroom or the more formal ex-
changes based on grade level, department, or small learning communities, these are
only successful because as teachers we understand teaching is about working together to help our students, not competition for better pay.* (Pechthalt 2007)

Teacher unions throughout the country have resisted merit pay precisely
because, they argue, it is based on insipid competition and therefore pits teachers against teachers when it comes to the best learning practices to be used with
students. If a teacher will receive a higher bonus by out-competing another
teacher, where is the incentive for collaborative problem solving, sharing, the
need to develop collaborative practices, and to work jointly with other teachers
to cut and paste creative ideas in an innovative, shared community? Merit pay,
claim those that oppose the idea, would effectively destroy collaboration at the
workplace and with it teacher excellence and student achievement. If teachers
knew that higher student test scores would result in higher pay, why would anyone want to share ideas with their colleagues? Furthermore, argue opponents, rewarding educators based on student test scores further exacerbates the "teach to
the test" syndrome that has narrowed the curriculum and dulled the educational
experience for both students and teachers. It could also create conditions that
would encourage cheating, as has happened across the nation. Also, argue opponents to the idea, merit pay would create a disincentive for the very teachers we
want going into the most challenging schools and communities. Such teachers
might want to move to the most affluent schools because the monetary rewards
would be greater. This could have a devastating impact in our poorest communities for it would further stratify schools along racial and class lines and actually
work to increase inequality.

Not so, says Steven Wilson, the exact opposite is true: collective bargaining
and unions destroy school communities and their culture:

*Not only does collective bargaining promote bureaucracy, its adversarial premise—
that, unless protected, staff will be exploited by management—also creates a culture
in which staff feel suspicious and chronically beleaguered.* (Wilson 2006)

Wilson's ideology is in keeping with the ideological rationalism of the market
fundamentalism that promotes the idea of human beings as simply calculating individuals, simplified selves with only their own self-interests at heart. Create a
deregulated system, they argue, where teachers can be unleashed to satisfy their
own selfish needs and all boats will rise.

Perhaps the position can be summed up best by UTLA spokesman, Joshua
Pechthalt:

*From a labor perspective merit pay would also divide the work force and in the long
run lessen our ability to fight collectively to improve public education. If salaries*

were not simply based on years of experience and number of college credits earned or additional services provided, the teaching force at any workplace would be more stratified (differentiated) and much less willing to stand together during a conflict with school site management or during a contract struggle. The role of the union would be seriously compromised. (Pechthalt 2007)

And that is the point; divide-and-conquer tactics are favorable from the point of view of those running the Washington D.C. or New Orleans "reconstruction" efforts in school charterization, just as they are for any business or entity seeking to increase productivity and maintain autocratic control. These entities like to pit worker against worker, preventing their understanding of their common-class interests while at the same time assuring, in this case, that teachers will not organize and make "unreasonable" demands (like shared decision making through collective bargaining), thereby presenting another "obstacle" to structural reformers like Vallas and Pastorek. It is part and parcel of the Darwinian, "go it alone individualism" that is at the heart of the privatization agenda and the unions know this, which is why they resist.

However, this sentiment is not shared by Ronald Corwin and Joseph Schneider, from Ohio State University and the National Policy Board for Educational Administration. Corwin and Schneider are no friends to the choice movement but they make the point that:

Teacher unions generally oppose contracts that permit differentiated assignments and pay scales. They fear that unethical principals will punish strong teachers who question their leadership by giving them un-desireable assignments. They also believe that most principals are unqualified to evaluate teacher performance, so they demand a single salary schedule for all teachers. Obviously, the teacher's unions have some justification for their positions. But consequences are creating a system of "rich schools and poor schools" within most districts. The better, more experienced teachers eventually use their senority to settle into schools serving the higher income students, leaving the new, less experienced teachers to serve the schools with the neediest students. (Corwin and Schneider 2007)

They go even one step further:

Since state laws generally exclude charter schools from union contracts, they can offer teachers special incentives in exchange for their commitment to specialize and to work in non-traditional settings. Meaningful incentives—including money, prestige and opportunity to wield influence—should be offered to teachers and principals willing to work in schools with special missions. In particular, teachers should be rewarded when their students progress to the point when they are prepared to move to other schools and programs. Teachers who can make these students successful should be acknowledged and rewarded, if they can't they shouldn't be retained as faculty in these schools. We are not proposing that teachers who are working with less advantaged children should be held to the same testing outcomes as teachers in more advantaged schools. We are talking only about rewarding improvement, taking the students' circumstances in account. (Ibid.)

From the point of view of teacher unions and their supporters, environments of competition, merit pay, and individual bonus incentives creates a malleable labor force for employers and assures that control and power remain the providence of the employer, in this case the new contract, charter school providers, and the small cabal that is responsible for running them. The new Teach for America graduating class will no doubt be seeped in a new culture and ideology that claims that competition among teachers increases student performance, while collectivism works to vitiate any true and meaningful reforms. They will be asked to look at their labor as teachers more as "caregivers" than as teacher professionals, which is why they will be called on to "sacrifice" both time and control in the new educational paradigm. With more and more charterization in store for the city of New Orleans and with these charters increasingly being contracted out to profit or nonprofit EMOs to operate as "providers," the last thing that the new reformers want is an organized labor force that would demand higher wages and benefits, which then serve to lower private profits while at the same time reducing autocratic control at the bargaining table. The plan being launched in New Orleans, according to many observers, is counting on low labor costs and autocratic control—a high turnover rate among teachers is simply collateral damage for the new providers who will run the increasingly charterized school system.

Teacher Unions and Academic Achievement

Opponents of teacher unions say they raise the cost of education and more importantly, hurt the very constituencies they have been designed to support, namely the students and teachers. According to Jay P. Greene, long time privatization pundit:

Those lit(erature) reviews find that unionization raises the cost of education by about 8% to 15%. In addition, they find that unionization tends to hurt the academic achievement of high-achieving and low-achieving students while benefiting more typical students found in the middle of the ability distribution. (Greene 2009)

Greene relies on the study done by Caroline Hoxby a Harvard economist who advocates free-market reforms and who has looked at charter school achievement among students for years. She argued that achievement among students in charter schools is higher than those of students in regular traditional public schools but her study is widely refuted for its methodology (The School Choice Hoax). The implication that can be drawn from her study is that unions are partly to blame if not wholly to blame. The argument can be summed up this way, according to the Brookings Institute in a publication they published entitled "Teachers Unions: Do They Help or Hurt Education Reform":

> *Critics of unions who argue that teacher unions are impeding school reform, and that since the introduction of collective bargaining in the late 1960s unions have moved to steadily control public education and to stifle important changes that would make schools more flexible and responsive. The critics regard unions as too powerful, gobbling up the prerogatives of management, and contracts as being too constraining, too negative in their effect. The implicit argument sometimes made explicit, is that management unfettered by the restrictions of collective bargaining can do a much better job, and our schools would be better. And so the conclusion, of course, is that the role of unions in collective bargaining should be reduced or eliminated.* (Brookings Institute 2000)

Terry Moe, senior fellow at the Hoover Institute, a professor of political science at Stanford University and longtime advocate for the privatization of education, when asked about teacher unions schools:

> *Okay. Now, so what are the fundamental interests of teachers unions? Well, we can argue about that. But they do have interests. And the key to understanding their behavior is finding out what those interests are, and follow them through. And so what I would say is the basic interests of teachers unions are that they want to promote the material well being and the job security of their members, teachers, and they want to maintain and increase their own membership as unions, their resources, and their power, the most basic things. It doesn't make them bad, it makes them like all the other groups that are out there. We're just trying to characterize their basic interests.* (Ibid.)

Moe and those who agree with him have been working to do away with teacher unions for years claiming they control schools and tie well-meaning reformers hands. This is why they admire and invite the charter school movement. They understand that the laws governing newly opened charters, not conversions, create "at will" employment for teaching staff, who can be fired outright or after a small contractual time period, who have no rights, no grievance outlet, and no collective bargaining guarantees. Moe and his colleagues wish to see schools run by unfettered market forces and those market forces, the argument goes, will assure democracy and this democracy will translate into higher student achievement through higher scores on standardized tests. Moe continues:

> *I think this is an absolutely fundamental issue and problem on its face. The schools are supposed to be democratically controlled, and if you read this article and read some other works on this new union movement, new unionism, basically it's an endorsement, a collaborationist model, or what political scientists would call a corporatist model in which the schools are basically run by the administration and the*

unions through these joint committees or whatever which meet on a variety of different issues, and basically run the schools. Nobody elected the unions. Why is it that this is an appropriate way for a democracy to control the schools? The schools are supposed to be run by elected officials who are responsible to constituencies. To the extent that the unions play an established, powerful role in that process, they are getting in the way of democratic control. And I think it does require real attention and justification because, on its face, it appears to be quite inconsistent with democratic control of the schools. (Ibid.)

In the educational reconstruction efforts currently underway in New Orleans, as well as elsewhere in the country where the charter experiment is being been conducted on a massive scale, democracy and a social contract is the last thing that administrators and key policymakers want. That is why negotiating with teachers' unions, public disclosure and transparency are problematic for them.

In Washington, D.C., the other site for "educational reform" through charterization in the city's "Renaissance 2010" program, School Chancellor Michelle Rhee is in control of the cities educational reform efforts where three out of every ten schools is now a charter school and she is outspoken about her position against unions. According to PBS, online *News hour*'s reporter, John Merrow:

She'd like to offer teachers the chance to earn six-figure salaries, if they give up job security, tenure. To change the way teachers are hired, fired and compensated in Washington, D.C., Michelle Rhee does not need the national press. She needs support from D.C.'s 4,000 teachers. (Merrow, under "Media Attention Hinders Rhee's Efforts to Reach Out to D.C. Teachers")

Perhaps it is the arrogance of the newly birthed managerial elite that upset the Washington, D.C. teachers and much of the public when, in December 2008, Rhee made the cover of *Time* magazine, standing in an empty classroom holding a broom. The metaphor elicited a strong reaction from D.C.'s teachers and many parents. Comment of George Parker, president of the Washington Teachers' Union:

This one shot gave the picture of, "Look, just sweep them all out. Get rid of them all." It was an insult to the hard work that our teachers perform every day. (Ibid.)

In the same interview with Merrow, teacher Randy Brown summed up what most teachers in Washington, D.C. were thinking at the time:

You can't really be accountable when you're undermined. They (management) don't believe in you. They've lost their confidence in their teachers. (Ibid.)

From the point of view of the teachers who labor in the classrooms with students each and every day, the question is not, "Do labor unions hurt the academic achievement of students?" but "Do the managers who run and operate the schools hurt the academic performance of students through attacks on teachers?" Evidently for many, the answer is yes, for the recent organizing efforts on behalf and by charter school teachers could be just the tip of the iceberg for teachers' unions in the burgeoning charter movement experiment in Washington, D.C. Chancellor Rhee might find that her own sanctimony, rhetoric, and actions might be the best organizer the union has.

Teacher Tenure and Educational Reform

Cynthia D. Prince, found that principals complain that teacher seniority rules within union contracts do not allow them to move experienced teachers to schools and classrooms where they are most needed. This is a complaint echoed by many administrators and educational observers. Principals can veto a teacher's request to move or stay at certain schools, but they rarely do.Why? According to some it is the time and money involved in the lengthy grievances filed by teachers not in agreement with the administrations plans. Teacher transfers have long been the subject of collective bargaining agreements. In Philadelphia, before 2002 when the state took over the schools, the union contract granted teachers, not principals, the right to control any assignments or transfers between schools (Spiri 2001). In the new charterized experiment in New Orleans there is no seniority and that pleases Vallas and Pastorek just fine, for it means they can control who teaches—where, when and how.

In a recent article in the *Los Angeles Times,* Steve Lopez a reporter for the *Times,* writing about the United Teachers of Los Angeles and the 5,500 pink slips that went to the teachers noted in 2009 due to budget cuts:

> . . . *what union President A.J. Duffy won't admit, as he raises a stink, is that when good teachers are on the chopping block and burned-out teachers are protected, it's because of his union's contract. Simply put, the UTLA contract—like a lot of others in the state—requires that the last hired are the first fired. And let's not let the district off the hook. It agreed to this arrangement, which ensures that when pink slips go out, there's no distinction between excellence and mediocrity. (Lopez 2009)*

Steve Barr, founder of Green Dot, the rapidly growing nonprofit EMO, feels the same way. He says the union has two primary purposes that have nothing to do with educating children: preserving prohibitively expensive lifetime benefits for teachers and their families, and allowing more senior teachers to work where they want rather than where they're needed, with tenure making even the burnouts untouchable (Ibid.).

This argument is hardly new. But is it true? According to Chancellor Rhee, who oversees the ever-growing charterized Washington D.C. school system, it most certainly is. Under the current D.C. contract with the district, teachers get seniority after two years. With tenure, if they lose their job, they can apply for positions at other schools in the system. Tenured teachers can be fired only for cause, such as receiving a poor evaluation or committing an act that subjects them to discipline. Rhee wants to change all of this. In a 2008 article in the *Washington Post* on the issue of seniority entitled, "Teacher Contract Would End Seniority: Union Is Reviewing Proposal from Rhee," *Washington Post* staff writer Dion Haynes commented on the controversy that now swirls in Washington D.C. over seniority rules:

> *Under the proposed contract, teachers would give up seniority in exchange for annual raises of about 6 percent, more personal-leave days and more money for supplies. In the last contract, which expired in the fall, teachers received a 10 percent raise over two years.*
>
> *Rhee "does want to infuse some new blood [into the schools]. She wants to make it attractive for young people coming in to advance," said the union member . . . "We've come to realize we're going to have to give in to her."* (Haynes, under "Teacher Contract Would End Seniority")

The controversy over seniority rights for unionized teachers is heating up all over the nation in the midst of the economic crisis and disastrous cutbacks that face public schools. These disastrous cutbacks, argue many opposed to removing seniority rights for teachers, form the "disaster economics" that are making it environmentally possible to renegotiate seniority rights for teachers or get rid of them completely, as Rhee wishes to do. In fact, Rhee has found a little-known District policy that may allow her to restrict seniority rights without any rule changes. Dion Haynes writes in the *Washington Post,* in 2008:

> *Rhee can restrict seniority rights through a little-used District law that allows principals to diminish seniority rankings and use them among several other factors—including evaluations, military service and whether the teacher is in a high-demand area such as math or special education—to make changes during staff cuts.* (Haynes, under "Rhee Seeks Tenure Pay Swap for Teachers")

More and more districts are looking for such loopholes in their laws to do away with seniority rights for teachers and, of course, charter schools seek to keep their workforce nonunion in an attempt to avoid the controversy altogether.

Teacher Tenure and Student Achievement

According to a 2008 *Time* magazine article:

> *Roughly 2.3 million public school teachers in the U.S. have tenure—a perk reserved for the noblest of professions (professors and judges also enjoy such rights). The problem with tenure, Rhee and other critics say, is that it inadvertently protects incompetent teachers from being fired. The Teach for America alumna, who oversees*

some 50,000 students and 5,000 teachers, has sparked controversy in the capital by proposing a new contract allowing teachers to earn as much as $130,000 a year if they forgo their tenure rights (a teacher's salary, on average, is less than $48,000; most start out making $32,000). (Stephey 2008)

Though tenure doesn't guarantee lifetime employment, it does make firing teachers a difficult and costly process, one that involves the union, the school board, the principal, the judicial system and thousands of dollars in legal fees. In most states, a tenured teacher can't be dismissed until charges are filed and months of evaluations, hearings and appeals have occurred. Meanwhile, school districts must shell out thousands of dollars for paid leave and substitute instructors. The system is deliberately slow and cumbersome, in order to dissuade school boards and parents from ousting a teacher for personal or political motives. (Ibid.)

This, according to many conservative pundits and school administrators, is the core of the matter. They argue that unions make it difficult to fire poor teachers and in doing so they protect and shield incompetency and this serves to shelter current school systems from reforming. *Time:*

Some school districts have resorted to separation agreements, buyouts that effectively pay a teacher to leave his or her job. The practice has evolved as a way to avoid the extensive hearings and appeals required by union contracts and state-labor laws in firing a tenured teacher. (Costs can run as high as $100,000). Other districts simply transfer inadequate teachers to other schools in what Calif. Gov. Arnold Schwarzenegger has called "the dance of the lemons." Former Mass. Gov. William Weld tried to pass legislation requiring teachers to take competency tests every five years, a move that triggered a number of complaints from local teachers' unions who called the bill adversarial and intrusive. Weld defended himself by explaining his stance as "anti-slob teacher," not "anti-teacher." (Ibid.)

Not all states have tenure requirements. In 1997, Oregon abolished tenure and replaced it with 2-year renewable contracts and a rehabilitation program for underachieving instructors. Other states like Connecticut, New York, and Michigan have simply eliminated the word "tenure" (from the Latin *tenere,* meaning to hold or keep) from the books while retaining the due-process rights it embodies. In Toledo, Ohio, officials have adopted a more creative approach by establishing a mentoring program to improve teacher performance. Fifteen surrounding communities have already copied the idea.

What is the response from teachers who feel they have been unfairly targeted in the tenure controversy? Perhaps this can be found by looking at Hill's report on the symposium on the future of teacher unions and charter schools:

Union leaders were particularly concerned about "at-will" employment of teachers in charter schools. To union leaders, "at will" means capricious and oppressive. Charter leaders argued that teachers employed "at will" have the same rights under state and federal law as employees in private companies and nonprofits, including legal protections about being fired without just cause. Even though most charters employ teachers on renewable one-year contracts, union leaders are convinced that some charter school managers use the threat of non-renewal to intimidate and drive out perfectly good teachers. Differences about the status of teachers broaden the gulf between the two sides. Some charter leaders claimed that charter and private schools can anticipate teacher turnover and yet have strong, stable teacher leadership and collaborative working environments. Union leaders claimed that such practices discourage investment in teacher skills and make all but a few teachers into disposable help. (Hill 2001)

As the report noted, charter leaders claim that such "reforms" are necessary if a school must pay salaries out of a fixed budget, while union leaders replied that no school's staffing decisions should be driven by how much a teacher's salary is set at. Charter leaders countered that they have no choice but to make staffing decisions in this way since their funding is based on the number of students they enroll. Unlike district-run schools, they argue, whose salaries are covered no matter how high they are, charter schools can pay salaries only up to the limit of what they receive in income, which is determined entirely by enrollment. But is this the real issue or is the real issue how we fund education in the United States and whether this funding should be based on regressive property taxes or a commitment by the nation to educational funding? And if funding is such a problem then how can a city like New Orleans afford such exorbitant salaries for the technocrats, like Pastorek or Vallas, to operate and manage the system?

Many teachers argue tenure has become a conservative scapegoat for a whole slew of educational and financial ills responsible for the dismal test scores and disappointing graduation rates in U.S. schools. According to them, abolishing tenure doesn't address growing inequality, problems of poverty, underfunding, lack of health care, family problems, overcrowding, or improving students' home environments and communities. They claim that despite more than a century of social progress, the need to protect teachers from the whims or tyrannical actions of administrators, remains as important as ever.

On the other side, the management of anti-union charter schools insist that the only acceptable standard of employment is "at-will employment," under which an employee can be dismissed at any time for any reason whatsoever. At-will employment was a common law creation of American state courts at the end of the nineteenth century when the economic doctrine of laissez-faire capitalism was being read into the Constitution and law, with courts striking down child labor laws, minimum wage laws, and laws restricting the length of the workday and week as violations of the 5th and 14th amendment rights to property.

The debate over tenure has been a hot and deeply contested one, but also a discussion devoid of historical understanding. Any understanding of contemporary tenure status for teachers and the arguments for and against tenure must be tied to historical understanding that gave rise to the movement towards tenure in the first place. The start of the tenure was part of the progressive era politics and the concurrent labor movement and labor struggles during the late nineteenth century age of industrial capitalism. Imbued with the spirit of collectivism and the need to demand protection from parents and administrators who would try to dictate lesson plans or exclude controversial materials like *Huck Finn* from reading lists, teachers, much like their counterparts, the industrial steel and auto workers who fought against unsafe working conditions and unlivable wages, were part of the growing working class consciousness that gripped the nation at the turn of the nineteenth century. The National Educator's Association (NEA) was founded in 1887 when nearly 10,000 teachers from across the country met in Chicago for the first-ever conference of what was to become one of the country's most powerful teachers' unions. At that historical meeting, the topic of "teacher's tenure" led the agenda. By the end of the nineteenth century, tenure had become a controversial issue that some politicians preferred to avoid. In 1900, the Democratic Party of New York shamed their rivals in the *New York Times* for taking up the issue:

> *We deprecate the tendency manifested by the Republican party of dragging the public school system of the state into politics.* (Stephey 2008)

In 1910, New Jersey became the first state to pass tenure legislation when it granted fair-dismissal rights to college professors. The women's suffrage movement of the 1920s revealed the cost to women for not having tenure, as Diane Ravitch alluded to briefly—female teachers could be fired for getting married or getting pregnant or wearing pants; it was at this time that tenure rights were extended to elementary and high school teachers as well. And there was also the issue of academic freedom for teachers, what they could teach or not teach in the public schools and what materials could they use or not use. Yet as the *Times* article notes, academic freedom is already currently in jeopardy:

> *thanks to the rigid testing requirements put in place by the No Child Left Behind Act, the academic freedom that tenure was meant to protect has been severely curtailed.* (Ibid.)

One might also add that this is thanks to "the managed curriculum" and "best practices" the new providers are requiring and tethering to the rigid standardized testing. The tenure track for college professors can require a record of published research and probationary periods of up to 10 years, but K-12 teachers (in some states) can win tenure after working as little as two years. The *Times* article notes:

> *In unionized schools, the prevailing standard for dismissal is just cause—there must be a good reason, such as the malfeasance in the performance of one's job, for an*

employee to be dismissed; unionized teachers are not "at will" employees. This is the general standard used in workplaces with union representation and in the civil service sector. Under the just cause standard, there are due process appeals for employees who believe that they have been dismissed without a good reason. Tenure really can be seen as the right to due process, under a just cause standard and before an impartial hearing body, when one is dismissed; it is granted after a period of probation during which the bearer of the right has demonstrated a mastery of the job. Since tenure is a protection of academic freedom which pre-dates collective bargaining in public education, it is generally written into education law. (Ibid.)

In a *Times* magazine article "Laying Siege to Seniority" Sam Allis wrote, 18 years ago:

Tenure for 2.3 million public school teachers, one of the sacred cows in American education, is under attack. For decades, thanks to strong union contracts and ingrained notions of academic freedom, underpaid school teachers could at least console themselves with the fact that they were pretty well assured of job security for life. But after years of dismal school performance, and under the strictures of shrinking budgets, legislators are suddenly reneging on the deal. "Professionalism and tenure are antithetical," says Chester Finn Jr., a former Assistant Secretary of Education and a proponent of free-market solutions to educational problems. "Teachers can't have it both ways." (Allis 1991)

It is noteworthy once again, to mention Washington D.C.'s experiment with the contract charterization of its schools. Chancellor Rhee not only opposes seniority, but she is looking for ways to erase tenure rights as well. Dion Haynes, the reporter for the *Washington Post* wrote recently about the proposal for pay scales for teachers that Rhee has introduced to the public and the unions:

Under the proposal, the school system would establish two pay tiers, red and green, said the union members, who spoke on condition of anonymity because the talks are confidential. Teachers in the red tier would receive traditional raises and would maintain tenure. Those who voluntarily go into the green tier would receive thousands of dollars in bonuses and raises, funded with foundation grants, for relinquishing tenure. Teachers in the green tier would be reviewed yearly and would be allowed to continue in their jobs only if they passed an evaluation and boosted students' test scores, the union members said.

    Under Rhee's proposal, raises to the green tier would be more than the 19 percent increase over five years she is proposing for all teachers, the union members said. (Haynes 2009)

However Rhee may not be successful as many new charter school providers, profit or nonprofit, have found that they must work with unions in order for there to be any success. Green Dot, the nonprofit EMO, stated in their online newsletter that what is clearly driving reform is their relationship with teachers' unions:

> *A key constituent in Green Dot's organization is the teachers union. Green Dot is the only non-district public school operator in California that has unionized teachers. Green Dot's teachers have organized as the Asociacion de Maestros Unidos (AMU), a CTA/NEA affiliate. Key reforms embodied in the AMU contract include: teachers have explicit say in school policy and curriculum; no tenure or seniority preference; a professional work day rather than defined minutes; and flexibility to adjust the contract in critical areas over time. Green Dot was able to achieve these reforms by establishing a relationship of mutual trust with the teachers union and committing to pay its teachers above the average of comparable schools' pay scales. In doing so, Green Dot and AMU share a unique relationship in the world of labor relations, one that is characterized by collaboration and a mutual interest in improving public education.* (Green Dot 2007)

Charter laws and education laws vary from state to state, but most jurisdictions, such as California and New York, do not include charter school teachers in the legal protections of the right of tenure. Consequently, unionized charter schools have to establish their own parallel system of due process for the protection of educator rights. This is what Green Dot did in conjunction with the United Teacher's Federation in New York. This is hardly unprecedented.

California charter school teachers, for example, start outside of the legal protections of tenure. The California Teachers Association local in the Green Dot Charter Schools negotiated a contract with the two essential elements of a tenure system: (1) a just cause standard, and (2) due process before an impartial arbitrator. The Green Dot contract provides that:

> *"No unit member shall be disciplined, non-renewed, dismissed, reduce in rank or compensation without just cause." Article XIV lays out a procedure for complaints and grievances that culminates in a hearing before an independent arbitrator with the power to make decisions binding on the school management.* (Casey, under "Steve Barr Welcome to Our World")

Educators in most private post-secondary institutions have tenure of this very type, and in many cases, without it ever being memorialized in a collective bargaining agreement.

As the charter school movement continues to grow, and as the fiscal crisis facing cities and states put more pressure on teacher unions to abandon many of their time honored positions on seniority and tenure, for example, the public can look forward to more bargaining and negotiations over issues of merit pay, tenure and seniority, and unions in general. As one union member commented when asked if he would accept the higher teacher salaries offered by Rhee in exchange for tenure:

You may be trading off your future, your tenure, your job security. When you trade that, it seems to me you're not getting much. (Haynes, under "Rhee Seeks Tenure Pay Swap for Teachers")

Where would Rhee get the money to pay the increased salaries being offered teachers in exchange for the "swap of tenure"? The city is broke so according to two union members in Washington D.C., Rhee wants to use donations from The Bill & Melinda Gates Foundation, Michael & Susan Dell Foundation, and Broad Foundation, in part, to pay for the raises and bonuses. Officials from the Gates and Broad foundations would not comment on proposed future funding (Ibid.) but one wonders how this is all sustainable, or if anyone would object to the idea of increasingly funding public services and schools with the gravitas of an education oriented philanthropic movement. Despite not being part of negotiations with teachers over swapping pay increases for tenure, they will have financial clout. As we saw with the KIPP organizing effort where David Levin co-founder of KIPP changed his mind about recognizing the union bargaining unit authorized by his teachers, financial and political clout, in these cases, could be the same.

It is not surprising then to see why the public teachers in New Orleans were targeted almost immediately after the hurricane, and efforts to implement free-market sweeping reforms were enacted. In his book, *Fixing Urban Schools* (Hill, Brookings Institute Press, 1998), Hill had spoken of the need to retrain teachers and the problem of teacher unions, and New Orleans charter administrators and city and state politicians would not let him down. To quote Saltman:

> *Despite the range of obvious failures of multiple public school privatization initiatives, the privatization advocates have hardly given up. In fact, the privatizers have become far more strategic. The new educational privatization might be termed "back door privatization" or maybe "smash and grab" privatization. A number of privatization schemes are being initiated through a process involving the dismantling of public schools followed by the opening of for-profit, charter, and deregulated public schools. These enterprises typically despise teachers unions, are hostile to local democratic governance and oversight, and have an unquenchable thirst for "experiments," especially with the private sector. These initiatives are informed by right wing think tanks and business organizations.* (Saltman 2007)

Recently, the Obama administration has called for the expansion of the charter school movement, much to the chagrin of many teachers unions. However, Obama's support for charter schools was accompanied by a call for the participation of the *Nation Education Association,* and the teachers unions in the development of charter schools. According to a recent blog by Lee Culpepper, who speaks for much of the conservative opposition to both the Obama administration and especially to the idea of the NEA involvement in charter schools, he likened the idea to that of a Trojan horse. Commenting on his blog, Culpepper echoed the sentiments of many who propose the privatization of education:

> *Like a modern day Odysseus, Obama is plotting to smuggle the National Education Association (NEA) into charter schools. But since charter school supporters would certainly not fall for a large wooden horse today, Obama has concocted a beguiling vow to double the amount of funding for charter schools. What better way to conceal NEA marauders and meddlesome bureaucrats than to stuff them inside deceptive government handouts?*
>
> *Should charter-school advocates ignore the mythology lesson and jubilantly drag the proposed cash inside their schools, they will surely awaken wishing that reality were only a drunken stupor. In the aftermath, they will realize too late that the NEA and bureaucrats have already toppled them. By then, administrators and the NEA will have charter schools mired in the same muck of central control, worthless regulations, and bureaucratic red tape that plagues so many traditional schools.* (Culpepper 2008)

Teacher Unions and Charter Schools

The Green Dot Charter School in New York City is run under a unique partnership between the Los Angeles EMO and the United Federation of Teachers, NYSUT's affiliate in New York City schools. According to an article in *New York Teacher* in 2008, unions are alive and well in many charter schools. A delegation of about 30 union-represented charter school teachers attended the National Charter Schools Conference in New Orleans during the summer break in 2008 to talk about charter schools and unions. The AFT, one of NYSUT's national affiliates, represents charter school staff in more than 70 schools across 10 states. Here in New York, more than a dozen charter schools are unionized in western New York, Albany, New York City, and Long Island. In New York City, the United Federation of Teachers, led by Randi Weingarten, has pioneered union-run charter schools, with two successful schools in Brooklyn. This fall, the union became the first in the nation to partner with a charter school EMO, Green Dot Public Schools, to open a new high school in the South Bronx. Weingarten commented on the union relationship with Green Dot:

> *We embraced the idea of a partnership with Green Dot because of its work with students and its respect for teachers and their unions.* (Saunders 2008)

The NEA states on its Web site:

> *NEA believes that charter schools and other nontraditional public school options have the potential to facilitate education reforms and develop new and creative teaching methods that can be replicated in traditional public schools for the benefit of all children. Whether charter schools will fulfill this potential depends on how*

charter schools are designed and implemented, including the oversight and assistance provided by charter authorizers. (National Education Association, under "Charter Schools")

They go on, however, to state a clear policy regarding the charter school movement:

State laws and regulations governing charter schools vary widely. NEA's state affiliates have positions on charter schools that are appropriate to the situation in their states. NEA's policy statement sets forth broad parameters and minimum criteria by which to evaluate state charter laws. For example:

A charter should be granted only if the proposed school intends to offer an educational experience that is qualitatively different from what is available in traditional public schools.

Local school boards should have the authority to grant or deny charter applications; the process should be open to the public, and applicants should have the right to appeal to a state agency decisions to deny or revoke a charter.

Charter school funding should not disproportionately divert resources from traditional public schools.

Charter schools should be monitored on a continuing basis and should be subject to modification or closure if children or the public interest is at risk.

Private schools should not be allowed to convert to public charter schools, and private for-profit entities should not be eligible to receive a charter.

Charter schools should be subject to the same public sector labor relations statutes as traditional public schools, and charter school employees should have the same collective bargaining rights as their counterparts in traditional public schools. (Ibid.)

Teachers continue to be enthused with the idea of a unionized charter school. Tara Shaleesh. a member of the United Federation of Teachers' Alliance of Charter Teachers and Staff in New York City:

I've got the best of both worlds. I've got the professionalism that comes with a union and the flexibility of a charter. (Ibid.)

Liz Fisher, a first-grade teacher at Pembroke Pines Charter Elementary in Florida, went even further arguing at the conference of charter school teachers:

There are so many misconceptions about the union. I'm here to tell you joining the Broward Teachers' Union has made our great school an even better place to work. The teachers just wanted a voice: Nothing more, nothing less. We wanted a say in professional development, hiring, evaluations, helping struggling colleagues. It's been a success story for us. We now have very little turnover and one common interest: the kids. (Ibid.)

But not all charter school management would agree. In a recent *Examiner* article, author Karen Piper noted the hesitancy of charter school providers to recognize unions, and the case of Civitas CEO, Simon Hess:

> One can sense the hesitation from Civitas Schools CEO Simon Hess. Like many other charter school leaders, Hess is concerned that a union presence would inhibit the schools' ability to offer longer school days or let go of teachers who don't make the grade. This is what he says about not having a union: It's a gift—this blank slate. We have this amazing opportunity to design schools that can actually be successful in meeting the needs of our students. (Piper 2009)

The keynote speaker at a recent National Charter Schools Conference was Michelle Bodden, who is leading the UFT Elementary Charter School after a long history of leadership with the UFT and as a NYSUT Board member. She said student achievement is high when educators are treated fairly, with respect, and have a voice in their practice. She went on to argue:

> We know some people in the charter movement are out to prove that competition makes schools better. And they're out to prove that non-union schools are more successful. Well, we know better. In New York and elsewhere, unionized charter schools consistently rank among the state's best and that's not by accident.
> So let's put to rest the big lie about charter schools and teacher unions. You are living proof that unionized charter schools work. And you're living proof that you can have the best of both worlds: the innovation that comes with working at a charter and the professional workplace that comes along with being in a union. (Ibid.)

Charter schools, Bodden pointed out, were the vision of legendary union leader Al Shanker who popularized the concept when he launched the charter school idea 20 years ago. But Shanker could never have envisioned the radical changes charter schools would bring and the unintended consequences they would have for many teachers and students. This seemed to be born out by some charter school teachers at the Progressive Policy Institute Symposium on the Future of Charter Schools and Teacher Unions in May of 2006. Paul Hill, reporting for the National Charter Research Project on the symposium:

> There was also a strong contingent of Minnesota and Wisconsin-based individuals, some identified with charter schools and others with unions, who told about schools run as teacher cooperatives, where teachers function as both labor and management. These examples include both charter schools and district-run schools that have received waivers from their local teachers unions. (Hill et al. 2006)

Schools run as "teacher cooperatives" are not what are sought after by the new social engineers who base their faith on market fundamentalism; on the contrary, they seek to construct a school system based on contract charters that are over-seen by public agencies and run by providers; schools where teachers have little or no say so in the "best practices" or the "managed curriculum" they are asked to employ or impart.

Union and Anti-Union Charter Agreement

A report by the AFT regarding charter schools states:

> *The crisis of confidence in public schools is well known. Public agenda polls (1994 and 1995) indicate that most Americans believe that students today are not achiev-ing as well as they could, as well as students from other nations, or as well as they need to for their—and the country's—future success.*
>
> *Public education is in ferment. There is much dissatisfaction with the current system. Many people believe that the school system is a moribund and highly bu-reaucratic monopoly—indifferent to criticism, captive to union interests, unwilling to change, and unaccountable to the public. Cries for reform, greater accountability, and more parental choice are everywhere . . . Thus, in an era of widespread discon-tent with public education, a belief in the efficacy of competition, and a climate of deregulation and cries for more accountability and local control, it is no accident that we see a growing demand for reforming the education system, in general, and cries for private school vouchers, the privatization of public schools, and the growth of the charter school movement in particular.* (American Federation of Teachers, un-der "AFT's Criteria for Good Charter School Legislation")

Those statements are similar to those made by the NEA, the largest teachers' union in the United States:

> *Our challenge is clear: Instead of relegating teachers to the role of production work-ers—with no say in organizing their schools for excellence—we need to enlist teach-ers as full partners, indeed, as co-managers of their schools. Instead of contracts that reduce flexibility and restrict change, we—and our schools—need contracts that empower and enable . . . This new collaboration is not about sleeping with the enemy. It is about waking up to our shared stake in reinvigorating the public educa-tion enterprise. It is about educating children better, more effectively, and more am-bitiously.* (Chase 1997)

Both statements by two powerful teachers' unions reflect the current state of agreement between many anti-union charter school proponents and advocates of teachers' unions. Both anti-union charter school proponents and pro-union charter proponents believe that education is changing rapidly; both parties agree that educational unionism is based on antiquated relations between school ad-ministrators and teacher-workers and must be changed; and both agree that schools must change to meet the exigencies of the twenty-first century. Where they disagree is on the form and content of this transition and the role that teachers' unions will play in future relations between teacher-workers, students, parents, and school administrations.

Joe Nathan blames the unions for what he calls "the factory model" of production and management. Nathan argues that teachers' unions promote the idea that seniority should decide who gets a job and when a layoff occurs, who loses their job. According to Nathan, this model results in a situation whereby it is almost impossible to fire a teacher; thus, bad teachers find refuge in a system that protects incompetence. And according to Nathan and others who advance similar arguments, teachers' unions have a vested interest in maintaining their power and therefore oppose charter schools because they threaten that power. Now, they claim, with parents, teachers, politicians, and students embracing the charter concept, teachers' unions realize they cannot defeat the idea and therefore work to weaken the charter laws.

Both the AFT and the NEA would disagree. Although they would argue that mechanisms must be put in place to hold teachers accountable, both unions would claim that they are interested in the well-being of students first and foremost and that the protection of teachers is a means to that well-being. They support charter school legislation but wish to ensure that the legislation promotes the interests of both teachers and students. AFT clearly states:

> *AFT supports properly structured charter schools as a useful vehicle for school reform. For charter school legislation to be responsible, it must make sure that all children can participate; that the governance structure is collegial, professional, and democratic; that schools operate within the framework of state or nationally established standards, curriculum, and assessments for all students; and, that teachers have the professional authority to find appropriate ways to achieve those standards for their students.* (American Federation of Teachers, under "AFT Charter Report")

So unions support charter schools if those schools are responsible, if teachers have professional authority and governance authority, and if the charter schools are subject to some state or district regulation.

Many anti-union proponents of charter schools argue that teachers' unions continue to play a role in attempting to kill charter school legislation wherever and whenever the opportunity arises. One example involves the state of Minnesota where charter school proponent, Joe Nathan, argued that the Minnesota Federation of Teachers (MFT) opposed charter school reform when it first appeared in 1991. Yet a closer examination of the union's position shows that it was more complex and did not reflect opposition to the idea at all.

The MFT passed a resolution stating it would support Minnesota's charter school legislation if:

> *All teachers staffing the school hold a license under the provisions of the Board of Teaching All staff be part of the bargaining unit in the district that authorize (sic)*

the school. The school be required to comply with the master agreement of employee groups in the authorizing district and be it further resolved that only local districts be authorized to establish any style of alternative or chartered schools. (Minnesota Federation of Teachers)

Both the AFT and the NEA have been in agreement regarding the above issues. Although they agree with proponents of charter school reform regarding the idea of charter schools, they promote the development of clear and precise criteria to measure what they feel is a responsible charter school and how they feel such schools should operate.

Moreover, there are prominent national labor leaders who will admit "Charters are here to stay," just as there are charter managers who not only tolerate but promote the formation of unions in their schools. (Hill et al. 2006)

Thus, for the most part, disagreement between union proponents and anti-union charter school proponents is not over the idea of charter schools but over how the idea will be implemented, what laws charter schools will be susceptible to, and how they will operate and be held accountable. These issues are complex and often are not afforded the depth and scrutiny that they deserve. Media treatment of charter schools in this regard often stifles the debate and understanding of the issues by focusing on anti-union or pro-union dichotomies, which actually obfuscates the important issues facing charter schools as an educational reform movement.

Although the NEA supports charter schools as an educational reform initiative, it differs from anti-union charter school advocates on such issues as accountability. For both anti-union charter proponents and pro-union charter proponents, the issue of accountability and the amount and size of state oversight and regulation remain the discerning aspect between the two positions. NEA president Bob Chase has expressed his concern that:

"charter school laws without adequate accountability measures open the door to gross abuses that hurt students. Charter schools must serve their communities and be fully accountable to taxpayers. Charters can be vehicles for streamlining administration, increasing parental and community involvement, and expanding the menu of education choices and options." (National Education Association, under "Charter Schools Run by For-Profit Companies")

Some charter schools and unions do agree on incorporating teacher voices in the day-to-day management of charter schools. Paul Hill reporting on the 2006 symposium held between charter school supporters and teacher unions:

Most also agreed that institutions and teachers matter—incorporating teacher voice and promoting collaboration are vital to good schooling. The group united against a common enemy: the school district bureaucracy. Union leaders pointed out, and charter leaders agreed, that the cumbersome collective bargaining agreements common in urban districts are largely a response to big district bureaucracies

To many participants' surprise, the union leaders most open to charter schools agreed that mandatory transfer rules to protect senior teachers and other forms of standardization common in district-wide agreements were inappropriate for charters. They agreed with the one charter manager whose schools have all unionized that every charter school needs to be its own bargaining unit, and the contract should cover only those issues that teachers and management believe help them do their work better. Some of the most influential union leaders in the room agreed that unionization of charter schools transforms union members from employees in a traditional labor-management arrangement into a new status resembling that of partners in a professional services organization. (Hill et al. 2006)

Combating Privatization

Perhaps the main interest of teachers' unions with respect to the charter school debate is to maintain and protect the notion of public schools. Both the NEA and the AFT have expressed concern that charter schools could provide the basis for an alternative school system available to a select few—a veritable road to privatization. They argue for a public, common school as a way of sustaining a pluralistic society in which diverse peoples can live together (American Federation of Teachers, under "AFT's Criteria for Good Charter School Legislation"). Worrying about the creation of elite enclaves that promise to educate a small portion of U.S. students, teachers' unions have advocated public scrutiny of the idea along with public disclosure and accountability.

The privatization of public schools has been increasing for some time, with "the education industry," coined by EdVentures investment firm, is now said to total $680 billion in the United States. The stock value of thirty publicly traded educational companies is growing twice as fast as the Dow Jones average, and brokerage firms such as Lehman Brothers and Montgomery Securities have specialists who seek out venture capital for new forms of penetration into what was once exclusively public education (Light 1998). Entrepreneurs see a $700+ billion industry in education and hope to organize schools into chains in order to control staffing and instruction and create financial efficiencies that will curtail and hold down costs.

All of this activity is troubling to teachers' unions, which compare the privatization of education to the privatization of health care. In fact many teachers say, Wall Street itself has referred to what was once public education as education maintenance organizations (EMOs) and seems to be bent on doing for education what health maintenance organizations (HMOs) have done for health care delivery.

And Wall Street is not alone. The education industry and proposals for corporatizing education have the conservative economist Milton Friedman and other heavy hitters on their side. Friedman first proposed vouchers for schools in 1955 and forty years later, in an op-ed piece for the *Washington Post,* Friedman suggested that "such reconstruction [of schools] can be achieved only by privatizing a major segment of the educational system—i.e., by enabling a private-for-profit industry to develop that will ... offer effective competition to public schools."

Bringing profit-oriented interests to bear on what has been a public venture is rigorously opposed by both the AFT and the NEA. The philosophy is that schools should be run for people, not for profit. The commercialism of education, argue the teachers' unions, will further exacerbate an educational divide and will assure that universal education for all children will become dependent on profits and investments. The unions also argue that profit motivation in education would create more inequity between suburban and urban districts and would also create what the Center for Analysis of Commercialism in Education has called "cookie-cutter schools" whose lesson plans are generic, sanitized, and designed for a one-size-fits-all approach to curriculum development. This approach, in turn, would disempower teachers further, reducing them to mere delivery conduits for commercialized education. The unions insist that the one-size-fits-all educational approach would also create new authoritarian rules for teachers and would divorce them further from the conception and development of curriculum and good teaching practices. Paul Pastorek and Paul Vallas in New Orleans, on the other hand, see the "managed curriculum" tied to rigid standards as the answer to our children's future and the means to measure the competency of the new "providers," viewing teachers as instruments in the delivery of the curriculum, not authors of it.

Privatization has come to have multiple meanings within the charter school movement as well. Because the teachers' unions are opposed to all forms of privatization, it is important to itemize their disapproval by highlighting the multifaceted aspects of the privatization efforts. Calls for the privatization of education through vouchers are now the centerpiece of the conservative agenda of dismantling public programs and are termed "entitlements." The different forms of privatization and how they correlate with charter schools are of grave interest to the teachers' unions and will be as time goes on.

Charter Schools and Private Resources

In their efforts to start and maintain charter schools, several school founders have been forced to rely on private funds for start-up costs and initial running and operating costs. Paying rent, securing a mortgage, affording the initial cost of insurance, and often the cost of construction, as well as funding the day-to-day operation of a school, are all costly. The organizational structure of the charter school and its relationship to the overall district in which it operates play huge roles in determining the dependency of a charter school on private funds. The more independent a school is from the district, the more it will be forced to pay out of its own budget for everything from insurance to legal fees. A recent University of California, Los Angeles (UCLA) study of privatization and education in California found that many start-up schools tend to be small and have a limited student body. An enrollment of 180 students or less may not be enough to pay for capital expenses, salaries, and benefits as well as curricular materials and administrative overhead costs associated with a new school (Wells and Scott 1999). Freedom from district bureaucracy can be costly and can usually mean private fund-raising from community-based, corporate-based, or foundation-based money, and this movement toward privatization is troubling to the teachers' unions.

The UCLA study found that every charter school studied relied in some way on funding from private foundations, the state of California, or the business community. It also found that the wealthier schools were able to rely on parent volunteers to raise money and write grants whereas parents at the lower-income charter schools generally had less time and fewer social networks to help with such activities. As a result, the already overburdened administration and teaching staffs at the low-income charter schools wrote grants and solicited funds in addition to their other responsibilities. Also, these schools' ability to call on parent volunteers meant that teachers in the wealthier schools could concentrate on teaching instead of fund-raising.

The UCLA study was also particularly distressing to union advocates because it confirmed that many suburban or wealthy charter schools were able to raise funds from within their own communities. The study also found that in some communities, parents raised staggering sums of money for school programs that did not even exist in the lower-income schools. Using professional and association connections, many wealthier and suburban schools are able to obtain a great deal of monetary support for school programs and resources. Outside collateral collected by local fund-raisers, such events as Tupperware parties, and corporate sponsorships mean that some charter schools have received exorbitant amounts of money while others have not—thus exacerbating the inequities in public education. The study also found that while schools in wealthier communities can rely on local fund-raising, the lower-income schools often rely exclusively on corporate sponsorships, which leaves them beholden to corporations and other outside donors.

Another concern expressed by the unions focuses on the private-public partnerships that often provide huge endowments to some schools and not others. Wells Fargo, Apple Computers, and Hewlett-Packard represent just a few of the corporations that have engaged in substantial sponsorship through grants. And while many suburban charter schools can count on elaborate donations from such corporations, those in the lower-income districts find they often are left out of the corporate sponsorship loop.

For example, one urban school the UCLA study researched was started by a nonprofit private educational foundation. Foundation employees wrote and presented the charter to the school board, secured a building for the school, recruited students with the help of a community organization, and paid for the remodeling of the school's facilities. The foundation also hired the faculty, selected the members of the school's governing body, and chose the school's curriculum. A question arose as to the role of a "partnership" and "community control" as it appeared that the school was being operated and controlled by the private foundation. This situation, argue the teachers' unions, is antithetical to charter claims of fostering community and local decision making among teachers. From the point of view of the teachers' unions, this example of market-reform based policies points to a subtle privatization of education and the disparities that result when schooling is left to the forces of the private market. The unions insist that it is precisely this pernicious and encroaching privatization that is nibbling away at the notion of a common school in the United States.

As author Kenneth Saltman notes, many cities and municipalities have fought back against commercialism in school in general, limiting soft drinks and candy bars on campuses, stopping advertisements in textbooks, preventing billboards and advertising on school grounds, and the like. Recently, for example, it was reported in the newspaper *USA Today* that the corporation Scholastic, the longtime children's book publisher, has been the object of a petition drive among at least 1,262 teachers. The teachers all signed a petition put out by the Campaign for a Commercial Free Childhood. The petition is asking Scholastic to stop enlisting teachers as "salespeople" to sell toys to students. The watchdog group reported to *USA Today* in June of 2009 that its review of Scholastic's 2008 elementary and middle-school book clubs found that a third of the items for sale weren't books but instead were toys, trinkets and even lip gloss (Horovitz 2009). These petition drives and push for new laws have been accomplished as a result of citizens' struggles to attempt to seal off the public space from complete takeover by corporations and commercial interests and the good news for those who are interested in preserving the public forum, free from commercialism, is that efforts to limit privatization and commercialism have been working throughout the United States, despite the growth of forces seeking to dominate the public sphere. The struggle for the expansion of democratic ideals within the public sphere is part and parcel of the struggle against privatization in all its forms and this is essential to understand the charter school movement in general.

In a 2007 article by Kenneth Saltman, titled, "Schooling in Disaster Capitalism: How the Political Right is Using Disaster to Privatize Public Schooling," he argues that much of the privatization movement we have witnessed in education in the past 30 years has failed to radically alter education as it was intended. He points to the failed efforts of the voucher movement nationally. He also makes the point Alex Molnar et al. made in their most recent study of for-profit EMOs:

However, it has become apparent that only a few years later Educational Management Organizations (EMO), that seek to manage public schools for profit, have not overtaken public education (though EMOs are growing at an alarming rate of a five-fold increase in schools managed in six years). The biggest experiment in for-profit management of public schooling, The Edison Schools, continues as a symbol, according to the right-wing business press, of why running schools for profit on a vast scale is not profitable. (Molnar et al. 2008)

Saltman argues, much as Corwin and Schneider do in their book, *The School Choice Hoax:*

The charter school movement, which is fostering privatization by allowing for publicly-funded schools managed by for-profit companies, and is being pushed by massive federal funding under No Child Left Behind, has also taken a hit from NAEP scores that in traditional terms of achievement suggest charters do not score as high as the much maligned public schools. (Saltman 2007)

In light of the struggles by antiprivatization educators and their allies, privatization forces have for years been attempting to work their way into public education, but without the results they would have liked. Then along came Katrina. The point that Saltman makes is that around the world, disaster is providing the means for business to privatize public agencies and accumulate profit and this could be seen domestically no where better than in New Orleans:

The new predatory form of educational privatization aims to dismantle and then commodify particular public schools. This conservative movement threatens the development of public schools as necessary places that foster engaged critical citizenship. At the same time it undermines the public and democratic purposes of public education, it amasses vast profits for few, and even furthers U.S. foreign policy agendas. (Saltman 2007)

The reader no doubts hears overtones of John Dewey and this can only remind us of the historical debate between Dewey and his contemporary, Walter Lippmann as to the nature of education, its hopes, possibilities, and society's expectations.

Contracting for Specific Services

The teachers' unions are also wary of contracting out vital school services to private firms. With a host of entrepreneurs literally waiting to take advantage of the educational marketplace, the practice of contracting out specific services such as food services, insurance, curriculum development, maintenance, and networking is growing. And the for-profit companies that wish to enter into the educational marketplace are focusing primarily on charter schools for these contracting opportunities. Unions are especially concerned that public schools are beginning to contract out more and more regular services to these for-profit private firms. Numerous charter schools are avoiding the use of unionized public employees by beginning to contract out such services as district maintenance, and many charters opt to use private landscaping firms because those firms provide workers with no unions and no salary packages, which means the wages and benefits are less costly.

Amy Wells found in her study of one charter school in California that after the school contracted out its maintenance personnel to a private landscape company, the classified staff's union sued the school, arguing that the charter must use district employees. The charter school prevailed in court by successfully defending its right to hire the less-expensive private company to do the gardening and maintenance at the charter school (Wells and Scott 1999). Unions claim that because district maintenance is often provided by minority workers, who, because of their union affiliations, enjoy benefits, adequate compensation, and safe working conditions, the trend to contract out services to for-profit private firms raises disturbing questions about the future of these employees' working conditions and how they will be able to support their families.

In developing strategies for confronting "niche" contracting, i.e., privatization in specific educational arenas, which is now becoming more pervasive, the NEA, for one, is developing strategies and criteria that will judge private sector involvement in contracting out services. Even in light of this opposition and skepticism of private contracting, it is clear that the union has begun to capitulate to some privatization demands and now promotes what it terms "public/private arrangement" (National Education Association, under "Education, Investors, and Entrepreneurs"). Nowhere better can this be seen than in the city of New Orleans.

Unions on Charter Legislation

The ways in which privatization interacts with public schools in this time of decentralization are subtle and not generally known to the public, yet the corporatization of public schools is increasing rapidly. There is very little information about what is taking place at the local charter school. Unlike health care, in which case public debate has at least scratched the surface of the issue, public debate and forums for education have not embraced the privatization of public schools as a topic. The media has failed in its job of honest and thorough investigative reporting on the issue, looking instead to private think tanks and pundits for sound bites as to the efficacy of the free-market and the failure of "government-run schools," which they then more than not, deliver uncritically to public consumers.

Given some of the issues that have been discussed regarding charter schools, the AFT, like the NEA, has established criteria for judging the efficacy of specific charter school legislation in order to protect public education. Their criteria include public accountability for student achievement, accessibility to charter schools by all students, the empowerment of professional educators at the charter schools, local district approval of charter schools, and the conduct of business in accordance with any and all state laws that require that public business of any kind be conducted publicly (American Federation of Teachers, under "AFT Charter Report"). As charter school legislation can differ state by state, the AFT established strong national criteria for charter schools in order to focus on charter schools in the various states. Understanding the arguments of unions such as the AFT will help shed some light on the teachers' union positions regarding charter schools.

Standards and Accountability

Both the AFT and the NEA agree that charter schools should meet rigorous state standards. They argue in favor of state assessments and call upon all charter schools to be subjected to those assessments from state to state. However, they differ in their opposition to No Child Left Behind.

The AFT argues that given the current recognition of and emphasis on difference, commonalties within and among public charter schools would disappear if there were no national criteria to assess their accountability. The union worries that with the development of specific charter schools, say African American schools or gender-based schools, the notion of a common curriculum or a common school might disappear. It questions what might happen if students are shifted from one school to another with no consistent curriculum or standards bridging the various schools. Thus, the AFT goes so far as to call for statewide curriculum frameworks and statewide assessment systems, which would be applicable to all schools whether they were charter schools or not.

The NEA voices similar concerns, pointing to what it calls three types of accountability that are needed to hold charter schools accountable to the public good. The first accountability concern is fiscal. Fiscal accountability is understood by unions within the day-to-day operations of a particular charter school, and such matters are usually handled by the governing board of the school. Governance and leadership are essential for a successful system of accountability, so the NEA is concerned about governance accountability. The second criterion is pedagogical. According to the NEA:

> One formal aspect of pedagogical accountability is the use of state mandated exams as overall indicators of school quality. Although formal pedagogical measures are difficult for teachers and administrators to conceptualize and implement, Charter School Initiative Schools are developing assessment and evaluation tools with non-traditional quality indicators aligned with the school's distinct vision and mission.

These indicators include character development, service learning, research, au-tonomous learning, and cultural appreciation. Put another way, the schools are at-tempting to think about quality education on a broad scale that goes beyond state required standardized testing. (National Education Association, under "Charter Schools: NEA Calls for Stronger School Laws to Spur Innovation")

The third level of accountability is professional accountability, which is concerned with the standards used to assess a teacher's work. The NEA has de-veloped a teacher evaluation system for its sponsored charter schools that allows parents to sit in a classroom and make observations regarding instruction. This activity, according to the NEA, reinforces the notion that teachers are accountable to parents (Ibid.). The NEA also supports an internal accountability system for professional development and accountability. Advocating peer mentoring, re-treats, and volunteerism among teachers and administrators, the NEA claims that it supports a multidimensional professional accountability system for charter schools (Ibid.).

To ensure that the three accountability factors are included as criteria in evaluating charter schools, the NEA launched the Charter School Initiative (CSI) in 1995. This five-year research and development effort was designed to assist the union and its members interested in starting charter schools and to inform the NEA of proactive roles the union can play in school reform efforts.

In 1996, when assessing state standard development and charter school law requirements, the AFT found that the disparities between state accountability re-quirements were not only vast but, as the study noted, only eight of the twenty-five states with charter school legislation that were studied had state standards in all four core subjects (English, science, mathematics, and social studies) that met AFT criteria for accountability. Only seven of the twenty-five states required that charter schools meet the state standards for academic accountability. The study also found that although all states were wrestling with the development and re-finement of state standards, six states with charter school legislation did not re-quire that charter schools meet state standards (American Federation of Teachers, under "AFT's Criteria for Good Charter School Legislation," p. 2). With No Child Left Behind this is, of course, moot. But if history teaches us, and the Act is re-pealed or modified, assessment standards will emerge again on the unions' agenda.

From the point of view of the teachers' unions, the issues of accountability and standards are far more complicated than what has been put forth by charter school advocates. The teachers' unions argue that if charter schools are to really demonstrate their success and to have an impact on public school reform, they must show how their students perform on the same assessment tests given to all public school students. But is this punishing? Both the AFT and NEA argue that comparison data are essential for determining the progress of any school, let alone charter schools. If one agrees that the standards imposed through rigid state testing tied to No Child Left Behind is actually harming students not helping them, or at least it can be argued they are unauthentic assessments, then, yes, it would be. Perhaps it is here that teachers unions need to step back and begin to critically examine the tests and the legislative acts that authorize them and begin to seek to replace them with authentic assessment.

As for experimentation and accountability, both unions understand that change takes time. Legislation for charter schools generally gives them three to five years to demonstrate their efficacy, and only a handful of the schools across the United States have been operating for that period of time. Therefore, argue the unions, it is too early to tell if student achievement in these schools is greater than if the children had remained in their traditional public schools. Thus far, state laws do not require the collection of baseline data about charter schools that would be helpful in determining whether the charter schools have lived up to their claims. And, although charter schools offer a wide range of programs, most do not represent choices that are being tried for the first time. Virtually all the educational approaches and strategies that are being tried in charter schools have been around for decades and have been tried in the traditional public schools (Ibid.). So, at this juncture, there really are no sufficient data to determine if charter schools are reaching their goals and having a positive effect on public education. This is still true thirteen years after the AFT study.

In 1996, the AFT assessed the twenty-five states that had passed charter legislation and found that seventeen of the twenty-five required that charter schools use the same tests as the other schools to determine that students are meeting state goals for learning. From the union's vantage point, the absence of comparison data in eight of those charter schools is highly problematic and indicative of what happens when no standard accountability is required (American Federation of Teachers 1996c, 4). Today, thirteen years later there is still befuddlement as to why there is a controversy over student achievement and the claims made by a multitude of sides are disappointingly based on studies whose methodology is questionable if not outright biased.

Accessibility to Charter Schools

Both the NEA and the AFT believe that a public education is a human right and should be available to all people regardless of ethnicity, culture, race, gender, or sexual orientation. They argue that the backbone of democracy is built on public schools, and they argue that assessing public school access remains a large issue to be considered when assessing the efficacy of charter schools. Worried about the propensity of charter schools to create a multi tiered choice system, which discriminates against some students and not others, both the NEA and the AFT have argued the charter schools must be open to all students—including students with special needs. Furthermore, the unions contend, the charter schools must be tuition-free. The AFT agrees that charter schools can be diverse, appeal to different interests and talents that students might have, and offer varied and different educational strategies and instructional methods, but it is also strongly committed to the idea that despite this diversity, each charter school should be publicly open to all students and thus offer true public choice to U.S. students.

These concerns seem to have merit. In testifying at a legislative hearing in Massachusetts, Robin Foley, co-chair of the Worchester Advisory Council in that state, noted that while it took approximately twenty minutes for most families to get registered at the county's Seven Hills Charter School, special education families were left to sit for more than two hours. Three months later, she testified that at least two special needs children were not receiving services prescribed by their individualized education plan (McFarlane 1997). The Seven Hills Charter School is one of twenty-five authorized under the state charter law.

Because each state determines whether charter schools will serve targeted populations, impose academic requirements, or be restricted to grade level or program preferences, potential problems can arise as to how these restrictions operate to exclude students. One particularly troubling aspect unions point to is the issue regarding restrictions on attendance at charter schools. This issue often arises with the requirement at some charter schools that parents sign a contract guaranteeing a certain level of parental participation at the school, like the KIPP-run schools. A common feature of charter schools, the AFT maintains that this clause in many charter school admission requirements can have the deleterious effect of decreasing the enrollment of children from disadvantaged backgrounds. Many working-class families either cannot afford the time off work or do not have the transportation necessary to regularly participate in their children's schools, and the AFT is worried that parental involvement could be used to screen students based on race or socioeconomic class.

Admissions requirements and processes are another way in which charter schools are better able to shape who attends and who does not. Many charter schools operate on a first-come, first-served basis. Some require meetings and an interview with school officials, and the interview can be used to ensure that there is a fit between the charter school and the family. Although this type of screening might not be overt, in explaining the school's culture and through subtle manipulation administrators can steer students toward or away from a particular charter school.

Charter schools argue that admission requirements such as an interview process are essential to their success, arguing that they must filter applicants to ensure they share the same values and beliefs as the school. The schools want an environment in which everybody is committed to the school's goals and vision, and they see admission requirements and intake interviews as ways to construct that environment. In a 1997 study of charter schools in California, it was found that 44 percent of the ninety-eight charter schools surveyed cited student and/or parent involvement and commitment to the school's philosophy as a factor in denying admission. For start-up charter schools, the number was 50 percent; for conversions, it was 39 percent (SRI International 1997).

Another issue that concerns teachers' unions is how tuition or fees can be used to limit accessibility to charter schools. Although charter schools are prohibited from charging tuition, there is no prohibition on donations, and according to an AFT study on charter school legislation, some charter schools are attempting to collect quarterly "donations" from parents (SRI International 1997, 5). Although the donations are supposed to be voluntary, the teachers' unions worry that many parents who cannot or do not wish to contribute may feel intimidated or feel that their children may not be as welcome as other children at the charter school. Both the AFT and the NEA worry that a policy of donations is a thinly veiled attempt to impose tuition in an effort to deny accessibility to some charter schools.

And then there is the controversy surrounding the opening of the new charter school in 2007, the Khalil Gibran International Academy (KGIA) in New York, which like a great many charter schools, is coincidently funded by the Bill and Melinda Gates Foundation. The school, according to its proponents and founders, is a dual language school but before the school opened and continuing up until the present controversies are swirling around with suggestions that a dual language school such as KGIA, with a special curricular focus on Arabic as a second language and the associated culture, would be more inclined to adopt an uncritical approach to that particular experience. Furthermore, conservatives have argued, that with the schools special focus on Arab culture, it would be more apt to neglect the teaching of what we "Americans" have in common. Speaking for UFT teachers, Leo Casey of the UFT states why the union supported the opening of the Khalil Gibran International Academy Charter School in New York, even in light of the controversy surrounding conservative claims that it is a potential Madrassa:

As part of the New Visions school approval process, the UFT had an opportunity to examine the design of and plans for KGIA: our representatives carefully studied an application of scores of pages, and participated in the panel interview of the school planning team. We found that the school's mission was entirely consistent with the American civic creed, promoting values of non-violence, tolerance and cultural understanding. Based on these findings, we have supported KGIA at every stage in its development.

Our understanding of KGIA's mission separates us both from the New York tabloid press and from some in the blogosphere who have rushed to criticize our public position on the "intifada" issue. The mere fact that KGIA is a dual language Arabic school provides the tabloids with sufficient cause to label it a fundamentalist madrasa, and in a remarkable symmetry, our critics carelessly describe KGIA as a school dedicated to the promotion of "Islamic culture, history and language." In fact, KGIA's namesake Gibran was not even a Muslim. If KGIA was even remotely close to either fact-free description, it would never have received our support. We would not support a public school dedicated to the promotion of the beliefs of any faith community, be it Christian, Jewish, Islamic or another religious creed. (Casey, under "The Civic Purposes of Public Schools and the UFT's Support for Khalil Gibran International Academy")

With similar controversies surrounding the Ben Gamla Charter School in New York, which we looked at in chapter 4, the issue of ethnic or culturally focused charter schools is a controversy that can be expected to continue. With the AFT supporting KGIA, it would seem likely we can count on them to support Ben Gamla and other similar schools as well.

Teacher Professionalism

High-quality teaching, teacher accountability, and professional development are all essential aspects of quality charter schools. Both NEA policies and AFT policies call for teacher professionalism through the development of high-quality teacher preparation. And while many charter proponents advocate legislation that specifically allows teachers who do not necessarily have a state license to teach, across the board teachers' unions are adamant proponents of licensing requirements. Charter school advocates argue that they should be able to hire unlicensed teachers. They like to do this because unlicensed teachers do not "cost as much," they can be paid less in benefits, pensions and wages, not to mention be excluded from many union protections that exist for licensed teachers. The Education Policy Center at Michigan State University conducted a study by Marissa Burian-Fitzgerald, Michael Luekens and Gregory Strizek regarding teacher recruitment and teacher qualifications. The researchers found that when they looked at the qualifications of charter school teachers in comparison with the qualifications of those teachers at regular public schools, the percentage of teachers in traditional public schools were more apt to be certified than charter school teachers. The study also found that the percentage of math teachers in traditional public schools with college majors or minors in mathematics, compared with math teachers in charter schools was also higher. Furthermore, their study concluded that the percentage of traditional public school teachers with more than five years experience were greater than those teachers found in charter schools. However, the study also noted that the percentage of teachers who graduated from the most selective or highly selective colleges within the United States, were more likely to be found in charter schools as opposed to TPSs, as were science teachers with majors and/or minors in science (see Appendix D).

Yet teacher professionalism is not relegated merely to licensing and educational development. Involvement in decision making in such issues as curriculum development, the development of instructional strategies and methods, grouping of students, and implementation of instructional strategies all concern the teachers' unions. The unions argue that initial discussions regarding charter schools focused to some degree on the perception of teachers and the educational profession in general as professionals, and charter schools were a mechanism whereby teachers, parents, and students could negotiate with local school boards for the implementation of new and innovative experiments in education (Budde 1989). The NEA, in a 1998 study, found that teachers in charter schools like the freedom that these independent, experimental schools provide (Green 1998).

The AFT argues that amid all the rhetoric regarding the greater role that teachers play in charter schools and school governance and development, the facts bear little resemblance to the claims. Indeed, the AFT claims that the central role of highly qualified teachers in creating and governing charter schools has actually been undermined and points to two areas of concern—collective bargaining among and by teachers and teacher certification. Paul Hill also noted in his October 2006 symposium review:

> *Charter leaders were similarly vague about how a school that treated its teachers as commodities that could be easily replaced could survive or improve in a market environment.* (Hill et al. 2006)

With teachers increasingly looked at as commodities, or one of the main "costs of educational production," it is hard to disagree with teachers who feel they have been reduced to mere instruments that work to assure student performance on standardized tests.

Collective Bargaining and Charter Schools

The AFT found in one study of charter schools that of the twenty-five states that had charter school legislation at the time, fifteen states had passed legislation that prevented, restricted, or was silent regarding the rights of charter school employees to belong to the local school district collective bargaining unit or to be covered by a collective bargaining agreement (American Federation of Teachers, under "AFT Charter Report").

For teachers' unions, collective bargaining assures that employees receive retirement and health care benefits, can bargain for salaries, and can participate in the development of school policies and curriculum. Unions across the country have adopted different strategies as to how to bargain collectively with school districts, and the unions argue that eliminating the rights of employees to bargain collectively will not enhance teacher professionalism or student learning. In fact, they say the contrary is true. In schools where teachers have lost the opportunity for collective bargaining, they work more hours and have fewer benefits and lower salaries. Some reform efforts in the area of collective bargaining have occurred as a result of charter school legislation, including allowances for waivers of contract provisions and the application of special contract clauses designed to meet the needs of special programs at charter schools (American Federation of Teachers, under "State-by-State Analysis of Charter School Legislation").

Of course, anti-union charter proponents argue that collective bargaining stymies reform efforts such as charter schools, and charter schools have sought, in many states, to get waivers from contract terms, such as collective bargaining, that did not meet the needs of the staff in those schools. The argument is that unionization is a hindrance to a high-performing school district. The unions, of course, disagree and point to Japan, Germany, and France where there is a greater degree of unionization among educational workers and yet students in those countries outperform the students in schools in the United States where teachers and other educational staff are not nearly as unionized. The unions also make the argument that even within the boundaries of the United States, the performance of students relative to levels of unionization is positive (Eberts and Stone 1984).

And then there are points of view like those of Zeke M. Vanderhoek, a former middle-school teacher turned entrepreneur who will serve as the Equity Project Charter School's new principal when it opens in 2009. He is not against teachers, he says: on the contrary, he wants to do away with teacher's unions in entirety by paying teachers more. The school, located in Brooklyn, will serve 120 students in grade 5th through 8th. Vanderhoek is promising to pay $125,000-a-year salaries to teachers to attract the best and the brightest. In this way the issue of unions, collective bargaining, merit pay, and tenure become moot. How does he plan to do this? According to the *New York Times* who published a recent story about the school, Vanderhoek plans to not only make the $125,000 salaries available to teachers but he plans to do so by inverting the traditional hierarchy among teachers and administrators (the principal will earn only $90,000) and by cutting back on support staff, administrators, and technology. For their part, teachers will be expected to work longer hours and more months out of the year, but of course with no union contract and thus no real enforceable rights (Gootman 2008).

According to Vanderhoek:

I would much rather put a phenomenal, great teacher in a field with 30 kids and nothing else than take the mediocre teacher and give them half the number of students and give them all the technology in the world. (Ibid.)

Frederick M. Hess, director of education policy studies at the American Enterprise Institute says the experiment should be followed closely:

This is an approach that has not been tried in this way in American education, and it opens up a slew of fascinating opportunities. That $125,000 figure could have a catalytic effect. (Ibid.)

Randi Weingarten, president of the United Federation of Teachers, called the hefty salaries "a good experiment," but she noted that when teachers were not unionized, as most charter school teachers are not, their performance can be hampered by a lack of power in dealing with the principal. Weingarten, who favors unionization, expresses concern:

What happens the first time a teacher says something like, "I don't agree with you?"

The school's creator and first principal, Zeke M. Vanderhoek, contends that high salaries will attract the best teachers without the need for unions. He says he wants to put into practice the conclusion reached by a steadily growing body of research: that teacher quality—not star principals, laptop computers, or abundant electives—is the crucial ingredient for success. How will he fund the school? Vanderhoek says he would like to run the school perennially on a public budget but admits that without grants he would not be able to stay in business. He might have to look to The Bill and Melinda Gates Foundation or perhaps the Walton family for funds. Once again, the question of who will fund our schools emerges and with charter schools, it increasingly points to philanthropic forces, many of them the same forces who support anti-union organizing efforts by teachers. Where is the philanthropy in that?

Although anti-union charter proponents argue that collective bargaining is a barrier to educational reform, the teachers' unions remain adamant in their contention that attempts to eliminate collective bargaining have less to do with educational reform than with an all-out assault on the teachers' unions themselves.

Teacher Certification and Charter Schools

The previously cited AFT report on charter schools found that of the twenty-five states studied, only six required that all teachers be certified to teach in charter schools. Fifteen of the states allowed charter schools to hire noncertified teachers, and most of those fifteen states allowed all teachers in charter schools to be noncertified. However, Louisiana caps noncertified teachers at 25 percent of the teacher workforce; Delaware allows 35 percent of the teacher workforce to be noncertified; and Connecticut and New Hampshire permit up to 50 percent of the teachers to be noncertified (American Federation of Teachers, under "AFT's Criteria for Good Charter School Legislation"). This has all changed since the time of that study.

The most comprehensive look at charter school teacher certification requirements was done by the Education Commission of the States in 2008. The Commission looked at forty states and the District of Columbia and Puerto Rico, identified as states with charter legislation, and indicated state by state the laws governing teacher certification to teach in charter schools (See Also Appendix C).

Proponents of hiring noncertified teachers to teach in charter schools argue that opening the profession to many people talented in their own field would allow for improvement and innovation of teaching and learning. They point to the many retired professionals who wish to work with young minds in educational settings and argue that rigid teacher certification requirements prevent such people from teaching, which, in turn, they argue, hurts the students.

Yet the teachers' unions argue that it is not enough for an educator to know his or her subject matter. It is crucial, they insist, that educators have knowledge about how students learn and how to teach. Simply being knowledgeable in one's field, the teachers' unions argue, does not guarantee that students will gain knowledge. They claim that in order to be an effective educator, teachers must have background knowledge of child development, learning strategies, cognitive theories, and learning assessment. For this reason, they are adamant in their struggle to ensure that every state require that teachers be certified. And although the unions would agree that the certification requirements themselves need to be scrutinized and are less than perfect, at a minimum the requirements guarantee that teachers have been exposed to some courses and experiences that will help them teach students. The unions contend that reforming and strengthening certification requirements, not abandoning the requirements, is preferred (American Federation of Teachers, under "AFT's Criteria for Good Charter School Legislation")

Local Approval of Charter Schools

Another one of the arguments put forth in support of charter schools is they will help local school districts by providing competition, which, in turn, will force the traditional public schools to change the way they educate students. The teachers' unions, on the other hand, argue that if a charter school is isolated from the local district in which it operates the effect is fragmentation, which makes the achievement of common standards, supported by the unions, difficult if not impossible. Making charter schools the subject of local district approval, argue the AFT and the NEA, is crucial to making sure that local districts do not ignore the charter schools. Because some advocates of charter schools argue that local districts are reluctant to grant charters to applicant schools, the AFT maintains that to ensure a fair hearing to applicants and to promote a strong collaboration with and connection to local districts, charter school legislation should include an appeal process. (Ibid.)

Avoiding obstructionism by local school districts while at the same time requiring local education agencies to grant charters, is the goal of the AFT and the NEA. These unions argue that the charter legislation should contain language that identifies and specifically indicates requirements for public notice and public hearings as well as guidelines for approval or denial. The unions feel that public oversight and monitoring are essential to the success of charter schools. According to the NEA:

> The theory that underlies charters is that such freeing of public schools will hasten educational innovation, improve student achievement, create greater parental involvement, and promote improvement of public education in general. And the theory provides that if there's no educational improvement, the school will be held accountable and the school's charter won't be renewed. Thus, careful public oversight and accurate accountability measures are critical to the whole hypothesis of charter schools. (National Education Association, under "Charter Schools Run by For-Profit Companies")

However, of the twenty-five states studied by the AFT in 1996 that had passed charter legislation, only Arizona and Massachusetts bypassed the local education agency completely in granting charters. Seven states permitted other entities such as universities and state departments to grant charters in addition to local agencies. Colorado and North Carolina had a process spelled out in their charter legislation that allowed the charter applicant to appeal to the state should a charter not be granted by the local education agency (American Federation of Teachers, under "AFT's Criteria for Good Charter School Legislation"). This trend has accelerated today with many agencies, organizations and groups able to now grant charters, from unions to universities.

Public Accountability and Charter Schools

Both the NEA and the AFT are avid supporters of what are called "sunshine laws." Most states have these laws, which are designed to ensure that all public business is conducted in the open. The AFT and NEA contend that because charter schools are public schools, all meetings regarding the business of these schools should be open to public scrutiny. They claim that all information about a charter school, from its finances to its academic results, should be available to the general public. Yet as the AFT has noted:

> Accountability requirements differ widely from state to state. Although many states require charters to submit to an annual report, the states fail to define the contents of the report or require that the reports be made available to the public. Most states require annual audits to be submitted but fail to define the contents of those reports. Other states require charters to submit the same reports that district schools are required to submit . . . Our analysis of current charter school legislation, like our 1966 study, reveals considerable variation from state to state. (American Federation of Teachers, under "Charter School Update")

And as we saw when looking at private EMOs and for-profit independent providers, disclosure and transparency are not even legally required. From the viewpoint of the AFT and the NEA, variation from state to state provides no ability to set standards, no benchmarking ability, and thus no way to hold schools accountable. Setting guidelines for accountability procedures argue the unions, is essential to monitor charter schools and allow public oversight. At a minimum, maintains the AFT, states and/or the local communities in which charter schools are operating should be required to issue an annual report that includes information concerning:

> *How many charters there are and where they are located;*
> *Who attends the charter schools—demographic information about the student body, and information as to whether special needs students are enrolled;*
> *Who staffs these schools—the credentials of staff members;*
> *The student and staff turnover rate;*
> *The composition of the education program;*
> *Student performance on achievement tests used by the state and/or designed to assess progress of students in meeting state standards;*
> *Where the money comes from—a full accounting of all sources of revenues; and*
> *How the money has been spent—a financial accounting of all expenditures.*
> (American Federation of Teachers, under "AFT's Criteria for Good Charter School Legislation")

NEW ROLES AND RESPONSIBILITES FOR TEACHER UNIONS

In order to head in a new direction and embrace the emerging needs of our nation's children, many progressives argue that the teachers' unions must also change. They argue that unions must create and maintain a vision of equity for all students; that they must seek to defend public education and the rights of teachers; that teachers' unions must place a strong emphasis on professionalism and accountability; and that these unions must be committed to all children in the communities they serve by addressing issues of race, class, and gender discrimination if they mean that some students are excluded and others rewarded *(Peterson and Charney 1999)*.

With the rapid changes in the knowledge needs of citizens, education is changing in both form and content. Teachers' unions are one of the most powerful forces in education, and the direction they take will determine to some degree the nature of education and educational opportunities in the United States. Progressive educators argue that teachers' unions must begin to be involved with issues of social justice and anticorporate posturing and must begin to struggle with a multitude of unions in other industries to stave off attacks on unions and support the EFCA. Many progressive educators believe that privatization efforts constitute an all-out attack on public education and that this form of corporatization is taking place, not just in the arena of education, but in society at large. They argue that if teachers' unions are to transcend the past and truly embark on a road of social justice and equity for all students, they must join with other anticorporate and antiprivatization efforts that are taking place throughout the country.

Along with allying with others to achieve social justice, progressive educators argue that teachers' unions must, at a minimum, be implicated in:

> *Determining who enters the teaching profession;*
> *Designing mentoring programs where new teachers receive intensive guidance and help;*
> *Participating in a community outreach programs where teachers used public forums such as churches, temples, community centers, sororities, and such for purposes of engaging community members in supporting educational efforts;*
> *Developing self-monitoring measures that would assure that all teachers performed with high quality;*
> *Operating a teachers' development center where teachers taught and received educational units for their efforts;*
> *Designing programs that combated prejudice and racism and incorporating multicultural and gender concerns into curriculum;*
> *Working in an ongoing alliance with community members, unions from other professions, youth groups and public organizations in efforts to transform social maladies; and*
> *Holding membership meetings in an atmosphere of civility and inquiry whereby social issues could be addressed in more systematic and comprehensive ways.* (Ibid.)

This professional unionism, progressive educators contend, must maintain a focus on innovative reforms such as charter schools while remaining vigilant in its opposition to privatization. And, claim progressive educators, this professional unionism must be a social justice unionism grounded in a commitment to global and national struggles that go beyond the classroom to the global community at large. The struggle for equitable and high-performing schools for all students is tantamount to the struggles to achieve health care for all citizens. But can support for a system of contract charter schools really be in the best interests of teachers?

Nowhere is the issue of professional unionism more obvious than in the area of teacher accountability. Although accountability has been the focus of many anti-union advocates, social justice unionism would focus on transcending the industrial model whereby accountability is the responsibility of principals and supervisors, not teachers. Professional accountability, argue progressive educators, must look beyond simply individual teachers and their individual rights and also consider the broader issues facing teachers. Internal quality controls, argue professional union advocates, would transcend the industrial model of teachers' union relations while at the same time assuring that due process and collective bargaining stay intact.

The people who seek to transform unions as opposed to abolishing or destroying them, argue that the unions need to:

> *Define and measure quality—for students, teachers, and schools;*
> *Organize around individual schools and abandon school district organizing;*
> *Focus on building an external labor market for teachers that would allow them to keep their benefit protections and employment support services as they move from job to job, in or out of the district;*
> *Enable teachers to take roles traditionally left to district administrators;*
> *Support teachers in developing their skills;*
> *Award teachers higher salaries by creating incentives for acquiring new skills and expertise;*
> *Develop new strategies for ensuring employment security;*
> *Actively involve teachers in planning, policymaking, and resource allocation;*
> *Redefine teaching;*
> *Create authentic standards for student performance;*
> *Institute peer assistance; and*
> *Redefine curriculum and transform schools. (Kerchner, Koppich, and Weeres 1998)*

SUMMARY

Teachers' unions have been one of the most successful union efforts in the twentieth century. They have fought for professionalism and collective bargaining arrangements that have transformed education and the society within which we live. How charter schools are run, the legislation they operate under, and the accountability demanded of them will all be decided, in part, with the help of the teachers' unions. If the unions can advocate successfully for students and teachers and accept new forms of innovation and experimentation, they will succeed in transforming themselves and the systems within which they work. Charter schools provide one of the challenges and for many the opportunities that the teachers' unions will face as we enter the twenty-first century. Although what teachers and charter school proponents agreed at the May 2006 symposium held by the Progressive Policy Institute that what was needed was more empirical evidence in order to critically examine the role of unions in charter schools, they did agree that some of the major questions are summed up by the symposium participants are:

> *How does the charter school teaching force differ from the teaching force in the neighboring district's schools in terms of age, educational attainment, and measured ability? Are charter schools constantly disrupted by teacher turnover, or have they learned to stabilize instruction and build teacher skills despite turnover (or even benefit from it in some cases)? Are charter teachers more or less satisfied in*

their jobs than teachers in neighboring public schools (and in schools serving similar populations)? Do charter school teachers use their market power (their ability to leave jobs they do not like) to exert influence on schools? If so, how? Do parents use their market power (their ability to choose schools and leave those they do not like) to exert influence on schools? If so, how? How does at-will employment work in charter schools? What proportion of teachers are bullied or arbitrarily dismissed in charter schools? Do charter school leaders (principals) differ from regular public school leaders in their leadership style and openness to teacher input? Do unionized charter schools suffer more internal conflict and focus less on instruction than non-unionized schools? (Hill et al. 2006)

At the symposium held by the Progressive Policy Institute back in May 2006, American Federation of Teachers union leader, Randi Weingarten and charter advocate Ted Kolderie, harped on the main issue facing education today. Millions of children in America are not getting the education they need. Continuing with business as usual certainly will not bring new, innovative, and different approaches and results. People committed to public education all know that experiments with new ideas are essential to change a faltering system. This experimentation includes new methods and modes of employing teacher talent and time, as well as increasing student involvement and motivation in learning. The real issue is who will control the "experiments" and new and different approaches symposium members say are needed? Will entrepreneurship and market fundamentalism, with its narrow approach to human nature and individual freedom based on an ideology premised on the pursuit of rational self-interests, secure the nation's educational needs? Or will it, as it has done in the health care sector, create higher costs for the consumer and higher profits for those who control the new schools while leaving citizens isolated, segregated, and without the care and/or educational services they need? Is this bleak vision of the individual being embraced at the expense of concerns about wider socials issues? Do we need a private option plan for public education or is what is really needed a "New Deal" when it comes to funding education, training teachers, developing new and just collective bargaining agreements that put workers on par with their "employers," and teach students what John Dewey not so long ago counseled, to be good citizens? All of these questions, concerns, and more are being played out in an educational drama that currently surrounds charter schools, private providers, public managers, public policy makes, teachers, philanthropists, and the parent and students that education is designed to serve.

REFERENCES

Adams, S., J. Heywood, and R. Rothstein. "Teachers, Performance Pay and Accountability." Economic Policy Institute, 14 May 2009. http://www.epi.org/publications/entry/books-teachers_performance_pay_and_accountability/.

Allis, S. "Laying Siege to Seniority." *Time,* 23 December 1991. http://www.time.com /time/magazine/ article/0,9171,974502,00.html.

American Federation of Teachers. AFT Charter Report. Washington, DC, 1996. a.

———. AFT's Criteria for Good Charter School Legislation. Washington, DC, 1996b.

———. Charter School Update. Educational Policy Issues Policy Brief, no. 9. Washington, DC, June 1999, 2.

———. State-by-State Analysis of Charter School Legislation. Washington, DC, 25 February 2000.

Bronfirebrenner, K. "No Holds Barred: The Intensification of Employer Opposition to Organizing." Economic Policy Institute, 20 May 2009. http://www.americanrightsatwork.org/dmdocuments/ ARAWReports/noholdsbarred_factsheet.pdf.

Bronston, B. "Merit Pay for Teachers Garners Praise from Obama and Local Schools." *The Times-Picayune,* 14 March 2009. http://www.nola.com/news/index.ssf/2009/03/performance_ management.htm.

Brookings Institute. "Teachers Unions: Do They Help or Hurt Education Reform?" (2000). http://www.brookings.edu/events/2000/0411education.aspx.

Budde, R. *Education by Charter: Restructuring Schools and School Districts.* Andover, MA: Regional Laboratory for Educational Improvement of the Northeast and Islands, 1989.

Casey, L. "KIPP Teachers Organize." *EdWize,* 13 January 2009. http://www.edwize.org/kipp-teachers-organize.KJ

———. "Steve Barr Welcome To Our World." *Edwize,* 18 May 2007. http://www.edwize.org/steve-barr-welcome-to-our-world.

———. "The Civic Purposes of Public Schoos and the UFT's Support for Khalil Gibran International Academy." *EdWize,* 21 August 2007. http://www.edwize.org/the-civic-purposes-of-public-schools-and-the-ufts-support-for-khalil-gibran-international-academy.

Catalyst Chicago. "NLRB Declares Civitas Teachers Private Employees." District 299: The Chicago Schools Blog, 3 June 2009. http://www.catalyst-chicago.org/RUSSO/index.php/entry1890/ NLRB_Declares_Civaitas_Teachers_Private_Employees.

Chase, B. "The New Unionism: A Course for School Quality." Speech given by the president of the National Education Association to the National Press Club, 5 February 1997.

Corwin, R, and E.J. Schneider. *The School Choice Hoax: Fixing America's Schools.* Lanham, MD: Rowman and Littlefield Education, 2007.

Culpepper, L. "Trojan Horse Made of Charter School Money." September 2008. http://townhall. com/columnists/LeeCulpepper/2008/09/14/a_trojan_horse_made_of_charter-school_ money.

Duffett, A., S. Farkas, A. J. Rotherham, and E. Silva. "Waiting to Be Won Over: Teachers Speak on the Profession, Unions and Reform." *Education Sector Report,* 2008. http://www.education sector.org/usr_doc/WaitingToBeWonOver.pdf.

Eberts, R., and A. Stone. *Unions and Public Schools.* Lexington, MA: Lexington Books, 1984.

Education Commission of the States. State Notes. "Do Teachers in a Charter School Have to be Certified?" Denver, CO. 2008. http://mb2.ecs.org/reports/Report.aspx?id=93

Foster, J.B., R McChesney, 1. Stole, and H. Holleman. "The Sales Effort and Monolopy Capitalism." *Monthy Review,* 60 no.11. April 2009.

Gootman, E. "At Charter School, Higher Teacher Pay." 17 March 2008. http://www.nytimes. com/2008/03/07/nyregion/07charter.html?_r=1.

Green Dot newsletter. "Driving Reform." 24 July 2007. http://www.greendot.org/driving_reform.

Green, R. "Union Research Finds Teachers Pleased with Charters." *Associated Press,* 2 July 1998.

Greene, J. P. "This is the song that never ends." http://jaypgreene.com/2009/05/20/this-is-the-song-that-never-ends/.

Haynes, V.D. "Teacher Contract Would End Seniority: Union Is Reviewing Proposal from Rhee." *Washington Post,* 21 May 2008. pg. B02. http://www.washingtonpost.com/wp-dyn/content/article/2008/05/20/AR2008052001789.html.

———. "Rhee Seeks Tenure Pay Swap for Teachers." *Washington Post,* 2 July 2009. http://www.washingtonpost.com/wp-dyn/content/article/2008/07/02/AR2008070203498.html.

Hess, S. *Civitas' Letter From CEO to Parents Regarding Unionization,* (2009). http://www.civitas schools.org/assets/Letter%20to%20Civitas%20Community%206_3_09.pdf.

Hill, P. "American Youth Forum, It Takes a City: Getting Serious about Urban School Reform, a Forum." *American Youth Forum,* 14 May 2001. http://www.aypf.org/forumbriefs/2001/fb051401.htm).

Fixing Urban Schools. *Brookings Insitute* Press, 2008.

Hill, P. and J. Harvey. *Making School Reform Work,* (2004). Brookings Institute Press.

Hill, P., L. Rainey, and A. Rotherman. "The Future of Charter Shools and Teacher Unions: Results of a Symposium National Charter School Research Project." October 2006. http://www.ncsrp.org/downloads/charter_unions.pdf.

Horovitz, B. "Teachers Snub Scholastic's Toys." *USA Today,* 8 June 2009.

Jonsson, P. "Private Dollars Leading Recovery of New Orleans." *The Christian Science Monitor,* 27 June 2007. http://www.csmonitor.com/2007/0627/p01s06-usec.html?page=.

Keller, B. "NEA Grows More Strategic About Membership." *EDWeek,* 22 June 2005. http://www.edweek.org/login.html?source=http://www.edweek.org/ew/articles/2005/06/22/41nea.h24.html&destination=http://www.edweek.org/ew/articles/2005/06/22/41nea.h24.html&levelId=1000.

Kerchner, C., J. Koppich, and J. Weeres. *Taking Charge of Quality: How Teachers and Unions Can Revitalize Schools.* San Francisco, CA: Jossey-Bass, 1998.

Kirkpatrick, D. "Charter Schools vs. Teacher Unions: Irresistible Force vs. Immovable Object?" *Viewpoint,* Buckeye Institute, 14 September 2006. http://www.buckeyeinstitute.org/article/824.

Klein, N. *The Shock Doctrine: The Rise of Disaster Capitalism.* New York: Metropolitan Books, 2007.

LaborNerd. "Always Singin' the Same Old Song." 10 March 2009. http://labornerd.blogspot.com/2009/03/always-singin-same-old-song.html.

Lieberman, M. *Teacher Unions: How the NEA and AFT Sabotage Reform and Hold Parents, Students, Teachers, and Taxpayers Hostage to Bureaucracy.* New York: The Free Press, 1997.

Light, J. "The Education Industry: The Corporate Takeover of Public Schools." *Corporate Watch,* 8 July 1998.

Lopez, S. "Seniority, Not Quality, Counts Most at United Teachers of Los Angeles." *Los Angeles Times,* 25 March 2009. http://www.latimes.com/news/local/la-me-lopez25-2009mar25,0,4942695.column.

Lowe, R. "The Chicago Teacher's Federation and Its Legacy." In *Transforming Teacher Unions: Fighting for Better Schools,* 14. Eds. B. Peterson and M. Charney. Milwaukee: ReThinking Schools, 1999.

Maloney, S. "Pastorek Paycheck Dwarfs Other Gulf Educators." *New Orleans City Business,* 10 March 2008.

Masterson, K. "Wanted: A Few Bad Teachers In an Anti-Union Campaign, A Lobbyist Dubbed 'Dr. Evil' Promises $10,000 Apiece to Bad Apples." *Chicago Tribune,* 31 March 2008. http://archives.chicagotribune.com/2008/mar/31/news/chi-worst-teachersmar31.

Mathews, J. "Charter Schools' Big Experiment." *Washington Post,* 9 June 2008. http://www.washingtonpost.com/wp-dyn/content/article/2008/06/08/AR2008060802174.html.

McFarlane, C. "Charter Schools Facing Scrutiny over Special Education." *Telegram and Gazette,* 1 April 1997.

Medina, J. "Teachers Say Union Faces Resistance From Brooklyn Charter School." *New York Times,* 6 February 2009. http://www.nytimes.com/2009/02/07/education/07kipp.html?_r=4.

Merrow, J. "Media Attention Hinders Rhee's Efforts to Reach Out to D.C. Teachers." *PBS Newshour,* 5 May 2009. http://www.pbs.org/newshour/bb/education/jan-june09/dcschools_05-05.html.

———. "Charter Schools Exclude Special Education Students." *San Francisco Education Examiner,* 7 May 2009. http://www.examiner.com/x-356-SF-Education-Examiner~y2009m5d7-NewsHour-New-Orleans-charter-schools-exclude-special-education-students.

Minnesota Federation of Teachers. "Minutes of Executive Council Meeting." 20 April 1991.

Molnar, A., G. Miron, and J. Urschel. *Profiles of For-Profit Educational Management Organizations Tenth Annual Report.* (2008). http://epicpolicy.org/files/EMO0708.pdf.

Nathan, J. *Charter Schools: Creating Hope and Opportunity for American Education.* San Francisco: Jossey-Bass, Inc., 1996.

National Charter Research Project. "The Future of Charter Schools and Teachers Unions." October 2006. http://www.ncsrp.org/downloads/charter_unions.pdf

National Education Association. Charter Schools: NEA Calls for Stronger School Laws to Spur Innovation. Washington, DC, 3 April 1999, p. 6.

———. Charter Schools Run by For-Profit Companies. Washington, DC, 23 April 2000, pp. 1-2.

———. Education, Investors, and Entrepreneurs: A Framework for Understanding Contracting-Out Public Schools and Public School Services. Washington, DC, 1998.

———. *In Brief: For-Profit Management of Public Schools.* Washington, DC, 1998.

———. *Charter Schools.* 2004. http://www.nea.org/home/16332.htm.

National Right to Work newsletter. "Teacher Union Dons Sing 'Charter School Blues.'" October 2007. http://www.nrtwc.org/nl/nl200710p4.pdf.

Pechthalt, J. "No Merit to Merit Pay: The Latest Incarnation of NCLB Would Bring this Harmful Practice to Schools Nationwide." *United Teacher, volume XXXVII, No. 3,* 9 November 2007. http://www.utla.net/node/930.

People's Weekly World. "Teacher Union Organizes Three Charter Schools in Area Wide First." 6 April 2009. http://www.pww.org/article/articleview/15133/.

Peterson, B., and M. Charney, eds. *Transforming Teacher Unions: Fighting for Better Schools and Social Justice.* Milwaukee: ReThinking Schools, 1999.

Piper, K. "Charter School to Union: No Thanks, Teachers Are Not Public Employees?" *The Examiner.* 19 May 2009. http://www.examiner.com/x-2157-Charter-Schools-Examiner~y2009m5d19-Charter-school-to-union-No-thanksteachers-are-not-public-employees.

Ravitch, D. "Why Teacher Unions Are Good for Teachers and the Public." *AFT Educator,* Winter 2006-2007. http://www.aft.org/pubs-reports/american_educator/issues/winter06-07/includes/ravitch.htm.

Saltman, K. *Capitalizing on Disaster: Taking and Breaking Public Schools Cultural Politics and the Promise of Democracy.* Boulder, CO: Paradigm Publishers, 2007.

Saunders, S. "Unions Are Alive and Well in Many Charter Schools: Schools Flourish with Partnership." *New York Teacher,* 22 September 2008. http://www.nysut.org/cps/rde/xchg/nysut/hs.xsl/newyorkteacher_10946.htm.

Silverstein, K. "Labor's Last Stand: The Corporate Campaign to Kill the Employee Free Choice Act." *Harpers Magazine,* vol. 319, no. 1910 (July 2009).

Simon, D. "More New Orleans Schools to Convert to Charter Status." *Times-Picayune,* 22 December 2008. http://www.nola.com/news/index.ssf/2008/12/more_schools_to_join_new_orlea.html.

Spiri, M.H. "School Leadership and Reform: Case Studies of Philadelphia Principals." Consortium for Policy Research in Education. May 2001. http://www.cpre.org/Publications/children02.pdf.

SRI International. *Evaluation of Charter School Effectiveness*. Report prepared for the state of California Office of Legislative Analyst. Menlo Park, CA, 1997.

Stephey, M.J. "A Brief History of Tenure." *Time,* 17 November 2008. http://www.time.com/time/nation/article/0,8599,1859505,00.html.

Tough, P. "A Touchable Moment." *New York Times,* 17 August 2008.

United Teachers of New Orleans. "AFT UTNO/Charter School Frequently Asked Questions." http://la.aft.org/utno/index.cfm?action=article&articleID=6e8cfc79-5f13-45e3-b1ff-b257cdf50a63.

Viadero, D. "Report Points to Risks of Merit Pay for Teachers." *EdWeek,* vol. 28, no. 32, 14 May 2009. http://www.edweek.org/ew/articles/2009/05/13/32meritpay.h28.html.

Washington Post. "Obama Backs Merit Pay for Teachers." 4 June 2009. http://www.nypost.com/seven/03102009/news/nationalnews/obama_backs_merit_pay_for_teachers_158918.htm.

Wells, A., and J. Scott. *Evaluation of Privatization and Charter Schools*. UCLA Charter School Study Prepared for Conference on the National Center for the Study of Privatization in Education, New York: Columbia University Teachers College, April 1999.

Wells, A.S., ed. *Where Charter School Policy Fails*. New York: Teachers College Press, 2002.

Wilson, S. *Learning on the Job*. Cambridge, MA: Harvard University Press, 2006.

Winters, M. "KIPP vs. the Teachers' Unions In New York, a Key Battle to Preserve Charter Schools' Effectiveness." 16 April 2008. http://www.city-journal.org/2009/eon0416mw.html.

Chapter Eight

Organizations, Associations, and Government Agencies

The following are organizations, associations, and governmental agencies that provide information on charter schools and the charter school controversies.

The American Enterprise Institute for Public Policy
1150 Seventeenth Street, NW
Washington, DC 20036
202-862-5800; fax: 202-862-7177
e-mail: VRodman@aei.org

This well-known conservative think tank states that its purposes are to defend the principles and improve the institutions of American freedom and democratic capitalism—limited government, private enterprise, individual liberty and responsibility, vigilant and effective defense and foreign policies, political accountability, and open debate. Its work is addressed to government officials and legislators, teachers and students, business executives, professionals, journalists, and all citizens interested in a serious understanding of government policy, the economy, and important social and political developments.

American Federation of Teachers
555 New Jersey Avenue, NW
Washington, DC 20001
202-393-8642
www.aft.org

One of the largest teachers' unions in the United States, the American Federation of Teachers (AFT) is a good source for information about union positions regarding charter schools and activities in specific areas of the United States. AFT's former president, Albert Shanker, was a major figure in the ideological development of charter schools.

American Institutes for Research
3333 K Street, NW
Washington, DC 20007-3541
202-342-5000
www.air.org

The American Institutes for Research (AIR) is an independent, nonprofit organization that provides government and the private sector with services that promote high quality by applying and advancing the knowledge, theories, methods, and standards of the behavioral and social sciences to solve significant societal problems. Institutes are located throughout the United States, and AIR is responsible for research regarding charter schools.

Annenberg Institute for School Reform
Brown University
Box 1985
Providence, RI 02912
401-863-7990
www.annenberginstitute.org

The mission of the Annenberg Institute for School Reform is to develop, share, and act on knowledge that improves the conditions and outcomes of schooling in the United States, especially in urban communities and in schools serving underserved children. The institute currently focuses its programs in six initiative areas. It carries out its work through research and analysis, collaborations with partner organizations, support for local action, publications, and conferences. To help develop and refine its programming, the institute periodically convenes a program advisory group to review current activities and make recommendations for the future focus of the institute's work. The Coalition of Essential Schools has profited from a large Annenberg grant.

Arizona Charter Schools Association
7500 N. Dreamy Draw Drive, Suite 220
Phoenix, AZ 85020
602-944-0644
http://www.azcharters.org/

The Arizona Charter Schools Association is dedicated to supporting the efforts of Arizona's charter schools. The organization states it seeks to continually create and improve educational opportunities and charter schools for the students, families, and communities they serve.

Association of Educators in Private Practice

N7425 Switzke Road
Watertown, WI 53094
800-252-3280
e-mail: info@aepp.org

The Association of Educators in Private Practice (AEPP) is a growing nonprofit, national, and professional organization made up of private practice educators. The group's mission states that it is based on providing support for and advancement of the education of students; aiding and assisting educators in private practice in the performance of their lawful functions; enhancing the effectiveness and professionalism of educators in private practice; encouraging, sponsoring, and facilitating the intercommunication and sharing of ideas and issues identified as common and relevant to educators in private practice; and promoting the instruction and training of an educated citizenry. AEPP publishes a variety of materials for members and nonmembers, including an *Index of Opportunities,* an *AEPP Directory,* and a newsletter entitled *Enterprising Educators,* which is published in the fall and spring.

Building Excellent Schools

262 Washington Street, 7th Floor
Boston, MA 02108
617-227-4545
http://www.buildingexcellentschools.org/

Building Excellent Schools (BES) states that it serves as a national model for supporting excellence in public education through the national charter school movement. It focuses on improving urban education by providing support for designing, launching, and sustaining urban charter schools—independently managed public schools. Building Excellent Schools is guided by a set of core beliefs in its pursuit of excellent urban charter schools. BES believes that the greatest value for urban communities, desperately in need of strong educational options for their children, should be determined by student academic performance. School safety is critical, but it is not enough. Parental satisfaction is important, but it is not the bellwether of exemplary education. The most important question to ask in striving for academic excellence is: "How are students performing?"

California Charter Schools Association
250 E. 1st Street, Suite 1000
Los Angeles, CA 90012
213-244-1446
http://www.myschool.org

The California Charter Schools Association is California's largest charter school service organization. The association claims it is the public voice for its members and the charter school movement in California. The association's goal is to unite the charter school community behind a common vision by providing charter schools with the resources and support to take the movement to the next level. The association has four main areas of focus: Core Strength, Advocacy, Quality, and Leadership. The California Charter Schools Association advances the charter school movement through state and local advocacy, leadership on quality and extensive resources.

Center for Critical Thinking
Sonoma State University
P.O. Box 220
Dillon Beach, CA 94929
707-78-9100; fax: 707-878-9111
www.criticalthinking.org

The Center for Critical Thinking conducts advanced research and disseminates information on critical thinking. Each year it sponsors an international conference on critical thinking and educational reform. It has worked with the college board, the National Education Association, the U.S. Department of Education, and numerous colleges, universities, and school districts to facilitate the implementation of critical thinking instruction focused on intellectual standards. The Center supports the best educational practices in public and private schools.

Center for Education Reform
910 Seventeenth, NW, Suite 120
Washington, DC 20006
800-521-2118
www.edreform.com

The Center for Education Reform is a conservative organization that publishes newsletters and materials about education reform, including charter schools. It has links on its Web site to various federal and state educational agencies, and it provides research and guidance for those interested in education reform.

Center for School Change
Humphrey Institute, University of Minnesota
301 Nineteenth Avenue South
Minneapolis, MN 55455
612-626-1834
www.centerforschoolchange.org

The Center for School Change publishes reports on the concept of charter schools, policies that underlie the movement, and the laws that govern it. It is a useful source for anyone who is trying to create a charter school.

Center on Reinventing Public Education
University of Washington
Box 363060
Seattle, WA 98195-3060
206-685-2214
www.crpe.org/
e-mail: correspondence@rand.org

The Center on Reinventing Public Education states as its mission that it seeks to develop and evaluate methods of public oversight that can allow individual schools to be focused, effective, and accountable. The center's research program, which was established in 1993, centers on current governance arrangements in public education, and researchers have found that the most productive schools follow coherent instructional strategies in an environment free of regulation and compliance imperatives. The center pursues a national program of research and development on such proposals as charter schools, school contracting, school choice, and school system decentralization via alliances with the Brookings Institute, the RAND Corporation, Vanderbilt University, and the University of Chicago. The center also conducts research into reform initiatives in Washington State and the Seattle public schools.

Charter Schools Development Center
California State University Institute for Education Reform
California State University, Sacramento
6000 J Street
Sacramento, CA 95819-6018
916-278-4611
www.csus.edu
e-mail: epremach@calstate.edu

The Charter Schools Development Center (CSDC) is a nonprofit program housed at California State University at Sacramento. CSDC's stated goal is to help public education make the leap from being a highly regulated, process-based system to one that allows and encourages schools to be more creative, performance-based centers of effective teaching and learning. The center provides technical assistance to the charter school reform movement in California and nationally. Its staff has extensive hands-on experience in both charter school policy and school-based practice, and staff members are known for their in-depth and practical expertise in the most challenging aspects of charter school planning, operations, and oversight. They specifically provide assistance in how to plan and start a charter school; how to define and measure student and school performance; how to understand the roles and responsibilities of charter-granting agencies; and how to understand charter school finance and operations, school governance and leadership, and charter school laws and policy.

Charter Schools Development Corporation

7272 Park Circle Drive, Suite 265
Hanover, MD 21076
443-561-1280; fax: 443-561-1281
http://www.csdc.org/
email: info@csdc.org

CSDC was founded in 1997 as a non-profit corporation established to serve the charter school community. The organization claims the charter idea is the most dynamic, innovative, and fastest growing segment of American K-12 education, and the catalyst, through more competition and choice, for the systemic reform and improvement of poor performing traditional public schools. CSDC's stated mission is to promote excellence, innovation, and parental choice in public education by assisting public charter schools with their facilities financing needs, and to work at the public policy level to improve the laws governing the financing of charter school capital projects.

Charter Schools USA

6245 N. Federal Highway, 5th Floor
Fort Lauderdale, FL 33308
954-202-3500; fax: 954-202-3512
http://www.charterschoolsusa.com/

Charter Schools USA is a for-profit management enterprise that designs, develops and operates high performing public schools: committed to student achievement and supported by sound business practices. It also provides a choice for communities, parents, students, and professionals that foster educational excellence in America. Charter Schools USA founded in 1997, is an organization that has emerged as one of the nation's fastest growing and most successful education companies, with approximately 1,400 employees educating over 14,000 students across Florida. According to the organization, Charter Schools USA schools produce some of the strongest academic gains in reading and math in the nation based on state and federal standards. Charter Schools USA started the nation's first charter school in the workplace, the first municipal charter school, and the largest municipal charter middle-high school. Charter Schools USA currently operates 19 schools on 14 campuses.

Coalition of Essential Schools
1330 Broadway, Suite 600
Oakland, CA 94612
510-433-1451
www.essentialschools.org

The Coalition of Essential Schools is a growing national network of over 1,000 schools and twenty-four regional support centers. It has evolved from a centrally run organization to a decentralized network of regional centers that provide technical assistance and personalized support to schools.

Commercialism in Education Research
Commercialism in Education Research Unit
Division of Educational Leadership & Policy Studies
Mary Lou Fulton College of Education
Box 872411
Arizona State University
Tempe, AZ 85287-2411
480-965-1886; fax: 480-965-0303
http://www.schoolcommercialism.org
e-mail: epic.epru@gmail.com

The Commercialism in Education Research Unit (CERU) conducts research, disseminates information, and helps facilitate dialogue between the education community, policymakers, and the public at large about commercial activities in schools. CERU is the only national academic research unit dedicated to this topic. CERU is guided by the belief that mixing commercial activities with public education raises fundamental issues of public policy, curriculum content, the proper relationship of educators to the students entrusted to them, and the values that the schools embody. CERU is the successor of the Center for the Analysis of Commercialism in Education (CACE) at the University of Wisconsin-Milwaukee.

Consortium for Policy Research in Education
Graduate School of Education
Pennsylvania State University
University Park, PA 16802

814-863-2599
www.gv.psu.edu

The Consortium for Policy Research in Education (CPRE) was created in 1985 to bring together researchers from five of the leading universities to improve elementary and secondary education through research on policy, finance, school reform—including charter schools—and school governance. CPRE focuses on three essential components of educational reform: incorporating a set of policies and practices in education, maintaining meaningful incentives for individuals and the organization, and building the capacity of the individual and the organization to institute and sustain necessary changes.

Council of Chief State School Officers
1 Massachusetts Avenue, NW, Suite 700
Washington, DC 20001-1431
202-408-5505
www.ccsso.org

The Council of Chief State School Officers (CCSSO) is a nationwide, nonprofit organization composed of public officials who head the departments responsible for elementary and secondary education in the states, nonstate U.S. jurisdictions, the District of Columbia, and the Department of Defense's Education Activity Committee. In representing chief education officers, the CCSSO works on behalf of the state agencies that serve public school students throughout the nation. It hosts council partnerships, helps implement federal education programs, endorses council projects, and issues publications and news releases concerning educational reform efforts.

Council of the Great City Schools
1301 Pennsylvania Avenue, NW, Suite 702
Washington, DC 20004
202-393-2427
www.cgcs.org

The Council of the Great City Schools is a coalition of some fifty-seven of the nation's largest urban public school systems. Founded in 1956 and incorporated in 1961, the council works to promote urban education through legislation, research, media relations, management, technology, and special projects. The council serves as a voice for urban educators, provides ways to share information about promising practices, and addresses common concerns.

Council of Urban Boards of Education
1680 Duke Street
Alexandria, VA 22314

703-838-6720
www.nsba.org/cube
e-mail: cube@nsba.org

The Council of Urban Boards of Education was started in 1967 to address the unique needs of school board members serving the largest cities in the United States. The council gathers information, develops recommendations, and takes appropriate actions to improve the quality and equality of education.

Drexel University Foundations Technical Assistance Center for Public Charter Schools
133 Q Gaither Drive
Mount Laurel, NJ 08054
888-693-6675; 856-642-6330
www.drexel.edu

Drexel University Foundations Technical Assistance Center (TAC) for Public Charter Schools advocates and assists in the development of quality public charter schools in the mid-Atlantic region as well as the rest of the nation. TAC states that it fosters school improvement by providing technical support to charter school planning groups, application-writing groups, and operating charter schools. Additionally, TAC provides on-site expert educational leaders, makes referrals, conducts workshops and conferences, and promotes legislation for charter schools.

EdisonLearning
EdisonLearning, Inc.
521 Fifth Avenue, 11th Floor
New York, NY 10175
212-419-1600; fax: 212-419-1764

Formerly the Edison Project, EdisonLearning is a for-profit educational management organization (EMO) that has over the last 17 years experienced not only servicing but *operating* public schools in collaboration with districts, boards, and other authorities with whom we partner. EdisonLearning touts itself as the only education company that works hand-in-hand with thousands of principals, teachers, and families, every day.

Editorial Projects in Education (EPE) Research Center
Editorial Projects in Education Inc.
6935 Arlington Road, Suite 100
Bethesda, MD 20814-5233
800-346-1834; 301-280-3100
http://www.edweek.org/rc/

The EPE Research Center is a division of Editorial Projects in Education, the non-profit organization that publishes *Education Week*. With a staff of full-time researchers, the Research Center conducts annual policy surveys, collects data, and performs analyses that appear in the *Quality Counts, Technology Counts,* and *Diplomas Count* annual issues of *Education Week*. The Center also manages the Education Counts database of state policy indicators, releases periodic special reports on a variety of topics, and contributes data and analysis to coverage in *Education Week, Teacher Magazine,* and edweek.org.

Education Commission of the States
700 Broadway, #810
Denver, CO 80203-3442
303-299-3600
www.ecs.org

The Education Commission of the States (ECS) launches partnerships between corporate leaders and education policymakers to help shape the future of public education. The ECS provides initiatives on teacher quality, information about educational reforms, the latest news releases regarding issues in public education, and policy studies. The mission of the ECS is to help state leaders identity, develop, and implement a public policy for education that addresses current and future needs of a learning society.

Educational Policy Institute
EPI International/United States
Dr. Watson Scott Swail
2400 Princess Anne Road
Virginia Beach, VA 23456
757-430-2200
e-mail: wswail@educationalpolicy.org

EPI Australasia
Dr. Ian R Dobson
174 Wingrove Street
Fairfield Vic 3078
Australia
+61 (0) 419 514 232
e-mail: idobson@educationalpolicy.org

EPI Canada
Mr. Alex Usher

20 Maud Street, Suite 207
Toronto, Ontario M5V 2M5
Canada
416-848-0215
e-mail: ausher@educationalpolicy.org

The Educational Policy Research Unit (EPRU) conducts original research, provides independent analyses of research and policy documents, and facilitates the implementation of innovations in areas such as student performance standards, assessment, and curriculum. The EPRU disseminates its reports, analyses, and other documents to policy makers, educators, and the public. The EPRU at Arizona State University is the successor of the Education Policy Project at the University of Wisconsin-Milwaukee.

According to their mission statement the Educational Policy Institute seeks to expand educational opportunity for low-income and other historically underrepresented students through high-level research and analysis. The Institute believes that by providing educational leaders and policymakers with the information required to make prudent programmatic and policy decisions, we believe that the doors of opportunity can be further opened for all students, resulting in an increase in the number of students prepared for, enrolled in, and completing postsecondary education.

Educational Policy Research Unit
Education Policy Research Unit
Division of Educational Leadership & Policy Studies
Mary Lou Fulton College of Education
Box 872411
Arizona State University
Tempe, AZ 85287-2411
480-965-1886; fax: 480-965-0303
e-mail: epic.epru@gmail.com

Education and the Public Interest Center at the University at Boulder Colorado
Education and the Public Interest Center
School of Education, 249 UCB
University of Colorado
Boulder, Colorado 80309-0249
303-447-3747
e-mail: epic@colorado.edu

The Education and the Public Interest Center (EPIC) at the University of Colorado at Boulder partners with the Education Policy Research Unit (EPRU) and the

Commercialism in Education Research Unit at Arizona State University to produce public policy briefs. These centers provide a variety of audiences, both academic and public, with information, analysis, and insight to further democratic deliberation regarding educational policies.

FairTest
15 Court Square, Suite 820
Boston, MA 02108
857-350-8207
www.fairtest.org/
e-mail: info@fairtest.org

FairTest, the National Center for Fair and Open Testing, is an advocacy organization working to end the abuses, misuses, and flaws of standardized testing and to ensure that any evaluation of students and workers is fair, open, and educationally sound. The center places special emphasis on eliminating the racial, class, gender, and cultural barriers to equal opportunity posed by standardized tests and seeks to prevent any damage they might do to the quality of education. Based on four goals and principles, the center provides information, technical assistance, and advocacy services on a broad range of testing concerns. The focus is on three areas: kindergarten through grade twelve, university admissions, and employment tests, including teacher testing.

Florida Charter School Resource Center
University of South Florida, HMS 401
4202 E. Fowler Avenue
Tampa, FL 33620-8360
813-974-3858; fax: 813-974-7823

This resource center conducts workshops, develops technical assistance materials, and lends a wide variety of resources from its library for free to educators and charter school advocates.

Florida Department of Education
Office of Independent Education and Parental Choice
Turlington Building—Florida Department of Education
325 W. Gaines Street, Room 522
Tallahassee, FL 32399-0400
800-447-1636
www.floridaschoolchoice.org/Information/charter_schools/

The group's Web site claims that charter schools are public schools of choice, are very popular, and among the fastest growing school choice options in Florida. Since 1996, the number of charter schools in Florida has grown from 5 to 358 schools in 2007-2008. Charter school student enrollment for 2007-2008 was well over 100,000 students. Over 20 new charter schools have opened in the 2007-2008 school year.

The Hoover Institution
Stanford University
434 Galvez Mall
Stanford, CA 94305-6010
650-723-1754; 877-466-8374; fax: 650-723-1687
e-mail: horaney@hoover.stanford.edu

The Hoover Institution on War, Revolution and Peace, Stanford University, is a conservative public policy research center devoted to advanced study of politics, economics, and political economy—both domestic and foreign—as well as international affairs.

The Hudson Institute
1015 15th Street, NW, 6th Floor
Washington, DC 20005
202-974-2400; fax: 202-974-2410
e-mail: info@hudson.org

Conservatives Herman Kahn, Max Singer, and Oscar Ruebhausen founded Hudson Institute in 1961 in Croton-on-Hudson. The Hudson Institute promotes conservative, free-market thinking about the future regarding social and public policies.

Illinois Network of Charter Schools
20 E. Jackson Boulevard, Suite 1300
Chicago, IL 60604
312-235-0798; fax: 312-235-0679
www.incschools.org/
e-mail: info@incschools.org

The Illinois Network of Charter Schools (INCS) brings together students, parents, educators, and administrators who all share a common goal: to improve the quality of public education by promoting and strengthening charter schools throughout the State of Illinois. There are currently 39 charters in the state, serving more than 32,000 Illinois children at 76 campuses.

Imagine Schools
1005 North Glebe Road, Suite 610
Arlington, VA 22201
703-527-2600; fax: 703-527-0038
contactus@imagineschools.com

Imagine Schools is a for-profit educational maintenance organization (EMO) comprised mostly of teachers and administrative personnel that operates 73 public charter schools in 12 states and the District of Columbia. They serve around 37,000 students nationwide.

Knowledge is Power Program (KIPP)
KIPP Foundation
KIPP Foundation (head office)
345 Spear Street, Suite 510
San Francisco, CA 94105
415-399-1556; fax 415-348-0588

KIPP Foundation
20 E. Jackson Boulevard, Suite 1300
Chicago, IL 60604
312-291-0838; fax 312-291-0846

KIPP Foundation
505 8th Avenue, Suite 2207
New York, NY 10018
212-233-5477; fax 212-233-5454
866-345-KIPP / 866-345-5477
e-mail: info@kipp.org

KIPP schools is a nonprofit educational maintenance organization (EMO). According to their Web site: KIPP schools are free, open-enrollment, college-preparatory public schools where underserved students develop the knowledge, skills, and character traits needed to succeed in top quality high schools, colleges, and the competitive world beyond. There are currently 66 KIPP public schools in 19 states and the District of Columbia enrolling more than 16,000 students. Across the KIPP network, 65 of the existing 66 schools are charter schools. The majority of KIPP schools (more than 85 percent) are middle schools designed to serve fifth- through eighth-grade students. The remaining schools include seven high schools, six pre-kindergarten/elementary schools, and one pre-kindergarten through eighth-grade school.

Over 90 percent of KIPP students are African American or Hispanic/Latino, and more than 80 percent of KIPP students are eligible for the federal free and reduced-price meals program. Students are accepted regardless of prior academic record, conduct, or socioeconomic background. In 2000, Doris and Don Fisher, co-founders of Gap Inc., formed a unique partnership with Feinberg and Levin to replicate the success of the two original KIPP Academies through the non-profit KIPP Foundation. The KIPP Foundation focuses its efforts on recruiting, training, and supporting outstanding leaders to open new, locally run KIPP schools in high-need communities. The KIPP Foundation does not manage KIPP schools, but is responsible for supporting and monitoring school quality across the network. Each KIPP school is run independently by a KIPP-trained school leader and local board of directors.

Learning Point Associates
222 Richmond Street, Suite 300
Providence, RI 02903-4226
401-274-9548
www.learningpt.org

The Regional Educational Laboratories have ten networks serving geographic regions that span the nation. They work to ensure that people involved in educational improvement efforts at the local, state, and regional levels have access to the best available information from research and practice. With support from the U.S. Department of Education, the Regional Educational Laboratories work with state and local educators, community leaders, and policymakers to tackle difficult problems in education.

Little Hoover Commission
925 L Street, Suite 805
Sacramento, CA 95814
916-445-2125
www.lhc.ca.gov/
e-mail: littl.hoover@lhc.ca.org

The Little Hoover Commission is an independent state body that functions to promote efficiency, effectiveness, and economy in California state programs. The commission studies California legislation, publishes reports on state programs, and researches issues such as charter schools.

The Manhattan Institute for Policy Research
52 Vanderbilt Avenue
New York, NY 10017
212-599-7000; fax: 212-599-3494

The Manhattan Institute has been an important conservative and market-based driven force in shaping American political culture around ideas that seek to foster economic choice and individual responsibility. They have supported and publicized research on our era's most significant public policy issues such as taxes, health care, energy, the legal system, policing, crime, homeland security, urban life, education, race, culture, and many others.

MN (Minnesota) Association of Charter Schools

351 E. Kellogg Boulevard
St. Paul, MN 55101
651-789-3090; fax: 651-789-3098
http://www.mncharterschools.org

The Minnesota Association of Charter Schools (MACS) is a nonprofit, membership organization that was established in 1997. With a mission to advance quality and choice in public education, MACS advocates for charter schools and the charter movement, facilitates support for new and established schools, and promotes quality assurance in the charter school community.

Morrison Institute for Public Policy

School of Public Affairs
Arizona State University
P.O. Box 874405
Tempe, AZ 85287-4405
480-965-4525
www.asu.edu

The Morrison Institute for Public Policy, located at Arizona State University, researches public policy issues, informs policymakers, and advises leaders on choices and actions in the area of education. The institute provides information and expertise on issues in school reform.

National Alliance for Public Charter Schools

1101 14th Street, NW, Suite 801
Washington, DC 20005
202-289-2700; fax: 202-289-4009
http://www.publiccharters.org/

The National Alliance for Public Charter Schools is the national nonprofit organization committed to advancing the charter school movement. The organization states that the ultimate goal is to increase the number of high-performing charter schools available to all families, particularly low-income and minority families who currently don't have access to quality public schools. The Alliance provides assistance to state charter school associations and resource centers, develops and advocates for improved public policies, and serves as the united voice for this large and diverse movement.

National Association of Charter School Authorizers (NACSA)

105 W. Adams Street, Suite 1430
Chicago, IL 60603-6253

312-376-2300; fax: 312-376-2400
www.qualitycharters.org/
e-mail: info@qualitycharters.org

NACSA seeks to improve charter school authorizer capacity by improving state and local policies that define regulations and oversight of authorizers.

National Center for Fair and Open Testing (See FairTest)

National Center for Research on Evaluation, Standards, and Student Testing (CRESST)
CRESST/University of California, Los Angeles
Box 951522
300 Charles E. Young Drive
North Los Angeles, CA 90095-1522
310-206-1532; fax: 310-825-3883
www.cse.ucla.edu/

Funded by the U.S. Department of Education and the Office of Educational Research and Improvement, the Center for Research on Evaluation, Standards, and Student Testing (CRESST) conducts research on important topics related to educational testing from kindergarten through grade twelve.

National Center on Education and the Economy
P.O. Box 10391
Rochester, NY 14610
888-361-6233
www.ncee.org/
e-mail: info@ncee.org

The National Center on Education and the Economy concentrates on helping states and localities develop the capacity to design and implement their own education and training systems, systems that are suited to their history, culture, and unique needs. The center does not provide designs to be replicated; it provides resources for design.

National Center on Educational Outcomes
University of Minnesota
350 Elliott Hall
75 E. River Road
Minneapolis, MN 55455
612-626-1530; fax: 612-624-0879
www.education.umn.edu/nceo/

The National Center on Educational Outcomes was established in 1990 to provide national leadership in the identification of outcomes, indicators, and assessments to monitor educational results for all students, including students with disabilities.

National Charter Schools Institute
2520 S. University Park Drive
Suite Box 11
Mount Pleasant, MI 48858
989-774-2999
http://www.nationalcharterschools.org/
e-mail: info@nationalcharterschools.org

Since 2001, the National Charter Schools Institute has worked with authorizers, boards, school leaders, teachers, policymakers and others who are serious about identifying and implementing effective strategies that provide children with the world's best educational opportunities. The National Charter Schools Institute exists to cultivate the success of charter schooling. We work with teachers, school leaders, boards, authorizers, policymakers and others who are serious about identifying and implementing effective strategies for providing children with world class educational opportunities. It is a non-profit organization.

National Clearinghouse for Bilingual Education
George Washington University Center for the Study of
Language and Education
2121 K Street, NW, Suite 260
Washington, DC 20037
202-467-0867
www.ncela.gwu.edu/

The National Clearinghouse for Bilingual Education (NCBE) is funded by the U.S. Department of Education's Office of Bilingual Education and Minority Languages Affairs to collect, analyze, and disseminate information relating to the effective education of linguistically and culturally diverse learners in the United States. NCBE provides information through its Web site; produces a biweekly news bulletin, Newsline; and manages a topical electronic discussion group, NCBE Roundtable. As part of the U.S. Department of Education's technical assistance and information network, NCBE works with other service providers to provide access to high-quality information to assist states and local school districts in the development of programs and the implementation of strategies that will help all students work toward high academic standards.

National Conference of State Legislatures
444 N. Capitol Street, NW, Suite 515
Washington, DC 20001
202-624-5400
www.ncsl.org
e-mail: info@ncsl.org

The National Conference of State Legislatures provides legislative updates regarding charter school arguments, research, legislation, and trends.

National Educators Association
1201 Sixteenth Street, NW
Washington, DC 20036
202-833-4000
www.nea.org
e-mail: kbrilliant@nea.org

The National Educators Association is a federal organization of educators that is devoted to providing assistance and information regarding the state of public education in the United States.

National Heritage Academies
3850 Broadmoor Avenue, Suite 201
Grand Rapids, MI 49512
616-222-1700; fax: 616-575-6801
Parent Communications: 866-642-3676
e-mail: info@heritageacademies.com

National Heritage Academies (NHA) is an education maintenance organization (EMO) that partners with independent school boards that want to bring a charter school to their local community. NHA is hired by the board to manage, for a profit, all of the day-to-day operations of the school. They have gone from managing one school in 1995 to partnerships with boards at 57 schools in six states, serving over 35,000 students and families.

New American Schools
1560 Wilson Boulevard, Suite 901
Arlington, VA 22209
703-908-9500; fax: 703-908-0622
e-mail: info@nasdc.org

New American Schools is a dynamic coalition of teachers, administrators, parents, policymakers, community and business leaders, and experts from around the country who are committed to improving academic achievement for all students. The coalition works to change U.S. classrooms, schools, and school systems using designs—blueprints for reorganizing an entire school rather than a single program or grade level within it—and by providing assistance to help schools implement the designs successfully.

New York Charter School Resource Center
41 Robbins Avenue
Amityville, NY 11701
516-598-4426
www.nycharterschools.org

The New York Charter School Resource Center provides services for anyone interested in beginning a charter school in New York State. Its services include explaining and interpreting the state's charter law; helping potential school operators complete and submit charter applications; providing technical assistance for school design, curriculum, standards, and assessment; providing legal services; and maintaining databases on charter school activity throughout the United States.

New York Charter Schools Association
120 Broadway
Albany, NY 12204
518-694-3110; toll free: 888-465-4401
http://www.nycsa.org/

The New York Charter Schools Association promotes effective, efficient, and accountable charter schools by providing services that dramatically increase academic performance, and ensure financial stability; and creating a social and political climate that fosters the establishment and expansion of public school choice.

New York City Charter School Center
111 Broadway, Suite 604
New York, NY 10006
212-437-8300; fax: 212-227-2763
http://www.nycchartercenter.org/
e-mail: info@nycchartercenter.org

New York City Charter School Center is an independent, not-for-profit organization, launched in 2004 as a partnership between New York City and the philanthropic community. The mission of the New York City Charter School Center is to increase the number of high-quality charter schools and thereby improve public education in New York City. The Center is an advocate, bridge, and catalyst for charter schools, helping them to achieve academic and operational excellence and long-term sustainability.

Northwest Regional Educational Laboratory (NWREL)
101 SW Main Street, Suite 500
Portland, OR 97204
503-275-9500; 800-547-6339; fax: 503-275-0660
http://www.nwrel.org/charter/national.html

Since 1966, NWREL has been working to make a difference in students' lives and those who support their learning. NWREL is a private nonprofit working closely with schools, districts, and other agencies to develop creative and practical solutions to important educational challenges. The mission of the Northwest Regional Educational Laboratory (NWREL) is to improve learning by building capacity in schools, families, and communities through applied research and development.

Pacific Research Institute for Public Policy
755 Sansome Street, Suite 450
San Francisco, CA 94111
415-989-0833
www.pacificresearch.org

The Pacific Research Institute for Public Policy promotes the principles of individual freedom and personal responsibility. The institute believes these principles are best encouraged through policies that emphasize a free enterprise economy, private initiative, and limited government. By focusing on public policy issues such as education, the environment, law, economics, and social welfare, the institute strives to foster a better understanding of the principles of a free society among leaders in government, academe, the media, and the business community.

Progressive Policy Institute
Education Section
600 Pennsylvania Avenue, SE, Suite 400
Washington, DC 20003
202-546-0007
www.dlcppi.org

The mission of the Progressive Policy Institute is to define and promote a new progressive politics for the United States in the twenty-first century. Through its research, policies, and perspectives, the institute is fashioning a new governing philosophy and agenda for public innovation geared to the information age.

Project Zero
Harvard Graduate School of Education
321 Longfellow Hall
13 Appian Way

Cambridge, MA 02138
617-496-7097
pzweb.harvard.edu

Project Zero, a research group in the Harvard Graduate School of Education, has investigated the development of learning processes in children, adults, and organizations for over thirty-two years. Today, Project Zero is building on this research to help create communities of reflective, independent learners; to enhance deep understanding within disciplines; and to promote critical and creative thinking. Project Zero's mission is to understand and enhance learning, thinking, and creativity in the arts and other disciplines for individuals and institutions.

Resource Center for Charter Schools

209 N. Water Street, Suite 328
Corpus Christi, TX 78401
361-561-8675; fax: 361-561-8677
http://www.charterstexas.org/

Resource Center for Charter Schools (RCCS) supports the formation and successful operation of charter schools across Texas. The Center serves as an information resource, offers access to professional expertise and lends direct technical support through all stages of the charter school development. The mission of the Resource Center is to improve public education in Texas by supporting the successful operation of high-quality charter schools. This is done by providing information, access to professional expertise, and direct technical support. The primary goal of the Resource Center is to see that a significant number of established charter schools remain strong, viable, and effective. In addition to daily technical assistance, the RCCS offers conferences, workshops, a website and numerous publications for each charter, at no cost to operational charters.

SABIS Educational Systems, Inc.

SABIS® International Charter School
160 Joan Street
Springfield, MA 01129
413-783-2600; fax: 413-783-2555
http://www.sics-sabis.net
e-mail: sicsma@sabis.net

Sabis Educational Systems, Inc. is a for-profit international educational maintenance organization (EMO). According to its Web site, Sabis Educational Systems, Inc. includes an array of all-inclusive products and services designed for the management of Pre-K and K-12 schools, Sabis Educational, Inc. offers: complete curriculum aligned with state requirements; software systems to enhance efficiency and improve standards; ongoing academic quality control through computerized academic monitoring (SABIS AMS®) and automatically generated reports; concept-targeted, well-researched books supporting the SABIS® program; recruitment, training, and supervision of staff; cutting-edge research and development methods designed to optimize results; and extensive business management services. Following its incorporation, SABIS® Educational Systems, Inc., a company founded and based in Lebanon, established a range of schools starting in the private sector and expanding into the public sector. In 1995, the first of SABIS®'s U.S. charter schools was established in Springfield, Massachusetts. Functioning with a Board of Directors contracting with SABIS® for the day-to-day management and organization of the charter school, the SABIS® International Charter School (SICS) in Springfield set the bar for achievement in SABIS® charter schools to come. In the United States, SABIS® Educational Systems, Inc. currently operates 8 charter schools and one private school.

SERVE Leaders Institute

P.O. Box 5406
Greensboro, NC 27435
336-334-4729
www.serve.org

The SERVE Leaders Institute is funded by a U.S. Department of Education grant, and its purpose is to address the challenges that charter school innovators and leaders face in the charter school reform movement. The institute arranges retreat activities with the assistance of nationally recognized charter school leaders. The leadership program is based on and expands the understanding of educational training programs, continuous learning, result-driven evaluation models, and practical issues that face educators daily.

Southwest Educational Development Laboratory (SEDL)

4700 Mueller Boulevard
Austin, TX 78723
800-476-6861
www.sedl.org

The SEDL works to meet the information needs of decision-makers and policy-makers as they create policies to improve education in their states and localities. The laboratory focuses on basic areas of direct services and applied policy research and development. It offers policy, practical, and research information about priority education topics, advice on how to discuss educational issues, in-depth studies on charter schools, and information about charter school legislation. It also provides resources such as policy briefs, meeting summaries, and articles that address the topic of charter schools and other educational reform issues.

Sylvan Learning
Jennifer Gaegler
Public Relations Manager
Sylvan Learning, Inc.
1001 Fleet Street
Baltimore, MD 21212
410-843-8928; fax: 410-843-8057
e-mail: jennifer.gaegler@educate.com

Sylvan Learning was founded in 1979 and is North America's leading provider of private tutoring for children in grades pre-K through 12. Today, we are proud to have more than 1,100 centers conveniently located in neighborhoods across the United States and Canada. Each location delivers personalized tutoring programs to students—of all ages and skill levels—in every academic subject, including test preparation. Sylvan Learning is owned by Educate Services, Inc., a leading pre-K through 12 for-profit educational services company that delivers tutoring and other supplemental education services to students and their families.

Teach for America
Teach for America
315 W. 36th Street, 7th Floor
New York, NY 10018
https://www.teachforamerica.org

Teach For America is the national corps of outstanding recent college graduates and professionals of all academic majors and career interests who commit two years to teach in urban and rural public schools and become leaders in the effort to expand educational opportunity.

According to the organization's Web site: Our mission is to build the movement to eliminate educational inequity by enlisting our nation's most promising future leaders in the effort. In the short run, our corps members work relentlessly to ensure that more students growing up today in our country's lowest-income communities are given the educational opportunities they deserve. In the long run, our alumni are a powerful force of leaders working from inside education and from every other sector to effect the fundamental changes needed to ensure that all children have an equal chance in life.

Thomas Fordham Foundation
Manhattan Institute
1016 16th Street, NW, 8th Floor
Washington, DC 20036
202-223-5452
www.edexcellence.net
e-mail: fordham@dunst.com

The Thomas Fordham Foundation is a conservative organization that supports research, publications, and projects of national significance in elementary and secondary education reform as well as significant education reform projects in Dayton, Ohio, and its vicinity. The foundation is affiliated with the Manhattan Institute, a think tank whose mission is to design, develop, and make available information on educational reform.

U.S. Charter Schools
415-615-3221
http://www.uscharterschools.org/
e-mail: uscharterschools@wested.org

The US Charter Schools Web site is a valuable source of information and knowledge for charter school developers, operators, parents, researchers and policymakers. Specifically, this Web site provides a wide range of information and links to resources to guide charter schools in every phase of their development, from start-up, to expansion, and to renewal. It also provides a "Community Exchange" environment that allows for discussion and the exchange of ideas between schools and various support providers. Lastly, the site's State Profiles contain contact information for resource centers to assist parents who are interested in learning more about and/or enrolling their children in a charter school.

The US Charter Schools Web site is a place where charter school developers, authorizers, and operators can meet, exchange ideas, and accesses a valuable resource library. The Web site provides a wide range of information and links to resources to guide charter schools in every phase of their development—from start-up, to expansion, to renewal.

Currently the site is neither supported nor endorsed by the U.S. Department of Education.

U.S. Department of Education (ED)
U.S. Department of Education
400 Maryland Avenue, SW
Washington, D.C. 20202
800-872-5327
http://www.ed.gov/index.jhtml

ED was created in 1980 by combining different offices from a number of federal agencies. According to their Web site, ED's mission is to promote student achievement and preparation for global competitiveness by fostering educational excellence and ensuring equal access. ED's 4,200 employees and $68.6 billion budget are dedicated to: establishing policies on federal financial aid for education, and distributing as well as monitoring those funds; collecting data on America's schools and disseminating research; focusing national attention on key educational issues; and prohibiting discrimination and ensuring equal access to education.

Chapter Nine

Selected Print and Nonprint Resources

The works listed in this chapter are divided into two categories. The first, lists both popular and scholarly books, articles, speeches, and studies that deal with the topic of educational reform and, specifically, charter schools. These include law journals, labor reports, government publications, and books by individual authors. The second section contains nonprint resources such as Web sites and Internet research sites invested in the topic of charter schools.

PRINTED RESOURCES

Union Publications

The following publications are published by the American Federation of Teachers (AFT) and the National Education Association (NEA). The speeches by Albert Shanker, former AFT president, are also available through the AFT. The AFT can be reached by contacting its Web site, www.aft.org, or by writing to the American Federation of Teachers, 555 New Jersey Avenue, NW, Washington, DC 20001. The NEA has developed a charter school initiative with Andrea DiLorenzo and Kay Brilliant as its co-directors. They can be reached at adilorenzo@nea.org or kbrilliant@nea.org, or by writing to them directly at Charter School Initiative, Public Education Advocacy Center, National Education Association, 1201 Sixteenth Street, NW, Washington, DC 20036.
The following information can be found at this Web site:

American Federation of Teachers
555 New Jersey Avenue, NW
Washington, DC 20001
202-393-8642
www.aft.org

——. *The AFT Charter School Report.* Washington, DC, 2000.

In this report, the union issues what could be called "a report card" on charter schools. The publication examines the issue state by state.

——. *Charter School Briefing Packet.* Washington, DC, 1995.

A comprehensive report on what charter schools are doing and in which specific localities. The report contains controversies and critiques.

——. *Charter School Laws: Do They Measure Up?* Washington, DC, 1996.

In this report, the union examines charter school laws and how they operate from state to state.

——. *Making Standards Matter, 1996: An Annual, Fifty-State Report on Efforts To Raise Academic Standards.* Washington, DC, 1996.

This report makes recommendations for standards of operation for charter schools that the union has identified as being of utmost importance. The report then examines charter schools state by state to apply the standards in the interest of evaluating the charter schools studied.

——. *National Education Standards and Assessment.* Washington, DC, 1992.

This report, an AFT convention resolution, speaks to educational standards and how they should apply to all public schools, including charter schools.

——. *Resolution on Charter Schools.* Anaheim, CA, July 1994.

This resolution, adopted by the AFT national convention, states the union's position on the charter school movement. It brings to the forefront questions that citizens need to be asking when evaluating the concept of charter schools.

——. **"U.S. Education: The Task Before Us."** Washington, DC, 1992.

This report, an AFT convention resolution, addresses how schools must change and the formidable problems and issues that face school reform.

Shanker, A. **"Classrooms Held Hostage: Restoring Order in Our Schools."** Speech to the AFT Conference on Discipline and Safety. Washington, DC, 3 February 1995.

In this highly critical speech, Shanker speaks out against conditions in the classrooms and emphasizes how educational workers must begin to construct a curriculum that works for children.

——. **"Making Standards Count: The Case for Student Incentives."** Speech to a Brookings Institute Conference. Washington, DC, 18 May 1994.

Here, former AFT president Albert Shanker makes a plea for the types of standards we should be looking at when examining, evaluating, and analyzing both student and school achievement.

——. **Untitled Speech to the National Press Club.** Washington, DC, 31 March 1998.

In this speech, Shanker makes his claim for the charter school idea. He lays out his reasoning and in doing so, indicates significant movement in union embracement of the idea of charter schools.

——. **"Where We Stand, Every School a Charter."** *New York Times,* 11 December 1994.

In this article, Shanker calls on every school to become a charter school and argues that the charter school idea should be the benchmark for all public schools.

Government Publications

With the huge growth and development of charter schools throughout the United States, government publications that evaluate and discuss aspects of charter school legislation have become more available. The following items represent just some of the publications that are available through federal and state governments.

Bierlein, L. **Charter Schools: Initial Findings.** Denver, CO: Education Commission of the States, March 1996.

This report publishes initial findings on charter schools and looks at the regulations that have been waived by many schools and how they might be doing as public entities by monitoring charter school legislation to identify nuances in the law, state-by-state.

Bierlein, L., and M. Fulton. **Emerging Issues in Charter School Financing.** Policy brief on charter school financing. Denver, CO: Education Commission of the States, May 1996.
In this report, the focus of the commentary is on funding and financing. The policy brief examines some of the problems charter schools face in the area of financing.

Blackorby, J., K. Finnegan, and L. Anderson. **Evaluation of Charter School Effectiveness.** Report prepared for the state of California Office of Legislative Analyst. Menlo Park, CA: SRI International, 1997.

This report, prepared for the state government, presents an evaluation of the work of charter schools within the state of California.

Budde, R. **Education by Charter: Restructuring Our Schools and School Districts.** Andover, MA: Regional Laboratory for Educational Improvement of the Northeast and Islands, 1989.

This report serves as a proponent of the charter school idea and posits it as a significant reform measure that promises to save public schools.

Clayton Foundation for the Colorado Department of Education. **1997 Colorado Charter School Evaluation Study.** Denver, CO, 1997.

This study is specific to Colorado and examines the laws, governance procedures, and workings of the charter school movement in Colorado.

Commonwealth of Massachusetts Department of Education. *The Massachusetts Charter School Initiative: Expanding the Possibilities of Education.* Boston, MA, 1998.

A state-specific report that looks at one of the most controversial states to have adopted charter school legislation. Every aspect is examined as it promotes or retards the charter school movement.

District of Columbia Board of Education. *Charter School Application: 1996.* Washington, DC, June 1996.

The District of Columbia Board of Education has published an examination of the charter application that deals with what is contained in these applications and how they are dealt with by government agencies.

Education Commission of the States. *Clearinghouse Issues Brief: Charter Schools.* Denver, CO, January 1996.

A general discussion of charter schools with a focus on what is working and what is not.

———. *Clearinghouse Notes: Charter Schools.* Denver, CO, June 1994.

This report, the first of a series, attempts to examine the charter school movement as an educational reform movement.

Louisiana State Department of Education. *Charter Schools Demonstrate Their Ability to Increase Students' Scores Over Time.* 2007. http://edreform.com/accountability/states/CER_2009_AR_Louisiana.pdf.

This report argues that charter schools are increasing student test scores. LEAP scores correspond to one of five achievement ratings: Advanced, Mastery, Basic, Approaching Basic, and Unsatisfactory. In 2007, 76 percent of charter school students in grade four scored at the Basic level or above in math, whereas only 64 percent of students statewide achieved this level of proficiency. From 2004 to 2007, charter school students have improved steadily on their English Language Arts proficiency. In 2004, 59 percent of students scored at the Basic level or above, while that number jumped to 74 percent in 2007.

Medler, A., and J. Nathan. *Charter Schools: What Are They up To?* Denver, CO: Education Commission of the States, August 1995.

A highly favorable view of charter schools, this report of a 1995 survey, compiled with the help of charter activist Joe Nathan, looks at what charter schools were doing at the time.

RPP International, University of Massachusetts. *A Study of Charter Schools: First Year Report.* Washington, DC: U.S. Department of Education, 1997.

This first five-year report, issued by the University of Massachusetts, examines and analyzes what the charter movement has or has not accomplished.

Texas Board of Education. *Texas Open-Enrollment Charter Schools: Second Year Evaluation.* Austin, TX, 1997–1998.

This report looks specifically at the state of Texas, especially open enrollment charter schools and how they are progressing in accordance with state educational standards.

Urahn, S., and D. Stewart. *Minnesota Charter Schools.* Minneapolis, MN: Minnesota House of Representatives Research Department, December 1994.

State-specific, this report looks at one of the first states to pass charter legislation. The report seeks to understand how charter schools have changed educational policies and procedures in Minnesota.

U.S. Department of Education. *A Look at Charter Schools.* Washington, DC, March 1996.

The U.S. government examines charter schools as a reform movement in education. This work examines issues of race, class, admission policies, governance, and accountability.

——. *A Nation at Risk: Imperative for Education Reform.* Washington, DC: National Commission on Excellence in Education, 1983.

This famous report, produced during the Reagan years, sparked a new way of looking at schools and education and became a catalyst for educational reform controversies.

——. *A National Study of Charter Schools.* Washington, DC: Office of Educational Research and Improvement, 1998.

This national study of charter schools attempts to compare and contrast these schools throughout the United States.

——. *The State of Charter Schools 2000: Fourth Year Report.* Washington, DC, 2000.

This fourth report by the U.S. Department of Education is a continuation of previous examinations of the charter school movement and the political and financial problems that face charter schools.

——. *A Study of Charter Schools: Second Year Report.* Washington, DC, 1998.

This report by the Department of Education is essentially a report card on the charter school movement, and it points to problems and benefits.

U.S. Department of Education. *The Charter Schools Program.* 2 February 2009. http://www.ed.gov/programs/charter/index.html.

This program provides financial assistance for the planning, program design, and initial implementation of charter schools, and the dissemination of information on charter schools. Grants are available, on a competitive basis, to SEAs in states that have charter school laws; SEAs in turn make subgrants to developers of charter schools who have applied for a charter.

U.S. General Accounting Office. *Charter Schools: New Models for Public Schools Provide Opportunities and Challenges.* Washington, DC, 1995.

Because they are proposed as new models for change, this report examines charter schools as an antidote to what the Accounting Office sees as problems with public schools.

Private and Public Think Tank Publications

These publications are put out by various private and nonprofit organizations of different political and economic persuasions. They are "think tanks" precisely because they carry on research, information dissemination and public relations on behalf of their constituencies and serve as a forum for publication and research on various aspects of public affairs.

Becker, H., and K. Nakagawa. *Parent Involvement Contracts in California Charter Schools: Strategy for Education Improvement or Method of Exclusion?* Los Alamitos, CA: Southwest Regional Laboratory, April 1995.

This report advocates the participation of parents in charter school start-up and governance. It also looks at situations in which parents have been active in the charter school movement and the supposed consequences.

Berman, P., L. Diamond, and E. Premack. *Making Charter Schools Work.* Berkeley, CA: Institute for Policy Analysis and Research, June 1995.

Can charter schools work, and if so how? This report looks at the issues that fuel charter schools and what might be done to make the schools successful.

Bierlein, L., and L. Mulholland. *Charter School Update and Observations Regarding Initial Trends and Impacts.* Phoenix: Morrison Institute for Public Policy, April 1995.

Specifically looking at charter schools in Arizona, one of the most controversial states with charter school legislation, this report looks at the updates in practices and makes observations and evaluations.

——. *Comparing Charter School Laws.* Phoenix: Morrison Institute for Public Policy, September 1994.

State by state, this report compares and contrasts state charter school laws.

Buckley, J., and M. Schneider. *Charter Schools: Hope or Hype?* Princeton, NJ: Princeton, University Press. 2007.

The question at hand in this book is if charter schools can bring hope to inner-city students. The authors use extensive empirical data from the District of Columbia where less than 30 percent of schools are charter schools.

Carnegie Forum on Education and the Economy. *A Nation Prepared: Teachers for the 21st Century.* Hyattsville, MD, 1986.

Looking at teaching and learning in the twenty-first century, this report speaks to what is necessary for effective teaching and educational reform as we enter the new millennium.

Carnoy, M., R. Jacobsen, L. Mishel, and R. Rothstein. *The Charter School Dustup: Examing the Evidence on Enrollment and Achievement.* Washington, DC: Economic Policy Institute and Teacher's College Press. 2005.

This book looks critically at the evidence submitted to attest to the claims that enrollment and achievement is far better in charter schools.

Center for Research on Education Outcomes (CREDO). *Multiple Choice: Charter School Performance in 16 States.* Stanford University, June 2009. http://credo.stanford.edu/reports/MULTIPLE_CHOICE_CREDO.pdf.

This report presents a longitudinal student level analysis of charter school impacts on more than 70 percent of the students in charter schools in the United States. The scope of the study makes it the first national assessment of charter school impacts. The study reveals that a decent fraction of charter schools, 17 percent, provide superior education opportunities for their students. Nearly half of the charter schools nationwide have results that are no different from the local public school options and over a third, 37 percent, deliver learning results that are significantly worse than their student would have realized had they remained in traditional public schools. These findings underlie the parallel findings of significant state by state differences in charter school performance and in the national aggregate performance of charter schools. The policy challenge is how to deal constructively with varying levels of performance today and into the future.

Chubb, J., and T. Moe. *Politics, Markets, and America's Schools.* Washington, DC: Brookings Institute, 1990.

A landmark book and one thought to spark the voucher movement in education. In this book, Moe and Chubb argue against public schools and why they feel they cannot and do not work.

Cobb, J., and G. Glass. **"Ethnic Segregation in Arizona Charter Schools."** *Education Policy Analysis Archives* 7, no. 1 (14 January 1999): 1-39.

This report looks at the issue of segregation in Arizona charter schools and why it exists.

Corwin, R., and M. Dianda. *Vision and Reality: A First Year Look at California's Charter Schools.* Los Alamitos, CA: Southwest Regional Laboratory, May 1994.

This work looks at the claims, visions, and actual practice of charter schools in California.

Corwin, R., and J. Flaherty, eds. *Freedom and Innovation in California Charter Schools.* Los Alamitos, CA: Southwest Regional Laboratory, November 1995.

In this report the emphasis is on the type of freedom and innovation the authors believe charter schools offer. They also offer recommendations to strengthen charter schools by providing more freedom from government regulation.

Corwin, R., and E.J. Schneider. *The School Choice Hoax: Fixing America's Schools.* Lanham, MD: Roman and Littlefield Education. 2005.

In this book the authors attempt to debunk the entire idea behind charter schools. The authors argue that charter schools and vouchers should be combined as an ideology and practice in American education.

Finn, C., L. Bierlein, and B. Manno. *Charter Schools in Action: A First Look.* Washington, DC: Hudson Institute, January 1996.

A highly favorable look at charter schools in action. Chester Finn is a well-known advocate of privatized schooling and has embraced charter school movements as a beginning toward that end.

Ladner, M. *How "No Child Left Behind" Threatens Florida's Successful Education Reforms.* Washington, D.C. The Heritage Foundation, 7 January 2009. http://www.heritage.org/Research/Education/bg2226.cfm.

After seven years, author Matthew Ladner suggests evidence that No Child Left Behind, like previous federal interventions, has failed to yield meaningful improvements in students' learning. According to the author, NCLB has also highlighted the limits and unintended consequences of federal intervention.

McDonnel, L., and A. Pascal. *Teacher Unions and Educational Reforms.* Santa Monica, CA: RAND, April 1988.

This work discusses what the authors believe is the need for changing roles between unions and the movement toward educational reform. The report calls for a different role of unions in education.

McGree, K. *Charter Schools: Early Findings.* Austin, TX: Southwest Educational Development Laboratory, 1995.

This report looks at charter school developments and compares and contrasts what was believed when they began and what is actually known now.

——. *Redefining Education Governance: The Charter School Concept.* Austin, TX: Southwest Educational Development Laboratory, 1995.

In this book, the author looks critically at current educational power and control and proposes that charter schools offer a means to redefine how schools are governed and run.

Millot, M. *Autonomy, Accountability, and the Values of Public Education: A Comparative Assessment of Charter School Statutes Leading to Model Legislation.* Santa Monica, CA: RAND, December 1994.

This report is centered on accountability in education and examines the assessment of schools through the glass of charter school legislation and reality.

National Center on Education and the Economy. **"Tough Choices or Tough Times: The Report of the New Commission on the Skills of the American Workforce."** Jossey-Bass, 2008.

This report by the New Commission on the Skills of the American Workforce (NCEE), funded by the Bill and Melinda Gates Foundation, calls for a complete overhaul and restructuring of the educational system in America. It comes 22 years after the NCEE's report, "A Nation At Risk," which raised similar concerns in 1987.

Books and Journals

The explosion of the charter school idea in the United States has been followed by the publication of various journals and books that discuss and examine research and comment on charter schools. These books and journals are published by scholars in the area of public policy, educational policy, and socio-political policy. The publications are both profit and nonprofit journals and books.

Ascher, C., N. Fruchter, and R. Berne. ***Hard Lessons: Public Schools and Privatization.*** New York: Twentieth-Century Fund Press, 1996.

What have we learned about privatization and public schools? This book looks at the issue in a way that helps the reader see why the movement for privatization is taking place.

Broderick, C. **"Rocky Mountain Rift: In the Mile-High City of Denver, a Maverick School Board Challenges the State's Charter School Law."** *American School Board Journal* 182, no. 10 (October 1995): 32-34.

What happens when a charter school law is challenged? That is the emphasis of this journal article, in which discussion is centered on the state Colorado.

Carnoy, M. **"Do Vouchers Improve Education?"** Paper presented at the Ford Foundation Constituency Building for School Reform Initiative, New York, 1998.

This paper criticizes the idea of vouchers and asks if the voucher movement will improve education. The author presents his reasoning as to why it will not.

——. **"School Improvement: Is Privatization the Answer?"** In *Decentralization and School Improvement: Can We Fulfill the Promise?* pp. 1–20. Ed. J. H. and M. Carnoy. San Francisco, CA: Jossey-Bass, 1993.

Is privatization of schools the answer to what is ailing public schools? This book examines this question and more in an attempt to forge a comprehensive approach to school reform.

"Charter School News." *Education Week,* 2 February 2000.

This article provides contemporary news about what some charter schools are doing.

Eberts, R., and A. Stone. ***Unions and Public Schools.*** Lexington, MA: Lexington Books, 1984.

What is the role of unions in public schools? Should they have a role? Does the role need to be redefined? This book takes up these issues.

Education Week. "The Obama Education Plan: An Education Week Guide." Jossey-Bass 9 February 2009.

This book is a guide to the educational priorities and change to expect from the Obama administration.

Fine, M. *Democratizing Choice: Reinventing Public Education.* New York: City of University New York Graduate Center, 1993.

This famous author looks at urban schools and what they are doing with the charter concept. Her book gives readers the voices of teachers, administrators, parents, and students.

Gill, B.P., P.M. Timpane, K.E. Ross, and D.J. Brewer. *Rhetoric versus Reality: What we Know and What We need to Know About Vouchers and Charter Schools.* Santa Monica, CA: Rand, 2001.

Access, integration and civic socialization are looked at critically by the authors within the context of charter schools.

Giroux, H. *The Terror of NeoLiberalism: Authoritarianism and the Eclipse of Democracy*. Boulder, CO: Paradyme Publishers 2004.

In this book the author makes an economic argument for changing education as well as uses an economic framework for analyzing failing schools.

Hart, J. **"MCAS Scores of Charters Fail to Meet Expectations."** *Boston Globe,* 14 December 1998.

How many charter schools are actually functioning as planned? What about the ones that do not make it? This article looks at failing charter schools and discusses why they fail.

Kearney, C. P., and M. L. Arnold. **"Market Driven Schools and Educational Choices."** *Theory into Practice* 33, no. 1 (Spring 1994): 112–117.

Highly critical of market-driven schools, this article frames the issue in terms of choice and what that might mean for the nation's system of education.

Kozol, Jonathan. *The Shame of the Nation: The Restoration of Apartheid Schooling in America*. Three Rivers Press, August 1, 2006.

Using data from state and local agencies along with interviews with researchers and policy makers, Kozol documents how the desegregation of schools is worsening in America.

Lopez, A., A.S. Wells, and J.J. Holme. **"Creating Charter School Communities: Identity Building, Diversity, and Selectivity."** Paper presented at the annual meeting of the American Educational Research Association, San Diego, 1998.

In this paper, the authors look at issues of discrimination and racial practices in charter school admissions. They also examine the notion of diversity and selectivity as social constructs.

McGray, D. **"The Instigator."** The *New Yorker,* 10 May 2009.

In this article in the New Yorker, Green Dot EMO founder, Steve Barr is portrayed as is the hostile "takeover" of public schools in Los Angeles by Green Dot and their strategies for implementing strategies to target public high schools for further takeover. Barr explains that California lawmakers have created an option for schools to abandon the district for a charter arrangement if at least fifty percent of tenured teachers vote to secede.

Miron, G., and C. Nelson. ***What's Public About Charter Schools?: Lessons Learned About Choice and Accountability.*** Thousand Oaks, CA: Corwin Press Inc. 2002.

From student performance to charter schools as a "laboratory of significant reform," this book examines a wide number of claims regarding charter school efficacy.

Nathan, J. ***Charter Schools: Creating Hope and Opportunity for American Education.*** San Francisco: Jossey-Bass, 1996.

The best contemporary book favorable to the charter school idea, it discusses problems with public education and how charter schools can be constructed to overcome these perceived problems.

——. **"Possibilities, Problems, and Progress: Early Lessons from the Charter School Movement."** *Phi Delta Kappan* 78, no. 1 (September 1996): 18-23.

The article praises charter schools but also points out problems. The author is highly supportive of the idea of charter school reform.

National Center on Education and the Economy. **"Tough Choices or Tough Times: The Report of the New Commission on the Skills of the American Workforce."** Jossey-Bass, 2008.

Following an historical slew of reports on our nation's schools, this book looks at American education and advances the idea of moving beyond charter schools to a privatized system of schools, ending remediation and special education for low performance students, ending teacher pensions and retirement plans, ending high school for many minority and poor students as well as a host of other controversial suggestions.

Quaid, L. **"Obama Education Plan Speech: Stricter Standards, Charter Schools, Merit Pay."** *Huffington Post,* 10 March 2009. http://www.huffingtonpost.com/2009/03/10/obama-education-plan-spee_n_173405.html.

President Obama called for tying teachers' pay to student performance and expanding innovative charter schools, embracing ideas that have provoked hostility from members of teachers' unions. He also suggested longer school days—and years—to help American children compete in the world.

Rhim, L.M. **"Franchising Public Education: An Analysis of Charter Schools and Private Education Management Companies."** Paper presented at the American Education Research Association, San Diego, 1998.

This paper looks at educational maintenance organizations (EMOs). It specifically examines private management companies that make claims to run public schools with public funds.

Saltman, K. *Capitalizing on Disaster: Taking and Breaking Public Schools (Cultural Politics & the Promise of Democracy).* Paradigm Publishers, 30 September 2007.

Capitalizing on Disaster dissects the most powerful educational reforms and highlights their relationship to the rise of powerful think tanks and business groups.

——. *Schooling and the Politics of Disaster.* Routledge, 30 May 2007.

Schooling and the Politics of Disaster is the first volume to address how disaster is being used for a radical social and economic reengineering of education.

Scherer, M. M. **"New Options for Public Education."** *Educational Leadership* 54, no. 2 (October 1996): 14-26.

In this article, charter schools are presented as a new option for what ails U.S. education.

Semple, M. **"Legal Issues in Charter Schooling."** *School Administrator* 52, no. 8 (August 1995): 24-26.

In this article, the administrator of a one school is asked to consider the legal issues involved in running a charter school.

Sizer, T., G. Wood, L. Dingerson, A. Hanauer, Z. El-Amine, L. Glazer, D. French, B. Miner, L. Darling-Hammond, and K. Montgomery. *Keeping the Promise? The Debate over Charter Schools.* Milwaukee, WI: Rethinking Schools Limited. 2008.

In this book, a collection of authors look critically at the impact of charter schools on issues of educational equity, accessibility to schools, corporate control of providers, and issues surrounding student achievement.

Sweet, L. **"Cautious Response from Teachers' Union on Obama Merit Pay Plan."** *Suntimes News Group,* 10 March 2009. http://blogs.suntimes.com/sweet/2009/03/cautious_response_from_teacher.html.

While issuing a very cautious reaction to President Obama's call for teacher merit pay, Randi Weingarten, the President of the American Federation of Teachers (AFT), stated that AFT embraces the goals and aspirations outlined by President Obama when he called for providing all Americans with a comprehensive, competitive education that begins in early childhood and extends through their careers. The president's vision of education—and AFT's—includes world-class standards for all students, new and better tools for teachers, greater effort to recruit and retain good teachers, and competitive teacher salaries with innovative ways to reward teaching excellence. AFT states it also fully supports the president's call for shared responsibility for education—among public officials, school administrators, parents, students and teachers. Teachers want to make a difference in kids' lives, and they appreciate a president who shares that goal and will spend his political capital to provide the resources to make it happen.

Toch, T. **"Education Bazaar."** *U.S. World and News Report,* 27 April 1998.

Are we selling out our schools? What is this thing called educational reform? This article presents those issues clearly.

Tyack, D., and L. Cuban, L. ***Tinkering towards Utopia: A Century of Public School Reform.*** Cambridge, MA: Harvard University Press, 1995.

What have so-called educational reform efforts really accomplished? This book looks at educational reform movements, of which charter schools are just one form.

Vine, P. **"To Market, to Market: The School Business Sells Kids Short."** *Nation Magazine,* 8-15 September 1997.

This article makes the point that privatization is selling children short and ruining education. Highly controversial, but compelling in its argumentation.

Weil, D. ***Towards a Critical Multicultural Literacy.*** New York, NY: Peter Lang Publishing, Inc. 2000.

This book critically analyzes the role of public education and the curriculum reform movements.

Wells, A. ***Where Charter School Policy Fails: The Problems of Accountability and Equity.*** New York, NY: Teacher's College Press. 2002.

In this book, transparency and disclosure are discussed within the context of the charter school movement.

Wells, A. S., and R. L. Crain. ***Stepping over the Color Line: African American Students in White Suburban Schools.*** New Haven, CT: Yale University Press, 1997.

How are African Americans being served by the charter schools? What is their experience in public schools? This work examines the color issue in education.

Wilson, S. ***Learning on the Job: When Business Takes on Public Schools.*** Cambridge, MA: Harvard University Press, 2006.

In this book, former founder of Advantage Schools, Steve Wilson, speaks about his experiences and predictions of the future of private management of charter schools. The book gives the history of some leading players in the charter school management industry.

Winerip, M. **"Schools for Sale."** *New York Times Magazine,* 4 June 1998.

Are we selling our schools to think tanks, private managerial firms, private curriculum companies, and the like? This article examines the privatization of all aspects of schools.

Yamashiro, K., and L. Carlos. ***More on Charter Schools.*** San Francisco: WestEd, 1996.

A thoughtful and comprehensive discussion of charter schools as a movement and as a reality.

Yancey, P. ***Parents Founding Charter Schools: Dilemmas of Empowerment and Decentralization.*** New York, NY: Peter Lang Publishing, Inc. 2000.

In this book the author takes a nuance approach in interviewing many people who actually started charter schools and the problems and issues they faced.

Zollers, N., and A. Ramanathan. **"For Profit Charter Schools and Students with Disabilities."** *Phi Delta Kappan* (December 1998): 297.

What about students with disabilities? How are they faring in charter schools? This article examines the selectivity process for assuring equal access to charter schools for disabled persons.

NONPRINT RESOURCES

Nonprint resources for charter schools are best found on the Internet. Although many educational organizations and their Web sites are mentioned in Chapter 8, the following organizations and essays include more links that offer online information about public education, charter schools, and specific articles.

American Association of School Administrators
http://www.aasa.org

This organization is devoted to educational issues faced by the administrators and managers of schools.

America's Choice
http://www.americaschoice.org/

America's Choice began as a program of the National Center on Education and the Economy (NCEE), a not-for-profit organization headquartered in Washington, D.C. In the autumn of 2004, America's Choice was reorganized as a for profit subsidiary of the NCEE. Since its founding in 1988, the NCEE has been a leader of the educational standards movement in the United States, and the America's Choice program has become a premier provider of comprehensive school and instructional design services, technical assistance and teacher professional development. America's Choice began its work with 40 schools in 1998. Over the past nine years, over 1,000 schools nationwide—elementary, K-8, middle, and high schools—have adopted the design.

America's Choice Shows Promising Results, Author of New Maryland Report Says
Megan Greenwell, *Washington Post*, 6 December 2007; http://www.americas choice.org/acsitedassuccessinpg

Jack Jennings, the president and CEO of the Center on Education Policy, released a report on Maryland's efforts to improve struggling schools. The Center on Education Policy cited America's Choice as one of two programs beginning to have a positive impact in Prince George's County schools, as reported in the Washington Post. According to the report, the Maryland Department of Education eliminated six previously available intervention alternatives—including turnaround specialists.

American Federation of Teachers
www.aft.org

The American Federation of Teachers (AFT) was founded in 1910 to represent the economic, social, and professional interests of classroom teachers. It is an affiliated international union of the AFL-CIO. The AFT currently has more than 1.4 million members. They have organized teachers in 70 charter schools nationwide.

AFT ACTS Alliance of Charter Teachers and Staff
http://www.aftacts.org/

The AFT represents charter school teachers and support staff in over 70 charter schools across ten states. These educators recognize that the AFT and its affiliates have the experience and professionalism to help them achieve their goals.

AFT Reaffirms Commitment to Organizing Charter Schools, National Charter School Week

Janet Bass, 30 April–4 May 2007; http://www.aft.org/presscenter/releases/2007/043007.htm.

In recognition of National Charter School Week, the American Federation of Teachers reaffirms its commitment to quality, accountable public education, pledging it will intensify its nationwide effort to organize charter schools.

American Federation of Teachers' Largest Affiliate and Green Dot Public Schools Announce Contract Agreement for Green Dot New York Charter School

23 June 2009; http://www.aft.org/quest2009/downloads/monday/CharterEducators-notes.pdf.

The American Federation of Teachers' New York City affiliate and Green Dot Public Schools announced a three-year contract agreement for teachers at Green Dot New York Charter School in the Bronx, an agreement that AFT President Randi Weingarten said proves that unionized charter schools can be collaborative, innovative, and good for students and teachers.

Charter Schools Can Empower Teachers; The AFT and Charter Schools Today; The Bottom Line: What Happens in the Classroom Matters Most

6 May 2008; http://www.aft.org/topics/charters/index.htm.

The American Federation of Teachers strongly supports charter schools that embody the core values of public education and a democratic society: equal access for all students; high academic standards; accountability to parents and the public; a curriculum that promotes good citizenship; a commitment to helping all public schools improve; and a commitment to the employees' right to freely choose union representation. The following reports iterate the AFT's current position on issues salient to charter schools.

Frequently Asked Questions of the AFT ACTS Alliance

http://www.aftacts.org/index.php?option=com_content&task=view&id=14&Itemid=43

The AFT and Charter Schools

http://www.aftacts.org/index.php?option=com_content&task=view&id=13&Itemid=42

The American Federation of Teachers strongly supports charter schools that embody the core values of public education and a democratic society: equal access for all students; high academic standards; accountability to parents and the public; a curriculum that promotes good citizenship; a commitment to helping all public schools improve; and a commitment to the employees' right to freely choose union representation.

AFT Charter School Achievement on the 2005 National Assessment of Educational Progress
F. Howard Nelson and Nancy Van Meter, November 2005, http://www.aft. org/topics/charters/downloads/CharterSchoolAchievement_Nov2005.pdf

The following AFT report is the only comprehensive report available to the public that uses the 2005 National Assessment of Educational Progress (NAEP) to compare student achievement in charter schools with achievement in other public schools. In our report, NAEP results are reported exactly as they would be in an official NAEP report, including all data qualifications used by NAEP regarding statistical significance and data reporting standards.

Multiple Choice: Charter School Performance in 16 States.
15 June 2009; http://www.aft.org/presscenter/releases/2009/061509.htm.

Reacting to the CREDO report released in 2009, which provides a significant national snapshot of how charter schools are faring, revealing that while in a few cases charter schools do a good job, in most cases they perform no better and are frequently worse than traditional public schools, Randi Weingarten, president of The American Federation of Teachers reiterates that AFT has long supported the role that charter schools play as laboratories for innovation. However, she argues, the inconsistencies in the quality of charter schools should give pause to those who want to lift charter caps, particularly when they are not matched with calls for legislatures to increase accountability. "Multiple Choice" reinforces the AFT's position that charter schools are not the panacea they often are made out to be, and that our national focus must continue to include discussion of how to support and improve our regular public schools, where the majority of America's students attend.

No Experience Necessary: How the New Orleans School Takeover Experiment Devalues Experienced Teachers
June 2007; http://www.aft.org/presscenter/releases/downloads/NoExper Report_07.pdf.

In this AFT co-sponsored study, the union concludes that the firing of virtually all teachers and other school district staff in December 2005 prompted a mass exodus of experienced teachers. Before Katrina, well-credentialed veteran teachers were already in short supply in the city's schools, however, the post-Katrina education decisions made by Louisiana officials turned a preexisting challenge—retaining experienced teachers—into a full-blown crisis.

The shortage of experienced teachers is acute. Veteran teachers have returned to the city's public schools at only about half the rate of students. Veteran teachers make up only 48 percent of the teaching force in RSD's regular schools and only 45 percent of teachers in RSD's charter schools. In contrast, approximately three out of four teachers who work in noncharter schools of the Orleans Parish School Board are veterans (three or more years of experience).

Teacher pay does not appear to be the most significant factor in the shortage of seasoned teachers. In fact, the RSD pays teachers more than any other parish, and RSD's pay exceeds pay in Orleans Parish's traditional schools by roughly $4,000. Empirical evidence and extensive interviews of teachers suggest that the major issues driving the shortage are lack of respect, poor working conditions and having no real voice in decisions.

Unlike teachers in the neighboring parishes of Jefferson and St. Tammany, and in a vast majority of other states, teachers in New Orleans have no collective bargaining rights—the ability to have a legally recognized organization represent them on key issues. The required workday for many teachers in New Orleans is as much as one hour longer than for those in neighboring parishes. Class sizes in many New Orleans schools have reached disturbingly high levels. Job security is also an issue, according to the report.

Teachers at Three Chicago Charters Seek Union Recognition
3 April 2009; http://www.aft.org/news/2009/chicago-charters.htm.

Taking a historic step forward, the majority of teachers at three Chicago-area charter school campuses, joined by parents and community leaders, served notice on April 3 to their school officials, Mayor Richard M. Daley, Chicago school board members and the State of Illinois that they have formed a union. The teachers seek immediate recognition of their collective bargaining unit and a commitment by school officials to promptly bargain and settle a contract.

American Legislative Exchange Council
http://www.alec.org

The mission of the American Legislative Exchange Council is to advance the Jeffersonian principles of free markets, limited government, federalism, and individual liberty, through a nonpartisan public-private partnership of America's state legislators, members of the private sector, the federal government, and general public.

Report Card on American Education

Andrew T. LeFevre, 1 November 2006; http://www.alec.org/fileadmin/ 2006%20Ed%20Report%20Card_ALEC.pdf

The "Report Card on American Education," published by the American Legislative Exchange Council, uses controversial methods to draw some very controversial findings. The report presents readily available statistics to generate hundreds of tables and figures concerning each state's education "inputs," "outputs," and demographics. Interspersed among these tables are a mere dozen pages of analysis intended to support the conclusion, in the words of ALEC Executive Director Lori Roman, that per-pupil spending increases, pupil-to-teacher ratio reductions and raises for teachers "...are not going to make the difference in raising American student achievement to international standards. Empowering parents will" (p. 1). But many have argued that ineptness and naiveté in measurement and data analysis have thwarted any attempt to legitimately derive such conclusions.

The Buckeye Institute for Public Policy Decisions

http://www.buckeyeinstitute.org/

The Buckeye Institute is a conservative think-tank committed to research and analysis on educational issues.

The Financial Impact of Ohio's Charter Schools

Matthew Carr, 6 July 2006; http://epsl.asu.edu/epru/ttdocuments/EPRU-0607-402-OWI.pdf

This report claims that charter schools in the "Big Eight" urban school districts in Ohio are producing greater achievement gains, increasing revenues in the traditional public schools of these districts, and are operating at lower costs.

Public Charter Schools: A Great Value for Ohio's Public Education System

Matthew Carr and Beth Lear, 14 November 2008; http://www.buckeyeinstitute.org/charterschools.pdf

This Buckeye Institute policy brief sets out to document problems and inequities in charter school finance in Ohio, but it arguably falls short in providing a comprehensive presentation of evidence. For one thing, it incorrectly assumes that charter schools serve the same types of students and provide the same range of services, and it does so based on only partial revenues. To illustrate these problems, this review presents a comprehensive description of particular cost advantages and disadvantages that charter schools face. Such comprehensiveness is important for seeing through one-sided arguments from opponents or advocates that may not take into consideration the whole range of factors that affect the equitable distribution of revenues.

California Charter Schools Association

http://www.charterassociation.org

A network of charter schools and their advocates, this site has links to a multitude of parties interested in the charter movement.

Cato Institute

The Cato Institute is a libertarian think-tank devoted to public policy issues.

End It, Don't Mend It: What to Do with No Child Left Behind
Neal McCluskey and Andrew J. Coulson, 5 September 2007; http://www.cato.org/pubs/pas/Pa599.pdf

This new report from the Cato Institute begins with a solid analysis of No Child Left Behind's effects on student achievement, concluding that the law has narrowed the curriculum while failing to boost test scores. The report also includes a useful review of current debates on Capitol Hill, focusing on proposals that the authors believe offer little more than tinkering with the current law.

Markets vs. Monopolies in Education: A Global Review of the Evidence
Andrew Coulson, 10 September 2008; http://www.cato.org/pubs/pas/pa620.pdf

The Cato Institute report examines international evidence on outcomes from public and private education. The paper makes three key claims: private schools outperform public schools in "the overwhelming majority of cases"; private schools' superiority is greatest in countries where the education system has more market features; and "the implications for U.S. education policy are profound."

Cato Scholar Comments on Florida Court's Decision on Charter Schools
Andrew Coulson, 3 December 2008; http://www.cato.org/pressroom.php?display=ncomments&id=173

Florida's First District Appellate Court ruled in 2008 that only the state's public school districts have the right to approve and oversee charter schools; the court ruling struck down a prior 2006 law that created an alternative state-level charter authorization body. In this report Andrew Coulson of the Cato Institute argues that because traditional public school districts typically—and correctly—see charters as competitors for scarce public funding, and this ruling will allow them to once again protect their monopoly position by stifling the competition (the very problem the 2006 law was meant to address).

Can Charter Schools Yield Market-Like Results?

Andrew Coulson, 19 July 2009; http://www.cato-at-liberty.org/2006/07/19/can-charter-schools-yield-market-like-results/

This report argues that the charter-schooling model lacks some of the essential characteristics of effective markets.

Center on Reinventing Public Education
University of Washington
Box 363060
Seattle, WA 98195-3060
206-685-2214
www.crpe.org/

This center provides ideas on how schools might be reinvented to meet the needs of history. The site offers links and resources for people interested in the multitude of issues facing reform efforts in education.

Hopes, Fears, & Reality: A Balanced Look at American Charter Schools in 2008

Robin Lake, December 2008; http://www.crpe.org/cs/crpe/view/csr_pubs/255

This 2008 annual report published by the National Charter School Research Project offers new evidence and analysis about the state of the nation's public charter schools. In five essays, the report explores how well charters are doing, where they need to improve, and what can be learned from current research.

Charter School Resource Center
http://www.pioneerinstitute.org

This center devotes itself to providing all and any resources needed to those wishing to start a charter school.

Corporate Watch
http://www.corpwatch.org

Corporate Watch provides news, analysis, research tools, and action resources to respond to corporate activity around the globe. The organization talks with people who are directly affected by corporate abuses as well as with others fighting for corporate accountability, human rights, and social and environmental justice. As part of the independent media, Corporate Watch is free of corporate sponsorship. The parent organization is the Transnational Resource and Action Center (TRAC), based in San Francisco. Corporate Watch seeks to monitor the influence of corporations in all areas of education.

Editorial Projects In Education
http://www.indeed.com/cmp/Editorial-Projects-In-Education

Editorial Projects in Education Inc. (EPE) publishes Education Week and Teacher Magazine, and produces the award-winning edweek.org and AgentK-12.org. EPE's primary mission is to help raise the level of awareness and understanding among professionals and the public of important issues in American education. EPE covers local, state, and national news and issues from preschool through the 12th grade. EPE also provides periodic special reports on issues ranging from technology to textbooks, as well as books of special interest to educators.

Diplomas Count Report
Editorial Projects in Education, April 2008; http://www.washingtonpost.com/ac2/related/topic/Editorial+Projects+in+Education+Inc.?tid=informline

In this 2008 report the EPE research center found that 52 percent of public high school students in the nation's fifty biggest cities completed the full curriculum and graduated between 2003 and 2004 and that 1.2 million high school students drop out of school each year.

Education and the Public Interest Center
The Education and the Public Interest Center (EPIC) at the University of Colorado at Boulder partners with the Education Policy Research Unit (EPRU), at Arizona University in Tempe and the Commercialism in Education Research Unit (CERU) located as well at Arizona State University to produce policy briefs and think tank reviews. These centers work in tandem to provide a variety of audiences, both academic and public, with information, analysis, and insight to further democratic deliberation regarding educational policies.

EPIC and EPRU also created in 2007, the Education Policy Alliance, a nationwide network of university-based research centers and organizations.

Charter Schools
Gerald W. Bracey; http://epsl.asu.edu/epru/documents/cerai-00-26.htm

Charter schools enthusiasts have offered the hope that they would offer immediate and major improvements in education. This report argues that the actual outcomes have been much more modest.

Charter Schools' Performance and Accountability: A Disconnect
Gerald W. Bracey, George Mason University, Education Policy Studies Laboratory

This comprehensive review of national and state charter school evaluations argues that charter schools are rarely held accountable and, in general, perform no better than traditional public schools.

Charter Schools: The Smiling Face of Disinvestment
Alex Molnar, University of Wisconsin-Milwaukee

An award-winning 1996 article about the risks charter schools may pose to public education reform and to students.

Profiles of For-Profit Education Management Companies: 1998-1999
Alex Molnar, Jennifer Morales, and Alison Vander Wyst

A who's who of for-profit companies that manage public schools and charter schools. This list features the names and contact information for companies in the for-profit education arena, as well as the name and location of each school they run. The company profiles are updated annually as new information becomes available.

Profiles of For-Profit Education Management Companies: 1999-2000
Alex Molnar, Jennifer Morales, and Alison Vander Wyst; University of Wisconsin-Milwaukee

The second directory of for-profit education management companies published by CERAI and the Education Policy Project identifies 20 companies managing 230 schools in 21 states. This is the most complete directory available of the for-profit education management industry.

Profiles of For-Profit Education Management Companies: 2000-2001
Alex Molnar, Jennifer Morales, and Alison Vander Wyst; University of Wisconsin-Milwaukee

The third directory of for-profit Education Management Companies published by CACE and the Education Policy Project identifies 21 companies managing 285 schools in 22 states.

Profiles of For-Profit Education Management Companies: 2001-2002
John Hutchinson, Alex Molnar, Melissa Restori, and Glen Wilson; Arizona State University

The number of for-profit companies managing public schools in the United States soared 70 percent in the past year, according to data compiled by the

Education Policy Studies Laboratory. Profiles of For-Profit Education Management Companies, 2001-2002, is the most comprehensive resource available on the growth of so-called Education Management Organizations, or EMOs.

Profiles of For-Profit Education Management Organizations: 2002-2003
Daniel Allen, Alex Molnar, and Glen Wilson; Arizona State University

This annual report, in its fifth edition, found that 47 education management companies (EMOs) operate in 24 states and the District of Columbia enrolling some 190,000 students. The report is the most comprehensive resource on the for-profit education management industry.

Profiles of For-Profit Education Management Organizations: 2003-2004
Alex Molnar; Arizona State University

This annual report, in its sixth edition, found that 51 management companies (EMOs) operate in 28 states and the District of Columbia, enrolling some 200,400 students. The report is the most comprehensive resource on the for-profit education management industry.

Profiles of For-Profit Education Management Organizations: 2004-2005
David R. Garcia, Jamie Joanou, Brendan McEvoy, Alex Molnar, and Carolyn Sullivan; Arizona State University, Education Policy Studies Laboratory

This annual report, in its seventh edition, found that Education Management Organizations (EMOs) tend to focus on managing charter primary schools and on enrolling relatively large numbers of students in those schools. Fifty-nine EMOs operate in 24 states and the District of Columbia, enrolling some 239,766 students. The report is the most comprehensive resource on the for-profit education management industry.

Profiles of For-Profit Education Management Organizations: 2005-2006
David R. Garcia, and Alex Molnar; Arizona State University, Commercialism in Education Research Unit and Education Policy Research Unit

This annual report, in its eighth edition, found that Education Management Organizations (EMOs) are consolidating and shifting business models to meet the demand for supplemental education services. Large EMOs continue to focus on managing charter primary schools and enrolling relatively large numbers of students in those schools. Fifty-one EMOs operate in 28 states and the District of Columbia, enrolling some 237,179 students. The report is the most comprehensive resource on the for-profit education management industry.

Profiles of For-Profit Education Management Organizations: 2006-2007
Shannon Berry, David R. Garcia, Gary Miron, and Alex Molnar

This annual report, in its ninth edition, found that, despite repeated requests, several large, publicly funded Education Management Organizations (EMOs) failed to provide information about their schools or finances when queried by researchers. The data collected in the report suggest that the number of charter schools overall has increased and the number of EMO-run charter schools has stabilized or declined slightly. The number of students enrolled in charter schools has shown a slight decrease. The report is the most comprehensive resource on the for-profit education management industry.

Profiles of For-Profit Education Management Organizations: 2007-2008
Gary Miron, Alex Molnar, and Jessica Urschel

Education management organizations, or EMOs, emerged in the early 1990s in the context of widespread interest in so-called market-based school reform proposals. Proponents of EMOs claim that they will bring a much needed dose of entrepreneurial spirit and a competitive ethos to public education. Opponents worry that outsourcing to EMOs will result in already limited school resources being redirected for service fees and/or profits for another layer of administration. Opponents also have expressed concerns about public bodies relinquishing control or ownership of schools.

The data in the annual Profiles of For-Profit Education Management Organizations reports describe general trends in the for-profit EMO industry over time. They are intended for a broad audience including policymakers, educators, school district officials, and school board members who may use this information to learn more about current or potential contractors. Investors, persons involved in the education industry, and employees of EMOs may use Profiles reports to track changes, strategize for growth, and plan investments. Finally, Profiles reports are important resources for journalists, researchers, and anyone who seeks to study and learn about education management organizations.

Evaluating the Impact of Charter Schools on Student Achievement:
A Longitudinal Look at the Great Lakes States
Chris Coryn, Dawn Mackety, and Gary Miron; Western Michigan University

The aim of this study is to examine the impact of charter schools on student achievement in the Great Lakes states: Illinois, Indiana, Michigan, Minnesota, Ohio, and Wisconsin. This evaluation addresses two specific questions: How does student achievement in charter schools compare with student achievement in demographically similar, traditional public schools? Do charter schools show promise of being an effective strategy for improving student achievement over time, even if they are not yet outperforming traditional public schools? These re some of the questions the report discusses.

No Student Left Unsold
Alex Molnar; Arizona State University

The Sixth Annual Report on Schoolhouse Commercialism Trends, Year 2002-2003, finds that commercial activity remains firmly entrenched in American public schools as protest mounts from citizens and legislative efforts to rein it in.

Ohio Charter Schools Report False and Deceitful
Gary Miron, (269) 599-7965; gary.miron@wmich.edu, Kevin Welner, (303) 492-8370; kevin.welner@gmail.com; http://epicpolicy.org/newsletter/2008/12/ohio-charter-schools-report-false-and-deceitful

EPIC review claims that the financial analysis and claims are merely propagandistic appeals.

School Choice and Accountability
Gregg Garn, Ph.D., University of Oklahoma, Casey Cobb, Ph.D., University of Connecticut, March 2008; http://epicpolicy.org/files/CHOICE-04-Garn2.pdf

This policy brief explores the intersection of school choice and accountability. Based on a review of research since 1970, the authors first develop a typology of four distinct models of accountability: *bureaucratic, performance, market* and *professional.* They both define these and demonstrate how they are embedded in the school choice movement. Second, they examine several school choice options—vouchers and tax credits, charter schools, virtual/cyber schools, home schools and inter- and intra-district choice—and detail the varied accountability systems inherent in each. Third, they explore the impact of school choice programs on the accountability of traditional district schools. Finally, the report provides practical recommendations for policymakers and other interested parties.

Charter Ranking Roulette: An Analysis of Reports That Grade States' Charter School Laws
Wendy C. Chi, and Kevin G. Welnew, 12 February 2008; http://epicpolicy.org/publication/charter-ranking-roulette

Since 1996, the Center for Education Reform has released an annual report card, grading each state's charter school legislation and labeling as the "strongest" those laws placing the fewest and slightest restrictions on charter schools. While the Center for Education Reform rankings have undoubtedly been the most influential, at least four other systems have been developed. In this article, we analyze the different ranking systems, including a new approach we have developed in order to illustrate the arbitrariness of any given ranking system and to highlight some key charter school issues. We then investigate the general, popular phenomenon of rankings in the field of education, exploring the benefits, drawbacks, and appeal of such rankings.

School Choice: Evidence and Recommendations
Gary Miron, Kevin G. Welner, Patricia H. Hinchey, and Alex Molnar, eds., 20 March 2008; http://epsl.asu.edu/epru/documents/EPSL-0803-252-EPRU.pdf

Over the past decade, school choice has been examined by a number of books and other publications. This scholarly work typically examines only a single form of school choice. Looking at specific forms of choice, these efforts have provided valuable insights and information. Vouchers, magnet schools, and tax credit policies have each received appropriate attention, as have home schooling and, most recently, charter schools. Other forms of public school choice, as well as "virtual schools," has also been examined. Each type of choice carries with it different rules and different empirical effects, yet they unquestionably share commonalities. *School Choice: Evidence and Recommendations* is collection of 10 policy briefs, each of which comprehensively considers school choice. The briefs probe key choice issues, mustering evidence and developing cross-choice themes and insights.

The Friedman Foundation for Educational Choice
Reports on 10 state public opinion surveys on K-12 school choice, Various Authors, 14 October 2008; http://www.friedmanfoundation.org/friedman/research/ShowFilteredResearch.do?method=friedman

The Friedman Foundation for Educational Choice has published 10 state reports based on surveys of likely voters in those states. According to the reports, the surveys demonstrate state residents' endorsement of vouchers allowing parents to send children to private schools.

The Heartland Institute
http://www.heartland.org

The Heartland Institute is a national nonprofit research and education organization, tax exempt under Section 501(c)3 of the Internal Revenue Code, and founded in Chicago in 1984. It is not affiliated with any political party, business, or foundation. Heartland's mission is to discover, develop, and promote free-market solutions to social and economic problems. Such solutions include parental choice in education, choice and personal responsibility in health care, market-based approaches to environmental protection, privatization of public services, and deregulation in areas where property rights and markets do a better job than government bureaucracies.

Choice and Education across the States
Michael Van Winkle, 17 April 2008; http://www.heartland.org/pdf/22914.pdf

Choice and Education across the States, published by the Heartland Institute, is an advocacy document that assigns letter grades to states based on the extensiveness of each state's school choice system. The report asserts, based on questionable use of past research, that an increase in school choice will strengthen accountability and improve student achievement. It awards most states low grades, reflecting a desire for more school choice throughout the nation.

Labor Notes
http://www.labornotes.org

Labor Notes is a nonprofit organization for union activists founded in 1979. It is devoted to discussing conditions for educational workers and what proposals for change might mean to them. The organization publishes the monthly magazine *Labor Notes,* which contains news of the labor movement.

Mackinac Center for Public Policy
http://www.mackinac.org/

The Mackinac Center for Public Policy is a market-based research and educational institute devoted to improving the quality of life for all Michigan citizens by promoting sound solutions to state and local policy questions. The Mackinac Center assists policymakers, scholars, business people, the media, and the public by providing objective analysis of Michigan issues. The goal of all Center reports, commentaries, and educational programs is to equip Michigan citizens and other decision-makers to better evaluate policy options.

A School Privatization Primer for Michigan School Officials, Media and Residents
Michael D. LaFaive, 27 June 2007; http://www.mackinac.org/article.aspx?ID=8691

Issued by the Mackinac Center for Public Policy, "A School Privatization Primer for Michigan School Officials, Media and Residents" examines the "contracting out" of public school support services—specifically food, transportation, and custodial services. The report describes the prevalence of contracting out and sets forth the practical steps in hiring a contractor and the benefits in allowing districts to focus on their core mission of instruction. This information may help districts already committed to contracting out. The report presupposes that the practice is beneficial. It relies primarily on testimony from district officials as opposed to direct data or research.

Milton and Rose D. Friedman Foundation for Educational Choice
http://www.friedmanfoundation.org/

The Friedman Foundation for Educational Choice, a nonprofit organization established in 1996, was founded upon the ideals and theories of Nobel Laureate economist Milton Friedman and economist Rose D. Friedman.

The ABC's of School Choice
The Milton and Rose Friedman Foundation, 1 September 2007; http://www.friedmanfoundation.org/friedman/downloadFilc.do?id=102

A new annual report from the Milton and Rose Friedman Foundation is designed as a resource to provide ammunition for persuading people as to the merits of school choice. The report provides updated information on thirteen states and the District of Columbia with policies that approximate the Friedman Foundation's voucher-based version of school "choice." While the descriptive compendium of information is mostly accurate and somewhat useful, the report begins and ends with "Frequently Asked Questions," where the Foundation seeks to interpret the research on school choice issues for the lay reader.

School Choice by the Numbers: The Fiscal Effect of School Choice Programs 1990-2006
Susan Aud, 9 May 2007; http://www.friedmanfoundation.org/friedman/downloadFile.do?id=243

This review considers the recently released study by Susan Aud of the Milton & Rose D. Friedman Foundation, concerning the fiscal effects of school vouchers policies. Aud calculates the simple difference between, on the one hand, state and local government spending on students attending traditional public schools, and, on the other, the government spending on children opting for vouchers to private schools. Aud finds a cumulative savings of $444 million over a 15-year period nationwide.

The High Cost of Failing to Reform Public Education in Missouri
Brian J. Gottlob, 1 March 2006; http://www.friedmanfoundation.org/friedman/downloadFile.do?id=95

The High Cost of Failing to Reform Public Education in Indiana
Brian J. Gottlob, 1 October 2006; http://www.friedmanfoundation.org/friedman/downloadFile.do?id=97

The High Cost of Failing to Reform Public Education in Texas
Brian J. Gottlob, 1 February 2007; http://www.friedmanfoundation.org/friedman/downloadFile.do?id=107

The High Cost of South Carolina's Low Graduation Rates
Brian J. Gottlob, 1 June 2007; http://www.friedmanfoundation.org/friedman/downloadFile.do?id=250

The High Cost of Low Graduation Rates in North Carolina
Brian J. Gottlob, 25 October 2007; http://www.friedmanfoundation.org/friedman/downloadFile.do?id=256

Five sister reports indicated above and published by the Friedman Foundation over the past three years asserts that private-school voucher programs can reduce the social costs of dropping out while increasing graduation rates. The reports are state-specific, targeting five different states.

National Coalition of Education Activists
www.idealist.org

This coalition of activists attempts to unite people who are interested in realistic and progressive social change in education.

National Commission on Teaching and America's Future
http://www.nctaf.org/

The National Commission on Teaching and America's Future treats every issue that confronts education today. The Web site gives links and resources along with opportunities to contact key players and members in the educational arena.

Academic Benefits to Students: Large Scale Research Findings and Sources for Student Achievement Benefits of Small Schools
Susan Black, April 1996, 18, no. 4, pp. 31-33; ERIC #EJ522752

This study, conducted by Susan Black, strongly indicates that creating smaller, more personal, learner-central school environments can result in improved academic achievement for students.

Network of Educators on the Americas
http://www.teachingforchange.org

The Network of Educators on the Americas is a think tank that provides a multitude of information on everything from charter schools to educational reform in integration.

RAND Corporation
http://www.rand.org/

The RAND Corporation is a nonprofit institution that helps improve policy and decision making through research and analysis. For more than 60 years, the RAND Corporation has pursued its nonprofit mission by conducting research on important and complicated problems. Initially, RAND (the name of which was derived from a contraction of the term *research and development*) focused on issues of national security. Eventually, RAND expanded its intellectual reserves to offer insight into other areas, such as business, education, health, law, and science.

RAND Corporation, Research For Action, and Program on Education Policy and Governance; State Takeover, School Restructuring, Private Management, and Student Achievement in Philadelphia
Brian Gill, Ron Zimmer, Jolley Christman and Suzanne Blanc, 1 February 2007; http://www.rand.org/pubs/monographs/2007/RAND_MG533.pdf

In 2002, the state of Pennsylvania took charge of the Philadelphia public schools. Within months of the takeover, a newly created School Reform Commission had launched the nation's largest experiment in the private management of public schools. The commission, which replaced the local school board, turned over 45 elementary and middle schools to seven private for-profit and nonprofit managers. In addition, the school district, under a new CEO, implemented wide-ranging and ambitious reforms in district-managed schools. This monograph examines student achievement outcomes for the district as a whole and for privately managed and district-managed "restructured" schools during the first four years after the takeover (through spring 2006).

School Reform in Philadelphia: A Comparison of Student Achievement at Privately-Managed Schools with Student Achievement in Other District Schools
Paul Peterson, 10 April 2007; http://www.ksg.harvard.edu/pepg/PDF/Papers/PEPG07-03_Peterson.pdf

In 2002 the city of Philadelphia began a policy of restructuring its lowest-achieving elementary and middle schools. Eighty-six schools were included. In Philadelphia, the most prominent restructuring approaches shifted school management to either the district or one of several private providers. In

2007, after four years of this policy, two research reports were issued, one by RAND in collaboration with Research For Action (RAND-RFA) and one by the Program on Education Policy and Governance (PEPG). Both reports examined whether any positive effects on the math and reading achievement of students could be attributed to privately managed schools, district-managed schools, or neither. According to the RAND-RFA report, private management has had no cumulative effect on math or reading achievement, while district management has had a positive effect on math achievement but no effect on reading. According to the PEPG report, private management has had a positive effect on the percentage of students reaching "Basic" levels of performance in math and reading, while district management has generally had no effect.

Achievement and Attainment in Chicago Charter Schools
Kevin Booker, Brian Gill, Ron Zimmer, and Tim R. Sass, 2008; www.rand. org/pubs/technical_reports/TR585

Over the past decade, charter schools have been among the fastest-growing segments of the K-12 education sector in Chicago and across the country. This report addresses several key issues related to charter schools using student-level data provided by the Chicago Public Schools. Students leaving traditional public schools for charter schools in Chicago tend to look much like the peers they left behind, in both demographic characteristics and student achievement. Transfers to charter schools tend to slightly reduce racial stratification across the schools. Achievement trajectories suggest that, on average, charter schools' performance in raising student achievement is approximately on par with traditional public schools—except that charter schools do not do well in raising student achievement in their first year of operation. Chicago's charter high schools may produce substantial positive effects on ACT scores, the probability of graduating, and the probability of enrolling in college—but these positive effects are solidly evident only in the multi-grade charter high schools (those that include middle-school grades). The large, positive attainment results in Chicago suggest remarkable promise for (at least) multigrade charter high schools and demonstrate that evaluations limited to test scores may fail to capture important benefits of charter schools. If charter schools (or other multigrade high schools) have positive effects on graduation and college entry, they may make a substantial, long-term difference in the life prospects of their students.

ReThinking Schools: An Urban Educational Journal
www.rethinkingschools.org

ReThinking Schools: An Urban Education Journal is a nonprofit, independent journal advocating the reform of elementary and secondary public schools. Emphasis is placed on urban schools and issues of social justice, and the journal stresses a grassroots perspective combining theory and practice and linking classroom issues to broader policy concerns. It is an activist publication and encourages teachers, parents, and students to become involved in building quality public schools for all children. The journal is published by Milwaukee-area teachers and educators, and contributing writers are from around the country. Re-Thinking Schools focuses on local and national school reform.

Strong American Schools

http://www.strongamericanschools.org/

Strong American Schools, a project of Rockefeller Philanthropy Advisors, is a nonpartisan campaign supported by The Eli and Edythe Broad Foundation and the Bill & Melinda Gates Foundation promoting sound education policies for all Americans. Among their three point agenda is ending seniority and substituting merit pay for teachers based on standardized test scores, promoting national educational standards based on standardized tests, and a longer school day and school year.

Policy Primer

Strong American Schools, 5 November 2008; http://www.strongamerica schools.org/files/110508%20Updated%20Policy%20Primer.pdf

This report argues that with the culmination of the 2008 presidential election, to build support and leverage for educational change, a reform agenda is needed that focuses on three policy pillars: common education standards, an effective teacher in every classroom, and expanded learning time for students.

Teachers Union Reform Network of AFT-NEA Locals

http://www.turnexchange.net

An alliance of two powerful teachers' unions, this network attempts to frame the issue of educational reform in ideas central to teachers, parents, and educational workers.

Time Magazine.
How to Bring Our Schools Out of the 20th Century

Sonja Steptoe and Claudia Wallace, 9 December 2006; http://www.time.com/time/nation/article/0,8599,1568429,00.html

Arguing that competency in reading and math—the focus of so much No Child Left Behind (NCLB) testing—is the meager minimum, these *Time* magazine reports argue that scientific and technical skills are, likewise, utterly necessary but insufficient in today's educational agenda. The authors argue that today's economy demands not only a high-level competence in the traditional academic disciplines, but also what might be called twenty-first century skills. The report discusses, in detail, these twenty-first century competency skills that the authors believe the contemporary educational agenda must tackle to truly reform education.

Thomas B. Fordham Institute
http://www.edexcellence.net

The Thomas B. Fordham Institute is a Washington, D.C. conservative-based, nonprofit think tank dedicated to advancing educational excellence in America's K-12 schools. They claim to promote policies that strengthen accountability and expand education options for parents and families. Their reports examine issues such as No Child Left Behind, school choice, and teacher quality. Their sister nonprofit, the Thomas B. Fordham Foundation, sponsors charter schools in Ohio.

Fund the Child: Bringing Equity, Autonomy, and Portability to Ohio School Finance
Thomas B. Fordham Institute, along with Public Impact and the University of Dayton's School of Education and Allied Professions, 12 March 2008; http://www.edexcellence.net/doc/fund_the_child_ohio_031208.pdf

The newly released Thomas B. Fordham Institute report is the latest in a series of reports promoting the implementation of decentralized governance of public schooling coupled with student-based allocation of revenues to schools. Most notably, the current report suggests that Ohio should implement a fully state-funded system. Second, the current report avoids unfounded claims that research has found decentralized governance to necessarily improve student outcomes. Third, it takes a measured approach toward recommendations for implementing the reform, and it acknowledges the potential political influences that might compromise equity goals of weighted funding formulas.

Playing to Type? Mapping the Charter School Landscape
Dick M. Carpenter II, 3 May 2006; http://www.edexcellence.net/doc/Carpenter%20ProjectV2.pdf

This report developed a unique typology to compare charter schools types by their enrollment, demographic background of students, and performance.

An Open Letter to President Obama, Secretary Duncan and the 111th Congress
Chester E. Finn, Jr., and Michael Petrilli, 18 December 2008 http://www.edexcellence.net/detail/news.cfm?news_id=741&id=92

In an open letter to newly elected Barack Obama and newly appointed Secretary Duncan and the 11th Congress, the Thomas B. Fordham Institute appraises the current policy landscape and its main players, and outlines the ideal federal role in K-12 education.

Trinational Coalition in Defense of Public Education: Canada, United States, and Mexico
http://www.trinationalcoalition.org

This organization is committed to the support and continuance of public education. It is a North American organization that addresses issues in the United States, Canada, and Mexico.

Destroying Public Education in America
Stephen Lendman, 7 April 2008; http://www.trinationalcoalition.org/english/docs/Destroying%20Public%20Education%20in%20America.doc

In this controversial article, author Stephen Lendman claims that throughout Chicago, Louisiana, and indeed the country, inner city schools are being closed, remaining ones are neglected and decrepit, classroom sizes are increasing, and children and parents are being sacrificed on the altar of marketplace triumphalism. The article is highly critical of marketplace approaches to educational reform.

Appendix A

Title II Accountability Provisions of the Higher Education Act (HEA)

The Title II Accountability Provisions of the HEA has as its purpose to present the most current information for 50 states, the District of Columbia, Puerto Rico and outlying areas, on the implementation of the teacher quality provisions of Title II of the Higher Education Act of 1965, as amended (HEA) and the mandates of NCLB. It develops key definitions for terms, and uniform reporting methods related to the performance of elementary school and secondary school teacher preparation programs, as reprinted here.

SEC. 207. ACCOUNTABILITY FOR PROGRAMS THAT PREPARE TEACHERS.

(a) DEVELOPMENT OF DEFINITIONS AND REPORTING METHODS—Within 9 months of the date of enactment of the Higher Education Amendments of 1998, the Commissioner of the National Center for Education Statistics, in consultation with States and institutions of higher education, shall develop key definitions for terms, and uniform reporting methods (including the key definitions for the consistent reporting of pass rates), related to the performance of elementary school and secondary school teacher preparation programs.

(b) STATE REPORT CARD ON THE QUALITY OF TEACHER PREPARATION— Each State that receives funds under this Act shall provide to the Secretary, within 2 years of the date of enactment of the Higher Education Amendments of 1998, and annually thereafter, in a uniform and comprehensible manner that conforms with the definitions and methods established in subsection (a), a State report card on the quality of teacher preparation in the State, which shall include at least the following:

(1) A description of the teacher certification and licensure assessments, and any other certification and licensure requirements, used by the State;

(2) The standards and criteria that prospective teachers must meet in order to attain initial teacher certification or licensure and to be certified or licensed to teach particular subjects or in particular grades within the State;

(3) A description of the extent to which the assessments and requirements described in paragraph (1) are aligned with the State's standards and assessments for students;

(4) The percentage of teaching candidates who passed each of the assessments used by the State for teacher certification and licensure, and the passing score on each assessment that determines whether a candidate has passed that assessment;

(5) The percentage of teaching candidates who passed each of the assessments used by the State for teacher certification and licensure, disaggre-

gated and ranked, by the teacher preparation program in that State from which the teacher candidate received the candidate's most recent degree, which shall be made available widely and publicly;

(6) Information on the extent to which teachers in the State are given waivers of State certification or licensure requirements, including the proportion of such teachers distributed across high- and low-poverty school districts and across subject areas;

(7) A description of each State's alternative routes to teacher certification, if any, and the percentage of teachers certified through alternative certification routes who pass State teacher certification or licensure assessments;

(8) For each State, a description of proposed criteria for assessing the performance of teacher preparation programs within institutions of higher education in the State, including indicators of teacher candidate knowledge and skills; and

(9) Information on the extent to which teachers or prospective teachers in each State are required to take examinations or other assessments of their subject matter knowledge in the area or areas in which the teachers provide instruction, the standards established for passing any such assessments, and the extent to which teachers or prospective teachers are required to receive a passing score on such assessments in order to teach in specific subject areas or grade levels.

(c) INITIAL REPORT—

(1) IN GENERAL—Each State that receives funds under this Act, not later than 6 months of the date of enactment of the Higher Education Amendments of 1998 and in a uniform and comprehensible manner, shall submit to the Secretary the information described in paragraphs (1), (5), and (6) of subsection (b). Such information shall be compiled by the Secretary and submitted to the Committee on Labor and Human Resources of the Senate and the Committee on Education and the Workforce of the House of Representatives not later than 9 months after the date of enactment of the Higher Education Amendments of 1998.

(2) CONSTRUCTION—Nothing in this subsection shall be construed to require a State to gather information that is not in the possession of the State or the teacher preparation programs in the State, or readily available to the State or teacher preparation programs.

(d) REPORT OF THE SECRETARY ON THE QUALITY OF TEACHER PREPARATION—

(1) REPORT CARD—The Secretary shall provide to Congress, and publish and make widely available, a report card on teacher qualifications and preparation in the United States, including all the information reported in paragraphs (1) through (9) of subsection (b). Such report shall identify

States for which eligible States and eligible partnerships received a grant under this title. Such report shall be so provided, published and made available not later than 2 years 6 months after the date of enactment of the Higher Education Amendments of 1998 and annually thereafter.

(2) REPORT TO CONGRESS—The Secretary shall report to Congress:

(A) a comparison of States' efforts to improve teaching quality; and

(B) regarding the national mean and median scores on any standardized test that is used in more than 1 State for teacher certification or licensure.

(3) SPECIAL RULE—In the case of teacher preparation programs with fewer than 10 graduates taking any single initial teacher certification or licensure assessment during an academic year, the Secretary shall collect and publish information with respect to an average pass rate on State certification or licensure assessments taken over a 3-year period.

(e) COORDINATION—The Secretary, to the extent practicable, shall coordinate the information collected and published under this title among States for individuals who took State teacher certification or licensure assessments in a State other than the State in which the individual received the individual's most recent degree.

(f) INSTITUTIONAL REPORT CARDS ON THE QUALITY OF TEACHER PREPARATION—

(1) REPORT CARD—Each institution of higher education that conducts a teacher preparation program that enrolls students receiving Federal assistance under this Act, not later than 18 months after the date of enactment of the Higher Education Amendments of 1998 and annually thereafter, shall report to the State and the general public, in a uniform and comprehensible manner that conforms with the definitions and methods established under subsection (a), the following information:

(A) PASS RATE—

(i) For the most recent year for which the information is available, the pass rate of the institution's graduates on the teacher certification or licensure assessments of the State in which the institution is located, but only for those students who took those assessments within 3 years of completing the program;

(ii) A comparison of the program's pass rate with the average pass rate for programs in the State; and

(iii) In the case of teacher preparation programs with fewer than 10 graduates taking any single initial teacher certification or licensure assessment during an academic year, the institution shall collect and publish information with respect to an average pass rate on State certification or licensure assessments taken over a 3-year period.

(B) PROGRAM INFORMATION—The number of students in the program, the average number of hours of supervised practice teaching required for those in the program, and the faculty-student ratio in supervised practice teaching.

(C) STATEMENT—In States that approve or accredit teacher education programs, a statement of whether the institution's program is so approved or accredited.

(D) DESIGNATION AS LOW-PERFORMING—Whether the program has been designated as low-performing by the State under section 208(a).

(2) REQUIREMENT—The information described in paragraph (1) shall be reported through publications such as school catalogs and promotional materials sent to potential applicants, secondary school guidance counselors, and prospective employers of the institution's program graduates.

(3) FINES—In addition to the actions authorized in section 487(c), the Secretary may impose a fine not to exceed $25,000 on an institution of higher education for failure to provide the information described in this subsection in a timely or accurate manner.

SEC. 208. STATE FUNCTIONS.

(a) STATE ASSESSMENT—In order to receive funds under this Act, a State, not later than 2 years after the date of enactment of the Higher Education Amendments of 1998, shall have in place a procedure to identify, and assist, through the provision of technical assistance, low-performing programs of teacher preparation within institutions of higher education. Such State shall provide the Secretary an annual list of such low-performing institutions that includes an identification of those institutions at-risk of being placed on such list. Such levels of performance shall be determined solely by the State and may include criteria based upon information collected pursuant to this title. Such assessment shall be described in the report under section 207(b).

(b) TERMINATION OF ELIGIBILITY—Any institution of higher education that offers a program of teacher preparation in which the State has withdrawn the State's approval or terminated the State's financial support due to the low performance of the institution's teacher preparation program based upon the State assessment described in subsection (a):

(1) shall be ineligible for any funding for professional development activities awarded by the Department of Education; and

(2) shall not be permitted to accept or enroll any student that receives aid under title IV of this Act in the institution's teacher preparation program.

(c) NEGOTIATED RULEMAKING—If the Secretary develops any regulations implementing subsection (b)(2), the Secretary shall submit such proposed regulations to a negotiated rulemaking process, which shall include representatives of States, institutions of higher education, and educational and student organizations.

SEC. 209. GENERAL PROVISIONS.

(a) METHODS—In complying with sections 207 and 208, the Secretary shall ensure that States and institutions of higher education use fair and equitable methods in reporting and that the reporting methods protect the privacy of individuals.

(b) SPECIAL RULE—For each State in which there are no State certification or licensure assessments, or for States that do not set minimum performance levels on those assessments:
   (1) the Secretary shall, to the extent practicable, collect data comparable to the data required under this title from States, local educational agencies, institutions of higher education, or other entities that administer such assessments to teachers or prospective teachers; and
   (2) notwithstanding any other provision of this title, the Secretary shall use such data to carry out requirements of this title related to assessments or pass rates.

(c) LIMITATIONS—
   (1) FEDERAL CONTROL PROHIBITED—Nothing in this title shall be construed to permit, allow, encourage, or authorize any Federal control over any aspect of any private, religious, or home school, whether or not a home school is treated as a private school or home school under State law. This section shall not be construed to prohibit private, religious, or home schools from participation in programs or services under this title.
   (2) NO CHANGE IN STATE CONTROL ENCOURAGED OR REQUIRED—Nothing in this title shall be construed to encourage or require any change in a State's treatment of any private, religious, or home school, whether or not a home school is treated as a private school or home school under State law.
   (3) NATIONAL SYSTEM OF TEACHER CERTIFICATION PROHIBITED—Nothing in this title shall be construed to permit, allow, encourage, or authorize the Secretary to establish or support any national system of teacher certification.

Source: U.S. Department of Education. "Title II Accountability Provisions of the Higher Education Act." http://www.ed.gov/policy/highered/leg/tq-statute.html.

Appendix B

Education in America: State-by-State Scorecard

State-by-state	Inputs and Outputs			Education Reform Action		
	Per Pupil Spending[1] Lowest (1) to Highest (51)	Achievement[2] Rank	Graduation Rate Rank[3] (Graduation Rate %)	Charter School[4] Law CER Grade	School Choice[5]	Accountability Policy[6] post NCLB (point change pre-NCLB)
Alabama	8 ($6,300)	48	46 (60%)	No Law	none	4.0 (+0.7)
Alaska	44 ($9,870)	25	44 (60%)	34 (D)	public	n/a
Arizona	7 ($6,282)	33	30 (71%)	4 (A)	public, tax credits	3.4 (+1.1)
Arkansas	10 ($6,482)	41	25 (74%)	30 (C)	public	3.4 (+1.1)
California	25 ($7,552)	42	39 (65%)	7 (A)	public*	n/a
Colorado	20 ($7,384)	28	29 (72%)	8 (B)	public, public-private	3.8 (+0.7)
Connecticut	48 ($11,057)	17	7 (82%)	31(C)	public	n/a
Delaware	49 ($11,847)	51	41 (63%)	3 (A)	public	n/a
District of Columbia	43 ($9,693)	29	40 (65%)	1 (A)	public-private	3.7 (+0.8)
Florida	9 ($6,439)	43	43 (61%)	9 (B)	public*, tax credits	n/a
Georgia	27 ($7,774)	45	50 (56%)	16 (B)	public	4.1 (+1.2)
Hawaii	31 ($8,100)	46	32 (70%)	35 (D)	public*	3.3 (+1.7)
Idaho	3 ($6,081)	24	22 (74%)	23 (C)	public	3.4 (+1.2)
Illinois	33 ($8,287)	32	26 (73%)	28 (C)	public, tax credits	3.8 (+0.6)
Indiana	29 ($8,057)	26	23 (74%)	6 (A)	public*	n/a
Iowa	26 ($7,574)	9	2 (85%)	40 (F)	public, tax credits	n/a
Kansas	21 ($7,454)	22	18 (76%)	37 (D)	public*	n/a
Kentucky	13 ($6,661)	34	36 (69%)	No Law	public	3.8 (+0.5)
Louisiana	15 ($6,922)	47	42 (63%)	26 (C)	public	n/a
Maine	42 ($9,344)	18	24 (74%)	No Law	public-secular	3.3 (+1.5)
Maryland	41 ($9,153)	27	20 (75%)	36 (D)	none	n/a
Massachusetts	47 ($10,460)	1	28 (72%)	10 (B)	public*	3.8 (+0.7)
Michigan	37 ($8,781)	31	13 (77%)	5 (A)	public*	3.9 (+1.0)
Minnesota	32 ($8,109)	2	5 (84%)	2 (A)	public, tax credits	3.8 (+1.0)
Mississippi	2 ($5,792)	50	47 (59%)	41 (F)	public	n/a
Missouri	23 ($7,495)	19	15 (76%)	14 (B)	public	n/a
Montana	24 ($7,496)	4	16 (76%)	No Law	public	3.3 (+1.4)
Nebraska	30 ($8,074)	10	6 (84%)	No Law	public	n/a
Nevada	5 ($6,092)	38	38 (67%)	27 (C)	public*	n/a
New Hampshire	35 ($8,579)	3	11(79%)	29 (C)	public*	3.4 (+1.0)
New Jersey	51 ($12,568)	12	1 (88%)	20 (B)	public*	n/a
New Mexico	17 ($7,125)	49	48 (59%)	17 (B)	public*	3.9 (+0.8)
New York	50 (11,961)	23	49 (58%)	13 (B)	public*	4.1 (+0.5)
North Carolina	12 ($6,562)	30	35 (69%)	15 (B)	none	4.5 (+0.2)
North Dakota	14 ($6,870)	11	4 (85%)	No Law	public*	3.3 (+1.7)
Ohio	36 ($8,632)	15	9 (79%)	12 (B)	public-private (Cleveland), public*	4.1 (+0.9)
Oklahoma	4 ($6,092)	37	27 (72%)	21 (B)	public	n/a
Oregon	22 ($7,491)	14	31 (70%)	18 (B)	public*	n/a
Pennsylvania	39 ($8,997)	20	8 (81%)	11 (B)	public*, tax credits	4.0 (+0.8)
Rhode Island	45 ($10,349)	35	19 (75%)	39 (D)	public*	3.4 (+1.1)
South Carolina	16 ($7,040)	40	51 (54%)	24 (C)	public*	n/a
South Dakota	11 ($6,547)	7	10 (79%)	No Law	public	3.4 (+1.7)
Tennessee	6 ($6,118)	39	45 (60%)	32 (C)	public*	n/a
Texas	18 ($7,136)	36	37 (69%)	22 (C)	public*	4.3 (+0.5)
Utah	1 ($4,838)	21	14 (77%)	25 (C)	public	n/a
Vermont	46 ($10,454)	5	12 (78%)	No Law	public*, public-secular	3.5 (+1.4)
Virginia	28 ($7,822)	13	21 (75%)	38 (D)	none	4.1 (+1.0)
Washington	19 ($7,252)	8	34 (69%)	No Law	public	3.4 (+1.0)
West Virginia	34 ($8,319)	44	17 (76%)	No Law	public*	3.4 (+0.9)
Wisconsin	40 ($9,004)	6	3 (85%)	19 (B)	public-private (Milwaukee), public	3.6 (+1.0)
Wyoming	38 ($8,985)	16	33 (70%)	33 (D)	public*	n/a

[1] National Center for Education Statistics, http://nces.ed.gov/programs/digest/d05/tables/dt05_166.asp?referer=list

[2] American Legislative Exchange Council Report Card on Education 2006 by Andrew T. LeFevre, page 4. Ranking based on 2004 test scores on the SAT, the ACT assessment, and 2005 scores on the NAEP 8th grade mathematics and reading tests. http://www.alec.org/fileadmin/2006%20Ed%20Report%20Card_ALEC.pdf

[3] Most rates for class of 2003, from Leaving Boys Behind: Public High School Graduation Rates by Jay P. Greene, Ph.D., The Manhattan Institute for Policy Research, April 2006 http://www.manhattan-institute.org/html/cr_48.htm
DC and Hawaii Rates for class of 2001, from Public High School Graduation and College Readiness Rates in the United State by ibid., September 2003 http://www.manhattan-institute.org/html/ewp_03.htm;

[4] The Center for Education Reform, www.edreform.com, Raising the Bar on Charter School Laws: 2006 Ranking and Scorecard.

[5] School Choice Key: public = states that have enacted open enrollment laws, *indicates states that offer open enrollment but districts are not required to participate; public-private = publically funded voucher law including public, private, and parochial schools; public-secular = publically-funded voucher law that does not include parochial schools. (reference: The Heritage Foundation; Choices in Education http://www.heritage.org/research/education/schoolchoice/schoolchoice.cfm, Education Commission of the States: School Choice State Laws http://mb2.ecs.org/reports/Report.aspx?id=207)

[6] The Guide To State Standards, Tests, And Accountability Policies, published by Thomas B. Fordham Foundation and AccountabilityWorks. Evaluated accountability systems across 30 states, looking at six broad measures for each state's K-12 accountability system, including accountability policies both before and after No Child Left Behind, included here. Ratings were assigned on a 1-5 scale, with 5 as "outstanding," 4 as "solid," 3 as "fair," 2 as "poor," and 1 as "very poor." The authors note, "Prior to the passage of the No Child Left Behind act, [the 30 evaluated] state accountability policies on average were only fair, bordering on poor. NCLB, if properly implemented, would increase the average accountability ranking significantly."

Compiled by The Center for Education Reform, June 2007

Appendix C

Charter School Teacher Certification

This chart describes each state's charter school teacher certification policy; it does not include the 10 states that have not enacted charter school laws.

	Do charter school teachers have to be certified?
Alaska: Charter Schools (2005)	Yes.
Arizona: Charter Schools (2005)	No.
Arkansas: Charter Schools (2005)	Yes, unless a waiver is granted in the charter.
California: Charter Schools (2005)	Yes.
Colorado: Charter Schools (2005)	Yes, unless a waiver is granted in the charter.
Connecticut: Charter Schools (2005)	At least 50% of a charter school's teachers must have standard certification, and up to 50% of teachers in a charter school may have alternative certification or temporary certification and be working toward standard certification.
Delaware: Charter Schools (2005)	Yes, with exceptions.
District of Columbia: Charter Schools (2005)	No.
Florida: Charter Schools (2005)	Yes.
Georgia: Charter Schools (2005)	No.
Hawaii: Charter Schools (2005)	Yes.
Idaho: Charter Schools (2005)	Yes. Although teachers may apply for a waiver or any of the limited certification options as provided by the state board of education.
Illinois: Charter Schools (2005)	Charter schools may employ uncertified teachers if they have a bachelor's degree, five years' experience in the area of degree, a passing score on state teacher tests and evidence of professional growth. Mentoring must be provided to uncertified teachers. Beginning with the 2006-07 school year, at least 50% of the individuals employed in instructional positions by a charter school in Chicago established after April 16, 2003, shall hold teaching certificates and 75% of the individuals employed in instructional positions by a charter school in Chicago established before April 16, 2003, shall hold teaching certificates.

	Do charter school teachers have to be certified?
Indiana: Charter Schools (2005)	Teachers must either be certified or be in the process of obtaining a license to teach through the transition to teaching program. For those in the transition to teaching program, licenses must be obtained within three years of beginning to teach at a charter school.
Iowa: Charter Schools (2005)	Yes.
Kansas: Charter Schools (2005)	Yes.
Louisiana: Charter Schools (2005)	For most types of charter schools, up to 25% of a charter school's teachers may be uncertified if they meet other specific requirements. For low-performing schools that are converted to charter schools as part of the state's accountability system, beginning no later than the third year of operation, teachers in core subjects must be certified and teachers in other subjects may be uncertified if they meet other specific requirements.
Maryland: Charter Schools (2005)	Yes.
Massachusetts: Charter Schools (2005)	For Horace Mann charter schools, yes. For other commonwealth charter schools, no teacher shall be hired who is not certified unless the teacher has successfully passed the state teacher test.
Michigan: Charter Schools (2005)	Except as otherwise provided by law, yes. For example, faculty at a university or community college may teach in a charter school operated or authorized by that institution.
Minnesota: Charter Schools (2005)	Yes.
Mississippi: Charter Schools (2005)	Yes.
Missouri: Charter Schools (2005)	Up to 20% of full-time equivalent instructional staff may be filled by uncertified personnel.
Nevada: Charter Schools (2005)	Up to 30% of instructional staff may be non-licensed personnel. In a vocational charter school, up to 50% of instructional staff may be non-licensed personnel.
New Hampshire: Charter Schools (2005)	At least 50% of a charter school's teacher staff must be certified or have three years of teaching experience.
New Jersey: Charter Schools (2005)	Yes.
New Mexico: Charter Schools (2005)	Yes.
New York: Charter Schools (2005)	Up to 30% or five teachers are permitted to have other credentials, but uncertified teachers must meet specified criteria: at least three years of elementary, middle or secondary classroom

	Do charter school teachers have to be certified?
	teaching experience; tenured or tenure track college faculty; two years of satisfactory experience through the Teach for America program; or exceptional business, professional, artistic, athletic, or military experience.
North Carolina: Charter Schools (2005)	Up to 25% of teachers in grades kindergarten through five and up to 50% of teachers in grades six through twelve may be uncertified.
Ohio: Charter Schools (2005)	Yes, except that a charter school may engage uncertificated persons to teach up to twelve hours per week.
Oklahoma: Charter Schools (2005)	Yes, unless a waiver is granted in the charter.
Oregon: Charter Schools (2005)	At least one-half of a charter school's teachers must be licensed by the Teacher Standards and Practices Commission (TSPC), and the non-TSPC-licensed staff must be registered by TSPC.
Pennsylvania: Charter Schools (2005)	Up to 25% of teachers may be uncertified.
Puerto Rico: Charter Schools (2005)	Yes.
Rhode Island: Charter Schools (2005)	Yes.
South Carolina: Charter Schools (2005)	Up to 10% of teachers in conversions and 25% in start-ups may be uncertified. In either a new or converted charter school, a teacher teaching in the core academic areas of English/language arts, mathematics, science or social studies must be certified in those areas or possess a baccalaureate or graduate degree in the subject he or she is hired to teach.
Tennessee: Charter Schools (2005)	Yes.
Texas: Charter Schools (2005)	No.
Utah: Charter Schools (2005)	A charter school must employ teachers who are licensed or, on the basis of demonstrated competency, would qualify to teach under alternative certification or authorization programs.
Virginia: Charter Schools (2005)	Yes.
Wisconsin: Charter Schools (2005)	Yes. However, if search for licensed teachers is unsuccessful, a special charter school permit is available for persons with a bachelor's degree in their field who take six credits of training each year and are supervised by a teacher with a regular license.
Wyoming: Charter Schools (2005)	Yes.

Source: Education Commission of the States 2008

Appendix D

Qualifications of Charter School vs. Regular Public School Teachers

This chart compares the percentage of charter school teachers vs. traditional public school teachers who graduated from the most selective or highly-selective colleges within the United States

	Charter Schools	TPS	Difference Charter v. TPS
All teachers in US	14% (grad)	10% grad	4% grad
Percent of teachers with certification			
All schools	72	93	−21
Central city schools	65	93	−27
Urban fringe/large towns	78	94	−15
Rural small town	78	94	−16
Elementary	76	93	−17
Secondary	66	94	−28
Percentage of math teachers with college major/minors in mathematics			
All teachers	39	51	−13
Central city schools	42	51	−9
Urban fringe/large towns	34	52	−18
Rural/small town	38	49	−12
Elementary	28	27	1
Secondary	56	70	−15
Percentage of science teachers with college majors/minors in science			
All teachers	61	60	0
Central city schools	64	58	5
Urban fringe/large towns	56	63	−7
Rural/small town	68	58	10
Elementary	52	34	18
Secondary	67	78	−11
Percentage of teachers with more than five years experience			
All teachers	39	75	−36
Central city schools	34	75	−41
Urban fringe/large towns	40	73	−33
Rural small town	53	77	−24
Elementary	38	74	−36
Secondary	42	75	−33

Source: Burian-Fitzgerald, M., M.T. Luekens, and G.A. Strizek. "Less Red Tape or More Green Teachers: Charter School Autonomy and Teacher Qualifications." *Taking Account of Charter Schools: What's Happened and What's Next.* K Bulkley & P. Wohlsetter (Eds.). Teachers College Press, New York. (2004)

Appendix E

State Numbers: Schools, Students, and Year Chartered

All numbers in following four charts are self-reported and reflective of the 2008/2009 school year. They compare state-by-state, year of charter school enactment, number of charter schools and enrollment.

1. Statistics by State

State	Year Law Passed	# of Charter Schools	# of Students Enrolled
Alaska	1995	24	4,618
Arizona	1994	464	93,213
Arkansas	1995	28	4,300
California	1992	750	276,000
Colorado	1993	133	52,242
Connecticut	1996	16	3,573
Delaware	1995	18	8,626
District of Columbia	1995	83	19,733
Florida	1996	356	98,000
Georgia	1993	71	33,230
Hawaii	1994	27	5,812
Idaho	1998	28	9,578
Illinois	1996	42	16,898
Indiana	2001	49	15,581
Iowa	2002	10	2,686
Kansas	1994	27	1,610
Louisiana	1995	66	25,000
Maryland	2003	30	7,149
Massachusetts	1993	61	25,034
Michigan	1993	229	91,567
Minnesota	1991	168	28,034
Mississippi	1997	1	374
Missouri	1998	40	11,519
Nevada	1997	22	5,850
New Hampshire	1995	11	498
New Jersey	1996	53	15,557
New Mexico	1993	62	11,361
New York	1998	94	25,736
North Carolina	1996	98	30,892
Ohio	1997	315	76,967
Oklahoma	1999	15	4,649
Oregon	1999	87	12,000
Pennsylvania	1997	126	59,976
Puerto Rico	1993	121	NA
Rhode Island	1995	11	2,812
South Carolina	1996	31	5,423
Tennessee	2002	16	3,500
Texas	1995	427	113,760
Utah	1998	51	19,290
Virginia	1998	4	284
Wisconsin	1993	232	34,387
Wyoming	1995	3	238
Total		4,500	1,257,557

2. Statistics by Year

State	Year Law Passed	# of Charter Schools	# of Students Enrolled
Minnesota	1991	168	28,034
California	1992	750	276,000
Colorado	1993	133	52,242
Georgia	1993	71	33,230
Massachusetts	1993	61	25,034
Michigan	1993	229	91,567
New Mexico	1993	62	11,361
Puerto Rico	1993	121	NA
Wisconsin	1993	232	34,387
Arizona	1994	464	93,213
Hawaii	1994	27	5,812
Kansas	1994	27	1,610
Alaska	1995	24	4,618
Arkansas	1995	28	4,300
Delaware	1995	18	8,626
District of Columbia	1995	83	19,733
Louisiana	1995	66	25,000
New Hampshire	1995	11	498
Rhode Island	1995	11	2,812
Texas	1995	427	113,760
Wyoming	1995	3	238
Connecticut	1996	16	3,573
Florida	1996	356	98,000
Illinois	1996	42	16,898
New Jersey	1996	53	15,557
North Carolina	1996	98	30,892
South Carolina	1996	31	5,423
Mississippi	1997	1	374
Nevada	1997	22	5,850
Ohio	1997	315	76,967
Pennsylvania	1997	126	59,976
Idaho	1998	28	9,578
Missouri	1998	40	11,519
New York	1998	94	25,736
Utah	1998	51	19,290
Virginia	1998	4	284
Oklahoma	1999	15	4,649
Oregon	1999	87	12,000
Indiana	2001	49	15,581
Iowa	2002	10	2,686
Tennessee	2002	16	3,500
Maryland	2003	30	7,149
Total		4,500	1,257,557

3. Statistics by Number of Schools

State	Year Law Passed	# of Charter Schools	# of Students Enrolled
California	1992	750	276,000
Arizona	1994	464	93,213
Texas	1995	427	113,760
Florida	1996	356	98,000
Ohio	1997	315	76,967
Wisconsin	1993	232	34,387
Michigan	1993	229	91,567
Minnesota	1991	168	28,034
Colorado	1993	133	52,242
Pennsylvania	1997	126	59,976
Puerto Rico	1993	121	NA
North Carolina	1996	98	30,892
New York	1998	94	25,736
Oregon	1999	87	12,000
District of Columbia	1995	83	19,733
Georgia	1993	71	33,230
Louisiana	1995	66	25,000
New Mexico	1993	62	11,361
Massachusetts	1993	61	25,034
New Jersey	1996	53	15,557
Utah	1998	51	19,290
Indiana	2001	49	15,581
Illinois	1996	42	16,898
Missouri	1998	40	11,519
South Carolina	1996	31	5,423
Maryland	2003	30	7,149
Arkansas	1995	28	4,300
Idaho	1998	28	9,578
Hawaii	1994	27	5,812
Kansas	1994	27	1,610
Alaska	1995	24	4,618
Nevada	1997	22	5,850
Delaware	1995	18	8,626
Connecticut	1996	16	3,573
Tennessee	2002	16	3,500
Oklahoma	1999	15	4,649
New Hampshire	1995	11	498
Rhode Island	1995	11	2,812
Iowa	2002	10	2,686
Virginia	1998	4	284
Wyoming	1995	3	238
Mississippi	1997	1	374
Total		4,500	1,257,557

4. Statistics by Enrollment

State	Year Law Passed	# of Charter Schools	# of Students Enrolled
Puerto Rico	1993	121	NA
California	1992	750	276,000
Texas	1995	427	113,760
Florida	1996	356	98,000
Arizona	1994	464	93,213
Michigan	1993	229	91,567
Ohio	1997	315	76,967
Pennsylvania	1997	126	59,976
Colorado	1993	133	52,242
Wisconsin	1993	232	34,387
Georgia	1993	71	33,230
North Carolina	1996	98	30,892
Minnesota	1991	168	28,034
New York	1998	94	25,736
Massachusetts	1993	61	25,034
Louisiana	1995	66	25,000
District of Columbia	1995	83	19,733
Utah	1998	51	19,290
Illinois	1996	42	16,898
Indiana	2001	49	15,581
New Jersey	1996	53	15,557
Oregon	1999	87	12,000
Missouri	1998	40	11,519
New Mexico	1993	62	11,361
Idaho	1998	28	9,578
Delaware	1995	18	8,626
Maryland	2003	30	7,149
Nevada	1997	22	5,850
Hawaii	1994	27	5,812
South Carolina	1996	31	5,423
Oklahoma	1999	15	4,649
Alaska	1995	24	4,618
Arkansas	1995	28	4,300
Connecticut	1996	16	3,573
Tennessee	2002	16	3,500
Rhode Island	1995	11	2,812
Iowa	2002	10	2,686
Kansas	1994	27	1,610
New Hampshire	1995	11	498
Mississippi	1997	1	374
Virginia	1998	4	284
Wyoming	1995	3	238
Total		4,500	1,257,557

Source: State departments of educations and state charter school associations.

Introduction to Primary Documents

This section of Primary Documents is designed to provide the reader with additional information about the charter school movement and charter schools themselves—from historical background, charter applications and parental agreements, to success-story articles and charter school study results. This introduction offers additional insight on each of the 15 reprinted documents in this section.

History

The story of charter schools and the beginning of the charter school concept cannot be told without understanding the initial idea of charters first promoted by Ray Budde, a teacher and then junior high principal in East Lansing MI. In the late 1960s, he was teaching educational administration at the University of Massachusetts when the dean reorganized its school of education. Budde's interest in education grew to encompass organizational theory as it applied to public schools. **The document on page 547 offers background about both Ray Budde and the charter school concept he developed and supported.** It is difficult to infer what Budde might have thought of the charter school movement today but one thing can be sure, Budde was an active supporter of teachers and new and innovative organizational designs for public schools. His ideas, which attracted the interest of Albert Shanker in 1988, who was at that time the president of the American Federation of Teachers, culminated in the first charter experiment in Minnesota.

After Ray Budde proposed the idea of a charter school, Albert Shanker supported the idea at the National Press Club in 1988. **The document on page 551 shows that, although Shanker supported the idea of charter schools, his (and Ray Budde's) concept was wedded to strong teacher unions and participatory student, administrative, and parent democracy.** Many feel this is not what charter schools have developed into. Shanker supported teacher, parent, student and community-run charter schools that would rest their mantle on nations of participatory democratic decision-making.

Legislation

Directly after hurricane Katrina hit the city of New Orleans, charter school advocates moved decisively and quickly, immediately requesting what they termed "necessary deregulation" and waivers from the State of Louisiana to implement the beginning of what would be the largest charter school experiment in the country. **On page 558 is the response from Nina S. Rees, Assistant Deputy Secretary for Innovation and Improvement, to requests by Cecil J. Pickard, Superintendent of Education for the State Department of Education, for waivers to meet what he called the needs of students displaced by hurricanes.** The requested waivers to launch the charter school experiment were granted—one of the first legal acts passed before the state legislature took over 107 New Orleans public schools in late November of 2005.

The document on page 561 reflects the organizational make-up of the New Orleans public and charterized school system. With the growth of several new administrations, this chart represents the new organizational, or Diverse Strategy model, proposed by Paul T. Hill and implemented in hurricane-ravaged New Orleans almost directly following the hurricane.

Applications & Contracts

When applying to open a charter school, mandatory applications must be sent to the state for the request to be considered. Charter school applications vary from state to state. Once charter schools are opened, admission of students is often dependent on mandatory parental contracts. Opponents of such contracts argue that they serve as disincentives to parents from enrolling their children in charter schools, while proponents say these parental contracts not only involve parents in the responsibilities for their child, but also act as a legal and binding contract between school and parent. **See a charter school application, page 564, and a parental contract, page 570.**

In addition to parent contracts, many charter schools also require parent and family involvement as an important part of building a strong school community. **The mandatory contract on page 572 requires parents to perform five hours of volunteer service per school year.**

When considering which students to admit, some, usually more affluent, charter schools go beyond parental involvement and volunteer hours. **The document on page 573 shows how students are accepted on the basis of the applicant's total matrix score on an in-house test.** This includes reading and math scores as well as other items in the matrix explained in the document.

From Charter School Teachers

Many charter school teachers, upset with forced overtime, lack of health benefits, job security, lack of professional development and the inability to have a decisive voice, are beginning to organize teacher unions. **The article on page 579 looks at just some of the issues and points of view regarding the upsurge in the unionization efforts of teachers at charter schools nationwide.**

Additional voices of charter school teachers became known during an interview by Barbara Miner, *ReThinking Schools'* former managing editor, educational activist and writer. **Starting on page 582, these educators speak of the challenges they faced regarding No Child Left Behind and student testing, curriculum ideology and development, their opposition to for-profit charter schools and various other nonprofit retail charter models.** They also address issues with the decision-making processes they utilize in governing with parents, students, and the communities they serve.

In Los Angeles

The Instigator **on page 590 is an investigation into the project of Steve Barr, the brains behind the charter management organization Green Dot Public Schools.** Barr started Green Dot after being turned down to manage one of Los Angeles' worst performing urban high schools. He initiated a hostile takeover by forming parent groups and petitioning the board. Barr and the parents were successful.

Green Dot, a nonprofit educational maintenance organization, is also behind the August 25, 2009 move by the Los Angeles Unified School District to charterize one third, or 250, of its schools, with their management contracted out to nonprofit organizations like Green Dot, Alliance Schools and others. Green Dot is also involved in "Parent Revolution," a group of parents who have worked to lobby for more charter schools in Los Angeles. *The Instigator* tells the partial story of Steve Barr and how he has, along with others, revolutionized public education and the charter school movement in Los Angeles.

Research Studies

During his speech to the National Alliance of Public Charter Schools, Secretary of Education Arne Duncan called on the charter school movement to subtly police itself. **In the article on page 605, Duncan, citing the newly released CREDO study, warned advocates of charter schools that second and third rate charter school operators threaten the charter school movement,** a movement that President Barack Obama is in favor of nationwide. **On page 607 is the Executive Summary of the June 2009 study done by CREDO at Stanford University.** Entitled *Multiple Choice: Charter School Performance in 16 States,* this report compares the standardized testing scores from traditional public school students to student test performance at charter schools.

The article on page 615 announces the results from new research performed by the New York City Charter Schools Evaluation Project. Entitled *How New York City's Charter Schools Affect Achievement,* the report analyzes the achievement of 93 percent of the New York City charter school students who were enrolled in test-taking grades 2000–2008, by following the progress of "lotteried-in" and "lotteried-out" students. **The Introduction and Executive Summary of the report can be found on page 617.** You will read that, on average, a student who attended a charter school from Kindergarten through eighth grade would close about 86 percent of the "Scarsdale-Harlem achievement gap" in Math, and 66 percent in English. A student who attended fewer grades would improve by a commensurately smaller amount.

It should be noted that one of the academic problems with these studies is that the students and families who "lose" these admission lotteries are no longer like the students and families who "win." There is no basis for thinking that their views of their schools are like those of the lottery "winners." In fact, one could argue that this method of analysis *ensures* that the "winning" charter school students are being compared to students who did *not* want to go to the schools they attend.

Ray Budde and the Origins of the 'Charter Concept'

By Ted Kolderie
June 2005

When Ray Budde recently died, the news made the New York Times. This is not easy to do. The Times obituary page is reserved for people of special interest and of significant accomplishment. Susan Saulny, who covers education, wrote the story. It was reprinted elsewhere. On the West Coast, National Public Radio did an interview about it. So this was pretty special for the charter idea.

All the attention given to Ray Budde's passing did puzzle people, especially younger education policy leaders and charter movement leaders. "Who was Ray Budde? What did he have to do with chartering?"

It's an interesting story, important for what it says about the way ideas begin and spread and about the way movements grow and develop. And it helps to explain where the charter idea began, how it has evolved over time and where it may yet be headed.

BUDDE'S IDEAS AROUND CHARTERING FIRST APPEARED IN 1974

Ray Budde said he'd always had a strong interest in "the way things are organized" and in "how things work or don't work in organizations". He'd been a teacher, then a junior high principal in East Lansing MI. In the late 1960s he was teaching educational administration at the University of Massachusetts when the dean reorganized its school of education. He was interested in organizational theory, and in 1974 presented the Society for General Systems Research some ideas for the reorganization of school districts in a paper he titled *"Education by Charter."*

As he told the story many years later in a piece he wrote for The Kappan (September 1996) he asked colleagues and friends: "Does this make sense? Is it workable? Would a district be willing to give it a try?"

The response? Zero. Nobody thought there was a problem significant enough to require such a restructuring. The attitude then was: Get a good new program idea, do some in-service training. That'll do it. So Budde put the idea away and went on to other things.

Then came the 1980s: The *Nation At Risk* report and all the media attention and the Carnegie Forum report that followed. Suddenly everyone was talking 'restructuring'. So Ray dusted off his paper and in early 1988 got it published by the Northeast Regional Lab. He sent it around widely; even to then-President George H.W. Bush. Then he waited. And waited.

Ted Kolderie is Co-founder & Senior Associate, Education | Evolving. Reprinted with permission from Education | Evolving, http://www.educationevolving.org/pdf/Ray_Budde.

One Sunday in July Budde's wife Priscilla put down the newspaper and said: "Hey, Ray, you've made the New York Times!" And she showed him the column reporting the American Federation of Teachers' support for the idea of teachers setting up autonomous schools. AFT President Al Shanker had in fact floated the proposal in a talk at the National Press Club in the spring of that year. He said Ray Budde had the best name for these schools: "charter schools."

BUDDE'S IDEAS EXPANDED UPON, THEN JUMP TO MINNESOTA

Ray Budde's proposal was actually for a restructuring of the *district:* for moving from "a four-level line and staff organization" to "a two-level form in which groups of teachers would receive educational charters directly from the school board" and would carry the responsibility for instruction. It dealt with existing schools. It was the concept that Paul Hill later called the 'contract district'; that the Education Commission of the States later termed the 'all-charter district'.

Shanker expanded on this idea by proposing that teachers start schools *new* (though within existing school buildings). But like Budde, Shanker simply put his idea out there; did not move to implement it.

But, it didn't take long after Shanker's talk for implementation to begin in Minnesota. A study committee of the Citizens League, chaired by John Rollwagen, then CEO of Cray Research, soon picked up the idea that summer and fall. It further modified the concepts advanced by Budde and Shanker, envisioning a framework of state policy and the possibility of schools being authorized by the state as well as by a local board.

The League had a plan fairly well thought out by October 1988 when the Minneapolis Foundation brought Al Shanker to Minnesota for The Itasca Seminar. Two legislators present—Sen. Ember Reichgott and Rep. Ken Nelson—picked up the idea and, as legislators are wont to do, began thinking about legislation.

Sen. Reichgott's charter provision got into the Senate omnibus bill in 1989 and again in 1990. The House would not accept it. As the conference committee was breaking up in 1990 Rep. Becky Kelso went over to Reichgott and said, "If you'd like to try that charter program again next year I'd like to help you". And in 1991 Kelso and Nelson did get a—compromised—version through the House. The Senate agreed. Gov. Arne Carlson signed it into law.

Interestingly, in today's highly partisan environment—both in Minnesota and nationally—Reichgott, Nelson and Kelso were all Democrats; Carlson, a Republican, picked up on the public school choice initiatives advanced by his Democratic predecessor, Rudy Perpich, in the mid-to-late 1980s.

In 1992, California enacted a chartering program, in a somewhat different form. In 1993 six more states acted, introducing more variations on the original idea, including non-district authorizers (Michigan and Massachusetts) and a state-level appeal (Colorado).

In 1991, Minnesota's U.S. Senator Dave Durenberger, a Republican, brought the charter idea to Washington, joining forces with Connecticut's Democratic U.S. Senator Joseph Lieberman to introduce what became the Federal charter school grant program. That legislation, adopted in 1994 with strong support from the Clinton Administration, added further encouragement to states to pass and implement charter laws.

Through the 1990s the concept continued to evolve through new and amended laws in the states, including significant expansions on the original law adopted almost every year in Minnesota. Like LINUX, chartering helped create an 'open system' continually changed and improved by all those working on it.

BUDDE CAME TO ACCEPT AND SUPPORT EXPANSIONS ON HIS ORIGINAL IDEAS

As the new-schools idea spread, people asked Ray Budde how he felt about what had happened with his idea. For some years he would say: "This is not what I originally had in mind".

But by the time of his 1996 Kappan article his feelings had changed. "There are more powerful dynamics at work in creating a whole new school than in simply restructuring a department or starting a new program", he wrote. He saw that the states were creating an expanding movement "challenging the traditional form of organization of the local school district". Which of course was what he originally had in mind.

Ray Budde continued to hope the decentralized model would come to be used by districts, too; felt this was important to revitalizing district public education. Call it chartering or site-management, there is "a necessity of placing more decision-making at the school level, close to the classrooms", he wrote. He went on to note, "The charter schools movement was, indeed, the catalyst that brought about my writing *'Strengthen School-based Management by Chartering All Schools'*." That book was published in 1996.

Ray Budde had come to believe, he wrote me in 1992, that "there has to be a formal/legal change that would . . . remove power from most central office positions and flow funds directly to schools" and that these changes would have to be "grounded in state law".

The last letter I have from him came in January 1998, attaching "my second-to-last effort in education reform". Its 17 "Action Areas" urged continued transfer of real authority to schools, smaller schools, and the transfer of instructional responsibility to groups of teachers.

The 25-year body of work by this obscure teacher/administrator in New England was strikingly prescient. He saw clearly the limitation of, the essentially conservatism and defensiveness of, all organizations. Unusually and importantly, he was open-minded enough to accept—even champion—the changes and improvements in the concept that were made later by others.

This whole story is testimony to the usefulness of having people who think, creatively, about problems and about solutions. And to the importance of changing the structure of organizations and institutions. Structure matters.

The story running through the 25 years also makes clear how complex are the origins of major change. Asking, "Where did it start?" is like asking where a river starts. You have to go upstream, where you probably will find no single source, but a variety of little streams flowing together as they run.

Ray Budde's work was one of those upstream sources. One of the earliest ones. One of those that weren't afraid to change course as they continued flowing downstream.

APPLICATIONS OF CHARTERING BACK TO ITS 'TEACHER ORIGINS'

It's fascinating to watch the chartering concept now evolving in ways that return to the central role of teachers, so important to the early thinking of both Ray Budde and Al Shanker.

First in Minnesota and then in Milwaukee, teachers have been forming collegial partnerships, like those in other professional fields like medicine and law. The chartered school or (in Milwaukee) the board of education gives the teacher partnership the authority to organize the learning program of the school; the partnership in return accepts the responsibility for school and student success.

Like the charter concept itself, the idea of the teachers having responsibility for the school is 'a bumblebee'. All conventional option says the bumblebee cannot possibly fly. But it does. All conventional wisdom says schools must be run by administrators; says that the work of running the school would distract teachers from their instructional duties.

But as RAND found to its surprise in a recent study of chartered schools in Pennsylvania, those noninstructional duties apparently create a "sense of engagement" that in fact contributes to the success of student learning in the school.

The Milwaukee arrangement, in particular, accommodates the interests of board, teachers, parents and the union in a way I think would have delighted, and amazed, Albert Shanker. It simply took some time for the arrangement to evolve; some thinking, and some trying-things *new*.

Ray Budde's vision may yet be realized, in full, by those who follow and by those who now continue to expand and improve-upon his original good and sound ideas.

National Press Club Speech

**Albert Shanker, President, American Federation of Teachers
Washington, D.C.**

We'll help, but usually by doing more or even less of the same thing that didn't work. And that's the point of view that needs to be changed. I've said all this in order to bring you to the second reform movement in this country, a movement that has as its underlying view the notion that I just expressed in the story: namely, that we need an institution that responds to people in the best way other professions and institutions respond. It's a view that's reflected in the Carnegie report, in the vision at the very beginning of the report. It's a small reform movement, and it's very fragile. It's not something that you'll see in every school across the country; it's not something that every teacher or supervisor is talking about. It may very well be that neither the Carnegie report nor the few places where the second reform movement is happening would have happened if there hadn't been A Nation At Risk or these other reports and reforms. But nonetheless, even though they may owe a lot in terms of their history and existence to this first wave of reform, they're very different.

Those who are engaged in this type of reform are aware of the fact that 80 percent of the students do not learn well in traditional settings. That's true in the United States; that's true in England; it's true in France; true in Germany. And so these people, a small group of people in a small number of places across the country, are developing a bottom-up approach to reform. They are trying things out of their own experience, their own understanding of children, their own understanding of these conclusions. They're trying to build something new and they're trying to build something that will be different, that will be effective for more than the 10 or 15 or 20 percent of the students who have been able to learn throughout history. They're trying to reach that 80 percent of the students who have not been reached in the past. Some interesting things are happening in a number of places. They are all places where there is a strong collective bargaining relationship. You don't see these creative things happening where teachers don't have any voice or power or influence. These things are all happening in places where there is no external threat to the superintendent, or to the leader of the union, or to the union itself. These are people who can say, "We can take some chances, we can take some risks; because even if we lose some support, we are still going to lead here."

Excerpted from National Press Club Speech given by Albert Shanker, President, American Federation of Teachers, 31 March 1988. Reprinted with permission from Reuther Library, www.reuther.wayne.edu.

These mostly are places where the bread and butter issues—while they are never solved and people always want more—are in good shape and people feel "We've been treated pretty well. We don't have to spend every minute of the time thinking about the peeling paint or the falling plaster, or the lousy salaries, or the no toilet in the bathrooms," or something like that. It's not that they have everything they want, but it's no longer the only or main issue that's before them. These are also places where there's a strong union leader and there's a strong management leader and a relationship of trust or respect between them. In some of those systems there are also some" academics, some foundations, and some business people who work with them to help them change the rules, help them to negotiate with the terribly bureaucratic system. This is a radical and tiny movement. We can count its districts on the fingers of both hands. You've been reading about them, and they are not many. There's Dade County and there's Rochester, Toledo, Cincinnati, Pittsburgh, Hammond, Indiana, and some schools in New York City. I'm going to leave out two or three, but we're still not up to the fingers of the two hands. That's about what it is.

Then you can also add a few school networks, like those of Ted Sizer and those of John Goodlad, that are trying things that fit into this second reform movement approach. Then there are some individual schools or programs, like the Key School, schools-without-walls, cities-in-schools, and things like that. Now when it comes to the first, the major reform movement, there's a very big, thick book out of the U.S. Department of Education, The Nation Responds, to show you how extensive that movement is: every state, every locality—here's what's happening, here's what the kids are taking, here's the homework requirement, here's the teacher testing requirement, here are the changes. Yes, there's a huge, massive response to that first wave of reform. Fine, but the problem is that when it comes to documenting wave two, the movement concerned about reaching the 80 percent, not just succeeding a little better with the 20 percent, there's not a thick book; there's hardly a page full of places to talk about. Therefore, I would like to make a proposal today. The proposal is based on the notion that we have not moved reform fast enough; not the first wave—that's moving along very well—but the second one, that one that looks at trying to reach the 80 percent who are not making it. We can't wait until all the districts throughout the country have the strongest and the best bargaining relationships. We can't wait until there are more districts that have both charismatic union leaders and superintendents. We can't wait to find places where everyone feels free to risk things. The question is, can we come up with a proposal which will move us from five or six or seven or ten districts that are doing these very exciting things to reach many, many more students? Can we expand that number very rapidly; not from 10 to 20, but from 10 to 1,000 or 2,000 or 3,000? Can we put in a new policy mechanism that will give teachers and parents the right to "opt for" a new type of school, to "opt for" the second type of reform?

I believe that we do not have to wait for the impossible to create the possible. I do not believe that all the conditions have to be right throughout the system in order to do the possible. What is it that I propose to get us there? I propose that just as we said collective bargaining is the way of improving things system-wide for schools and for teachers, and just as within the last few years we have developed ways in which entire schools, by a method of consensus or majority vote, can decide to do things that are very different from the rest of the system and to move out of a lock-step situation—this union now needs to seek ways that will enable any group of teachers—let's say six or seven or eight or twelve teachers in any building—and any group of parents to opt for a different type of school. How would this work? The school district and the teacher union would develop a procedure that would encourage any group of six or more teachers to submit a proposal to create a new school. Do not think of a school as a building, and you can see how it works. Consider six or seven or twelve teachers in a school who say, "We've got an idea. We've got a way of doing something very different. We've got a way of reaching the kids that are now not being reached by what the school is doing."

That group of teachers could set up a school within that school which ultimately, if the procedure works and it's accepted, would be a totally autonomous school within that district. The district should create a panel that would be used to either approve or reject the teacher proposals that would come in. The panel could be a joint panel between the union and the board; it could include outsiders, or it might be a system in which the union and the board would separately have to ratify such proposals. What should the proposals look like? Obviously, I'm not going to lay down a master plan, because the whole point of this is to have people within a school develop their own proposals; so they are all going to be different. Schools all across the country now, unfortunately, look very much alike. These schools will look very different, and they should follow certain guidelines that don't tell you what the school is going to look like, but what you're going to look for in terms of approving such a proposal.

I would approve such a proposal if it included a plan for faculty decision making, for participative management; team teaching; a way for a teaching team to govern itself; and a provision that shows how such a submit would be organized so the teachers would no longer be isolated in the classroom throughout their professional lives, but would have the time to be available to share ideas and talk to and with each other. I would approve such a proposal if it showed how teachers would work with individual students, coaching rather than lecturing most of the time. I would also include the following: How would you design a school that would eliminate most of the harmful aspects of schools at the present time? We know that everybody learns at his or her own rate, but schools are organized so the kids better learn at the rate the teacher is talking, because otherwise they're not going to learn. We say that everyone learns at his own rate, but then we develop a system that says: You'd better learn at the same rate. I would approve a school in which kids are not placed in unfair competition with others—which is what we do now by age-grading but failing to recognize that the oldest kid in a class is a year older than the youngest. And then we find that the youngest kids in the early grades end up having a higher dropout rate and so forth years later, because they're convinced that they're dumber when actually they've only been competing with kids who are a lot older than they are.

I would approve a school that shows how, when children are trying to learn something, they would not be humiliated in front of the whole class. (Most people who didn't learn how to drive early on were probably taught by their husbands or wives or someone who they cared for—because it's a humiliating experience. Most of us are willing to pay for a driving instructor so that we don't have to face the consequences of personal humiliation. Kids are the same. They don't want to see their efforts at learning, especially when they're still groping and trying, exposed to someone else.) Can we come up with a plan for a school, which does that? Can we come up with a plan for a school, which doesn't require kids to do something that most adults can't do, which is to sit still for five or six hours a day listening to somebody talk? Most adults can't do it; most kids can't do it. Kids who are able to do it later become college graduates. That's the greatest educational requirement that we have. What about developing a plan which shows we understand that some kids don't learn right away by listening to someone talk or by reading a book, which are the only two ways the system uses to get kids to learn in school? What about a school in which there are videotapes and audio tapes and computers and simulation games, and one kid teaching another kid and volunteers within a school helping those kids—that is, a variety of different ways of learning, and its maximization?

What about a plan that says that learning mathematics or social studies is more than repeating and regurgitating back things on standardized examinations, that we're going to have a school that also develops creativity and other aspects of intelligence? Because the kids who do the best on these tests are not necessarily people who later on in life make the greatest contributions to society. (As a matter of fact, if you look at the Einsteins and the Churchills and the Edisons, they all had trouble in school, because they asked creative questions and they were considered wiseguys. They didn't care as much about the facts as they did about ideas.) I would also include a provision for cooperative learning, the notion that kids can sit around a table and help each other just as the kids help each other on a basketball team or a football team or a baseball team kids working with each other. The research on that is extremely strong. I would also ask the teachers who submit a plan to show that the group of kids that they're taking in reflects the composition of the entire school. That is, we are not talking about a school where all the advantaged kids or all the white kids or any other group is segregated to one group. The school would have to reflect the whole group. And then the teachers would have to show that they've done some thinking about what they want to show at the end of this.

They would have to think of some good goals and be able to get away from some of the standardized tests and look at some of the better things that the National Assessment of Educational Progress has done: goals such as, can kids read and understand an editorial in the newspaper when they're finished with this school? Can they look at an advertisement of a supermarket and understand what the shopping list is going to cost? Are they able to understand a railroad or a bus timetable? Can they write persuasively, argue, attack problems? Are they able to do a whole bunch of things? The school would announce in advance to the community what it is that it's trying to achieve and announce how it's going to test it, how it wants to prove what it can do. And then, finally, it would also admit something: that we really do not know just how to reach the 80 percent of these kids; that nobody has ever really educated all of them, and that therefore we are engaged in a search. It's a lot like trying to find a cure for the common cold, or for AIDS, or for cancer, or for a chip that we don't yet have.

Therefore, it is important to organize this school in such a way that people have a chance to keep records of what they have done, of what works and what doesn't work. And just as doctors are honored because, when they try something, they publish the results so that no one else need die of the same cure again, we need to honor those educators who try something and when it doesn't work, they inform all of us that it didn't work.

That's a picture of sort of a set of guidelines, of what I would look for in a school proposal if I were on one of these panels. I also would say that in order for such a school-within-a school to exist, the other teachers in the school and the principal would have to sign off and say, "We agree to it." It's very hard to have a submit like that working in a hostile environment. Six or twelve teachers ought to be able to say, "Here's our plan; it's a good idea." But they also ought to be able to say to the others: "Look, we're doing this in such a way that it's not going to hurt you and it's not going to upset you." And then they ought to get a budget, their per capita share of what a school spends on students, and be able to find different ways of spending the money.

This would be a school of choice; that is, no teacher would be forced to be in this submit, and neither would any parent be compelled to send a child to this school. It would be a way for parents and teachers to cooperate with each other, to build a new structure. It is also essential for there to be a guarantee that such a school would be left alone for five to ten years, provided that parents wanted to keep sending their kids there, teachers wanted to continue teaching there, and there were no precipitous drop in certain indicators. One of the things that discourages people from bringing about change in schools is the experience of having that effort stopped for no good reason. I hear this allover the country. Somebody says, Noh, Mr. Shanker, we tried something like that 15 years ago. We worked around the clock, and we worked weekends. We read and discussed books. I never worked so hard in my life. And then a new school board was elected or a new principal or superintendent came in and said, 'That's not my thing.'" And that's the end of the school or program.

You'll never get people to make that kind of commitment if our educational world is just filled with people who went through the disappointment of having been engaged and involved and committed to building something only to have it cut out from under them. There is a role in all this for the federal government, state government, the local government, the business community, and foundations. We do need some grants. It would not be operating money. These schools will have to operate on the same money that all other schools do. But these schools do need some technology, they will need some networking capacity, they will need time for teachers to meet after school and perhaps during weekends and summers to develop these programs. The teachers will need to attend conferences, and they will need training. And then probably we ought to develop some sort of a computerized, national network, a databank, so that some teacher in the eighth grade can say, "I used the following National Geographic videotape, it worked very well, and here are the questions I used." Other teachers could then dig into that and find the eight or twelve or fifteen ways that have been found by other teachers to work, and add their own comments. There's no reason why we can't build a national pool of teacher experience as part of this proposal. This proposal is not pie in the sky. It's small. The reason I'm proposing it is that I think it is almost impossible to change an entire school system. Why? We've got the same schools today that we had 100 or 200 years ago. There has been no shortage of reformers. Every couple of years the reformers come along. We've got to admit to ourselves that even though people have known that the system doesn't work, and even though there have always been reformers, it hasn't changed, and it hasn't changed because we're trying to change everybody at the same time. When you try to change everybody at the same time, you get tremendous amounts of resistance. Not only is that true of an entire school system, it's even true of an entire school. I know that, for instance, New York City has a provision, an excellent provision in its agreement, which says that if 75 percent of the teachers in a school vote to modify the union contract, they could do it, because they wanted to create better conditions. It's a marvelous provision, and in some schools it's happening. But in other schools, I hear that even if 80 percent of the people agree, they don't want to shove it down the throats of the other 20 percent, because it's very unpleasant to have lunch every day with one person at your table who says, "You're forcing me to do something that I didn't want to do." We've got to take that into account. That's reality, so we've got to give that 75 percent the chance to do something and leave alone the 25 percent who don't want to do it. At least the 75 percent will do something.

This is a way of getting around the question of, do you shove reform down people's throats, or do you try and change a whole state at once? You'll never do it. If you try to change a whole system at once, you won't do it, or you'll water it down so much it's meaningless. You can't even change a whole school at once. If you have a charismatic leader who holds everyone's hand so he develops consensus over one or two or three years, It will happen for a while, but it's very difficult. You have to wait for a magical person to come along and to work real hard with everybody, but then eventually that person leaves or gets burned out, and away it goes.

So we need to provide a policy mechanism to allow smaller groups of people to be able to do these things. The great advantage that this will have is that we could do this in practically every district in the country. People won't have to say, "Well, that's in Rochester or that's in Dade County or that's all the way at the other end of the district. They had ideal conditions. Someone or ones let them do it." There is hardly a school in this country where you can't find six or seven or eight or nine teachers who will sit together and come up with ideas that are quite different, and who will make this work. I would like to say that we in the American Federation of Teachers intend to make this work. We're going to go to each and everyone of our locals across the country. We're not going to ask them to change the whole system; we're not going to ask them to even change a whole school, though if they can great. We're going to say to them, "Make it possible for any group of six, seven, eight, nine, twelve or more teachers who want to do this to do it." There will be other teachers in that same building who will not do it but they will be talking about it and watching it. And if it works and I believe it will, over time, for this is no magic bullet but a way in which people can do things more intelligently and in a way that is not going to harm kids—I think that other teachers are going to say, "Hey, that looks pretty good to me. We'd like to try it next year." It's a way of building by example. It's a way not of shoving things down people's throats, but enlisting them in a movement and in a cause. I believe that this proposal will take us from the point where the number of real basic reform efforts can be counted on the fingers of two hands to a point where, if we meet here again a few years from now, we'll be able to talk about thousands and thousands of schools in this country where people are building a new type of school that reaches the overwhelming majority of our students.

Response to Louisiana's Request to Amend Charter Application

Letter Approving Louisiana Department of Education's Request for Waivers to Meet Needs of Students Displaced by Hurricanes
October 15, 2005

Dear Superintendent Picard:

I am writing in response to the waiver request that you submitted to the Department pursuant to the Louisiana Department of Education (LDE) grant under the U.S. Department of Education's Charter Schools Program (CSP). We are treating your request as a request to amend LDE's approved CSP grant application.

Under Section 5204(e) of the Elementary and Secondary Education Act (ESEA), as amended by the No Child Left Behind Act of 2001 (NCLB), the Secretary may grant a waiver if: (1) the waiver is requested in an approved application for funds under the CSP; and (2) the Secretary determines that granting the waiver will promote the purposes of the CSP. The LDE is a grantee under the CSP and submitted, on September 27, 2005, the following requests for the Department to waive a section of the Education Department General Administration Regulations (EDGAR) and certain provisions under the ESEA.

Waiver Request 1: Waive EDGAR 75.261(c)(2) in order for LDE to receive additional CSP funds during an extension period (a period after the original end of a grant period) to expedite the planning and implementation of charter schools to address the immediate educational needs of students displaced as a result of Hurricanes Katrina and Rita. This section prohibits eligible applicants from receiving additional Federal funds during an extension year.

The Department approves your request and waives 34 C.F.R. 75.261(c)(2) of EDGAR so that LDE can receive additional CSP funds during an extension period. This will enable LDE to expedite the planning and implementation of charter schools in the State to address the immediate educational needs of students displaced as a result of Hurricanes Katrina and Rita. This approval authorizes LDE to use the supplemental CSP funds the Department awarded Louisiana under its approved CSP application during the current extension period.

Waiver Request 2: Waive section 5202(d)(1) of the ESEA so that eligible applicants that have already received one CSP grant may receive a second grant in order to enroll students displaced as a result of Hurricanes Katrina and Rita. In addition, LDE requests a waiver of this section to allow eligible applicants that have already received one CSP grant and whose facilities have been damaged or destroyed by Hurricanes Katrina or Rita to receive a second CSP grant in order to plan, design, and implement a program for a school in recovery. This section prohibits an eligible applicant from receiving more than one CSP grant.

Reprinted from ED.gov, http://www.ed.gov/print/programs/charter/waiver101505.html.

The Department approves your request to waive Section 5202(d)(1) to allow eligible applicants that have already received one CSP grant to receive a second grant in order to enroll students displaced as a result of Hurricanes Katrina and Rita. This waiver also will enable eligible applicants that have already received one CSP grant and whose facilities have been damaged or destroyed by Hurricanes Katrina or Rita to plan, design, and implement programs to replace those damaged or lost as a result of these hurricanes. This approval authorizes LDE to award a second CSP grant to eligible applicants that received planning, program design, and implementation grants previously and are expanding significantly to enroll students displaced as a result of Hurricanes Katrina and Rita. In addition, this approval authorizes LDE to award a second CSP grant to eligible applicants that have received planning, program design, and implementation grants previously and are replacing programs damaged or lost as a result of these hurricanes.

Waiver Request 3: Waive section 5202(c)(2) of the ESEA in order to allow eligible applicants that were approved and had planned to open schools prior to Hurricanes Katrina and Rita the opportunity to complete a full 36-month grant period without deducting any time accrued under the original application. This section limits CSP grants to a maximum period of three years, no more than 18 months of which may be used for planning and program design and no more than two years of which may be used for the initial implementation of a charter school.

The Department approves your request to waive Section 5202(c)(2) to allow eligible applicants that were approved and had planned to open schools prior to Hurricanes Katrina and Rita, but whose facilities were damaged or destroyed as a result of these hurricanes, the opportunity to complete a full 36-month grant period while not deducting any time lost as a result of these hurricanes. This approval authorizes LDE to allow eligible applicants that received a CSP planning or implementation grant, but were interrupted in their projects, the opportunity to complete a full 36-month grant period of which not more than 18 months may be used for planning and program design and not more than two years for implementation.

Waiver Request 4: Waive section 5204(f)(3) of the ESEA in order to allow the use of subgrant funds for activities that are not considered planning, program design, or initial implementation of a charter school. This section limits the use of CSP funds to "post-award planning and design of the educational program" and "the initial implementation of the charter school." Examples of planning and program design activities include—

i. Refinement of the desired educational results and of the methods for measuring progress toward achieving those results; and
ii. Professional development of teachers and other staff who will work in the charter school.

Implementation activities may include—
i. Informing the community about the school;

ii. Acquiring necessary equipment and educational materials and supplies;

iii. Acquiring or developing curriculum materials; and

iv. Other initial operational costs that cannot be met from State or local sources.

The Department does not approve your request to waive section 5204(f)(3) to allow the use of subgrant funds for activities that are not considered to be post-award planning or design of the educational program or the initial implementation of a charter school. CSP funds may only be used for post-award planning and program design or the initial implementation of a charter school. These activities may include, but are not limited to, the examples provided in the statute. In addition, as recipients of Federal funds, the State and charter school must adhere to the cost principles set forth in OMB Circulars A-87 and A-122 in determining allowable costs.

In addition to your waiver requests, the State requested that any new or existing charter schools in Louisiana be allowed to adopt a weighted lottery to give priority to homeless and displaced students. Secretary Spellings has addressed this question in a Dear Colleague letter dated September 14, 2005, which authorizes States and their charter schools to conduct an expedited and weighted lottery for the specific purpose of educating students displaced as a result of Hurricane Katrina. A copy of the Secretary's Dear Colleague letter is enclosed for your review and guidance. This guidance also applies to students displaced as a result of Hurricane Rita.

Thank you for the support and care your department has demonstrated for students in the State of Louisiana displaced by Hurricanes Katrina and Rita. We look forward to continuing to work closely with Louisiana in expanding the number of high-quality charter schools. Please feel free to contact me should you need further assistance.

I am sending an identical response to Glenny Lee Buquet.

Sincerely,
Nina S. Rees
Assistant Deputy Secretary
for Innovation and Improvement

Board of Elementary and Secondary Education (BESE)

NEW ORLEANS PUBLIC SCHOOLS, 2009

Today's New Orleans public schools are split between traditional schools and charter schools, with both types reporting to several separate administrations. Here's how it will work for the upcoming school year: The state-run Recovery School District will directly run 22 schools, and oversee 20 charter schools. The Orleans Parish School Board will operate five traditional public schools, and oversee 12 charter schools. On the West Bank, the Algiers Charter Schools Association will oversee nine charter schools (though the Recovery District remains the official chartering authority for seven of the Algiers schools, and the School Board for the remaining two). Finally, the state's Board of Elementary and Secondary Education serves as the chartering authority for two charters. Charters differ from traditional public schools in that they operate independently; their budgets, curriculum choices and all other daily management decisions fall under the school's principal and an appointed board, rather than an elected board and administration dictating one-size-fits-all policies for large groups of schools.

Orleans Parish School Board New Orleans public schools

NOPS-Operated Schools

Mary Bethune Elementary (PK-8)
Benjamin Franklin Elementary Math & Science (PK-6)
McDonogh 35 High School (7-12)
Eleanor McMain High (7-12)
Orleans Parish PM School (7-12)

OPSB Charters

Audubon Charter (PK-8)
Alice Harte Elementary (K-8)*
Lake Forest Elementary (K-8)
Robert R. Moton Charter (PK-6)
Edward Hynes Charter (PK-4)
Edward Hynes Charter (5-8)
Einstein Charter (K-8)
Lusher Charter (K-5)
Lusher Charter (6-12)
Priestley Charter School (9-10)
Edna Karr High (9-12)*

Reprinted with permission from the Parent's Guide, authored by the New Orleans Parent Organizing Network.

Warren Easton Sr. High (9-12)
Ben Franklin High (9-12)
New Orleans Charter Math & Science High (9-12)

Independent BESE charters
Milestone/SABIS Charter (K-8)
International School of Lousiana (K-6)

Louisiana Department of Education Recovery School District
RSD-charter schools
Lafayette Academy (K-7)
Dwight D. Eisenhower Elementary (K-8)*
Harriet Tubman Elementary (K-8)*
McDonogh 32 Elementary (K-8)*
Fischer Elementary (PK-8)*
James M. Singleton Charter School (PK-8)
Martin Behrman Elementary (PK-8)*
McDonogh 15 KIPP School (PK-8)
S.J. Green Charter School (PK-8)
McDonogh 28 Elementary (K-8)
New Orleans Free School (PK-8)
Pierre A. Capdau Charter (PK-8)
Medard Nelson Charter (PK-8)
Dr. Martin Luther King Jr. Charter School for Science & Technology (PK-8)
Sophie B. Wright Charter School (4-8)
KIPP Believe College Prep (5-6)
Pierre A. Capdau Early College High (9-10)
O. Perry Walker High (9-12)*

Newly approved charters
KIPP Central City (5)
Langston Hughes (K-5)
Andrew Wilson Charter School Pelican Foundation (K-8)
Esperanza Charter School (K-8)
New Orleans College Prep (6)
Treme Charter School (PK-8)
N.O. Charter Middle School (K-8)
Technology High School (9-12)*

*Denotes Algiers Charter Schools Association (ACSA)

RSD-operated schools
Benjamin Banneker Elementary (PK-8)
Joseph A. Craig Elementary (PK-8)
John Dibert Elementary (PK-8)
Charles Drew Elementary (PK-8)
Paul Habans Elementary (PK-8)
Murray Henderson Elementary (PK-8)
James Johnson Elementary (PK-8)
Laurel Elementary (PK-8)
Live Oak Elementary (PK-8)
McDonogh 42 Elementary (PK-5)
Sarah T. Reed School (PK-12)
Rosenwald Elementary (PK-8)
A.P. Tureaud Elementary (K-5)
Albert Wicker Elementary (K-8)
Sylvanie Williams Elementary (PK-8)
Joseph T. Clark High (9-12)
Walter Cohen Senior High (9-10)
Frederick Douglass High (9-12)
John McDonogh High (9-12)
L.E. Rabouin High (9-12)
Sarah T. Reed School (9-12)
Schwartz Alternative School (6-12)
school for students removed from other schools because of behavior problems

Florida's Charter School Application

Please answer the following questions as thoroughly and clearly as possible in the sequence in which they appear. Following each question is a brief description of the standards which may be used to review your application. These review standards are not intended to be exhaustive or prescriptive, but rather should serve as a helpful guide as you attempt to formulate your response.

I.   ACADEMIC DESIGN

1) Mission:
  A. Describe the core philosophy or underlying purpose of the proposed school.

  B. Describe the target student population to be served, including student ages and grade levels at the school.

  What reviewers will look for: Clearly articulated vision for an innovative public school which will lead to improved educational outcomes and greater community ownership of the local school; consistency between mission and the educational programs as a means to achieve this.

2) Educational Program:
  A. Describe the educational program of the school, providing an overview of curriculum objectives and content of the main subject areas.

  B. Briefly outline the instructional methods to be used, including any distinctive instructional techniques to be employed. How will this pedagogy enhance student learning?

  C. Describe how your school will meet the needs of Exceptional Education students, including limited English proficient students.

  What reviewers will look for: Innovative teaching methods and curriculum approaches; substantive overview of curriculum; consistency between the mission, curriculum, and student population to be served; Compliance with applicable regulations to meet the needs of limited English proficient and special needs students in the school program.

3) Student Assessment:
  A. Describe your plan to assess student performance in the core academic areas. Please include the current baseline standard of achievement, the outcomes to be achieved and the method(s) of measurement to be used.

  B. Describe the methods used to identify the educational strengths and needs of students and the extent to which educational goals and performance standards are being met.

Florida Department of Education. Florida's Charter School Application. Available: http://www. uscharterschools.org/cs/r/view/uscs_rs/459.

C. Describe how students will, at a minimum, participate in the statewide assessment program.

D. For secondary charter schools, describe the method for determining that a student has satisfied the requirements for graduation in section 232.246, Florida Statutes.

What reviewers will look for: Commitment to high academic standards for all students; well-developed assessment mechanisms; understanding of the state assessment requirements.

II. **GOVERNANCE & MANAGEMENT**

1) **Profile of the Founding Board and/or Initial Incorporators:**

A. Describe the organizing group of initial incorporators that is working together to apply for a charter, including the names of the organizers, their background and experiences, and references for each.

B. Discuss any business arrangements or partnerships with existing schools, educational programs, businesses, or non-profit organizations.

What reviewers will look for: A well-balanced group which brings together people with a range of professional skills capable of the organizational, financial, pedagogical, legal, and other tasks required to open a functioning public school; local representation; meets requirements of law.

2) **School Governance:**

A. Describe the governance structure of the school, including the status of the charter school as a public or private employer as required in subsection (7) of the statute.

B. Describe the administrative management structure of the school.

C. Describe how the board of directors will be chosen and what steps will be taken to maintain continuity between the founding organizer's vision and that of the permanently established board of directors.

D. Describe the roles and responsibilities of the governing board, including the relationship of the governing board to teachers and administrators.

E. Discuss the proposed method for resolving conflicts between the governing board of the charter school and the sponsor.

F. Discuss the nature of parental involvement in decision-making matters.

G. Discuss how the charter school will comply with Florida statutes relating to public records and public meetings. (chapter 119, Florida Statues & s. 286.011, Florida Statues)

What reviewers will look for: Stable, effective, and comprehensive governance model; consistency with mission; clearly defined roles of the board and its interaction with staff; appropriate teacher and parent input in school decision-making; well developed, viable administrative management structure; knowledge of and compliance with public information laws.

3) **Length of Contract & Implementation Timetable:**

A. State the length of the initial charter term, up to 3 years. Technically, the charter may be terminated before that period, as described in subsection (10) of the charter statute. In any case, the charter school is subject to an annual review of academic progress.

B. Present a timetable for implementing the charter, which addresses the implementation of each element thereof and the date by which the charter shall be awarded in order to meet this timetable.

4) **Evidence of Support:**

A. Try to convey as clearly and concretely as possible the scope of community backing for the proposed charter school and its founding board. Document this community support among teachers, parents, students, community members and institutional leaders and others, through the use of letters of support, surveys, or other tangible means.

What reviewers will look for: Evidence that the founders inspire the confidence of their targeted community;evidence that the program provides an attractive educational alternative to students and parents; breadth of community support extending well beyond the core group of founders.

III. FINANCE & FACILITIES

1) **Facilities:**

A. Describe the facilities to be used and their location, or alternatively, describe your present options for a school building.

B. Demonstrate how this site would be a suitable facility for the proposed school, including any plans to renovate and bring facility into compliance with all applicable local building codes.

C. If applicable, discuss any progress, partnership developments, or other future steps towards acquisition of a school building.

D. Describe financing plans for facilities, if applicable.

What reviewers will look for: Progress toward identifying and acquiring an adequate school facility.

2) **Finances:**

A. Describe the financial management and internal accounting procedures of the school.

B. Present a budget for start-up expenses, covering only the planning and capital expenses necessary before school opening.

C. Present a 3-year budget covering all projected sources of revenue, both public and private, and planned expenditures.

    D. Do you plan to conduct any fund-raising efforts to generate capital or to supplement the per pupil allocations? If so, briefly explain.

    E. Explain the manner in which the school will be insured, including liability insurance.

What reviewers will look for: Sound financial planning; fiscal viability of the school.

3) Recruiting & Marketing Plan:

    A. Demonstrate how you will publicize the school to attract a sufficient pool of applicants.

    B. What steps will be taken to reach students representative of the racial and socio-economic diversity in the community, including typically "harder to reach" families?

What reviewers will look for: A solid plan to attract sufficient students to operate a school; effort to publicize the school to a broad audience in order to foster a student body representative of the local community; and recruitment efforts which seek to ensure a match between the school program and applicants' educational and personal needs.

IV. OPERATIONS

1) Admissions & Registration Plan:

    A. Describe the admissions procedures and dismissal procedures you will use.

    B. Describe the timetable to be used for registering & admitting students, including a plan for the admission lottery if the number of applicants exceeds the program capacity.

    C. Describe the ways in which the school will endeavor to achieve a racial/ethnic balance reflective of the community it serves.

    D. In the case of an existing school being converted to charter status, suggest alternative arrangements for current students who choose not to attend the charter school.

What reviewers will look for: Consistency with the mission of the school; a non-discriminatory admissions process; timely and realistic procedures for admitting students; compliance with charter school legislation.

2) Human Resource Information:

    A. Describe the standards to be used in the hiring process of teachers, administrators and other school staff.

    B. Describe your human resource policies governing: salaries, contracts, hiring & dismissal, and benefit packages.

    C. Describe how the qualifications of the teachers will be described to parents considering the charter school for their children, as required in the charter statute.

    D. What is the targeted staff size, staffing plan, and projected student-to-teacher ratio?

E. In the case of an existing school being converted to charter status, suggest alternative arrangements for current teachers who choose not to teach in the school after conversion. These suggestions may or may not be adopted by the local school board, which alone bears full responsibility for the placement of any of district employees who choose not to work in the charter school. (Any teacher choosing not to work in the charter school must be treated by the school board in accordance with the existing collective-bargaining agreement or with school board policy in the absence of a collective bargaining agreement.)

What reviewers will look for: High professional standards for teachers and other staff; commitment to professional development of staff; working conditions and compensation packages which will attract quality staff; compliance with labor laws , fingerprinting and background checks.

3) **Transportation:**

A. Discuss the plans for transporting students to and from school. What arrangements, if any, will be made with the local school district, private providers, or with parents?

B. Charter schools are responsible for providing transportation for students residing within a "reasonable distance" of the charter school. How has that reasonable distance been defined in your charter transportation plan? What factors helped form the basis for this distance determination?

C. Describe the policies which will help ensure that transportation is not a barrier to equal access for all students.

D. If the school district is under court-ordered desegregation, describe how that has been taken into account in the transportation plan.

What reviewers will look for: A workable, fair, non-discriminatory and cost-effective arrangement for safely transporting students to and from school.

V. **FINAL DOCUMENTATION**

Final documents to be submitted prior to the opening of the charter school. Approval of a charter school and a charter agreement may be granted prior to the final submission of these documents. However, final authorization to operate the charter school will almost certainly be contingent upon the submission of these (or similar) documents.

1) **Facilities Safety Approval:**

A. In order to demonstrate the safety and structural soundness of the school and compliance with applicable state minimum building codes and fire protection codes, please submit written documentation of:

- Inspection by a local building inspector;
- Inspection by local Fire Department;
- Compliance with all other federal and state health & safety laws and regulations.
  - **B.** Submit a final site plan.
2) **Final Governance Documents:**
   - **A.** Submit copies of the school's articles of incorporation, by-laws, contracts, and other documents required by applicable law.
   - **B.** Updated board members' names, addresses, phone numbers, resume's and disclosure information.
3) **Insurance, Final Budgets, & Other:**
   - **A.** Present your school's insurance coverage plans, including applicable health, general liability, property insurance, and Director's and Officer's liability coverage, if any.
   - **B.** Submit updated budgets.
   - **C.** Final school calendars.

Mater Academy Charter Middle-High School Parent Contract

Enrollment in Mater Academy signifies acceptance of our school's parent contract and other policies; copies of which follow:

- **I understand and will assure compliance** of the Mater Academy Student Code of Excellence, which has been given to me at the time of registration. Any infraction will result in a referral/SCAM form, which will be placed in my child's permanent record.
- **I understand that attendance is mandatory.** After an absence, the parent must send a handwritten note explaining the reason for their child's absence. Be aware that more than 5 or more unexcused absences within a semester course or 10 or more within an annual course will result in the withholding of a student's grade.
- **Arrival time is from 7:00 a.m. to 7:25 a.m.** The doors open at 7:15 a.m. Students must be in their seat by 7:30 a.m. Any student arriving after 7:35 a.m. will be issued a late pass in the cafetorium. Excessive tardiness will result in detentions and referrals.
- **Dismissal Time is 2:30 p.m.**

NOTE: THESE TIMES WILL BE STRICTLY ENFORCED FOR INSURANCE REASONS. WE ARE NOT RESPONSIBLE FOR STUDENTS ARRIVING AT SCHOOL BEFORE 7:00 am OR DEPARTING AFTER 2:30 p.m. (AS OUR INSURANCE COVERAGE ENDS AT THIS TIME). THE SCHOOL RESERVES THE RIGHT TO APPLY SANCTIONS TO STUDENTS WHO ARE ON CAMPUS AFTER 2:30 p.m. AND WHO DO NOT PARTICIPATE IN THE AFTER SCHOOL CARE PROGRAM, CLASSES, OR ARE PARTICIPATING IN A SCHOOL SPONSORED CLUB OR SPORT ACTIVITY.

- Parents who wish to pick up their child early (on a regular school day) need to provide proof of medical/dental appointment. **After 2:00 p.m., parents will not be permitted to pick up their children for early dismissal.**
- **Students are not allowed to bring any games, toys, or electronic devices from home into the classroom.** The teacher will confiscate any unauthorized items that my child may bring into the school. The teacher or administration may keep such items until the end of the school year. While the school will take every effort to protect such confiscated items, we cannot be responsible for lost or damaged items, we strongly recommend that parents ensure students do not bring such items to school.

http://materacademyhigh.dadeschools.net/studentservices/curriculumbulletin/parentcontract.html

- **Uniforms must be worn everyday as stated in the uniform policy. Please Note:** Students who are not wearing the correct uniform will be suspended indoors until they are in compliance with the policy. Repeat offenders may be suspended outdoors.
- **Satisfactory Academic Progress:** Students need to have a minimum Grade Point Average (GPA) of 2.0 to graduate from high school in the State of Florida. Also, this is the minimum requirement for participation in sports and activities. Mater Academy as part of our Code of Excellence will enforce stricter rules. Any student failing to achieve this minimum requirement at the end of any nine week period will be placed on a Progress Monitoring Plan (PMP).If there is no improvement at the end of the semester, the AIP will be reviewed. Parents are responsible for the implementation of all aspects of the plan.
- Each family is required to complete 30 volunteer hours or the equivalent prior to the last day of school. Failure to complete the 30 hours by the designated date will result in the non-registration of the student for the following school year.

The Neighborhood House Charter School Family Learning Contract

At NHCS, we strongly believe that there needs to be a strong partnership between home and school to educate our children. By choosing to send your child to NHCS, you have decided to be an active participant in your child's education. Therefore, we have outlined the requirements for your child to attend the Neighborhood House Charter School and be a successful student.

This is an agreement between the family of (child's name) _____ and Neighborhood House Charter School. This agreement is in effect for the academic school year of _____. By signing the Family Learning Contract you agree to adhere to the following:

- Attend all academic meetings to discuss their child's progress and goals.
- Notify the main office immediately (within 24 hours) if the phone number or address changes and provide up-to-date emergency and medical information.
- Read the Family Handbook and abide by the policies and guidelines set forth.
- Complete at least 5 hours of volunteer service at the school. (See Volunteer Resource Form.)
- Stay informed and up-to-date about events and issues at school by reading notices, newsletters, emails, posted announcements, and checking in periodically with staff.
- Respond promptly (within 2 school days) to school communications, including permission slips, email, phone messages, etc.
- Support your child at home to ensure his/her needs are met in school by arriving on time, completing homework assignments on time, completing home reading, and following the recommendations of the classroom teachers/advisors.

By signing this contract I fully agree with the terms outlined. Furthermore, I understand that by fulfilling these requirements I am helping my child succeed at the Neighborhood House Charter School.

Non-compliance with this contract may result in a meeting with the Headmaster to determine the appropriateness of your child's placement at NHCS. Failure to comply may also impact eligibility for scholarships or other financial assistance available through NHCS.

Signature_____   Date _____

"It's backed by 30 years of research. When families are involved, children do better in school. The schools do better too."

—Parents are Powerful
Center for Law and Education

---

http://www.neighborhoodhousecharterschool.org/pdf/fam_learn_contract.pdf

Lusher Charter School Application

**Applications must be presented IN PERSON from 9-11am or 2-4:30pm
by Friday, December 5th.
Late applications will only be processed if there are no applicants
on the waiting list.**

Applications for Grades K-5 will NOT be processed unless they contain all of the following:

___ Completed Lusher Charter School Grades K-5 application form

___ Completed Arts Profile - *Students applying for grades 3-5 are expected to complete this form themselves. Younger students should have a parent fill out the form for them.*

___ Copy of student's birth certificate – *Bring original and copy*

___ Copy of parent/legal guardian's Driver's License or State ID – *Bring original and copy*

___ Copy of **FINAL 2007-2008** and **1st Quarter 2008-2009 report cards** for students applying for 2nd-5th Grade - *Bring original and copy*

___ Students who need testing accommodations scheduled must submit a copy of their **504 Accommodations IAP** or the accommodations page of their **Special Education IEP**.

___ Students with a Tulane University affiliation must complete the Tulane Verification Form.

___ One #10 white business envelope with 42¢ postage stamp – **DO NOT ADDRESS ENVELOPE**

ALL APPLICANTS WILL BE TESTED. THERE WILL BE NO RETESTING FOR ANY REASON.
Please advise us if your child is not English proficient or needs accommodations for testing.

Additional requirements for KINDERGARTEN and FIRST GRADE APPLICANTS ONLY:

___ **Parent attendance at a Curriculum Meeting.** Meetings are scheduled on Thursday, January 15, 2009 at 9:00 a.m. and Wednesday, January 21, 2009, at 6:00 p.m. Parents/guardians can attend either meeting. Contact the school if you are currently living out of town.

___ Completed **Parent Questionnaire**. It will only be distributed at the Curriculum Meetings listed above.

Additional requirements for FIFTH GRADE APPLICANTS ONLY:

___ Students applying for 5th grade who are transferring from a private school or are home schooled must provide proof that they have passed the LEAP test or that they have signed up to take it.

---

http://lusherschool.org.

OPEN HOUSE

A presentation for all families of potential new students will be held on Thursday, November 13, 2008 at 9:00 a.m. All interested parents can learn more about Lusher Charter School and have their questions answered. You are invited to attend Morning Meeting at 8:20 a.m. and then proceed to the school cafeteria at 9:00 a.m.

ADMISSIONS – If your child is accepted for admission, you must provide the information listed below at New Student Registration, Monday, May 11, 2009. Your family must also be living in Orleans Parish by this date.

___ Completed registration packet

___ Three (3) current proofs of residence in **Orleans Parish** – *Bring originals and copies Acceptable proofs of residence include: Utility bills (electric, water, cable/internet service), Homestead Exemption, Orleans Parish tax bill, homeowner's insurance, medical insurance, auto insurance, or check stub from employer. Renters must submit name, address and phone number of landlord. Proofs should be dated within 30 days of submission to the school.*

___ If you are not the student's birth parent, please provide court documentation showing legal guardianship of child. – *Bring original and copy*

___ Copy of your child's Social Security Card – *Bring original and copy*

___ Copy of your child's Immunization Record – *Bring original and copy*

___ Copy of current IEP or Progress Report for Gifted/Talented/Special Education students

___ Copy of current IAP for 504 students

K-5 ADMISSIONS MATRIX

MATRIX POINTS	GPA Grades 2-5	MATH %TILE All Grades	READING %TILE All Grades	ARTS PROFILE & APPLICATION All Grades	PARENT INVOLVEMENT Grades K-1
10	3.5-4.00	90-99	90-99	**3 points** if turned in completed and on time	**4 points** for attending Curriculum Meeting
9		80-89	80-89		
8	3.0-3.49	70-79	70-79		
7	2.5-2.99	60-69	60-69		
6	2.3-2.49	55-59	55-59		**3 points** for completing Questionnaire given at meeting
5	2.0-2.29	50-54	50-54		
4		40-49	40-49		
0	0.0-1.99	0-39	0-39		

Acceptance to Lusher Charter School will be determined by the applicant's total matrix score.

For students applying for Grades 2nd–5th, the score is composed of GPA (maximum of 10 points), Math %tile, Reading %tile (maximum of 10 points each) and turning in the completed application packet on time (3 points). Students must score **28 out of the 33 points** possible to be eligible to participate in the two-tiered* process for acceptance.

For students applying for Kindergarten–1st, the score is composed of Math %tile, Reading %tile (maximum of 10 points each), the completed application packet (3 points), attending the curriculum meeting (4 points) and filling out the questionnaire (3 points). Students must score **20 out of the 30 points** possible to be eligible to participate in the two-tiered* process for acceptance.

*TWO-TIERED SELECTION PROCESS

First Tier – Qualified applicants are ranked by their total matrix score and a percentage of available openings at each grade level will be filled by students with the highest matrix score. If a lottery is required due to students having the same score for the last available spots, the parent/guardian will be notified.

Second Tier – A percentage of the remaining available openings at each grade level will be filled through a lottery drawing of all remaining qualified applicants. Qualified students not accepted at the time of the lottery will go on a waiting list.

As per our charter application, a certain number of openings will be reserved for children of Tulane University affiliated parents as long as the students qualify for acceptance.

If you have any questions about the Lusher Charter School application process for grades K– 5, please contact the school office at 7315 Willow Street, phone: (504)862-5110 or FAX: (504)309-4171.

FOR OFFICE USE ONLY

____ Date Received	____ Report Card (2nd-5th) _____	GPA ____
____ Birth Certificate	____ Parent Questionnaire (K-1st)	PQx ____
____ Parent/Guardian ID	____ Arts Profile	APx ____
____ IEP or 504 IAP	____ Test Scores _____%	Read ____
____ Sibling _____	____ Test Scores _____%	Math ____
____ Affiliate _____		MATRIX ____

LUSHER CHARTER SCHOOL APPLICATION
2009-2010 SCHOOL YEAR   GRADES K-5 ONLY
DEADLINE: 4:30 p.m., Friday, December 5, 2008

GENERAL INSTRUCTIONS: Applications for K–5 should be submitted in person from 9:00-11:00 a.m. and 2:00-4:30 p.m. to the office at 7315 Willow St. Late applications will be processed only if vacancies exist.

PLEASE PRINT ALL INFORMATION

STUDENT INFORMATION

_____   _____

Last Name, First Name & Middle Name   Grade Applying For
(Print exactly as name appears on birth certificate.)

_____   _____

Current Street Address   City   State   Zip   Home Phone No.

Date of Birth (MM/DD/YY) _____   Sex: ___M ___F   Race/Ethnicity _____

PARENT/LEGAL GUARDIAN INFORMATION

_____   _____

Parent/Legal Guardian 1 (Full Name)   Parent/Legal Guardian 2 (Full Name)

_____   _____

Relationship to Student   Relationship to Student

_____   _____

Address if Different from Student   Address if Different from Student

_____   _____

Cell Phone   Cell Phone

_____   _____

e-mail   e-mail

EDUCATION HISTORY

Current school (2008-2009) _____ Current grade_____

List all previous schools (list city/state if outside New Orleans) _____

_____

Please check educational designations applying to the applicant (will not affect matrix score):

____ Special Education (1508)   ____ Talented in _____ with IEP

____ Gifted with IEP   ____ 504 IAP

____ English as a Second Language (ESL)

____ Primary Home Language Other than English (PHLOTE)

____ I suspect that my child may qualify for special education services. Explain: _____

____ Check here if your child has ever had behavior problems, which includes suspensions, expulsions and behavior plans or contracts. Please explain:

_____

_____

_____

All applicants will be tested

____ My child needs special testing considerations because he/she has an IEP or 504 IAP.

If your child is applying for Kindergarten and has siblings currently enrolled at Lusher, list below:

_____

As per our charter, a certain number of openings will be reserved for children of qualifying Tulane University affiliated applicants. Please complete Tulane Affiliate Verification Form.

____ Check here if parent/guardian is a full-time student or employee of Tulane University.

If your child is applying for 5th grade, please read and initial.

____ I understand it is necessary for my child to take the LEAP test during this school year (2008-09). I agree to provide his/her LEAP scores by the end of this school year.

Please read carefully and initial.

____ I certify that I am legally responsible for the child for whom the application is being made and have the legal right to apply, on behalf of the child, for admission and to register the child if admission is offered. *If you are not the student's birth parent, please provide a Certified True copy of the Transfer of Custody/Legal Guardianship.* A notarized statement is NOT considered proof of guardianship.

____ I have responded to all sections of this application and certify that all the information is true to the best of my knowledge. I understand that falsification of any part of this application will render it ineligible and any admission offered would thereby be revoked.

____ I understand that it is my responsibility to **schedule a testing date** for my child **by Friday, January 30, 2009.**

____ I understand that it is my responsibility to notify the school of any special testing accommodations my child may need **at the time I turn in the completed application.**

____ I understand that if my child cannot keep the testing date assigned, it is my responsibility to contact the school and re-schedule for a later date.

____ I understand that **retests will not be administered.**

_____   _____

Signature of Parent/Legal Guardian   Date

Applications and all material submitted are property of Lusher Charter School.
Applicants are responsible for maintaining copies of all documents submitted.

LUSHER CHARTER SCHOOL APPLICATION
2009-2010 SCHOOL YEAR
K-5 ARTS PROFILE

Student Name _____   Date _____

Parent Name _____   Grade Applying For _____

Arts are central to learning at Lusher. Each applicant is required to submit an Arts Profile indicating past experiences in the arts, interest in the arts, and desire to participate in a high academic program including many varied art activities to extend learning. Please answer the following questions as completely as possible. Your answers must be submitted on this form: however, additional information may be attached to this form. Answers may be typed or handwritten. *Students applying for grades 3-5 are expected to complete this form themselves. Younger students should have a parent fill out the form for them.*

1. What prior experiences have you had in the arts? (Examples could include, but not be limited to: art, dance, music or drama lessons, participation in arts performances or exhibitions, special arts classes or trips, and/or informal art activities undertaken independently.)

2. What are your interests in the arts? Describe an art activity that you pursued on your own, or give any other information that you feel indicates your personal interest in the arts.

3. Why do you want to participate in a high academic program that puts the arts at the core of the curriculum along with language, math, science and social studies?

As Charter Schools Unionize, Many Debate Effect

By Sam Dillon
July 27, 2009

CHICAGO—Dissatisfied with long hours, churning turnover and, in some cases, lower pay than instructors at other public schools, an increasing number of teachers at charter schools are unionizing.

Labor organizing that began two years ago at seven charter schools in Florida has proliferated over the last year to at least a dozen more charters from Massachusetts and New York to California and Oregon.

Charter schools, which are publicly financed but managed by groups separate from school districts, have been a mainstay of the education reform movement and widely embraced by parents. Because most of the nation's 4,600 charter schools operate without unions, they have been freer to innovate, their advocates say, allowing them to lengthen the class day, dismiss underperforming teachers at will, and experiment with merit pay and other changes that are often banned by work rules governing traditional public schools.

"Charter schools have been too successful for the unions to ignore," said Elizabeth D. Purvis, executive director of the Chicago International Charter School, where teachers voted last month to unionize 3 of its 12 campuses.

President Obama has been especially assertive in championing charter schools. On Friday, he and the education secretary, Arne Duncan, announced a competition for $4.35 billion in federal financing for states that ease restrictions on charter schools and adopt some charter-like standards for other schools—like linking teacher pay to student achievement.

But the unionization effort raises questions about whether unions will strengthen the charter movement by stabilizing its young, often transient teaching force, or weaken it by preventing administrators from firing ineffective teachers and imposing changes they say help raise achievement, like an extended school year.

"A charter school is a more fragile host than a school district," said Paul T. Hill, director of the Center on Reinventing Public Education at the University of Washington. "Labor unrest in a charter school can wipe it out fast. It won't go well for unions if the schools they organize decline in quality or go bust."

Unions are not entirely new to charter schools. Teachers at hundreds of charter schools in Wisconsin, California and elsewhere have long been union members, not because they signed up, but because of local laws, like those that extend union status to all schools in a state or district.

Steve Barr, the founder of one large charter network, Green Dot, said his group operates its 17 charter schools in Los Angeles and one in the Bronx with union staff because it makes sense in the heavily unionized environment of public education.

In recent months, teachers have won union recognition at schools including the Boston Conservatory Lab School, a school in Brooklyn that is part of the Knowledge Is Power Program, an Afro-centric school in Philadelphia, four campuses in the Accelerated School network in Los Angeles, and a Montessori school in Oregon. Moves toward unionizing have revealed greater teacher unrest than was previously known.

"I was frustrated with all the turnover among staff, with the lack of teacher input, with working longer and harder than teachers at other schools and earning less," said Jennifer Gilley, a social studies teacher at the Ralph Ellison Campus of the Chicago International Charter School, who said she made $38,000 as a base salary as a starting teacher, compared with about $43,500 paid by the Chicago Public Schools.

The potential for further unionization of charter schools is a matter of debate.

"They'll have a success here and there," said Todd Ziebarth, a vice president of the National Alliance for Public Charter Schools. "But unionized charters will continue to be a small part of the movement."

Randi Weingarten, president of the American Federation of Teachers, called the gains of the past year "a precursor."

"You're going to see far more union representation in charter schools," Ms. Weingarten said. "We had a group of schools that were basically unorganized, groups of teachers wanting a voice, a union willing to start organizing them, and now money in our organizing budget to back that up. And all of that has come together in the last 6 to 12 months."

She quoted Albert Shanker, her union's founder, as saying charter schools should be "incubators of good instructional practice."

"I'm adding to the argument," Ms. Weingarten said. "Let them be incubators of good labor practice."

The largest teachers union, the National Education Association, has no national charter organizing campaign. But some of its state affiliates have helped charters unionize.

Some recently unionized charters say they are feeling their way forward.

The Knowledge Is Power Program, known as KIPP, which operates 82 mostly high-performing charter schools nationwide, is facing first-time negotiations with teachers at its KIPP Amp Academy in Brooklyn, where teachers this spring won affiliation with the United Federation of Teachers.

KIPP is also facing demands for higher pay at its high-performing Ujima Village Academy in Baltimore, which has been unionized under Maryland law since its founding.

"Our schools had largely been left alone," said Steve Mancini, a KIPP spokesman. "Now we're getting all this union attention." One goal KIPP will seek in negotiations in New York and Baltimore, Mr. Mancini said, is to preserve the principals' right to mold their teams.

Whether KIPP can maintain that posture in its negotiations remains to be seen. Another question is whether the strains of unionization will affect the culture of collegiality that has helped charter schools prosper.

Here in Chicago, where students at several Chicago International campuses have scores among the city's highest for nonselective schools, teachers began organizing last fall after an administrator increased workloads to six classes a day from five, said Emily Mueller, a Spanish teacher at Northtown Academy.

"We were really proud of the scores, and still are," Ms. Mueller said. "But the workload, teaching 160 kids a day, it wasn't sustainable. You can't put out the kind of energy we were putting out for our kids year after year."

Some teachers disagreed. Theresa Furr, a second-grade teacher at the Wrightwood campus, said she opposed unionization.

"Every meeting I went to," Ms. Furr said, "it was always 'What can we get?' and never 'How is this going to make our students' education better?' "

For Joyce Pae, an English teacher at Ralph Ellison, the decision was agonizing. Her concerns over what she saw as chaotic turnover and inconsistency in allocating merit pay led her to join the drive. But after school leaders began paying more attention to teachers' views, she said, she voted against unionization in June.

Union teachers won the vote, 73-49.

"If nothing else," Ms. Pae said, "this experience has really helped teachers feel empowered."

Lessons from the Ground: Interviews with Charter School Educators

By Barbara Miner

The following is condensed from interviews with educators from three community-based charter schools. Those interviewed are:

Debbie Wei, *principal of The Folk Arts—Cultural Treasures Charter School (FACTS) in Philadelphia.* FACTS opened in September 2005, chartered by Asian Americans United in association with the Philadelphia Folklore Project, two long-established community organizations. The goal was a multiracial K-8 school serving the specific needs of immigrant populations, fostering an appreciation of learning, culture, and community, and implementing an art-based, culturally sensitive curriculum. Website: www.factsweb.org.

Rob van Nood, *teacher, 3rd-4th-5th Intermediate Grades, Trillium Charter School in Portland, Ore.* Trillium was founded in 2002 by parents and teachers with educational philosophies rooted in the democratic school/freeschool movement. A K-12 school with a tuition-based preschool, Trillium describes itself as a "democratically structured environment that fosters students' natural curiosity, creativity, and self-awareness. Students learn to take initiative and assume responsibility for their own learning, which supports constructive interaction with the local, regional, and global community." Website: www.trilliumcharterschool.org.

Linda Ohmans, *former principal of The Next Step/El Proximo Paso in Washington, D.C.* The Next Step was started by the Latin American Youth Center, a 26-year-old educational and social service organization. Opening in 1998, the school serves students ages 14-21, with a special focus on teen parents and young people who have dropped out of other schools. It believes that young people learn best in small schools, with a curriculum relevant to their lives and a staff sensitive to the student's culture and the obstacles students face as they try to stay in school. Ohmans was the school's principal from its founding until November 2006. Website: www.laycdc.org/charterschools/nextstep.html.

Why did you opt for a charter over a traditional public school? Were there specific union or district regulations you wanted to avoid?

Wei: It took us a long time to decide because we had all these concerns about how charters were being used by the right and by privatization interests. But we had been so frustrated with education reform within the district. You would go through these protracted struggles, finally get what you want, and then the superintendent would change, or the principal would change, and everything you fought for would be deep-sixed. We couldn't attain lasting, sustained change in any place that we organized.

Used with permission from Keeping the Promise? The Debate Over Charter Schools. *Published by Rethinking Schools. www.rethinkingschools.org. Barbara Miner is a writer and editor for newspapers, magazines, and books. A columnist for* Rethinking Schools *magazine, she writes often on education and other social issues. Her writing has appeared in the* New York Times *to the* Nation, *the* Progressive, ColorLines, Milwaukee Magazine, *and the* Milwaukee Journal Sentinel.

Another problem was the inability of schools to choose teachers. The Philly union contract was a straight-up seniority system and it didn't matter if you created this particular vision, because you were basically beholden to the seniority system and whoever felt like coming in could come in.

A third factor was the district's failure to meet the needs of immigrant kids and their families. We won a lawsuit against the district, basically around inequitable access to education for non-English speaking students, and that suit was filed in 1985. Twenty years later, they are still working in committee to address the issues raised. We were not suing for money but equitable services. But that was when I was young and naive. Now I realize that when you ask for equitable services in an underfunded district that doesn't work for poor students, immigrants and nonimmigrant alike, asking for equity goes only so far.

Van Nood: The founding people were part of what was called the Sunnyside Cooperative School. It was a public elementary and middle school, but it was located in another elementary school's building and the principal of that school had a very different philosophy of education. There was constant tension and a lot of families left. A group of teachers and several parents with children in the school felt that given the tensions, the school would not be able to maintain a progressive vision. So they decided to try a charter.

In terms of district and union rules, the main issue had to do with being able to hire staff who fit with our philosophy. Before we were charter, you had people on staff who were either not understanding the school's philosophy or didn't care. They had moved into the position because there was an opening. The district allowed the school to develop its own philosophy, but if you don't have the right staff, that doesn't work.

Personally, I am pro-union and that was one of the hardest things for me to accept coming to the charter school. I gave up the union so I could teach the way I want to teach.

Ohmans: At the time we applied to be a charter school, I was the director of the teen parent program at the Latin American Youth Center. The program was a combination of social service support for teen mothers and an educational program geared toward young parents either learning English and hopefully going back to a regular school, or passing the GED. It had been working really well for five years, and the director of the Youth center pushed the idea of converting to a charter school. We didn't even know what that meant, it was all so new. But it seemed that what we were doing in the teen parent program was alternative education and that was an ideal of charter schools at the time. It didn't have anything to do with union and district regulations.

We also had the idea, and I think people still have the idea, that it would be great if there were a way that the school could be a model for other public schools in the district. One of the reasons we are able to keep the kids in the school is that we provide a variety of social services supports, and that could be a model. We work closely with other neighborhood agencies, health clinics; we help students find daycare; we provide stipends so the girls can pay their own babysitters at home; we have two social workers—and we had five years of experience in knowing the extra support that teen mothers need.

What have you gained by operating independently of the public school system?
Wei: One of the things we gained was the power to come out from under the district's mandated curriculum. Philly's public schools were taken over by the state and are run by this School Reform Commission. Philly doesn't have a superintendent, but we have a CEO and a business model, with a mandated core curriculum tied to test preparation. As a charter, we can not only hire our own teachers but also implement our curriculum according to our mission and our respect for language and culture and social justice. As it stands in the district right now, we would not have been able to do that.

Van Nood: Problems with the district's curricular approach is a big part of why I came to Trillium. Within the Portland district, there has been a strong standardized testing push in the last 10 years, coupled with mandated programs. One friend in the Portland public schools told me that under the district's mandates, there are tight restrictions on what you can use to teach reading because of their contract with an international textbook publisher. Say you are doing a reading unit that involves bread; this person was afraid to even bring in someone who is a baker, or show a video, unless it came from the textbook publisher. At Trillium, in contrast, we can build a curriculum based on individual students' needs and interests.

Most important, however, is that we have been able to build a school run by the people involved in it every day—the students, staff, and parents.

Ohmans: Control of the curriculum is one of the most important issues for us, as well. We place a strong focus on using the experiences and stories of our students to shape the curriculum. We use their life stories to teach writing, U.S. history, reading comprehension, and English as a Second Language, as well as to inspire other areas of study and provide the connections that the students need to stay in school. Portfolio assessments have become an anchor for our school and are increasingly driving our instruction. To help keep students in school, we have a work experience program that includes workshops on how to get and keep a job, job shadowing, and paid internships. We believe so strongly in this connection between the curriculum and the real world that we have a full-time staff person dedicated to the program.

Our curriculum is constantly in motion because so are our students. The curricular freedoms come with challenges, but the freedom also inspires creativity.

What are your student demographics?

Wei: The school had about 400 students in 2007-08 in K-7, with plans to expand to K-8 next year. All our students are accepted through a straight-up lottery. Sixty percent of the students are Asian (Chinese, Indonesian, Vietnamese, Cambodian, Lao), 35 percent are African-American, and about 5 percent are Latino immigrants, although some are African immigrants from Liberia. And there are a handful of white students. Overall, 92 percent of our students qualify for free or reduced lunch. About 30 percent of the students are English language learners, with all teachers trained to provide ELL support; about 10 percent of the students require special education services, although the special ed figures are hard to know for sure because there are students we think may require special services, but have not yet been formally identified.

Van Nood: We admit students through a lottery, unless they have a sibling already at the school, and then they get first priority. We also ask that parents and the students spend a day at the school before they come, just so they understand the school's philosophy. About 35-40 percent of our students are low-income and qualify for the federal lunch program, about 16-20 percent are special ed, and less than 1 percent are English language learners. Overall, about 75 percent of our students are white and 25 percent students of color. In the 2007-08 year we have about 320 students in K-12, with an additional 40 in the preschool.

Ohmans: About 85 percent of our students are Latino, primarily from Central America, and 15 percent are African-American. Occasionally, there have been Asian students. In the 2007-08 school year, about 13 percent of the students receive special education services, 80 percent are English language learners, and 99 percent receive free or reduced lunch. The school has about 84 students. We're one of the smallest of the charter schools in D.C., but we think our current enrollment is about right for what we want to do.

What are your relations with the broader community?

Wei: When we decided to do a charter, we specifically chose to locate it in Philadelphia's Chinatown. One of the reasons was the lack of publicly funded institutions in the community. There is no traditional public school in Chinatown, no health center, no recreation center. We have 4,000 residents and about a quarter are youth and there are no such facilities. On top of that there is gentrification that is pushing out families. So we wanted a strong public institution in our community.

A few years back, Asian Americans United worked with others to defeat a proposal for a baseball stadium in Chinatown. In fact, our school is located in the footprint of that proposed stadium.

It is hard for folks to do things in the community when they don't control the properties, but in this case we had a community businessman who owned the space, was concerned about gentrification, and wanted to build a community institution. He got a lot of offers to turn his space into condos or hotels. When we approached him he said he would hold the building for us if we could get the charter. He took on the risk and helped with the renovation of the building. He said, "If this is the only way we will get an institution in the community, I will do it." It's a nice story because it highlights certain things about our school and its centeredness in the community. Because of gentrification, we would not have been able to afford a place for the school if Mr. Wong had not stepped forward.

Van Nood: Our school is open to anyone in Portland, and our community is centered on our educational philosophy. We also have a community representative on our board. Within the school, we have a strong emphasis on democratic decision-making and student and staff say in the school. The staff, led by the director, makes most of the decisions about the school program; for instance we decide what classes will be taught, who will teach them, the schedule, and so forth. Staff meetings are run collectively, with rotating responsibilities, and most decisions are made as a group. The staff and students created the school constitution, which is modeled after the U.S. Constitution and puts a lot of power in the hands of staff and students.

Ohmans: We are affiliated with the Latin American Youth Center, which was founded in the late 1960s, and our school is located in their building. In addition, one of our board members is from the Youth Center, and a couple of others are community representatives. Our relationship to the Youth Center and to the community make us very different from charters that are part of a national franchise.

Our connection to the Youth Center also allows us to tap into their programs, so under the same roof we have a number of wraparound services such as a counseling program and after-school activities.

What about staffing issues such as certification and teacher turnover?

Wei: Our teachers are not part of the union, although by law they have comparable healthcare benefits. By law, up to 25 percent of the charter school teachers do not have to be certified but in our school, 95 percent are certified. We are actually like the haven for progressive teachers who can't take it anymore in the Philadelphia district.

Van Nood: When we became a charter, flexibility in certification was a big issue, partly because we wanted to bring in staff that were experienced in different areas, especially community-based people, but who might not be certified. While certification fluctuates from year to year, about 75 percent of our staff are certified and have a master's degree.

We are not part of the union, and, as with other charters, pay and benefits are decided by the school. The founders of Trillium want a good pay scale, and for newer and midlevel teachers the pay and benefits are comparable to what Portland offers. We haven't been able to have as high a ceiling for top pay, however.

Staff turnover was somewhat of an issue the first several years. We were a startup charter and, on both sides, people wanted to make sure there was a good fit. In recent years, turnover has not been an issue. I know a lot of charters have had problems with so many beginning teachers, without enough veterans to provide support and help keep things stable. We've been lucky because we have about half and half, in terms of younger versus experienced teachers.

Ohmans: Most of the teachers are certified, most have masters', and all but two are bilingual. Math and science have always been the hardest positions to fill. In terms of staff turnover, it has been very, very low. There are lots of reasons, but one is that we want our salaries to be competitive with the public schools; we pay about $1,000 a year less, partly because our school is so small that we have little budget flexibility. Hopefully, our teaching environment and the voice the teachers have in the operation of the school make up for that. We also raise our pay scale when the public teachers get a raise.

How has the federal No Child Left Behind (NCLB) act affected your school?
Wei: The mandated testing is a big issue. We do certain types of test preparation, because kids can't walk into a test and do well if they have never seen standardized tests before. NCLB has also cost us money in the sense that there is communication required to go home and we are not reimbursed for any of the costs—in particular because we routinely translate documents into four languages: Chinese, Indonesian, Vietnamese, and Spanish. And then there's the issue of how Adequate Yearly Progress is determined. We have not met AYP in any given year, partly because we're so new and a lot of our students are playing catch-up. Last year we didn't make AYP because of our African-American subgroup, so we are looking hard at achievement gap issues. Also, the state keeps changing what you need to meet AYP.

Ohmans: For our students, NCLB hasn't had a huge impact. You need a certain number of students to have a testing subgroup, and we rarely have enough, partly because we have such a wide range of ages and, for different reasons, our population is very transient, and also because we're a small school. So we've been able to keep a focus on shaping our curriculum around our students' needs.

How do you relate to the public school system or other charters? How are the lessons you have learned transmitted to other schools?

Wei: Overall in Pennsylvania, the conservatives and Republicans pushed charter schools. The schools themselves tend to be a mixed bag—in terms of the number of charter schools as a group in Philadelphia, we constitute the second largest district in the state. There are a number of charters that, quality- wise, are not very good. And there are a number that are very good. All of the charters tend to be safer than the Philadelphia public schools. In terms of philosophy, there are schools that speak to the cultural or political needs of the students and communities they serve, but there are also the Edison and KIPP type schools.

I have informal contact with some of the more progressive charters, and there are a few I email a lot.

One principal I communicate with a lot called me this weekend. They have an Indonesian student whose family is slated for deportation. She knew we had a lot of experience working around immigrant rights and picked my brains about how to do organizing work on behalf of the family. There's a lot of that kind of informal support that I have with a few schools.

There has been some talk of trying to coordinate professional development among the charters, but that hasn't happened. People are so overwhelmed trying to keep their schools going. We pay fees for this charter school coalition in the state, but their politics are a lot more conservative than ours. Actually, a lot of the charter schools are more conservative than we are. So, it's great to have a coalition for some things, but we aren't all necessarily kindred spirits.

Van Nood: One of the directives of the charter school law in Oregon is that charter schools will attempt to bring what they have learned to other schools. But we haven't had much direct contact with other public schools because it's hard to find avenues for that. We moved into a new location this year and in the old location, we tried to have a relationship with the middle school there but it didn't really go anywhere for a lot of reasons. For one, the principal was open to a conversation, but wasn't overly excited about making it happen. And it was a struggling middle school, which is now being reconstituted as an all-girls high school. So it already had its own struggles and there wasn't the time to build a partnership.

There aren't any formal structures, so everything has to be done by the schools themselves. Trillium got a federal dissemination grant and we hosted several conferences to talk about what we are doing. But for the most part, the people who come are from charter schools, whether in Portland or other districts.

At this point, there's not a lot of interaction with the Portland public schools. My sense is that some in the professional teaching community see us as a kind of thorn in the sides of the schools, and think we are stealing their kids away, stealing their resources, and so forth. They don't greet us with open arms. There is more of an interest from families, especially when they feel their kids aren't making it and need other options.

As far as charters, we are a bit in a bubble in Portland, so I feel I can talk positively about charter schools. In Portland, we don't have a lot of the Edisons or other commercially oriented charters. Portland charters are pretty progressive philosophically, and not into scripted, back-to-basic curriculums.

Overall, we are trying to prevent Edison-type schools from coming into the state. We don't feel we have much in common with the conservative, privatization charters and don't want them to gain a foothold in the state.

Ohmans: Our contact with other schools is minimal. There has never been any mechanism to share what we are doing, either with traditional public schools or charter schools. We had cordial relations with other charters, but we didn't share much in common. Our situation was somewhat unique. When we started we had this beautiful space to move into in the Latin American Youth Center building—everything was there, from the security, to the accounting, to the janitorial services. Other charters, meanwhile, were looking around for decent space, sometimes temporarily housed in a church basement or something like that. For most new charters, finding space is an incredibly consuming problem. In addition, we work with high school students, the only charter to do so in that beginning stage. Finally, our students are primarily Latino although admission is open to any student who applies on a first-come, first-served basis. That's not true of a lot of the charters.

While we never saw ourselves as promoting a model to be replicated, at the same time when we realize something works we often find ourselves saying, 'Gee, there's no reason this couldn't be done elsewhere.' There's no reason, for instance, why a high school of 3,000 students couldn't be divided up into schools of 1,000 each. Or no reason not to have more social counselors and other support services, which are absolutely critical for young parents. Or no reason not to have a strong bilingual program where students can be taught core academic classes in Spanish at the same time they are learning English as a second language.

A strong point of our school—and there's no reason why it couldn't happen in other schools—is that there is a sense of ownership among the staff. Everyone feels responsible for how the school turns out.

The Instigator

A crusader's plan to remake failing schools

by Douglas McGray

May 11, 2009

Steve Barr stood in the breezeway at Alain Leroy Locke High School, at the edge of the Watts neighborhood of Los Angeles, on a February morning. He's more than six feet tall, with white-gray hair that's perpetually unkempt, and the bulk of an ex-jock. Beside him was Ramon Cortines—neat, in a trim suit—the Los Angeles Unified School District's new superintendent. Cortines had to be thinking about last May, when, as a senior deputy superintendent, he had visited under very different circumstances. That was when a tangle between two rival cliques near an outdoor vending machine turned into a fight that spread to every corner of the schoolyard. Police sent more than a dozen squad cars and surged across the campus in riot gear, as teachers grabbed kids on the margins and whisked them into locked classrooms.

The school's test scores had been among the worst in the state. In recent years, seventy-five per cent of incoming freshmen had dropped out. Only about three per cent graduated with enough credits to apply to a California state university. Two years ago, Barr had asked L.A.U.S.D. to give his charter-school-management organization, Green Dot Public Schools, control of Locke, and let him help the district turn it around. When the district refused, Green Dot became the first charter group in the country to seize a high school in a hostile takeover. ("He's a revolutionary," Nelson Smith, the president and C.E.O. of the National Alliance for Public Charter Schools, said.) Locke reopened in September, four months after the riot, as a half-dozen Green Dot schools.

"Last year, there was graffiti everywhere," Barr said. "You'd see kids everywhere—they'd be out here gambling. You'd smell weed." He recalled hearing movies playing in classroom after classroom: "People called it ghetto cineplex." Barr and Cortines walked to the quad, where the riot had started. The cracked pavement had been replaced by a lawn of thick green grass, lined with newly planted olive trees.

"It's night and day," Cortines said.

In the past decade, Barr has opened seventeen charter high schools—small, locally managed institutions that aim for a high degree of teacher autonomy and parent involvement—in some of the poorest neighborhoods in Los Angeles, as well as one in the Bronx. His charter-school group is now California's largest, by enrollment, and one of its most successful. Green Dot schools take kids who, in most cases, test far below grade level and send nearly eighty per cent of them to

---

Reprinted with author's permission. Douglas McGray is an Irvine Fellow at the New America Foundation. Article previously published in the New Yorker, *May 11, 2009.*

college. (Only forty-seven per cent of L.A.U.S.D. students graduate with a high-school diploma.) As of 2006, Green Dot's standardized-test scores were almost twenty per cent higher than L.A. Unified's average, and, adjusting for student demographics, the state Department of Education grades their performance a nine on a scale of one to ten; L.A.U.S.D. schools rate only a five.

Barr himself has a colorful reputation. He drives a decommissioned police car, a Crown Victoria with floodlights, which he bought from a friend, the former Fox executive who launched the network's reality show "Cops." ("It's faster than anything on the road," he told me, and when he wants to change lanes "people move out of the way.") He met his wife, an Alaskan radio reporter twenty years his junior, at a Burning Man festival seven years ago, and married her in Las Vegas three weeks later. And this is how he talks about working with what is arguably the country's most troubled big-city school system: "You ever see that movie 'Man on Fire,' with Denzel Washington? There's a scene in the movie where the police chief of Mexico City gets kidnapped by Denzel Washington. He wakes up, he's on the hood of his car under the underpass, in his boxers, his hands tied. Denzel Washington starts asking him questions, he's not getting the answers he wants, so he walks away from him, and leaves a bomb stuck up his ass." Barr laughed. "I don't want to blow up L.A.U.S.D.'s ass. But what will it take to get this system to serve who they need to serve? It's going to take that kind of aggressiveness."

Green Dot's ascent stems mostly from Barr's skill as an instigator and an organizer. Outrageous rhetoric is a big part of that, and it's not uncalculated. "It takes a certain amount of panache to call the head of the union a pig f*****," Ted Mitchell, the president of the California State Board of Education, said. (Those weren't Barr's words exactly.) "Steve has this 'Oh, shucks, you know me—I can't control my mouth' persona. It allows him to get away with murder." But, Mitchell points out, "he's a public curmudgeon and a private negotiator." And he has built Green Dot to be a political force unlike anything else in the world of education. For instance, Barr runs the only large charter organization in the country that has embraced unionized teachers and a collectively bargained contract—an unnecessary hassle, if his aim was to run a few schools, but a source of leverage for Green Dot's main purpose, which is to push for citywide change. "I don't see how you tip a system with a hundred per cent unionized labor without unionized labor," he said.

First period at Locke was ending. Kids swarmed the halls, shoving and laughing and posturing and flirting for every last second of their five minutes of freedom. Barr was quiet with Cortines, almost solicitous. Cortines, for his part, seemed eager for peace. After years of failed attempts to fix Locke, nobody could ignore how much Green Dot had accomplished in a matter of months.

Another fight between Barr and L.A.U.S.D. seemed inevitable, though. After Cortines left, Barr said, "Ray and I have had conversations about Fremont High School," another large troubled school, in South Los Angeles. But Cortines, he knew, was hesitant. "I've been clear that we can talk," Cortines told me later. "I can't necessarily deliver. I still think we have to look at the evidence from Locke." Data like test scores, graduation rates, and student retention won't be available until later this year.

Barr doesn't want to hear it. "Nobody can tell me that a small, autonomous, well-funded school, where the parents are involved, where accountability is put on that staff, is not the right way to go," he said. "We get along really well, but I get fucking impatient."

Cortines didn't know that Barr was already planning his next assault on the district, one he described to me as "Armageddon." He planned to target five to ten of the largest, worst-performing schools in Los Angeles, and then submit a hundred charters for new schools to be clustered around them. Then he would give the district a choice: it could either dissolve most of the central bureaucracy, and turn over hiring, firing, and spending decisions to neighborhood schools, or surrender leadership of the schools to Green Dot. If the district refused both options, Barr would open his new schools and begin stealing thousands of students, and the millions of dollars in funding that follow them. "If I take ten Locke High Schools, they can't survive," he said.

But, just weeks after Cortines's visit to Locke, Barr got a call from the new Secretary of Education, Arne Duncan. He flew to Washington, D.C., at the end of March, for what he expected to be a social visit. At the meeting, Duncan revealed that he was interested in committing several billion dollars of the education stimulus package to a Locke-style takeover and transformation of the lowest-performing one per cent of schools across the country, at least four thousand of them, in the next several years. The Department of Education would favor districts that agreed to partner with an outside group, like Green Dot. "You seem to have cracked the code," Duncan told Barr.

Duncan was interested in the fact that Barr was targeting high schools, not elementary or middle schools. "The toughest work in urban education today is what you do with large failing high schools," Duncan told me. These schools get less study and less attention from charter groups and education reformers, most of whom feel that ninth grade is too late to begin saving kids. "Teach for America, NewSchools Venture Fund, the Broad Foundation—all these folks are doing extraordinary work in public education," Duncan said. "Nobody national is turning around large failing high schools."

When Barr got back to Los Angeles, he told me, "We're being asked, 'Could you guys do five schools in L.A. next year? Could you expand beyond L.A.?' If you'd asked a month ago, 'What about Green Dot America?,' I would have said, 'No way.' But if this President wants to get after it I'm going to reconsider."

Barr opened his first school in August of 2000, at the edge of Lennox, a poor, mostly Spanish-speaking community near Los Angeles International Airport, under a landing path. The local high school, Hawthorne, was a few miles away. "Where the Beach Boys went," Barr said. "Now it's a dropout factory."

He announced plans for the school at a middle-school gymnasium crowded with families. "I told the parents, 'When you come to this school, seven thousand dollars follows you' "—the rough sum that California paid a charter school to educate a child. " 'That's your money. I will treat that like tuition.' " He promised them a school that was safe, local, and accountable. He said he'd need their help. And he gave everyone his home phone number and said that they could call him anytime. By the end of the night, he had a hundred and forty kids committed to his ninth-grade class. Suddenly, he said, "I started shaking."

"I'm standing in front of these parents, who have no money—all they have is their kids," he recalled. "And they're trusting me. I didn't have a facility yet, and I didn't have a staff. It was February, and school was opening in August. I walked out to the parking lot and threw up."

Opening a school was an unlikely move for Barr. He had done fundraising for California politicians, helped organize the Olympic-torch relay before the 1984 Summer Games, and spent three years as an on-air television reporter. He co-founded Rock the Vote, and worked on Bill Clinton's 1992 Presidential campaign. But he'd never thought much about education. In fact, he'd been a mediocre student.

Barr was born in 1959, just south of San Francisco, and lived with his mother in Monterey, near the military base, where she worked as a dental assistant and a cocktail waitress. When he was six, he and his younger brother spent a year in foster care. Later, they made their home in a trailer in Missouri, before moving back to California.

In school, Barr was a good athlete, and popular. Every teacher knew his name. His brother, Mike, was quiet and overweight. Mike tried playing in the band for a while. ("Why do you give the chubby kid a tuba?" Barr asked, sighing. "Do you know how hilarious it is seeing a chubby kid try to get on the bus with a tuba?") But soon Mike got lost in their large high school. Steve graduated, and went on to the University of California at Santa Barbara. Mike dropped out, and never really settled into an adult life. Eventually, he was in a motorcycle accident. After a series of surgeries, he lost his leg. He won a settlement, but that attracted the wrong friends. "You take a poor kid who has problems and give him a lot of money . . ." Barr said. When Barr was thirty-two, Mike died of a drug overdose. His mother died shortly afterward, and Barr began to drift.

He discovered charter schools by accident. When President Clinton went to San Carlos to visit California's first charter school, Barr tagged along, and encountered the school's founder, Don Shalvey, and a Silicon Valley businessman, Reed Hastings, who had just founded Netflix. Shalvey and Hastings were about to draw up a ballot initiative that would increase the number of charter schools in California. Barr decided to help. "He came out of nowhere," Hastings said. And he brought a very different approach. He persuaded them, for instance, to try to make peace with the California Teachers Association. "He helped us realize we were perhaps overly simplistic in demonizing the union as the enemy," Hastings said. "It turned out C.T.A. was open to a stronger charter law."

As Barr worked on the campaign, he started to think about his own years in school, and his brother's. High school, he decided, was the point where their lives diverged. When the charter-school measure passed, he broke up with his girlfriend, moved out of their apartment, gave up his convertible, and rented a decrepit place in Venice, sight unseen. He moved in on Christmas morning, to a room strewn with needles, vomit, and feces. "I'm thirty-nine, I'm alone," he said. "Merry fucking Christmas." He tied his chocolate Lab, Jerry Brown, in the corner, put on the Harry Belafonte album his mother used to play every Saturday morning, when they did chores together, and scrubbed the apartment.

A year and a half later, he opened Animo Leadership Charter High School, near Lennox. (He said that in Spanish *animo* can mean "courage" or "valor," but he prefers a Mexican surfing buddy's translation: "Get off your ass.") He hired five of his seven teachers straight out of college and rented classrooms at a night school. When one of the teachers quit in the first couple of weeks, he replaced her with his office manager. Barr worked mostly without pay for the next few years, spending the last of his savings and his brother's settlement, and doing such damage to his finances that Costco revoked his membership. He pitched in a lot himself. "Maybe the most fun I had was going to test-drive school buses," he said.

And he starting a surfing club. "There were a handful of kids at the school who were really fricking cool but weren't being reached somehow," he said. "There was a kid named Ricky. He was smart, charismatic. All the girls loved this guy. There was another girl named Stephanie, who I think had a crush on Ricky." They agreed to find twenty-five kids who would show up before school, at 6 A.M.

"We were driving to the South Bay, Manhattan Beach. It was real quiet," Barr recalled. "Halfway out there, one of the kids said, 'Mr. Barr, do you have to know how to swim to surf?'" Half the kids couldn't. Barr put his head in his hands and laughed.

"The Manhattan Beach school system, they actually have surfing in gym class, so you have all these blond-haired, blue-eyed kids in the water," Barr continued. "And here come these kids from Lennox. The Lennox surf team." He mimicked a slow, tough walk. "Their gear's a little off, you know, they're all Latino, and a couple of black kids. I remember them getting triple takes."

At the end of its first chaotic year, Barr's school beat Hawthorne High School in every measurable outcome. "When the scores come out, I have to call Shalvey"—Barr's charter-school mentor—"and ask him, 'Are they good?'" Barr said. "'Cause I don't f***** know. I don't know how to read test scores." The night school eventually moved, and Animo Leadership took over the entire campus. Last year, *U.S. News & World Report* ranked it among the top hundred public high schools in the country.

A pair of skinny Latino boys with shoulder-length hair cruised down Locke's breezeway on their skateboards. Zeus Cubias, an assistant principal, turned and glared. It was a few minutes after the last bell, and the two kids had swapped their uniform polos for black band T-shirts.

"What did I tell you? Don't act the fool," Cubias said sternly, as the boys picked up their skateboards. He turned to the taller boy. "Especially when you're wearing a Guns N' Roses shirt. Don't embarrass the shirt." The boy laughed. "Next time, I'm taking boards," Cubias said.

Cubias is compact and athletic, with floppy hair, a tidy beard, and three earrings. "I'd be doing the same thing when I was a kid," he admitted. He grew up just a few blocks down the street, and graduated from Locke, class of '92. He showed me his freshman yearbook. "Here's the Jheri Curl mullet," he said, flipping through the faces. "Ghetto business in the front, ghetto party in the back. And here's me, sporting my own mullet."

The high school opened in 1967, two years after the Watts riots. Named for Alain Leroy Locke, the country's first African-American Rhodes Scholar, it was set on a twenty-six-acre plot near the edge of the neighborhood, and was meant to be a symbol of rebirth. But by the time Cubias was a freshman, jobs and middle-class families had disappeared; the school, like the neighborhood, became infamous. Security guards with metal-detecting wands would interrupt class to spot-check boys.

As a freshman, Cubias landed in remedial and English as a Second Language classes. "I had a Spanish name," he said. Most Latinos in Watts were recent immigrants, and there were so many kids, and so few counsellors, that it was hard to keep everyone straight. Locke had grown huge. Los Angeles went more than thirty years without building a new high school, even as the city's population swelled; schools like Locke, meant for about fifteen hundred kids, doubled their enrollment, packing classrooms and erecting cheap, prefabricated units in their parking lots. Cubias ditched class a lot and got bad grades. But a substitute covering his English class thought he seemed out of place and recommended him for an honors class. When he showed up the first day, he recalled, he met a girl with black hair and *ojos tapatíos*—almond-shaped eyes—who carried a novel wherever she went. He was smitten. "I had heard about kids who read books, but they were, like, mythical," Cubias said, laughing. He asked a counsellor to give him the same class schedule as the girl, and in that instant he passed from one world to another. She took all honors classes, on her way to graduating as valedictorian.

"These poor high schools, you have an Advanced Placement track, and the teachers only believe in triage, so they put the kids who have a chance in that track," Barr explained. "It's built on the back of the other three tracks."

Cubias ended up scoring a 5 on his A.P. calculus exam, which no Locke student had ever done before, and went to the University of California at Santa Barbara. Even before he left Locke, he knew that he wanted to come back and teach there. "Now, I'm bilingual, and a math teacher, with a University of California certification," Cubias said. "In this district, I'm gold." But when he first went downtown to apply for a teaching position and said that he wanted a job at Locke he was told, "You don't have to teach there. You're qualified to teach at this place, or this place, or this place."

The interviewer thought she was doing him a favor. "These schools like Locke and Fremont and Jordan, they just get the leftovers," Cubias said. Locke would have substitutes covering unfilled teaching positions well into the school year. New hires were often uninspiring and unprepared. "Damn the day the University of Phoenix started offering teaching credentials," he added.

In the spring of 2007, a rumor spread through the school. Teachers and parents were summoned to a community meeting at the middle school down the street. The room was packed. Cubias took a seat near the front. The superintendent at the time got up to speak. He said that the district was interested in handing over leadership of Locke High School to a charter organization, Green Dot.

For Cubias, this was worse than neglect—to be abandoned by the district and relegated to some white guy he'd never met. "We'll see about that," he said.

The sudden announcement stunned United Teachers Los Angeles, the neighborhood, and Locke's staff, even the principal. Almost immediately, the superintendent began shying away from the deal. Barr had learned by now to have a backup plan ready. If the district refused to give him Locke, he'd just open a bunch of Green Dot schools in Watts and take the kids.

Green Dot had become more professional since Barr's early days at Animo Leadership. But it had also become more radical. When case-study writers from Harvard Business School asked Barr to describe the inspiration behind Green Dot's model, he didn't cite other schools; he named the Student Nonviolent Coordinating Committee. He hired an opposition researcher to investigate Green Dot and see what enemies might use against him. He started a citywide group called the Los Angeles Parents Union, an activist alternative to the Parent-Teacher Association, in the hope of mobilizing foot soldiers for Green Dot's escalating war against the district. He even put a school-board member on his payroll—"a mole," Barr said—to report back on closed meetings. Judged purely on test scores, or scholastic reputation, another group, Alliance for College-Ready Public Schools, is probably the premier charter-school-management organization in Los Angeles. "They're brilliant about academics," Barr said. But, as a political organization that happens to run great schools, Green Dot is unique.

As Barr became more political, he began to worry about the limits of the charter movement. "There's this cult around charter schools," Barr said. "They're not even close to being the answer." Opening a new school like Animo Leadership takes an enormous amount of effort and money. Barr has to find a big building in the right neighborhood, and convert it into classrooms, and fill it with new teachers and administrators, and sell the idea to parents and community leaders. This is all before any public dollars arrive. Four years after Barr started Animo Leadership, he had a nice school of about five hundred students. But that barely registered in a district with around seven hundred thousand. Barr began to covet district schools with thousands of students. (Locke had almost three thousand.) "We were trying to figure out how to get out of the charter-school business, and how to get into the helping-schools-transform business," he said.

Barr tested a new strategy at Jefferson High School, a place that is much like Locke, a few miles to the north. In 2005, over the course of a year, he met with the superintendent to try to negotiate a deal to transform the institution into a series of small autonomous schools. When talks broke down, Barr hired a field staff from the neighborhood. They worked out of a housing project across the street from the school and collected ten thousand signatures from local parents. When the district still balked, Barr gathered a thousand parents and marched to L.A.U.S.D.'s central office, towing the paperwork for five new Green Dot schools in little red wagons. Jefferson remained an L.A.U.S.D. school. But the following fall more than half of its incoming freshmen entered the lottery for a spot at one of Barr's schools. "When Green Dot was able to walk into a neighborhood, build strong coalitions with neighborhood groups, and begin to drain the school, I think that sent a shock wave through the system," Ted Mitchell, the president of the State Board of Education, said.

Barr was ready to do the same thing at Locke. "What I didn't foresee was the teachers rising up," he said. A group from the school—Zeus Cubias and a few others—sent word that they wanted a meeting. Barr agreed to meet them at a nearby community center. Fifty or sixty teachers sat on one side, in a semicircle; Barr sat alone, facing them.

"Locke is a cash cow," he explained to them. It attracted more state and federal funding than schools in richer neighborhoods—"money-that's-thrown-at-a-failed-school kind of money," he said. "According to our analysis, only about sixty per cent of that money makes it into the classroom."

A gigantic district like L.A.U.S.D. has layer upon layer of bureaucracy. Locke had two full-time employees who painted over graffiti. Bathroom monitors were contractually limited to bathroom-related supervision. Locke often came in well under budget, yet students still shared textbooks, because the surplus was locked up in some unnecessary line item. Byzantine chains of accountability made it almost impossible to isolate problems and fix them.

"There was yelling back and forth," Barr said. "A lot of the time I just sat there, let them work their shit out. A young Latino math teacher, big guy, f****** six foot five, he broke down and started crying." The teacher feared that although Green Dot might get more kids to college, the most vulnerable kids, the hardest cases, might slip away. It's a big knock against charter schools—sometimes fair, sometimes unfair—that only a traditional public school teaches all kids. "We bombarded him," Cubias said. Barr came back with the same answer again and again: "How will it be worse than what you have now?"

Even if they agreed about the district's ills, many teachers worried about Green Dot's contract. At around thirty pages, it would be only a tenth as long as their contract with L.A.U.S.D. "Union contracts are written in response to bad systems," Barr said. (A. J. Duffy, the president of United Teachers Los Angeles, counters, "Our view of a decent contract is it will provide longevity of teaching staff." Too many charter schools, he argues, churn through young teachers.) Green Dot offered no tenure and no lifetime benefits. But salaries would be about ten per cent higher; it spends more than sixty per cent of its staff budget on teacher salaries, a good deal more than L.A.U.S.D., Green Dot claims. Green Dot's union—affiliated with the statewide teachers' association rather than with the more defensive one in Los Angeles—would protect them from arbitrary dismissal. And Barr promised teachers more freedom in the classroom. At his schools, the principals lay out firm curricular guidelines, in keeping with California state standards and Green Dot benchmarks, but teachers are free to huddle, and decide what to teach and how to teach it, for the most part, as long as students pass quarterly assessments.

"After about five and a half hours, one teacher said, 'Let's face it, the only time the district comes out here is when a kid gets killed,' " Barr recalled. "Another teacher said, 'And the only time our union comes out is when Green Dot's mentioned.' Somebody said, 'What can we do?' "

Barr explained that California lawmakers had created an option for schools to abandon the district for a charter arrangement if at least fifty per cent of tenured teachers vote to secede. "We'd be interested in that," Barr said.

Barr had a stack of petition forms sent to the school. Cubias, an English teacher named Bruce Smith, and the principal, Frank Wells, began circulating them. Barr wasn't sure he had the votes. Locke's young teachers were mostly untenured and ineligible. The older faculty tended to be deeply skeptical of what Barr was selling. "A lot of these teachers have been on the front lines during the whole demise of our public education system," he said. "Now, every year or two, there's some new reform. You get reform fatigue: 'Oh, God, another God-damned bright idea from the business world.' " Out of a total tenured faculty of seventy-three, Barr needed thirty-seven votes to take the school. That meant all the eligible younger teachers and a decent number of the older ones. Smith and Wells started canvassing between bells. "It was a sneaky inside job, but there was no other way to do it," Smith said.

District administrators were furious. They sent school police to find Wells and escort him off school property. But it was too late: Barr's allies had the signatures. Two days later, television crews gathered across the street for a press conference. Kids milled around and stared. Smith sneaked into a bathroom to write a speech. "I've got security guards carrying walkie-talkies, saying, 'He's walking down the hall,' " Smith recalled. "I'm pretty nervous." He hid in a stall, and scribbled notes for his remarks on an index card: "Do what we're doing: take back your schools."

Within days, the district and the teachers' union counterattacked. "To take over a whole school—it was scandalous!" Karen Wickhorst, a French teacher and, at the time, a site representative for United Teachers Los Angeles, recently recalled. "A big public school! It was so underhanded."

The district banned Barr from the school and summoned teachers to a meeting. Duffy, the union president, and the district's regional administrator addressed the teachers. "They scared the shit out of everyone," Barr said. Seventeen teachers revoked their signatures.

Barr set up a war room at Green Dot's offices. He wrote the number "17" on a whiteboard. Organizers mapped out the teachers who had rescinded their votes—their issues, their biases—as well as new teachers they might swing. "It was like chasing down Senate votes," Barr said. He got up at five, and met teachers at a doughnut shop before school. He went to their houses for dinner, and showed up at church on Sunday. Allies would sneak him onto the school grounds through a back gate, and he'd hold court in a gym teacher's office.

They got all seventeen votes back—but not one more. And Barr began to look ahead. "After the press conference, a dozen different schools contacted me," he said. They were ready to lead their own insurrections. "If I'd been prepared, I could have run the table," Barr said.

Some of his closest confidants, though, worried that even one big high school might be too many. "Most people around him, including me, said, 'Oh, man, Locke is going to kill you,' " Reed Hastings, of Netflix, said. "Creating new schools is easy politics. It's ribbon-cutting, it's new opportunities. Taking over a school—it's district property, those are union jobs. I was afraid he would put in a lot of effort and not succeed. Or he'd get the conversion done and the difficulty of running the school would overwhelm him. And if he did a bad job it would be a black mark for everyone."

A tall girl, her hair pulled back tightly in a ponytail, reached up to tape a bright hand-painted poster ("Valentines Day Candygrams") above a row of lockers.

"You're showing your butt crack," a boy walking by said.

"So? Everyone has one."

"I don't."

"Idiot." She rolled her eyes. The boy looked back over his shoulder and grinned.

Locke's hallways are now filled with these handmade signs—for dances, tryouts, movie nights, college tours. They used to be banned; kids would vandalize them. Instead, there was graffiti. "Everywhere you walked," Shannan Burrell, a junior, said. "About six out of ten, it was gang tags."

Shannan is curvy and baby-faced, with rosy brown skin. Her hair was in a bright-purple wrap. She lived nearby, with her mother, in a yellow house, close enough to walk to school in the morning (keeping quiet, looking straight ahead) but outside Locke's immediate neighborhood, which was a good thing. "It's dirty," she said. "Gangbangers out 24/7." She wears a necklace that spells out the name "Jerome" in curling, glittering script. He was her best friend, before he was shot and killed around the corner, when she was in ninth grade. "It was random," she said softly. "He was a schoolboy, for real."

When she entered Locke, three years ago, she liked it. "It was fun—wandering around the halls, around the campus," she said. "Just wilding out." She'd drop into classroom after classroom, looking for friends. "Like 'Come outside real quick,' " she said, laughing. "Quick" usually meant for the rest of class. "And we wouldn't just go to our lunch—we'd go to all of them," she said. "Why are we going to go to class if nobody ever says nothing?" But in her sophomore year she started getting in fights. "I felt like, at Locke, you have to earn your reputation," she explained. "And I earned mine, after like my third fight. But then, after that, it seemed like girls wanted to challenge me. So it got worse." She fought once or twice a week. Her grades were terrible.

She was eating with the football players, in the shade of the quad's only tree, when the riot began. Suddenly, everyone around her was fighting. A boy she'd never seen before punched her. "I wanted to cry, bad," she said. "But it ain't inside me to cry." Instead, she fought back. A few weeks later, she left her mother's house and moved in with her adult sister, about an hour away. But in the fall she decided to go back to Locke. She'd heard that there were going to be changes.

Old-timers and union loyalists who left Locke after the takeover insisted that Green Dot would find a way to weed out problem kids. Others, such as Cubias, worried that uniforms and the promise of tougher discipline would simply keep bad kids away. But teachers and administrators went out into the neighborhood to visit hundreds of parents and students and encourage them to reënroll. Eighty-five per cent of Locke students returned. (In a normal year, only seventy per cent would come back from summer break.) That meant hundreds more than either Green Dot or the city had projected.

"When I got to school, I was laughing at everyone else—I was, like, 'Ha, you got on a uniform,' " Shannan said. "They're, like, 'Ha, you got on a uniform, too!' " Green Dot split the incoming ninth grade into five new small schools, like the schools around Jefferson. Three of them ended up in buildings off campus; the other two were in Locke's prefabricated units, walled off by tall black fences. Then they split the upper three grades into two academies, one for each wing of Locke's original building. Each school had its own bell schedule, its own lunch period, its own entrance, and its own color polo shirt. Shannan drew white.

Locke's teachers were all dismissed and asked to reapply. Only about thirty per cent got their jobs back. Shannan's English teacher, Mr. Sully, was one of them. "He just, he a nice teacher," she said. "He keep you on your toes. If you ain't doing something, he'll make you do something." Dozens of kids told me this—that teachers make them do stuff now, whether they want to or not. Almost immediately, Shannan stopped ditching. For one thing, she couldn't get away with it anymore. ("They don't play," she said.) She stopped fighting, too.

Sully passed a new novel out to Shannan's class—"a book called 'The Bluest Eye,' " Shannan said. She was unimpressed with the cover and the first page. "I was like, 'Mr. Sully, this book about to be stooopid.' And he said, 'What did I say?' And I said, 'O.K., I won't use "stupid," but this book is about to be not interesting.' He sat me down and had a strong conversation with me." She agreed to give it a few pages. Then the character Claudia, a fighter, made her first appearance. "I hear her talk about beating up a girl name Rosemary, a little white girl. I was like, 'Oh, I'm going to read this!' " She giggled. "It's turned out to be a good book," she said. "That's the funny thing."

"There is no secret curriculum-and-instruction sauce at Green Dot at all," Don Shalvey said. "Steve hires good people. They're just doing old-school schooling."

Shannan doesn't like every class. Physics, she said, is boring. So is a test-preparation and college-readiness class, mandatory for most Green Dot students. But she tries to do the work now. When I asked her why, she thought about it for a long time. "Honestly, it didn't matter how you did before," she said. "Wasn't nobody really looking at Locke kids"—meaning to go to college. That's not true, of course, but it felt true to Shannan. "Now, if I make a bad grade, I'm like, 'Please, can I make it up?' "

There are problems that Green Dot can't fix on its own, however. According to Cubias, at least forty per cent of Locke's students come from single-parent households. "Another fifteen per cent are in foster care," he said. Green Dot requires parents to get involved at school, a minimum of thirty-five hours a year, but they can't make every parent a good influence. (Recently, after a girl tangled with a classmate, an assistant principal called the girl's mother, and when the woman showed up she started screaming at the other student.) Security can stop neighborhood gangs from tagging the halls or hoisting couches up to Locke's roof, which was a hangout last year, but they can't keep gangs out of kids' lives.

I made plans to attend classes with Shannan the next day, but when I arrived at her first-period class, English with Mr. Sully, she wasn't there. I called her house after school. The phone line was dead. (Her mother, a quiet, serious woman, has been out of work for at least two years. Her father has been in jail since around the time Shannan was a toddler.) When we finally talked, her voice was so flat that I didn't recognize it.

"I'm not going to be in school this week," she said. "I have to take care of family business."

"Did someone get hurt?" I asked.

"Yes."

"Was it a car accident or something?"

"Much worse," she said. "It's not something I want to talk about." Several days passed before she returned to classes.

There remain problems to address inside Locke, too. Fall semester was difficult. "We made so many mistakes," Cubias said. September was almost wholly devoted to coping with the crush of unexpected students. Administrators struggled to find good teachers who were still on the job market. Clubs and activities suffered. "It's hard to see incremental changes," a new principal, Veronica Coleman, said. "That turned into some low-level frustration for both students and teachers."

Sully told me that Locke is significantly calmer, and administrators are more present. And Green Dot got rid of the teachers who did little for students. But the takeover also chased away some good, experienced staff. Locke's overwhelmingly new and mostly young faculty members are learning how to work together. Sully still has problems with chronic truancy. He still sees kids out of uniform. And when Locke's test scores, their first since the takeover, come back this fall they are almost certain to be the lowest among Barr's schools. Sully guesses that the school might see a small bounce, but anything more than that would surprise him. Kids in Locke's upper grades have spent as many as three years in one of the city's worst academic environments. And, for the first time at a Green Dot school, there is no lottery process for admission. There is no waiting list. Locke is serving every kid in the neighborhood, including ones whose parents, in another neighborhood, would never research alternatives to the big traditional school. "Every child who is in his other schools is there because they have an advocate," Cortines said. "Not so at Locke. They took the whole population."

Even security remains a challenge. Green Dot blanketed the schoolyard with guards from a private security firm, club-bouncer burly, carrying handguns and pepper spray. Gangs have nowhere near the profile they once did, and fights, once a daily occurrence, are rare. Still, in mid-April, a student was shot, across the street, just before first period. And guards have occasionally displayed a heavy hand. Twice this year, they pepper-sprayed students; in both cases, Cubias said, they should have been able to cool the kids down before it came to that, but they were trained to secure facilities, not to supervise adolescents.

Yet, when I wandered around campus during lunch periods and between classes, looking for disgruntled kids, I never found any.

"The whole atmosphere is different," a Latino boy, sketching graffiti in a notebook, said. "The teachers pay more attention to you."

"You actually get through the lessons you're supposed to get through," Jamie, an African-American girl with straightened swept-back hair, said, as she picked at French fries with her friend Andrea.

"I noticed that, too," Andrea said.

"Last year, my grades got so bad—I got four D's! My will to get good grades improved," Jamie said.

"Will Locke be perfect?" Cortines asked. "I don't care. If they make mistakes, they'll find a way to do things differently. What we do in regular schools is keep doing the same thing, even if it doesn't work."

Barr is always talking about "the tribes." Union leaders and reformers, in his view, spend too much time fighting one another instead of finding common interests. Charter groups and unions agree on limiting central bureaucracy, giving teachers fewer students and more freedom, and concentrating funds in the classroom, but they mostly go at each other over tenure and the right to unionize. Ultimately, Barr's project isn't about fixing one broken school; he thinks he can resolve that impasse. His grander ambitions, as much as Green Dot's experience in Watts, are what brought him to Arne Duncan's office in March.

Duncan asked Barr what it would take to break up and remake thousands of large failing schools. "One, you have to reconstitute," Barr told him—that is, fire everyone and make them reapply or transfer elsewhere in the district. "Arne didn't seem to flinch at that," he said. "Second, if we can figure out a national union partnership, we can take away some of the opposition." Duncan asked Barr if he could persuade Randi Weingarten, the president of the American Federation of Teachers, to support the idea. "I'd love to do that," she told Barr, but she also expressed concerns. "She said, 'I can't be seen as coming in and firing all these teachers.' " So they talked about alternatives, like transferring teachers or using stimulus money for buyouts.

Cortines has also agreed in principle to a partnership in Los Angeles. "We'll find out very quickly what he thinks a partnership is," Barr said. "I think a partnership is Locke, period." Federal money, Barr noted, and an alliance with the national union "will force Mr. Duffy"—the U.T.L.A. president—"to come along." Green Dot could take over as many as five Los Angeles schools in 2010, and maybe more.

This month, Barr expects to meet again with Weingarten and her staff and outline plans for a Green Dot America, a national school-turnaround partnership between Green Dot and the A.F.T. Their first city would most likely be Washington, D.C. "If we're successful there, we'll get the attention of a lot of lawmakers," Barr said.

There are risks for Barr in this kind of expansion. It will be months, and maybe years, before there's hard evidence about what Green Dot has accomplished at Locke. And that one takeover put a real strain on the organization. "If they were to take over another high school in Los Angeles, they could handle that," Steve Seleznow, the deputy director of education for the Gates Foundation, said. "I'm not sure they have the capacity to do five at once." Then he paused. "I'm sure Steve has the *appetite* for it," he added, and laughed. Barr's impatience and his willingness to overextend himself are a bigger part of Green Dot's institutional culture than any theory of education.

In the meantime, Barr and his supporters continue to campaign. On a recent morning, outside 135th Street Elementary School, in Gardena, near Watts, a gregarious woman with a streak of gray through her black curls, wearing a Los Angeles Parents Union sweatshirt, passed a sheet of paper to a young Latino man in a Sears Appliance Repair jacket. He was accompanied by two little girls with matching Hannah Montana backpacks. "Would you like to sign a petition to transform Perry Middle School and Gardena High School?" she asked. She waved down a car that showed no sign of stopping, and bent over at the window when it did. "Do you have time to sign my petition to transform Perry Middle School and Gardena High School?" she asked. Immediately, the driver pulled over. Organizers are now in many neighborhoods, targeting elementary schools, telling parents that they have time to blow up and rebuild their middle schools and high schools before their kids enroll.

Everyone signed up. It's like that whenever she goes out. "People know something is wrong," she told me. "But they think it's their kids. Or it's their neighborhood. Or it's because they're poor. If we have to, we'll build a whole bunch of little charters around the school and take the students," the woman said, loud enough for half the block to hear. "We're going to get the change one way or another."

Education Chief to Warn Advocates That Inferior Charter Schools Harm the Effort

By Sam Dillon
June 22, 2009

The Obama administration has made opening more charter schools a big part of its plans for improving the nation's education system, but Education Secretary Arne Duncan will warn advocates of the schools on Monday that low-quality institutions are giving their movement a black eye.

"The charter movement is putting itself at risk by allowing too many second-rate and third-rate schools to exist," Mr. Duncan says in prepared remarks that he is scheduled to deliver in Washington at the annual gathering of the National Alliance for Public Charter Schools.

In an interview, Mr. Duncan said he would use the address to praise innovations made by high-quality charter schools, urge charter leaders to become more active in weeding out bad apples in their movement and invite the leaders to help out in the administration's broad effort to remake several thousand of the nation's worst public schools.

Since 1991, when educators founded the first charter school in Minnesota, 4,600 have opened; they now educate some 1.4 million of the nation's 50 million public school students, according to Education Department figures. The schools are financed with taxpayer money but operate free of many curricular requirements and other regulations that apply to traditional public schools.

Mr. Duncan's speech will come at a pivotal moment for the charter school movement. The Obama administration has been working to persuade state legislatures to lift caps on the number of charter schools.

At the same time, the movement is smarting from the release last week of a report by Stanford University researchers that found that although some charter schools were doing an excellent job, many students in charter schools were not faring as well as students in traditional public schools.

"The charter movement is one of the most profound changes in American education, bringing tremendous new options to underserved communities," Mr. Duncan is to say in the speech, the text of which was provided to The New York Times by his advisers.

But, the speech says, states should scrutinize plans for new charter schools to allow only high-quality ones to open. In exchange for the autonomy that states extend to charter schools, states should demand "absolute, unequivocal accountability," the speech says, and close charter schools that fail to lift student achievement.

Mr. Duncan's speech calls the Stanford report—which singles out Arizona, Florida, Minnesota, New Mexico, Ohio and Texas as states that have done little to hold poorly run charter schools accountable—"a wake-up call."

"Charter authorizers need to do a better job of holding schools accountable," the speech says. (Mr. Duncan is to note exceptions like the California Charter Schools Association, which last week announced a plan to establish and enforce academic performance standards for charter schools.)

The Stanford study, by the Center for Research on Education Outcomes, used student achievement data from 15 states and the District of Columbia to gauge whether students who attended charter schools had fared better than they would if they had attended a traditional public school.

"The study reveals that a decent fraction of charter schools, 17 percent, provide superior education opportunities for their students," the report says. "Nearly half of the charter schools nationwide have results that are no different from the local public school options, and over a third, 37 percent, deliver learning results that are significantly worse than their students would have realized had they remained in traditional public schools."

Reports on charter schools often arouse impassioned debates, because charter schools in some cities have drawn millions of dollars in taxpayer money away from traditional public schools, and because many operate with nonunion teachers. The Stanford study was no exception; some charter school advocates asserted that it was slanted to favor traditional public schools.

Nelson Smith, president of the charter school alliance, said that the authors of the Stanford study could have phrased their findings more positively, with no loss of accuracy, but that he considered the center a "very credible outfit" and its director, Margaret Raymond, "an esteemed researcher."

Mr. Smith praised the administration's efforts to increase financing for charter school startups.

"To a remarkable extent, they are walking the walk," he said. "They've been very clear on the need to stimulate the growth of quality charters."

Mr. Duncan has been working to build a national effort to restructure 5,000 chronically failing public schools, which turn out middle school students who cannot read and most of the nation's high school dropouts. In his speech, he will urge states, school districts, nonprofit groups, teachers' unions and charter organizations "to get in the business of turning around our lowest-performing schools."

"Over the coming years," the speech says, "America needs to find 5,000 high-energy, hero principals to take over these struggling schools, and a quarter of a million great teachers who are willing to do the toughest work in public education."

Mr. Smith said he believed that some charter school operators would react favorably to Mr. Duncan's call, but only if they were given flexibility over hiring and firing teachers, structuring student learning time and other issues.

"They have to be able to maintain the integrity of the charter model," Mr. Smith said.

Center for Research on Educational Outcomes

Multiple Choice: Charter School Performance in 16 States

INTRODUCTION

As charter schools play an increasingly central role in education reform agendas across the United States, it becomes more important to have current and comprehensible analysis about how well they do educating their students. Thanks to progress in student data systems and regular student achievement testing, it is possible to examine student learning in charter schools and compare it to the experience the students would have had in the traditional public schools (TPS) they would otherwise have attended. This report presents a longitudinal student-level analysis of charter school impacts on more than 70 percent of the students in charter schools in the United States. The scope of the study makes it the first national assessment of charter school impacts.

Charter schools are permitted to select their focus, environment and operations and wide diversity exists across the sector. This study provides an overview that aggregates charter schools in different ways to examine different facets of their impact on student academic growth.

The group portrait shows wide variation in performance. The study reveals that a decent fraction of charter schools, 17 percent, provide superior education opportunities for their students. Nearly half of the charter schools nationwide have results that are no different from the local public school options and over a third, 37 percent, deliver learning results that are significantly worse than their student would have realized had they remained in traditional public schools. These findings underlie the parallel findings of significant state-by-state differences in charter school performance and in the national aggregate performance of charter schools. The policy challenge is how to deal constructively with varying levels of performance today and into the future.

PROJECT APPROACH

CREDO has partnered with 15 states and the District of Columbia to consolidate longitudinal student-level achievement data for the purposes of creating a national pooled analysis of the impact of charter schooling on student learn-

---

"Multiple Choice: Charter School Performance in 16 States, June 2009 Report." Center For Research on Education Outcomes (CREDO).

ing gains. For each charter school student, a virtual twin is created based on students who match the charter student's demographics, English language proficiency and participation in special education or subsidized lunch programs. Virtual twins were developed for 84 percent of all the students in charter schools. The resulting matched longitudinal comparison is used to test whether students who attend charter schools fare better than if they had instead attended traditional public schools in their community. The outcome of interest is academic learning gains in reading and math, measured in standard deviation units. Student academic learning gains on reading and math state achievement tests were examined in three ways: a pooled nationwide analysis of charter school impacts, a state-by-state analysis of charter school results, and an examination of the performance of charter schools against their local alternatives.

In all cases, the outcome of interest is the magnitude of student learning that occurs in charter school students compared to their traditional public school virtual twins. Each analysis looks at the impact of a variety of factors on charter school student learning: the state where the student resides, the school's grade-span, the student's background, time in charter schools, and a number of policy characteristics of the charter school environment.

SUMMARY OF FINDINGS

Charter school performance is a complex and difficult matter to assess. Each of the three analyses revealed distinct facets of charter school performance. In increasing levels of aggregation, from the head-to-head comparisons within communities to the pooled national analysis, the results are presented below.

When the effect of charter schools on student learning is compared to the experience the students would have realized in their local traditional public schools, the result can be graphed in a point-in-time Quality Curve that relates the average math growth in each charter school to the performance their students would have realized in traditional public schools in their immediate community, as measured by the experience of their virtual twins. The Quality Curve displays the distribution of individual charter school performance relative to their TPS counterparts. A score of "0" means there is no difference between the charter school performance and that of their TPS comparison group. More positive values indicate increasingly better performance of charters relative to traditional public school effects and negative values indicate that charter school effects are worse than what was observed for the traditional public school effects.

Charter School Market Fixed Effects Quality Curve

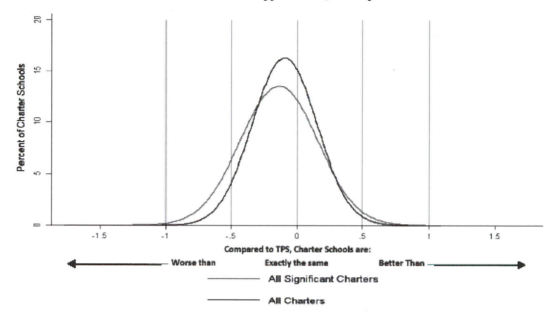

The Quality Curve results are sobering:

- Of the 2403 charter schools reflected on the curve, 46 percent of charter schools have math gains that are statistically indistinguishable from the average growth among their TPS comparisons.
- Charters whose math growth exceeded their TPS equivalent growth by a significant amount account for 17 percent of the total.
- The remaining group, 37 percent of charter schools, posted math gains that were significantly below what their students would have seen if they enrolled in local traditional public schools instead.

The state-by-state analysis showed the following:

- The effectiveness of charter schools was found to vary widely by state. The variation was over and above existing differences among states in their academic results.

  States with significantly higher learning gains for charter school students than would have occurred in traditional schools include:

  o Arkansas
  o Colorado (Denver)
  o Illinois (Chicago)

> o Louisiana
> o Missouri

The gains in growth ranged from .02 Standard deviations in Illinois (Chicago) to .07 standard deviations in Colorado (Denver).

States that demonstrated lower average charter school student growth than their peers in traditional schools included:

> o Arizona
> o Florida
> o Minnesota
> o New Mexico
> o Ohio
> o Texas

In this group, the marginal shift ranged from −.01 in Arizona to −.06 standard deviations in Ohio.

Four states had mixed results or were no different than the gains for traditional school peers:

> o California
> o District of Columbia
> o Georgia
> o North Carolina

- The academic success of charter school students was found to be affected by the contours of the charter policies under which their schools operate.
- States that have limits on the number of charter schools permitted to operate, known as caps, realize significantly lower academic growth than states without caps, around .03 standard deviations.
- States that empower multiple entities to act as charter school authorizers realize significantly lower growth in academic learning in their students, on the order of −.08 standard deviations. While more research is needed into the causal mechanism, it appears that charter school operators are able to identify and choose the more permissive entity to provide them oversight.
- Where state charter legislation provides an avenue for appeals of adverse decisions on applications or renewals, students realize a small but significant gain in learning, about .02 standard deviations.

To put variation in state results in context, the average charter school gains in reading and math were plotted against the 2007 4th Grade NAEP state averages. The position of the states relative to the national NAEP average and relative to average learning gains tees up important questions about school quality in general and charter school quality specifically.

Charter Growth Compared to 2007 NAEP State by State—Reading

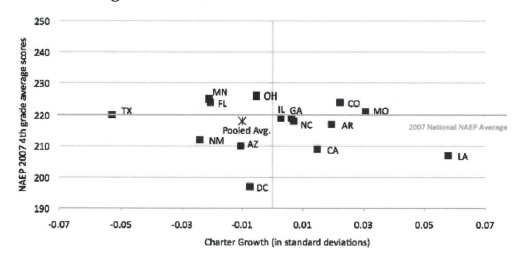

Charter Growth Compared to 2007 NAEP Score by State—Math

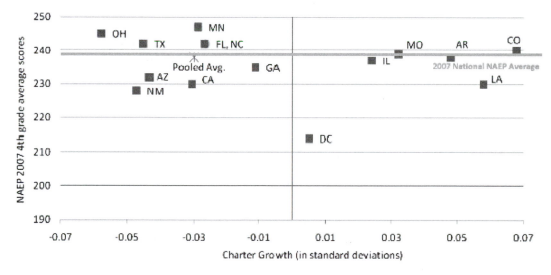

The analysis of total charter school effects, pooled student-level data from all of the participating states and examined the aggregate effect of charter schools on student learning. The national pooled analysis of charter school impacts showed the following results:

- Charter school students on average see a decrease in their academic growth in reading of .01 standard deviations compared to their traditional school peers. In math, their learning lags by .03 standard deviations on average. While the magnitude of these effects is small, they are both statistically significant.
- The effects for charter school students are consistent across the spectrum of starting positions. In reading, charter school learning gains are smaller for all students but those whose starting scores are in the lowest or highest deciles. For math, the effect is consistent across the entire range.
- Charter students in elementary and middle school grades have significantly higher rates of learning than their peers in traditional public schools, but students in charter high schools and charter multi-level schools have significantly worse results.
- Charter schools have different impacts on students based on their family backgrounds. For Blacks and Hispanics, their learning gains are significantly worse than that of their traditional school twins. However, charter schools are found to have better academic growth results for students in poverty. English Language Learners realize significantly better learning gains in charter schools. Students in Special Education programs have about the same outcomes.
- Students do better in charter schools over time. First year charter students on average experience a decline in learning, which may reflect a combination of mobility effects and the experience of a charter school in its early years. Second and third years in charter schools see a significant reversal to positive gains.

POLICY IMPLICATIONS

As of 2009, more than 4700 charter schools enroll over 1.4 million children in 40 states and the District of Columbia. The ranks of charters grow by hundreds each year. Even so, more than 365,000 names linger on charter school wait lists[1]. After more than fifteen years, there is no doubt that both supply and demand in the charter sector are strong.

In some ways, however, charter schools are just beginning to come into their own. Charter schools have become a rallying cry for education reformers

---

[1]National Alliance for Public Charter Schools As of June 3, 2009: http://www.publiccharters.org/aboutschools/benefits

across the country, with every expectation that they will continue to figure prominently in national educational strategy in the months and years to come. And yet, this study reveals in unmistakable terms that, in the aggregate, charter students are not faring as well as their TPS counterparts. Further, tremendous variation in academic quality among charters is the norm, not the exception. The problem of quality is the most pressing issue that charter schools and their supporters face. The study findings reported here give the first wide-angle view of the charter school landscape in the United States. It is the first time a sufficiently large body of student-level data has been compiled to create findings that could be considered "national" in scope. More important, they provide a broad common yardstick to support on-going conversations about quality and performance. For the first time, the dialog about charter school quality can be married to empirical evidence about performance. Further development of performance measures in forums like the Building Charter School Quality initiative could be greatly enhanced with complementary multi-state analysis such as this first report.

It is important to note that the news for charter schools has some encouraging facets. In our nationally pooled sample, two subgroups fare better in charters than in the traditional system: students in poverty and ELL students. This is no small feat. In these cases, our numbers indicate that charter students who fall into these categories are outperforming their TPS counterparts in both reading and math. These populations, then, have clearly been well served by the introduction of charters into the education landscape. These findings are particularly heartening for the charter advocates who target the most challenging educational populations or strive to improve education options in the most difficult communities. Charter schools that are organized around a mission to teach the most economically disadvantaged students in particular seem to have developed expertise in serving these communities. We applaud their efforts, and recommend that schools or school models demonstrating success be further studied with an eye toward the notoriously difficult process of replication. Further, even for student subgroups in charters that had aggregate learning gains lagging behind their TPS peers, the analysis revealed charter schools in at least one state that demonstrated positive academic growth relative to TPS peers. These higher performers also have lessons to share that could improve the performance of the larger community of charters schools.

The flip-side of this insight should not be ignored either. Students not in poverty and students who are not English language learners on average do notably worse than the same students who remain in the traditional public school system. Additional work is needed to determine the reasons underlying this phenomenon. Perhaps these students are "off-mission" in the schools they attend. Perhaps they are left behind in otherwise high-performing charter schools, or perhaps these findings are a reflection of a large pool of generally underperforming schools. Whatever the reason, the policy community needs to be aware of this dichotomy, and greater attention should be paid to the large number of students not being well served in charter schools.

In addition, we know now that first year charter students suffer a sharp decline in academic growth. Equipped with this knowledge, charter school operators can perhaps take appropriate steps to mitigate or reverse this "first year effect." Despite promising results in a number of states and within certain subgroups, the overall findings of this report indicate a disturbing—and far-reaching—subset of poorly performing charter schools. If the charter school movement is to flourish, or indeed to deliver on promises made by proponents, a deliberate and sustained effort to increase the proportion of high quality schools is essential. The replication of successful school models is one important element of this effort. On the other side of the equation, however, authorizers must be willing and able to fulfill their end of the original charter school bargain: accountability in exchange for flexibility. When schools consistently fail, they should be closed.

Though simple in formulation, this task has proven to be extremely difficult in practice. Simply put, neither market mechanisms nor regulatory oversight been a sufficient force to deal with underperforming schools. At present there appears to be an authorizing crisis in the charter school sector. For a number of reasons—many of them understandable—authorizers find it difficult to close poorly performing schools. Despite low test scores, failing charter schools often have powerful and persuasive supporters in their communities who feel strongly that shutting down *this* school does not serve the best interests of currently enrolled students. Evidence of financial insolvency or corrupt governance structure, less easy to dispute or defend, is much more likely to lead to school closures than poor academic performance. And yet, as this report demonstrates, the apparent reluctance of authorizers to close underperforming charters ultimately reflects poorly on charter schools as a whole. More importantly, it hurts students.

Charter schools are already expected to maintain transparency with regard to their operations and academic records, giving authorizers full access. We propose that authorizers be expected to do the same. True accountability demands that the public know the status of each school in an authorizer's portfolio, and that we be able to gauge authorizer performance just as authorizers currently gauge charter performance. To this end, we suggest the adoption of a national set of performance metrics, collected uniformly by all authorizers in order to provide a common base line by which we can compare the performance of charter schools and actions of authorizers across state lines. Using these metrics, Authorizer Report Cards would provide full transparency and put pressure on authorizers to act in clear cases of failure.

The charter school movement to date has concentrated its formidable resources and energy on removing barriers to charter school entry into the market. It is time to concentrate equally on removing the barriers to exit.

Charter Schools Pass Key Test in Study

By John Hechinger and Ianthe Jeanne Dugan
September 22, 2009

New York City students who win a lottery to enroll in charter schools outperform those who don't win spots and go on to attend traditional schools, according to new research to be released Tuesday.

The study, led by Stanford University economics Prof. Caroline Hoxby, is likely to fire up the movement to push states and school districts to expand charter schools—one of the centerpieces of President Barack Obama's education strategy.

Among students who had spent their academic careers in charter schools, the average eighth grader in Ms. Hoxby's study had a state mathematics test score of 680, compared with 650 for those in traditional schools. The tests are generally scored on a roughly 500 to 800 scale, with 650 representing proficiency.

Ms. Hoxby's study found that the charter-school students, who tend to come from poor and disadvantaged families, scored almost as well as students in the affluent Scarsdale school district in the suburbs north of the city. The English test results showed a similar pattern. The study also found students were more likely to earn a state Regents diploma, given to higher-achieving students, the longer they attended charter schools.

This year, the Renaissance Charter School in Queens and the Democracy Prep Charter School in Harlem each had 1,500 applicants for 80 seats. Rennaissance co-principal Stacey Gauthier says 90% of students achieve proficiency in the state test and end up going to college. "We have to perform well or we lose our charter," she says. "It makes us step up our game."

Randi Weingarten, president of the American Federation of Teachers, argued that New York City's charter schools aren't representative of the nation's, because the state caps charter schools and agencies vet them thoroughly before authorizing them, assuring they are of higher quality than elsewhere.

Charter schools are publicly funded schools, typically with nonunion teachers, that are granted more freedom by states in curriculum and hiring, and are often promoted as a way to turn around failing schools.

Critics of charter schools have long argued that any higher test scores were not necessarily attributable to anything the schools were doing, but to the students themselves, on the premise that only the most motivated students and families elected charters. Ms. Hoxby's study sought to address that argument by comparing students who attend charters directly with similarly motivated students—those who sought to attend charters but were denied a seat through a random lottery. She concluded the charters did have a positive effect.

Charter supporters, including many conservatives, have often cited the school-choice research of Ms. Hoxby, a well-known economist who is also a fellow at Stanford's right-leaning Hoover Institution.

New York City's 99 charter schools are concentrated in poorer neighborhoods such as Harlem and the South Bronx. Some 30,000 students attend and another 40,000 are on waiting lists—a small fraction of the 1.1 million students in the nation's largest school district.

Ms. Hoxby's study noted a strong correlation between achievement and charter programs with the following practices: a longer school day, merit pay for teachers and a disciplinary policy that punishes small infractions and rewards courtesy.

"We want to make New York City the Silicon Valley of charter schools," says schools Chancellor Joel Klein, who supports lifting statewide caps. "This study shows that when districts aren't antagonistic to charter schools, and instead welcome them, the results are very powerful."

But Ms. Weingarten, the union leader, cited another study this year from the Center for Research on Education Outcomes—also at Stanford—that looked at charters in 16 states and found that half did no better than traditional schools, and more than a third performed worse.

Pierina Arias, an Ecuadorean immigrant, turned to the Renaissance charter after her twins were rejected by a private school because they didn't speak English. "I was crying," says Ms. Arias. "I didn't know what to do." The twins won charter admission in a lottery, recently graduated with honors and are both in college, she says.

Patricia Hesselbach won a place in Democracy Prep's lottery for her 14-year-old daughter, Ayanna Mason, now a ninth grader. She had been at a traditional public school and needed to take outside courses to keep up with such basics as reading, her mother says. At Democracy Prep, Ms. Hasselbach says, her daughter is thriving. "They hold them to high expectations, and make sure they have discipline and dedication," Ms. Hesselbach says.

But Cynthia Lee, a hospital manager in Harlem, entered ten lotteries to get her 13-year-old daughter into Democracy Prep and didn't win a place. So, the single mother enrolled her daughter in a Catholic school for $3,100 a year. "I had no choice," she says. "I'd rather pay every last dime than put her in a public school."

New York City's Charter Schools Evaluation Project

How New York City's Charter Schools Affect Achievement

The New York City Charter Schools Evaluation Project is a multi-year study in which nearly all of the city's charter schools are participating. This is the second report in the study and analyzes achievement and other data from the 2000-01 school year up through the 2007-08 school year. The next report in the study will analyze achievement up through the 2008-09 school year. The previous report (July 2007) and a technical report may be downloaded from the following site: www.nber.org/~schools/charterschoolseval.

This *report* (August 2009) analyzes the achievement of 93 percent of the New York City charter school students who were enrolled in test-taking grades (grades 3 through 12) in 2000-01 through 2007-08. The remaining students are not covered by this report for one of two reasons. 5 percent of charter school students in test-taking grades were enrolled in schools that opened from 2006-07 onwards. Their achievement will be covered by the next report of the New York City Charter Schools Evaluation Project. 2 percent of charter school students in test-taking grades were enrolled in schools that declined to participate in the study.

The most distinctive feature of the study is that charter schools' effects on achievement are estimated by the best available, "gold standard" method: lotteries. 94 percent of charter school students in New York City are admitted to a school after having participated in a random lottery for school places. This is because the city's charter schools are required to hold lotteries whenever there are more applicants than places, and the charter schools are routinely oversubscribed. In a lottery-based study like this one, each charter school's applicants are randomly divided into the "lotteried-in" (who attend charter schools) and the "lotteried-out" (who remain in the regular public schools. These two groups of students are essentially identical at the time of the lottery. They are not identical just on dimensions that we can readily observe, such as race, ethnicity, gender, poverty, limited English, and disability. They are also identical on dimensions that we cannot readily observe like motivation and their family's interest in education. The lotteried-in and lotteried-out students who participated in the same lottery are identical on these subtle dimensions because *they all applied* to the charter school. They are separated only by a random number.

We follow the progress of lotteried-in and lotteried-out students. We compute the effect that charter schools have on their students' achievement by com-

Hoxby, Caroline M., Sonali Murarka, and Jenny Kang. "How New York City's Charter Schools Affect Achievement, August 2009 Report." Second report in series. Cambridge, MA: New York City Charter Schools Evaluation Project, September 2009.

paring the lotteried-in students to their lotteried-out counterparts. This is a true "apples-to-apples" comparison. Lottery-based studies are scientific and reliable. There are no other methods of studying the achievement of charter school students that have reliability that is "in the same ballpark" (details below).

The New York City Charter Schools Evaluation Project reports on the city's charter schools *in the aggregate*. We do not identify individual charter schools with their individual results. However, we do describe the variation in charter schools' performance in this report, and we show the association between charter schools' policies and their effects on achievement. In general, it is important to remember that charter schools differ, and no charter school is a mirror image of the aggregate results.

The New York City Charter Schools Evaluation Project is funded by a grant from the Institute for Education Sciences, which is the research arm of the United States Department of Education. The study would not be possible without the generous cooperation and help of the New York City Department of Education, the New York City Charter School Center, and the charter schools located in New York City. More information about the project may be found in the Frequently Asked Questions.

EXECUTIVE SUMMARY

The distinctive feature of this study is that charter schools' effects on achievement are estimated by the best available, "gold standard" method: lotteries. 94 percent of charter school students in New York City are admitted to a school after having participated in a random lottery for school places. In a lottery-based study like this one, each charter school's applicants are randomly divided into the "lotteried-in" (who attend charter schools) and the "lotteried-out" (who remain in the regular public schools). These two groups of students are identical not just on dimensions that we can readily observe, such as race, ethnicity, gender, poverty, limited English, and disability. They are also identical on dimensions that we cannot readily observe like motivation and their family's interest in education. The lotteried-in and lotteried-out students who participated in the same lottery are identical on these subtle dimensions because *they all applied* to the charter school. They are separated only by a random number.

We follow the progress of lotteried-in and lotteried-out students. We compute the effect that charter schools have on their students' achievement by comparing the lotteried-in students to their lotteried-out counterparts. This is a true "apples-to-apples" comparison. Lottery-based studies are scientific and reliable. There are no other methods of studying the achievement of charter school students that have similar reliability.

The key findings of this report are as follows.

- Charter school applicants are much more likely to be black and much less likely to be Asian or white than the average student in New York City's traditional public schools. [Chapter II]
- Charter school applicants are more likely to be poor than the average student in New York City's traditional public schools. [Chapter II]
- Charter schools' lotteries appear to be truly random, as they are designed to be. Our tests for randomness are based on students' race, ethnicity, gender, prior test scores, free and reduced-price lunch participation, special education participation, and English Learner status. [Chapter II]
- Students who actually enroll in charter schools appear to be a random subset of the students who were admitted. [Chapter II]
- Lottery-based analysis of charter schools' effects on achievement is, by far, the most reliable method of evaluation. It is the only method that reliably eliminates "selection biases" which occur if students who apply to charter schools are more disadvantaged, more motivated, or different in any other way than students who do not apply. [Chapter III]
- On average, a student who attended a charter school for all of grades kindergarten through eight would close about 86 percent of the "Scarsdale-Harlem achievement gap" in math and 66 percent of the achievement gap in English. A student who attended fewer grades would improve by a commensurately smaller amount. [Chapter IV]
- On average, a lotteried-out student who stayed in the traditional public schools for all of grades kindergarten through eight would stay on grade level but would not close the "Scarsdale-Harlem achievement gap" by much. However, the lotteried-out students' performance <u>does</u> improve and <u>is</u> better than the norm in the U.S. where, as a rule, disadvantaged students fall further behind as they age. [Chapter IV]
- Compared to his lotteried-out counterpart, a student who attends a charter high school has Regents examination scores that are about 3 points higher for each year he spends in the charter school before taking the test. For instance, a student who took the English Comprehensive exam after three years in charter school would score about 9 points higher. [Chapter IV]
- A student who attends a charter high school is about 7 percent more likely to earn a Regents diploma by age 20 for each year he spends in that school. For instance, a student who spent grades ten through twelve in charter high school would have about a 21 percent higher probability of getting a Regents diploma. [Chapter IV]
- The following policies are associated with a charter school's having better effects on achievement. We emphasize that these are merely associa-

tions and do not necessarily indicate that these policies *cause* achievement to improve.

- a long school year;
- a greater number of minutes devoted to English during each school day;
- a small rewards/small penalties disciplinary policy;
- teacher pay based somewhat on performance or duties, as opposed to a traditional pay scale based strictly on seniority and credentials;
- a mission statement that emphasizes academic performance, as opposed to other goals. [Chapter V]

Index

About the Author

Danny Weil is a public interest attorney who has authored numerous books on educational policy and curriculum development, including the first edition of *Charter Schools: A Reference Handbook*. He also served as the acquisition editor for ABC-CLIO Publishing's series, Contemporary Education Issues.

A former bilingual elementary school teacher in South Central Los Angeles, he also taught migrant children, and helped found Pimeria Alta Charter School in Arizona where he served on the board. Dr. Weil holds a Ph.D. in both Education and Law, and teaches critical thinking and philosophy at Allan Hancock Junior College in California.